Time and

Relational Theory

Temporal Databases in

the Relational Model and SQL

C. J. Date
Hugh Darwen
Nikos A. Lorentzos

Cover Image: Lord's Cricket Ground
Text design: C. J. Date
Acquiring Editor: Steve Elliot
Editorial Project Manager: Kaitlin Herbert
Project Manager: Mohana Natarajan
Designer: Matthew Limbert

Morgan Kaufmann is an imprint of Elsevier
225 Wyman Street, Waltham, MA 02451, USA

Notices

Library of Congress Cataloging-in-Publication Data
Application Submitted

British Library Cataloguing-in-Publication Data
A catalogue record for this book is available from the British Library

ISBN: 978-0-12-800631-3

For information on all MK publications, visit our website at www.mkp.com

This book has been manufactured using Print On Demand technology. Each copy is produced to order and is limited to black ink. The online version of this book will show color figures where appropriate.

The cover illustration is the famous weathervane "Old Father Time" from Lord's Cricket Ground in London.

———— ◆◆◆◆◆ ————

*What, then, is time? I know well enough what it is,
provided that nobody asks me; but if I am asked what it is and try to explain,
I am baffled.*

—Saint Augustine of Hippo:
Confessions (397)

*The distinction between past, present, and future
is only a stubbornly persistent illusion.*

—Albert Einstein:
Letter to the family of Michele Besso (1955)

Time is what keeps everything from happening at once.

—Ray Cummings:
The Girl in the Golden Atom (1922)

Time is what happens when nothing else does.

—Richard Feynman (attrib.)

*Time present and time past
Are both perhaps present in time future,
And time future contained in time past.*

—T. S. Eliot:
Burnt Norton (1936)

About the Authors

C. J. Date is an independent author, lecturer, researcher, and consultant, specializing in relational database technology. He is best known for his book *An Introduction to Database Systems* (8th edition, Addison-Wesley, 2004), which has sold some 900,000 copies at the time of writing and is used by several hundred colleges and universities worldwide. He is also the author or coauthor of numerous other books on database management. He was inducted into the Computing Industry Hall of Fame in 2004. He enjoys a reputation that is second to none for his ability to explain complex technical subjects in a clear and understandable fashion.

Hugh Darwen was employed in IBM's software development divisions from 1967 to 2004. In the early part of his career, he was involved in DBMS development; from 1978 to 1982, he was one of the chief architects of an IBM product called Business System 12, a product that faithfully embraced the principles of the relational model. He was an active participant in the development of the international SQL standard (and related standards) from 1988 to 2004. Based in the U.K., he currently teaches relational database theory at Warwick University and is a tutor and course development consultant for the Open University. He has written two books on database management as well as coauthoring several others with C. J. Date. He has received honorary degrees from the University of Wolverhampton and the Open University.

Nikos A. Lorentzos is a Professor at the Agricultural University of Athens. He is mainly known for his research in temporal (also spatiotemporal) databases. He has participated in relevant European Union funded projects (prime researcher for the development of a temporal DBMS). The temporal model he has proposed has been extensively evaluated by independent researchers with positive comments; it is described in books addressed to university students, it has been the basis of PhDs undertaken in Europe, it has attracted the interest of DBMS developers, and it has had impact on international standards, as witnessed by the fact that SQL:2011 includes temporal characteristics proposed exclusively in his research. He is coeditor of the book *Spatiotemporal Databases: The Chorochronos Approach* (spatiotemporal databases). He is active in temporal, spatial, and spatiotemporal databases as well as in the development of decision support and expert systems in the forestry and agricultural domains.

Contents

Preface

This book is a major revision—in fact, a total rewrite—of an earlier one by the same authors. That earlier book was published by Morgan Kaufmann in 2003, under the title *Temporal Data and the Relational Model*. But the present book is so different from the previous one (except, to some extent, in its overall structure) that it doesn't seem reasonable to refer to it as just a second edition. (We've even given it a different title, partly for that reason.) As a consequence, we won't make any attempt in the text to call out specific points of difference with respect to that earlier book. Nor will we do what's usually done with the preface to a new edition, which is first to repeat the preface from the previous edition and then to explain what's changed in the new one. In other words, what you're reading right now is, to all intents and purposes, the preface to a brand new book.

So what exactly is "temporal data"? Well, a temporal database system is one that includes special support for the time dimension; in other words, it's a system that provides special facilities for storing, querying, and updating historical and/or future data. Database management systems (DBMSs for short) as classically understood aren't temporal in this sense—they provide little or no special support for temporal data at all. However, this situation is beginning to change, for the following reasons among others:

■ Disks and other secondary storage media have become cheap enough that keeping large volumes of temporal data is now a practical possibility.

■ As a consequence, data warehouses have become increasingly widespread.

■ Hence, users of those warehouses have begun to find themselves faced with temporal data problems, and they've begun to feel the need for solutions to those problems.

■ In order to address those problems, certain temporal features have been incorporated into the most recent version of the SQL standard ("SQL:2011," so called because it was ratified in late 2011).

■ Accordingly, vendors of conventional DBMS products have also begun to add temporal support to those products (there's a huge market opportunity here).

Here are some examples of application scenarios where such temporal support is very definitely needed. The examples are taken, with permission, from "A Matter of Time: Temporal Data Management in DB2 10," by Cynthia Saracco, Matthias Nicola, and Lenisha Gandhi (see Appendix F for further details):

1. An internal audit requires a financial institution to report on changes made to a client's records over the past five years.

2. A lawsuit prompts a hospital to reassess its knowledge of a patient's medical condition just before a new treatment was ordered.

3. A client challenges an insurance agency's resolution of a claim involving a car accident. The agency needs to determine the policy terms that were in effect when the accident occurred.

4. An online travel agency wants to detect inconsistencies in itineraries. For example, if someone books a hotel in Rome for eight days and reserves a car in New York for three of those days, the agency would like to flag the situation for review.

5. A retailer needs to ensure that no more than one discount is offered for a given product during a given period of time.

6. A client inquiry reveals a data entry error involving the introductory interest rate on a credit card. The bank needs to correct the error, retroactively, and compute a new balance if necessary.

That same paper by Saracco, Nicola, and Gandhi also gives some indication of the development benefits to be obtained from the availability of "native" temporal support in the DBMS (IBM's DB2 product, in the case at hand):

> The DB2 temporal support reduced coding requirements by more than 90% over homegrown implementations. Implementing just the core logic in SQL stored procedures or Java required 16 and 45 times as many lines of code, respectively, as the equivalent SQL statements using the DB2 temporal features. Also, it took less than an hour to develop and test those DB2 statements. By contrast, the homegrown approaches required 4-5 weeks to code and test, and they provided only a subset of the temporal support built into DB2. Thus, providing truly equivalent support through a homegrown implementation would likely take months.

Now, research into temporal databases isn't new—technical papers on the subject have been appearing in the literature ever since the beginning of the 1980s, if not earlier. However, much of that research ultimately proved unproductive: It turned out to be excessively complicated, or it led to logical inconsistencies, or it failed to solve certain aspects of the problem, or it was unsatisfactory for some other reason. So we'll have little to say about that research in this book (apart from a few remarks in Chapter 19 and in the annotation to some of the references in Appendix F). Instead, we'll focus on what we regard as a much more promising approach, one that's firmly rooted in the relational model of data, which those others mostly aren't, or weren't. Of course, it's precisely because of its strong relational foundations that we believe the approach we favor will stand the test of time (as it were!). And since the approach in question is directly and primarily due to one of the present authors (Lorentzos), the book can be regarded as authoritative.

The book also includes much original material resulting from continuing investigations by all three authors, material that's currently documented nowhere else at all. Examples include new database design techniques; a new normal form; new relational operators; new update operators; a new approach to the problem of temporal "granularity"; and support for "cyclic point types."[1] Overall, therefore, the book can be seen as, among other things, an abstract blueprint for the design of a temporal DBMS and the language interface to such a DBMS. In other words, it's forward looking, in the sense that it describes not only how temporal DBMSs might and do work today, but also, and more importantly, how we think they should and will work in the future.

One further point: Although this book concentrates on temporal data as such, many of the concepts are actually of much wider applicability. To be specific, the basic data construct involved is the *interval*, and intervals don't necessarily have to be temporal in nature. (On the other hand, certain of the ideas discussed are indeed specifically temporal ones: for example, the notion sometimes referred to, informally, as "the moving point *now*.")

Structure of the Book

The body of the book is divided into four major parts:

I.   A Review of Relational Concepts
II. Laying the Foundations
III. Building on the Foundations
IV. SQL Support

To elaborate:

■ Part I (three chapters) provides a refresher course on the relational model, with the emphasis on aspects that don't seem to be as widely appreciated as they might be. It also introduces the language **Tutorial D**—note the boldface name—which we'll be using in coding examples throughout the book.

■ Part II (eight chapters) covers basic temporal concepts and principles. It explains some of the problems that temporal data seems to give rise to, with reference to queries and

---

[1] All of the technical features described in this preface as "new" might more accurately be described as "new, except possibly (and to some partial extent) to readers of this book's 2003 predecessor *Temporal Data and the Relational Model*." *Note:* In this connection, we'd like to mention a couple of prototypes, MighTyD and SIRA_PRISE, that have implemented many of the features described in that earlier book: Details of those prototypes and much related material can be found on the website *www.thethirdmanifesto.com*.

integrity constraints in particular, and it describes some important new operators that can help in formulating those queries and constraints. *Note:* We should immediately explain that those new operators are all, in the last analysis, just shorthand for certain combinations of operators that can already be expressed using the traditional relational algebra. However, the shorthands in question turn out to be extremely useful ones—not just because they simplify the formulation of queries and constraints (a laudable goal in itself, of course), but also, more importantly, because they serve to raise the level of abstraction, and hence the overall level of discourse, regarding temporal issues in general.

■ Part III (seven chapters) covers a range of more advanced temporal concepts and principles. In effect, it shows how the ideas introduced in Part II can be applied to such matters as temporal database design, temporal database updates, the formulation of temporal database constraints, and a variety of more specialized topics.

■ Part IV (one long chapter) describes the temporal features of the SQL standard.

In addition to the foregoing, there are six appendixes, covering (as appendixes are wont to do) a somewhat mixed bag of topics. Appendixes A-C discuss possible extensions to certain of the notions introduced in the body of the book. Appendix D provides an abbreviated grammar, for reference purposes, for the language **Tutorial D**. Appendix E discusses implementation and optimization issues. Finally, as already indicated, Appendix F gives an annotated and consolidated list of references for the entire book. *Note:* Talking of references, we should explain that throughout the book such references take the form of numbers in square brackets. For example, "[2]" refers to the second publication mentioned in that appendix: namely, the paper "Maintaining Knowledge about Temporal Intervals," by James F. Allen, which was published in *CACM 26*, No. 11, in November 1983.[2]

Note: Parts II, III, and IV, at least, are definitely not meant for "dipping." Rather, they're meant to be read in sequence as written—if you skip a section or a chapter, you're likely to have difficulty with later material. While this state of affairs might seem a little undesirable in general, the fact is that temporal data does seem to suffer from certain innate complexities, and the book necessarily reflects some of those complexities. What's more, it's only fair to warn you that, beginning with Chapter 12 (the first chapter in Part III), you might notice a definite *increase* in complexity. At the same time, you should be aware that the full picture doesn't really begin to emerge until that same Chapter 12. Please note too that this isn't a closed subject!—several interesting research issues remain. Such issues are touched on and appropriately flagged at pertinent points in the book.

Last, a couple of remarks regarding our use of terminology:

---

[2] *CACM = Communications of the ACM.*

1. Other than in Part IV, we adhere almost exclusively to the formal relational terms *relation*, *tuple*, *attribute*, etc., instead of using their SQL counterparts *table*, *row*, *column*, etc. In our opinion, those SQL terms have done the cause of genuine understanding a serious disservice over the years. Besides, the constructs referred to by those terms include many deviations from relational theory, such as duplicate rows, left to right column ordering, and nulls, and we certainly don't want to give the impression that we might condone such deviations.

2. We've been forced to introduce our own terminology for several concepts—"packed form," "U_ operators," "U_keys," "sixth normal form," and others—precisely because the concepts themselves are new (for the most part, at least). However, we've tried in every case to choose terms that are appropriate and make good intuitive sense, and we haven't intentionally used familiar terms in unfamiliar ways. We apologize if our choice of terms causes you any unnecessary difficulties.

Intended Readership

Who should read this book? Well, in at least one sense the book is quite definitely not self-contained—it does assume you're professionally interested in database technology and are reasonably well acquainted with conventional database theory and practice. However, we've tried to define and explain, as carefully as possible, any concepts that might be thought novel. In fact, we've done the same for several concepts that really shouldn't be novel at all but don't seem to be as widely understood as they might be (relation variables, also known as *relvars*, are an obvious case in point here). We've also included a set of exercises, with answers, at the end of each chapter. In other words, we've tried to make the book suitable for both reference and tutorial purposes. Our intended audience is thus just about anyone with a serious interest in database technology, including but not limited to the following:

- Database language designers and standardizers

- DBMS product implementers and other vendor personnel

- Data and database administrators

- "Information modelers" and database designers

- Application designers and developers

- Computer science professors specializing in database issues

- Database students, both graduate and undergraduate

- People responsible for DBMS product evaluation and acquisition

- Technically aware end users

The only background knowledge required is a general understanding of data management concepts and issues (including in particular a basic familiarity with the relational model) and, for Part IV, a general knowledge of SQL.

Note: There are currently few college courses, if any, that include coverage of temporal data. Because of what we see as the growing demand for proper temporal support, however, we can expect such courses to appear in the near future. We believe this book can serve as the text for such a course. For academic readers in particular, therefore (students as well as teachers), we should make it clear that we've tried to present the foundations of the temporal database field in a way that's clear, precise, correct, and uncluttered by the baggage—not to say mistakes—that usually, and regrettably, seem to accompany commercial implementations. Thus, we believe the book provides an opportunity to acquire a firm understanding of that crucial foundation material, without being distracted by irrelevancies.

Acknowledgments

First of all, we're pleased to be able to acknowledge the many friends and colleagues, too numerous to mention individually, who gave encouragement, participated in discussions and research, offered comments (both written and oral) on various drafts of this book and other publications, or helped in a variety of other ways. We'd also like to acknowledge the many conference and seminar attendees, again too numerous to mention individually, who have expressed support for the ideas contained herein. A special vote of thanks goes to our early reviewers Georgia Garani, Erwin Smout, Dimitri Souflis, Rios Viqueira, and Dave Voorhis. We'd also like to thank Cynthia Saracco, Matthias Nicola, and Lenisha Gandhi for permission to quote from their paper "A Matter of Time: Temporal Data Management in DB2 10" in this preface, and Krishna Kulkarni and Jan-Eike Michels for permission to quote from their paper "Temporal Features in SQL:2011" in Chapter 19 (also for their help in answering various technical questions in connection with—and in Krishna's case reviewing—that chapter). Finally, we are grateful to Andrea Dierna, Steve Elliott, and Kaitlin Herbert, and to all of the other staff at Morgan Kaufmann, for their assistance and their high standards of professionalism. It has been a pleasure to work with them.

Nikos Lorentzos adds: I would like to thank my mother Efrosini, who knows better than anyone how endlessly busy my work keeps me, and Aliki Galati who has always encouraged me in my research. I would also like to express a strong debt of gratitude to Mike Sykes, the first person to express an interest in my work on temporal databases. Thanks to Mike, I came in contact with Hugh Darwen, with whom I have had many fruitful discussions on this topic. And thanks to

Hugh, I finally met Chris Date, who has done a great job on this book. I am most grateful to my coauthors, Hugh and Chris, for our fruitful collaboration.

Hugh Darwen adds: I began my study of temporal database issues in the mid 1990s in connection with my work in UKDBL, the working group that formulates U.K. contributions to the development of the international SQL standard. I was joined in that study by my UKDBL colleague Mike Sykes, and together we began to search for alternatives to the temporal proposals then being considered by the SQL standards committee. It was Mike who first discovered the work of Nikos Lorentzos, and I am profoundly grateful to him for realizing that it was not only exactly what he had been looking for but also what he knew *I* had been looking for. (Mike had been looking for an approach based on intervals in general rather than just time intervals in particular. I had been looking for an approach that did not depart from the relational model.)

　　Various university contacts in the U.K. were helpful during my initial study period. I would especially like to thank Babis Theodoulidis of the University of Manchester Institute of Science and Technology for setting up a meeting between academics (including Nikos Lorentzos) and members of UKDBL. My subsequent education in the temporal field benefited greatly from discussions with people at IBM's Almaden Research Center, especially Cliff Leung and later Bob Lyle. Finally, I must mention the participants at the June 1997 workshop on temporal databases in Dagstuhl, Germany, whose output was reference [55]. There were too many for me to name them individually, but I am grateful to them all for what struck me as a most informative, productive, stimulating, lively, and friendly event.

Chris Date adds: Once again I'd like to thank my wife Lindy for her support throughout the production of this book, as well as all of its predecessors. I'd also like to acknowledge the debt I owe my coauthors—Nikos, for doing such a good job of laying the theoretical foundations for the approach described in this book; Hugh, for his persistence in trying to persuade me that I ought to take an interest in temporal database matters in general and Nikos's work in particular; and both Nikos and Hugh for their efforts in reviewing the numerous iterations this manuscript went through and their patience in correcting my many early errors and misconceptions.

C. J. Date (*Healdsburg, California*)
Hugh Darwen (*Shrewley, England*)
Nikos A. Lorentzos (*Athens, Greece*)
2014

Part I

A REVIEW OF

RELATIONAL CONCEPTS

This book assumes a basic familiarity with the relational model. Thus, this first part is intended merely as a quick refresher course on that model; in effect, it summarizes, and serves as a reference source for, material you'll be expected to know when we get to the temporal discussions in Parts II, III, and IV. It consists of three chapters:

1. Types and Relations

2. Relational Algebra

3. Relation Variables

Of course, tutorials on the relational model and related matters can be found in many places (see, e.g., references [28], [42], and [45]); thus, if you're familiar with any of those references, you probably don't need to read this part of the book in detail. However, if your knowledge of the relational model derives from other sources—especially ones based on SQL—then you probably do need to read these chapters fairly carefully, because they emphasize numerous important topics that such sources typically don't. Such topics include:

- "Possible representations," selectors, and THE_ operators

- Relation types

- Relation values vs. relation variables

- Predicates and propositions

- Relation valued attributes

- Relational assignment

- The fundamental role of constraints

- Less well known but important operators such as EXTEND, MATCHING, and NOT MATCHING

and many others.

Note: Chapter 1 also introduces the suppliers-and-shipments database, which serves as the basis for almost all of the examples in later chapters. Even if you decide just to skim this part of the book, therefore, you should at least take a look at that sample database before moving on to Part II.

Chapter 1

T y p e s   a n d   R e l a t i o n s

What type of relation do you mean?

—Anon.:
Where Bugs Go

The relational model is, of course, defined in terms of relations, and relations in turn are defined in terms of types. This first chapter explains these two constructs in detail. First, however, it introduces the running example.

THE RUNNING EXAMPLE

Most of the examples in this book are based on the well known suppliers-and-parts database—or, more precisely, on a simplified version of that database that we refer to as *suppliers and shipments*. Fig. 1.1 shows a set of sample values for that simplified database (and please note that we'll be assuming those specific sample values in examples throughout this part of the book, barring explicit statements to the contrary). *Note:* In case you happen to be familiar with the more usual version of this database as discussed in, e.g., reference [45], we explain here briefly what the simplifications consist of:

- First of all, we've dropped the parts relvar P entirely (hence the revised name "suppliers and shipments"). *Note:* The term *relvar* is short for *relation variable*. Relation variables are discussed in detail in Chapter 3.

- Second, we've removed attribute QTY ("quantity") from the shipments relvar SP, leaving just attributes SNO and PNO.

- Third, we (re)interpret that revised SP relvar thus: "Supplier SNO is *currently able* to supply part PNO." In other words, instead of standing for *actual* shipments of parts by suppliers, as it did in, e.g., reference [45], relvar SP now stands for what might be called *potential* shipments—i.e., the *ability* of certain suppliers to supply certain parts.

S

SNO	SNAME	STATUS	CITY
S1	Smith	20	London
S2	Jones	10	Paris
S3	Blake	30	Paris
S4	Clark	20	London
S5	Adams	30	Athens

SP

SNO	PNO
S1	P1
S1	P2
S1	P3
S1	P4
S1	P5
S1	P6
S2	P1
S2	P2
S3	P2
S4	P2
S4	P4
S4	P5

Fig. 1.1: The suppliers-and-shipments database (first version)–sample values

Overall, then, the database is meant to be interpreted as follows:

■ Relvar S represents *suppliers under contract*. Each such supplier has a supplier number (SNO), unique to that supplier; a supplier name (SNAME), not necessarily unique (though the sample SNAME values shown in Fig. 1.1 do happen to be unique); a status or rating value (STATUS); and a location (CITY). *Note:* In the rest of this book we'll refer to "suppliers under contract," most of the time, as just *suppliers* for short.

■ Relvar SP represents *potential shipments*—it shows which suppliers are capable of supplying, or shipping, which parts. Obviously, the combination of SNO and PNO values for a given "potential shipment" is unique to that shipment. *Note:* In the rest of this book we'll take the liberty of referring to "potential shipments"—somewhat inaccurately, but very conveniently—as just *shipments* for short. Also, we'll assume it's possible for a given supplier to be under contract at some time and yet not actually be able to supply any parts at that time (supplier S5 is a case in point, given the sample values of Fig. 1.1).

Here for purposes of reference are formal definitions for the example, expressed in a language called **Tutorial D**—or, rather, in a version of that language that's been tailored slightly in order to suit the purposes of this book. **Tutorial D** is a computationally complete programming language with fully integrated database functionality and, we believe, more or less self-explanatory syntax. It was introduced in the first (1998) edition of reference [52] as a vehicle for teaching database concepts. All coding examples in this book are expressed in that language or certain specified extensions thereto (except, of course, for the SQL-specific examples in Part IV).

```
TYPE SNO ... ;
TYPE PNO ... ;
TYPE NAME ... ;

VAR S BASE
     RELATION
        { SNO     SNO ,
          SNAME   NAME ,
          STATUS  INTEGER ,
          CITY    CHAR }
     KEY { SNO } ;

VAR SP BASE
     RELATION
        { SNO SNO ,
          PNO PNO }
     KEY { SNO , PNO }
     FOREIGN KEY { SNO } REFERENCES S ;
```

To elaborate briefly (note, however, that all of the technical issues illustrated by this example and discussed in outline below will be explained in more detail either later in this chapter or somewhere in the next two):

■ The first three lines are type definitions (shown here in outline only; further details are given in the section "Types," immediately following the present section). The specified types—SNO, PNO, and NAME—are *user defined* types, and they're used in the definitions of attributes SNO and SNAME in relvar S and attributes SNO and PNO in relvar SP. By contrast, attributes STATUS and CITY in relvar S are of *system* defined types—namely, INTEGER (integers) and CHAR (character strings of arbitrary length), respectively—and, of course, no explicit type definitions are needed for such types. *Note:* In what follows, we'll assume the availability of another system defined type also: namely, type BOOLEAN (truth values), consisting of just the two values TRUE and FALSE.

■ The next seven lines constitute the definition of relvar S. The keyword VAR indicates that the statement overall defines a variable. The variable in question is called S. The keyword BASE indicates the kind of variable being defined; it stands for "base relvar," which is the kind of relvar S is. *Note:* Relvars come in several different varieties, of which the most important are (a) *base*, or *real*, relvars and (b) *virtual* relvars, also called *views*. In this book, however, we'll have little to say regarding virtual relvars until we get to Chapter 15; prior to that point, therefore, we'll adopt the simplifying assumption that the unqualified term *relvar* always means a base relvar specifically, unless the context demands otherwise.

■ Within the definition for relvar S, lines 2–6 specify the type of the variable being defined. The keyword RELATION shows it's a relation type, and the next four lines specify the corresponding attributes, where each attribute consists of the applicable attribute name together with the name of the corresponding type. The complete set of attribute specifications is enclosed in braces. No significance attaches to the order in which the attributes are specified within those braces. *Note:* For a general explanation of how braces are used in **Tutorial D**, please see Appendix D.

■ Line 7 of the definition for relvar S defines {SNO} to be a key for that relvar.

■ The last six lines constitute the definition of relvar SP. The definition follows the same general pattern as that for relvar S; the only new construct is the foreign key specification in the last line, which defines {SNO} to be a foreign key in relvar SP referencing the "target" key {SNO} in relvar S. Note, incidentally, that relvar SP is "all key."

TYPES

Relations in the relational model are defined over *types* (also known as *domains*—the terms are interchangeable, but we'll stay with *types*). Types are discussed in the present section, relations are discussed in the next.

What exactly is a type? Among other things, it's *a set of values*. Examples include:

■ The set of all integers (type INTEGER)

■ The set of all character strings (type CHAR)

■ The set of all supplier numbers (type SNO)

Aside: Instead of saying that (e.g.) type INTEGER is the set of *all* integers, it would be more correct to say it's the set of all integers that are capable of representation in the computer system under consideration. Obviously there'll be some integers that are beyond the representational capability of any given system. In what follows, however, we won't usually bother to be quite so precise. *End of aside*.

Every *value* has, or is of, some type; in fact, every value is of exactly one type.[1] Moreover:

■ Every *variable* is defined, or "declared," to be of some type, meaning that every possible value of the variable in question is a value of the type in question.

■ Every *attribute* of every relation is declared to be of some type, meaning that every possible value of the attribute in question is a value of the type in question.

---

[1] Except possibly if type inheritance is supported, in which case a given value might have more than one type. Even then, however, the value will still have exactly one *most specific* type. Type inheritance is discussed further in Chapter 18.

■ Every *operator* that returns a result is declared to be of some type, meaning that every possible result that can be returned by an invocation of the operator in question is a value of the type in question. *Note:* An operator that returns a result is called a *read-only* operator; an operator that returns no result but updates one or more of its arguments instead is called an *update* operator. Examples of both kinds are given in the subsection "User Defined Operators" later in this section. Further, let *Op* be an update operator. Since an invocation of *Op* doesn't denote a value, *Op* doesn't have a declared type (though its parameters do—see the bullet item immediately following).

■ Every *parameter* of every operator is declared to be of some type, meaning that every possible argument that can be substituted for the parameter in question is a value or variable of the type in question. Note that it must be a variable if the operator in question is an update operator and the argument corresponding to the parameter in question will be updated by an invocation of the operator in question.

■ More generally, every *expression* is declared to be of some type—namely, the type declared for the outermost operator (necessarily a read-only operator) involved in the expression in question, or equivalently the type of the value denoted by that expression.

Aside: The remarks concerning operators and parameters in the two bullet items immediately preceding require some slight refinement if the operator in question is *polymorphic*. An operator is said to be polymorphic if it's defined in terms of some parameter *P* and the argument corresponding to *P* can be of different types on different invocations. The equality operator "=" is an obvious example: We can compare values of *any* type for equality (just so long as the values in question are both of the same type), and so "=" is polymorphic—it applies to integers, and character strings, and supplier numbers, and in fact to values of every type. Analogous remarks apply to the assignment operator ":="; indeed, we follow reference [49] in requiring both "=" and ":=" to be defined for every type. Further examples of polymorphic operators include aggregate operators such as SUM and MAX (see Chapter 2); operators of the relational algebra such as UNION and JOIN (again, see Chapter 2); and the operators defined for intervals in Part II of this book. *End of aside.*

Any given type is either *system defined* or *user defined*.[2] As previously noted, of the types mentioned in connection with the running example, types INTEGER, CHAR, and BOOLEAN

---

[2] This sentence is only an approximation to the truth. A more accurate statement would be: *Nongenerated* types—see the next section—are either system defined or user defined (the concept of system vs. user defined doesn't apply to generated types). Note that relation types in particular are generated types (again, see the next section). So are tuple types, incidentally.

are system defined (or so we assume for the purposes of this book, at any rate), and types SNO, NAME, and PNO are user defined.

Next, any type whatsoever, regardless of whether it's system or user defined, can be used as the basis for defining variables, attributes, operators, and parameters. Well ... there are two small exceptions to this statement, both of them having to do with attribute types specifically:

- First, the relational model expressly prohibits relations in the database from having attributes of any pointer type—meaning in particular, albeit a little loosely, that no relation in the database is allowed to have an attribute whose values are pointers to tuples in the database. *Note:* Relations and tuples are discussed in the next section.

- The second limitation is a little harder to state, but what it boils down to is this: If relation *r* has heading *H*, then no attribute of *r* can be defined in terms of a relation or tuple type that has that same heading *H*, at any level of nesting. *Note:* Headings too are discussed in the next section.

Next, it's usual to think of types, informally, as being either *scalar* or *nonscalar*. Loosely, a type is scalar if it has no user visible components and nonscalar otherwise—and values, variables, attributes, operators, parameters, and expressions of some type *T* are scalar or nonscalar according as type *T* itself is scalar or nonscalar. For example:

- Type INTEGER is a scalar type (it has no user visible components); hence, values, variables, and so on of type INTEGER are also all scalar.

- Relation and tuple types are nonscalar (the pertinent user visible components being the corresponding attributes); hence, relation and tuple values, variables, and so on are also all nonscalar.

That said, we must emphasize that these notions are quite informal. In particular, the relational model nowhere relies on the scalar vs. nonscalar distinction in any formal sense. In this book, however, we do appeal to it informally from time to time, because we do find it at least intuitively useful.[3] To be specific, we use the term *scalar* in connection with types that are neither tuple nor relation types, and the term *nonscalar* in connection with types that *are* either tuple or relation types.[4]

---

[3] Occasionally, anyway. Actually we won't be using it all that much except in this first chapter.

[4] This sentence too is only an approximation to the truth. A more accurate statement would be: Nongenerated types are scalar; generated types (e.g., relation types) are typically nonscalar, but don't have to be. An example of a scalar generated type is the SQL type CHAR(25). See reference [42] for further explanation.

Aside: Another term you'll sometimes hear used to mean "scalar" is *encapsulated.* Be aware, however, that this term is also used—especially in object oriented contexts—to refer to the physical bundling, or packaging, of code and data (or operator definitions and data representation definitions, to be more precise about the matter). But to use the term in this latter sense is to mix model and implementation considerations; clearly the user shouldn't care, and shouldn't need to care, whether code and data are physically bundled together or are kept separate. See reference [36] for further discussion. *End of aside.*

Following on from the foregoing, we need to explain that although scalar types have no user visible components, they do have what are called *possible representations* ("possreps" for short), and those possible representations are user visible and do have user visible components, as we'll see in a moment. Don't be misled, however: Those user visible components aren't components of the type, they're components of the possrep. The type itself is still scalar in the sense explained above.

By way of illustration, suppose we have a user defined scalar type called QTY ("quantity"). Assume for the sake of the example that a possible representation called QPR is declared for this type that says, in effect, that quantities can "possibly be represented" by positive integers, as indicated here:

```
TYPE QTY POSSREP QPR { Q INTEGER CONSTRAINT Q ≥ 1 ... } ;
```

Then the specified possrep certainly does have user visible components—in fact, it has exactly one such component, Q, of type INTEGER—but, to repeat, quantities per se do not.

Here's a more complicated example that illustrates the same point:

```
TYPE POINT      /* geometric points in two-dimensional space */
     POSSREP CARTESIAN { X RATIONAL , Y RATIONAL ... }
     POSSREP POLAR { RHO RATIONAL , THETA RATIONAL ... } ;
```

Type POINT has two distinct possreps, CARTESIAN and POLAR, reflecting the fact that points in two-dimensional space can indeed "possibly be represented" by either cartesian or polar coordinates. Each of those possreps in turn has two components, both of which are of type RATIONAL ("rational numbers").[5] Note carefully, however, that, to say it again, type POINT per se is still scalar—it has no user visible components. Note too that the *physical* representation of POINT values, in the particular implementation at hand, might be cartesian coordinates, or it might be polar coordinates, or it might be something else entirely. In other words, possible representations (which are, to repeat, user visible) are indeed only possible ones; physical representations are an implementation matter merely and should never be visible to the user.

---

[5] We follow reference [52] in preferring RATIONAL over the more usual REAL as the name of this type.

Next, be aware that each POSSREP specification causes automatic definition of the following more or less self-explanatory operators:

- One *selector* operator, which allows the user to select, or specify, a value of the type in question by supplying a value for each component of the possible representation in question

- A set of *THE_* operators (one such for each component of the possible representation in question), which allow the user to access components of the corresponding possible representation of values of the type in question

   Aside: When we say a POSSREP specification causes "automatic definition" of such operators, what we mean is this: Whatever agency—possibly the system, possibly some human user—is responsible for implementing the type in question is also responsible for implementing those operators; moreover, until those operators have been implemented, the process of implementing the type can't be regarded as complete. *End of aside.*

We adopt certain naming conventions in connection with the foregoing operators. To be specific, we adopt the conventions that (a) selectors have the same name as the corresponding possrep, and (b) THE_ operators have names of the form THE_*C*, where *C* is the name of the corresponding component of the corresponding possrep. Thus, type QTY has one selector, called QPR, and one THE_ operator, called THE_Q. By contrast, type POINT has two selectors, called CARTESIAN and POLAR; it also has two THE_ operators corresponding to the CARTESIAN possrep, called THE_X and THE_Y, and two THE_ operators corresponding to the POLAR possrep, called THE_RHO and THE_THETA. Here are some sample invocations:

```
QPR ( 250 )
/* returns the quantity corresponding to the integer 250  */

THE_Q ( QX )
/* returns the integer corresponding to the quantity      */
/* value in QX, where QX is a variable of type QTY         */

CARTESIAN ( 5.0 , -2.5 )
/* returns the point with x = 5.0 and y = -2.5             */

CARTESIAN ( X1 , Y1 )
/* returns the point with x = X1 and y = Y1, where X1 and */
/* Y1 are variables of type RATIONAL                       */

POLAR ( 1.7 , 2.0 )
/* returns the point with rho = 1.7 and theta = 2.0        */

THE_X ( P )
/* returns the x coordinate of the point value in P,       */
/* where P is a variable of type POINT                     */
```

```
THE_RHO ( P )
/* returns the rho coordinate of the point value in P,    */
/* where P is a variable of type POINT                    */

THE_Y ( exp )
/* returns the y coordinate of the point denoted by the   */
/* expression exp (which must be of type POINT)           */
```

We adopt another naming convention also: If type *T* has a possrep with no explicitly declared name, then that possrep is named *T* by default. By way of example, we could simplify the definition of type QTY by omitting the possrep name QPR, thus:

```
TYPE QTY POSSREP { Q INTEGER CONSTRAINT Q ≥ 1 ... } ;
```

And then we could simplify the first selector invocation in the foregoing list of examples to the following more user friendly form:

```
QTY ( 250 )
/* returns the quantity corresponding to the integer 250 */
```

Note: As several of the foregoing examples should be sufficient to suggest, selectors—or selector *invocations*, rather—are a generalization of the more familiar concept of a literal.[6] In fact, all literals are selector invocations; however, not all selector invocations are literals. To be specific, a selector invocation is a literal if and only if its argument expressions are all literals in turn. Thus, of the selector invocations shown above, QTY (250) (or QPR (250)), CARTESIAN (5.0,–2.5), and POLAR (1.7,2.0) are literals and the others aren't.

User Defined Operators

The foregoing discussion of THE_ operators in particular touches on another crucial issue: namely, the fact that the type concept includes the associated notion of the operators that apply to values and variables of the type in question. (By definition, values and variables of a given type can be operated upon only by means of the operators defined in connection with that type.) For example, in the case of the system defined type INTEGER:

---

[6] The concept might be familiar, but it seems to be quite difficult to find a good definition for it in the literature. Here's our own preferred definition: A literal is a symbol that denotes a value that's fixed and determined by the symbol in question (and the type of that value is also fixed and determined by the symbol in question). Loosely, we can say a literal is *self-defining*. Here are some **Tutorial D** examples:

```
FALSE                        /* a literal of type BOOLEAN  */
4                            /* a literal of type INTEGER  */
2.7                          /* a literal of type RATIONAL */
'ABC'                        /* a literal of type CHAR     */
SNO ( 'S1' )                 /* a literal of type SNO      */
CARTESIAN ( 5.0 , -2.5 )     /* a literal of type POINT    */
```

- The system defines operators ":=", "=", ">", and so on, for assigning and comparing integers.

- It also defines operators "+", "*", and so on, for performing arithmetic on integers.

- It does *not* define operators "| |" (concatenate), SUBSTR (substring), and so on, for performing string operations on integers. In other words, string operations on integers aren't supported.

By way of another example, consider the user defined type SNO. Then whoever actually defines that type will certainly define ":=" and "=" operators, and perhaps ">" and "<" operators as well, for assigning and comparing supplier numbers. However, that user will probably not define operators "+", "*", and so on, which means that arithmetic on supplier numbers won't be supported.

We see, therefore, that users will necessarily have the ability to define their own operators. This fact isn't particularly relevant to the primary topic of the present book—at least, it won't be until we get to Chapter 18—but we show a few examples here in order to give some idea as to what such a feature might look like. First, here's the definition for a user defined operator called ABS ("absolute value") for the system defined type INTEGER:

```
OPERATOR ABS ( I INTEGER ) RETURNS INTEGER ;
   RETURN ( IF I ≥ 0 THEN +I ELSE −I END IF ) ;
END OPERATOR ;
```

This operator is declared to be of type INTEGER (i.e., it returns an integer when it's invoked), and it has just one parameter, I, which is also of declared type INTEGER.

By way of a second example, here's the definition for an operator DIST ("distance between") for the user defined type POINT:

```
OPERATOR DIST ( P1 POINT , P2 POINT ) RETURNS RATIONAL ;
   RETURN ( SQRT ( ( THE_X ( P1 ) − THE_X ( P2 ) ) ↑ 2 +
                   ( THE_Y ( P1 ) − THE_Y ( P2 ) ) ↑ 2 ) ) ;
END OPERATOR ;
```

This operator is of declared type RATIONAL; it has two parameters, P1 and P2, both of declared type POINT. (We're assuming for the sake of the example that the operator SQRT returns a rational number result, representing the nonnegative square root of its nonnegative rational number argument. The symbol "↑" means "raise to the power of.")

Now, ABS and DIST are both read-only operators. Here by contrast is an example of a definition for an update operator called REFLECT:

```
OPERATOR REFLECT ( P POINT ) UPDATES { P } ;
    THE_X ( P )   :=  - THE_X ( P ) ,
    THE_Y ( P )   :=  - THE_Y ( P ) ;
END OPERATOR ;
```

This operator has just one parameter P, of declared type POINT, and that parameter is "subject to update" (meaning that when the operator is invoked, it updates the argument variable corresponding to that parameter). It doesn't return a result, and thus has no declared type. *Note:* This example also illustrates the use of (a) multiple assignment and (b) THE_ operators on the left side of an assignment ("THE_ pseudovariables"). Multiple assignment is discussed in Chapter 3, also in reference [48]. As for THE_ pseudovariables, for the purposes of this book we take them to be self-explanatory. A detailed explanation of pseudovariables in general and THE_ pseudovariables in particular can be found in that same reference [48].

Type Constraints

Every type definition includes, implicitly or explicitly, a corresponding type constraint, which is a specification of the set of values that make up that type. Now, in the case of system defined types, it's the system that provides that specification, and there's not much more to be said. So let's focus for the moment on user defined types. Here once again is the type definition for the user defined type QTY, but now shown complete (we've numbered the lines for purposes of subsequent reference):

```
1.   TYPE QTY
2.       POSSREP QTY
3.           { Q INTEGER
4.               CONSTRAINT Q ≥ 1 AND Q ≤ 5000 } ;
```

Explanation:

■ Line 1 just says we're defining a type called QTY.

■ Line 2 says quantities have a possible representation also called QTY. (In fact, of course, the possrep name QTY would have been assumed by default if no possrep name had been specified explicitly.)

■ Line 3 says possrep QTY has a single component, called Q, which is of type INTEGER.

■ Finally, line 4 says those integers must lie in the range 1 to 5000 inclusive. Thus, lines 2-4 taken together define valid quantities to be, precisely, those values that can possibly be represented by integers in the specified range, and it's that definition that constitutes the type constraint for type QTY. Observe, therefore, that such constraints are specified not in terms of the type as such but, rather, in terms of a possrep for the type. Indeed, one of the reasons (not the only one) for requiring the possrep concept in the first place is precisely to serve as a vehicle for formulating type constraints, as the example suggests.

By way of a second example, here's a variation on the POINT type definition from a few pages back:

```
TYPE CPOINT POSSREP { X RATIONAL , Y RATIONAL
                      CONSTRAINT SQRT ( X ↑ 2 + Y ↑ 2 ) ≤ 100.0 } ;
```

The CONSTRAINT specification here says (in effect) that the only points we're interested in are those that lie on or inside a circle with center the origin and radius 100.

Type constraints are checked whenever some selector is invoked. For example, with reference to type QTY as defined above, the expression QTY (250) is an invocation of the QTY selector, and that invocation succeeds. By contrast, the expression QTY (6000) is also such an invocation, but it fails. In fact, it should be obvious that we can never tolerate an expression that's supposed to denote a value of some type *T* but in fact doesn't; after all, "a value of type *T* that's not a value of type *T*" is a contradiction in terms. Since, ultimately, the only way *any* expression can yield a value of type *T* is by virtue of some invocation of some selector for type *T*, it follows that no variable can ever be assigned a value that's not of the right type.

RELATIONS

Relations are made up of tuples, and so, in order to come up with a definition of exactly what a relation is, we first need to say what a tuple is:

Definition: Let *T1*, *T2*, ..., *Tn* ($n \geq 0$) be type names, not necessarily all distinct. Associate with each *Ti* a distinct *attribute name*, *Ai*; each of the *n* attribute-name : type-name pairs that results is an **attribute**. Associate with each attribute *Ai* an *attribute value*, *vi*, of type *Ti*; each of the *n* attribute : value pairs that results is a *component*. Then the set—call it *t*—of all *n* components thus defined is a *tuple value* (or just a **tuple** for short) over the attributes *A1*, *A2*, ..., *An*. The value *n* is the **degree** of *t*; a tuple of degree one is *unary*, a tuple of degree two is *binary*, a tuple of degree three is *ternary*, ..., and more generally a tuple of degree *n* is *n-ary*. The set *H* of all *n* attributes is the **heading** of *t* (and the degree and attributes of *t* are, respectively, the degree and attributes of *H*).

And here now is a precise definition of the term *relation*:

Definition: Let *H* be a tuple heading, and let *t1, t2, ..., tm* (*m* ≥ 0) be distinct tuples all with heading *H*. Then the combination—call it *r*—of *H* and the set of tuples {*t1, t2, ..., tm*} is a *relation value* (or just a **relation** for short) over the attributes *A1, A2, ..., An*, where *A1, A2, ..., An* are all of the attributes in *H*. The **heading** of *r* is *H*; *r* has the same attributes (and hence the same attribute names and types) and the same degree as that heading does. The set of tuples {*t1, t2, ..., tm*} is the **body** of *r*. The value *m* is the **cardinality** of *r*.

Points arising from these definitions:

■ In terms of the usual tabular picture of a relation—see, e.g., the two examples in Fig. 1.1—the row of column names denotes the heading and the data rows denote the body. *Note:* Strictly speaking, the rows of column names in such pictures should therefore include the relevant type names; similarly, the data rows should include the relevant attribute names. In practice, however, it's usual to omit those type and attribute names as we did in Fig. 1.1 (and as we'll continue to do throughout the rest of the book).

■ Following on from the previous point, observe that of course there's a logical difference[7] between an attribute name and an attribute per se. Informally, however, we often use expressions such as "attribute *A*"—indeed, we've done so several times in this chapter already, as you might have noticed—but such expressions must of course be understood as meaning the attribute whose *name* is *A* (and whose type has been left unspecified).

■ Observe now that a relation does not directly contain its tuples—it contains a body, and that body in turn contains those tuples. Informally, however, it's convenient to talk as if relations did contain their tuples directly, and we'll follow this simplifying convention throughout this book. In particular, we'll often use the term "empty relation," a little loosely, to mean a relation whose body is empty.

■ A relation of degree one is said to be *unary,* a relation of degree two *binary,* a relation of degree three *ternary, ...,* and a relation of degree *n n-ary*. A relation of degree zero is said to be *nullary*.[8] *Note:* Perhaps we should say a little more about the nullary case, since the concept might be unfamiliar to you. In fact there are exactly two nullary relations, one that contains just one tuple (necessarily with no components, and hence a nullary tuple or *0-tuple*—see the bullet item immediately following), and one that's empty and thus contains no tuples at all. Following reference [25], we refer to these two relations colloquially as TABLE_DEE and TABLE_DUM, respectively. We'll meet them again, many times, in later chapters.

---

[7] This useful term derives from Wittgenstein's dictum to the effect that ***all logical differences are big differences.*** For further discussion, see reference [38].

[8] Nothing to do with SQL-style nulls, please note! We'll be discussing nulls, briefly, in just a few moments.

Aside: For the benefit of readers who might not be native English speakers, we should explain that the names TABLE_DEE and TABLE_DUM are basically just wordplay on Tweedledee and Tweedledum, who were originally characters in a children's nursery rhyme and were subsequently incorporated into *Through the Looking-Glass and What Alice Found There*, by Lewis Carroll. TABLE_DEE is the one with just one tuple, TABLE_DUM is the empty one. *End of aside.*

■ The term *n-tuple* is sometimes used in place of *tuple* (and so we sometimes speak of, e.g., 2-tuples, 4-tuples, 0-tuples, etc.). However, it's usual to drop the "*n-*" prefix and speak of just *tuples*, unqualified. The terms *pair*, *triple*, etc., are also used on occasion.

■ No relation ever contains any duplicate tuples.[9] *Note:* We should explain precisely what we mean by the term "duplicate tuples." Here's a definition:

Definition: Tuples t and t' are **duplicates** of one another if and only if they have exactly the same attributes $A1, A2, ..., An$ and, for all i ($i = 1, 2, ..., n$), the value for Ai in t is equal to the value for Ai in t'. Furthermore—this might seem obvious but it needs to be said—tuples t and t' are **equal** to each other (i.e., $t = t'$ is true) if and only if they're duplicates of each other, meaning they're in fact the very same tuple.

The concept of tuple equality is relevant in numerous contexts, including, for example, the definitions of *key* and *foreign key* (see Chapter 3) and the definition of relational operators such as join (see Chapter 2).

Incidentally, note that it's an immediate consequence of the foregoing definition that all 0-tuples are duplicates of one another. For this reason, we're justified in talking in terms of *the* 0-tuple instead of "a" 0-tuple, and indeed we usually do.

■ There's no top to bottom ordering to the tuples of a relation (pictures like Fig. 1.1 notwithstanding).

■ There's no left to right ordering to the attributes of a tuple or relation (pictures like Fig. 1.1 notwithstanding).

■ Every tuple of every relation contains exactly one value, of the appropriate type, for each attribute of the relation in question (in other words, relations are always *normalized* or, equivalently, in *first normal form*, 1NF). *Note:* As you probably know, much of the

---

[9] Of course, SQL tables can contain duplicate rows and thus aren't relations, in general. Please note, therefore, that in this book we always use the term *relation* to mean a relation as such—without duplicate tuples, by definition—and not an SQL-style table. Please note further that—again by definition—relational operations (projection and union in particular) always produce a result without duplicate tuples, as we'll see in Chapter 2.

literature talks about—and SQL products in particular support—the use of what are called "nulls" in attribute positions to indicate that some value is missing for some reason. However, since by definition nulls aren't values, the notion of a "tuple" containing nulls is a contradiction in terms. A "tuple" that contains nulls isn't a tuple!—and a "relation" that contains such a "tuple" isn't a relation. In other words, *relations never contain nulls*. (In fact, we categorically reject the concept of nulls, at least as that concept is usually understood. A detailed justification for this position can be found in reference [37]. See also references [23], [24], [34], and [90], among many others.)

■ If relation *r* has heading *H*, then that relation *r* is of type RELATION *H* (and the name of that type is, precisely, "RELATION *H*"). In fact, RELATION here is a *type generator* (see the subsection "Relation Types Revisited," later in this section), and RELATION *H* is a specific relation type—namely, the type produced by invoking that type generator with heading *H* as argument. And type RELATION *H* is said to have the same heading, degree, and attributes as every relation of that type does.

■ Note carefully that, by definition, a relation is a value (a nonscalar value, of course, with a set of user visible components). Fig. 1.1, for example, shows two such values. For emphasis, we sometimes speak of "relation values" explicitly, but we usually abbreviate that term to simply *relations* (just as we usually abbreviate, e.g., "integer values" to simply *integers*). See Chapter 3 for further discussion of this and related matters. *Note:* All of the remarks in this bullet item apply to tuples also, mutatis mutandis.[10]

■ Finally, if tuple *t* has heading *H*, then that tuple *t* is of type TUPLE *H* (and the name of that type is, precisely, "TUPLE *H*"). In fact, TUPLE here is a type generator (again, see the subsection "Relation Types Revisited"), and TUPLE *H* is a specific tuple type—namely, the type produced by invoking that type generator with heading *H* as argument. And type TUPLE *H* is said to have the same heading, degree, and attributes as every tuple of that type does. *Note:* If tuple *t* has heading *H*, we also say, a trifle informally, that tuple *t* "conforms to" heading *H*. Note that if relation *r* is of type RELATION *H*, then every tuple in *r* is of type TUPLE *H* and thus conforms to heading *H*.

Relation Valued Attributes

To repeat, any type whatsoever—apart from the two exceptions noted in the section "Types" earlier—can be used as the basis for defining attributes of relations. In particular, relation types can be used for this purpose. (So too can tuple types.) Thus, attributes can be *relation valued*,

---

[10] In case you're not familiar with the useful expression *mutatis mutandis*, we offer a brief explanation here. Essentially, it means *with all necessary changes having been made* (and it can save a great deal of writing). In the case at hand, for example, the necessary changes are as follows: In the first sentence, replace "relation" by "tuple"; delete the second sentence; and in what was the third sentence (now the second), replace "relation values" by "tuple values" and *"relations"* by *"tuples."*

meaning we can have relations with attributes whose values are relations in turn. An example of such a relation is shown, in outline, in Fig. 1.2.

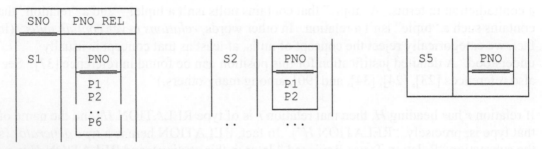

Fig. 1.2: A relation with a relation valued attribute (RVA)

Relations and Their Meaning

Note: The topic of this subsection is of crucial importance. We'll be appealing to it repeatedly in the chapters to come, as you'll quickly discover.

Given a relation *r*, the heading of *r* can be regarded as denoting a certain *predicate*, or in other words a *truth valued function*. Like all functions, that predicate has a set of parameters, and, because it's truth valued, it returns a boolean value—TRUE or FALSE—when it's invoked (i.e., when arguments are substituted for those parameters). The predicate corresponding to relation *r* is the *relation predicate* for *r*. Further, each tuple in the body of *r* can be regarded as denoting a certain proposition (where a *proposition* is a statement that's unconditionally either true or false).[11] The propositions in question represent invocations, or "instantiations," of the relation predicate, obtained from that predicate by using values from the pertinent tuple as arguments to be substituted for the parameters. By way of example, consider the suppliers relation shown in Fig. 1.1. For that relation, the predicate, when expressed in the form of an English sentence, looks something like this:

> *Supplier SNO is under contract, is named SNAME, has status STATUS, and is located in city CITY*

(the parameters here are SNO, SNAME, STATUS, and CITY, corresponding of course to the attributes of the relation). And the corresponding propositions, again when expressed as English sentences, are:

> *Supplier S1 is under contract, is named Smith, has status 20, and is located in city London*

---

[11] Don't make the mistake of thinking that propositions must always be true. For example, *2+2 = 5* is a proposition, but it's a false one.

(obtained by substituting the SNO value S1, the NAME value Smith, the INTEGER value 20, and the CHAR value London for the appropriate parameters);

> *Supplier S2 is under contract, is named Jones, has status 10, and is located in city Paris*

(obtained by substituting the SNO value S2, the NAME value Jones, the INTEGER value 10, and the CHAR value Paris for the appropriate parameters); and so on.

More generally, we can say the predicate corresponding to a given relation is *the intended interpretation*, or *meaning*, for that relation. And the propositions corresponding to tuples appearing in that relation are understood by convention to be ones that evaluate to TRUE. In other words, we subscribe, noncontroversially, to what's called *The Closed World Assumption*. Here's a definition:

> **Definition:** Let relation *r* have predicate *P*. Then ***The Closed World Assumption*** (CWA) says: If tuple *t* appears in *r*, then the instantiation *p* of *P* corresponding to *t* is assumed to be true; conversely, if tuple *t* has the same heading as *r* but doesn't appear in *r*, then the instantiation *p* of *P* corresponding to *t* is assumed to be false. In other words, a tuple appears in relation *r* if and only if it satisfies the predicate for *r*.

To say it another way: If relation *r* has predicate *P*, then the body of *r* contains *all* and *only* those tuples that correspond to instantiations of *P* that evaluate to TRUE.

By the way, it's important to understand that *every* relation has an associated predicate, including in particular relations that are defined in terms of others by means of relational operators such as projection and join (see Chapter 2). For example, suppose we project the suppliers relation shown in Fig. 1.1 over the SNO, SNAME, and STATUS attributes (thereby effectively removing the CITY attribute). Then the predicate for the relation that results looks something like this:

> ***There exists some city CITY such that*** *supplier SNO is under contract, is named SNAME, has status STATUS, and is located in city CITY.*

Observe that (as required) this predicate does have three parameters, not four, corresponding to the three attributes of the relation—CITY is now no longer a parameter but a *bound variable* instead, thanks to the fact that it's *quantified* by the phrase "there exists some city." *Note:* Another and perhaps clearer way of making the same point (i.e., that the predicate has three parameters, not four) is to observe that the predicate as stated is logically equivalent to this one:

> *Supplier SNO is under contract, is named SNAME, has status STATUS, and is located somewhere (i.e., in some unspecified city).*

This version of the predicate very clearly has just three parameters.

Relation Types Revisited

Earlier in this section, we said that if a given relation has heading *H*, then that relation is of type—relation type, that is—RELATION *H*. For example, the type of the suppliers relation from our running example is:

```
RELATION { SNO SNO , SNAME NAME , STATUS INTEGER , CITY CHAR }
```

Of course, no significance attaches to the order in which the attributes happen to be specified within those enclosing braces, because there's no left to right ordering to the attributes of a relation.

Now, there's quite a bit more to be said about relation types in general; first, however, we need to take a closer look at tuple types. Let *t* be a tuple within the suppliers relation. Then *t* is of the following tuple type:

```
TUPLE { SNO SNO , SNAME NAME , STATUS INTEGER , CITY CHAR }
```

(where, again, no significance attaches to the order in which the attributes are specified within the enclosing braces).

Observe now that, in contrast to the user defined scalar types SNO, NAME, and PNO, the foregoing tuple type—let's call it STT—is *not* defined by means of a TYPE statement as such. Rather, the fact that the specified attribute types (SNO, NAME, INTEGER, and CHAR, in the case at hand) all exist is sufficient to ensure that type STT exists as well, albeit implicitly. In fact, *every* tuple type *TT* exists implicitly, just so long as every attribute of that tuple type *TT* is of some type that's known to the system. For definiteness, however, let's concentrate here on tuple type STT specifically:

- Since there's no TYPE statement for that type, there's no associated possible representation ("possrep") either.

- Since there's no possrep for that type, there aren't any associated THE_ operators either.

- However, there *is* an associated selector operator (in fact, *every* type has at least one associated selector). The easiest way to explain what an invocation of such a selector looks like is to show a simple BNF grammar fragment:[12]

---

[12] This grammar fragment contains the first mention in this book of the useful term *commalist*, which we'll be using quite a lot in the pages ahead. It can be defined as follows: Let *xyz* be some syntactic construct (e.g., "component"). Then the term *xyz commalist* denotes a sequence of zero or more *xyz*'s in which (a) each pair of adjacent *xyz*'s is separated by a comma, as well as zero or more spaces before or after the comma or both; (b) the first *xyz* is preceded by zero or more spaces; and (c) the last *xyz* is followed by zero or more spaces.

```
<tuple selector invocation>
    ::=    TUPLE { <component commalist> }

<component>
    ::=    <attribute name> <expression>
```

Here's an example for tuple type STT:

```
TUPLE { SNO SNO ( 'S1' ) , SNAME NAME ( 'Smith' ) ,
                              STATUS 20 , CITY 'London' }
```

This example is actually a tuple *literal* (which is a special case, of course)—it's a literal because all of its component attribute values are specified as literals in turn—and it denotes precisely the tuple for supplier S1 from the suppliers relation as shown in Fig. 1.1. Of course, the order in which the components are specified is irrelevant.

> *Aside:* When we say here that, e.g., the expression SNO ('S1') is a literal, we're making tacit assumptions to the effect that (a) type SNO has a possrep also called—very likely by default—SNO, and further that (b) the possrep in question has a single component, of type CHAR. Similar remarks apply to types NAME and PNO also. *End of aside.*

Here's another example, in which by contrast the component attribute values are mostly not specified as literals:

```
TUPLE { SNO SX , SNAME NMX , STATUS STX + 5 , CITY 'London' }
```

Here, presumably, SX is a variable of type SNO, NMX is a variable of type NAME, and STX is a variable of type INTEGER.

One last point regarding tuple type STT: The fact is, that type—like all tuple types, at least so far as we're concerned—is actually a *generated* type. A generated type is a type that's obtained by invoking some *type generator* (in the example, the type generator is, specifically, TUPLE). You can think of a type generator as a special kind of operator; it's special because (a) it returns a type instead of a value, and (b) it's invoked at compile time instead of run time. For example, most programming languages support a type generator called ARRAY, which lets users define a variety of specific array types. In such a language, for example, the expression

```
ARRAY [ 1..10 ] OF INTEGER
```

might constitute an invocation of that type generator that returns a type consisting of all one-dimensional arrays with integer elements and with lower bound 1 and upper bound 10. In the same kind of way, the expression

```
TUPLE { SNO SNO , SNAME NAME , STATUS INTEGER , CITY CHAR }
```

constitutes an invocation of the TUPLE type generator, and it returns a type consisting of all tuples whose attributes have the specified names and types—in other words, tuple type STT.

Turning now to relation types, almost everything we've been saying regarding tuple types applies to relation types as well, mutatis mutandis. For example, the relation type

```
RELATION { SNO SNO , SNAME NAME , STATUS INTEGER , CITY CHAR }
```

—let's call it SRT—is also not defined by means of a TYPE statement as such. Instead, the fact that the specified attribute types all exist is sufficient to ensure that type SRT exists as well, albeit implicitly. In fact, every relation type *RT* exists implicitly, just so long as every attribute of that relation type *RT* is of some type that's known to the system. For definiteness, however, let's concentrate here on type SRT specifically:

- Since there's no TYPE statement for that type, there's no associated possible representation ("possrep") either.

- Since there's no possrep for that type, there aren't any associated THE_ operators either.

- However, an associated selector operator does exist, and again the easiest way to explain it is by way of a simple BNF grammar fragment:[13]

```
<relation selector invocation>
    ::=    RELATION [ <heading> ] <body>

<heading>
    ::=    { <attribute name commalist> }

<body>
    ::=    { <tuple expression commalist> }
```

Here's an example for relation type SRT:

```
RELATION
    { TUPLE { SNO SNO ( 'S1' ) , SNAME NAME ( 'Smith' ) ,
                                STATUS 20 , CITY 'London' } ,
      TUPLE { SNO SNO ( 'S2' ) , SNAME NAME ( 'Jones' ) ,
                                STATUS 10 , CITY 'Paris'  } ,
      TUPLE { SNO SNO ( 'S3' ) , SNAME NAME ( 'Blake' ) ,
                                STATUS 30 , CITY 'Paris'  } ,
      TUPLE { SNO SNO ( 'S4' ) , SNAME NAME ( 'Clark' ) ,
                                STATUS 20 , CITY 'London' } ,
      TUPLE { SNO SNO ( 'S5' ) , SNAME NAME ( 'Adams' ) ,
                                STATUS 30 , CITY 'Athens' } } ;
```

---

[13] In accordance with usual convention, we use brackets "[" and "]" in BNF grammar fragments, here and throughout this book, to mean the material they enclose is optional (barring explicit statements to the contrary, of course).

This example is actually a relation literal (because the tuples that make up the body are all specified by means of literals in turn), and it denotes precisely the suppliers relation as shown in Fig. 1.1. (Of course, the order in which the tuples are specified is irrelevant. However, those tuples must certainly all be of the same tuple type—type STT, in fact, in the case at hand.) No explicit heading has been specified in this example, because the pertinent heading can obviously be inferred from the body. In fact, an explicit heading need be specified in a relation selector invocation if and only if the associated body is empty.

Providing an example in which the tuples are specified not as literals but as more general expressions is left as an exercise.

Finally, relation type SRT (like all relation types, in fact) is actually a generated type. That is, the expression

```
RELATION { SNO SNO , SNAME NAME , STATUS INTEGER , CITY CHAR }
```

constitutes an invocation of the RELATION type generator, and it returns a type consisting of all relations with the specified heading—in other words, relation type SRT.

EXERCISES

1.1   Explain in your own words the terms *type*, *possible representation*, and *selector*.

1.2   Explain the difference between scalar and nonscalar types.

1.3   What's a literal?

1.4   Write a **Tutorial D** definition for a read-only operator called DOUBLE that takes an integer and doubles it.

1.5   Repeat Exercise 1.4 but make the operator an update operator instead (i.e., the effect of invoking the operator should be to double the value assigned to a specified variable).

1.6   Define the terms *heading*, *attribute*, *body*, *tuple*, *cardinality*, and *degree*. By the way, the following facts are worth bearing in mind:

  a.   Every subset of a heading is a heading.

  b.   Every subset of a body is a body.

  c.   Every subset of a tuple is a tuple.

Aside: The term *subset* and various related terms are often used somewhat imprecisely in informal writing, and we therefore offer some brief (but accurate) definitions here. Let *A* and *B* be sets. Then "*A* is a subset of *B*" (or "*A* is included in *B*"), written $A \subseteq B$, means every element of *A* is also an element of *B*. By contrast, "*A* is a *proper* subset of *B*" (or "*A* is *properly* included in *B*"), written $A \subset B$, means *A* is a subset of *B* but there exists at least one element of *B* that isn't also an element of *A*. So every set is a subset of itself, but no set is a proper subset of itself.

All of the foregoing applies to supersets also, mutatis mutandis. Thus, "*B* is a superset of *A*" (or "*B* includes *A*"), written $B \supseteq A$, means the same as "*A* is a subset of *B*." Similarly, "*B* is a proper superset of *A*" (or "*B* properly includes *A*"), written $B \supset A$, means the same as "*A* is a proper subset of *B*." So every set is a superset of itself, but no set is a proper superset of itself. *End of aside.*

1.7   State as precisely as you can what it means for two tuples *t* and *t'* to be duplicates of each other.

1.8   What's a relation valued attribute?

1.9   Explain the term *relation predicate*.

1.10 Explain *The Closed World Assumption*.

1.11 What's a type generator?

1.12 Give an example of (a) a tuple literal, (b) a relation literal.

ANSWERS

Most of the exercises in this chapter are really just review questions, and answers can be found in the body of the chapter. Here we give answers to Exercises 1.4 and 1.5 only.

1.4
```
OPERATOR DOUBLE ( N INTEGER ) RETURNS INTEGER ;
    RETURN ( 2 * N ) ;
END OPERATOR ;
```

1.5
```
OPERATOR DOUBLE ( N INTEGER ) UPDATES { N } ;
    N := 2 * N ;
END OPERATOR ;
```

Chapter 2

Relational Algebra

In poetry and algebra we have the pure idea
elaborated and expressed through the vehicle of language.
—James Joseph Sylvester (attrib.)

The relational model includes an open ended set of generic read-only operators known collectively as *the relational algebra.*[1] In this chapter, we define the operators we'll be relying on most heavily in the pages to come; we also give a few examples, but only where we think the operators in question might be unfamiliar to you. Each operator takes zero or more relations as its operands and returns another relation as its result.[2] (In case you're wondering, the zero case arises in connection with the so called *n*-adic operators, q.v.) *Note:* The—very important!—fact that the result is another relation is referred to as the relational *closure* property. It's that property that, among other things, allows us to write nested relational expressions.

RENAME

Definition: Let relation *r* have an attribute called *A* and no attribute called *B*. Then the expression *r* RENAME {*A* AS *B*} denotes an (attribute) **renaming** of *r*, and it returns the relation with heading identical to that of *r* except that attribute *A* in that heading is renamed *B*, and body identical to that of *r* except that all references to *A* in that body—more precisely, in tuples in that body—are replaced by references to *B*.

As a matter of user convenience, **Tutorial D** also supports a multiple form of RENAME, which allows several renamings to be done in parallel ("simultaneously"). For example:

```
SP RENAME { SNO AS SNUM , PNO AS PNUM }
```

---

[1] To say the operators are generic means they're available for all possible relations (speaking a trifle loosely)—it's not as if we need, say, one join operator to join suppliers and shipments and a whole different join operator to join employees and departments. And the reason the operators are generic in this sense is precisely that they're associated with the RELATION type generator (they're part of the package, as it were).

[2] Except for the relational comparison operators (discussed in a section of their own toward the end of the chapter), which return a truth value, not a relation.

RESTRICT

Definition: Let *r* be a relation and let *bx* be a restriction condition on *r* (i.e., a boolean expression in which every attribute reference identifies some attribute of *r* and there are no references to any other relation). Then the expression *r* WHERE *bx* denotes the **restriction** of *r* according to *bx*, and it returns the relation with heading the same as that of *r* and body consisting of all tuples of *r* for which *bx* evaluates to TRUE.

As a matter of user convenience, real languages (including both **Tutorial D** and SQL in particular) typically allow WHERE conditions to be more general than simple restriction conditions as defined above. An example appears in the section "EXTEND *bis*" later in this chapter, and another appears in the section "Relational Comparisons."

PROJECT

Definition: Let {*A1*, *A2*, ..., *An*} be a subset of the heading of relation *r*. Then the expression *r*{*A1,A2,...,An*} denotes the **projection** of *r* on {*A1*, *A2*, ..., *An*}, and it returns the relation with heading {*A1,A2,...,An*} and body consisting of all tuples *t* such that there exists a tuple in *r* that has the same values for attributes *A1*, *A2*, ..., *An* as *t* does.

As a matter of user convenience, **Tutorial D** allows projection operations to be expressed in terms of the attributes to be removed instead of the ones to be retained. For example, the following **Tutorial D** expressions are logically equivalent:

```
S { SNO , SNAME , CITY }
S { ALL BUT STATUS }
```

Note: **Tutorial D** supports this ALL BUT syntax not just for projection but all throughout the language—essentially wherever it makes sense to do so.

Aside: Actually, the definition given above for projection isn't quite as precise as it might be. If {*A1,A2,...,An*} is, as stated, a subset of the heading of relation *r*, then by definition each of those *Ai*'s is an attribute name : type name pair. But in the projection expression *r*{*A1,A2,...,An*}, each of those *Ai*'s is just an attribute name. (The syntax works because attribute names are unique within the pertinent heading.) And then, when we say {*A1,A2,...,An*} is the heading of the result of the projection, each of those *Ai*'s is supposed to denote an attribute name : type name pair once again. So there's a kind of punning going on here—the very same symbol *Ai* is being used to denote different things in different contexts.

Similar remarks apply elsewhere in this chapter, and indeed throughout this book. Also—generalizing from such remarks—please note that the term *attribute* must sometimes be understood as meaning an attribute name rather than an attribute as such, and the term *heading* must sometimes be understood as meaning a set of attribute names rather than a set of attributes as such. Apologies if you find this state of affairs confusing, but in fact it's pretty standard practice. *End of aside.*

UNION, INTERSECT, AND MINUS

Let relations *r1* and *r2* be of the same type *T*. Then:

Definition: The expression *r1* UNION *r2* denotes the **union** of *r1* and *r2*, and it returns the relation of type *T* with body the set of all tuples *t* such that *t* appears in *r1* or *r2* or both.

Definition: The expression *r1* INTERSECT *r2* denotes the **intersection** of *r1* and *r2*, and it returns the relation of type *T* with body the set of all tuples *t* such that *t* appears in both *r1* and *r2*.

Definition: The expression *r1* MINUS *r2* denotes the **difference** between *r1* and *r2* (in that order), and it returns the relation of type *T* with body the set of all tuples *t* such that *t* appears in *r1* and not in *r2*.

Example: The following **Tutorial D** expression represents the natural language query "Get supplier numbers for suppliers currently unable to supply any parts at all":[3]

```
S { SNO } MINUS SP { SNO }
```

Suppose, however, that the supplier number attribute in SP were called SNUM instead of SNO. Then the projections S{SNO} and SP{SNUM} would be of different types. In order to be able to form the required difference, therefore, we'd have to rename at least one of those supplier number attributes first—e.g., as follows:

```
S { SNO } MINUS ( SP RENAME { SNUM AS SNO } ) { SNO }
```

Some Formal Properties

Union is commutative, associative, and idempotent. *Commutative* here means *r1* UNION *r2* and *r2* UNION *r1* are equivalent (this property follows immediately from the fact that the operator

---

[3]We choose not to get into details in this book of **Tutorial D** operator precedence rules in general. As this example suggests, however, we do find it convenient to assign high precedence to the projection operator in particular.

definition is symmetric in *r1* and *r2*). *Associative* means *r1* UNION (*r2* UNION *r3*) and (*r1* UNION *r2*) UNION *r3* are equivalent, so the parentheses aren't needed and both of these expressions can be simplified to just *r1* UNION *r2* UNION *r3*. *Idempotent* means *r* UNION *r* reduces to simply *r*.

The foregoing paragraph applies to intersection also, mutatis mutandis; that is, intersection too is commutative, associative, and idempotent. However, it doesn't apply to difference, for which none of the three properties holds.

Note: Partly because UNION and INTERSECT do enjoy the foregoing formal properties, it turns out to be possible, and desirable, to define *n*-adic versions of those operators. To be specific, let relations *r1*, *r2*, ..., *rn* ($n \geq 0$) all be of the same type *T*. Then:

Definition: The expression UNION {*r1*,*r2*,...,*rn*} denotes the **union** of *r1*, *r2*, ..., *rn*, and it returns the relation of type *T* with body the set of all tuples *t* such that *t* appears in at least one of *r1*, *r2*, ..., *rn*. *Note:* If *n* = 0, then (a) some syntactic mechanism, not shown here, is needed to specify the pertinent type *T*, and (b) the result is the empty relation of that type (i.e., the unique relation of type *T* whose body contains no tuples at all).

Definition: The expression INTERSECT {*r1*,*r2*,...,*rn*} denotes the **intersection** of *r1*, *r2*, ..., *rn*, and it returns the relation of type *T* with body the set of all tuples *t* such that *t* appears in each of *r1*, *r2*, ..., *rn*. *Note:* If *n* = 0, then (a) some syntactic mechanism, not shown here, is needed to specify the pertinent type *T*, and (b) the result is the universal relation of that type (i.e., the unique relation of type *T* whose body contains all possible tuples of type TUPLE *H*, where *H* is the heading of type *T*).

D_UNION and I_MINUS

D_UNION ("disjoint union") and I_MINUS ("included minus") are variants on the regular UNION and MINUS operators that can be useful on occasion (especially in connection with update operations—see Chapter 3). Let relations *r1* and *r2* be of the same type. Then:

Definition: If *r1* and *r2* have any tuples in common, then the expression *r1* D_UNION *r2* is undefined; otherwise it denotes the **disjoint union** of *r1* and *r2*, and it reduces to *r1* UNION *r2*. *Note:* An *n*-adic version of D_UNION can be defined too, but we omit the details here, since they're essentially obvious.

Definition: If some tuple appears in *r2* and not in *r1*, then the expression *r1* I_MINUS *r2* is undefined; otherwise it denotes the **included difference** between *r1* and *r2* (in that order), and it reduces to *r1* MINUS *r2*.

JOIN

Before we define JOIN as such, it's helpful to introduce the concept of *joinability*. Briefly, relations *r1* and *r2* are *joinable* if and only if attributes with the same name are of the same type, meaning, formally speaking, that they're the very same attribute.[4] So let relations *r1* and *r2* be joinable. Then:

> **Definition:** The expression *r1* JOIN *r2* denotes the **join** of *r1* and *r2*, and it returns the relation with heading the set theory union of the headings of *r1* and *r2* and body the set of all tuples *t* such that *t* is the set theory union of a tuple of *r1* and a tuple of *r2*.

Cartesian Product

It's easy to see that cartesian product (product for short) is a special case of join, but we give the definition for completeness:

> **Definition:** If relations *r1* and *r2* have any attribute names in common, then the expression *r1* TIMES *r2* is undefined; otherwise, it denotes the **product** of *r1* and *r2*, and it reduces to *r1* JOIN *r2*.

Tutorial D does support TIMES, but it does so mainly for psychological reasons. For simplicity, therefore, we'll ignore it in what follows, except for the occasional remark here and there.

Intersection Revisited

It's easy to see that intersection too is a special case of join; to be specific, *r1* JOIN *r2* is equivalent to *r1* INTERSECT *r2* if and only if *r1* and *r2* are of the same type. In fact, INTERSECT, like TIMES, is supported in **Tutorial D** mainly for psychological reasons. In this case, however, the benefits of explicit support are perhaps more obvious, and (partly for such reasons) we'll definitely have more to say about INTERSECT as such in later chapters.

Formal Properties

Like union and intersection, join is commutative, associative, and idempotent. Thus, *r1* JOIN *r2* and *r2* JOIN *r1* are equivalent; *r1* JOIN (*r2* JOIN *r3*) and (*r1* JOIN *r2*) JOIN *r3* are also equivalent, so the parentheses aren't needed and both of these expressions can be simplified to

---

[4] Two points here: First, the notion of joinability, despite the name, is applicable in various other contexts in addition to join as such, as we'll soon see. (Also, note that another way to define it is: Relations *r1* and *r2* are joinable if and only if the set theory union of their headings is a valid heading.) Second, the notion readily extends to any number of relations, thus: Relations *r1, r2, ..., rn* ($n \geq 0$) are joinable if and only if, for all *i* and *j*, relations *ri* and *rj* are joinable ($1 \leq i \leq n, 1 \leq j \leq n$).

just *r1* JOIN *r2* JOIN *r3*; and *r* JOIN *r* reduces to simply *r*. And it's possible, and desirable, to define an *n*-adic version of the operator. To be specific, let relations *r1*, *r2*, ..., *rn* ($n \geq 0$) be joinable. Then:

> **Definition:** The expression JOIN {*r1,r2,...,rn*} denotes the **join** of *r1*, *r2*, ..., *rn*, and it's defined as follows: If $n = 0$, the result is TABLE_DEE;[5] if $n = 1$, the result is *r1*; otherwise, choose any two distinct relations *ri* and *rj* from *r1*, *r2*, ..., *rn* and replace them by their join *ri* JOIN *rj*, and repeat this process until there's just one relation *r* left, which is the final result.

MATCHING AND NOT MATCHING

Let relations *r1* and *r2* be joinable. Then:

> **Definition:** The expression *r1* MATCHING *r2* denotes the **semijoin** of *r1* with *r2* (in that order), and it returns the projection of *r1* JOIN *r2* on all of the attributes of *r1*.

> **Definition:** The expression *r1* NOT MATCHING *r2* denotes the **semidifference** between *r1* and *r2* (in that order), and it returns the relation denoted by the expression *r1* MINUS (*r1* MATCHING *r2*).

> *Note:* If *r1* and *r2* aren't just joinable but are in fact of the same type, then *r1* NOT MATCHING *r2* reduces to *r1* MINUS *r2*. In other words, regular difference is a special case of semidifference.

EXTEND

EXTEND comes in two forms. Here's a definition of the first:

> **Definition:** Let relation *r* not have an attribute called *A*. Then the expression EXTEND *r* : {*A* := *exp*} denotes an **extension** of *r*, and it returns the relation with heading the heading of *r* extended with attribute *A* and body the set of all tuples *t* such that *t* is a tuple of *r* extended with a value for *A* that's computed by evaluating the expression *exp* on that tuple of *r*.

Here's a simple example (the query is "For each supplier, get full supplier information, together with a TRIPLE value that's equal to three times the supplier's status"):

---

[5] Just to remind you, TABLE_DEE is the unique relation of degree zero and cardinality one (see Chapter 1).

```
EXTEND S : { TRIPLE := 3 * STATUS }
```

Here's the result:

SNO	SNAME	STATUS	CITY	TRIPLE
S1	Smith	20	London	60
S2	Jones	10	Paris	30
S3	Blake	30	Paris	90
S4	Clark	20	London	60
S5	Adams	30	Athens	90

The second form of EXTEND differs from the first only in that the target attribute, in the attribute assignment in braces, isn't a "new" attribute as it is in the first form—instead, it's an attribute that already exists in the relation that's being extended. For example:

```
EXTEND S : { STATUS := 3 * STATUS }
```

Here's the result:

SNO	SNAME	STATUS	CITY
S1	Smith	60	London
S2	Jones	30	Paris
S3	Blake	90	Paris
S4	Clark	60	London
S5	Adams	90	Athens

For completeness, here's the definition:

Definition: Let relation r have an attribute called A. Then the expression EXTEND r : $\{A := exp\}$ denotes an **extension** of r, and it returns the relation with heading the same as that of r and body the set of all tuples t such that t is derived from a tuple of r by replacing the value of A by a value that's computed by evaluating the expression exp on that tuple of r.[6]

---

[6] This second form of EXTEND is sometimes referred to as the "what if" form, because it can be used to explore what happens if certain changes are made to the database without actually having to make (and subsequently unmake, possibly) the changes in question. Note, however, that in this case the input relation isn't exactly being "extended" in the usual sense, and it might be nice to find a better keyword than EXTEND for the purpose. But we'll stay with EXTEND in this book.

As a matter of user convenience, **Tutorial D** also supports a multiple form of EXTEND, which allows several attribute assignments to be done in parallel ("simultaneously"). For example:

```
EXTEND S : { TRIPLE := 3 * STATUS ,
             STATUS := STATUS + 5 ,
             CITY := 'Oslo' }
```

Here's the result:

SNO	SNAME	STATUS	CITY	TRIPLE
S1	Smith	25	Oslo	60
S2	Jones	15	Oslo	30
S3	Blake	35	Oslo	90
S4	Clark	25	Oslo	60
S5	Adams	35	Oslo	90

IMAGE RELATIONS

An image relation is, loosely, the "image" within some relation *r* of some tuple (usually but not necessarily a tuple within some distinct relation *r'*). For example, given our usual suppliers-and-shipments database, the following is the image within the shipments relation of the tuple in the suppliers relation for supplier S4:

PNO
P2
P4
P5

Clearly, this particular image relation can be obtained by evaluating the following expression (a projection of a restriction):

```
( SP WHERE SNO = SNO ( 'S4' ) ) { PNO }
```

But image relations in general are such a useful and widely applicable concept that it's desirable to define a shorthand for them, and so we do. Here's an example to illustrate:

```
EXTEND S : { PNO_REL := !!SP }
```

In this expression, the subexpression !!SP—pronounced "bang bang SP" or "double bang SP"—is an *image relation reference*, and it denotes the image relation within SP corresponding to "the current tuple" of S (i.e., it denotes that restriction of SP having the same values for common attributes as that current tuple, projected over all but those common attributes).[7] Thus, the foregoing expression is evaluated as follows:

- The expression overall (EXTEND S ...) denotes a certain extension of the suppliers relation. You can imagine that extension being done a tuple at a time in some arbitrary sequence. Consider one such tuple, say the tuple for supplier S*x*. For that tuple, then, the expression !!SP denotes the corresponding image relation within the shipments relation. For example, if S*x* is S4, it denotes the relation shown at the beginning of this section.

- So the new attribute PNO_REL is relation valued—recall from Chapter 1 that relation valued attributes are certainly legal—and the value for that attribute for supplier S*x* is precisely the corresponding image relation.

Here's the overall result (in outline):

SNO	SNAME	STATUS	CITY	PNO_REL
S1	Smith	20	London	PNO P1 P2 .. P6
..	.....	..	......	..
S5	Adams	30	Athens	PNO

GROUP AND UNGROUP

To repeat, relation valued attributes (RVAs for short) are certainly legal. So consider Fig. 2.1, which shows (a) a relation *r1* without any RVAs—it's a simplified version of our usual shipments relation—and (b) another relation *r2* that does have an RVA. Observe that relations *r1* and *r2* are clearly not the same as one another but that, equally clearly, they do both represent the same information.

---

[7] For a more formal and precise definition, see reference [40].

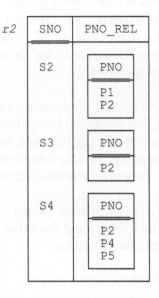

Fig. 2.1: Relations *r1* and *r2* represent the same information

Here are the corresponding predicates:

r1:   *Supplier SNO is able to supply part PNO.*

r2:   *Supplier SNO is able to supply part p, if and only if p appears as a PNO value in some tuple in the body of relation PNO_REL.*[8]

And here for the record are the corresponding types:

r1:   RELATION { SNO SNO , PNO PNO }

r2:   RELATION { SNO SNO , PNO_REL RELATION { PNO PNO } }

Now, we obviously need a way to map between relations without RVAs (like *r1*) and corresponding relations with them (like *r2*), and that's the purpose of the GROUP and UNGROUP operators. For example, given relations *r1* and *r2* from Fig. 2.1, the expression

        r1 GROUP { PNO } AS PNO_REL

---

[8] The fact that the predicate for *r2* is rather more complicated than that for *r1* gives some idea as to why RVAs are usually contraindicated. However, they do have their uses, as we'll see in Chapter 9 in particular.

effectively maps *r1* to *r2*; likewise, the expression

```
r2 UNGROUP PNO_REL
```

effectively maps *r2* to *r1*.

In order to define the GROUP and UNGROUP operators more formally, it's convenient first to introduce two auxiliary operators called WRAP and UNWRAP. Basically, WRAP wraps up specified attributes of a given relation into a single attribute that's tuple valued, and UNWRAP does the opposite. For example, given relation *r1* from Fig. 2.1, the expression

```
r1 WRAP { PNO } AS PNO_TUP
```

produces the relation *r3* shown in Fig. 2.2, and then the expression

```
r3 UNWRAP PNO_TUP
```

produces relation *r1* again. (Please note that the PNO_TUP values in relation *r3* are tuples, not relations—PNO_TUP is a tuple valued attribute, not a relation valued attribute.)

Fig. 2.2: Relation *r3* = *r1* WRAP {PNO} AS PNO_TUP

Here now are definitions of these various operators. *Note:* We give these definitions mainly for completeness; they might be a little difficult to understand, at least on a first reading.

Definition: Let relation *r* have attributes called *A1, A2, ..., Am, B1, B2, ..., Bn* (only), and let *BT* be an attribute name that's distinct from that of every attribute *Ai* ($1 \leq i \leq m$). Then the expression *r* WRAP {*B1,B2,...,Bn*} AS *BT* denotes the **wrapping** of *r* on

{*B1,B2,...,Bn*}, and it returns the relation denoted by the expression (EXTEND *r* : {*BT* := TUPLE {*B1 B1, B2 B2, ..., Bn Bn*}}){*A1,A2,...,Am,BT*}.

Definition: Let relation *r* have attributes called *A1, A2, ..., Am,* and *BT* (only), and let attribute *BT* be tuple valued and have attributes called *B1, B2, ..., Bn* (only); further, let no *Ai* have the same name as any *Bj* ($1 \le i \le m$, $1 \le j \le n$). Then the expression *r* UNWRAP *BT* denotes the **unwrapping** of *r* on *BT*, and it returns the relation denoted by the expression (EXTEND *r* : {*B1* := *B1* FROM *BT*, *B2* := *B2* FROM *BT*, ..., *Bn* := *Bn* FROM *BT*}){ALL BUT *BT*}.

Note: This latter definition makes use of expressions of the form *X* FROM *tx*, where *X* is an attribute name and *tx* is a tuple expression. Such an expression is, of course, defined to return the value of attribute *X* from the tuple denoted by *tx*.[9]

Definition: Let the heading of relation *r* be partitioned into subsets *A* = {*A1,A2,...,Am*} and *B* = {*B1,B2 ...,Bn*}; also, let *BR* be an attribute name that's distinct from that of every attribute *Ai* ($1 \le i \le m$). Then the expression *r* GROUP {*B1,B2,...,Bn*} AS *BR* denotes the **grouping** of *r* on {*B1,B2,...,Bn*}, and it returns a relation *s* with heading{*A1,A2,...,Am,BR*}, where *BR* is a relation valued attribute with heading {*B1,B2,...,Bn*}. The body of *s* is defined as follows. Let *x* be the result of *r* WRAP {*B1,B2,...,Bn*} AS *BT*. For each distinct *A* value *a* in *x*, let *br* be the relation whose tuples are all and only those *BT* values from tuples in *x* in which the *A* value is *a*; let *t* be a tuple with heading { *A1,A2,...,Am,BR* } with *A* value *a* and *BR* value *br*; then, and only then, *t* is a tuple of *s*.

Definition: Let relation *s* have a relation valued attribute *BR* with heading {*B1,B2,...,Bn*}, and let *A* = {*A1,A2,...,Am*} be all of the attributes of *s* other than *BR*; also, let no *Ai* have the same name as any *Bj* ($1 \le i \le m$, $1 \le j \le n$). Then the expression *s* UNGROUP *BR* denotes the **ungrouping** of *s* on *BR*, and it returns a relation *r* with heading {*A1,A2,...,Am, B1,B2,...,Bn*}. The body of *r* is defined as follows. Let *x* be a relation with heading {*A1,A2,...,Am,BT*}, where *BT* is a tuple valued attribute with heading {*B1,B2,...,Bn*}, and body defined as follows: For each tuple of *s*, *x* contains one tuple (*t*, say) for each tuple in the *BR* value in that *s* tuple; each such tuple *t* contains an *A* value equal to the *A* value from the *s* tuple in question and a *BT* value equal to some tuple from the *BR* value in the *s* tuple in question. Let *x* contain no other tuples. Then *r* is the result of *x* UNWRAP *BT*.

Note, incidentally, that given some relation *r* and some grouping of *r*, there's always an inverse ungrouping that yields *r* again; however, the converse isn't necessarily so. The following example illustrates the point. Consider the relation—call it *r1*—shown on the left in Fig. 2.3,

---

[9] And here's as good a place as any to mention the operator TUPLE FROM *rx*, which returns the sole tuple from the relation— which must be of cardinality one—denoted by the relational expression *rx*.

and note in particular that the PNO_REL value in that relation for supplier S2 is empty. The expression *r1* UNGROUP PNO_REL yields the relation *r2* shown in the middle of the figure. And the expression *r2* GROUP {PNO} AS PNO_REL then yields the relation *r3* shown on the right, which is obviously not the same as the original relation *r1*.

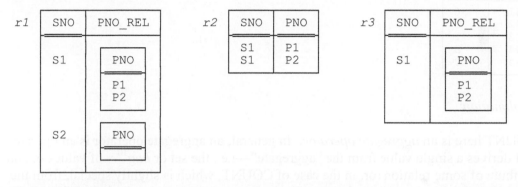

Fig. 2.3: UNGROUP and GROUP aren't necessarily inverses

Note: Refer again to Fig. 2.1. Here again is the expression that derives relation *r2* from relation *r1*:

```
r1 GROUP { PNO } AS PNO_REL
```

As you might have realized, the following expression will produce exactly the same result:

```
EXTEND r1 { SNO } : { PNO_REL := !!r1 }
```

Indeed, as this example suggests, GROUP can actually be defined in terms of EXTEND and image relations. What's more, the same goes for UNGROUP as well. We choose not to show those definitions here, but you can find them if you're interested in reference [46]. Of course, we're not suggesting we get rid of our useful GROUP and UNGROUP operators—but it's at least interesting, and perhaps pedagogically helpful, to note that the semantics of GROUP and UNGROUP can in fact be explained in such a manner.

EXTEND *bis*

EXTEND and image relations can be used together to perform *summarizations*. Here's an example (the query is "For each supplier, get the supplier number and a count of the number of parts that supplier supplies"):

```
EXTEND S { SNO } : { PCT := COUNT ( !!SP ) }
```

Here's the result:

SNO	PCT
S1	6
S2	2
S3	1
S4	3
S5	0

Explanation:

- COUNT here is an *aggregate operator*. In general, an aggregate operator is an operator that derives a single value from the "aggregate"—i.e., the set or *bag*[10]—of values of some attribute of some relation (or, in the case of COUNT, which is slightly special, from the "aggregate" that's the entire relation). Typical aggregate operators include COUNT, SUM, AVG, MAX, MIN, AND, and OR (where SUM and AVG apply only to aggregates of numeric values; MAX and MIN apply only to aggregates of values for which the operators ">" and "<" are defined; and AND and OR apply only to aggregates of boolean values).

- As already indicated, the expression overall in the example—i.e., the EXTEND invocation—denotes a certain summarization. Loosely, to perform a summarization on some given relation *r* means, for each tuple of *r*, (a) to identify some corresponding image relation, and then (b) to perform some aggregation over that image relation—which is, of course, exactly what we did in the example.

Here's another example (note the syntax of the AVG invocation in particular):

```
EXTEND S { CITY } : { AVT := AVG ( !!S , STATUS ) }
```

Result:

CITY	AVT
London	20
Paris	20
Athens	30

---

[10] A *bag*, also known as a *multiset*, is like a set but permits duplicates.

Tutorial D also allows aggregate operator invocations to appear in WHERE conditions, as in the following example (the query is "Get suppliers able to supply two or more distinct parts"):

```
S WHERE COUNT ( !!SP ) > 1
```

Note: This expression isn't a proper relational restriction as such because the boolean expression (i.e., the WHERE condition) isn't a restriction condition as such. However, the expression overall can be regarded as shorthand for the following:

```
( ( EXTEND S : { x := COUNT ( !!SP ) } WHERE x > 1 ) { ALL BUT x }
```

And the boolean expression (i.e., the WHERE condition) in this latter formulation *is* a proper restriction condition, of course.

RELATIONAL COMPARISONS

As noted in Chapter 1, the "=" comparison operator is—in fact, must be—defined for every type, and relation types are no exception to this rule. That is, given two relations *r1* and *r2* of the same type *T*, we must certainly be able to test whether they're equal. For example:

```
S { SNO } = SP { SNO }
```

The left comparand here is the projection of suppliers on SNO, the right comparand is the projection of shipments on SNO, and the comparison gives TRUE if these two projections are equal, FALSE otherwise. (Given our usual sample values, it gives FALSE, of course.)

The comparison operators "≠", "⊆" (is included in), "⊂" (is properly included in), "⊇" (includes), and "⊃" (properly includes) should obviously all be supported as well. Here's another example, illustrating the use of "⊃":

```
S { SNO } ⊃ SP { SNO }
```

The meaning of this expression, considerably paraphrased, is: "Some suppliers supply no parts at all" (which, please note, does necessarily evaluate to either TRUE or FALSE).

Aside: There's a tiny technical issue here that might be bothering you. The operators of the relational algebra are supposed to form a closed system, in the sense that the result of every such operator is supposed to be a relation. But the result of the relational comparison operators is, of course, not a relation but a truth value. Thus, it's not clear that these operators should be considered part of the algebra as such (writers differ on this issue). However, the important point as far as we're concerned is simply that the operators are certainly available, regardless of whether we consider them part of the algebra as such. *End of aside*.

Here now is an example of the use of a relational comparison in formulating a fairly complicated (but realistic) query:

```
S WHERE ( !!SP ) { PNO } ⊇ ( SP WHERE SNO = SNO ( 'S2' ) ) { PNO }
```

The query is "Get supplier information for suppliers who supply all parts supplied by supplier S2."

One very common requirement is to be able to perform an "=" comparison between some given relation r and the corresponding empty relation (i.e., the unique empty relation of the same type as r)—in other words, a test to see whether r is empty. So we define a shorthand:

```
IS_EMPTY ( r )
```

This expression is defined to return TRUE if r is empty and FALSE otherwise. It can be regarded as shorthand for the following:

```
r = ( r WHERE FALSE )
```

(It's also equivalent to $r\{\ \} = $ TABLE_DUM.) The inverse operator is useful too:

```
IS_NOT_EMPTY ( r )
```

This expression is equivalent to NOT (IS_EMPTY(r)), or $r\{\ \} = $ TABLE_DEE.

FORMULATING EXPRESSIONS ONE STEP AT A TIME

Consider the following expression (the query is "Get pairs of supplier numbers such that the suppliers concerned are in the same city"):

```
( ( ( S RENAME { SNO AS XNO } ) { XNO , CITY } JOIN
    ( S RENAME { SNO AS YNO } ) { YNO , CITY } )
                                WHERE XNO < YNO ) { XNO , YNO }
```

The result has two "supplier number" attributes, called XNO and YNO. *Note:* The purpose of the condition XNO < YNO is twofold—it eliminates pairs of supplier numbers of the form (x,x), and it guarantees that the pairs (x,y) and (y,x) won't both appear. Of course, we're assuming here that the operator "<" has been defined in connection with type SNO.

We now show another formulation of the query in order to show how **Tutorial D**'s WITH construct can be used to simplify the business of formulating what might otherwise be considered rather complicated expressions:

```
WITH ( t1 := ( S RENAME { SNO AS XNO } ) { XNO , CITY } ,
       t2 := ( S RENAME { SNO AS YNO } ) { YNO , CITY } ,
       t3 := t1 JOIN t2 ,
       t4 := t3 WHERE XNO < YNO ) :
t4 { XNO , YNO }
```

WITH isn't an operator as such, it's just a syntactic device that lets us introduce names for subexpressions and thereby lets us see the trees as well as the forest (as it were). As the example suggests, a WITH specification consists of the keyword WITH followed by a parenthesized commalist of assignments of the form *name := expression*, that parenthesized commalist then being followed by a colon. For each such assignment, the specified expression is evaluated and the result is effectively assigned to a temporary variable with the specified name. Also, since the assignments are effectively performed in sequence as written, any given assignment is allowed to refer to names introduced earlier within the same commalist.

Note: **Tutorial D** allows WITH specifications on statements as well as on expressions. Here's a simple example (the statement here is a relational assignment statement—see Chapter 3 for further explanation):

```
WITH ( X := RELATION { TUPLE { SNO SNO ( 'S5' ) ,
                               PNO PNO ( 'P6' ) } } ) :
SP := SP UNION X ;
```

RELATIONAL COMPLETENESS

We began this chapter by saying the set of algebraic operators was open ended. That's true, but what we didn't say was that the operators in question, taken together, are supposed to be at least *relationally complete* [22]. Relational completeness is a basic measure of the expressive capability of a language. If a language is relationally complete, then it means—speaking *very* loosely, please note!—that queries of arbitrary complexity can be formulated in that language without having to resort to branching or iterative loops. And in order to be relationally complete, it's sufficient that the language in question support, directly or indirectly, all of the following operators: restriction, projection, JOIN, UNION, NOT MATCHING, and EXTEND (first version), together with the relational inclusion operator "⊆".

EXERCISES

2.1   Write algebraic expressions for the following queries:

a.   Get all shipments.

b.   Get supplier numbers for suppliers able to supply part P1.

c.   Get part numbers for parts capable of being supplied by a supplier in London.

d.   Get part numbers for parts capable of being supplied, but not by a supplier in London.

e.   Get part numbers for parts capable of being supplied by either a supplier in London or a supplier in Paris or both.

f.   Get pairs of part numbers such that some supplier is able to supply both of the indicated parts.

g.   For each supplier in Paris, get the supplier number and the total number of parts capable of being supplied by the supplier in question.

h.   Get supplier numbers for suppliers with a status lower than that of supplier S1.

i.   Get supplier numbers for suppliers whose city is first in the alphabetic list of such cities.

j.   Get part numbers for parts capable of being supplied by all suppliers in London.

k.   Get supplier number / part number pairs such that the indicated supplier is unable to supply the indicated part.

l.   Get pairs of supplier numbers for suppliers who are able to supply exactly the same set of parts each.

2.2   Consider the following definitions for the relvars in a courses-and-students database:[11]

```
VAR COURSE BASE RELATION
  { COURSENO    COURSENO ,
    CNAME       NAME ,
    AVAILABLE   DATE }
  KEY { COURSENO } ;
```

---

[11] Note that many exercises in subsequent chapters make use of this database or some variant thereof.

```
VAR STUDENT BASE RELATION
  { STUDENTNO   STUDENTNO ,
    SNAME       NAME ,
    REGISTERED DATE }
  KEY { STUDENTNO } ;

VAR ENROLLMENT BASE RELATION
  { COURSENO   COURSENO ,
    STUDENTNO STUDENTNO ,
    ENROLLED   DATE }
  KEY { COURSENO , STUDENTNO }
  FOREIGN KEY { COURSENO } REFERENCES COURSE
  FOREIGN KEY { STUDENTNO } REFERENCES STUDENT ;
```

Types COURSENO and STUDENTNO are user defined, type DATE is built in. You can assume these types each have an associated selector operator with the same name, each one taking a single argument of type CHAR and returning a value of the appropriate type. The predicates for the relvars are as follows:

- COURSE: *Course COURSENO, named CNAME, became available at the university on date AVAILABLE.*

- STUDENT: *Student STUDENTNO, named SNAME, registered with the university on date REGISTERED.*

- ENROLLMENT: *Student STUDENTNO enrolled on course COURSENO on date ENROLLED.*

a. Write a query to get student number and name for students who are enrolled on all the courses student ST2 is enrolled on.

b. Consider the following expression:

```
( ( STUDENT WHERE STUDENTNO = STUDENTNO ( 'ST1' ) ) JOIN COURSE )
                                        WHERE AVAILABLE > REGISTERED
```

Write a predicate for the relation denoted by this expression.

ANSWERS

2.1 The following solutions aren't the only ones possible. *Note:* This remark applies to many of the solutions provided in this book; we won't bother to keep repeating it, however, letting this one disclaimer do duty for all.

a. SP

b. (SP WHERE PNO = PNO ('P1')) { SNO }

c. (SP MATCHING (S WHERE CITY = 'London')){ PNO }

d. (SP NOT MATCHING (S WHERE CITY = 'London')) { PNO }

e. (SP MATCHING (S WHERE CITY = 'London' OR CITY = 'Paris')) { PNO }

f. (JOIN { SP RENAME { PNO AS XNO } , SP RENAME { PNO AS YNO } })
                                               { XNO , YNO }

g. EXTEND (S WHERE CITY = 'Paris') { SNO } : { PCT := COUNT (!!SP) }

h. (S WHERE STATUS < STATUS FROM (TUPLE FROM
                            (S WHERE SNO = SNO ('S1')))) { SNO }

i. (S WHERE CITY = MIN (S , CITY)) { SNO }

j. (P WHERE !!SP { SNO } ⊇ (S WHERE CITY = 'London') { SNO }) { PNO }

k. (S { SNO } JOIN SP { PNO }) MINUS SP

l. ((((SP GROUP { PNO } AS X }) RENAME { SNO AS XNO }) JOIN
        ((SP GROUP { PNO } AS X }) RENAME { SNO AS YNO })))
                                               { XNO , YNO }

2.2

a. (STUDENT WHERE (!!ENROLLMENT) { COURSENO } ⊇
        (ENROLLMENT WHERE STUDENTNO = STUDENTNO ('ST2')) { COURSENO })
                                               { STUDENTNO , SNAME }

b. Predicate: *Student STUDENTNO has student number ST1, is named SNAME, and registered on date REGISTERED; course COURSENO is named CNAME and became available on date AVAILABLE; and AVAILABLE is more recent than REGISTERED.*

Note: What this exercise illustrates is the following. Recall from Chapter 1 that every relation does have a predicate. Well, the predicate for the relation denoted by some operational expression can be obtained from the predicates for the operands (relations) involved in that expression, together with the semantics of the operators involved in that expression. For example, if relations *r1* and *r2* have predicates *p1* and *p2*, respectively, then the relation denoted by *r1* JOIN *r2* has predicate *p1* AND *p2*. For further discussion of such matters, see, e.g., reference [28].

Chapter 3

Relation Variables

A golden key can open any door.

—late 16th century proverb

It's an unfortunate fact that the term *relation* has long been used in the database literature—indeed, it still is used—to mean two quite different things. To be specific, it's used to mean both a relation *value* and a relation *variable*. But there's a clear logical difference here! What's more, certain properties commonly thought of as properties of relation values—e.g., the property of having keys, and the property of possibly having foreign keys, and most especially the property of being updatable—are more correctly seen as properties of relation variables instead. This chapter elaborates on such matters.

RELATIONS vs. RELVARS

Consider the suppliers-and-shipments database from Fig. 1.1 once again. Now, what that figure clearly shows is two relation values: namely, the relation values that happen to appear in the database at some particular time. But, of course, if we were to look at the database at some different time, then we would probably see two different relation values. In other words, the objects referred to as S and SP in that figure are really variables: *relation* variables, to be precise, or in other words variables whose permitted values are relation values (different relation values at different times). For example, suppose relation variable S currently has the value shown in Fig. 1.1, and suppose we now delete the tuples for suppliers in Paris:

```
DELETE S WHERE CITY = 'Paris' ;
```

Here's the result:

SNO	SNAME	STATUS	CITY
S1	Smith	20	London
S4	Clark	20	London
S5	Adams	30	Athens

Conceptually, what's happened here is that the old relation value of S has been replaced en bloc by an entirely new relation value. Of course, the old value (with five tuples) and the new one (with three) are somewhat similar, but they certainly are different values. Indeed, the DELETE operation just shown is basically shorthand for the following *relational assignment*:

```
S := S MINUS ( S WHERE CITY = 'Paris' ) ;
```

As in all assignments, what's going on here, conceptually speaking, is that (a) the *source expression* on the right side is evaluated, and (b) the result of that evaluation is then assigned to the *target variable* on the left side.[1] Thus, the net effect is, as already stated, to replace the "old" value of S by a "new" one, or in other words to update the variable S.[2]

In analogous fashion, of course, the relational INSERT and UPDATE operators are also just shorthand for certain relational assignments. In the case of INSERT, for example, the expression on the right side of that assignment represents the union of (a) the current value of the target relation variable and (b) a relation value containing the tuples to be inserted (see the section "Relational Assignment" for further discussion). Thus, while **Tutorial D** certainly does support the familiar INSERT, DELETE, and UPDATE operators on relation variables, it expressly recognizes that those operators are all just shorthand (albeit very convenient shorthand) for certain relational assignments.

Back to relation variables as such. Given the crucial importance of the logical difference between relation variables and relation values, we'll take great care throughout this book to distinguish between the two. That is, we'll be very careful to talk in terms of relation variables, not relation values, when it really is relation variables that we mean, and in terms of relation values, not relation variables, when it really is relation values that we mean. That said, however, we now add that—as previously noted in Chapter 1—we'll abbreviate *relation value*, most of the time, to *relation*, unqualified (just as we abbreviate *integer value* most of the time to simply *integer*). And we'll abbreviate *relation variable* most of the time to **relvar**; for example, we'll say the suppliers-and-shipments database contains two relvars.[3]

Relvar Definitions

Here now, repeated from Chapter 1 for ease of reference, are the definitions of relvars S and SP from our running example:

---

[1] Of course, the left side of an assignment must consist of a variable reference specifically (i.e., a variable name, syntactically speaking). Variables are updatable by definition (values, of course, aren't); in the final analysis, in fact, to say that V is a variable is to say that V can serve as the target for an assignment operation, no more and no less.

[2] We follow convention throughout this book in using the generic term *update* to refer to the INSERT, DELETE, and UPDATE (and relational assignment) operators considered collectively. When we want to refer to the UPDATE operator as such, we'll set it in all caps as just shown.

[3] More precisely, two "real" or base relvars, so called to distinguish them from so called "virtual" relvars or views (see the section "Views" later in this chapter).

```
VAR S BASE RELATION { SNO SNO , SNAME NAME , STATUS INTEGER , CITY CHAR }
    KEY { SNO } ;

VAR SP BASE RELATION { SNO SNO , PNO PNO )
    KEY { SNO , PNO }
    FOREIGN KEY { SNO } REFERENCES S ;
```

We remind you that any given relvar is declared to be of some specific relation type—and, of course, all possible values of that relvar (i.e., all relations that can possibly be assigned to that relvar) are of that same type, necessarily. For example, the type of both relvar S and all possible "supplier relations" is, precisely,

```
RELATION { SNO SNO , SNAME NAME , STATUS INTEGER , CITY CHAR }
```

Also, the terms *heading*, *body*, *attribute*, *tuple*, *cardinality*, and *degree*, defined in Chapter 1 for relation values, can all be interpreted in the obvious way to apply to relation variables or relvars as well. (In the case of *body*, *tuple*, and *cardinality*, the terms must be understood as applying to the relation that happens to be the current value of the relvar in question.)

Furthermore, relvars, like relation values, also have a corresponding *predicate* (called the *relvar predicate* for the relvar in question): namely, the predicate that's common to all of the relations that are possible values of the relvar in question. In the case of the suppliers relvar S, for example, the relvar predicate is (to repeat from Chapter 1):

Supplier SNO is under contract, is named SNAME, has status STATUS, and is located in city CITY.

Finally, we remind you of *The Closed World Assumption*, which we discussed in Chapter 1 in connection with relations but in fact applies (perhaps more importantly) to relvars as well. Here again is the definition, but expressed now in terms of relvars rather than relations:

Definition: Let relvar *R* have predicate *P*. Then *The Closed World Assumption* (CWA) says: If tuple *t* appears in *R* at time *T*, then the instantiation *p* of *P* corresponding to *t* is assumed to be true at time *T*; conversely, if tuple *t* has the same heading as *R* but doesn't appear in *R* at time *T*, then the instantiation *p* of *P* corresponding to *t* is assumed to be false at time *T*. In other words, a tuple appears in relvar *R* at a given time *T* if and only if it satisfies the predicate for *R* at that time *T*.

RELATIONAL ASSIGNMENT

An explicit relational assignment as such takes the form:

```
R := rx
```

Here *R* is a relvar reference (syntactically, just a relvar name); *rx* is a relational expression; and the assignment works by assigning the relation *r* denoted by *rx* to the relvar *R*. Of course, *r* and *R* must be of the same relation type.

So now we can explain the syntax and semantics of the INSERT, DELETE, and UPDATE shorthands. First, however, we need to stress the point that these operators (as well as relational assignment), since they're all update operators, aren't operators of the relational algebra as such (recall from Chapter 2 that the operators of the relational algebra are all, by definition, read-only operators specifically). However, they can certainly be explained—in fact, they're defined—in terms of such algebraic operators. For example, the INSERT statement

```
INSERT R rx ;
```

is shorthand for the following explicit relational assignment:

```
R := R UNION rx ;
```

Observe now that the foregoing definition of INSERT in terms of union implies that, other things being equal, an attempt to insert "a tuple that already exists"—i.e., an INSERT in which the relations denoted by *R* and *rx* aren't disjoint—will succeed. (It won't insert any duplicate tuples, of course—it just won't have any effect as far as those existing tuples are concerned.) For such reasons, we define a variant on INSERT called D_INSERT ("disjoint INSERT"), with syntax as follows:

```
D_INSERT R rx ;
```

This statement is shorthand for:

```
R := R D_UNION rx ;
```

Recall from Chapter 2 that D_UNION—"disjoint union"—is just like regular union, except that it's undefined if its operand relations have any tuples in common. It follows that an attempt to use D_INSERT to insert a tuple that already exists will fail (and an exception will be raised).

Turning now to DELETE, the DELETE statement

```
DELETE R rx ;
```

is shorthand for the following explicit assignment:

```
R := R MINUS rx ;
```

Note: The foregoing is the most general form of DELETE. But the DELETE example in the previous section—

```
DELETE S WHERE CITY = 'Paris' ;
```

—took the simpler form "DELETE *R* WHERE *bx*." Now, that simpler form (which is actually the form most commonly encountered in practice) can be regarded as shorthand for a DELETE of the form "DELETE *R rx*" in which *rx* in turn takes the form "*R* WHERE *bx*". However, an alternative and arguably simpler expansion for that common special form is:

```
R := R WHERE NOT ( bx )
```

Thus, we could alternatively say the DELETE in the example is shorthand for:

```
S := S WHERE NOT ( CITY = 'Paris' ) ;
```

We'll be appealing to this alternative expansion from time to time in the chapters to come.

Now, the foregoing definition (i.e., of a DELETE of the form "DELETE *R rx*") implies that, other things being equal, an attempt to delete "a tuple that doesn't exist"—i.e., a DELETE in which the relation denoted by *rx* isn't wholly included in the relation denoted by *R*—will succeed. For that reason, we define a variant on DELETE called I_DELETE ("included DELETE"), with syntax as follows:

```
I_DELETE R rx ;
```

This statement is shorthand for:

```
R := R I_MINUS rx ;
```

Recall from Chapter 2 that I_MINUS—"included minus"—is just like regular minus, except that it's undefined if some tuple appears in its second operand relation and not in its first. It follows that an attempt to use I_DELETE to delete a tuple that doesn't exist will fail, and an exception will be raised. (Note, however, that a DELETE of the form "DELETE *R* WHERE *bx*" can never attempt to delete "a tuple that doesn't exist," and no I_DELETE analog is needed in this case.)

As for UPDATE, the statement

```
UPDATE R WHERE bx : { A := ax } ;
```

is shorthand for the following explicit assignment:

```
R := ( R WHERE NOT ( bx ) )
       UNION
     ( EXTEND ( R WHERE bx ) : { A := ax } ) ;
```

A here is, of course, an attribute reference—syntactically, just an attribute name—denoting an attribute of relvar *R*. As for the EXTEND in which that reference appears, note that it's of the "what if" form (see Chapter 2 if you need to refresh your memory regarding this possibility).

Note: You might be wondering whether we could, or should, define a variant form of UPDATE, analogous to the D_INSERT and I_DELETE operators discussed above. For reasons beyond the scope of this book, however, such an operator doesn't seem to make much sense.

Finally, we observe that assignment operations in general are required to satisfy what's called *The Assignment Principle*. Here's the definition:

> **Definition:** *The Assignment Principle* states that after assignment of value *v* to variable *V*, the comparison *v* = *V* must evaluate to TRUE.

Of course, this principle actually applies to assignments of all kinds—in fact, as you can see, it's more or less the definition of assignment—but for the purposes of this book it's sufficient to note that it applies to relational assignments in particular.

KEYS

> **Definition:** Let *K* be a subset of the heading of relvar *R*. Then *K* is a **key** (also known as a *candidate* key) for *R* if and only if it possesses both of the following properties:
>
> 1. **Uniqueness:** No relation that can legally be assigned to *R* has two distinct tuples with the same value for *K*.
>
> 2. **Irreducibility:** No proper subset of *K* has the uniqueness property.
>
> If *K* consists of *n* attributes, then *n* is the **degree** of *K*.

Note that every relvar does have at least one key (why?). Note too that keys are sets of attributes, not attributes per se (even when the set in question consists of just one attribute), because they're defined to be a subset—not necessarily a proper subset—of the pertinent heading.[4] Thus, the sole key for relvar S is {SNO} (note the braces), not SNO; likewise, the sole key for relvar SP is {SNO,PNO}. (In fact, as noted in Chapter 1, this latter relvar is "all key.") In other words, relvar S is subject to the *key constraint* that {SNO} is a key for that relvar; likewise, relvar SP is subject to the key constraint that it's all key.

By the way, observe that {SNAME} isn't a key for relvar S, even though the SNAME values shown in Fig. 1.1 do happen to be unique. The point is, there's no key constraint in effect that says supplier names *have* to be unique.

---

[4] It follows that key values are tuples; in fact, any given key value is a "subtuple"—i.e., a subset of the tuple in which it appears.

A remark on primary keys: If relvar R has more than one key (which is certainly possible), then it's usual, though not required, to single out one of those keys and call it "primary." And if relvar R has just one key, it's also usual, but not required, to call that key "primary." For reasons discussed in reference [43], we don't insist on this practice; however, we don't prohibit it either, and indeed we usually adopt it in our own examples. In particular, we assume, where it makes any difference, that {SNO} is the primary key for relvar S and {SNO,PNO} is the primary key for relvar SP. And in figures like Fig. 1.1, we adopt the convention of identifying primary keys by "double underlining" the attributes that constitute the key in question. Note, however, that **Tutorial D** actually has no syntax for distinguishing between primary and other keys. *End of remark.*

Functional Dependencies

Definition: Let X and Y be subsets of the heading of relvar R. Then the **functional dependency** $X \rightarrow Y$ holds in R if and only if, in every relation that's a possible value of R, whenever two tuples have the same value for X, they also have the same value for Y.[5]

For example, suppose there's a rule in effect in the suppliers-and-shipments world that says that if two suppliers are located in the same city at the same time, then they must have the same status at that time. Then the functional dependency (FD for short)

```
{ CITY }  →{ STATUS }
```

would hold in relvar S. Note in particular that if K is a key for relvar R and Z is any subset of the heading of R, then the FD $K \rightarrow Z$ necessarily holds in R (why, exactly?)—in other words, every key constraint implies certain FD constraints, necessarily. See the section "Database Constraints" later in the chapter for further discussion of constraints in general.

FOREIGN KEYS

In our running example, {SNO} in relvar SP is a foreign key, referencing the sole key {SNO} in relvar S. What this means is that if, at some given time T, relvar SP contains a tuple in which the SNO value is (let's say) S3, then relvar S must contain a tuple at that same time T in which the SNO value is S3 as well. Here's a definition:

Definition: Let relvars $R2$ and $R1$ (not necessarily distinct) be such that:

---

[5] And at the risk of laboring the point, we stress the fact that like key values, those X and Y values are (sub)tuples.

1.   *K* is a key for *R1*.

2.   *FK* is a subset of the heading of *R2*.

3.   At any given time, every *FK* value in *R2* is required to be equal to the *K* value in some (necessarily unique) tuple in *R1*.[6]

Then *FK* is a **foreign key** in *R2*, referencing *K* in *R1*. And if *FK* consists of *n* attributes, then *n* is the **degree** of *FK*.

Actually the foregoing definition is considerably simplified, but it's good enough for present purposes. Note, however, that it does tacitly assume that *K* and *FK* each consist of the very same attributes. That is (to spell the point out), every attribute in each of *K* and *FK* must have the same name and be of the same type as the corresponding attribute in the other; formally, in fact, they must be the very same attribute—which means that, in practice, the syntax for foreign key specifications might need to include some kind of support for attribute renaming (see, e.g., reference [42] for further discussion). *Terminology*:

■ Relvars *R2* and *R1* in the definition are the *referencing* relvar and the *referenced* (or *target*) relvar, respectively.

■ A particular tuple *t2* in *R2* and the corresponding tuple *t1* in *R1* are a *referencing* tuple and the corresponding *referenced* (or *target*) tuple, respectively.

■ Key *K* in *R1* is the *referenced* (or *target*) key.

■ The constraint that, at any given time, every *FK* value in *R2* is required to be equal to the *K* value in some tuple in *R1* is a *foreign key constraint* or *referential constraint*.

■ The rule that no foreign key constraint must ever be violated is the *referential integrity rule*.

In our running example, any attempt to delete a supplier tuple must fail if it would otherwise leave any "dangling references"—i.e., references in relvar SP to the supplier tuple that now no longer exists.[7]

---

[6] And yes, those *K* and *FK* values are (sub)tuples.

[7] In practice, systems often allow a "cascade delete rule" to be specified in connection with foreign keys. If such a rule were specified in the case at hand, a DELETE on S would "cascade" to cause an automatic DELETE on SP as well—to be specific, a DELETE for all SP tuples with the same supplier number as any tuple being deleted from S—as a consequence of which no violation of the referential constraint would in fact occur.

DATABASE CONSTRAINTS

A database constraint, or just a *constraint* for short,[8] is, loosely, a boolean expression that (a) mentions no variables except database relvars and (b) must evaluate to TRUE (because if it evaluates to FALSE, there must be something wrong with the database). Any attempt to update the database in such a way as to cause some constraint to evaluate to FALSE must therefore fail—and, in the relational model, fail immediately, meaning an exception must be raised as soon as the update is attempted. *Note:* This requirement (i.e., that constraint violations be detected immediately) is sometimes called **The Golden Rule**. Observe that it's a consequence of this rule that no user ever sees the database in an inconsistent state, where an inconsistent state is, by definition, a state of the database that violates at least one known constraint.

Of course, we've discussed key constraints and foreign key constraints (also functional dependencies) already. Such constraints are extremely important, but they're also rather simple. Constraints of arbitrary complexity are possible, however, and do indeed occur in practice (sometimes they're called *business rules*). Let's consider a few examples:[9]

1. Supplier status values must be in the range 1 to 100 inclusive.

   ```
   CONSTRAINT CX1 IS_EMPTY ( S WHERE STATUS < 1 OR STATUS > 100 ) ;
   ```

   Alternatively:

   ```
   CONSTRAINT CX1 AND ( S , STATUS ≥ 1 AND STATUS ≤ 100 ) ;
   ```

   Explanation: AND here is an aggregate operator (we mentioned it in Chapter 2, but gave no examples there). It works on aggregates of boolean values, returning the logical AND of the boolean values in the aggregate in question.[10] In the example, the aggregate contains one boolean value for each tuple in the suppliers relation, that value being computed by evaluating the boolean expression STATUS ≥ 1 AND STATUS ≤ 100 against the tuple in question. *Note:* When used in the context of a constraint, as in this example, AND might conveniently be pronounced "for all." For example, the second formulation above of Constraint CX1 might intuitively be read as follows: "For all suppliers, the status must be greater than or equal to 1 and less than or equal to 100."

---

[8] Also known as an *integrity* constraint. *Note:* Constraints (or integrity constraints) in general are usually taken to include type constraints (see Chapter 1) as well as database constraints. Here and for the remainder of this book, however, we deliberately limit our attention to database constraints only, barring explicit statements to the contrary.

[9] The discussion that follows (which is deliberately a little terse) is based on one that originally appeared in reference [45].

[10] Note that AND returns TRUE if its aggregate operand happens to be empty.

2. Suppliers in London must have status 20.

```
CONSTRAINT CX2 IS_EMPTY ( S WHERE CITY = 'London' AND STATUS ≠ 20 ) ;
```

3. Supplier numbers must be unique.

```
CONSTRAINT CX3 COUNT ( S ) = COUNT ( S { SNO } ) ;
```

In other words, {SNO} is a key for relvar S. In practice, of course, we would almost certainly specify this constraint not by means of an explicit CONSTRAINT statement as shown, but rather by means of an appropriate KEY specification on the definition of relvar S. But it's interesting to note that such a specification is really nothing more than shorthand for something that can be expressed, albeit more longwindedly, using that explicit CONSTRAINT syntax.

Aside: It would be more accurate to say Constraint CX3 means {SNO} is a *superkey* for relvar S. Loosely, a superkey is a superset—not necessarily a proper superset, of course— of a key; thus, all keys are superkeys, but "most" superkeys aren't keys. Superkeys satisfy the key uniqueness requirement but not necessarily the key irreducibility requirement. In the case at hand, of course, the superkey in fact does satisfy the irreducibility requirement and is thus indeed a key after all. *End of aside.*

4. Suppliers with status less than 20 mustn't supply part P6.

```
CONSTRAINT CX4
    IS_EMPTY ( ( S JOIN SP ) WHERE STATUS < 20 AND PNO = PNO ( 'P6' ) ) ;
```

This constraint involves (better: *interrelates*) two distinct relvars, S and SP. In general, a constraint might involve, or interrelate, any number of distinct relvars. *Terminology*: A constraint that involves just a single relvar is known, informally, as a relvar constraint (sometimes a single-relvar constraint, for emphasis); a constraint that involves two or more distinct relvars is known, informally, as a multirelvar constraint. Constraints CX1-CX3 are all single-relvar constraints, while Constraint CX4 is a multirelvar constraint.

5. Every supplier number in SP must also appear in S.

```
CONSTRAINT CX5 SP { SNO } ⊆ S { SNO } ;
```

This example is also a multirelvar constraint, and what it means is that {SNO} in relvar SP is a foreign key, referencing relvar S. In practice, of course, we would almost certainly specify this constraint not by means of an explicit CONSTRAINT statement as shown, but rather by means of an appropriate FOREIGN KEY specification as part of the statement that defines relvar SP. But as with Example 3 above, it's interesting to note that such a specification is really nothing more than shorthand[11] for something that can be expressed using that explicit CONSTRAINT syntax.

Note finally that database constraints do apply specifically to relvars, not relations (which is why we discuss them in this chapter, of course). Why? Because, by definition, they constrain updates—that is, the only way they can be violated is by means of some update operation—and, again by definition, updates apply to variables, not values.

Multiple Assignment

Suppose the suppliers-and-shipments database is subject to a constraint to the effect that every supplier in London must be able to supply part P1:

```
CONSTRAINT CX6 IS_EMPTY
     ( ( S WHERE CITY = 'London ) NOT MATCHING
                            ( SP WHERE PNO = PNO ( 'P1' ) ) ) ;
```

Given this constraint, it's clear that if we insert a new London supplier, say supplier number S6, into relvar S, then we also need to insert a shipment with supplier number S6 and part number P1 into relvar SP. The trouble is, if we try to do the INSERT on S first, it'll fail on a violation of Constraint CX6, and if we try to do the INSERT on SP first, it'll fail on a violation of Constraint CX5 (the foreign key constraint). So what we need to do is perform both updates at the same time, as it were—i.e., as a single combined operation. In other words, we need to perform a *multiple assignment*, like this:

```
INSERT S  RELATION { TUPLE { SNO SNO ( 'S6' ) , ... , CITY 'London' } } ,
INSERT SP RELATION { TUPLE { SNO SNO ( 'S6' ) , PNO PNO ( 'P1' ) } } ;
```

(Note the comma separator, which means the two INSERTs are part of the same overall statement.) Of course, INSERT is really assignment, so the foregoing "double INSERT" is really shorthand for a double assignment that, in outline, looks like this:

```
S := ... , SP := ... ;
```

This double assignment assigns one value to relvar S and another to relvar SP, both as part of the same overall operation. And—important!—no constraint checking is done until the end of the statement is reached (i.e., until the semicolon, in effect).

In outline, the semantics of multiple assignment are as follows: First, the source expressions on the right sides of the individual assignments are evaluated; second, those individual assignments are executed; last, any applicable constraints are checked. Observe in particular, therefore, that—precisely because the source expressions are all evaluated before any

---

[11] Well ... actually it's longer than what it's supposed to be shorthand for.

of the individual assignments are executed—none of those individual assignments can depend on the result of any other, and so the sequence in which they're executed is irrelevant (you can think of them as being executed in parallel, or "simultaneously," if you like).

> *Aside:* The foregoing explanation requires some slight refinement in the case where two or more of the individual assignments specify the same target variable. In effect, what happens in such a situation (i.e., if two or more of the individual assignments do specify the same target variable) is that those particular assignments are executed in sequence as written. For further details, see reference [48]. *End of aside.*

VIEWS

As noted in Chapter 2, the operators of the relational algebra are all read-only and thus apply, by definition, to relation values specifically. In particular, of course, they apply to the values that happen to be the current values of relation variables. As a consequence, it obviously makes sense to write an expression such as

```
S { SNO , CITY }
```

and to read it as "the projection of relvar S on the SNO and CITY attributes"—meaning the projection on those attributes of *the current value of* relvar S (the result of that operation, of course, being a certain relation value).[12] Occasionally, however, it's convenient to use expressions like "the projection of relvar S on the SNO and CITY attributes" in a slightly different sense. In particular, we might want to define a *view* (also called a *virtual relvar*) SC of the suppliers relvar that consists of just the SNO and CITY attributes of that relvar, like this:

```
VAR SC VIRTUAL ( S { SNO , CITY } ) KEY { SNO } ;
```

In this example, we might say, loosely but very conveniently, that relvar SC is "the projection on SNO and CITY of relvar S"—meaning, more precisely, that the value of relvar SC at any given time is the projection on SNO and CITY of the value of relvar S at the time in question. In a sense, therefore, we can talk in terms of projections of relvars per se, rather than just in terms of projections of current values of relvars. We hope this kind of dual usage on our part won't cause you any confusion.

We'll have comparatively little to say on the topic of views in this book; however, we should at least explain that from the user's point of view—pardon the pun—views are supposed to behave just like base relvars. In fact, there's another principle involved here:

---

[12] As an obvious but important special case of this point, a relvar reference such as "S" is a perfectly legitimate relational expression, denoting the relation that's the current value of the specified relvar. (Actually, of course, we've made use of this fact repeatedly in examples prior to this point, both in this chapter and in Chapters 1 and 2.)

Definition: *The Principle of Interchangeability* (of views and base relvars) states that there must be no arbitrary and unnecessary distinctions between base relvars and views; in other words, views should—as far as possible—"look and feel" just like base relvars as far as users are concerned.

See reference [44] for further discussion.

THE RELATIONAL MODEL

We close this chapter with a formal, and deliberately somewhat terse, definition of the relational model, based on one given and discussed in detail in reference [45] and elsewhere. Here it is:

Definition: The **relational model** consists of five components:

1. An open ended collection of **types**, including type BOOLEAN in particular

2. A **relation type generator** and an intended interpretation for relations of types generated thereby

3. Facilities for defining **relation variables** of such generated relation types

4. A **relational assignment** operator for assigning relation values to such relation variables

5. A relationally complete, but otherwise open ended, collection of **generic relational operators** for deriving relation values from other relation values

The material of this chapter and its two predecessors should be sufficient to explain most if not all of the foregoing definition. If you need further clarification, please see reference [45].

EXERCISES

3.1   Write CONSTRAINT statements for the suppliers-and-shipments database to express the following requirements:

a.   No Paris supplier can have status 20.

b.   No two suppliers can be located in the same city.

c. At most one supplier can be located in Athens at any one time.

d. There must exist at least one London supplier.

e. The average supplier status must be at least 10.

f. No London supplier must be capable of supplying part P2.

3.2   With reference to the courses-and-students database from Exercise 2.2 in Chapter 2, write a constraint to express the fact that no student can be enrolled on a course prior to that course's becoming available or prior to that student's registration with the university.

ANSWERS

3.1

a. `CONSTRAINT CX31a IS_EMPTY ( S WHERE CITY = 'Paris' AND STATUS = 20 ) ;`

b. `CONSTRAINT CX31b COUNT ( S ) = COUNT ( S { CITY } ) ;`

c. `CONSTRAINT CX31c COUNT ( S WHERE CITY = 'Athens' ) < 2 ;`

d. `CONSTRAINT CX31d IS_NOT_EMPTY ( S WHERE CITY = 'London' ) ;`

e. ```
CONSTRAINT CX31e
     CASE
         WHEN IS_EMPTY (S) THEN TRUE
         ELSE AVG (S , STATUS) ≥ 10
     END CASE ;
```

f.  ```
CONSTRAINT CX31f IS_EMPTY ( ( S JOIN SP )
                  WHERE CITY = 'London' AND PNO = PNO ( 'P2' ) ) ;
```

3.2   ```
CONSTRAINT CX32 IS_EMPTY (JOIN { COURSE , STUDENT , ENROLLMENT }
                WHERE ENROLLED < AVAILABLE OR ENROLLED < REGISTERED) ;
```
```

Part II

LAYING THE FOUNDATIONS

The purpose of this part of the book is to explain basic temporal database principles—i.e., the basic concepts and fundamental theory underlying temporal data and temporal databases. It consists of the following chapters (which, as stated in the preface, are definitely meant to be read in sequence as written):

4. Time and the Database

5. What's the Problem?

6. Intervals

7. Interval Operators

8. The EXPAND and COLLAPSE Operators

9. The PACK and UNPACK Operators I: The Single-Attribute Case

10. The PACK and UNPACK Operators II: The Multiattribute Case

11. Generalizing the Algebraic Operators

The titles give some idea as to the scope of each chapter. Further specifics are given near the end of the section "Temporal Databases" in Chapter 4.

Chapter 4

Time and the Database

Eternity's a terrible thought.
I mean, where's it all going to end?

—Tom Stoppard:
Rosencrantz and Guildenstern Are Dead (1967)

We're now ready to begin our investigation into what a temporal database might look like and how such a database might best be managed. We start by considering in broad terms just what it is—if anything—that distinguishes a temporal database from any other kind of database.

TEMPORAL DATABASES

A temporal database can be thought of, loosely, as a database that contains historical data instead of or in addition to current data. Such databases have been under active investigation since at least the beginning of the 1980s—perhaps earlier. Some of those investigations have taken the extreme position that data in such a database, once inserted, should never be deleted or changed in any way, in which case the database can be thought of, again loosely, as containing historical data only. (Some data warehouses adopt this approach, at least to a first approximation.) Conventional databases, by contrast, are typically at the other extreme; a conventional database typically contains current data only, and data in such a database is changed or deleted as soon as the propositions represented by that data cease to be true. (Refer to Chapter 1, subsection titled "Relations and Their Meaning," if you need to refresh your memory regarding the important idea that the data in a database can be thought of as a collection of true propositions.) In what follows, we'll occasionally refer to such a database explicitly as *nontemporal*, in order to emphasize the fact that it contains current data only.[1]

The suppliers-and-shipments database of Chapters 1-3 is a nontemporal database in the foregoing sense. Consider Fig. 1.1 once again, which shows some sample values for that database. That figure shows among other things that the status of supplier S1 is currently 20. By contrast, a temporal version of that database might show not only that the status of that supplier

---

[1] Nontemporal databases are sometimes called *snapshot* databases in the literature. We don't much care for this term, however, because "snapshot" has often been used in the past (and still is used) to refer to the database as it appears or appeared at some specific point in time. In other words, the term very reasonably can be, and is, applied to *any* database, temporal or otherwise.

is currently 20, but also that it has been 20 ever since July 1st last year, and perhaps that it was 15 from April 5th to June 30th last year, and so on. Thus, the propositions in a nontemporal database are generally thought of as referring to the current state of affairs (i.e., the state of affairs"now," when the database is actually inspected). In fact, even if they're thought of as referring to some time other than "now," it makes no real difference to the way the data is managed and used. As we'll see over the next few chapters, however, the way the data is managed and used in a temporal database differs in a variety of ways from the way it's managed and used in a nontemporal one (a fact that accounts for the existence of this book, of course).

The distinguishing feature of a temporal database is, naturally, time itself. Temporal database research has therefore involved a certain amount of investigation into the nature of time as such. Here are some of the questions that have been explored:

- Does time have a beginning or an end?

- Is time is a continuum, or is it divided into discrete quanta?

- How can we best characterize the important concept "*now*" (sometimes known as "the moving point *now*")?

But these questions, interesting though they might be in themselves, aren't intrinsically database questions as such, and we therefore won't delve very deeply into them in this book. Instead, we'll simply make what we hope are reasonable assumptions as we proceed. This approach allows us to concentrate on matters that are more directly relevant to our overall aim. However, we note that parts of that temporal research do possess certain interesting generalizations; that is, ideas developed originally or primarily to support temporal data in particular have been found to have application in other important areas as well. We'll touch on this point again from time to time in subsequent chapters.

Out of all that research, the ideas we focus on in this book represent what we regard—naturally enough, since the ideas in question are due primarily to one of the present authors (Lorentzos)[2]—as the most satisfactory and most promising part. What do we mean by "most promising"? Well, it's unfortunately the case that for a long time the research community was divided over how best to address the temporal database problem. (Indeed, in some respects it still is.) In a nutshell:

- Some people proposed a very specialized approach to the problem, one that treats temporal data as special and involves some departure from relational principles (see below).

---

[2] Be warned, however, that over questions of nomenclature and similar matters we depart (quite extensively, in fact) from previous publications by Lorentzos on the same subject.

■ Others, the present writers included, favored an approach that most definitely does *not* depart from relational principles but treats temporal data as far as possible just like data of any other kind.

The departure in question—i.e., from relational principles—consists primarily in representing timestamps by means of "hidden attributes" instead of by conventional relational attributes in the usual way. (The attributes are hidden in the sense that they're not directly visible to the user in the usual way and can't be referenced by simple attribute names in the usual way.) We believe such a scheme is unwise. Indeed, it's clear that "hidden attributes" aren't true relational attributes, "relations" that contain such "attributes" aren't true relations, and the overall approach constitutes a clear violation of Codd's *Information Principle*. Some of the consequences of such violation are explained in detail in reference [29].

> *Aside:* In case you might be unfamiliar with it, we digress for a moment to say a few words about *The Information Principle*. The principle was originally formulated by Codd—inventor of the relational model—in the following terms, more or less: *The entire information content of the database at any given time is represented in one and only one way: namely, as explicit values in attribute positions in tuples in relations.* Or perhaps more precisely: *The database contains relvars, and nothing but relvars.* In other words, relation variables are the only kind of variable permitted in a relational database; all other kinds, scalar variables or tuple variables or any other kind, are explicitly prohibited.
> The essential simplicity of the relational model derives in large part from this principle. Indeed, Codd referred to it (the principle) on more than one occasion as *the* fundamental principle underlying the relational model. Certainly it's true that any violation of it should be seen as a serious matter. An extended discussion of some of the consequences of such violation can be found in references [42] and [45], but what they boil down to is this: If the database contains *N* different kinds of variables, then *N* different sets of operators are needed for dealing with them. And if the database is relational, then *N* = 1, which is the minimum. *End of aside.*

Now, if (as we saw in Chapter 1) data in general can be regarded as an encoded representation of propositions, then temporal data in particular can be regarded as an encoded representation of timestamped propositions—by which we mean propositions that involve one or more values of some timestamp type. It follows that in a temporal database (under the extreme interpretation of that term, according to which all of the data is temporal), every proposition is timestamped in the foregoing sense. We might therefore define a temporal relation to be one in which each tuple contains at least one timestamp (i.e., the relation heading contains at least one attribute of some timestamp type); we might further define a temporal relvar to be one whose heading is that of some temporal relation; and we might finally define a temporal database to be one in which all of the relvars are temporal ones. *Note:* We're being deliberately vague here as to what the timestamps we're talking about might look like in actual practice. We'll take up this issue in Chapters 5 and (especially) 6.

Having just offered a reasonably precise definition of a temporal database (in its extreme form), we now dismiss that definition as not very useful! We dismiss it because even if the relvars in the database are indeed all temporal ones, many relations that can be derived from that database won't be temporal in the foregoing sense. For example, the answer to the query "Get the names of all employees we've ever hired" might be obtained from some temporal database, but the result would clearly not be a temporal relation as defined above. And it would be a strange DBMS indeed—certainly not a relational one—that would let us obtain query results that couldn't themselves be kept in the database.

From this point forward, therefore, we take a temporal database to be one that does include some temporal data but isn't necessarily limited to temporal data only. The chapters in this part of the book discuss such databases in detail. The plan for those chapters is as follows:

- The remainder of the present chapter and Chapter 5 together set the scene for subsequent chapters. In particular, Chapter 5 shows why temporal data does seem to require special treatment, at least in certain respects.

- Chapter 6 introduces *intervals* as a convenient basis for timestamping certain kinds of data (i.e., as a basis for defining what we've been referring to in the last few paragraphs as "timestamp types").

- Chapters 7 and 8 then discuss a variety of operators for dealing with such intervals and sets containing such intervals.

- Finally, Chapters 9 and 10 introduce some important new operators for dealing with relations with interval valued attributes, and Chapter 11 considers some of the consequences of those operators for the conventional relational algebra.

By the way, it's important to understand that—with just one exception, the interval type generator introduced in Chapter 6, along with its associated generic operators and generic constraints—all of the new constructs to be discussed in this part of the book (and the next part, too) are essentially just shorthand. That is, they can all be expressed—albeit only very longwindedly, in most cases—in terms of features already available in a relationally complete language such as **Tutorial D**. Thus, the approach to temporal databases that we advocate involves *no* changes to the classical relational model—though it does involve certain generalizations, as we'll see in Chapter 11 and later chapters, and as already indicated it does also involve the introduction of a new type generator. With regard to this latter point, however, we note that the question as to which types and type generators are supported is essentially orthogonal to the question of support for the relational model itself. That is, the relational model merely requires that *some* types be made available, somehow, in order that relations might be defined over them; nowhere does it prescribe exactly what types have to be supported.[3]

TIMESTAMPED PROPOSITIONS

We're now in a position to begin our investigation into some of the issues surrounding temporal databases. We start by appealing to the way people typically express timestamped propositions in natural language. Here are three simple examples (labeled *p1-p3* for purposes of subsequent reference):

p1:   Supplier S1 was appointed—i.e., placed under contract—**on** July 1st, 2012.

p2:   Supplier S1 has been under contract **since** July 1st, 2012.

p3:   Supplier S1 was under contract **during** the interval from July 1st, 2012, to the present day.

Each of these three propositions represents a possible interpretation for a tuple—call it *t*—that looks like this (as you can see, that tuple has two attributes, SNO and FROM, with values the supplier number S1 and the timestamp July 1st, 2012, respectively):

SNO	FROM
S1	July 1st, 2012

Any of the three interpretations might be appropriate if tuple *t* appeared in some relation in some database that represented the state of affairs in some enterprise. The boldface prepositions **on**, **since**, and **during** characterize the three interpretations.

Now, although we've said there are three possible interpretations, it could be argued that they all say the same thing, albeit in slightly different ways. Indeed, we do take propositions *p2* and *p3* to be equivalent, but not *p1*. For consider:

- ■ *p1* clearly implies that supplier S1 was not under contract on the date (June 30th, 2012) immediately preceding the specified appointment date;[4] *p2* neither states that fact nor implies it.

---

[3] Except for type BOOLEAN and the type generator RELATION, both of which must be supported for obvious reasons.

[4] At least, such would be the normal interpretation. But natural language is so often imprecise! The appointment on July 1st might have been a renewal, and supplier S1 might have been under contract on June 30th after all. For the sake of the present discussion, however, we assume the normal interpretation.

■ Suppose today ("the present day") is July 1st, 2013. Then *p2* clearly states that supplier S1 was under contract on every day from July 1st, 2012 to July 1st, 2013, inclusive; *p1* neither states *that* fact, nor implies it.

Thus, neither of *p1* and *p2* implies the other, and they're certainly not equivalent.

That said, tuples in conventional databases often do contain things like "date of appointment," and propositions like *p2* (or *p3*) often are the intended interpretation. If such is the case here, however—i.e., if *p1* is meant to be equivalent to *p2* and *p3* after all—then the given formulation isn't quite adequate to the task. We can improve it by rephrasing it thus:

p1:   Supplier S1 was most recently appointed on July 1st, 2012, and the contract hasn't subsequently been terminated.

What's more, if this version of *p1* really is what tuple *t* is supposed to mean, then *p2* in its present form isn't really adequate either—it needs to be rephrased thus:

p2:   Supplier S1 wasn't under contract on June 30th, 2012, but has been so ever since July 1st, 2012.

Of course, *p3* needs an analogous clarification:

p3:   Supplier S1 wasn't under contract on June 30th, 2012, but has been so throughout the interval from July 1st, 2012, to the present day.

Observe now that *p1* expresses a time **at** which a certain event took place, while *p2* and *p3* express an interval of time **during** which a certain state persisted. We've deliberately chosen an example in which a certain *state* might be inferred from information regarding a certain *event*: Since the event—i.e., the most recent appointment of supplier S1—occurred on July 1st, 2012 (and the contract hasn't subsequently been terminated), that supplier has been in the state of being under contract from that date to the present day. Conventional database technology can handle time instants (times **at** which events occur) reasonably well; however, it can't handle time intervals (intervals **during** which states persist) very well at all, as we'll see in the next chapter.

Now, events from which states *can't* be inferred aren't very interesting from the point of view of temporal data in general. For example, the statement "Lightning struck at 2:30 pm last Tuesday" is certainly a timestamped proposition, but—from the point of view of temporal data in general, at any rate—it's not a very interesting one. To be more specific, the timestamp in this example has almost none of the special properties, and displays almost none of the special kinds of behavior, that (as we'll see over the next few chapters) apply to temporal data in general. For such reasons, we'll have little to say from this point forward regarding propositions like the one in the lightning example.

To return to propositions *p1-p3*: Observe now that, although *p2* and *p3* are logically equivalent, they're significantly different in form; in other words, the predicates of which they're instantiations (see Chapter 1) are significantly different. To be specific, *p3* explicitly refers to a specific time *interval*, with a specific begin point and specific end point, while *p2* refers only to a specific time *instant*. As a consequence, the form of *p2* can't be used for historical records, while that of *p3* can[5]—provided, of course, that we replace the phrase "the present day" in that proposition by some explicit date, say July 1st, 2013. The corresponding predicates (call them *P2* and *P3*, respectively) look something like this:

P2: Supplier S*x* has been under contract since date *d*.

P3: Supplier S*x* was under contract during the interval from date *b* to date *e*.

Note: For simplicity, we ignore for the moment the various clarifications discussed earlier, although those clarifications would certainly be needed in practice. See the further remarks on this subject at the very end of this chapter.

We conclude from the foregoing that the concept of ***during*** is very important for historical records. Indeed, that concept pervades the next several chapters, as we'll soon see.[6]

We close this section by noting that, despite our repeated use of terms such as "historical data" and "historical records," temporal databases might quite reasonably contain information about the future as well as, or instead of, the past. For example, we might wish to document the fact that supplier S1 *will be* under contract during the interval from date *b* to date *e*, where *e* is a date in the future, and *b* might be as well. Thus, we'll take the terms *temporal* and *historical* to include the future in this way throughout this book, unless the context demands otherwise. We'll also offer a few comments on the question of recording information about the future specifically, at suitable points in the text.

VALID TIME vs. TRANSACTION TIME

In a conventional (nontemporal) database, anything can be updated, barring explicit edicts to the contrary. But if *historical* data can be updated, we find ourselves faced with the possibility that, apparently, history can be changed! What of this possibility?

Well, it's important to understand that, obviously, the database doesn't contain "the real world" as such; instead, it contains our *knowledge of*, or *beliefs about*, the real world.[7] And while it's perfectly reasonable to assert that the past is immutable and history as such can never

---

[5] These remarks are based on the empirical observation that most interesting historical records do involve intervals, not instants.

[6] It's tempting to describe those chapters, therefore, as an investigation into the possibility of building a During Machine.

[7] More precisely, it contains a *representation* of those beliefs. For simplicity, we talk throughout this book as if the database contained not just representations of information but information per se, though such talk is more than a little loose.

change, it's equally reasonable to assert that our beliefs about it *can* change—indeed, they often do. In a database context, therefore, when we speak of "updating history," what we really mean is updating our *beliefs about* history, not updating history as such—though the distinction is often blurred, and even confused, in informal contexts, as you might imagine.

In the temporal database literature, the terms *valid time* and *transaction time* are used in an attempt to get at the foregoing distinction [103]. We don't particularly care for these terms ourselves (their meanings can hardly be said to "leap off the page," as it were), and we won't be using them much in the chapters to come; however, the distinction as such is important, and it does merit some discussion. So consider the following simple example. Let *p* be the proposition "Supplier S1 was under contract." Suppose it's our current understanding that this state of affairs obtained from July 1st, 2012, to June 30th, 2013, and we therefore insert the following tuple into some relvar in the database:

SNO	FROM	TO
S1	July 1st, 2012	June 30th, 2013

Note very carefully that this tuple does *not* correspond to proposition *p*. Rather, it corresponds to what might be called a *timestamped extension* of *p* that can be stated thus:

Supplier S1 was under contract—that's *p*—***from July 1st, 2012, to June 30th, 2013***.

And the literature would refer to the timestamp here—i.e., the interval from July 1st, 2012, to June 30th, 2013—as the *valid time* for the original proposition *p*. Thus, the valid time for *p* in this example is the interval of time during which (according to our current beliefs) *p* was in fact true. *Note:* We're assuming here for simplicity that the specified interval (from July 1st, 2012, to June 30th, 2013) is the *only* interval during which the specified supplier was under contract. In general, however, the valid time for a given proposition will consist of a set of intervals, not just a single interval as such. For example, if it's our understanding that supplier S1 was also under contract previously from January 1st, 2010, to March 30th, 2011, then the relevant valid time would clearly involve two intervals, not just one. But we'll continue to assume for the remainder of this section, for simplicity, that valid times are indeed just single intervals.

Suppose we now learn that supplier S1's contract in fact began on *June* 1st, not July 1st, 2012, and we therefore replace the original tuple by one that looks like this:

SNO	FROM	TO
S1	June 1st, 2012	June 30th, 2013

Now, this change has no effect on proposition *p* as such, of course—it merely changes the associated timestamp (i.e., it reflects our revised understanding, to the effect that supplier S1 was in fact under contract from June 1st, 2012, to June 30th, 2013). Thus, the valid time for proposition *p* is now the interval from June 1st, 2012, to June 30th, 2013, and we've just "updated our beliefs about history." What we've certainly not done, however, is update history as such; the update we've just performed *does not* and *cannot* change the historical fact that the database previously showed supplier S1 as under contract from July (not June) 1st, 2012.

Finally, suppose we discover a mistake was made and supplier S1 was in fact never under contract at all, and we therefore delete the foregoing tuple entirely. Proposition *p* is now known to be false; as a consequence, there's now no valid time associated with it at all.[8]

Now suppose the original tuple was inserted at time *t1* and replaced at time *t2*, and that replacement tuple was then deleted at time *t3*. Then the literature would say the interval from *t1* to *t2* was the *transaction time*—not for proposition *p* as such, but rather for the *timestamped extension* of *p* with valid time July 1st, 2012, to June 30th, 2013; that is, the interval from *t1* to *t2* is the time during which the database asserted that this particular timestamped extension of *p* was true. Likewise, the literature would say the interval from *t2* to *t3* was the transaction time for the timestamped extension of *p* with valid time June 1st, 2012, to June 30th, 2013; that is, the interval from *t2* to *t3* is the time during which the database asserted that *that* particular timestamped extension of *p* was true.[9] *Note:* Again we're simplifying matters somewhat; in general, transaction times, like valid times, are sets of intervals, not individual intervals as such. For example, if the database additionally showed the first of the foregoing timestamped extensions of *p* as being true during the interval from *t4* to *t5*, then the relevant transaction time would clearly involve two intervals instead of one.

We'll have a great deal more to say about these matters in Chapter 17. Prior to that point, it's sufficient to stress the fact that—as our examples have suggested—*valid times can be updated, but transaction times can't.* (Valid times reflect our beliefs about history, and those beliefs can change; transaction times, by contrast, reflect history as such, and history can't change. Indeed, as we'll see in Chapter 17, transaction times are managed by the system anyway, not by some human user.) Largely for such reasons, all of our discussions from this point forward will concern themselves with valid times only (what's more, they'll do so only implicitly, for the most part), until we get to Chapter 17.

SOME FUNDAMENTAL QUESTIONS

The references in the foregoing discussions to intervals of time tacitly introduce a simple but fundamental idea: namely, the idea that an interval with begin time *b* and end time *e* can be

---

[8] More precisely, the valid time is now *an empty set* (of intervals).

[9] Of course, the first of these two transaction times isn't exactly the interval from *t1* to *t2* but, rather, the interval from *t1* to "just before" *t2* (and similarly for the second). For simplicity, however, we'll ignore such niceties, until further notice.

thought of as *the set of all times t such that b ≤ t ≤ e* (where "<" means "earlier than," of course). Though "obvious," this simple notion has numerous far reaching consequences, as we'll see in the chapters to come. It also leads directly to a series of fairly fundamental questions!—indeed, some of those questions might already have occurred to you. For example:

1. Doesn't the expression "all times *t* such that $b ≤ t ≤ e$" raise the specter of infinite sets and all of the conceptual and computational difficulties such sets suffer from?

   Answer: Well, yes, it does appear to, but we dismiss the specter and circumvent the difficulties by adopting the assumption—except briefly in Appendix B—that the "timeline" consists of a finite contiguous sequence of discrete indivisible *time quanta* (where a time quantum is the smallest time unit the system is capable of representing). The interval with begin time *b* and end time *e* is a section of that timeline and thus also consists of a finite contiguous sequence of such quanta, a fortiori.

   Note: Much of the literature refers to a time quantum as a *chronon*. However, it then typically goes on to define a chronon as an interval—see, e.g., reference [62]—implying that chronons have a begin point and an end point, and perhaps further points in between, and so aren't indivisible after all. (What exactly are those various "points" in such an interval? What else can they be but chronons?) We find some confusion here and therefore choose to avoid the term.

2. Propositions *p1-p3* as discussed in the section "Timestamped Propositions" above seem to assume that time quanta are days, but surely the system supports time units all the way down to tiny fractions of a second. If S1 was a supplier on July 1st, 2012, but not on June 30th, 2012, what's to be done about the presumed interval of time from the beginning of the day July 1st, 2012, up to the very instant of appointment, during which S1 was still not officially under contract?

   Answer: We need to distinguish carefully between time quanta as such, which are the smallest time units the system is capable of representing, and the time units that are relevant for some particular purpose, which might be days, or months, or milliseconds, or any other unit of measure that makes sense. We call these latter units *time points* (or just *points* for short) in order to stress the fact that, at least for the purpose at hand, they too are considered to be indivisible. Now, we might say informally that a time point is a section of the timeline—i.e., a sequence of time quanta—that stretches from one "boundary" quantum to the next (e.g., from midnight on one day to midnight on the next). We might therefore say, again informally, that time points have a duration (one day, in the foregoing example). Formally, however, time points are indeed points: They're indivisible, and the concept of duration doesn't apply to them.

   Note: Much of the literature uses the term *granule* to refer to something like a time point as just defined (see, e.g., reference [6]). As with the term *chronon*, however, it then typically goes on (unfortunately) to say that a granule is an interval ... We therefore choose to avoid the term *granule* also.[10] We do, however, sometimes make informal use of the related term *granularity*, which refers to the "size" of the applicable time point, or equivalently to the "size" of the gap between adjacent points. Thus, we might say in our example that the granularity is one day, meaning we're ignoring (in this context) the fact that a day is made up of hours, which are made up of minutes, and so on. Such notions can be expressed only by recourse to finer levels of granularity.

By the way, the term *granularity* does tend to suggest that in any given context all points and gaps are the same size. This assumption isn't necessarily valid when we extend our temporal ideas to nontemporal data, as discussed in Chapter 6; in fact, it isn't always valid for temporal data, either (for example, different months are of different duration). See Chapter 18 for further discussion.

3. Given, then, that the timeline can be regarded for some specific purpose as a finite and contiguous sequence of time points, we can refer unambiguously to the time point immediately succeeding or preceding any given point—right?

    Answer: Yes, up to a point—the point in question being, of course, the end of time! And down to a point, too—the beginning of time. As far as we're concerned, the beginning of time is a time point that has no predecessor (it might perhaps correspond to cosmologists' best estimate of the very moment of the Big Bang), and the end of time is a time point that has no successor. To repeat, the timeline is a *finite* sequence of discrete points.
    Note: In Appendix A, we'll briefly consider the possibility of a "timeline" that's *cyclic* and thus has no beginning and no end. Elsewhere, however, we'll assume that time does indeed have a beginning and an end.

4. If some relvar currently contains a tuple representing the fact that supplier S1 was under contract from July 1st, 2012 to June 30th, 2013, doesn't *The Closed World Assumption*—see Chapters 1 and 3—demand that the relvar in question also contain, for example, a tuple representing the fact that supplier S1 was under contract from July 2nd, 2012, until June 29th, 2013, and a whole host of other tuples representing further trivial consequences of the fact represented by the original tuple?

    Answer: Good point! Clearly, we need a more constraining predicate as our general interpretation of such tuples:

---

[10] The confusion over whether chronons and granules are intervals seems to us to stem from a confusion over intuition vs. formalism. An intuitive belief about the way the world works is one thing; a formal model is something else entirely. In particular, we might believe the timeline is continuous and infinite, but we nevertheless model it for computing purposes as discrete and finite. (There's an obvious parallel here with real numbers, incidentally: The real number line is likewise continuous and infinite, but we model it for computing purposes as discrete and finite.)

Supplier Sx was under contract throughout the interval from date b to date e, but not throughout any interval that properly includes that interval.[11]

In other words, we take *during* to mean "**throughout and not immediately before or immediately after** (the interval in question)." In similar fashion, we take *since* to mean "**ever since and not immediately before** (the point in question)." Thus, please note that henceforth we'll use these terms in these specific senses only (barring explicit statements to the contrary, of course).

We close this section, and this chapter, with some final remarks regarding the running example. To be specific, from this point forward we'll assume, realistically enough, that:

a.   No supplier can end one contract on one day and begin another on the very next day.

b.   No supplier can be under two distinct contracts at the same time.

c.   Supplier contracts can be open ended—that is, a supplier can be currently under contract and the end date for that contract can be currently unknown.

EXERCISES

4.1   What's a timestamped proposition? Give some examples.

4.2   Distinguish between valid time and transaction time.

4.3   What's a time quantum? What's a time point?

4.4   What do you understand by the term *granularity*?

4.5   What do you understand by the terms *beginning of time* and *end of time*?

ANSWERS

The exercises in this chapter are all just review questions, and suitable answers can be found in the body of the chapter.

---

[11] The notion of one interval properly including another is defined formally in Chapter 7. For now, we just assume it makes good intuitive sense.

Chapter 5

What's the Problem?

Nothing puzzles me more than time and space;
and yet nothing troubles me less, as I never think about them.

—Charles Lamb:
Letter to Thomas Manning (1810)

In this chapter, we use the suppliers-and-shipments database as a basis for illustrating some of the problems that arise when we try to add temporal features to a conventional (nontemporal) database. We deliberately add those features in a piecemeal fashion.

REVISING THE RUNNING EXAMPLE

Actually, the first change we want to make isn't a temporal one at all (nor is it an addition); rather, it's a matter of simplification. To be specific, we simplify relvar S, the suppliers relvar, by dropping all of the attributes except attribute SNO. The predicate for this revised—and dramatically simplified!—relvar is thus just: *Supplier SNO is under contract.* (The predicate for SP remains unchanged, of course.) Fig. 5.1, a simplified version of Fig. 1.1, shows a set of sample values for the database after this revision has been applied.

S
SNO
S1
S2
S3
S4
S5

SP	
SNO	PNO
S1	P1
S1	P2
S1	P3
S1	P4
S1	P5
S1	P6
S2	P1
S2	P2
S3	P2
S4	P2
S4	P4
S4	P5

Fig. 5.1: Simplified suppliers-and-shipments database—sample values

As already indicated, this simplified database is still a purely conventional one—it involves no temporal aspects at all. *Note:* In case you're thinking it's surely much *too* simple, we'd like to assure you that in fact it's perfectly adequate as a basis for illustrating almost all of the points we want to make in this part of the book, and we'll stay with it until further notice. In fact, *not* simplifying the database in the manner indicated would lead to certain problems that we don't wish to get into at this juncture. We'll consider those problems in Part III of this book.

SAMPLE CONSTRAINTS AND QUERIES

We now proceed to consider some sample constraints and queries against the database of Fig. 5.1. In the two sections following this one (also in the next chapter, to some extent), we'll see what happens to those constraints and queries when that database is extended to incorporate various temporal features.

Constraints (nontemporal database, Fig. 5.1): The only constraints we want to consider here are the pertinent key and foreign key constraints. Just to remind you, {SNO} is the sole key for relvar S; {SNO,PNO} is the sole key for relvar SP (in fact, S and SP are now both "all key"); and {SNO} is a foreign key in relvar SP, referencing the sole key of relvar S.

Queries (nontemporal database, Fig. 5.1): We consider just two queries, both of them very simple:

- **Query A:** Get supplier numbers for suppliers who are currently able to supply at least one part. **Tutorial D** formulation:

```
SP { SNO }
```

- **Query B:** Get supplier numbers for suppliers who are currently unable to supply any parts at all. **Tutorial D** formulation:

```
S { SNO } MINUS SP { SNO }
```

Observe that Query A involves a simple projection and Query B involves the difference between two such projections. When we consider temporal analogs of these two queries in Chapter 9, we'll find they involve "temporal" analogs of these operators (and you probably won't be surprised to learn in Chapter 11 that similar "temporal" analogs of other relational operators can be defined as well).

Aside: In the case of Query B, the first projection is actually an *identity* projection (the expression "S {SNO}" is logically equivalent to just "S"). We show it as an explicit projection for reasons of clarity. Furthermore, the query overall could alternatively, and arguably more simply, have been formulated thus:

```
S NOT MATCHING SP
```

However, it suits our purposes better to stay with the formulation shown previously, involving MINUS. *End of aside.*

SEMITEMPORALIZING THE EXAMPLE

As previously noted, we plan to proceed gently and make our temporal revisions to the database in a piecemeal fashion. The first such revision involves "semitemporalizing" (so to speak) relvars S and SP by adding a timestamp attribute, SINCE, to each and renaming the relvars accordingly. See Fig. 5.2.

S_SINCE

SNO	SINCE
S1	d04
S2	d07
S3	d03
S4	d04
S5	d02

SP_SINCE

SNO	PNO	SINCE
S1	P1	d04
S1	P2	d05
S1	P3	d09
S1	P4	d05
S1	P5	d04
S1	P6	d06
S2	P1	d08
S2	P2	d09
S3	P2	d08
S4	P2	d06
S4	P4	d04
S4	P5	d05

Fig. 5.2: Simplified suppliers-and-shipments database (semitemporal version)—
sample values

For simplicity, we don't show real timestamps in Fig. 5.2; instead, we use symbols of the form *d01*, *d02*, etc. (where the "*d*" can conveniently be pronounced "day"), a convention to which we adhere throughout this book. (Note that most of our examples in the next few chapters do make use of time points that are days specifically; the applicable granularity in all of those examples is thus one day.) We assume that day 1 immediately precedes day 2, day 2 immediately precedes day 3, and so on; also, as you can see, we drop insignificant leading zeros from expressions such as "day 1."

The predicate for relvar S_SINCE is:

Supplier SNO has been under contract ever since day SINCE, and not on the day immediately before day SINCE.

And the predicate for relvar SP_SINCE is:

Supplier SNO has been able to supply part PNO ever since day SINCE, and not on the day immediately before day SINCE.

(We deliberately spell these predicates out fairly precisely here, just to remind you of the need to be careful when stating intended interpretations. We won't always bother to be quite so precise, however, appealing instead for the most part to our tightened interpretations of the terms *since* and *during* as explained at the very end of Chapter 4.)

Constraints (semitemporal database, Fig. 5.2): The key and foreign key constraints for the semitemporal database of Fig. 5.2 are the same as they were for the original nontemporal database of Fig. 5.1. Thus, the relvar definitions might look as follows:

```
VAR S_SINCE BASE RELATION { SNO SNO , SINCE DATE }
    KEY { SNO } ;

VAR SP_SINCE BASE RELATION { SNO SNO , PNO PNO , SINCE DATE }
    KEY { SNO , PNO }
    FOREIGN KEY { SNO } REFERENCES S_SINCE ;
```

We've defined the two SINCE attributes to be of type DATE, which we take to be a system defined type representing calendar dates (by which we mean dates—points on the timeline—that are accurate to the day and are constrained by the usual calendar rules, implying among other things that, e.g., "April 31st, 2015" and "February 29th, 2100" aren't valid dates).

But the foregoing definitions are inadequate as they stand. To be specific, we need an additional constraint, over and above the foreign key constraint from SP_SINCE to S_SINCE, to reflect the fact that no supplier can supply any part before that supplier is under contract:

```
CONSTRAINT XST1 /* "extra semitemporal constraint no. 1" */
    IS_EMPTY ( ( ( SP_SINCE RENAME { SINCE AS SPS } ) JOIN
               ( S_SINCE  RENAME { SINCE AS SS  } ) )
                                      WHERE SPS < SS ) ;
```

The intuition behind this formulation is that if tuple *sp* in SP_SINCE references tuple *s* in S_SINCE, then the SINCE value in *sp* mustn't be less than that in *s*. We observe that, given a semitemporal database like that of Fig. 5.2, we'll probably need to state many constraints of the same general and rather cumbersome nature as Constraint XST1, and we'll soon begin to wish we had some convenient shorthand for the purpose.

Queries (semitemporal database, Fig. 5.2): We now consider, not Queries A and B as such (i.e., as those queries were stated in the previous section), but rather certain semitemporal analogs of those queries.

■ **Query A:** Get supplier numbers for suppliers who are currently able to supply at least one part, showing in each case the date since when they've been able to do so.

If supplier S*x* is currently able to supply any parts at all, then clearly S*x* has been able to supply at least one part since the earliest SINCE date shown for that supplier in relvar SP_SINCE (e.g., if S*x* is S1, that earliest SINCE date is *d04*). Here then is a **Tutorial D** formulation of the query:

```
EXTEND SP_SINCE { SNO } : { SINCE := MIN ( !!SP_SINCE , SINCE ) }
```

Here's the result:

SNO	SINCE
S1	*d04*
S2	*d08*
S3	*d08*
S4	*d04*

■ **Query B:** Get supplier numbers for suppliers who are currently unable to supply any parts at all, showing in each case the date since when they've been unable to do so.

In our sample data there's just one supplier, supplier S5, who's currently unable to supply any parts at all. However, we can't discover the date since when that supplier has been unable to supply any parts, because there isn't enough information in the database; to say it again, the database is still only *semi*temporal. For example, suppose the current day is day 10. Then it might be the case that supplier S5 was able to supply at least one part from as early as day 2, when that supplier was first placed under contract, right up to as late as day 9; or, going to the other extreme, it might be the case that supplier S5 has never been able to supply any parts at all.

In order to have any hope of answering Query B, therefore, we must complete the "temporalizing" of our database (or the SP portion of it, at any rate). To be more precise, we must keep *historical records* in the database to show which suppliers were able to supply which parts when, as described in the section immediately following.

FULLY TEMPORALIZING THE EXAMPLE

Fig. 5.3 shows a "fully temporalized" version of suppliers and shipments.[1] Observe that the SINCE attributes have become FROM attributes, and each relvar has acquired an additional timestamp attribute called TO (and for that reason we've replaced "_SINCE" by "_FROM_TO" in the relvar names). The FROM and TO attributes together express the notion of an interval of time during which, according to our current beliefs, some proposition was true. *Note:* We've assumed for definiteness that today is day 10, and so we've shown *d10* as the TO value for each tuple that pertains to the current state of affairs. However, that assumption might, and indeed should, immediately lead you to wonder what mechanism could cause all of those *d10*'s to be replaced by *d11*'s on the stroke of midnight (as it were) on day 10. Well, we'll have to set this issue aside for the time being. We'll return to it in Chapter 12.

S_FROM_TO

SNO	FROM	TO
S1	*d04*	*d10*
S2	*d02*	*d04*
S2	*d07*	*d10*
S3	*d03*	*d10*
S4	*d04*	*d10*
S5	*d02*	*d10*

SP_FROM_TO

SNO	PNO	FROM	TO
S1	P1	*d04*	*d10*
S1	P2	*d05*	*d10*
S1	P3	*d09*	*d10*
S1	P4	*d05*	*d10*
S1	P5	*d04*	*d10*
S1	P6	*d06*	*d10*
S2	P1	*d02*	*d04*
S2	P1	*d08*	*d10*
S2	P2	*d03*	*d03*
S2	P2	*d09*	*d10*
S3	P2	*d08*	*d10*
S4	P2	*d06*	*d09*
S4	P4	*d04*	*d08*
S4	P5	*d05*	*d10*

Fig. 5.3: Simplified suppliers-and-shipments database (first fully temporal version, using explicit FROM and TO attributes)—sample values

Because we're now keeping historical records, there are more tuples in this database than there were in either of its predecessors, as you can see. In fact, the fully temporal database of Fig. 5.3 includes all of the information from the semitemporal one of Fig. 5.2—except that, purely for the sake of the example, we've shown the TO value for two of supplier S4's shipments as a date prior to the current date (i.e., we've converted those two shipments from "current" to past or "historical" information). That fully temporal database also includes historical information concerning an earlier interval of time, from *d02* to *d04*, during which supplier S2 was also under contract and able to supply certain parts. The predicate for S_FROM_TO is:

---

[1] At least, it shows a first attempt at such a version. A more satisfactory attempt will be described in the next chapter.

Supplier SNO was under contract throughout the interval from day FROM to day TO, and not throughout any interval that properly includes that interval.

And the predicate for SP_FROM_TO is:

Supplier SNO was able to supply part PNO throughout the interval from day FROM to day TO, and not throughout any interval that properly includes that interval.

Constraints (fully temporal database, Fig. 5.3): First of all, we need to guard against the absurdity of a FROM-TO pair appearing in which the TO value is less than the FROM value:

```
CONSTRAINT S_FROM_TO_OK IS_EMPTY ( S_FROM_TO WHERE TO < FROM ) ;

CONSTRAINT SP_FROM_TO_OK IS_EMPTY ( SP_FROM_TO WHERE TO < FROM ) ;
```

Next, observe from the double underlining in Fig. 5.3 that we've included the FROM attribute in the primary keys for both relvars. (Note that {SNO} alone is *not* a key for S_FROM_TO, nor is {SNO,PNO} a key for SP_FROM_TO.) But observe also that we could equally well have included the TO attributes in those keys instead of the FROM attributes; in fact, relvars S_FROM_TO and SP_FROM_TO both have two keys and are good examples of relvars for which there's no obvious reason to choose one of those keys as primary. We make the choices we do in Fig. 5.3 purely for the sake of definiteness, not for any good logical reason.
   Here then are the relvar definitions:

```
VAR S_FROM_TO BASE RELATION { SNO SNO , FROM DATE , TO DATE }
    KEY { SNO , FROM }
    KEY { SNO , TO } ;

VAR SP_FROM_TO BASE RELATION { SNO SNO , PNO PNO , FROM DATE , TO DATE }
    KEY { SNO , PNO , FROM }
    KEY { SNO , PNO , TO } ;
```

However, the constraints we've discussed so far—the two "_FROM_TO_OK" constraints and the four KEY constraints—are still inadequate in themselves to capture everything we'd like them to.[2] Consider relvar S_FROM_TO, for example. Obviously, if there's a tuple for supplier S*x* in that relvar with FROM value *f* and TO value *t*, we want there *not* to be a tuple for supplier S*x* in that same relvar indicating that S*x* was under contract on the day immediately before *f* or the day immediately after *t*. By way of example, consider supplier S1, for whom we have just one S_FROM_TO tuple, with FROM = *d04* and TO = *d10*:

---

[2] In particular, you might be wondering about the lack of any FOREIGN KEY specification for relvar SP. We'll get to that issue in a little while.

SNO	FROM	TO
S1	d04	d10

The mere fact that {SNO,FROM} is a key for relvar S_FROM_TO is clearly insufficient to prevent the appearance of an additional "overlapping" S1 tuple with (say) FROM = *d02* and TO = *d06*:

SNO	FROM	TO
S1	d02	d06

Observe that if this additional tuple did appear, the relvar would be in violation of its own predicate (because the previous tuple implies among other things that supplier S1 wasn't under contract on day 3, while the "overlapping" tuple implies that supplier S1 *was* under contract on day 3, and we would thus have a contradiction on our hands). Clearly, what we'd like is for these two S1 tuples to be merged into one, with FROM = *d02* and TO = *d10*:

SNO	FROM	TO
S1	d02	d10

Now, you might already have guessed that this idea of merging tuples is going to turn out to be very important. Indeed, *not* merging tuples in the foregoing example would be almost as bad as permitting duplicates! Duplicates amount to "saying the same thing twice." And those two tuples for supplier S1 with overlapping FROM-TO intervals do indeed "say the same thing twice"; to be specific, they both say among other things that supplier S1 was under contract on days 4, 5, and 6. We'll revisit this issue and discuss it in detail in Chapter 13.

Next, the fact that {SNO,FROM} is a key for S_FROM_TO is also insufficient to prevent the appearance of an additional "abutting" S1 tuple with (say) FROM = *d02* and TO = *d03*:

SNO	FROM	TO
S1	d02	d03

If this tuple did appear, the relvar would again be in violation of its own predicate (the original tuple implies among other things that supplier S1 wasn't under contract on day 3, while the "abutting" tuple implies that supplier S1 *was* under contract on day 3, and so again we would have a contradiction on our hands). As before, then, what we'd like is for the two tuples in question to be merged into one—the same one as before, in fact:

SNO	FROM	TO
S1	d02	d10

Again, we'll revisit this issue and discuss it in detail in Chapter 13.

Here then is a constraint that does prohibit such overlapping and abutting:

```
CONSTRAINT XFT1
    IS_EMPTY ( ( ( S_FROM_TO RENAME { FROM AS F1 , TO AS T1 } ) JOIN
                 ( S_FROM_TO RENAME { FROM AS F2 , TO AS T2 } ) )
                        WHERE ( T1 ≥ F2 AND T2 ≥ F1 ) )
                        OR ( F2 = T1+1 OR F1 = T2+1 ) ) ;
```

With this example, we begin to see the problem. This constraint is quite complicated!—not to mention the fact that we've taken the gross liberty of writing (e.g.) T1+1 to designate the immediate successor of the day denoted by T1, a point we'll come back to in the next chapter. Furthermore, we observe that, given a fully temporal database like that of Fig. 5.3, we'll probably need to state many constraints of the same general nature as constraint XFT1, and again we'll surely wish we had some good shorthand for the purpose.[3]

> *Aside:* In Chapter 13, we'll refer to the possibility that tuples might overlap in the foregoing sense as a *redundancy* problem (because it amounts to "saying the same thing twice"). Analogously, we'll refer to the possibility that tuples might abut in the foregoing sense as a *circumlocution* problem (because it amounts to taking two tuples to say what could be said with one). As already indicated, both of these problems give rise in turn to a *contradiction* problem, in the sense that the relvar might be in violation of its own predicate and might thereby imply, in effect, that some proposition and its negation are both true. What's more, it's going to turn out when we get to Chapter 13 that (in general) another kind of contradiction is possible, too; however, our running example in its present form is too simple to illustrate that second kind. *End of aside.*

Next, observe that {SNO,FROM} in relvar SP_FROM_TO is *not* a foreign key from that relvar to relvar S_FROM_TO, even though it does involve the same attributes as one of the keys—in fact, the one we arbitrarily chose to be the primary key—of this latter relvar. (It's not a foreign key because it's possible for an {SNO,FROM} value to appear in SP_FROM_TO and

---

[3] In fact, there's yet another problem with constraint XFT1 as stated: namely, what happens to the expression T1+1 if T1 happens to denote "the end of time"?

not in S_FROM_TO, as a glance at Fig. 5.3 will quickly confirm.)[4] On the other hand, we certainly do need to ensure that if a given supplier is represented in relvar SP_FROM_TO, then that same supplier is also represented in relvar S_FROM_TO:

```
CONSTRAINT XFT2 SP_FROM_TO { SNO } ⊆ S_FROM_TO { SNO } ;
```

This constraint is an example of an *inclusion dependency* [10]. Inclusion dependencies can be regarded as a generalization of foreign key constraints. And it should be clear that any fully temporal database like that of Fig. 5.3 is likely to involve a large number of such dependencies.

Constraint XFT2 is still not enough, however; we also need to ensure that if relvar SP_FROM_TO shows some supplier as being able to supply some part during some interval of time, then relvar S_FROM_TO shows that same supplier as being under contract throughout that same interval of time (this is an example of what in Chapter 14 we'll be calling a *denseness* constraint). Two attempts at formulating this constraint—the first of which is incorrect, please note—are shown below. *We recommend strongly that you try producing a formulation of your own before reading any further*.

━━━━━ ◆◆◆◆◆ ━━━━━

Here then is a first attempt (*Warning: Incorrect!*):

```
CONSTRAINT XFT3
    IS_EMPTY ( ( S_FROM_TO  RENAME { FROM AS SF , TO AS ST } ) JOIN
               ( SP_FROM_TO RENAME { FROM AS SPF , TO AS SPT } ) )
                        WHERE SPF < SF OR SPT > ST ) ;
```

The intuition behind this formulation is that if tuples *s* and *sp*, in relvars S_FROM_TO and SP_FROM_TO, respectively, correspond to the same supplier, then the FROM-TO interval in *s* must encompass that in *sp*. As the comment indicates, however, both the intuition and the formulation are incorrect, or at least incomplete. To see why, let relvars S_FROM_TO and SP_FROM_TO be as shown in Fig. 5.3, except that SP_FROM_TO contains an additional tuple for supplier S2 with (say) FROM = *d03* and TO = *d04*:

SNO	PNO	FROM	TO
S2	...	*d03*	*d04*

Such an arrangement is clearly consistent (since supplier S2 was under contract from day 2 to day 4), and yet constraint XFT3 as stated above would actually prohibit it—because (a) the result of the join would contain a tuple for supplier S2 with SF = *d07*, ST = *d10*, SPF = *d03*, and

---

[4] Analogous remarks apply to {SNO,TO}, of course.

SPT = *d04*; (b) the comparison SPF < SF would give TRUE for this tuple; (c) the IS_EMPTY test overall would therefore give FALSE; and (d) the constraint would thereby be violated.

Here by contrast is a correct formulation:

```
CONSTRAINT XFT3
   COUNT ( SP_FROM_TO { SNO , FROM , TO } ) =
   COUNT ( ( ( SP_FROM_TO
                  RENAME { FROM AS SPF , TO AS SPT } ) { SNO , SPF , SPT }
               JOIN
               ( S_FROM_TO
                  RENAME { FROM AS SF , TO AS ST } ) )
                                        WHERE SF ≤ SPF AND ST ≥ SPT ) ;
```

The (correct) intuition here is that if relvar SP_FROM_TO contains a tuple showing supplier S*x* as able to supply some specific part from day *spf* to day *spt*, then relvar S_FROM_TO must contain exactly one tuple showing supplier S*x* as being under contract throughout that interval. (Note that we're assuming here that *all* of the constraints discussed previously are in effect!) A detailed explanation follows:

- The constraint overall requires two counts to be equal.

- The first is a count of the number of distinct propositions of the form "S*x* was able to supply some part from day *spf* to day *spt*" implied by relvar SP_FROM_TO. Let that count be *N*.

- The second is a count of the number of tuples contained in a certain restriction of a certain join. The join in question should contain at least one tuple for each of the *N* propositions of the form "S*x* was under contract from day *sf* to day *st* and was able to supply some part from day *spf* to day *spt*" implied by relvar SP_FROM_TO. The subsequent restriction should then eliminate all but one of those tuples for each of those *N* propositions.

Now, you might have had some difficulty in following the foregoing explanation. Even if you didn't, you'll surely recognize that once again the constraint is quite complex, and yet once again we'll surely need to state many constraints of that same general nature, given a fully temporal database like that of Fig. 5.3. Once again, therefore, we'll surely wish we had some good shorthand available.

So much for constraints. We turn now to queries.

Queries (fully temporal database, Fig. 5.3): Here then are fully temporal analogs of Queries A and B:

- **Query A:** Get SNO-FROM-TO triples for suppliers who have been able to supply at least one part during at least one interval of time, where FROM and TO together designate a maximal interval during which supplier SNO was in fact able to supply at least one part. *Note:* We use the term *maximal interval* here as a convenient shorthand to mean (in the case at hand) that supplier SNO was unable to supply any part at all on the day immediately before FROM or immediately after TO. Note too that the result of the query might contain several tuples for the same supplier (but with different intervals, of course; moreover, those different intervals will neither abut nor overlap).

■ **Query B:** Get SNO-FROM-TO triples for suppliers who have been unable to supply any parts at all during at least one interval of time, where FROM and TO together designate a maximal interval during which supplier SNO was in fact unable to supply any parts at all. (Again the result might contain several tuples for the same supplier.)

Well, you might like to take a little time to convince yourself that, like us, you'd really rather not even attempt these queries! If you do make the effort, however, the fact that they *can* be expressed, albeit exceedingly laboriously, will (or should) eventually emerge, but it'll surely be obvious that some kind of shorthand is highly desirable.

In a nutshell, then, the problem of temporal data is that it quickly leads to constraints and queries[5] that are unreasonably complex to express: unreasonably complex, that is, unless the system provides some well designed shorthands, which commercially available DBMSs typically don't.[6] In the next chapter, therefore, we'll begin our search for such a set of "well designed shorthands."

EXERCISES

5.1   State as precisely as you can the predicates for:

a.   Relvars S and SP as illustrated in Fig. 5.1

b.   Relvars S_SINCE and SP_SINCE as illustrated in Fig. 5.2

c.   Relvars S_FROM_TO and SP_FROM_TO as illustrated in Fig. 5.3

---

[5] Not to mention updates. You might have noticed that this chapter—deliberately, of course—has had absolutely nothing to say about updates, prior to this point. (Well, actually that's not quite true—the chapter *has* discussed constraints at some length, showing how complicated they can be in a temporal database, and, as you'd expect, complications in constraints can lead to concomitant complications in updates.) But the fact is, updates on temporal data can quickly become very complex indeed, and we don't yet have enough of the groundwork in place to illustrate that complexity properly. We'll discuss it in detail, of course, in a later chapter (Chapter 16).

[6] And this is as good a place as any to warn you that most of the ideas we'll be describing in the next several chapters unfortunately remain unimplemented in commercial database systems at the time of writing. What's more, most of those ideas have no counterpart in the current (2011) version of the SQL standard either (see Part IV).

5.2   Explain the redundancy and circumlocution problems in your own words.

5.3   Write **Tutorial D** expressions for the following queries on the database of Fig. 5.2:

a. Get supplier numbers for suppliers who are currently able to supply at least two different parts, showing in each case the date since when they've been able to do so.

b. Get supplier numbers for suppliers who are currently unable to supply at least two different parts, showing in each case the date since when they've been unable to do so.

What about analogs of these two queries on the database of Fig.5.3? At least try to state such analogs in natural language, even if you decide you'd rather not attempt to come up with any corresponding **Tutorial D** formulations.

ANSWERS

5.1   See the body of the chapter. *Note:* Actually there's a point here that might be bothering you. Consider relvar S_FROM_TO, for example, for which we said the predicate was *Supplier SNO was under contract throughout the interval from day FROM to day TO, and not throughout any interval that properly includes that interval.* Now, in the sample value for that relvar shown in Fig. 5.3, we used day 10 (i.e., *d10*) as the TO value in tuples that pertained to the current state of affairs—and that phrase "the current state of affairs" implies, or at least rather strongly suggests, that the very same state of affairs might continue to exist on day 11. But if it does, then the relvar will be in violation of its own predicate!—because the interval from, say, day 4 to day 11 clearly "properly includes" the interval from day 4 to day 10. Well, we did say in the body of the chapter that we'd have to set aside, for now, the issue of using a definite value such as *d10* in such a manner. But the present discussion can be seen as a strong argument (a strong argument, that is, in addition to other arguments to be presented later in the book) for *not* using definite values such as *d10* in such a manner.

5.2   See the section "Fully Temporalizing the Example" in the body of the chapter.

5.3

```
a.  WITH ( t1 := SP_SINCE RENAME { PNO AS XNO , SINCE AS XS } ,
           t2 := SP_SINCE RENAME { PNO AS YNO , SINCE AS YS } ,
           t3 := t1 JOIN t2 ,
           t4 := t3 WHERE XNO ≠ YNO AND XS ≤ YS ) :
    EXTEND t4 { SNO } : { SINCE := MIN ( !!t4 , YS ) }
```

b. This query can't be fully answered using only the "semitemporal" database of Fig. 5.2. However, we can at least get supplier numbers for suppliers who are currently unable to supply at least two different parts:

```
WITH ( t1 := SP_SINCE RENAME { PNO AS XNO , SINCE AS XS } ,
       t2 := SP_SINCE RENAME { PNO AS YNO , SINCE AS YS } ,
       t3 := t1 JOIN t2 ,
       t4 := t3 WHERE XNO ≠ YNO ) :
S { SNO } NOT MATCHING t4
```

Analogous queries for the database of Fig. 5.3, expressed in natural language, are:

a. Get SNO-FROM-TO triples such that FROM and TO together designate a maximal interval during which supplier SNO was able supply at least two different parts.

b. Get SNO-FROM-TO triples such that FROM and TO together designate a maximal interval during which supplier SNO was unable supply at least two different parts.

Chapter 6

Intervals

Lucid intervals and happy pauses

—Francis Bacon:
History of King Henry VII (1622)

We're now ready to embark on our development of an appropriate set of constructs for dealing properly with temporal data. The first and most fundamental step is to recognize the need to deal with intervals as such—i.e., the need to treat them as values in their own right, instead of as pairs of separate FROM and TO values as in the previous chapter.

WHAT'S AN INTERVAL?

Take another look at Fig. 5.3 in Chapter 5. According to that figure, supplier S1 was able to supply part P1 during the interval from day 4 to day 10. But what does "the interval from day 4 to day 10" mean? It's clear that days 5, 6, 7, 8, and 9 are included—but what about days 4 and 10 themselves? It turns out that if some interval *i* is described as stretching "from *b* to *e*," sometimes we want to consider the points *b* and *e* as part of *i* and sometimes we don't. If we do want to consider *b* as part of *i*, we say *i* is closed at its beginning, otherwise we say it's open at its beginning. Likewise, if we want to consider *e* as part of *i*, we say *i* is closed at its end, otherwise we say it's open at its end.

    Conventionally, therefore, we denote an interval by a pair of points *b* and *e* separated by a colon,[1] preceded by an opening bracket or parenthesis and followed by a closing bracket or parenthesis. We use a bracket where we want the closed interpretation, a parenthesis where we want the open one. There are thus four distinct ways to denote the specific interval that runs from the "begin point" day 4 to the "end point" day 10, inclusive:

```
[d04:d10]
[d04:d11)
(d03:d10]
(d03:d11)
```

---

[1] Other separators—e.g., commas, hyphens—are also used in the literature. We prefer colons because commas can make intervals look like subscripts and hyphens can look like minus signs.

Now, you might think it odd to use, say, an opening bracket with a closing parenthesis. In fact, however, there are good reasons to allow all four styles. Indeed, the closed:open style—i.e., closed at the beginning and open at the end, as in, e.g., [*d04:d11*)—is the style most often used in practice. But the closed:closed style, as in, e.g., [*d04:d10*], is surely the most intuitive, and it's the one we'll favor throughout what follows. *Note:* To see why the closed:open style might be advantageous, consider the operation of splitting the interval [*d04:d11*) immediately before, say, day 7. The result is the abutting pair of intervals [*d04:d07*) and [*d07:d11*).

Now, given that an interval such as [*d04:d10*] can be considered as a value in its own right, it clearly makes sense to combine the FROM and TO attributes of each of the relvars of Fig. 5.3 into a single attribute, DURING, whose values are drawn from some interval type (see the section "Point and Interval Types" later in this chapter). Fig. 6.1 shows what happens to our running example if we adopt this approach (note the relvar name changes):

S_DURING

SNO	DURING
S1	[*d04:d10*]
S2	[*d02:d04*]
S2	[*d07:d10*]
S3	[*d03:d10*]
S4	[*d04:d10*]
S5	[*d02:d10*]

SP_DURING

SNO	PNO	DURING
S1	P1	[*d04:d10*]
S1	P2	[*d05:d10*]
S1	P3	[*d09:d10*]
S1	P4	[*d05:d10*]
S1	P5	[*d04:d10*]
S1	P6	[*d06:d10*]
S2	P1	[*d02:d04*]
S2	P1	[*d08:d10*]
S2	P2	[*d03:d03*]
S2	P2	[*d09:d10*]
S3	P2	[*d08:d10*]
S4	P2	[*d06:d09*]
S4	P4	[*d04:d08*]
S4	P5	[*d05:d10*]

Fig. 6.1: Simplified suppliers-and-shipments database (second fully temporal version, using intervals)–sample values

The predicate for S_DURING is:

Supplier SNO was under contract throughout the interval from the day that's the begin point of DURING to the day that's the end point of DURING, inclusive, and not throughout any interval that properly includes that interval.

And the predicate for SP_DURING is:

Supplier SNO was able to supply part PNO throughout the interval from the day that's the begin point of DURING to the day that's the end point of DURING, inclusive, and not throughout any interval that properly includes that interval.

The idea of replacing the pair of attributes FROM and TO by the single attribute DURING has a number of immediate advantages. Here are some of them:

■ It avoids the problem (if it really is a problem) of having to make an arbitrary choice as to which of two keys should be regarded as primary. For example, relvar S_FROM_TO had two keys, {SNO,FROM} and {SNO,TO}, but relvar S_DURING has just one, {SNO,DURING}, which we can therefore designate as primary if we want to without any undesirable arbitrariness.[2] Similarly, relvar SP_FROM_TO also had two keys but relvar SP_DURING has just one, {SNO,PNO,DURING}, which again we can designate as primary if we want to.

■ It also avoids the problem of having to know whether the FROM-TO intervals in the previous version of the database (Fig. 5.3) are to be interpreted as closed or open with respect to FROM and TO. In Chapter 5, those intervals were implicitly taken to be closed with respect to both FROM and TO. But now, e.g., [*d04*:*d10*], [*d04*:*d11*), (*d03*:*d10*], and (*d03*:*d11*) are four distinct "possible representations" of the very same interval, and we can use whichever of these four styles we like—whichever one best serves our purposes at the time.[3] If we like, we can even mix styles and show, e.g., the DURING values for suppliers S1 and S4 in S_DURING as [*d04*:*d10*] and (*d03*:*d11*), respectively, even though those two values are actually identical. *Note:* Refer to Chapter 1 if you need to refresh your memory regarding the concept of possible representations.

■ Yet another advantage is that constraints "to guard against the absurdity of a FROM-TO pair in which the TO value is less than the FROM value" (as we put it in the previous chapter) are no longer necessary, because the constraint FROM ≤ TO is implicit in the very notion of an interval type. That is, those explicit constraints of the form FROM ≤ TO are all effectively replaced by a generic constraint that implicitly applies to intervals of each and every specific interval type. Those specific interval types are defined by means of invocations of the interval type generator (again, see the section "Point and Interval Types," later), and that generic constraint can be thought of as being associated with that type generator, just as the generic interval operators to be discussed later in this chapter and in the next can also be thought of as being associated with that type generator.

Other advantages will become clear over the next few chapters.

---

[2] In any case, reducing the number of keys is probably a good thing in its own right.

[3] This claim is correct in general, but we do need to point out the following exceptions. Let *i* be the closed:closed interval [*b*:*e*]. Then *i* can't be represented in either the open:closed or open:open style if *b* is "the beginning of time"; likewise, *i* can't be represented in either the closed:open or open:open style if *e* is "the end of time." The closed:closed style, by contrast, is capable of representing all possible intervals; indeed, it's the only style that does have this desirable property.

As for the constraints and queries discussed in the previous chapter, it should be clear that direct analogs of those constraints and queries can be formulated against the database of Fig. 6.1, just so long as we have a way of accessing the begin and end points of any given interval (once again, see the section "Point and Interval Types"). We won't bother to show such formulations, however, since it's precisely part of our goal to come up with a better way of dealing with such matters—a way, that is, of expressing such constraints and queries that involves something better than just direct analogs of those earlier formulations. We'll discuss such a better way in subsequent chapters; to be specific, we'll deal with queries in Chapters 9-11 (and again in Chapter 15) and constraints in Chapters 13 and 14.

One final remark: We should stress the point, implicit in much of what we've been saying already, that intervals as discussed in this chapter are scalar values—they have no user visible components. (The begin and end points for a given interval are components of a certain possible representation of that interval, not components of that interval as such.) Another way of saying the same thing is to say that intervals are "encapsulated" (but see reference [36]).

APPLICATIONS OF INTERVALS

The interval concept is the key to addressing the problems raised in the previous chapter; in other words, intervals are the abstraction we need for dealing with temporal data satisfactorily. Before we start getting into details of temporal intervals as such, however, we want to emphasize the fact that the interval concept is actually of much wider applicability; that is, there are many other applications for intervals, applications in which the intervals aren't necessarily temporal ones as such (see, e.g., reference [75]). Here are a few examples:

- Tax brackets are represented by taxable income ranges—i.e., intervals whose contained points are money values.

- Machines are built to operate within certain temperature and voltage ranges—i.e., intervals whose contained points are temperatures and voltages, respectively.

- Animals vary in the range of frequencies of light and sound waves to which their eyes and ears are receptive.

- Various natural phenomena occur and can be measured in ranges in depth of soil or sea or height above sea level.

And so on. And although our focus in this book is, for the most part, on temporal intervals specifically, many of our discussions are relevant to intervals in general, not just to temporal ones in particular. However, we'll consider certain specifically temporal issues in Part III of this book, when we get to the chapters that discuss temporal database design and various related matters.

Note: All of the intervals discussed so far can be thought of as one-dimensional. Given two one-dimensional intervals, however, we might sometimes want to consider them in combination as forming a two-dimensional interval. For example, a rectangular plot of ground might be thought of as a two-dimensional interval, because it is, by definition, an object with length and width, each of which is basically a one-dimensional interval measured along some axis. And, of course, we can extend this idea to any number of dimensions. For example, a (rather simple!) building might be regarded as a three-dimensional interval: It's an object with length, width, and height, or in other words a *cuboid*. (More realistically, a building might be regarded as a set of such cuboids that overlap in various ways.) And so on. In what follows, however, we'll restrict our attention to one-dimensional intervals specifically (barring explicit statements to the contrary), and we'll omit the "one-dimensional" qualifier for simplicity.

POINT AND INTERVAL TYPES

Our discussion of intervals so far has been mostly intuitive in nature. Now we need to address the issue a little more formally. We begin by considering the interval [*d04:d10*] once again; let's agree to refer to it as "the interval value *i*," or just interval *i* for short. In accordance with our running convention, the points that make up interval *i*—namely, *d04*, *d05*, ..., and *d10*—are all, specifically, days. For the sake of the example, therefore, let's assume those points are in fact all values of type DATE, where (as in the previous chapter) type DATE represents calendar dates, accurate to the day. Then type DATE is said to be the *point type* for interval *i*.

But how exactly do we know the points in *i*, in sequence, are the ones we said they were (namely, *d04*, *d05*, ..., *d10*)? Well, we certainly know that *i* includes its begin and end points *d04* and *d10*, by definition. We also know that *i* consists of a set of points arranged in accordance with some agreed ordering. So if we're to determine the complete set of points in *i* in their proper sequence, we first need to determine the point—informally, let's refer to it as *d04*+1— that immediately follows the begin point *d04* according to that agreed ordering. That point *d04*+1 is the *successor* of *d04* according to that ordering, and the function by which that successor is determined is the corresponding *successor function*. In the case at hand, where the point type is DATE, the successor function is basically "next day" (meaning "add one day to the given date")—i.e., it's a function that, given a DATE value *d*, returns the DATE value that's the immediate successor of *d*. *Note:* If *d*+1 is the successor of *d* in some ordering, then of course *d* is the *predecessor* of *d*+1 in that same ordering. Informally, we sometimes refer to the predecessor of *d* as *d*−1.

Having determined that *d04*+1 is the successor of *d04*, we must next determine whether *d04*+1 comes after the end point *d10* according to that same agreed ordering. If it doesn't, then *d04*+1 is indeed a point in *i* = [*d04:d10*], and we must now consider the next point, *d04*+2. Repeating this process until we come to the first point *d04*+*n* (actually *d04*+7, or in other words *d11*) that comes after *d10*—or, just possibly, until we come to "the last day" (see below)—we'll discover every point, in sequence, in *i* = [*d04:d10*].

More generally, let interval *i* = [*b:e*], where *b* and *e* are again values of type DATE, and the same "next day" successor function applies. Then there are, of course, a couple of special cases to consider:

■   *b* = "the first day" (i.e., the point corresponding to "the beginning of time," which has no predecessor). The expression *b*−1 is undefined in this case.

■   *e* = "the last day" (i.e., the point corresponding to "the end of time," which has no successor). The expression *e*+1 is undefined in this case.

So, as the foregoing discussion should be sufficient to suggest, we have the following:

Definition: Type *T* is usable as a **point type** if all of the following are defined for it:

a.   A *total ordering*, according to which the operator ">" (greater than) is defined for every pair of values *v1* and *v2* of type *T*, such that if *v1* and *v2* are distinct, exactly one of the expressions *v1* > *v2* and *v2* > *v1* returns TRUE and the other returns FALSE

b.   Niladic *first* and *last* operators, which return the smallest (first) and largest (last) value of type *T*, respectively, according to the aforementioned ordering

c.   Monadic *next* and *prior* operators, which return the successor (if it exists) and predecessor (if it exists), respectively, of any given value of type *T* according to the aforementioned ordering

Points arising (pardon the pun):

■   The *next* operator is the successor function, of course. Also, as already noted, *next* and *prior* are undefined if their argument—the given value of point type *T*—is in fact the last or first value, respectively, of that type *T*.

■   As we know from Chapter 1, the "=" operator is certainly defined for any given point type *T*. Given that ">" is defined as well, therefore (and given also the availability of the boolean operator NOT), we can assume without loss of generality that all of the usual comparison operators—"=", "≠", ">", "≥", "<", and "≤"—are in fact available for all pairs of values of type *T*.

We now make an important assumption. To be specific, we assume until further notice that *the successor function is unique*; in other words, if *T* is a point type, then *T* has exactly one successor function. Now, this assumption might seem reasonable at first glance—but is it? Consider type DATE once again. In practice, we don't always want to deal with dates that are accurate to the day. For example, U.S. presidential administrations are usually specified in terms of dates that are accurate only to the year (e.g., "Gerald R. Ford, 1974-1977"), and the same is true for reigns of monarchs and the like. It follows that we might want to consider two distinct successor functions for type DATE, "next day" and "next year" (note that these two functions correspond informally to two distinct DATE *granularities*—see Chapter 4). Such considerations muddy the picture considerably, as you might expect. We therefore choose to defer detailed discussion of them to a later chapter (Chapter 18); until then, we'll simply stay with our "unique successor function" assumption. Please understand, however, that certain of the concepts and issues discussed prior to Chapter 18 will need to be revisited (and extended slightly, in some cases) when we get to that chapter.

To get back to our example of the interval *i* = [*d04*:*d10*], we can now pin down the type of that value precisely, as follows:

- First, of course, it's of some interval type, and that fact by itself is sufficient to determine the generic interval operators that are available for the interval value in question (just as to say that, e.g., some value is of some relation type is sufficient to determine the generic relational operators—restrict, project, and so on—that are available for the relation value in question). A few such operators are discussed later in this section, and more are discussed in Chapter 7.

- Second, the interval value in question is, specifically, an interval from one DATE value to another, and—thanks to our "unique successor function" assumption—that fact is sufficient to determine the specific set of values that together constitute the interval type in question: It's precisely the set of intervals of the form [*b*:*e*], where *b* and *e* are values of type DATE and, by definition, $b \leq e$.

In other words, we can say the specific type of the interval value *i* = [*d04*:*d10*] is, precisely, INTERVAL_DATE, where:

- INTERVAL is a type generator, and INTERVAL_DATE represents a specific invocation of that type generator.

- DATE is, as already explained, the point type for this interval type; i.e., intervals of this specific interval type are made up of points of this specific point type.

Here by way of illustration are a couple more examples of interval types:

■ INTERVAL_INTEGER

The point type here is INTEGER; the successor function is "next integer" (i.e., "add one"), and values of this interval type are intervals of the form [*b*:*e*], where *b* and *e* are values of type INTEGER (and *b* ≤ *e*).

■ INTERVAL_MONEY

MONEY here is—let's assume—a type that represents monetary amounts measured in dollars and cents. The successor function is "add one cent." Values of this interval type are intervals of the form [*b*:*e*], where *b* and *e* are values of type MONEY (and *b* ≤ *e*).

And here (at last!) is a formal definition of the term *interval*:

Definition: Let *T* be a point type. Then an *interval value* (or just an **interval** for short) *i* of type INTERVAL_*T* is a value for which two monadic operators, BEGIN and END, and one dyadic operator, "∈", are defined, such that:

a.   BEGIN (*i*) and END (*i*) both return a value of type *T*.

b.   BEGIN (*i*) ≤ END (*i*).

c.   If *p* is a value of type *T*, then *p* ∈ *i* is true if and only if BEGIN (*i*) ≤ *p* and *p* ≤ END (*i*) are both true. *Note:* Of course, "∈" here is just a variant on the conventional set membership operator. The expression "*p* ∈ *i*" can be pronounced as "*p* belongs to *i*" or "*p* is contained in *i*" or, more simply, just "*p* [is] in *i*."

Points arising:

■ Observe that intervals are always nonempty—i.e., there's always at least one point in any given interval.

■ Intervals *i1* and *i2* of the same interval type are equal—i.e., *i1* = *i2* is true—if and only if BEGIN (*i1*) = BEGIN (*i2*) and END (*i1*) = END (*i2*) are both true (see Chapter 7 for further discussion).

■ As noted earlier, the begin and end points for a given interval together constitute a possible representation for that interval. In **Tutorial D**, therefore, we would normally refer to those BEGIN and END operators as THE_BEGIN and THE_END, respectively (see Chapter 1). However, we use BEGIN and END in this book for consistency with other writings in this field.

■ By the same token, an expression of the form "[*b:e*]" can be thought of, informally, as an interval selector invocation. We'll have a little more to say in the next chapter as to what interval selectors (as well as the crucially important successor and predecessor functions) might look like in a real language.

■ An interval *i* for which BEGIN (*i*) = END (*i*) is true is called a *unit interval*. In other words, a unit interval is an interval that contains exactly one value of the associated point type; for example, the interval [*d04:d04*] is a unit interval of type INTERVAL_DATE.

To close this section, here are definitions for relvars S_DURING and SP_DURING:

```
VAR S_DURING BASE RELATION
  { SNO SNO , DURING INTERVAL_DATE }
    KEY { SNO , DURING } ;

VAR SP_DURING BASE RELATION
  { SNO SNO , PNO PNO , DURING INTERVAL_DATE }
    KEY { SNO , PNO , DURING } ;
```

Please note, however, that these definitions are very incomplete! We'll come back and elaborate on them in Chapters 13 and 14.

A MORE SEARCHING EXAMPLE

Relvars S_DURING and SP_DURING both have just one interval attribute, called DURING in both cases. However, it's certainly possible for a relvar to have two or more such attributes. For example:

■ Suppose, not unreasonably, that there's a total ordering on part numbers, such that P1 < P2 < P3 (etc.)—more precisely, suppose type PNO can legitimately be used as a point type— and suppose further that we wish our database to show that certain suppliers were able to supply certain *ranges* of parts during certain intervals of time.

■ Then relvar SP_DURING could well have two interval attributes, DURING and PARTS (say), where DURING is as before and PARTS indicates the corresponding part ranges.

To avoid confusion, let's refer to this revised version of the relvar as S_PARTS_DURING instead of SP_DURING. A sample value is shown in Fig. 6.2. *Note:* That sample value is deliberately not meant to correspond in any particular way to the sample value shown for relvar SP_DURING in Fig. 6.1.

S_PARTS_DURING

SNO	PARTS	DURING
S1	[P1:P3]	[d01:d04]
S1	[P2:P4]	[d07:d08]
S1	[P5:P6]	[d09:d09]
S2	[P1:P1]	[d08:d09]
S2	[P1:P2]	[d08:d08]
S2	[P3:P4]	[d07:d08]
S3	[P2:P4]	[d01:d04]
S3	[P3:P5]	[d01:d04]
S3	[P2:P4]	[d05:d06]
S3	[P2:P4]	[d06:d09]
S4	[P3:P4]	[d05:d08]

Fig. 6.2: A relvar with two interval attributes (S_PARTS_DURING)—sample value

Here's the predicate for S_PARTS_DURING:

Throughout the interval from the begin point of DURING to the end point of DURING, inclusive, supplier SNO was able to supply every part PNO in the interval from the begin point of PARTS to the end point of PARTS, inclusive.

Observe that, with respect to attribute DURING, this predicate *doesn't* include text of the form "and not throughout any interval that properly includes that interval"; nor does it include any analogous text with respect to attribute PARTS. Indeed, you might have noticed that the sample value in Fig. 6.2 suffers—again deliberately, of course—from certain redundancies; for example, it tells us twice that supplier S3 was able to supply part P4 on days 1 to 4 inclusive. (The point is, of course, that if the predicate did include text of the form "and not throughout any interval that properly includes that interval," then such redundancies couldn't occur. We'll have a lot more to say about such issues in later chapters—in Chapters 10 and 13 in particular.)

Aside: Actually, given the predicate as stated, the relation shown in Fig. 6.2 can't possibly be a legitimate value for the relvar. At best it's incomplete. The reason is as follows: Since the predicate does indeed not include text of the form "not throughout any interval that properly includes that interval," it follows that if, e.g., the sole tuple shown for supplier S4 appears, then numerous additional tuples for supplier S4 ought by rights to appear as well: one saying supplier S4 supplies parts P3 and P4 on day 5, one saying supplier S4 supplies parts P3 and P4 on days 5 and 6, one saying supplier S4 supplies part P3 on days 5 and 6, and so on, for a grand total of 30 tuples altogether—and that's just for supplier S4! For space reasons, however, we certainly don't want to expand the figure to show all of those "missing" tuples; for simplicity, therefore, we adopt the fiction—where it makes any difference—that the relation shown in the figure does in fact constitute a legitimate value for the relvar after all. *End of aside.*

In the remainder of the book we'll occasionally make use of examples based on relvar S_PARTS_DURING instead of our more usual relvar SP_DURING. Meanwhile, here are a few final points to close the present chapter:

■ Relvar S_PARTS_DURING has two interval attributes, but only one of them represents temporal intervals specifically. Here by contrast is a relvar (in outline) with two distinct interval attributes, both of them representing temporal intervals specifically:

```
EMP { ENO , PRIMARY , SECONDARY }
```

Here attributes PRIMARY and SECONDARY show the intervals of time during which the employee identified by ENO received his or her primary and secondary education, respectively.

■ Second, note that even if we had no *relvars* (like EMP or S_PARTS_DURING) with two or more interval attributes, we'd still need to be able to deal with *relations*—i.e., relation values—with two or more such attributes. For example, as soon as we join the two relations *r1* {*A,B*} and *r2* {*A,C*}, where *B* and *C* are interval attributes, we obtain a relation with two such attributes.

■ Third, we could extend the S_PARTS_DURING example to one with three interval attributes by replacing attribute SNO by an attribute SUPPLIERS showing supplier number ranges (assuming type SNO is also a legitimate point type, of course). Here's a sample value:

SUPPLIERS	PARTS	DURING
[S1:S2]	[P2:P3]	[*d03*:*d04*]
[S2:S3]	[P3:P4]	[*d04*:*d05*]

In general, there's obviously no reason why a relation (or a relvar) shouldn't have any number of interval attributes. What's more, it's possible, as the foregoing example also demonstrates, to have a relation or relvar with interval attributes only (i.e., every attribute is of some interval type).

EXERCISES

6.1   State the predicates, as precisely as you can, for relvars S_DURING and SP_DURING from Fig. 6.1.

6.2   List as many advantages as you can think of in favor of replacing FROM-TO attribute pairs by individual DURING attributes.

6.3   Give some examples of your own of nontemporal intervals, over and above the ones listed earlier in the chapter.

6.4   Define the terms *point type* and *interval type*. Complete the following sentence in your own words: "Type *T* is usable as a point type if ... ."

6.5   Is a singleton scalar type—i.e., one containing just a single scalar value—a valid point type? What about the empty scalar type (i.e., the scalar type containing no values at all, called *omega* in reference [51])?

6.6   Let *i* be an interval. What do the expressions BEGIN (*i*), END (*i*), and *p* ∈ *i* return?

6.7   What's a unit interval?

6.8   Give a plausible predicate for the relation with three interval attributes shown at the end of the section "A More Searching Example."

6.9   Give examples of your own of (a) a relation or relvar with two interval attributes; (b) a relation or relvar with three.

6.10 The following relvar definitions are for a considerably extended version of the courses-and-students database from Exercise 2.2 in Chapter 2:

```
VAR COURSE BASE RELATION
  { COURSENO   COURSENO ,
    CNAME      NAME ,
    AVAILABLE DATE }
  KEY { COURSENO } ;

VAR CANCELED_COURSE BASE RELATION
  { COURSENO COURSENO ,
    CANCELED DATE }
  KEY { COURSENO }
  FOREIGN KEY { COURSENO } REFERENCES COURSE ;
```

```
VAR STUDENT BASE RELATION
  { STUDENTNO   STUDENTNO ,
    SNAME       NAME ,
    REGISTERED DATE }
  KEY { STUDENTNO , REGISTERED } ;

VAR UNREG_STUDENT BASE RELATION
  { STUDENTNO     STUDENTNO ,
    UNREGISTERED DATE }
  KEY { STUDENTNO , UNREGISTERED } ;

VAR ENROLLMENT BASE RELATION
  { COURSENO   COURSENO ,
    STUDENTNO STUDENTNO ,
    ENROLLED   DATE }
  KEY { COURSENO , STUDENTNO }
  FOREIGN KEY { COURSENO } REFERENCES COURSE
  FOREIGN KEY { STUDENTNO } REFERENCES STUDENT ;

VAR COMPLETED_COURSE BASE RELATION
  { COURSENO   COURSENO ,
    STUDENTNO STUDENTNO ,
    COMPLETED DATE ,
    GRADE       GRADE }
  KEY { COURSENO , STUDENTNO }
  FOREIGN KEY { COURSENO } REFERENCES COURSE ;
```

The predicates are as follows:

- **COURSE:** *Course COURSENO, named CNAME, became available on date AVAILABLE.*

- **CANCELED_COURSE:** *Course COURSENO ceased to be available on date CANCELED.*

- **STUDENT:** *Student STUDENTNO, named SNAME, registered with the university on date REGISTERED.*

- **UNREG_STUDENT:** *Student STUDENTNO left the university on date UNREGISTERED.*

- **ENROLLMENT:** *Student STUDENTNO enrolled on course COURSENO on date ENROLLED.*

- **COMPLETED_COURSE:** *Student STUDENTNO completed course COURSENO on date COMPLETED, achieving grade GRADE.*

a. Assuming this database constitutes a record of the relevant part of a typical university's business, what additional constraints (expressed in natural language) might be required?

b. Suppose we decide to add the following relvar, with the intent (eventually) of using it to replace relvar COMPLETED_COURSE:

```
VAR STUDIED BASE RELATION
   { COURSENO  COURSENO ,
     STUDENTNO STUDENTNO ,
     DURING    INTERVAL_DATE ,
     GRADE     GRADE }
  KEY { COURSENO , STUDENTNO }
  FOREIGN KEY { COURSENO } REFERENCES COURSE ;
```

The predicate is:

Student STUDENTNO studied course COURSENO throughout interval DURING (and not throughout any interval that properly includes that interval), achieving grade GRADE.

Write a query, using relvars ENROLLMENT and COMPLETED_COURSE, whose result corresponds to exactly this predicate (and can therefore usefully be assigned to relvar STUDIED).

c. Write a definition for a relvar called COURSE_AVAILABILITY that combines relvars COURSE and CANCELED_COURSE analogously to the way STUDIED combined relvars ENROLLMENT and COMPLETED_COURSE in part b. of this exercise.

d. Write a query that makes use of relvars STUDENT and UNREG_STUDENT to obtain the entire student registration history of the university. The heading of the result should look like this:

```
{ STUDENTNO STUDENTNO , SNAME NAME , REG_DURING INTERVAL_DATE }
```

The value of END (REG_DURING) for current registrations should be set to "the last day," which we assume—see Chapter 7—can be denoted LAST_DATE ( ).

ANSWERS

6.1 See the section "What's an Interval?" in the body of the chapter.

6.2 See the section "What's an Interval?" in the body of the chapter.

6.3 Here are some possibilities:

■ Intervals of exam scores, such as those determining grades for a course

■ Intervals of page numbers, such as those found in an index to a book

■ Intervals of chapter numbers, such as the constituent chapters of parts of a book

■ Intervals of latitude, such as those within which certain winds blow

■ Salary ranges, such as those agreed for different job levels

■ Intervals of house numbers such as, in some countries, those of buildings on the same block in some street

■ Intervals of letters of the alphabet, such as those indicating the contents of the different volumes of an encyclopedia

6.4   See the section "Point and Interval Types" in the body of the chapter.

6.5   Yes, a singleton scalar type is a valid point type, even though none of its values has a successor. Let *PT* be such a type, and let *p* be the sole value of that type. Then the *first* and *last* operators both return *p*, and the *next* and *prior* operators always fail. *Note:* The interval type INTERVAL_*PT* is a singleton type also, of course—it contains just the unit interval [*p*:*p*].

   As for the empty scalar type, believe it or not, it too satisfies the requirements for a point type!—vacuously so, however, because if the point type is empty, then the corresponding interval type will necessarily be empty as well. Of course, the operators *first*, *last*, *next*, *prior*, BEGIN, END, and "∈"will all be undefined in this case.

6.6   See the section "Point and Interval Types" in the body of the chapter.

6.7   A unit interval is an interval *i* for which BEGIN (*i*) = END (*i*) is true.

6.8   *Throughout the interval from the begin point of DURING to the end point of DURING, inclusive, every supplier SNO in the interval from the begin point of SUPPLIERS to the end point of SUPPLIERS, inclusive, was able to supply every part PNO in the interval from the begin point of PARTS to the end point of PARTS, inclusive.*[4]

---

[4] But if the predicate is no more and no less than as stated here, then the sample value shown for the relvar at the end of the section "A More Searching Example" (like the sample value shown for relvar S_PARTS_DURING in that same section) is certainly incomplete.

6.9 *No answer provided.*

6.10

a. Here are some reasonable possibilities:

■ A course can be canceled only if it's currently available.

■ A student can register only if he or she isn't already registered.

■ A student can enroll in a course only if he or she is currently registered, the course is currently available, and he or she isn't already enrolled in the course.

■ A student can become "unregistered" only if he or she is currently registered.

■ A student can complete a course only if the student is currently enrolled in the course.

Note that the following constraint *doesn't* need to be added, because it's implied by the KEY specification for relvar COURSE:

■ A course can become available only if it's not already available.

b.
```
( EXTEND ( ENROLLMENT JOIN COMPLETED_COURSE ) :
            { DURING := INTERVAL_DATE ( ⁻[ ENROLLED : COMPLETED ] ) } )
                        { COURSENO , STUDENTNO , DURING , GRADE }
```

Note: The expression INTERVAL_DATE ([ENROLLED:COMPLETED]) here is an interval selector invocation (see Chapter 7).

c.
```
VAR COURSE_AVAILABILITY BASE RELATION
    { COURSENO COURSENO , CNAME NAME , DURING INTERVAL_DATE }
      KEY { COURSENO } ;
```

d.
```
WITH ( t1 := EXTEND STUDENT : { UNREGISTERED := LAST_DATE ( ) }
                                    { STUDENTNO , UNREGISTERED } ,
          t2 := t1 UNION UNREG_STUDENT ,
          t3 := t2 JOIN STUDENT ,
          t4 := t3 WHERE UNREGISTERED ≥ REGISTERED ,
          t5 := EXTEND t4 { STUDENTNO , SNAME , REGISTERED } :
                          { UNREGISTERED := MIN ( !!t4 , UNREGISTERED ) } ,
          t6 := EXTEND t5 : { REG_DURING :=
                          INTERVAL_DATE ( [ REGISTERED : UNREGISTERED ] ) } :
      t6 { STUDENTNO , SNAME , REG_DURING }
```

Chapter 7

Interval Operators

What Nature provides is the intervals.

—Paul Hindemith:
The Craft of Musical Composition (1937)

In this chapter we discuss a number of useful operators that apply to intervals. Most if not all of the operators in question are described in the literature, under a variety of different names. The names we use ourselves are the ones that seem most satisfactory to us, of course, but you should at least be aware that other names do appear in the literature, and we'll mention some of those alternative names from time to time in the pages ahead.

NOTATION

We adopt and extend the notation from Chapter 6, as follows:

- Let T be a point type and let p be a value of type T. Then we use the expressions $p+1$, $p+2$, etc., to denote the value that's the successor of p, the value that's the successor of $p+1$, and so on. Of course, this notation is only informal; a real language would have to provide some kind of explicit *next* operator. When we need to refer to that formal operator explicitly, we'll call it NEXT_T—thus, NEXT_T (p) returns $p+1$, NEXT_T (NEXT_T (p)) returns $p+2$, and so on. Observe, therefore, that the formal *next* operator has an explicit "_T" qualifier (and the same is true for the formal *prior*, *first*, *last*, and *interval selector* operators, as we'll see in a moment). We'll explain why that qualifier is necessary in Chapter 18.

- We also use, again informally, the expressions $p-1$, $p-2$, etc., to denote the value whose successor is p, the value whose successor is $p-1$, etc. A real language would have to provide an explicit *prior* operator, which we'll call PRIOR_T; PRIOR_T (p) returns $p-1$, PRIOR_T (PRIOR_T (p)) returns $p-2$, and so on.

- We also need niladic FIRST_T and LAST_T operators; FIRST_T ( ) and LAST_T ( ) return the "first" and "last" value, respectively, of type T.

■ The interval type corresponding to point type *T* is INTERVAL_*T*. Informally, we use the expression [*p1*:*pn*] to denote the interval whose contained points are exactly *p1*, *p1*+1, *p1*+2, ..., *pn* (1 ≤ *n*). In fact, of course, an expression such as [*p1*:*pn*] can be regarded as informal syntax for an interval selector invocation (indeed, we already said as much in Chapter 6). A real language would have to provide some kind of explicit syntax for such invocations, as in, e.g., INTERVAL_*T* ([*p1*:*pn*]), and we'll use this latter, more formal, notation in examples later in the book.[1]

■ We also refer occasionally to the other styles for intervals (closed:open, open:closed, and open:open) discussed briefly in Chapter 6. Here's an example, just to remind you. Let the point type be INTEGER (so the corresponding interval type is INTERVAL_INTEGER). Then the (informal) expressions [3:5], [3:6), (2:5], and (2:6) all denote the exact same interval: namely, the interval whose contained points are exactly 3, 4, and 5. The respective formal analogs of these expressions are as follows:

```
INTERVAL_INTEGER ( [ 3 : 5 ] )
INTERVAL_INTEGER ( [ 3 : 6 ) )
INTERVAL_INTEGER ( ( 2 : 5 ] )
INTERVAL_INTEGER ( ( 2 : 6 ) )
```

We remind you also of the operators BEGIN, END, and "∈" from Chapter 6. For convenience, we repeat the definitions here (slightly reworded in each case). Let *i* be the interval [*b*:*e*] of type INTERVAL_*T* and let *p* be a value of type *T*. Then BEGIN (*i*) returns *b*; END (*i*) returns *e*; and *p* ∈ *i* returns TRUE if and only if *b* ≤ *p* and *p* ≤ *e* both return TRUE. We also define:

■ PRE (*i*), which returns *b*−1

■ POST (*i*), which returns *e*+1

■ *i* ∋ *p* (read "*i* contains *p*"), which returns TRUE if and only if *p* ∈ *i* returns TRUE

Observe that PRE (*i*) is undefined if *b* is the first value of type *T*, and POST (*i*) is undefined if *e* is the last value of type *T*. Of course, PRE (*i*) and POST (*i*) are effectively just shorthand for PRIOR_*T* (BEGIN (*i*)) and NEXT_*T* (END (*i*)), respectively. *Note:* POST has been called STOP in the literature [62]. PRE might thus analogously be called START, but doesn't usually seem to be defined at all. We prefer the names PRE and POST because they're more obviously distinct from BEGIN and END and because we find them intuitively clearer as well.

Finally:

---

[1] Actually we've already seen an example of this more formal notation in the answer to Exercise 6.10c in Chapter 6.

■ Let *i* be the unit interval [*p:p*] of type INTERVAL_*T*. Then POINT FROM *i* returns the point value *p*. *Note:* If *i* isn't a unit interval, POINT FROM *i* is undefined (and an exception is raised). On the other hand, if *i* is a unit interval, POINT FROM *i*, BEGIN (*i*), and END (*i*) all return the same value.

INTERVAL COMPARISONS

A variety of operators can be defined for comparing intervals to see whether two intervals are equal, whether they overlap, and so on. In this section, we describe several such operators, giving in each case a formal definition together with an intuitive picture to illustrate the functionality. *Note:* The operators in question are often referred to collectively as *Allen's operators*, most of them having first been proposed (in effect) by Allen in reference [2]—though in fact the definitions we give below, which are of course the ones we find the most useful, tend to differ somewhat from Allen's original definitions, at least at the detailed level.

Here and throughout the remainder of this chapter, we take *i1* and *i2* to be the intervals [*b1:e1*] and [*b2:e2*], respectively, both of the same type INTERVAL_*T*. Note that, in order for the various operators to be defined in the first place, the two intervals must indeed be of the same interval type and so must be defined over the same point type.

Equals ("="): As we already know from Chapter 6, *i1* = *i2* is true if and only if *b1* = *b2* and *e1* = *e2* are both true.

Includes ("⊇") and included in ("⊆"): *i1* ⊇ *i2* is true if and only if *b1* ≤ *b2* and *e1* ≥ *e2* are both true; *i2* ⊆ *i1* is true if and only if *i1* ⊇ *i2* is true. *Note:* Reference [2] refers to "⊇" and "⊆" as *contains* and *during*, respectively.

Properly includes ("⊃") and **properly included in ("⊂")**: *i1* ⊃ *i2* is true if and only if *i1* ⊇ *i2* is true and *i1* = *i2* is false; *i2* ⊂ *i1* is true if and only if *i1* ⊃ *i2* is true. *Note:* The picture just used to illustrate "⊇" and "⊆" in fact illustrates the "proper" versions of these operators ("⊃" and "⊂", respectively). Here it is again:

```
b1                                    e1
├───────────── i1 ─────────────┤

        b2                e2
        ├─────── i2 ───────┤
```

BEFORE and AFTER: *i1* BEFORE *i2* is true if and only if *e1* < *b2* is true; *i2* AFTER *i1* is true if and only if *i1* BEFORE *i2* is true.

```
b1                      e1       b2                      e2
├────────── i1 ─────────┤        ├────────── i2 ─────────┤
```

OVERLAPS: *i1* OVERLAPS *i2* is true if and only if *b1* ≤ *e2* and *b2* ≤ *e1* are both true (it follows that *i2* OVERLAPS *i1* is true if and only if *i1* OVERLAPS *i2* is true).[2]

```
b1                            e1
├─────────────── i1 ──────────┤

        b2                e2
        ├─────── i2 ───────┤
```

MEETS: *i1* MEETS *i2* is true if and only if *b2* = *e1*+1 is true or *b1* = *e2*+1 is true (it follows that *i2* MEETS *i1* is true if and only if *i1* MEETS *i2* is true).[3]

```
b1                      e1b2                     e2
├────────── i1 ─────────┤├────────── i2 ─────────┤
```

---

[2] It also follows as a special case of the foregoing that if either *i1* ⊇ *i2* or *i2* ⊇ *i1* is true, then *i1* OVERLAPS *i2* is true as well.

[3] We referred to meeting as *abutting* in Chapter 5.

MERGES: *i1* MERGES *i2* is true if and only if *i1* OVERLAPS *i2* is true or *i1* MEETS *i2* is true (it follows that *i2* MERGES *i1* is true if and only if *i1* MERGES *i2* is true). *Note:* This operator was first defined in reference [70], not reference [2]. The keyword MERGES is perhaps not very good from the standpoint of intuition, but it's hard to find one that catches the sense better and yet is equally succinct. That sense is, of course, "overlaps or meets."

```
b1                             e1
├──────────── i1 ──────────────┤

                    b2              e2
                    ├────── i2 ──────┤
```

Or:

```
b1                                      e1b2          e2
├──────────────── i1 ──────────────────┤├────── i2 ──────┤
```

BEGINS: *i1* BEGINS *i2* is true if and only if *b1* = *b2* and *e1* ∈ *i2* are both true. *Note:* Reference [2] uses the keyword *starts* in place of BEGINS.

```
b1                       e1
├────────── i1 ──────────┤

b2                               e2
├──────────── i2 ──────────────┤
```

ENDS: *i1* ENDS *i2* is true if and only if *e1* = *e2* and *b1* ∈ *i2* are both true. *Note:* Reference [2] uses the keyword *finishes* in place of ENDS.

```
          b1                   e1
          ├────────── i1 ──────┤

b2                             e2
├──────────────── i2 ──────────┤
```

Negated forms of the foregoing operators can usefully be defined as well; for example, *i1* NOT OVERLAPS *i2* is true if and only if *i1* OVERLAPS *i2* is false. (Of course, "NOT =" is just "≠"; likewise, "NOT ⊇", "NOT ⊆", "NOT ⊃", and "NOT ⊂" are just "⊂", "⊃", "⊆", and "⊇", respectively. Also, NOT OVERLAPS might reasonably be spelled DISJOINT.)[4]

We observe that the operator "⊃" in particular allows us to give a precise definition for the term *maximal interval*, which we used several times in Chapter 5:

> **Definition:** Let *P* be a predicate whose sole parameter is of some interval type. Then interval *i* is **maximal** with respect to *P* if and only if *i* satisfies *P* and no *j* such that *j* ⊃ *i* satisfies *P*. *Note:* The qualifier "with respect to *P*" can be omitted if *P* is understood.

By way of a simple but typical example, consider relvar S_DURING once again. Here's the predicate we gave for that relvar in Chapter 6:

> *Supplier SNO was under contract throughout the interval from the day that's the begin point of DURING to the day that's the end point of DURING, inclusive, and not throughout any interval that properly includes that interval.*

Using the concept of maximal intervals as just defined, we can now simplify this predicate considerably, thus:

> *DURING denotes a maximal interval of days throughout which supplier SNO was under contract.*

"SET OPERATORS"

Clearly, an interval, if we ignore the ordering, can be regarded as a set of points, and the set operators UNION, INTERSECT, and MINUS are thus directly applicable. However, those operators, although they'll certainly always return a set, won't always return an interval (after all, an interval isn't just a set of points—rather, it's a set of *contiguous* points). As an extreme example, if intervals *i1* and *i2* are disjoint, then their intersection *i1* INTERSECT *i2* will be empty, and intervals as such are never empty. Thus, it makes sense to impose certain limitations on the operands to the interval versions of those set operators, in order to guarantee that the result isn't just some set of points but is, rather, an interval specifically.

We begin by defining a couple of auxiliary operators, MAX and MIN (essentially just variants on the aggregate operators of the same name). Let *p1* and *p2* be values of the same type *T* and let "<" be defined for that type. Then:

- MAX {*p1,p2*} returns *p2* if *p1* < *p2* is true and *p1* otherwise.

---

[4] Definitions of still more interval comparison operators are given in the annotation to reference [2] in Appendix F.

■ MIN {*p1,p2*} returns *p1* if *p1* < *p2* is true and *p2* otherwise.

Now let *i1* and *i2* be values of the same interval type. Then we have:

UNION: *i1* UNION *i2* returns [MIN{*b1,b2*}:MAX{*e1,e2*}] if *i1* MERGES *i2* is true and is otherwise undefined.

```
b1                          e1
├──────────── i1 ───────────┤
                b2                          e2
                ├────────── i2 ──────────┤
b1                                          e2
├───────────────── i1 UNION i2 ──────────────┤
```

Incidentally, note that interval union, unlike set theory union (unlike the union operator of the relational algebra also) has no corresponding identity value. (If it had one, it would be the empty interval of the applicable type, and intervals are never empty.)

Aside: In case you're not familiar with the concept of an identity value, here's a definition. Let *Op* be a commutative dyadic operator, and assume for definiteness that *Op* is expressed in infix style. If there exists a value *i* such that *i Op v* and *v Op i* are both equal to *v* for all possible values *v*, then *i* is the *identity*, or *identity value*, with respect to *Op*. *End of aside*.

INTERSECT: *i1* INTERSECT *i2* returns [MAX{*b1,b2*}:MIN{*e1,e2*}] if *i1* OVERLAPS *i2* is true and is otherwise undefined.

```
b1                          e1
├──────────── i1 ───────────┤
                b2                          e2
                ├────────── i2 ──────────┤
                b2          e1
                ├───────────┤
                     └──── i1 INTERSECT i2
```

MINUS: *i1* MINUS *i2* returns [*b1*:MIN{*b2*–1,*e1*}] if *b1* < *b2* and *e1* ≤ *e2* are both true, [MAX{*e2*+1,*b1*}:*e1*] if *b1* ≥ *b2* and *e1* > *e2* are both true, and is otherwise undefined. Note, therefore, that *i1* MINUS *i2* is defined if and only if (a) *i1* and *i2* are disjoint (in which case *i1* MINUS *i2* reduces to simply *i1*), or (b) *i1* contains either *b2* or *e2* but not both, or (c) exactly one of *i2* BEGINS *i1* and *i2* ENDS *i1* is true. (The following picture illustrates case (b) only; development of pictures to illustrate the other cases—and perhaps the cases where MINUS isn't defined, too—is left as an exercise. Also, what happens exactly if *b2* > *b1* and *e2* < *e1* are both true or *b1* > *b2* and *e1* < *e2* are both true?)

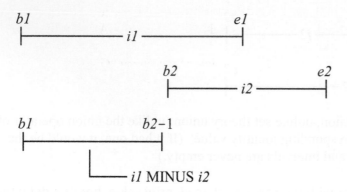

Note: Reference [70] calls the interval UNION and INTERSECT operators MERGE and INTERVSECT, respectively (it doesn't discuss an interval MINUS operator). Observe that if *i1* INTERSECT *i2* is defined, then *i1* UNION *i2* is certainly defined, but the converse is false (i.e., some pairs of intervals—which ones, exactly?—have a union but no intersection). Observe also that *i1* MINUS *i2* is sometimes defined when *i1* UNION *i2* and *i1* INTERSECT *i2* aren't, and vice versa. (It follows, incidentally, that certain identities that hold for the set operators in general—for example, *s1* INTERSECT *s2* ≡ *s1* MINUS (*s1* MINUS *s2*)—don't necessarily hold for the interval analogs of those operators.)[5]

Finally, we define the operator COUNT (*i*), which returns a count of the number of points in interval *i* (in other words, it returns the cardinality—sometimes called the *length* or *duration*— of that interval). For example, if *i* is the interval [*d03*:*d07*], of type INTERVAL_DATE, then COUNT (*i*) is 5.

---

[5] The symbol "≡" can be read as "is equivalent to" or "is identically equal to."

QUERIES

The operators discussed in previous sections are of course available for use in all of the usual contexts, including queries in particular. Let's look at some examples. Consider the database of Fig. 6.1 (the fully temporal version with intervals, where the relvars are S_DURING and SP_DURING). Consider also this query: "Get supplier numbers for suppliers who were able to supply part P2 on day 8." Here's a possible formulation:

```
( SP_DURING WHERE PNO = PNO ( 'P2' ) AND d08 ∈ DURING ) { SNO }
```

This expression should be pretty much self-explanatory; we note, however, that in a real language the reference to day 8 ("*d08*") in the WHERE condition would have to be replaced by an appropriate DATE selector invocation. For example, if "day 8" is actually April 30th, 2013, that date selector invocation might look like this: DATE ('2013/4/30').[6]

By way of another example, here's a possible formulation of the query "Get pairs of suppliers who were able to supply the same part at the same time":

```
WITH ( t1 := SP_DURING RENAME { SNO AS XNO , DURING AS XD } ,
       t2 := SP_DURING RENAME { SNO AS YNO , DURING AS YD } ,
       t3 := t1 JOIN t2 ,
       t4 := t3 WHERE XD OVERLAPS YD ,
       t5 := t4 WHERE XNO < YNO ) :
t5 { XNO , YNO }
```

Explanation: Recall from Chapter 2 that WITH isn't an operator as such, it's just a syntactic device that lets us introduce names for subexpressions, thereby enabling us to formulate what might otherwise be rather complicated expressions one step at a time.[7] Thus:

- *t1* is just the current value of SP_DURING, except that attributes SNO and DURING are renamed XNO and XD, respectively.

- *t2* is the same except that the new attribute names are YNO and YD.

- *t3* is the join of *t1* and *t2* (over part numbers, because PNO is the only attribute common to *t1* and *t2*, thanks to the renaming steps).

- *t4* is the restriction of *t3* to just those tuples where the XD and YD intervals overlap (meaning the suppliers in question weren't just able to supply the same part but in fact were able to supply the same part at the same time, as required).

---

[6] In SQL it would be DATE '2013-4-30'.

[7] In fact we used WITH in the answers to some of the exercises in Chapters 5 and 6, as you might recall.

■ *t5* is the restriction of *t4* to just those tuples where supplier number XNO is less than supplier number YNO. The purpose of this step is twofold: It eliminates pairs of supplier numbers of the form (*x,x*), and it guarantees that the pairs (*x,y*) and (*y,x*) don't both appear. Of course, as noted in Chapter 2, the operator "<" must be defined for type SNO in order for this step to be legitimate.

■ The final projection of *t5* on XNO and YNO produces the desired result.

As a third example, suppose we want to get, not just pairs of suppliers who were able to supply the same part at the same time, but the parts and times in question as well. Here then is a possible formulation:

```
WITH ( t1 := SP_DURING RENAME { SNO AS XNO , DURING AS XD } ,
       t2 := SP_DURING RENAME { SNO AS YNO , DURING AS YD } ,
       t3 := t1 JOIN t2 ,
       t4 := t3 WHERE XD OVERLAPS YD ,
       t5 := t4 WHERE XNO < YNO ,
       t6 := EXTEND t5 : { DURING := XD INTERSECT YD } ) :
t6 { XNO , YNO , PNO , DURING }
```

Explanation: Relations *t1-t5* are exactly as they were in the previous example. The EXTEND step then computes the relevant intervals, and the final projection produces the desired result.

CONCLUDING REMARKS

We close this chapter by stressing the fact that all of the operators on intervals we've been discussing—BEGIN, END, PRE, POST, POINT FROM, "∈" and "∋", Allen's operators, and interval UNION, INTERSECT, MINUS, and COUNT—are generic, in the sense that they apply to all possible intervals. Of course, the operators are generic precisely because they're associated with the INTERVAL type generator (just as the operators of the relational algebra are generic because they're associated with the RELATION type generator, as pointed out in Chapter 6). In other words, these operators are *polymorphic*—see the remarks on this topic in the section "Types" in Chapter 1—and the kind of polymorphism they exhibit is *generic polymorphism*.

Aside: In fact, the UNION, INTERSECT, and MINUS operators in particular exhibit another kind of polymorphism also. By defining these operators—or operators with these names, rather—to apply to both intervals and relations, we've *overloaded* those operator names. What this means is as follows (let's concentrate on UNION, just to be definite): In reality, there are two distinct operators here, one for intervals and the other for relations. However, we've chosen to give those two operators the same name. And such a state of affairs is described in the literature (by some writers, at any rate) as an example of *overloading polymorphism.*

We note also that there's at least one further kind of polymorphism, called *inclusion polymorphism,* which we'll be discussing in Chapter 18. *End of aside.*

EXERCISES

7.1   We pointed out in the body of the chapter that the interval version of UNION has no identity value. But what about INTERSECT and MINUS?

7.2   We pointed out in the body of the chapter that the set theory identity *s1* INTERSECT *s2* ≡ *s1* MINUS (*s1* MINUS *s2*) ceases to hold, in general, if *s1* and *s2* aren't sets but intervals. Why so?

7.3   Let *i* be a value of type INTERVAL_INTEGER. Write an expression denoting the interval resulting from extending *i* by its own length in both directions (e.g., [5:7] becomes [2:10]). In what circumstances will evaluation of your expression fail at run time?

7.4   Again let *i* be a value of type INTERVAL_INTEGER. Write an expression denoting the interval representing the middle third of *i*. You can assume COUNT (*i*) is a multiple of three.

7.5   Let *i1*, *i2*, and *i3* be intervals such that there's a single interval *i4* consisting of every point *p* such that *p* ∈ *i1* or *p* ∈ *i2* or *p* ∈ *i3*. Write an expression defining *i4* in terms of *i1*, *i2*, and *i3*. *Warning*: There's a trap here.

7.6   Given the relvar STUDIED from Exercise 6.10b in Chapter 6, write an expression that, when evaluated, shows for every grade the average length of study for all students who achieved that grade. *Note:* We assume for the sake of this exercise that students complete courses at their own pace.

7.7   Given relvars as follows (the semantics are meant to be self-explanatory)—

```
FEDERAL_GOVT { PRESIDENT , PARTY , DURING }
STATE_GOVT   { GOVERNOR , STATE , PARTY , DURING }
```

—write an expression to produce a result with attributes PRESIDENT, GOVERNOR, STATE, PARTY, and DURING, such that a tuple appears in this result if and only if the specified president and specified state governor both belong to the specified party and have overlapping periods of administration (and DURING specifies exactly the overlap in question).

ANSWERS

7.1 The identity value for INTERSECT is what might be called the *universal interval* of the applicable type (i.e., the interval [FIRST_*T* ( ):LAST_*T* ( )], where *T* is the applicable point type. MINUS has no identity value (nor does it in set theory, of course).

7.2 Let *i1* and *i2* be intervals of the same type, and let *i2* be properly included in *i1*. Then *i1* INTERSECT *i2* returns *i2*, but *i1* MINUS *i2* is undefined—and so therefore is *i1* MINUS (*i1* MINUS *i2*) a fortiori. Note, however, that the identity does hold so long as *i1* MINUS (*i1* MINUS *i2*) is defined.

7.3
```
INTERVAL_INTEGER ( [ BEGIN ( i ) - COUNT ( i ) :
                     END ( i ) + COUNT ( i ) ] )
```

Evaluation of this expression will fail at run time if either of the following expressions evaluates to TRUE:

```
BEGIN ( i ) < FIRST_INTEGER ( ) + COUNT ( i )

END ( i )   > LAST_INTEGER ( )  - COUNT ( i )
```

7.4
```
INTERVAL_INTEGER ( [ BEGIN ( i ) + ( COUNT ( i ) / 3 ) :
                     END ( i )   - ( COUNT ( i ) / 3 ) ] )
```

7.5
```
INTERVAL_INTEGER
  ( [ MIN { MIN { BEGIN ( i1 ) , BEGIN ( i2 ) } , BEGIN ( i3 ) } :
      MAX { MAX { END ( i1 )   , END ( i2 )   } , END ( i3 )   } ] )
```

We've assumed for definiteness here that INTEGER is the underlying point type. The trap is this: Under the stated conditions, it can't be guaranteed that, e.g., *i1* UNION *i2* is defined, and so an expression of the form (*i1* UNION *i2*) UNION *i3* isn't guaranteed to work.

7.6
```
( EXTEND STUDIED { GRADE } :
      { ALS := AVG ( !!STUDIED , COUNT ( DURING ) ) } { GRADE , ALS }
```

7.7
```
WITH ( fg := FEDERAL_GOVT RENAME { DURING AS FD } ,
       sg := STATE_GOVT RENAME { DURING AS SD } ,
       t1 := fg JOIN sg ,
       t2 := t1 WHERE FD OVERLAPS SD ,
       t3 := EXTEND t2 : { DURING := FD INTERSECT SD } ) :
  t3 { ALL BUT FD , SD }
```

Chapter 8

The EXPAND and COLLAPSE

Operators

Then all collapsed, and the great shroud of the sea rolled on
as it rolled five thousand years ago.

—Herman Melville:
Moby-Dick (1851)

In Chapters 6 and 7, we encountered a variety of generic operators—BEGIN, PRE, OVERLAPS, MERGES, UNION, and so on—that applied to intervals (or pairs of intervals, rather, in most cases). In this chapter, we meet two more generic operators, which we call EXPAND and COLLAPSE, respectively.[1] Unlike BEGIN, PRE, and the rest, however, these two operators apply not to intervals as such but rather to sets of intervals. More specifically, each of those operators (a) takes a set of intervals all of the same type as its input and (b) returns another set of intervals of that same type as its result.

PRELIMINARY REMARKS

The result sets produced by EXPAND and COLLAPSE can each be regarded as a particular *canonical form* for the corresponding input set—and the canonical forms in question both have an important role to play in the solutions we're at last beginning to approach to the problems we identified in Chapters 4 and 5. *Note:* It might help to state up front that each of those two canonical forms has the property that every point represented in some interval in the input set is represented exactly once—i.e., as part of exactly one interval—in the corresponding result set.

> *Aside:* The notion of canonical form is central to many branches of mathematics and related disciplines. In case you're unfamiliar with it, we digress for a moment to explain it briefly. The basic idea is this: Given a set *s1*, together with a stated notion of equivalence

---

[1] Other names appear in the literature, earlier writings by the present authors included.

among the elements of that set, subset *s2* of *s1* is *a set of canonical forms* for *s1* if and only if every element *a1* of *s1* is equivalent, under that notion of equivalence, to just one element *a2* of *s2* (and that element *a2* is *a canonical form* for the element *a1*). We can also say, a trifle loosely, that the set *s2* taken as a whole is a canonical form for the set *s1* as such. Various "interesting" properties that apply to *s1* also apply to *s2*, mutatis mutandis; thus, we can study just the "small" set *s2*, not the "large" set *s1*, in order to prove a variety of interesting theorems or results. Here's a simple example:

- Let *s1* be the set of nonnegative integers {0,1,2,...}.

- Define equivalence among elements of *s1* as follows: Elements *a* and *b* are equivalent if and only if they leave the same remainder on division by five. Thus, e.g., the integers 8, 13, 18, 23, etc., are all equivalent to 3 (as is 3 itself, of course).

- Under this definition of equivalence, then, *s2* is the set {0,1,2,3,4}—every element of *s1* is equivalent to just one of these five integers, and each of these five is in fact the canonical form for an infinite number of elements of *s1*. Note in particular that *s2* here is finite, whereas *s1* is infinite.

- As for an "interesting" property that applies in this example, let *a1*, *b1*, and *c1* be any three elements of *s1*, and let their canonical forms in *s2* be *a2*, *b2*, and *c2*, respectively. Then the product *b1* * *c1* is equivalent to *a1* if and only if the product *b2* * *c2* is equivalent to *a2*.

End of aside.

The applicability of the foregoing ideas to sets of intervals in particular is explained in the next two sections.

EXPANDED FORM

As already indicated, the objects we wish to study are sets of intervals,[2] where the intervals in question are all of the same interval type and are thus necessarily defined over the same point type. Let *X1* and *X2* be two such sets. Then we define the necessary notion of equivalence thus:

---

[2] At the risk of confusing you, we stress that these sets aren't the sets *s1* and *s2* mentioned in the aside explaining the notion of canonical form in general; rather, they're the elements that make up those sets.

Definition: Sets *X1* and *X2* are **equivalent** if and only if the set of all points contained in intervals in *X1* is equal to the set of all points contained in intervals in *X2*.

By way of example, let *X1* and *X2* be as follows:

```
{ [d01:d01] , [d03:d05] , [d04:d06] }                    /*  X1  */

{ [d01:d01] , [d03:d04] , [d05:d05] , [d05:d06] }        /*  X2  */
```

Clearly, *X1* and *X2* aren't equal—they're not the same set. However, it's easy to see they're equivalent under the foregoing definition, because the set of all points *p* such that *p* is contained in some interval in *X1* is equal to the set of all points *p* such that *p* is contained in some interval in *X2*. The set of points in question is, obviously enough, this set:

```
{ d01 , d03 , d04 , d05 , d06 }
```

For reasons that'll quickly become apparent, however, we're interested not so much in this set of points as such, but rather in the corresponding set of *unit intervals* (let's call it *X3*):

```
{ [d01:d01] , [d03:d03] , [d04:d04] , [d05:d05] , [d06:d06] }
```

X3 here is clearly equivalent to each of *X1* and *X2*; in fact, it's the *expanded form* of each of those sets. Here's the definition:

Definition: Let *X* be a set of intervals all of the same type. Then the **expanded form** of *X* is the set of all intervals—more precisely, the set of all unit intervals—of the form [*p*:*p*] such that *p* is a point in some interval in *X*.

From this definition, it should be clear that if *X* is a set of intervals all of the same type, then:

■ An expanded form of *X* always exists.

■ That expanded form is equivalent to *X*.

■ That expanded form is unique.

Observe in particular that if *X* is empty, then the expanded form of *X* is empty too.

The expanded form of *X* is one possible canonical form for *X*. To be specific, it's that unique equivalent set whose contained intervals are all of the minimum possible length (i.e., one). Intuitively, the expanded form of *X* allows us to focus on the information content of *X* at an atomic level, without having to worry about the many different ways that information might be bundled together into "clumps."

Note: The concept of expanded form allows us to restate our original definition of equivalence more succinctly, thus:

> **Definition:** Two sets of intervals are **equivalent** if and only if they have the same expanded form.

As an exercise, consider the projections on DURING of the relations shown as values of relvars S_DURING and SP_DURING in Fig. 6.1 in Chapter 6. Are the sets of intervals in those two projections equivalent? What are the corresponding expanded forms?

COLLAPSED FORM

The sets *X1*, *X2*, and *X3* discussed in the previous section all have different cardinalities. In fact, it so happens in that particular example that *X3*, the expanded form, is the one whose cardinality is the greatest. However, it's easy to find another set *X4* that has the same expanded form—i.e., that's equivalent to *X1* and *X2*—but has cardinality greater than that of *X3*. One such set *X4* (not the only one possible) is:

> { [d01:d01] , [d03:d03] , [d03:d04] , [d03:d05] , [d03:d06] ,
>   [d04:d04] , [d04:d05] , [d04:d06] }

It's also easy to find the much more interesting set *X5* that has the same expanded form and the *minimum possible* cardinality:

> { [d01:d01] , [d03:d06] }

X5 is the *collapsed form* of *X1* (also of *X2*, *X3*, and *X4*). Here's the definition:

Definition: Let *X* be a set of intervals all of the same type. Then the **collapsed form** of *X* is the set *Y* of intervals of the same type such that:

■ *X* and *Y* have the same expanded form.

■ No two distinct intervals *i1* and *i2* in *Y* are such that *i1* MERGES *i2* is true (recall that MERGES means "overlaps or meets"). Equivalently, no two distinct intervals *i1* and *i2* in *Y* are such that *i1* UNION *i2* is defined.

Note: It follows from this latter point that *Y* can be computed from *X* by successively replacing pairs of intervals in *X* by their union (assuming their union is defined, of course) until no further such replacements are possible. It also follows that no two distinct intervals *i1* and *i2* in *Y* are such that *i1* INTERSECT *i2* is defined, either.

Aside: The intersection *i1* INTERSECT *i2* is likewise not defined for any pair of intervals *i1* and *i2* in the *expanded* form of *X*; however, the union *i1* UNION *i2* might be. To be specific, *i1* UNION *i2* will be defined for such a pair of intervals if and only if the (necessarily unique) points *p1* and *p2* in *i1* and *i2*, respectively, are such that one is the immediate successor of the other. *End of aside.*

The collapsed form of X is another possible canonical form for X. To be specific, it's that unique equivalent set that has the minimum possible cardinality. Intuitively, the collapsed form of X allows us to focus on the information content of X in a compressed ("clumped") form, without having to worry about the possibility that distinct "clumps" might meet or overlap.

Note that—as indeed we've already seen—many distinct sets can have the same collapsed form. Also, it should be clear from the foregoing definition that if X is a set of intervals all of the same type, then:

■ A collapsed form of X always exists.

■ That collapsed form is equivalent to X.

■ That collapsed form is unique.

Observe in particular that if X is empty, then the collapsed form of X is empty too.

Note: The concept of collapsed form also allows us to restate our original definition of equivalence more succinctly, thus:

Definition: Two sets of intervals are **equivalent** if and only if they have the same collapsed form.

As an exercise, again consider the projections on DURING of the relations shown as values of relvars S_DURING and SP_DURING in Fig. 6.1 in Chapter 6; more specifically, consider the sets of intervals in those two projections. What are the corresponding expanded forms?

OPERATOR DEFINITIONS

We can now define the EXPAND and COLLAPSE operators:

Definition: Let X be a set of intervals all of the same type. Then EXPAND (X) returns the expanded form of X and COLLAPSE (X) returns the collapsed form of X.

Note in particular that:

■ If *X* has cardinality zero, the result does so too (for both EXPAND and COLLAPSE).

■ If *X* has cardinality one, the result is equal to *X* for COLLAPSE, but not for EXPAND (unless the sole interval in *X* happens to be a unit interval).

By the way, don't make the mistake of thinking that EXPAND and COLLAPSE are inverses of each other. For example, let *X1* be the set

```
{ [d01:d01] , [d03:d05] , [d04:d06] }
```

(as previously). If we expand this set and then collapse the result, we necessarily obtain the collapsed form *X5*:

```
{ [d01:d01] , [d03:d06] }
```

And if we collapse the original set *X1* and then expand the result, we (again necessarily) obtain the expanded form *X3*:

```
{ [d01:d01] , [d03:d03] , [d04:d04] , [d05:d05] , [d06:d06] }
```

In other words, neither EXPAND (COLLAPSE (*X*)) nor COLLAPSE (EXPAND (*X*)) is identically equal to *X*, in general (though they're both *equivalent* to *X*, of course). Indeed, it's easy to see that the following identities hold:

```
EXPAND ( COLLAPSE ( X ) )    ≡   EXPAND ( X )

COLLAPSE ( EXPAND ( X ) )    ≡   COLLAPSE ( X )
```

The following identities clearly hold as well:

```
EXPAND ( EXPAND ( X ) )       ≡   EXPAND ( X )

COLLAPSE ( COLLAPSE ( X ) )   ≡   COLLAPSE ( X )
```

It follows from all of these identities that the first operation in evaluating any of the expressions shown on the left side of the "≡" symbol can simply be ignored, a fact that could be useful for optimization purposes (especially when that first operation is EXPAND).

Alternative Definitions

Note: This subsection is included primarily for completeness. It requires an elementary understanding of the quantifiers of predicate logic (see, e.g., reference [45]). However, it can safely be skipped without interfering with the overall flow.

We now give alternative definitions of the EXPAND and COLLAPSE operators in order to show that—like so much else discussed in this book—they're really just shorthand. First EXPAND. Let X be a set of intervals all of the same type, IT say, and let i and j be intervals of type IT. Let i = [b:e]. Then we have:

> EXPAND (X) $\overset{\text{def}}{=}$ { i : b = e AND EXISTS j ∈ X (b ∈ j) }

In other words, EXPAND (X) is the set of all intervals i of type IT such that (a) the begin and end points of i are one and the same, and (b) the point in question is contained within at least one interval in X. (The symbol "$\overset{\text{def}}{=}$" means "is defined as.") Note that we've extended our use of the set membership operator "∈" to apply not just to a point and an interval ("b ∈ j"), but also to an interval and a set of intervals ("j ∈ X"); in fact, we're *overloading* "∈" here (see the remarks on this notion near the end of Chapter 7).

COLLAPSE is rather more complicated. Again, let X be a set of intervals all of the same type IT; also, let the underlying point type be T. Let i, $i1$, $i2$, and j be intervals of type IT; let p be a point of type T; and let i = [b:e], $i1$ = [$b1$:$e1$], and $i2$ = [$b2$:$e2$]. Then we have:

```
1.    COLLAPSE ( X )    def
2.      { i : FORALL p ∈ i ( EXISTS j ∈ X ( p ∈ j ) )
3.          AND
4.          EXISTS i1 ∈ X ( EXISTS i2 ∈ X
5.              ( b = b1 AND e = e2 AND b1 ≤ b2 AND e1 ≤ e2
6.              AND
7.              IF b2 ≠ FIRST_T ( ) THEN
8.                  IF e1 < PRE ( i2 ) THEN
9.                      FORALL p ∈ ( e1 : b2 )
10.                         ( EXISTS j ∈ X ( p ∈ j ) ) END IF END IF
11.             AND
12.             FORALL p ∈ i
13.                 ( IF p ≠ FIRST_T ( ) THEN
14.                     NOT EXISTS j ∈ X ( PRE ( i ) ∈ j ) END IF
15.                 AND
16.                 IF p ≠ LAST_T ( ) THEN
17.                     NOT EXISTS j ∈ X ( POST ( i ) ∈ j ) END IF ) ) )
18.     }
```

Explanation:

- Line 2 ensures that if interval i appears in COLLAPSE (X), then every point p in i must also appear in at least one interval j in X. *Note:* Of course, the converse is true as well—every point in some interval j in X must also appear in some i in COLLAPSE (X)—but this requirement is taken care of implicitly by the remaining lines taken together.

- Lines 4-5 ensure that the begin point of i is the begin point $b1$ of some interval $i1$ in X and the end point of i is the end point $e2$ of some interval $i2$ in X ($i1$ and $i2$ not necessarily distinct). The condition $b1 \leq b2$ AND $e1 \leq e2$ in line 5 ensures that $i1$ neither begins nor ends after $i2$ does, so we can say definitively that BEGIN (i) is $b1$ and END (i) is $e2$.

■ Lines 7-10 ensure that every point between intervals $i1$ and $i2$ is in fact a point in some interval in X, so that merging $i1$ and $i2$ to form i is legitimate. By the way, note the use of open:open notation in line 9, avoiding the rather more complicated expression "[POST $(i1)$: PRE $(i2)$]" that use of closed:closed notation would have entailed.

■ Lines 12-14 ensure that there's no interval in X containing the predecessor $b-1$ of BEGIN (i)—because if there were, it should have been merged with i.

■ Lines (12 and) 16-17 ensure likewise that there's no interval in X containing the successor $e+1$ of END (i), for essentially similar reasons.

UNARY RELATIONS

Now, you might have noticed that we've been indulging in a tiny sleight of hand in this chapter so far. To be specific, we've described two operators, EXPAND and COLLAPSE, that apply to sets—sets of intervals, to be specific[3]—but the relational model deals with relations, not general sets, and EXPAND and COLLAPSE as described so far are thus not a good fit with that model. So we have a little tidying up to do, and that's the purpose of this section.

We begin by observing that of course any set of values all of the same type can easily be converted to a unary relation. To be specific, if $v1$, $v2$, ..., vn are distinct values of the same type T, then the relation selector invocation

```
RELATION { A T } { TUPLE { A v1 } ,
                   TUPLE { A v2 } ,
                   .......
                   TUPLE { A vn } }
```

produces this relation:

---

[3] Actually the operators can be generalized to apply to sets containing other kinds of values in place of intervals as such. This possibility is briefly explored in Appendix C.

Note: Relation selectors were discussed in Chapter 1. Just to remind you, the specification {A *T*} in the example defines the heading for the relation being selected. Such a specification can always be omitted from a given relation selector invocation unless the given set of values *v1*, *v2*, ..., *vn* happens to be empty. If such were the case in the foregoing example, the relation selector invocation shown would degenerate to just RELATION {A *T*} { }.

In order to stay within the framework of the relational model, therefore, what we need to do—and of course what we *can* do, without loss of generality—is replace the EXPAND and COLLAPSE operators as previously described by versions in which the argument is specified as a unary relation instead of just a set. Replacing the operators as just suggested is straightforward, of course. To be specific, the unary relation versions of the operators are essentially similar to the set versions as previously described, except that the input and output, instead of just being sets of intervals, are now unary relations whose tuples contain those intervals as such. For example, suppose the input relation (*r*, say) looks like this:

```
┌─────────────┐
│ DURING      │
├─────────────┤
│ [d06:d09]   │
│ [d04:d08]   │
│ [d05:d10]   │
│ [d01:d01]   │
└─────────────┘
```

Then EXPAND (*r*) and COLLAPSE (*r*) produce results that look like this (EXPAND on the left, COLLAPSE on the right):

```
┌─────────────┐        ┌─────────────┐
│ DURING      │        │ DURING      │
├─────────────┤        ├─────────────┤
│ [d01:d01]   │        │ [d01:d01]   │
│ [d04:d04]   │        │ [d04:d10]   │
│ [d05:d05]   │        └─────────────┘
│ [d06:d06]   │
│ [d07:d07]   │
│ [d08:d08]   │
│ [d09:d09]   │
│ [d10:d10]   │
└─────────────┘
```

We can also define a notion of equivalence for such unary relations. To be specific, two such relations are equivalent if and only if they have the same expanded form (or the same collapsed form).

Finally, please note that we take all references to EXPAND and COLLAPSE throughout the remainder of this book as references to the versions just defined for unary relations, barring explicit statements to the contrary. However, please note also that certain of those "explicit statements to the contrary" appear in the section immediately following!

NULLARY RELATIONS

For reasons that should become clear in Chapters 10 and (especially) 11, it turns out to be highly desirable to define versions of EXPAND and COLLAPSE that work on nullary relations instead of unary ones. Just to remind you, a nullary relation is one that has no attributes, and there are exactly two such:

■ TABLE_DEE, which contains just one tuple (necessarily the 0-tuple, which is the unique tuple with no components)

■ TABLE_DUM, which contains no tuples at all

Of course, a nullary relation can't possibly contain intervals—more precisely, it can't contain tuples that contain intervals—but this fact need not deter us. To be specific, we simply define the result of expanding or collapsing a nullary relation, reasonably enough, to be equal to the input in both cases. For example, COLLAPSE (TABLE_DEE) returns TABLE_DEE, and EXPAND (TABLE_DUM) returns TABLE_DUM. Note that it follows from this definition, again reasonably enough, that two nullary relations are equivalent if and only if they're equal.

We close this section, and this chapter, by observing that EXPAND and COLLAPSE as we've defined them are still not quite what we need to deal with temporal data; they're still just another stepping stone on the way, so to speak. The point is, those operators work on unary (or nullary) relations, and what we're going to need are operators that work on general *n*-ary relations instead—in particular, on *n*-ary relations with interval attributes. We'll introduce such operators in the next chapter.

EXERCISES

8.1   (*Repeated from the body of the chapter.*) Consider the projections on DURING of the relations shown as values of relvars S_DURING and SP_DURING in Fig. 6.1 in Chapter 6; more specifically, consider the sets of intervals in those two projections. Are those two sets equivalent? What are the corresponding expanded and collapsed forms?

8.2   Let MOD3 be the type whose values are the integers 0, 1, and 2. Consider the type RELATION {DURING INTERVAL_MOD3}. How many relations *xr* of this type satisfy the condition EXPAND (*xr*) = *xr*? List every relation *cr* of this type satisfying the condition COLLAPSE (*cr*) = *cr*.

ANSWERS

8.1   Here first are the expanded and collapsed forms of the projection of S_DURING on DURING:

```
┌─────────────────┐          ┌─────────────────┐
│ DURING          │          │ DURING          │
├─────────────────┤          ├─────────────────┤
│ [d02:d02]       │          │   [d02:d10]     │
│ [d03:d03]       │          └─────────────────┘
│ [d04:d04]       │
│ [d05:d05]       │
│ [d06:d06]       │
│ [d07:d07]       │
│ [d08:d08]       │
│ [d09:d09]       │
│ [d10:d10]       │
└─────────────────┘
```

The expanded form is on the left and the collapsed form is on the right, of course. And it's easy to see that the expanded and collapsed forms of the projection of SP_DURING on DURING are identical to the foregoing, whence it follows that the two projections are indeed equivalent.

8.2   Note first that there are precisely six intervals of type INTERVAL_MOD3, as follows:

```
[0:0]   [0:1]   [0:2]   [1:1]   [1:2]   [2:2]
```

It follows that there are precisely $2^6 = 64$ relations of the specified type. Then:

- A relation of the specified type will be equal to its expanded form if and only if all of the DURING values it contains are unit intervals. There are precisely eight such relations:

```
┌───────────┐   ┌───────────┐   ┌───────────┐   ┌───────────┐
│ DURING    │   │ DURING    │   │ DURING    │   │ DURING    │
╞═══════════╡   ├───────────┤   ├───────────┤   ├───────────┤
└───────────┘   │  [0:0]    │   │  [1:1]    │   │  [2:2]    │
                └───────────┘   └───────────┘   └───────────┘

┌───────────┐   ┌───────────┐   ┌───────────┐   ┌───────────┐
│ DURING    │   │ DURING    │   │ DURING    │   │ DURING    │
├───────────┤   ├───────────┤   ├───────────┤   ├───────────┤
│  [0:0]    │   │  [1:1]    │   │  [2:2]    │   │  [0:0]    │
│  [1:1]    │   │  [2:2]    │   │  [0:0]    │   │  [1:1]    │
└───────────┘   └───────────┘   └───────────┘   │  [2:2]    │
                                                └───────────┘
```

- A relation of the specified type will be equal to its collapsed form if and only if it contains no overlapping or abutting DURING values. Again there are precisely eight such relations:

```
┌─────────────┐   ┌─────────────┐   ┌─────────────┐   ┌─────────────┐
│   DURING    │   │   DURING    │   │   DURING    │   │   DURING    │
├─────────────┤   ├─────────────┤   ├─────────────┤   ├─────────────┤
│             │   │    [0:0]    │   │    [1:1]    │   │    [2:2]    │
└─────────────┘   └─────────────┘   └─────────────┘   └─────────────┘


┌─────────────┐   ┌─────────────┐   ┌─────────────┐   ┌─────────────┐
│   DURING    │   │   DURING    │   │   DURING    │   │   DURING    │
├─────────────┤   ├─────────────┤   ├─────────────┤   ├─────────────┤
│    [0:1]    │   │    [1:2]    │   │    [0:2]    │   │    [0:0]    │
│             │   │             │   │             │   │    [2:2]    │
└─────────────┘   └─────────────┘   └─────────────┘   └─────────────┘
```

Chapter 9

The PACK and UNPACK Operators

I : The Single–Attribute Case

Relations are simply a tedious pack.

—Oscar Wilde:
A Woman of No Importance (1893)

As indicated at the end of Chapter 8, the purpose of the present chapter is to introduce and describe certain relational operators that build on the operators COLLAPSE and EXPAND discussed in that previous chapter. The operators in question are called PACK and UNPACK, respectively;[1] PACK builds on COLLAPSE and UNPACK builds on EXPAND.

PRELIMINARY EXAMPLES

We begin with a couple of preliminary examples that should help you understand the detailed discussions to appear in subsequent sections. Consider the following relation (let's call it *r*):[2]

SNO	DURING
S2	[d02:d04]
S2	[d03:d05]
S4	[d02:d05]
S4	[d04:d06]
S4	[d09:d10]

"Packing" relation *r* on its interval attribute DURING—which we express formally as PACK *r* ON (DURING)—gives the following *packed form* of the relation:

---

[1] As with COLLAPSE and EXPAND, other names appear in the literature, earlier writings by the present authors included.

[2] You might be thinking *r* is a possible value for relvar S_DURING from Chapter 6, but actually it can't be, because it's not consistent with the predicate for that relvar. Indeed, this chapter and the next five, as well as Chapter16, are all concerned in large part with what's involved in avoiding such inconsistencies.

SNO	DURING
S2	[*d02:d05*]
S4	[*d02:d06*]
S4	[*d09:d10*]

Informally, this result consists of a restructured version of the original relation *r*; it represents the same information as *r*—in fact, it's formally *equivalent* to *r*, in a sense to be explained in Chapter 10—but the representation has been restructured in such a way that no two DURING intervals for a given supplier either meet or overlap. The effect of that restructuring, or *packing*, is thus to let us view the information content of *r* in a clumped form, without having to worry about the possibility that distinct clumps might meet or overlap. The relevance of COLLAPSE to such restructuring should be obvious.[3]

Analogously, unpacking that same original relation *r* on DURING, which we express formally as UNPACK *r* ON (DURING), gives the following *unpacked form* of the relation:

SNO	DURING
S2	[*d02:d02*]
S2	[*d03:d03*]
S2	[*d04:d04*]
S2	[*d05:d05*]
S4	[*d02:d02*]
S4	[*d03:d03*]
S4	[*d04:d04*]
S4	[*d05:d05*]
S4	[*d06:d06*]
S4	[*d09:d09*]
S4	[*d10:d10*]

Informally, this result also consists of a restructured version of the original relation *r*; it represents the same information as *r*—again, it's formally equivalent to *r*—but the representation has been restructured in such a way that every DURING value is a unit interval specifically. The effect of that restructuring, or *unpacking*, is thus to let us view the information content of *r* at an atomic level, without having to worry about the many different ways in which that information might be bundled together into clumps. The relevance of EXPAND to such restructuring should be obvious.[4]

---

[3] It's worth noting that the DURING values are now maximal intervals, and hence that this restructured version of the relation (unlike the original version) does satisfy the predicate for—and is therefore a possible value for—relvar S_DURING.

[4] The predicate satisfied by this unpacked form of the relation is *Supplier SNO was under contract on day d, where day d is the sole day contained in the interval DURING* (i.e., DURING is a unit interval).

In the next two sections, we explain the PACK and UNPACK operators in detail. Our explanations are based on examples that are based in turn on Queries A and B from the very end of Chapter 5. Just to remind you, here first are slightly simplified restatements of those queries:

Queries (fully temporal database with FROM-TO pairs, Fig. 5.3):

■ **Query A:** Get SNO-FROM-TO triples such that FROM and TO together designate a maximal interval during which supplier SNO was able to supply at least one part. *Note:* We remind you that the term *maximal interval*, in the case at hand, means that supplier SNO was unable to supply any part at all on the day immediately before FROM or immediately after TO. We remind you also that the result of the query might contain several tuples for the same supplier (but with different intervals, of course; moreover, those different intervals will neither meet nor overlap).

■ **Query B:** Get SNO-FROM-TO triples such that FROM and TO together designate a maximal interval during which supplier SNO was unable to supply any parts at all. *Note:* Again the result might contain several tuples for the same supplier.

Of course, we need to restate these queries in terms of the database of Fig. 6.1 (i.e., the version of the database containing intervals as such, instead of explicit FROM-TO pairs. For convenience, however, we first repeat in Fig. 9.1 the sample values from Fig. 6.1:

S_DURING

SNO	DURING
S1	[*d04:d10*]
S2	[*d02:d04*]
S2	[*d07:d10*]
S3	[*d03:d10*]
S4	[*d04:d10*]
S5	[*d02:d10*]

SP_DURING

SNO	PNO	DURING
S1	P1	[*d04:d10*]
S1	P2	[*d05:d10*]
S1	P3	[*d09:d10*]
S1	P4	[*d05:d10*]
S1	P5	[*d04:d10*]
S1	P6	[*d06:d10*]
S2	P1	[*d02:d04*]
S2	P1	[*d08:d10*]
S2	P2	[*d03:d03*]
S2	P2	[*d09:d10*]
S3	P2	[*d08:d10*]
S4	P2	[*d06:d09*]
S4	P4	[*d04:d08*]
S4	P5	[*d05:d10*]

Fig. 9.1: Simplified suppliers-and-shipments database (fully temporal version using intervals)—sample values

Now we can restate the queries:

Queries (fully temporal database with DURING intervals, Fig. 9.1):

- **Query A:** Get SNO-DURING pairs such that DURING designates a maximal interval during which supplier SNO was able to supply at least one part.

- **Query B:** Get SNO-DURING pairs such that DURING designates a maximal interval during which supplier SNO was unable to supply any parts at all.

It might help to show the results of these queries, given the sample values from Fig. 9.1. Here they are—Query A on the left, Query B on the right:

SNO	DURING
S1	[d04:d10]
S2	[d02:d04]
S2	[d08:d10]
S3	[d08:d10]
S4	[d04:d10]

SNO	DURING
S2	[d07:d07]
S3	[d03:d07]
S5	[d02:d10]

In what follows, we'll refer to these two result relations as *ResultA* and *ResultB*, respectively. Observe in particular that the DURING values in these relations are all maximal intervals.

PACKED FORM

We now focus on Query A specifically. First of all, it's intuitively obvious that Query A can be answered from SP_DURING alone—we don't need to inspect S_DURING at all. Now, you might recall that the very first version of the query, which applied to the nontemporal version of the database (Fig. 5.1) and was discussed in Chapter 5, involved a simple projection operation on SP. So you might not be surprised to learn that the restated version of the query for the database of Fig. 9.1 is going to involve an operator on SP_DURING that some writers like to call "temporal projection"—though we hasten to add that we don't much care for this nomenclature ourselves, because the operator doesn't apply only to temporal intervals as such.

Be that as it may, we'll build up our formulation of the query one step at a time, using **Tutorial D**'s WITH construct. Here's the first step:

```
WITH ( t1 := SP_DURING { SNO , DURING } ) :
```

This step simply projects away part numbers, which are irrelevant to the query under consideration, and introduces the name *t1* for the result of that projection. So here's *t1* (observe in particular that certain tuples in this result derive from more than one tuple in SP_DURING— in other words, the projection has "eliminated duplicates," to use the common parlance):

SNO	DURING
S1	[*d04:d10*]
S1	[*d05:d10*]
S1	[*d09:d10*]
S1	[*d06:d10*]
S2	[*d02:d04*]
S2	[*d08:d10*]
S2	[*d03:d03*]
S2	[*d09:d10*]
S3	[*d08:d10*]
S4	[*d06:d09*]
S4	[*d04:d08*]
S4	[*d05:d10*]

Observe next that *t1* contains redundant information; for example, it tells us three times that supplier S1 was able to supply something on day 6. By contrast, the desired result, *ResultA*, contains no such redundancies. Now, as you've probably realized, that desired result is in fact the packed form of *t1* on DURING—and please note very carefully that a DURING value for a given supplier in that packed form doesn't necessarily exist as a DURING value for that supplier in the relation *t1* from which that packed form is derived. In our example, this remark applies to supplier S4 in particular (but to supplier S4 only, as it happens).

Now, we'll eventually reach a point where we can obtain that desired result by means of a simple expression of the form:

```
PACK t1 ON ( DURING )
```

As already indicated, however, we want to build up to that point gradually. The next step is:

```
WITH ( t2 := t1 GROUP { DURING } AS X ) :
```

Aside: The source expression on the right of the ":=" symbol in the assignment here could equally well have been the following EXTEND expression:

```
EXTEND t1 { SNO } : { X := !!t1 }
```

In other words, the X value corresponding to any given tuple *t* of *t1* is, precisely, the image relation within *t1* itself of the SNO value in that tuple *t*. *End of aside.*

So here's *t2* (note in particular that attribute X is relation valued):

SNO	X
S1	DURING [d04:d10] [d05:d10] [d09:d10] [d06:d10]
S2	DURING [d02:d04] [d08:d10] [d03:d03] [d09:d10]

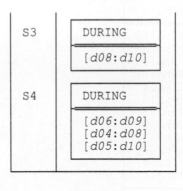

SNO	X
S3	DURING [d08:d10]
S4	DURING [d06:d09] [d04:d08] [d05:d10]

Next, we replace each of those X values by its collapsed form, using the "what if" form of EXTEND and the COLLAPSE operator from the previous chapter:

```
WITH ( t3 := EXTEND t2 : { X := COLLAPSE ( X ) } ) :
```

Here's *t3*:

SNO	X
S1	DURING [d04:d10]
S2	DURING [d02:d04] [d08:d10]
S3	DURING [d08:d10]
S4	DURING [d04:d10]

Finally, we ungroup:

```
t3 UNGROUP X
```

And this ungrouping yields the relation we earlier called *ResultA*. Thus, bringing all of the steps together and simplifying slightly, *ResultA* is the result of evaluating this expression:

```
WITH ( t1 := SP_DURING { SNO , DURING } ,
       t2 := t1 GROUP { DURING } AS X ,
       t3 := EXTEND t2 : { X := COLLAPSE ( X ) } ) :
t3 UNGROUP X
```

Now, it would obviously be desirable to be able to get from *t1* to *ResultA* in a single operation. To that end, we introduce (at last!) our new PACK operator. Here's the definition:

Definition (*single-attribute PACK*): Let relation *r* have an interval attribute *A*. Then the expression PACK *r* ON (*A*) denotes the **packing** of *r* on *A*, and it's defined to be shorthand for the following:

```
WITH ( r1 := r GROUP { A } AS X ,
       r2 := EXTEND r1 : { X := COLLAPSE ( X ) } ) :
r2 UNGROUP X
```

And it's clear from this definition that, as claimed earlier, PACK is really just shorthand—but of course it's extremely useful shorthand. It should also be clear (but it might help to spell the point out explicitly) that packing a relation on some attribute *A* involves *partitioning* that relation on all of its attributes apart from *A*. For instance, consider relation *t1* from the example we used above to explain the packing process. That relation had attributes SNO and DURING, and when we packed it on DURING, we effectively formed a partition consisting of the tuples for supplier S1, another consisting of the tuples for supplier S2, and so on. (Note, however, that there's no suggestion that each such partition will contribute just one tuple to the final packed result. That is, the expression PACK *r* ON (*A*) might return a result with several tuples for any given value of *B*, where *B* is all of the attributes of *r* apart from *A*. By way of example, see relation *ResultA* above, which has two tuples for supplier S2.)

To get back to Query A, we can now offer the following as a reasonably concise formulation of that query:

```
PACK SP_DURING { SNO , DURING } ON ( DURING )
```

As indicated earlier, the overall operation denoted by this expression is an example of what's sometimes called *temporal projection* (see, e.g., reference [62]). To be specific, it's the "temporal projection" of SP_DURING on SNO and DURING. We'll have quite a lot more to say about such "temporal" operators in general in Chapter 11.

UNPACKED FORM

We turn now to Query B ("Get SNO-DURING pairs such that DURING designates a maximal interval during which supplier SNO was unable to supply any parts at all"). Intuitively, it should be clear that, unlike Query A, this one can't be answered from SP_DURING alone—we need to inspect S_DURING as well. In fact, as you might recall, the very first version of this query, for the nontemporal version of the database, involved taking the difference between ... well, not exactly S and SP as such, but, rather, certain projections of S and SP. But, ignoring this point of detail for the moment, if now you're expecting to see something that might be called a "temporal difference," then of course you're right. What's more, as you might also be expecting, while "temporal projection" involved the PACK operator, "temporal difference" is going to involve the UNPACK operator. (Actually it's going to involve PACK as well, as we'll see.)

In essence, then, what we need to do for Query B is look for SNO-DURING pairs that (a) are either contained in or implied by S_DURING and (b) are neither contained in nor implied by SP_DURING, because (speaking very loosely):

- SNO-DURING pairs that are contained in or implied by S_DURING show when suppliers were under contract.

- SNO-DURING pairs that are contained in or implied by SP_DURING show when suppliers were able to supply something.

- The difference between the first of these two sets of SNO-DURING pairs and the second (in that order) shows when suppliers were under contract but unable to supply anything.

This brief outline should be sufficient to suggest, correctly, that (again in essence) what we need to do is perform a couple of unpack operations and then take the difference between the results. So first let's introduce the UNPACK operator:

Definition (*single-attribute UNPACK*): Let relation *r* have an interval attribute *A*. Then the expression UNPACK *r* ON (*A*) denotes the **unpacking** of *r* on *A*, and it's defined to be shorthand for the following:

```
WITH ( r1 := r GROUP { A } AS X ,
       r2 := EXTEND r1 : { X := EXPAND ( X ) } ) :
r2 UNGROUP X
```

As you can see, this definition is identical to that for PACK, except for the appearance of EXPAND rather than COLLAPSE in the second line of the expansion.

Returning to Query B, we can obtain the left operand we need (i.e., SNO-DURING pairs that are contained in or implied by S_DURING) as follows:

```
UNPACK S_DURING { SNO , DURING } ON ( DURING )
```

(Of course, the subexpression S_DURING {SNO,DURING} here could be simplified to just S_DURING, since that projection is in fact an identity projection. We show the projection explicitly for reasons of clarity.) Here's the expanded form of this UNPACK:

```
WITH ( r1 := S_DURING { SNO , DURING } GROUP { DURING } AS X ,
       r2 := EXTEND r1 : { X := EXPAND ( X ) } ) :
r2 UNGROUP X
```

Given the sample data of Fig. 9.1, the result of this expression—let's call it *u1*—looks like this:

SNO	DURING
S1	[d04:d04]
S1	[d05:d05]
S1	[d06:d06]
S1	[d07:d07]
S1	[d08:d08]
S1	[d09:d09]
S1	[d10:d10]
S2	[d02:d02]
S2	[d03:d03]
S2	[d04:d04]
S2	[d07:d07]
S2	[d08:d08]
S2	[d09:d09]
S2	[d10:d10]
S3	[d03:d03]
S3	[d04:d04]
S3	[d05:d05]
S3	[d06:d06]
S3	[d07:d07]
S3	[d08:d08]
S3	[d09:d09]
S3	[d10:d10]

SNO	DURING
S4	[d04:d04]
S4	[d05:d05]
S4	[d06:d06]
S4	[d07:d07]
S4	[d08:d08]
S4	[d09:d09]
S4	[d10:d10]
S5	[d02:d02]
S5	[d03:d03]
S5	[d04:d04]
S5	[d05:d05]
S5	[d06:d06]
S5	[d07:d07]
S5	[d08:d08]
S5	[d09:d09]
S5	[d10:d10]

Relation *u1* is the *unpacked form* of S_DURING on DURING, and it's the left operand for the difference operation we're gradually building up to. Of course, the right operand (i.e., SNO-DURING pairs that are contained in or implied by SP_DURING) is obtained in like fashion:

```
UNPACK SP_DURING { SNO , DURING } ON ( DURING )
```

The result of this expression—let's call it *u2*—looks like this:

SNO	DURING
S1	[d04:d04]
S1	[d05:d05]
S1	[d06:d06]
S1	[d07:d07]
S1	[d08:d08]
S1	[d09:d09]
S1	[d10:d10]
S2	[d02:d02]
S2	[d03:d03]
S2	[d04:d04]
S2	[d08:d08]
S2	[d09:d09]
S2	[d10:d10]

SNO	DURING
S3	[d08:d08]
S3	[d09:d09]
S3	[d10:d10]
S4	[d04:d04]
S4	[d05:d05]
S4	[d06:d06]
S4	[d07:d07]
S4	[d08:d08]
S4	[d09:d09]
S4	[d10:d10]

Now we can form the difference:[5]

```
u1 MINUS u2
```

The result of this expression, *u3* say, looks like this:

SNO	DURING
S2	[d07:d07]
S3	[d03:d03]
S3	[d04:d04]
S3	[d05:d05]
S3	[d06:d06]
S3	[d07:d07]

SNO	DURING
S5	[d02:d02]
S5	[d03:d03]
S5	[d04:d04]
S5	[d05:d05]
S5	[d06:d06]
S5	[d07:d07]
S5	[d08:d08]
S5	[d09:d09]
S5	[d10:d10]

Finally, we pack *u3* on DURING to obtain the desired overall result:

```
PACK u3 ON ( DURING )
```

And that final result is, of course, exactly *ResultB* as shown previously:

SNO	DURING
S2	[d07:d07]
S3	[d03:d07]
S5	[d02:d10]

---

[5] We could have used NOT MATCHING here in place of MINUS, thus: *u1* NOT MATCHING *u2*.

Here then is a formulation of Query B as a single expression:[6]

```
PACK
    ( ( UNPACK S_DURING { SNO , DURING } ON ( DURING ) )
      MINUS
      ( UNPACK SP_DURING { SNO , DURING } ON ( DURING ) ) )
ON ( DURING )
```

As already noted, the overall operation denoted by this expression is an example of what's sometimes called *temporal difference*. More precisely, it's a "temporal difference" between (a) the projection of S_DURING on SNO and DURING and (b) the projection of SP_DURING on SNO and DURING (in that order). Again, we'll have much more to say on such matters in Chapter 11; here we content ourselves with a few fairly obvious remarks regarding the semantics of the PACK and UNPACK operators as such. Here first is a repeat of the formal definition of UNPACK:

```
UNPACK r ON ( A ) ≝
    WITH ( r1 := r GROUP { A } AS X ,
           r2 := EXTEND r1 : { X := EXPAND ( X ) } ) :
    r2 UNGROUP X
```

Observe now that:

■ Unpacking *r* on *A* (just like packing *r* on *A*) involves partitioning *r* on all of its attributes apart from *A*.

■ Like PACK, UNPACK is really just shorthand; in particular, it's defined in terms of the EXPAND operator from Chapter 8.

■ Like the operators COLLAPSE and EXPAND on which they're based, PACK and UNPACK are *not* inverses of each other. That is, neither of the expressions

```
UNPACK ( PACK r ON ( A ) ) ON ( A )
```

and

```
PACK ( UNPACK r ON ( A ) ) ON ( A )
```

is guaranteed to return *r*, in general. In fact, the following identities clearly hold:

---

[6] Again we could have used NOT MATCHING in place of MINUS. In fact, if we did, then the two projections on SNO and DURING wouldn't be necessary.

```
UNPACK ( PACK r ON ( A ) ) ON ( A )  ≡  UNPACK r ON ( A )

PACK ( UNPACK r ON ( A ) ) ON ( A )  ≡  PACK r ON ( A )
```

It follows that the first operation in a PACK-then-UNPACK or UNPACK-then-PACK sequence on some given relation can simply be ignored, a fact that could be useful for optimization purposes (especially when that first operation is UNPACK).[7]

■ The following identities clearly hold as well:

```
UNPACK ( UNPACK ( r ) ON ( A ) ) ON ( A )  ≡  UNPACK ( r ) ON ( A )

PACK ( PACK ( r ) ON ( A ) ) ON ( A )  ≡  PACK ( r ) ON ( A )
```

FURTHER QUERIES

In this section, we give some further examples of the use of PACK and UNPACK in formulating queries. We assume the result is required in packed form in each case.

Our first example is deliberately not a temporal one. We're given a relvar NHW, with attributes NAME, HEIGHT, and WEIGHT, giving the height and weight of certain persons. (You might like to try writing out a sample value for this relvar and using that sample value as a basis for understanding what's being asked for in the following query, also for illustrating the steps in the subsequent explanation.) The query is "For each weight represented in NHW, get every range of heights such that for each such range *hr* and for each height in *hr* there's at least one person represented in NHW who's of that height and weight." Possible formulation:

```
PACK
   ( ( EXTEND NHW { HEIGHT , WEIGHT } :
                 { HR := INTERVAL_HEIGHT ( [ HEIGHT : HEIGHT ] ) } )
                                                  { WEIGHT , HR } )
ON ( HR )
```

Explanation: We begin by projecting NHW over HEIGHT and WEIGHT, thereby obtaining all height : weight pairs in the original relation (i.e., all height : weight pairs such that there's at least one person of that height and weight). We then extend that projection by introducing another attribute, HR, whose value in any given tuple is a unit interval of the form [*h:h*], where *h* is the HEIGHT value in that same tuple (note the invocation of the interval selector INTERVAL_HEIGHT). We then project away the HEIGHT attribute and pack the result on HR. The final result is a relation with two attributes, WEIGHT and HR, and predicate as follows:

---

[7] Actually, when we get to the slightly more formal and extended treatment of these matters in the next chapter, we're going to *define* PACK to do a preliminary UNPACK anyway. But in the case at hand, where the packing and unpacking are done on the basis of just a single attribute, it's easy to see the preliminary UNPACK can simply be ignored.

HR denotes a maximal interval of heights such that, for all heights h in HR, there exists at least one person p such that p has height h and weight WEIGHT.

Note carefully that this example is indeed, as stated, not a temporal one—the intervals involved represent ranges of heights, not ranges of temporal values. To be specific, they're of type INTERVAL_HEIGHT, where HEIGHT is the applicable point type.

By way of a second example, consider relvar SP_DURING once again (Fig. 9.1). At any given time, if there are any shipments at all at that time, then there's some part number *pmax* such that, at that time, (a) at least one supplier is able to supply part *pmax*, but (b) no supplier is able to supply any part with a part number greater than *pmax*. (Obviously we're assuming here that the operator ">" is defined for values of type PNO.) So consider the query "For each part number that has ever been such a *pmax* value, get that part number together with the interval(s) during which it actually was that *pmax* value." Here's a possible formulation:

```
WITH ( t1 := UNPACK SP_DURING ON ( DURING ) ,
       t2 := EXTEND t1 { DURING } : { PMAX := MAX ( !!t1 , PNO ) } ) :
PACK t2 ON ( DURING )
```

Our third and last example is based on relvar S_PARTS_DURING from the section "A More Searching Example" in Chapter 6. For convenience, we show a sample value for that relvar in Fig. 9.2 (a repeat of Fig. 6.2):[8]

S_PARTS_DURING

SNO	PARTS	DURING
S1	[P1:P3]	[d01:d04]
S1	[P2:P4]	[d07:d08]
S1	[P5:P6]	[d09:d09]
S2	[P1:P1]	[d08:d09]
S2	[P1:P2]	[d08:d08]
S2	[P3:P4]	[d07:d08]
S3	[P2:P4]	[d01:d04]
S3	[P3:P5]	[d01:d04]
S3	[P2:P4]	[d05:d06]
S3	[P2:P4]	[d06:d09]
S4	[P3:P4]	[d05:d08]

Fig. 9.2: A relvar with two interval attributes (S_PARTS_DURING)—sample value

---

[8] Of course, relvar S_PARTS_DURING has two interval attributes, not just one. In keeping with the subject matter and title of this chapter, however, the only packing and unpacking we'll be doing here will be on the basis of just a single attribute. Chapter 10 will examine the question of packing and unpacking on two attributes or more. *Note:* We remind you also from Chapter 6 that the sample value shown is actually incomplete, but this fact doesn't materially affect the discussion in any way.

Consider the query "For each part that has ever been capable of being supplied by supplier S3, get the part number and the applicable intervals of time." Given the values shown in Fig. 9.2, the desired result looks like this:

PNO	DURING
P2	[*d01:d09*]
P3	[*d01:d09*]
P4	[*d01:d09*]
P5	[*d01:d04*]

Here's a possible formulation of this query (note the reliance in line 4 on the fact that, thanks to the UNPACK in line 3, PARTS values in *t3* are unit intervals):

```
WITH ( t1 := S_PARTS_DURING WHERE SNO = SNO ( 'S3' ) ,
       t2 := t1 { PARTS , DURING } ,
       t3 := UNPACK t2 ON ( PARTS ) ,
       t4 := EXTEND t3 : { PNO := POINT FROM PARTS } ,
       t5 := t4 { PNO , DURING } ) :
PACK t5 ON ( DURING )
```

EXERCISES

9.1   Give a formulation of the query just discussed—"For each part that has ever been capable of being supplied by supplier S3, get the part number and the applicable intervals of time"—using our usual relvar SP_DURING instead of S_PARTS_DURING.

9.2   Give formulations of the query "For each day on which some part has been capable of being supplied by supplier S3, get that day and the applicable ranges of parts," using (a) relvar SP_DURING; (b) relvar S_PARTS_DURING.

9.3   Can you find a pair of relations *r1* and *r2* such that the unpacked form of *r1* is a proper subset of the unpacked form of *r2* but the packed form of *r1* is a proper superset of the packed form of *r2* (where the packing and unpacking operations are done on the basis of the same attribute in every case, of course)?

ANSWERS

9.1
```
WITH ( t1 := SP_DURING WHERE SNO = SNO ( 'S3' ) ,
       t2 := t1 { PNO , DURING } ) :
PACK t2 ON ( DURING )
```

Note: If we can rely on relvar SP_DURING being kept in packed form—see Chapter 13—the final PACK step here will be unnecessary (why, exactly?).

9.2

a.
```
WITH ( t1 := SP_DURING WHERE SNO = SNO ( 'S3' ) ,
       t2 := t1 { PNO , DURING } ,
       t3 := UNPACK t2 ON ( DURING ) ,
       t4 := EXTEND t3 : { DAY := POINT FROM DURING } ,
       t5 := EXTEND t4 : { PARTS := INTERVAL_DATE ( [ DAY : DAY ] ) } ) :
PACK t5 { DAY , PARTS } ON ( PARTS )
```

b. One solution here (perhaps not the most efficient) is just to unpack S_PARTS_DURING on PARTS; then, if *t0* is the result of that UNPACK, the solution to Exercise 9.2a applies directly, with *t0* playing the role of SP_DURING. Alternatively:

```
WITH ( t1 := S_PARTS_DURING WHERE SNO = SNO ( 'S3' ) ,
       t2 := t1 { PARTS , DURING } ,
       t3 := UNPACK t2 ON ( DURING ) ,
       t4 := EXTEND t3 : { DAY := POINT FROM DURING } ,
PACK t4 { DAY , PARTS } ON ( PARTS )
```

9.3   A simple example is as follows:

r1

SNO	DURING
S1	[d01:d01]
S1	[d03:d03]

r2

SNO	DURING
S1	[d01:d01]
S1	[d02:d02]
S1	[d03:d03]

Chapter 10

The PACK and UNPACK Operators

II : The Multiattribute Case

In Nature there are neither rewards nor punishments—
there are consequences.

—Robert G. Ingersoll:
Some Reasons Why (1881)

In their simplest form—certainly the form in which they're most likely to be encountered in practice—PACK and UNPACK each operate in terms of just one interval attribute, exactly as described in the previous chapter. As we know, however, it's possible for a relation to have more than one such attribute. For that reason, it's desirable to generalize the operators in such a way as to allow the packing and unpacking to be done on *any subset of* the attributes of the relation in question (just so long as every attribute in that subset is interval valued, of course). What's more, it turns out that such generalizations have a number of consequences and ramifications that aren't always immediately obvious; indeed, they can be very confusing. Such matters are the subject of the present chapter.

PACKING AND UNPACKING ON NO ATTRIBUTES

As just noted, we wish to extend the PACK and UNPACK operators to operate in terms of any subset of the interval attributes of the relation in question. The first case to consider is the one in which the subset in question is empty (the empty set is a subset of every set, of course).[1] As we'll see in the next chapter, the ability to pack or unpack a relation on no attributes at all is going to turn out, perhaps surprisingly, to be rather important. The syntax is as follows:

```
PACK r ON ( )

UNPACK r ON ( )
```

---

[1] Observe that there's no violation here of the requirement that every attribute in the subset be an interval attribute specifically. Certainly the packing and unpacking aren't being done on the basis of any attribute that's *not* an interval attribute.

We define the result of each of these expressions to be simply *r*, and justify this definition as follows. First, PACK. Consider the expression:

```
WITH ( r1 := r GROUP { } AS X ,
       r2 := EXTEND r1 : { X := COLLAPSE ( X ) } ) :
r2 UNGROUP X
```

As you can see, this expression is identical to our usual expansion for PACK *r* ON (*A*)— see Chapter 9—except that the first step (the grouping step) specifies "GROUP { }" instead of "GROUP {*A*}." Thus, the semantics are as follows:

■ The first (grouping) step gives an intermediate result *r1* with the same cardinality as *r* and with heading the same as that of *r* except that it contains an additional attribute *X*, which is relation valued. (In general, the result of *r* GROUP {*A1,A2,...,An*} AS *B* has degree *nr−n*+1, where *nr* is the degree of *r*. If *n* = 0, therefore, the slightly counterintuitive effect is indeed to add an attribute to the heading.) The relations that are values of *X* have degree zero; i.e., they're nullary relations. Furthermore, each of those relations is TABLE_DEE, not TABLE_DUM, because every tuple of *r*—in fact, *every* tuple, regardless of whether or not it's a tuple of *r*—effectively includes the 0-tuple as its value for that subtuple that corresponds to the empty set of attributes [25]. Thus, each tuple in *r1* effectively consists of the corresponding tuple from *r* extended with the *X* value TABLE_DEE.

■ The next step effectively gives an intermediate result *r2* that's identical to *r1* (recall from Chapter 8 that collapsing TABLE_DEE returns TABLE_DEE).

■ The final (ungrouping) step then effectively replaces each tuple *t* in *r2* by its set theory union with the 0-tuple, returning the relation so obtained as the overall result. But, of course, the set theory union of any tuple *t* with the 0-tuple is simply tuple *t* itself. Thus, the final result is identical to relation *r*.

Turning now to UNPACK, UNPACK *r* ON ( ) is shorthand for the following:

```
WITH ( r1 := r GROUP { } AS X ,
     ( r2 := EXTEND r1 : { X := EXPAND ( X ) } ) :
r2 UNGROUP X
```

By an argument analogous to that for PACK above, this expression is readily seen to evaluate to *r* as well.

Note: One obvious consequence of the foregoing definitions is that unpacking some relation *r* on no attributes and then packing the result, also on no attributes, returns *r*. We'll be appealing to this seemingly rather trivial observation in the section "Packing on Two or More

Attributes" later in the chapter; however, its real significance won't become apparent until we get to the final section of Chapter 11.

UNPACKING ON TWO OR MORE ATTRIBUTES

Now we turn to the question of packing and unpacking relations on more than one attribute. For reasons that'll become clear in the next section, it's convenient to deal with UNPACK first. We begin by considering the case of unpacking on exactly two attributes.

Let *r* be a relation with two interval attributes A1 and A2 (possibly other attributes as well, interval valued or otherwise). Just to be definite, suppose *r* looks like this:

A1	A2
[P1:P1]	[*d08*:*d09*]
[P1:P2]	[*d08*:*d08*]
[P3:P4]	[*d07*:*d08*]

This relation is in fact the restriction of the relation shown in Fig. 9.2—a hypothetical sample value for relvar S_PARTS_DURING—to just the tuples for supplier S2, projected over PARTS and DURING, except that we've renamed those two attributes A1 and A2, respectively. (Actually, we could have retained the SNO attribute if we'd wanted to—it would have made essentially no difference to the analysis that follows.)

Now consider the following expression:

```
UNPACK ( UNPACK r ON ( A1 ) ) ON ( A2 )
```

The inner expression UNPACK *r* ON (A1) yields:

A1	A2
[P1:P1]	[*d08*:*d09*]
[P1:P1]	[*d08*:*d08*]
[P2:P2]	[*d08*:*d08*]
[P3:P3]	[*d07*:*d08*]
[P4:P4]	[*d07*:*d08*]

Unpacking this relation on A2 then yields:

A1	A2
[P1:P1]	[d08:d08]
[P1:P1]	[d09:d09]
[P2:P2]	[d08:d08]
[P3:P3]	[d07:d07]
[P3:P3]	[d08:d08]
[P4:P4]	[d07:d07]
[P4:P4]	[d08:d08]

Now let's see what happens if we do the two unpackings in the reverse order—i.e., consider the following expression:

```
UNPACK ( UNPACK r ON ( A2 ) ) ON ( A1 )
```

The inner expression UNPACK *r* ON (A2) yields:

A1	A2
[P1:P1]	[d08:d08]
[P1:P1]	[d09:d09]
[P1:P2]	[d08:d08]
[P3:P4]	[d07:d07]
[P3:P4]	[d08:d08]

Unpacking this relation on A1 then yields:

A1	A2
[P1:P1]	[d08:d08]
[P1:P1]	[d09:d09]
[P2:P2]	[d08:d08]
[P3:P3]	[d07:d07]
[P4:P4]	[d07:d07]
[P3:P3]	[d08:d08]
[P4:P4]	[d08:d08]

And this overall result is readily seen to be the same as before.[2] In fact, it's easy to see that if *r* is any relation with interval attributes *A1* and *A2,* then the following identity holds:

```
UNPACK ( UNPACK r ON ( A1 ) ) ON ( A2 )   ≡
UNPACK ( UNPACK r ON ( A2 ) ) ON ( A1 )
```

---

[2] The tuples are shown in a slightly different order, but that's simply because the mental algorithm we followed in producing the result—when we "played DBMS," as it were—happened to produce them in a different order.

(Working through the foregoing example in detail should be sufficient to give you the necessary insight as to why this identity holds.) Indeed, it's easy to see more generally that if r has interval attributes $A1, A2, ..., An$, then unpacking r on those attributes one at a time in any order whatsoever will always yield the same overall result. We therefore propose the following extended definition:

> **Definition** (*multiattribute UNPACK*): Let relation r have interval attributes $A1, A2, ..., An$ (possibly other attributes as well, interval valued or otherwise), where n is greater than one. Then the expression UNPACK r ON $(A1, A2, ..., An)$ denotes the **unpacking** of r on $A1$, $A2, ..., An$, and it's defined to be shorthand for the following—
>
> ```
> UNPACK ( ... ( UNPACK ( UNPACK r ON ( B1 ) ) ON ( B2 ) ) ... ) ON ( Bn )
> ```
>
> —where the sequence of attribute names $B1, B2, ..., Bn$ consists of some arbitrary permutation of the specified sequence of attribute names $A1, A2, ..., An$.[3]

Note: The commalist $A1, A2, ..., An$ in the expression UNPACK r ON $(A1, A2, ..., An)$ actually denotes a set, not a sequence, of attribute names (since the sequence as such is irrelevant). In **Tutorial D**, therefore, we would normally enclose it in braces, not parentheses. As we'll see in the next section, however, parentheses are *required* in the case of PACK—that is, the sequence in which the attribute names are specified is significant for PACK—and we thus felt it would be more user friendly to use parentheses instead of braces in the case of UNPACK as well, but then to state explicitly that for UNPACK the sequence is arbitrary.

PACKING ON TWO OR MORE ATTRIBUTES

We turn now to PACK. Here we proceed a little differently. In fact, for reasons we hope will shortly become clear, we begin with a definition instead an example:

> **Definition** (*multiattribute PACK*): Let relation r have interval attributes $A1, A2, ..., An$ (possibly other attributes as well, interval valued or otherwise), where n is greater than one.[4] Then the expression PACK r ON $(A1, A2, ..., An)$ denotes the **packing** of r on $A1$, $A2, ..., An$ (in that order), and it's defined to be shorthand for the following—

---

[3] We've said n must be greater than one, but that requirement can in fact be dropped (we include it only to make the definition parallel that given for multiattribute PACK in the next section), because (a) if $n = 0$, the expansion reduces to UNPACK r ON ( ), which we've already defined to return simply r, and (b) if $n = 1$ it reduces to UNPACK r ON $(B1)$, which returns a result as defined in the previous chapter (Chapter 9).

[4] But we're going to show that the requirement that n be greater than one can be dropped here, too.

```
PACK ( ... ( PACK ( PACK r' ON ( A1 ) ) ON ( A2 ) ) ... ) ON ( An )
```

—where *r'* is the relation denoted by the expression UNPACK *r* ON (*A1, A2, ..., An*).

Observe, therefore, that we define PACK to operate by first *un*packing the specified relation on all of the specified attributes (in some arbitrary order, of course), and then packing it on those same attributes, in the order specified. Thus, for example, the expression

```
PACK r ON ( A1 , A2 )
```

is defined to be shorthand for the expression

```
PACK ( PACK ( UNPACK r ON ( A1 , A2 ) ) ON ( A1 ) ) ON ( A2 )
```

In other words, the original PACK invocation PACK *r* ON (*A1,A2*) is evaluated by first unpacking relation *r* on *A1* and *A2*, then packing the result on *A1*, and finally packing *that* result on *A2*.

Note: You might be forgiven for thinking the foregoing definition is circular, since it's apparently defining the PACK operator in terms of itself. But it isn't. Rather, all of the references to PACK in the formal expansion are, as you can see, references to the single-attribute version of that operator, which was defined in Chapter 9. (As for the implicit reference to UNPACK—this time on several attributes, not just one—that's a reference to UNPACK as defined in the previous section.) Thus, there's in fact no circularity involved.

Now, before we consider the question of packing on two or more attributes in detail, we ought really to convince ourselves that the definition given above for packing on *n* attributes is at least consistent with the definitions previously given for *n* = 1 (in Chapter 9) and *n* = 0 (earlier in the present chapter). In other words, let's see what happens if we drop the requirement that *n* be greater than one. Consider first the case *n* = 1, for which the text of the definition given above reduces to:

Let relation *r* have an interval attribute *A* (possibly other attributes as well, interval valued or otherwise). Then the expression PACK *r* ON (*A*) denotes the packing of *r* on *A*, and it's defined to be shorthand for the following:

```
PACK ( UNPACK r ON ( A ) ) ON ( A )
```

As we saw in Chapter 9, however, this expression reduces to just PACK *r* ON (*A*)—i.e., the initial UNPACK can be ignored—and so we see that PACK as defined in Chapter 9 is indeed a special case of PACK as defined above, at the start of the present section.

Aside: You might also be worried about an apparent inefficiency in the definition for packing on *n* attributes. For example, it looks as if the expression PACK *r* ON (*A1,A2*) has to be evaluated by first (a) doing an UNPACK of *r* on (*A1,A2*); then, (b) packing the result of the previous step on *A1*, which apparently involves another preliminary UNPACK on *A1*; finally, (c) packing the result of the previous step on *A2*, which apparently involves yet another preliminary UNPACK. Again, however, we observe that the initial UNPACK can be ignored in an UNPACK-then-PACK sequence, just so long as the unpacking and packing are being done on the basis of a single attribute. Thus, the UNPACKs in steps (b) and (c) here can simply be ignored. *End of aside*.

What about the case $n = 0$? Here the text of the definition given above reduces to:

Let *r* be a relation. Then the expression PACK *r* ON ( ) denotes the packing of *r* on no attributes, and it's defined to be shorthand for the following:

```
PACK ( UNPACK r ON ( ) ) ON ( )
```

As we saw earlier in this chapter, however, UNPACK *r* ON ( ) and PACK *r* ON ( ) both return *r*, and so PACK on no attributes too is just a special case of PACK as defined at the start of the present section.

Now let's consider the question of packing on two attributes. Let *r* be a relation with two interval attributes A1 and A2 (possibly other attributes as well, interval valued or otherwise). Just to be definite, suppose *r* looks like this:

A1	A2
[P2:P4]	[d01:d04]
[P3:P5]	[d01:d04]
[P2:P4]	[d05:d06]
[P2:P4]	[d06:d09]

This relation is in fact the restriction of the relation shown in Fig. 9.2—a hypothetical sample value for relvar S_PARTS_DURING—to just those tuples for supplier S3, projected over PARTS and DURING, except that we've renamed those two attributes A1 and A2, respectively. (As in the case of the UNPACK discussion in the previous section, we could have retained the SNO attribute if we had wanted to—it would have made essentially no difference to the analysis that follows.)

Now consider the following expression:

```
PACK r ON ( A1 , A2 )
```

Here first is the result of evaluating the implicit UNPACK *r* ON (A1,A2) that lies at the heart of the expansion of this expression:

A1	A2
[P2:P2]	[*d01:d01*]
[P2:P2]	[*d02:d02*]
[P2:P2]	[*d03:d03*]
[P2:P2]	[*d04:d04*]
[P3:P3]	[*d01:d01*]
[P3:P3]	[*d02:d02*]
[P3:P3]	[*d03:d03*]
[P3:P3]	[*d04:d04*]
[P4:P4]	[*d01:d01*]
[P4:P4]	[*d02:d02*]
[P4:P4]	[*d03:d03*]
[P4:P4]	[*d04:d04*]
[P5:P5]	[*d01:d01*]
[P5:P5]	[*d02:d02*]
[P5:P5]	[*d03:d03*]
[P5:P5]	[*d04:d04*]

A1	A2
[P2:P2]	[*d05:d05*]
[P2:P2]	[*d06:d06*]
[P3:P3]	[*d05:d05*]
[P3:P3]	[*d06:d06*]
[P4:P4]	[*d05:d05*]
[P4:P4]	[*d06:d06*]
[P2:P2]	[*d07:d07*]
[P2:P2]	[*d08:d08*]
[P2:P2]	[*d09:d09*]
[P3:P3]	[*d07:d07*]
[P3:P3]	[*d08:d08*]
[P3:P3]	[*d09:d09*]
[P4:P4]	[*d07:d07*]
[P4:P4]	[*d08:d08*]
[P4:P4]	[*d09:d09*]

Packing this relation on A1 yields:

A1	A2
[P2:P5]	[*d01:d01*]
[P2:P5]	[*d02:d02*]
[P2:P5]	[*d03:d03*]
[P2:P5]	[*d04:d04*]
[P2:P4]	[*d05:d05*]
[P2:P4]	[*d06:d06*]
[P2:P4]	[*d07:d07*]
[P2:P4]	[*d08:d08*]
[P2:P4]	[*d09:d09*]

And packing *this* relation on A2 then yields:

A1	A2
[P2:P5]	[*d01:d04*]
[P2:P4]	[*d05:d09*]

Now we consider what happens if we do the two packings in the reverse order—i.e., we consider the following expression:

```
PACK r ON ( A2 , A1 )
```

First of all, the implicit UNPACK yields the same relation as before, of course. Packing that relation on A2 then yields:

A1	A2
[P2:P2]	[d01:d09]
[P3:P3]	[d01:d09]
[P4:P4]	[d01:d09]
[P5:P5]	[d01:d04]

And packing *this* relation on A1 then yields:

A1	A2
[P2:P4]	[d01:d09]
[P5:P5]	[d01:d04]

And this final result is clearly not the same as before. Thus we see that if *r* is a relation with interval attributes *A1* and *A2*, then

```
PACK r ON ( A1 , A2 )   ≢   PACK r ON ( A2 , A1 )
```

(in general). Of course, an analogous remark applies to an arbitrary relation *r* with *n* interval attributes *A1*, *A2*, ..., *An* for arbitrary *n* > 1. That's why, in the general syntax proposed earlier—

```
PACK r ON ( A1 , A2 , ... , An )
```

—the sequence of attribute names matters (and that's why we enclose it in parentheses instead of braces).

A Graphical Representation

We've just seen an example in which we obtained different results from (a) packing a certain relation *r* on attributes A1 then A2 and (b) packing that same relation *r* on attributes A2 then A1. Such examples lend themselves to a simple pictorial—i.e., graphical, or geometric— interpretation that some readers might find helpful. We explain the basic idea in terms of that same example. Here again is the original relation *r* (but now we've added some tuple labels):

	A1	A2
x1	[P2:P4]	[d01:d04]
x2	[P3:P5]	[d01:d04]
x3	[P2:P4]	[d05:d06]
x4	[P2:P4]	[d06:d09]

We can represent this relation by means of a two-dimensional graph with A1 values shown vertically and A2 values shown horizontally (see Fig. 10.1, where shaded rectangles correspond to tuples *x1-x4* as indicated and heavy shading shows where tuples overlap, as it were):

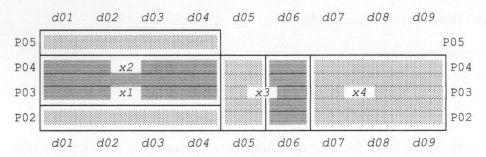

Fig. 10.1: Graphical representation of relation *r*

Packing *r* on A1 then A2 gives the following relation (again we've added some tuple labels):

	A1	A2
y1	[P2:P5]	[d01:d04]
y2	[P2:P4]	[d05:d09]

The corresponding graph is as shown in Fig. 10.2:

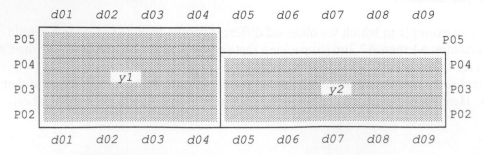

Fig. 10.2: Packing *r* on A1 then A2

By contrast, packing *r* on A2 then A1 gives—

	A1	A2
z1	[P2:P4]	[*d01*:*d09*]
z2	[P5:P5]	[*d01*:*d04*]

—for which the corresponding graph is as shown in Fig. 10.3:

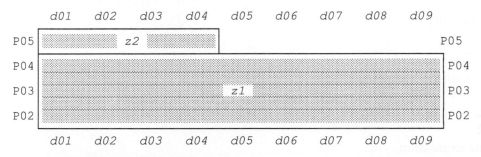

Fig. 10.3: Packing *r* on A2 then A1

As you can see, the two packed forms both cover the same area of the graph by means of two nonoverlapping rectangles (corresponding to nonoverlapping tuples), but they do so in two different ways. In other words, the fact that (a) the problem *Cover the shaded area of the graph by two nonoverlapping rectangles* has two different solutions offers some good insight into why (b) relation *r* has two different "fully packed" forms.

Further examples of such graphs can be found in Appendix E.

A LOGICAL DIFFERENCE

As noted at the beginning of this chapter, the full consequences of generalizing PACK and UNPACK as we've been doing—i.e., to allow packing and unpacking to be done on any subset of the interval attributes of the relation in question—aren't always immediately obvious. One of those consequences is as follows. Consider once again the relation *r* we used in the previous section to demonstrate that, at least for PACK, the order (i.e., of attribute names) matters:

A1	A2
[P2:P4]	[d01:d04]
[P3:P5]	[d01:d04]
[P2:P4]	[d05:d06]
[P2:P4]	[d06:d09]

■ As we saw in the previous section, the expression

```
PACK r ON ( A1 , A2 )
```

yields this result:

A1	A2
[P2:P5]	[d01:d04]
[P2:P4]	[d05:d09]

In fact, the expression

```
PACK ( PACK r ON ( A1 ) ) ON ( A2 )
```

yields the same result, as you can—and, we strongly suggest, you should—confirm for yourself.

■ By contrast, the expression

```
PACK r ON ( A2 , A1 )
```

yields this result (as we also saw in the previous section):

A1	A2
[P2:P4]	[d01:d09]
[P5:P5]	[d01:d04]

But the expression

```
PACK ( PACK r ON ( A2 ) ) ON ( A1 )
```

does *not* yield this same result. Instead, as you can—and, we again strongly suggest, you should—confirm for yourself, it yields this relation:

A1	A2
[P2:P4]	[*d01:d09*]
[P3:P5]	[*d01:d04*]

Note: Drawing the graph corresponding to this latter relation might help you appreciate what's going on here. In fact, in examples from this point forward you might always want to consider drawing such graphs, if you find them helpful.

So the first message from this example is that (to generalize slightly) the expressions

```
PACK r ON ( A1 , A2 , ... , An )
```

and

```
PACK ( ... ( PACK ( PACK r ON ( A1 ) ) ON ( A2 ) ) ... ) ON ( An )
```

aren't logically equivalent, in general. (Just to remind you, the first expression involves a preliminary "total UNPACK"—i.e., an UNPACK of *r* on (*A1,A2,...,An*)—while the second doesn't.)

To return to the second bullet item above, the difference between the two results is this: Where the relation produced by PACK *r* ON (A2,A1) has the interval [P5:P5], the relation produced by PACK (PACK *r* ON (A2)) ON (A1) has the interval [P3:P5] instead. Thus, this latter relation effectively tells us twice that parts P3 and P4 appear in combination with days 1, 2, 3, and 4; in other words, it contains some redundancy. The former relation, by contrast, doesn't. And this state of affairs explains why we define multiattribute PACK the way we do, with a preliminary total UNPACK, instead of—as might seem on the face of it more "natural"—just as a sequence of single-attribute PACKs: We do so because that definition is guaranteed to eliminate redundancy, which the apparently more natural definition isn't. See the section "Some Remarks on Redundancy" later in this chapter for further discussion.

EQUIVALENCE OF RELATIONS

Consider yet again the relation *r* we used earlier to demonstrate that, for PACK, order matters:

A1	A2
[P2:P4]	[*d01:d04*]
[P3:P5]	[*d01:d04*]
[P2:P4]	[*d05:d06*]
[P2:P4]	[*d06:d09*]

Here again are the relations that result from evaluating the expressions PACK *r* ON (A1,A2) and PACK *r* ON (A2,A1), now shown side by side (relation *left* corresponds to packing on A1 then A2, relation *right* to packing on A2 then A1):

left

A1	A2
[P2:P5]	[d01:d04]
[P2:P4]	[d05:d09]

right

A1	A2
[P2:P4]	[d01:d09]
[P5:P5]	[d01:d04]

Now, relations *left* and *right* certainly aren't equal, but they're at least *equivalent*, in a sense which we now explain. Loosely, we can say they both represent the same information; however, they do so from two different points of view, as it were. To be more specific, *left* shows the ranges of parts (A1) corresponding to given intervals of time (A2), while *right* shows the intervals of time (A2) corresponding to given ranges of parts (A1).[5] Tightening these remarks up slightly, we obtain the predicates:

Left: *Every day in the interval A2 (and not day PRE(A2) or day POST(A2)) corresponds to every part in the range A1 (and not to part PRE(A1) or part POST(A1)).*

Right: *Every part in the range A1 (and not part PRE(A1) or part POST(A1)) corresponds to every day in the interval A2 (and not to day PRE(A2) or day POST(A2)).*

Observe in particular, therefore, that:

■ In *left*, if two distinct tuples contain part ranges that meet or overlap, then the associated time intervals don't overlap (though they might meet). Likewise, in *right*, if two distinct tuples contain time intervals that meet or overlap, then the associated part ranges don't overlap (though they might meet).

■ In *left*, if two distinct tuples contain the same time interval, then the associated part ranges neither meet nor overlap. Likewise, in *right*, if two distinct tuples contain the same part range, then the associated time intervals neither meet nor overlap.[6]

---

[5] It's relevant to repeat here the point that, as we saw in Figs. 10.2 and 10.3, the corresponding graphs both cover the same area with two nonoverlapping rectangles, but they do so in two different ways.

[6] Relations *left* and *right* are unfortunately too simple to illustrate the points being made in this second bullet item, but those points are valid in general, as later examples will show.

Thus, both relations are nonredundant—i.e., neither of them displays the kind of redundancy we identified in the previous section (and will be discussing further in the next).

> *Aside:* You might have noticed that *left* has at most one tuple for any given day, while *right* has at most one tuple for any given part. However, this state of affairs is a fluke. To be more precise, if relation *r* has interval attributes *A1, A2, ..., An*, then it's *not* necessarily guaranteed that the result of PACK *r* ON *(A1,A2,...,An)* will contain just one tuple for each point *p* that's contained in at least one interval that's an *An* value somewhere in the original relation *r*. (You might want to read that sentence again.) We'll see a counterexample in the section "Some Remarks on Redundancy," later. *End of aside.*

Of course, the foregoing difference in interpretation between *left* and *right* is perhaps more significant from a psychological perspective than it is from a logical one. Also, of course, it's a trivial matter—conceptually speaking, at any rate—to convert either relation into the other. For example, the following expression will effectively convert *left* into *right*:

```
PACK left ON ( A2 , A1 )
```

With the foregoing discussion by way of motivation, we can now define the notion of equivalence for *n*-ary relations as follows:

> **Definition:** Let *r1* and *r2* be relations of the same type, and let attributes *A1, A2, ..., An* of those two relations be interval valued. Then *r1* and *r2* are **equivalent** with respect to *A1, A2,..., An* if and only if the results of UNPACK *r1* ON *(A1,A2,...,An)* and UNPACK *r2* ON *(A1,A2,...,An)* are equal. *Note:* The qualification "with respect to *A1, A2, ..., An*" can be omitted if attributes *A1, A2, ..., An* are understood.

Observe, incidentally, that if *r1* and *r2* are equal, then they're certainly equivalent—with respect to every possible subset of their attributes, in fact, just so long as every attribute in the subset in question is interval valued.

EXPAND AND COLLAPSE REVISITED

The following example (repeated from the section "Unary Relations" in Chapter 8) shows a relation *r* containing just one attribute, which is interval valued, together with the corresponding expanded and collapsed forms:

```
         r                    EXPAND(r)              COLLAPSE(r)
  ┌─────────────┐         ┌─────────────┐         ┌─────────────┐
  │   DURING    │         │   DURING    │         │   DURING    │
  ├═════════════┤         ├═════════════┤         ├═════════════┤
  │  [d06:d09]  │         │  [d01:d01]  │         │  [d01:d01]  │
  │  [d04:d08]  │         │  [d04:d04]  │         │  [d04:d10]  │
  │  [d05:d10]  │         │  [d05:d05]  │         └─────────────┘
  │  [d01:d01]  │         │  [d06:d06]  │
  └─────────────┘         │  [d07:d07]  │
                          │  [d08:d08]  │
                          │  [d09:d09]  │
                          │  [d10:d10]  │
                          └─────────────┘
```

Consider now what happens if we unpack *r* on DURING. Since there's just one interval attribute, the definition from Chapter 9 applies, and so we have:

```
UNPACK r ON ( DURING )  ≝
     WITH ( r1 := r GROUP { DURING } AS X ,
            r2 := EXTEND r1 : { X := EXPAND ( X ) } ) :
     r2 UNGROUP X
```

Hence:

■ The GROUP step gives an intermediate result *r1* that looks like this (observe that it has degree and cardinality both one—attribute *X* is a relation valued attribute or RVA—and the single value it contains is exactly relation *r*):

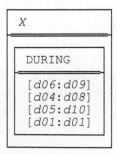

■ The EXTEND step gives an intermediate result *r2* that looks like this (observe that it too has degree and cardinality both one, and the single value it contains is exactly the expanded form of relation *r*):

```
┌─────────────────────┐
│ X                   │
│ ╞═════════════════╡ │
│ ┌─────────────────┐ │
│ │ DURING          │ │
│ │ ╞═════════════╡ │ │
│ │ [d01:d01]       │ │
│ │ [d04:d04]       │ │
│ │ [d05:d05]       │ │
│ │ [d06:d06]       │ │
│ │ [d07:d07]       │ │
│ │ [d08:d08]       │ │
│ │ [d09:d09]       │ │
│ │ [d10:d10]       │ │
│ └─────────────────┘ │
└─────────────────────┘
```

■ The UNGROUP step then produces the final result, which is exactly EXPAND (*r*).

In other words, EXPAND is just a special case of UNPACK! Thus, there was no logical need to introduce the EXPAND operator at all—we could have called it UNPACK right from the outset, in Chapter 8. Rightly or wrongly, however, we judged that it would have been too confusing to do so, since it would have meant we would have to say something along the lines of "We now introduce an operator called UNPACK that we need as a stepping stone on the way to defining an operator called UNPACK." Be that as it may, from this point forward we'll drop our references to EXPAND as such and talk in terms of UNPACK only.

Analogously, it turns out that—as you'll surely be expecting—COLLAPSE is just a special case of PACK. It's not worth going through the detailed argument here (though you might like to have a go at producing that argument for yourself); suffice it to say that from this point forward we'll drop our references to COLLAPSE as such and talk in terms of PACK only.

SOME REMARKS ON REDUNDANCY

Here's yet another example that bears close examination. Let relation *r* be as follows:

A1	A2
[P3:P8]	[d01:d04]
[P5:P9]	[d03:d08]
[P1:P7]	[d07:d10]

Then the results of PACK *r* ON (A1,A2) and PACK *r* ON (A2,A1) are as shown here (and once again we recommend that you verify these results for yourself):

PACK *r* ON (A1,A2)

A1	A2
[P3:P8]	[d01:d02]
[P3:P9]	[d03:d04]
[P5:P9]	[d05:d06]
[P1:P9]	[d07:d08]
[P1:P7]	[d09:d10]

PACK *r* ON (A2,A1)

A1	A2
[P3:P4]	[d01:d04]
[P1:P4]	[d07:d10]
[P5:P7]	[d01:d10]
[P8:P8]	[d01:d08]
[P9:P9]	[d03:d08]

The interesting thing about this example isn't so much that the two packed forms are different once again (though they are), but rather that—perhaps somewhat counterintuitively—they both have cardinality greater than that of the original relation! Thus, while the original relation certainly involves some redundancy (for example, it tells us twice that part P5 appears in combination with day 3), it's in a sense more compact than the two packed forms, even though those packed forms don't display that same kind of redundancy.[7]

So what does it mean for a relation to display, or not to display, redundancy in the foregoing sense? Well, here's a definition:

Definition: Let relation *r* have interval attributes *A1, A2, ..., An* (possibly other attributes as well, interval valued or otherwise). Let *u* be the relation that results from unpacking *r* on all of those attributes *A1, A2, ..., An*. Then, if every tuple in *u* derives from exactly one tuple in *r*, *r* is **nonredundant** (or *redundancy free*) with respect to *A1, A2, ..., An*; otherwise *r* is **redundant** with respect to *A1, A2, ..., An*. *Note:* The qualification "with respect to *A1, A2, ..., An*" can be omitted if attributes *A1, A2, ..., An* are understood.

For example, the relation *r* shown at the beginning of this section is redundant with respect to attributes A1 and A2, because if we perform a "total unpack" of that relation—i.e., if we unpack it on A1 and A2—then the result contains the following tuple among many others:

A1	A2
[P5:P5]	[d03:d03]

And this tuple derives from both of the following tuples of *r*:

A1	A2
[P3:P8]	[d01:d04]

A1	A2
[P5:P9]	[d03:d08]

---

[7] So *pack* might not be the best name for the operator, since packing a relation isn't guaranteed to make it smaller, as it were. But *pack* is our preferred term nevertheless.

By contrast, PACK *r* ON (A1,A2) and PACK *r* ON (A2,A1)—i.e., both of the fully packed forms of the original relation *r*—are nonredundant in the foregoing sense. (*Exercise:* Check this claim.) In general, in fact, any fully packed form of any relation is guaranteed to be free of redundancy in the foregoing sense.

The foregoing example also raises a couple of further points:

- First, note that the result of PACK *r* ON (A2,A1) contains two distinct tuples corresponding to part number P3 (also two distinct tuples corresponding to part number P4). Thus, we have here—as promised in the section "Equivalence of Relations" earlier—an example to show that the result of PACK *r* ON (*A1,A2,...,An*) is *not* guaranteed to contain just one tuple for each point *p* that's contained in at least one interval that's an *An* value somewhere in the original relation *r*.

- Second, note that although the two fully packed forms in the example both have cardinality greater than that of the original relation, they do at least both have the same cardinality. Again, however, this state of affairs is a fluke. By way of a counterexample, let relation *r* be as follows:

A1	A2
[P1:P2]	[d01:d02]
[P1:P4]	[d03:d04]
[P3:P4]	[d05:d06]

Then packing this relation on (A1,A2) returns the original relation *r*, with cardinality three. By contrast, packing it on (A2,A1) returns the following relation, with cardinality two:

A1	A2
[P1:P2]	[d01:d04]
[P3:P4]	[d03:d06]

However, returning to the previous example (the one from the beginning of this section), we see that if *r* is a relation and *FP* is the set of all fully packed forms of *r*, then there isn't in general just one relation *fp* in *FP* with *minimum* cardinality—i.e., with cardinality less than that of all other relations *fp'* (*fp'* ≠ *fp*) in *FP*. It follows that, if we regard each *fp* in *FP* as a canonical form of *r*, then there's no canonical form *fp* in general that's somehow "more canonical" than all the rest.

A MORE COMPLEX EXAMPLE

We conclude this chapter by briefly examining an example involving three interval attributes. Consider the following relation *r* (which is identical to the relation shown at the very end of Chapter 6, except that we've renamed the attributes A1, A2, and A3 for simplicity):

A1	A2	A3
[S1:S2]	[P2:P3]	[d03:d04]
[S2:S3]	[P3:P4]	[d04:d05]

This relation has six fully packed forms, which we now show:

PACK *r* ON (A1,A2,A3)

A1	A2	A3
[S1:S2]	[P2:P3]	[d03:d03]
[S1:S2]	[P2:P2]	[d04:d04]
[S1:S3]	[P3:P3]	[d04:d04]
[S2:S3]	[P3:P4]	[d05:d05]
[S2:S3]	[P4:P4]	[d04:d04]

PACK *r* ON (A1,A3,A2)

A1	A2	A3
[S1:S2]	[P2:P2]	[d03:d04]
[S1:S2]	[P3:P3]	[d03:d03]
[S1:S3]	[P3:P3]	[d04:d04]
[S2:S3]	[P3:P3]	[d05:d05]
[S2:S3]	[P4:P4]	[d04:d05]

PACK *r* ON (A2,A1,A3)

A1	A2	A3
[S1:S2]	[P2:P3]	[d03:d03]
[S1:S1]	[P2:P3]	[d04:d04]
[S2:S2]	[P2:P4]	[d04:d04]
[S2:S3]	[P3:P4]	[d05:d05]
[S3:S3]	[P3:P4]	[d04:d04]

PACK `r` ON `(A2,A3,A1)`

A1	A2	A3
[S1:S1]	[P2:P3]	[d03:d04]
[S2:S2]	[P2:P3]	[d03:d03]
[S2:S2]	[P2:P4]	[d04:d04]
[S2:S2]	[P3:P4]	[d05:d05]
[S3:S3]	[P3:P4]	[d04:d05]

PACK `r` ON `(A3,A1,A2)`

A1	A2	A3
[S1:S2]	[P2:P2]	[d03:d04]
[S1:S1]	[P3:P3]	[d03:d04]
[S2:S2]	[P3:P3]	[d03:d05]
[S2:S3]	[P4:P4]	[d04:d05]
[S3:S3]	[P3:P3]	[d04:d05]

PACK `r` ON `(A3,A2,A1)`

A1	A2	A3
[S1:S1]	[P2:P3]	[d03:d04]
[S2:S2]	[P2:P2]	[d03:d04]
[S2:S2]	[P3:P3]	[d03:d05]
[S2:S2]	[P4:P4]	[d04:d05]
[S3:S3]	[P3:P4]	[d04:d05]

All of these relations have the same cardinality, as it happens, though that cardinality is greater than that of the original relation. Of course, they're all redundancy free.

EXERCISES

10.1 If relation *r* is in packed form (on attributes *A1*, *A2*, ..., *An*, say), is it true that every restriction of *r* is also in that same packed form?

10.2 What exactly does it mean to say some relation *r* is redundancy free with respect to attributes *A1*, *A2*, ..., *An*?

10.3 Let relation *r* be as follows:

A1	A2
[P2:P4]	[d05:d06]
[P3:P5]	[d01:d04]
[P1:P4]	[d06:d08]
[P2:P4]	[d01:d04]

Show the result of PACK *r* ON (A1,A2) and PACK *r* ON (A2,A1).

10.4 Let relation *r* be as follows:

A1	A2	A3
[S2:S4]	[P2:P3]	[d03:d04]
[S2:S3]	[P3:P5]	[d04:d05]
[S3:S4]	[P3:P4]	[d03:d04]

Show all fully packed forms of *r* (where by *fully packed* we mean the relation is packed on all of its attributes A1, A2, and A3, in some order).

10.5 Let *T* be a type consisting of all positive integers in the range [1: *n*]. Find the smallest value for *n* such that relations *r1* and *r2* of type

```
RELATION { A1 INTERVAL_T , A2 INTERVAL_T }
```

exist that satisfy all of the following conditions a.-f.:

a. *r1* ≠ *r2*

b. UNPACK *r1* ON (A1 , A2) = UNPACK *r2* ON (A1 , A2)

c. *r1* ≠ PACK *r1* ON (A1 , A2)

d. *r2* ≠ PACK *r2* ON (A1 , A2)

e. COUNT (*r1*) = COUNT (*r2*)

f. There's no relation *r3* of the same type as *r1* and *r2* such that the following expression evaluates to TRUE:

```
UNPACK r3 ON ( A1 , A2 ) = UNPACK r1 ON ( A1 , A2 )
AND COUNT ( r3 ) < COUNT ( r1 )
```

What do you conclude from this exercise?

ANSWERS

10.1 Yes, it is.

10.2 See the section "Some Remarks on Redundancy" in the body of the chapter.

10.3 PACK r ON (A1,A2)

A1	A2
[P2:P4]	[d05:d05]
[P1:P4]	[d06:d08]
[P2:P5]	[d01:d04]

PACK r ON (A2,A1)

A1	A2
[P2:P4]	[d01:d08]
[P5:P5]	[d01:d04]
[P1:P1]	[d06:d08]

10.4 PACK r ON (A1,A2,A3)

A1	A2	A3
[S2:S4]	[P2:P3]	[d03:d03]
[S2:S4]	[P2:P4]	[d04:d04]
[S2:S3]	[P3:P5]	[d05:d05]
[S2:S3]	[P5:P5]	[d04:d04]
[S3:S4]	[P4:P4]	[d03:d03]

PACK r ON (A1,A3,A2)

A1	A2	A3
[S2:S4]	[P2:P3]	[d03:d04]
[S2:S3]	[P3:P4]	[d05:d05]
[S2:S4]	[P4:P4]	[d04:d04]
[32:S3]	[P5:P5]	[d04:d05]
[S3:S4]	[P4:P4]	[d03:d03]

PACK r ON (A2,A1,A3)

A1	A2	A3
[S2:S2]	[P2:P3]	[d03:d03]
[S2:S3]	[P2:P5]	[d04:d04]
[S3:S4]	[P2:P4]	[d03:d03]
[S4:S4]	[P2:P4]	[d04:d04]
[S2:S3]	[P3:P5]	[d05:d05]

PACK *r* ON (A2,A3,A1)

A1	A2	A3
[S2:S2]	[P2:P3]	[*d03:d03*]
[S2:S3]	[P2:P5]	[*d04:d04*]
[S3:S3]	[P2:P4]	[*d03:d03*]
[S4:S4]	[P2:P4]	[*d03:d04*]
[S2:S3]	[P3:P5]	[*d05:d05*]

PACK *r* ON (A3,A1,A2)

A1	A2	A3
[S2:S4]	[P2:P2]	[*d03:d04*]
[S2:S3]	[P3:P3]	[*d03:d05*]
[S4:S4]	[P3:P4]	[*d03:d04*]
[S2:S2]	[P4:P4]	[*d04:d05*]
[S2:S3]	[P5:P5]	[*d04:d05*]
[S3:S3]	[P4:P4]	[*d03:d05*]

PACK *r* ON (A3,A2,A1)

A1	A2	A3
[S2:S3]	[P2:P2]	[*d03:d04*]
[S2:S2]	[P3:P3]	[*d03:d05*]
[S3:S3]	[P3:P4]	[*d03:d05*]
[S2:S2]	[P4:P5]	[*d04:d05*]
[S3:S3]	[P5:P5]	[*d04:d05*]
[S4:S4]	[P2:P4]	[*d03:d04*]

10.5 Suppose *n* = 1. Then:

■ Type INTERVAL_*T* has just one value—the unit interval [1:1].

■ All relations of the specified type are thus in unpacked form (in fact, there are exactly two such relations), and so conditions a. and b. can't both be satisfied.

■ We remark as an aside that all relations of the specified type are also in packed form, since their cardinality is less than two in every case, and conditions c. and d. can't be satisfied either. Nor can conditions a. and e.

It follows that *n* = 1 is impossible. So suppose *n* = 2. Then:

■ Type INTERVAL_*T* has exactly three values—[1:1], [1:2], and [2:2].

■ It follows that there are exactly nine distinct tuples that can appear in relations of the specified type, and therefore exactly $2^9 = 512$ relations of that type.

■ Of those 512 relations, we can eliminate all in which the attribute value [1:2] fails to appear, because all such relations are in unpacked form, and conditions a. and b. thus can't possibly both be satisfied by two such relations.

■ We can also eliminate all relations of cardinality less than two, because all relations of cardinality less than two are in unpacked form; thus (again) conditions a. and b. can't possibly both be satisfied by two such relations.

■ Observe now that there are exactly five tuples of the relevant type in which either A1 = [1:2] or A2 = [1:2]:

A1	A2
[1:2]	[1:1]

A1	A2
[1:2]	[1:2]

A1	A2
[1:2]	[2:2]

A1	A2
[1:1]	[1:2]

A1	A2
[2:2]	[1:2]

It can be seen by inspection that no relation that contains just one of these five tuples and just one other tuple is in packed form, and moreover that the packed form of each such relation contains just a single tuple. It follows that even if we can find two relations of the type at hand with cardinality greater than one that satisfy conditions a.-e., they would fail to satisfy condition f. because their packed form is of cardinality one.

It follows that $n = 2$ is also impossible. We now show that there does exist a pair of relations satisfying the given conditions when $n = 3$. Consider the following relations *r1* and *r2*:

r1

A1	A2
[1:2] [1:3]	[1:2] [2:2]

r2

A1	A2
[1:2] [2:3]	[1:2] [2:2]

■ Conditions a. and e. are clearly satisfied. Condition b. is also satisfied, because the unpacked form *u* of both *r1* and *r2* is as follows:

u

A1	A2
[1:1]	[1:1]
[1:1]	[2:2]
[2:2]	[1:1]
[2:2]	[2:2]
[3:3]	[2:2]

■ Conditions c. and d. are also satisfied, because packing *u* on (A1,A2) yields:

A1	A2
[1:2]	[1:1]
[1:3]	[2:2]

(which is distinct from both *r1* and *r2*). As an aside, we note that packing *u* on (A2,A1) yields yet another distinct relation:

A1	A2
[1:2]	[1:2]
[3:3]	[2:2]

■ Condition f. is satisfied because every relation of cardinality one is in packed form and the packed form of *r1* and *r2* is of cardinality two. Thus, no relation of cardinality one, when unpacked, can yield the unpacked form of *r1*.

We conclude from this exercise that, given a certain relation *u* in unpacked form and the set *Ru* of relations whose unpacked form is *u*, in general there's no unique member of *Ru* whose cardinality is less than that of all of the other members of *Ru*, except possibly when some fully packed form of *u* has that property. In other words (and indeed as noted in the body of the chapter), there's no third canonical form in addition to packed and unpacked forms that's based on minimum cardinality alone. (Of course, there's obviously no canonical form based on *maximum* cardinality alone, because the unpacked form always has that property.)

Chapter 11

Generalizing

the Algebraic Operators

To generalize is to be an idiot.

—William Blake:
Annotations to Sir Joshua Reynolds's Discourses (c. 1798)

In Chapters 9 and 10, we saw how expressions that would have been quite complex and cumbersome to formulate in terms of the original relational algebra could be made much less so—indeed, much more user friendly and manageable—by means of the PACK and UNPACK shorthands. But PACK and UNPACK as such are still not the end of the story. To be specific, PACK and UNPACK can be used as a basis for defining still further shorthands at a still higher level of abstraction. Such further shorthands are the subject of the present chapter. *Note:* For convenience, we show our running example once again in Fig. 11.1. As usual, coding examples will be based on these sample values, barring explicit statements to the contrary.

S_DURING

SNO	DURING
S1	[d04:d10]
S2	[d02:d04]
S2	[d07:d10]
S3	[d03:d10]
S4	[d04:d10]
S5	[d02:d10]

SP_DURING

SNO	PNO	DURING
S1	P1	[d04:d10]
S1	P2	[d05:d10]
S1	P3	[d09:d10]
S1	P4	[d05:d10]
S1	P5	[d04:d10]
S1	P6	[d06:d10]
S2	P1	[d02:d04]
S2	P1	[d08:d10]
S2	P2	[d03:d03]
S2	P2	[d09:d10]
S3	P2	[d08:d10]
S4	P2	[d06:d09]
S4	P4	[d04:d08]
S4	P5	[d05:d10]

Fig. 11.1: The running example repeated

A MOTIVATING EXAMPLE

Here's Query B once again, repeated from Chapter 9:

■ **Query B:** Get SNO-DURING pairs such that DURING designates a maximal interval during which supplier SNO was unable to supply any parts at all.

And here again is the "temporal difference" formulation of this query, also repeated from Chapter 9:

```
PACK
    ( ( UNPACK S_DURING { SNO , DURING } ON ( DURING ) )
        MINUS
      ( UNPACK SP_DURING { SNO , DURING } ON ( DURING ) ) )
ON ( DURING )
```

As you can see, this expression overall is effectively asking for the following sequence of operations to be performed:

1. Unpack both operands.

2. Take the difference.

3. Pack the result.

Now, it turns out that the general pattern illustrated by this example—unpack certain input relation(s), perform some relational operation on the resulting unpacked form(s), and then pack the result of that operation—occurs so frequently that the possibility of defining a shorthand seems worth investigation. What's more (bonus!), such a shorthand offers the possibility of better performance. Consider in particular what happens with intervals of large cardinality (note that such intervals are likely to be commonplace if the contained points are of fine granularity, such as milliseconds or even microseconds). When such intervals are involved, the output from UNPACK can be very large in comparison to the input. Thus, if the system were actually to materialize such unpacked relations (and then perform the appropriate relational operation on the unpacked versions, and then pack the result), the query might "run forever" or run out of memory. By contrast, expressing the overall requirement as a single operation might let the optimizer choose a more efficient implementation, one that doesn't require materialization of those intermediate unpacked results (see Appendix E). So let's investigate.

DYADIC OPERATORS

It should be clear that shorthands of the kind we have in mind can in principle be defined for all of the conventional relational operators. In this section, however, we limit our attention to the dyadic operators specifically—in other words, the operators UNION, INTERSECT, and MINUS; D_UNION and I_MINUS; JOIN; and MATCHING and NOT MATCHING. *Note:* Relational comparisons are dyadic operators too, of course, but we defer treatment of relational comparison operators to a section of their own.

UNION, INTERSECT, and MINUS

Since we began this chapter with a brief look at "temporal difference," let's complete our treatment of that operator first. Here's a definition:

> **Definition:** Let relations *r1* and *r2* be of the same type *T*, and let *ACL* be a commalist of attribute names in which every attribute mentioned (a) is one of type *T*'s component attributes and (b) is of some interval type. Then the expression USING (*ACL*) : *r1* MINUS *r2* denotes the **U_difference** with respect to *ACL* between *r1* and *r2* (in that order), and it's defined to be shorthand for the following:

```
PACK
    ( ( UNPACK r1 ON ( ACL ) )
        MINUS
      ( UNPACK r2 ON ( ACL ) ) )
ON ( ACL )
```

Points arising:

■ The qualification "with respect to *ACL*" can be omitted if the commalist *ACL* is understood. Do note, however, that if *IA* is the set of all of type *T*'s component attributes that are interval valued, then in general there's a distinct U_difference between *r1* and *r2* (in that order) for each distinct permutation of the attributes in each subset of *IA*. *Note:* Analogous remarks apply to all of the operators to be defined in this chapter, and we won't bother to keep repeating them, instead letting this one paragraph do duty for all.

■ In our discussion of the motivating example in the previous section, we referred to the operator just defined as "temporal difference." As noted in Chapter 9, however, we don't much care for this terminology, because the operator doesn't apply just to temporal intervals as such. Until further notice, therefore, we'll call it U_difference—U for USING[1]—or simply U_MINUS for short.

---

[1] Or for unpacking, if you like—unpacking being, in a sense, the most important step in the sequence "unpack the operands, take the difference, pack the result."

■ In what follows, we'll be defining several further U_ operators. In all cases, the syntax takes the following form:

```
USING ( ACL ) : exp
```

Please be aware, however, that this syntax is used in this book for expository purposes only. It hasn't been checked for syntactic soundness.

Aside: For readers who might be familiar with "temporal statement modifiers" as described in, e.g., reference [8], we wish to stress that our USING specifications aren't the same thing. Loosely speaking, temporal statement modifiers are supposed to apply to every operator involved in the expression or statement to which they're attached. Our USING specifications, by contrast, apply only to the *outermost* operator of the expression to which they're attached.[2] For example, in the U_difference USING (*ACL*) : *r1* MINUS *r2*, the USING specification applies to the MINUS operator as such, not to any operators that might be invoked during evaluation of the expressions denoting *r1* and *r2*. See the revised formulation of Query B shown below for an illustration of this point.

These observations raise another point, however—namely, what in general *is* "the outermost operator" in an arbitrary **Tutorial D** expression? The answer to this question clearly depends on **Tutorial D**'s operator precedence rules, details of which (as noted in Chapter 2) we prefer not to provide in this book.[3] In our examples, therefore, we'll always use parentheses and/or WITH specifications, if and as necessary, in order to avoid any possibility of ambiguity. *End of aside.*

Here then is a shorthand formulation for Query B:

```
USING ( DURING ) :
      S_DURING { SNO , DURING } MINUS SP_DURING { SNO , DURING }
```

Explanation: First, the projections of S_DURING and SP_DURING on SNO and DURING are computed. (The first of these is an identity projection, of course.) Those projections are then unpacked on DURING; the difference between those unpacked results is computed; and that difference is then packed on DURING.[4]

---

[2] Like "temporal statement modifiers," USING specifications can be attached to statements as well as expressions. This possibility is discussed in Chapter 16.

[3] We remind you, though, that we find it convenient to assign high precedence to projection in particular.

[4] We could have used U_semidifference in place of U_difference in this example, thus: USING (DURING) : S_DURING NOT MATCHING SP_DURING. U_semidifference is discussed later in this section.

It's interesting to note, by the way, that (unlike the regular MINUS operator) U_MINUS can produce a result whose cardinality is greater than that of its left operand. For example, let *r1* and *r2* be as follows:

Then USING (A) : *r1* MINUS *r2* gives:

```
A

[d02:d02]
[d04:d04]
```

Now we turn to U_UNION. Here's the definition:

Definition: Let relations *r1* and *r2* be of the same type *T*, and let *ACL* be a commalist of attribute names in which every attribute mentioned (a) is one of type *T*'s component attributes and (b) is of some interval type. Then the expression USING (*ACL*) : *r1* UNION *r2* denotes the **U_union** with respect to *ACL* of *r1* and *r2*, and it's defined to be shorthand for the following:

```
PACK
    ( ( UNPACK r1 ON ( ACL ) )
        UNION
      ( UNPACK r2 ON ( ACL ) ) )
ON ( ACL )
```

Actually there's no need to do those preliminary UNPACKs in this particular case. That is, the U_UNION expansion can be simplified to just:

```
PACK ( r1 UNION r2 ) ON ( ACL )
```

It's not hard to see why this simplification is possible, but you can try working through an example if you need to convince yourself. *Note:* Similar simplifications are possible with several of the other U_ operators as well. We won't bother to spell out the specifics in this chapter, however; instead, we refer you to Appendix E, where such matters are discussed in detail.

Unlike the regular UNION operator, U_UNION can produce a result whose cardinality is less than that of either of its operands. For example, let *r1* and *r2* be as follows:

```
r1                          r2
┌──────────────┐            ┌──────────────┐
│ A            │            │ A            │
├──────────────┤            ├──────────────┤
│ [d02:d02]    │            │ [d03:d03]    │
│ [d04:d04]    │            │ [d04:d04]    │
└──────────────┘            └──────────────┘
```

Then USING (A) : *r1* UNION *r2* gives:

```
┌──────────────┐
│ A            │
├──────────────┤
│ [d02:d04]    │
└──────────────┘
```

Finally we turn to U_INTERSECT:

Definition: Let relations *r1* and *r2* be of the same type *T*, and let *ACL* be a commalist of attribute names in which every attribute mentioned (a) is one of type *T*'s component attributes and (b) is of some interval type. Then the expression USING (*ACL*) : *r1* INTERSECT *r2* denotes the **U_intersection** with respect to *ACL* of *r1* and *r2*, and it's defined to be shorthand for the following:

```
PACK
    ( ( UNPACK r1 ON ( ACL ) )
        INTERSECT
      ( UNPACK r2 ON ( ACL ) ) )
ON ( ACL )
```

Unlike the regular INTERSECT operator, U_INTERSECT can produce a result whose cardinality is greater than that of either of its operands. For example, let *r1* and *r2* be as follows:

```
r1                          r2
┌──────────────┐            ┌──────────────┐
│ A            │            │ A            │
├──────────────┤            ├──────────────┤
│ [d01:d07]    │            │ [d02:d02]    │
│ [d12:d12]    │            │ [d04:d07]    │
│ [d14:d17]    │            │ [d10:d17]    │
└──────────────┘            └──────────────┘
```

Then USING (A) : *r1* INTERSECT *r2* gives:

```
A
[d02:d02]
[d04:d07]
[d12:d12]
[d14:d17]
```

D_UNION and I_MINUS

U_ versions of D_UNION and I_MINUS certainly make sense, though the nomenclature gets a little clumsy. Once again let relations *r1* and *r2* be of the same type *T*, and let *ACL* be a commalist of attribute names in which every attribute mentioned (a) is one of type *T*'s component attributes and (b) is of some interval type. Then:

Definition: The expression USING (*ACL*) : *r1* D_UNION *r2* denotes the **disjoint U_union** with respect to *ACL* of *r1* and *r2*, and it's defined to be shorthand for the following:

```
PACK
    ( ( UNPACK r1 ON ( ACL ) )
        D_UNION
        ( UNPACK r2 ON ( ACL ) ) )
ON ( ACL )
```

Definition: The expression USING (*ACL*) : *r1* I_MINUS *r2* denotes the **included U_difference** with respect to *ACL* between *r1* and *r2* (in that order), and it's defined to be shorthand for the following:

```
PACK
    ( ( UNPACK r1 ON ( ACL ) )
        I_MINUS
        ( UNPACK r2 ON ( ACL ) ) )
ON ( ACL )
```

Examples:

■ Let *r1* and *r2* be as follows:

```
r1                      r2
A                       A
[d01:d03]               [d03:d04]
```

Then USING (A) : *r1* D_UNION *r2* is undefined. But if the sole A value in *r2* had been [*d04*:*d04*] instead of [*d03*:*d04*], the result would have been:

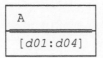

■ Again let *r1* and *r2* be as follows:

Then USING (A) : *r1* I_MINUS *r2* is undefined. But if the sole A value in *r2* had been [*d03*:*d03*] instead of [*d03*:*d04*], the result would have been:

```
A
━━━━━━━━
[d01:d02]
```

JOIN

Definition: Let relations *r1* and *r2* be joinable, and let *ACL* be a commalist of attribute names in which every attribute mentioned (a) is an attribute of both *r1* and *r2* and (b) is of some interval type. Then the expression USING (*ACL*) : *r1* JOIN *r2* denotes the **U_join** with respect to *ACL* of *r1* and *r2*, and it's defined to be shorthand for the following:

```
PACK
    ( ( UNPACK r1 ON ( ACL ) )
        JOIN
      ( UNPACK r2 ON ( ACL ) ) )
ON ( ACL )
```

Note: If *r1* and *r2* are of the same type, then U_JOIN degenerates (as would surely be expected) to U_INTERSECT.

In order to illustrate the use of U_JOIN, suppose we have, in addition to our usual relvars S_DURING and SP_DURING, another relvar S_CITY_DURING—see Chapter 12—with attributes {SNO,CITY,DURING}, key {SNO,DURING}, and predicate as follows:

DURING denotes a maximal interval of days throughout which supplier SNO was located in city CITY.

Now consider the query "Get SNO-CITY-PNO-DURING tuples such that supplier SNO was both (a) located in city CITY, and (b) able to supply part PNO, throughout interval DURING, where DURING contains day 4." Here's a possible formulation of that query:

```
( USING ( DURING ) : S_CITY_DURING JOIN SP_DURING ) WHERE d04 ∈ DURING
```

Observe that this formulation involves a U_join followed by a *regular* restrict.

> *Aside:* If we were to project attribute DURING away from the result of the foregoing query, the resulting projection would represent what's sometimes called a *snapshot* of the database—or, more precisely, a snapshot of a certain portion of the database—as of a certain point in time (day 4, in the case at hand). Such *snapshot queries* are needed quite often in practice. (By the way, don't confuse "a snapshot of the database" with "a snapshot database"! See footnote 1 in Chapter 4 for a brief explanation of this latter term.) *End of aside.*

One last point on U_join: Since TIMES is a special case of JOIN, we could obviously define a U_TIMES operator too if we wanted to, of the form USING (*ACL*) : *r1* TIMES *r2*. However, *ACL* here would necessarily be empty, and U_TIMES would thus effectively be indistinguishable from the regular TIMES operator (see the section "The Regular Operators Revisited" at the end of the chapter). But we might still want to support such an operator, if only for completeness.

MATCHING and NOT MATCHING

Let relations *r1* and *r2* be joinable, and let *ACL* be a commalist of attribute names in which every attribute mentioned (a) is an attribute of both *r1* and *r2* and (b) is of some interval type. Then:

Definition: The expression USING (*ACL*) : *r1* MATCHING *r2* denotes the **U_semijoin** with respect to *ACL* of *r1* and *r2*, and it's defined to be shorthand for the following:

```
PACK
    ( ( UNPACK r1 ON ( ACL ) )
        MATCHING
      ( UNPACK r2 ON ( ACL ) ) )
ON ( ACL )
```

Definition: The expression USING (*ACL*) : *r1* NOT MATCHING *r2* denotes the **U_semidifference** with respect to *ACL* between *r1* and *r2* (in that order), and it's defined to be shorthand for the following:

```
PACK
    ( ( UNPACK r1 ON ( ACL ) )
        NOT MATCHING
      ( UNPACK r2 ON ( ACL ) ) )
ON ( ACL )
```

Let's focus on MATCHING for a moment. Let *A1*, *A2*, ..., *An* be all of the attributes of relation *r1*. As you'll recall from Chapter 2, then, the expression *r1* MATCHING *r2* is shorthand for the following:

```
( ( r1 JOIN r2 ) { A1 , A2 ,..., An } )
```

(outer parentheses shown for reasons of clarity). However, the expression USING (*ACL*) : *r1* MATCHING *r2* is *not* shorthand for USING (*ACL*) : ((*r1* JOIN *r2*) {*A1,A2,...,An*}). Instead, it's shorthand for:

```
USING ( ACL ) : ( ( USING ( ACL ) : r1 JOIN r2 ) { A1 ,A2 ,..., An } )
```

The outer USING here applies to the projection, the inner one to the join. In other words, where a regular semijoin is a regular projection of a regular join, a U_semijoin is a U_projection of a U_join. *Note:* U_join has already been discussed. As for U_projection, see the section "Monadic Operators," later.

In similar fashion, the expression USING (*ACL*) : *r1* NOT MATCHING *r2* is shorthand for:

```
USING ( ACL ) : ( r1 MINUS ( USING ( ACL ) : r1 MATCHING r2 ) )
```

(a U_difference in which the second operand is a U_semijoin).

n-ADIC OPERATORS

Several of the operators discussed in the section "Dyadic Operators" above have *n*-adic analogs; to be specific, the operators UNION, INTERSECT, D_UNION, and JOIN all do. (So does TIMES, of course.) So we can define U_ versions of these operators that (a) involve unpacking all *n* of the relations involved, (b) applying the regular *n*-adic operator to those *n* unpacked forms, and then (c) packing the result. Here for example is a definition for *n*-adic U_JOIN (the definitions for the other operators follow the same general pattern, and we omit the specifics here):

Definition: Let relations *r1*, *r2*, ..., *rn* be joinable, and let *ACL* be a commalist of attribute names in which every attribute mentioned (a) is an attribute of each of *r1*, *r2*, ..., *rn* and (b) is of some interval type. Then the expression USING (*ACL*) : JOIN {*r1,r2,...,rn*} denotes the **U_join** with respect to *ACL* of *r1*, *r2*, ..., *rn*, and it's defined to be shorthand for the following:

```
PACK
    ( JOIN { UNPACK r1 ON ( ACL ) ,
             UNPACK r2 ON ( ACL ) ,
             .............       ,
             UNPACK rn ON ( ACL ) } )
ON ( ACL )
```

MONADIC OPERATORS

We turn now to U_ versions of the monadic operators RENAME, restrict, project, EXTEND, GROUP, and UNGROUP.

RENAME

Definition: Let *r* be a relation, let *ACL* be a commalist of attribute names in which every attribute mentioned (a) is an attribute of *r* and (b) is of some interval type, and let *r* have an attribute called *A* (not mentioned in *ACL*) and no attribute called *B*. Then the expression USING (*ACL*) : *r* RENAME {*A* AS *B*} denotes an (attribute) **U_renaming** of *r*, and it's defined to be shorthand for the following:

```
PACK
    ( ( UNPACK r ON ( ACL ) ) RENAME { A AS B } )
ON ( ACL )
```

Of course, this expression reduces to just:

```
PACK ( r RENAME { A AS B } ) ON ( ACL )
```

Note: We include a definition of U_renaming here mainly for reasons of completeness, not because we expect such an operator to be very much used in practice.

Restrict

Definition: Let *r* be a relation, let *ACL* be a commalist of attribute names in which every attribute mentioned (a) is an attribute of *r* and (b) is of some interval type, and let *bx* be a restriction condition on *r*. Then the expression USING (*ACL*) : *r* WHERE *bx* denotes the

U_restriction with respect to *ACL* of *r* according to *bx*, and it's defined to be shorthand for the following:

```
PACK
    ( ( UNPACK r ON ( ACL ) ) WHERE bx )
ON ( ACL )
```

Observe that the preliminary UNPACK here applies to *r* per se, not to the restriction *r* WHERE *bx*. Here's an example:

```
USING ( DURING ) :
        S_DURING WHERE DURING ⊆ INTERVAL_DATE ( [ d03 : d07 ] )
```

Note the difference between this U_restrict and the following regular restrict:

```
S_DURING WHERE DURING ⊆ INTERVAL_DATE ( [ d03 : d07 ] )
```

Suppose, for example, that relvar S_DURING currently contains just two tuples, as follows:

SNO	DURING
S2	[d01:d03]
S2	[d05:d09]

Then the regular restrict just shown will return an empty result, while the U_restrict will return a result of cardinality two, thus (regular restrict on the left, U_restrict on the right):

SNO	DURING

SNO	DURING
S2	[d03:d03]
S2	[d05:d07]

Unlike regular restrict, U_restrict can produce a result with cardinality greater than that of its input. For example, suppose again that relvar S_DURING contains just the two tuples for supplier S2 shown above, and consider the following U_restrict:

```
USING ( DURING ) :
        S_DURING WHERE DURING = INTERVAL_DATE ( [ d02 : d02 ] )
                OR     DURING = INTERVAL_DATE ( [ d05 : d05 ] )
                OR     DURING = INTERVAL_DATE ( [ d07 : d07 ] )
```

Here's the result:

SNO	DURING
S2	[d02:d02]
S2	[d05:d05]
S2	[d07:d07]

Project

Definition: Let *r* be a relation, let *ACL* be a commalist of attribute names in which every attribute mentioned (a) is an attribute of *r* and (b) is of some interval type, and let *BCL* be a commalist of attribute names such that every attribute mentioned in *ACL* is also mentioned in *BCL*. Then the expression USING (*ACL*) : *r* {*BCL*} denotes the **U_projection** with respect to *ACL* of *r* on *BCL*, and it's defined to be shorthand for the following:

```
PACK
    ( ( UNPACK r ON ( ACL ) ) { BCL } )
ON ( ACL )
```

By way of an example, recall Query A from Chapter 9:

■ **Query A:** Get SNO-DURING pairs such that DURING designates a maximal interval during which supplier SNO was able to supply at least one part.

Here's a formulation for this query using U_project (as noted in Chapter 10, it's an example of what's sometimes called "temporal projection"):

```
USING ( DURING ) : SP_DURING { SNO , DURING }
```

EXTEND

By now the pattern should be familiar:

Definition: Let *r* be a relation, and let *ACL* be a commalist of attribute names in which every attribute mentioned (a) is an attribute of *r* and (b) is of some interval type. Then the expression USING (*ACL*) : EXTEND *r* : {*A* := *exp*} denotes a **U_extension** with respect to *ACL* of *r*, and it's defined to be shorthand for the following:

```
PACK
    ( ( EXTEND ( UNPACK r ON ( ACL ) ) : { A := exp } )
ON ( ACL )
```

Unlike the regular EXTEND operator, U_EXTEND can return a result with cardinality either greater or less than that of its input.[5] Suppose, for example, that relvar S_DURING currently contains just two tuples, as follows:

SNO	DURING
S2	[d01:d05]
S2	[d03:d04]

Then the first of the following U_EXTENDs will return a relation of cardinality five and the second will return a relation of cardinality one:

```
USING ( DURING ) : EXTEND S_DURING : { X := BEGIN ( DURING ) }

USING ( DURING ) : EXTEND S_DURING : { Y := COUNT ( DURING ) }
```

Here are the results:

SNO	DURING	X
S2	[d01:d01]	d01
S2	[d02:d02]	d02
S2	[d03:d03]	d03
S2	[d04:d04]	d04
S2	[d05:d05]	d05

SNO	DURING	Y
S2	[d01:d05]	1

Note: The expression BEGIN (DURING) in the first of the foregoing U_EXTENDs is equivalent to, and might more clearly have been replaced by, POINT FROM DURING.

Recall now the following example from the discussion of image relations in Chapter 2:

```
EXTEND S : { PNO_REL := !!SP }
```

Suppose we replace those references to S and SP by references to S_DURING and SP_DURING, respectively, and prefix the whole thing with USING (DURING), like this:

```
USING ( DURING ) : EXTEND S_DURING : { PNO_REL := !!SP_DURING }
```

What happens? Well, this is a U_EXTEND, and the initial UNPACK is thus done on the relation being extended—i.e., the relation that's the current value of S_DURING. Next, a

---

[5] Actually, the "what if" version of the regular EXTEND operator can also return a result with cardinality less than—but never greater than—that of its input. *Exercise*: When exactly might this phenomenon occur?

regular extension is done on that unpacked relation, and the result is then packed again. Here's the result of the initial UNPACK (in outline):

SNO	DURING
S1	[d04:d04]
..	...
S1	[d10:d10]
S2	[d02:d02]
..	...
S2	[d04:d04]
S2	[d07:d07]
..	...
S2	[d10:d10]

SNO	DURING
S3	[d03:d03]
..	...
S3	[d10:d10]
S4	[d04:d04]
..	...
S4	[d10:d10]
S5	[d02:d02]
..	...
S5	[d10:d10]

Let's call this unpacked relation *u*. Now, if you'll take a look at Fig. 6.1 in Chapter 6 or Fig. 9.1 in Chapter 9, you'll see that the only tuple in SP_DURING "matching"—i.e., with the same SNO and DURING values as—some tuple in *u* is this one:

SNO	PNO	DURING
S2	P2	[d03:d03]

In effect, therefore, every tuple in *u* is extended with a PNO_REL value that's an empty relation, with the sole exception of the tuple with supplier number S2 and DURING value the interval [*d03*:*d03*], which gets a PNO_REL value that's a relation with heading {PNO} and body containing just a tuple for part number P2. Thus, the final PACK yields a result containing:

- For each tuple in S_DURING with SNO value not S2, a copy of that tuple extended with a PNO_REL value consisting of a relation with heading {PNO} and body empty

- For the tuple in S_DURING with SNO value S2 and DURING value [*d07*:*d10*], a copy of that tuple extended with a PNO_REL value consisting of a relation with heading {PNO} and body empty

- For the tuple in S_DURING with SNO value S2 and DURING value [*d02*:*d04*], three separate tuples that look like this:

SNO	DURING	PNO_REL
S2	[*d02*:*d02*]	PNO ———

SNO	DURING	PNO_REL
S2	[*d03*:*d03*]	PNO ——— P2

SNO	DURING	PNO_REL
S2	[*d04*:*d04*]	PNO ———

Now, this overall result is probably not what was wanted! Probably we'd have liked SP_DURING, as well as S_DURING, to be unpacked before the extension is done—but that's not the way U_EXTEND works. (It's not the way it works because the operator is monadic, and the implicit UNPACK therefore applies, as it does in the case of restrict, to the sole relation operand: namely, the relation being extended.) Thus, a more reasonable, or more useful (?), version of the query might look like this:

```
USING ( DURING ) : EXTEND S_DURING :
     { PNO_REL := !!( UNPACK SP_DURING ON ( DURING ) ) }
```

A pictorial (tabular) representation of the result of this expression—*r*, say—would be much too large to show here in its entirety, but you might like to confirm for yourself that the only tuples relation *r* contains, for supplier S1 in particular, are as follows:

■ A tuple with DURING value [*d04*:*d04*] and PNO_REL value consisting of a relation with heading {PNO} and body containing tuples for part numbers P1 and P5

■ A tuple with DURING value [*d05*:*d05*] and PNO_REL value consisting of a relation with heading {PNO} and body containing tuples for part numbers P1, P2, P4, and P5

■ A tuple with DURING value [*d06*:*d08*] and PNO_REL value consisting of a relation with heading {PNO} and body containing tuples for part numbers P1, P2, P4, P5, and P6

- A tuple with DURING value [*d09*:*d10*] and PNO_REL value consisting of a relation with heading {PNO} and body containing tuples for part numbers P1, P2, P3, P4, P5, and P6

Let's look at another example. Recall this query from Chapter 9:

- At any given time, if there are any shipments at all at that time, then there's some part number *pmax* such that, at that time, (a) at least one supplier is able to supply part *pmax*, but (b) no supplier is able to supply any part with a part number greater than *pmax*. So, for each part number that has ever been such a *pmax* value, get that part number together with the interval(s) during which it actually was that *pmax* value.

Just to remind you, here's the formulation we gave in Chapter 9:

```
WITH ( t1 := UNPACK SP_DURING ON ( DURING ) ,
       t2 := EXTEND t1 { DURING } : { PMAX := MAX ( !!t1 , PNO ) } ) :
PACK t2 ON ( DURING )
```

Here by contrast is a formulation using U_EXTEND:

```
WITH ( t1 := UNPACK SP_DURING ON ( DURING ) ) :
USING ( DURING ) :
      EXTEND SP_DURING { DURING } : { PMAX := MAX ( !!t1 , PNO ) }
```

As you'll probably agree, this latter formulation isn't much of an improvement on the Chapter 9 version (if it's an improvement at all, that is). Indeed, what this example tends to suggest—and the same goes for the example immediately preceding this one—is that there might be scope here for defining a further shorthand of some kind.

> *Aside:* **Tutorial D** currently supports an explicit SUMMARIZE operator that's expressly intended for queries of the kind under discussion. Now, there were, and are, good reasons to prefer EXTEND and image relations over SUMMARIZE in general (see reference [40])—in fact, SUMMARIZE can actually be defined in terms of EXTEND and image relations. But one advantage SUMMARIZE clearly does have over EXTEND, at least in the present context, is that it's a dyadic operator; in other words, it's explicitly defined to take two relational operands. Thus, it would be reasonable to define a U_SUMMARIZE operator that would genuinely be useful for queries like the one under discussion.[6] Here's a putative U_SUMMARIZE version of that query:
>
> ```
> USING ( DURING ) : SUMMARIZE SP_DURING PER ( SP_DURING { DURING } ) :
>                                        { PMAX := MAX ( PNO ) }
> ```

---

[6] On the other hand, it wouldn't help with examples like the one discussed immediately prior to the present one.

The two relational operands here are (a) the current value of SP_DURING ("the SUMMARIZE relation") and (b) the current value of the projection of SP_DURING on DURING ("the PER relation"). Thus, what the U_SUMMARIZE does is this: First, it unpacks both of these relations on DURING. Second, for each DURING value—a unit interval— in the unpacked form of the PER relation, it appends the corresponding PMAX value, which it computes by examining all tuples with that DURING value in the unpacked form of the SUMMARIZE relation (the result of this step is a relation with attributes DURING and PMAX). Finally, it packs the result on DURING again. *End of aside.*

Observe now that the foregoing discussion (i.e., of the *pmax* example) has to do specifically with aggregate operator invocations that appear within an attribute assignment within a U_EXTEND invocation. But exactly analogous considerations apply to aggregate operator invocations within a WHERE condition in a restriction. We omit detailed examination of this latter case here, however, since (as we saw in Chapter 2) it's defined in terms of the former case anyway.

GROUP and UNGROUP

Definition: Let r be a relation; let ACL be a commalist of attribute names in which every attribute mentioned (a) is an attribute of r and (b) is of some interval type, let BCL be a commalist of attribute names in which every attribute mentioned is an attribute of r not mentioned in ACL; and let X be an attribute name that's distinct from that of every attribute of r apart possibly from those attributes mentioned in BCL. Then the expression USING (ACL) : r GROUP {BCL} AS X denotes the **U_grouping** with respect to ACL of r on BCL, and it's defined to be shorthand for the following:

```
PACK
    ( ( UNPACK r ON ( ACL ) ) GROUP { BCL } AS X )
ON ( ACL )
```

Definition: Let r be a relation, let r have a relation valued attribute B, and let ACL be a commalist of attribute names in which every attribute mentioned (a) is an attribute of r and (b) is of some interval type. Then the expression USING (ACL) : r UNGROUP B denotes the **U_ungrouping** with respect to ACL of r on B, and it's defined to be shorthand for the following:

```
PACK
    ( ( UNPACK r ON ( ACL ) ) UNGROUP B )
ON ( ACL )
```

Here's a U_GROUP example. Let the current value of relvar SP_DURING be as follows:

SNO	PNO	DURING
S2	P1	[*d08*:*d10*]
S2	P2	[*d09*:*d10*]
S4	P2	[*d07*:*d09*]
S4	P4	[*d07*:*d08*]

Then the expression

```
USING ( DURING ) : SP_DURING GROUP { PNO } AS PNO_REL
```

yields the following result:

SNO	DURING	PNO_REL		SNO	DURING	PNO_REL
S2	[*d08*:*d08*]	PNO / P1		S4	[*d07*:*d08*]	PNO / P2 / P4
S2	[*d09*:*d10*]	PNO / P1 / P2		S4	[*d09*:*d09*]	PNO / P2

Exercise: Show that the foregoing U_GROUP expression is logically equivalent to the following (and hence, in effect, that U_GROUP can be defined in terms of U_EXTEND):

```
USING ( DURING ) : EXTEND SP_DURING { SNO , DURING } :
                 { PNO_REL := !!( UNPACK SP_DURING ON ( DURING ) ) }
```

As for U_UNGROUP, we leave it as another exercise to show that if *r* is the result of the foregoing U_GROUP example, then the expression

```
USING ( DURING ) : r UNGROUP PNO_REL
```

returns the value of SP_DURING shown as the input relation for the U_GROUP example discussed above.

We remark without going into details that, like U_GROUP, U_UNGROUP too can be defined in terms of U_EXTEND.

RELATIONAL COMPARISONS

The syntax of a regular relational comparison is basically as follows—

```
r1 compop r2
```

—where *r1* and *r2* are relations of the same type *T* and *compop* is one of the following:

=   ≠   ⊆   ⊂   ⊇   ⊃

Now, when relations *r1* and *r2* involve any interval attributes, what we often want to do is compare, not those relations per se, but certain unpacked versions of those relations. To that end, we introduce U_ versions of the regular comparison operators:

Definition: Let relations *r1* and *r2* be of the same type *T*, and let *ACL* be a commalist of attribute names in which every attribute mentioned (a) is one of type *T*'s component attributes and (b) is of some interval type. Then the expression USING (*ACL*) : *r1 compop r2* (where *compop* is any of the regular relational comparison operators) denotes a **U_comparison** with respect to *ACL* between *r1* and *r2*, and it's defined to be shorthand for the following:

```
( UNPACK r1 ON ( ACL ) ) compop ( UNPACK r2 ON ( ACL ) )
```

Note that there's no question of performing a final PACK step here, because the result of a comparison is a truth value, not a relation. By way of example, let *r1* and *r2* be as follows:

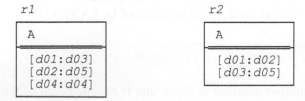

```
r1                          r2
A                           A
[d01:d03]                   [d01:d02]
[d02:d05]                   [d03:d05]
[d04:d04]
```

Then *r1* = *r2* is clearly false, but USING (A) : *r1* = *r2* is true. *Note:* When (as in this example) *compop* is "=", the U_comparison is, of course, U_equality. And U_equality in turn is precisely the equivalence operator we defined for *n*-ary relations in Chapter 10.

THE UNDERLYING INTUITION

In this section, we briefly discuss an alternative way of thinking about relations with interval attributes and the U_ operators on such relations as discussed in this chapter so far. Suppose the current value of relvar S_DURING is the relation shown here (let's call it *r*):

SNO	DURING
S1	[*d04*:*d06*]
S2	[*d02*:*d04*]
S2	[*d06*:*d07*]
S3	[*d05*:*d07*]
S4	[*d03*:*d05*]

The intended interpretation for this relation, just to remind you, is that the indicated supplier was under contract throughout the indicated interval.

    Observe now that the set of time points in DURING intervals in this relation *r* is exactly the following set:

{ *d02* , *d03* , *d04* , *d05* , *d06* , *d07* }

    The cardinality of this set is six. Thus, we can think of relation *r* as effectively specifying the overall state of affairs, regarding who was under contract, at each of those six separate points in time. In other words, we can think of *r* as a kind of shorthand for a sequence of six separate relations, one for each of the six time points in question (where the sequence in question is chronological, of course). Those six relations—let's label them *r02*, *r03*, ..., *r07* in the obvious way—look like this:

r02	*r03*	*r04*	*r05*	*r06*	*r07*
SNO	SNO	SNO	SNO	SNO	SNO
S2	S2 S4	S1 S2 S4	S1 S3 S4	S1 S2 S3	S2 S3

For example, relation *r03* shows that suppliers S2 and S4 (only) were under contract on day 3. And, of course, that relation is obtained from relation *r* by (a) restricting *r* to just those tuples in which the DURING interval contains the value *d03* and then (b) projecting the result of that restriction on attribute SNO.

    It follows from the foregoing that we can imagine an operator that produces the sequence of relations *r02*, *r03*, ..., *r07* from relation *r*. Similarly, we can imagine an inverse operator that takes the sequence of relations *r02*, *r03*, ..., *r07* and gives us back relation *r* once again.[7] For the sake of the present discussion, then, let's refer to those two operators as REL_TO_SEQ and SEQ_TO_REL, respectively.

Now we can explain the intuition behind the various U_operators. For definiteness, let's consider the operator U_JOIN specifically. Then the basic idea is that, first, for each individual point (each individual *time* point, in the foregoing example), the pertinent underlying operator— i.e., JOIN, in the case of U_JOIN—is applied to the pair of relations that correspond to that particular point value; second, the results of all of those individual operations are then put back together again appropriately. Thus, the operation of U_JOIN, for example, can be thought of, loosely, as doing a regular join on a point by point basis. (By way of another example, the U_equality comparison operator can be thought of, again loosely, as doing a regular equality comparison on a point by point basis.)

In order to see how the foregoing works out in more detail, let's consider the case of U_JOIN a little more closely. Let the relations to be U_joined be *r1* and *r2*. Conceptually, then, what happens is the following:

- Let *P1* be the set of all point values in intervals in *r1*. REL_TO_SEQ is applied to *r1* to yield a sequence *Q1* of relations, one for each point value in *P1*.

- Let *P2* be the set of all point values in intervals in *r2* (note that *P1* and *P2* will be distinct sets, in general). REL_TO_SEQ is applied to *r2* to yield a sequence *Q2* of relations, one for each point value in *P2*.

- Let *P* be the union of *P1* and *P2*, and let the points in *P*, in sequence according to the ordering defined for the pertinent point type, be *p1*, *p2*, ..., *pn*.

- For all points *pi* in *P* (*i* = 1, 2, ..., *n*), if *pi* appears in *P1* and not *P2*, an empty relation of the same type as *r2* and corresponding to *pi* is inserted into *Q2*; similarly, if *pi* appears in *P2* and not in *P1*, an empty relation of the same type as *r1* and corresponding to *pi* is inserted into *Q1*. *Note:* This step is necessary merely to ensure that the join operations in the next step are all well defined.

- For all *i* (*i* = 1, 2, ..., *n*), the relations in *Q1* and *Q2* corresponding to point *pi* are joined together. The net result is a sequence *Q* of *n* relations resulting from those joins.

- SEQ_TO_REL is applied to *Q* to yield the desired overall result.

---

[7] Of course, SEQ_TO_REL would also need to know the time point corresponding to each relation in the sequence.

THE REGULAR OPERATORS REVISITED

Consider once again the U_MINUS definition from the section "Dyadic Operators" earlier in this chapter. Just to remind you, we defined USING (*ACL*) : *r1* MINUS *r2* to be shorthand for:

```
PACK
     ( ( UNPACK r1 ON ( ACL ) )
          MINUS
       ( UNPACK r2 ON ( ACL ) ) )
ON ( ACL )
```

Now suppose *ACL* is empty (i.e., specifies no attributes at all), so that the U_MINUS invocation becomes:

```
USING ( ) : r1 MINUS r2
```

Then the expansion becomes

```
PACK
     ( ( UNPACK r1 ON ( ) )
          MINUS
       ( UNPACK r2 ON ( ) ) )
ON ( )
```

Recall now from Chapter 10 that UNPACK *r* ON ( ) and PACK *r* ON ( ) both reduce to just *r*. Thus, the entire expression reduces to just

```
r1 MINUS r2
```

In other words, the regular relational MINUS operator is essentially just a special case of U_MINUS! Thus, if we redefine the syntax of the regular MINUS operator as follows[8]—

```
[ USING ( ACL ) : ] r1 MINUS r2
```

—and if we allow the USING specification (and colon separator) to be omitted if and only if *ACL* is empty, then we no longer have any need to talk about a special U_MINUS operator at all: All MINUS invocations effectively become U_MINUS invocations, and we can generalize the semantics of the MINUS operator accordingly.

Analogous remarks apply to all of the other regular operators we've been talking about in this chapter (relational comparisons included): In all cases, the regular operator is basically just that special case of the corresponding U_ operator in which the USING specification mentions no attributes at all, and we can allow that specification and the colon separator to be omitted in

---

[8] We remind you that we use brackets "[" and "]" in BNF grammar fragments, here and throughout this book, to mean the material they enclose is optional (barring explicit statements to the contrary, of course).

such a case. To put it another way, the U_ operators are all just straightforward generalizations of their regular counterparts. Thus, we no longer need to talk explicitly about U_ operators, as such, at all (and we no longer will, except when we want to do so for reasons of clarity or emphasis). Instead, all we need do is recognize that the regular operators permit, but don't require, an additional operand when they're applied to relations with interval attributes. Please note carefully, therefore, that throughout the rest of the book, we'll take all references to relational operators and relational comparisons to refer to the generalized versions as described in the present chapter (unless the context demands otherwise). For clarity and emphasis, however, we'll occasionally use the explicit qualifiers *regular* (or *classical*) and *generalized*, as applicable, when referring to those operators and comparisons. As already noted, we'll also sometimes use an explicit "U_" qualifier in such references for the same reason.

EXERCISES

11.1 In the body of the chapter we defined U_ versions of the regular relational operators, including operators like MATCHING that are fundamentally just shorthand. But what about the PACK and UNPACK shorthands? Would U_PACK and U_UNPACK operators make sense?

11.2 Does the following identity hold?

```
USING ( ACL ) : r1 INTERSECT r2 ≡
       USING ( ACL ) : r1 MINUS ( USING ( ACL ) : r1 MINUS r2 )
```

11.3 Consider the operator U_JOIN. Assume for simplicity that the packing and unpacking are to be done on the basis of a single attribute *A*. Confirm that the following identity holds:

```
USING ( A ) : r1 JOIN r2 ≡
       WITH ( t1 := r1 RENAME { A AS X } ,
              t2 := r2 RENAME { A AS Y } ,
              t3 := t1 JOIN t2 ,
              t4 := t3 WHERE X OVERLAPS Y ,
              t5 := EXTEND t4 : { A := X INTERSECT Y } ,
              t6 := T5 { ALL BUT X , Y } ) :
       PACK t6 ON ( A )
```

Confirm also that if *r1* and *r2* are initially packed on *A*, the final PACK step is unnecessary.

ANSWERS

11.1 Such operators wouldn't make a lot of sense (though that's not necessarily a good reason for failing to support them, of course). Consider, e.g., a hypothetical U_PACK operator; more specifically, consider the following hypothetical expression:

```
USING ( DURING ) : PACK S_DURING ON ( DURING )
```

Presumably this expression would be defined to be shorthand for:

```
PACK
     ( UNPACK ( PACK S_DURING ON ( DURING ) ) ON ( DURING ) )
ON ( DURING )
```

And, of course, this expression reduces to simply PACK S_DURING ON (DURING). *Note:* In similar fashion, the expression USING (*ACL*) : !!*r*, if supported, would be equivalent to PACK !!*r* ON (*ACL*).

11.2 Yes, it does!

11.3 In essence, we need to show that the following identity holds:

```
( UNPACK r1 ON ( A ) )  JOIN  ( UNPACK r2 ON ( A ) )   ≡   UNPACK t6 ON ( A )
```

Let *B1* be all of the attributes of *r1* apart from *A*, let *B2* be all of the attributes of *r2* apart from *A*, and let *B* be the set theory union of *B1* and *B2*. Then:

- Let *B* be empty. Then *t6* has just one attribute, *A*, and the *A* values in its body consist of all possible intersections of an *A* value from *r1* and an *A* value from *r2*. It follows that, loosely speaking, the unpacked form of *t6* consists of every unit interval [*p*:*p*] such that *p* is contained in at least one of those intersections. And it's clear that, speaking even more loosely, the join of the unpacked forms of *r1* and *r2* consists of exactly those same unit intervals. Thus, the identity does hold in this simple case.

- Now let *B* be nonempty. If we partition *r1* and *r2* on the basis of *B1* values and *B2* values, respectively, we can apply an argument analogous to that given above to each pair of partitions, one each from *r1* and *r2*. Hence the identity holds in all cases.

Proof that the final PACK step is unnecessary if r1 and r2 are initially packed: Note first that if the *A* value *a* appears in *t6*, then *a* is the intersection of some *A* value *x* appearing in *r1* and some *A* value *y* appearing in *r2*; thus $a \subseteq x$. Now let *B*, *B1*, and *B2* be as above. Further, let *C* be the set theory intersection of *B1* and *B2*, let *D* be the set theory difference between *B1* and *B2* in that order, and let *E* be the set theory difference between *B2* and *B1* in that order. In other words, *C* is the other common attributes of *r1* and *r2* apart from *A*, *D* is the other attributes of *r1*, and *E* is the other attributes of *r2*.

Now let $t = (a,c,d,e)$ and $t' = (a',c,d,e)$ be tuples in *t6*, where $a \neq a'$. (Here we use a shorthand notation for tuples that we take to be self-explanatory.) Then there must exist tuples $(x,c,d) \in r1$ and $(x',c,d) \in r1$ such that $a \subseteq x$ and $a' \subseteq x'$. But *r1* is packed on *A*, so these latter tuples neither meet nor overlap. Hence, since $a \subseteq x$ and $a' \subseteq x'$, tuples *t* and *t'* neither meet nor overlap. Hence *t6* is packed.

Points arising: First, we've now effectively discovered an algorithm for computing a U_join that involves no packing or unpacking at all; the algorithm works just so long as the input relations are initially packed. Second, the algorithm doesn't in fact require both input relations to be packed—it's sufficient that at least one of them be so. See Appendix E for further discussion.

Part III

BUILDING ON THE FOUNDATIONS

This part of the book uses the concepts introduced in Part II as a basis for investigating a variety of more advanced aspects of temporal database support—in particular, the question of temporal database design, which turns out to involve quite a lot of complexity, at least potentially. There are seven chapters (which, as with Part II, are definitely meant to be read in sequence as written):

Chapter 12

D a t a b a s e   D e s i g n

I : S t r u c t u r e

How dangerous it always is to reason from insufficient data.
—Arthur Conan Doyle:
The Adventure of the Speckled Band (1891)

Database design isn't just a matter of pinning down relvars and their attributes—the associated constraints are crucial too. But there's so much to say about constraints in general in the temporal context that to include that topic in this chapter would make the chapter far too long and unwieldy. For that reason, we've spread our discussion of design issues across three chapters, as follows:

■ The present chapter is concerned mainly just with structure, or in other words with relvars and their attributes—though even here there'll unavoidably be quite a lot of discussion of constraints as well, especially in the section "A New Normal Form."

■ Chapters 13 and 14 then discuss constraints as such: Chapter 13 discusses keys and what might be called "key like" constraints, and Chapter 14 discusses general constraints.

Note: For obvious reasons, the unqualified term *design* should be taken throughout this chapter and the next two as referring to temporal database design specifically, unless the context demands otherwise.

THE RUNNING EXAMPLE REVISITED

Up to this point, our sample relvars S_DURING and SP_DURING have served us well, clearly demonstrating the need for interval types and the desirability of special operators for dealing with interval data. Obviously enough, however, those relvars are extremely simple in structure—and S_DURING, at least, is really *too* simple to serve as a basis for a proper investigation into design issues. So let's now go all the way back to our original *non*temporal relvars S and SP from Chapter 1. Here again are the original relvar definitions:

```
VAR S BASE RELATION
  { SNO     SNO ,
    SNAME   NAME ,
    STATUS  INTEGER ,
    CITY    CHAR }
  KEY { SNO } ;

VAR SP BASE RELATION
  { SNO SNO ,
    PNO PNO }
  KEY { SNO , PNO }
  FOREIGN KEY { SNO } REFERENCES S ;
```

Now let's concentrate on relvar S specifically until further notice (we'll come back to SP at the very end of the chapter). Just to remind you, the predicate for relvar S is:

Supplier SNO is under contract, is named SNAME, has status STATUS, and is located in city CITY.

However, noting that relvar S is subject to the constraint that {SNO} is a key—and hence that there's a functional dependency from {SNO} to each of {SNAME}, {STATUS}, and {CITY}— we can observe that the following more precise statement is in fact the case:

The supplier identified by SNO is under exactly one contract, has exactly one name SNAME, has exactly one status STATUS, and is located in exactly one city CITY.

In what follows we won't always bother to spell matters out quite so carefully, but we'll certainly rely on the fact that such more careful statements do in fact apply, and hence that in the case at hand, for example, a given supplier does have exactly one name, one status, and one city at any one time.

Now suppose we want to design a temporal analog of this nontemporal relvar. How can we do this? The most obvious approach, of course, is just to add an appropriate timestamp attribute—a "since" attribute if we merely want to "semitemporalize" the design, or a "during" attribute if we want to temporalize it fully, as follows (semitemporal on the left, fully temporal on the right):

```
VAR SSSC_SINCE BASE RELATION          VAR SSSC_DURING BASE RELATION
  { SNO     SNO ,                       { SNO     SNO ,
    SNAME   NAME ,                         SNAME   NAME ,
    STATUS  INTEGER ,                      STATUS  INTEGER ,
    CITY    CHAR ,                         CITY    CHAR ,
    SINCE   DATE }                         DURING  INTERVAL_DATE }
  KEY { SNO } ;                         KEY { SNO , DURING } ;
```

Note the revised relvar names and, in the case of relvar SSSC_DURING, the revised KEY specification as well.[1] *Terminology*: We'll refer to SSSC_SINCE and SSSC_DURING as a "since relvar" and a "during relvar," respectively; loosely speaking, a since relvar is one that contains current information, while a during relvar is one that contains historical information. Please note immediately that these characterizations are, as indicated, both fairly loose; we'll tighten them up later, in the sections "Since Relvars Only" and "During Relvars Only," respectively. However, we do find them—the characterizations, that is—useful from an intuitive point of view, and we'll appeal to them from time to time in what follows.

Now, it's easy to see (and subsequent sections will show) that relvars SSSC_SINCE and SSSC_DURING are in fact both very badly designed; that is, simply adding a timestamp attribute of some kind to a nontemporal relvar is *not* a good way to do temporal design.[2] So what would a good design look like? Well, the answer to this question depends on whether we want a fully temporal design or merely a semitemporal one:

■ If a semitemporal design is all we want, then all we need to do, in terms of our example, is revise the structure of relvar SSSC_SINCE appropriately. But it turns out that the revisions in question are quite straightforward, and they're discussed in the next section.

■ Alternatively, if a fully temporal design is our target, then we need to revise the structure of relvar SSSC_DURING instead—and here it turns out that the revisions we need are rather more drastic. To be specific, we propose that, in general, such relvars be subjected to

a.   "Vertical" decomposition, to deal with the fact that different "properties" of the same "entity" typically vary at different rates,

and preferably also to

b.   "Horizontal" decomposition, to deal with the fact that there's a logical difference between current and historical information.

But first things first. Here's the plan for the chapter. In the next section ("Since Relvars Only"), we consider relvars like SSSC_SINCE and make some recommendations for dealing

---

[1] In order to head off certain questions that might already be occurring to you, we repeat that we'll have a lot more to say about key constraints and related matters in the next two chapters.

[2] Which raises an interesting question in passing: namely, how does one draw an E/R ("entity/relationship") diagram for a temporal database? In this connection, you might like to ponder the following lightly edited remarks from reference [108], which are, as you'll observe, quite clearly at odds with our own position on this matter: "In the approach we espouse, we initially ignore the time-varying nature of the applications. We focus on capturing the *current reality* and temporally ignore any history that may be useful to capture. This selective amnesia somewhat simplifies what is often a highly complex task of capturing the full semantics. An added benefit is that existing design methodologies apply in full. Only after the full design is complete do we augment the E/R schema with time-varying semantics."

with that comparatively simple case. Then, in the subsequent section ("During Relvars Only"), we consider relvars like SSSC_DURING; that discussion leads to the proposed vertical decomposition, which we consider in detail in a section of its own ("A New Normal Form"). We then go on to discuss "the moving point *now*" and the special problems caused by that construct. As we'll see, those problems can occur in connection with during relvars even if vertical decomposition is done, and it's that fact that leads to the proposed horizontal decomposition, which is considered in detail in the section "Both Since and During Relvars."

One further preliminary point: The wording of the previous paragraph might be taken to suggest that a given database has to follow one of the various design approaches exclusively (since relvars only, during relvars only, or a mixture of both). In practice, of course, any combination can be used; that is, some "entities" and their corresponding "properties" might be represented by since relvars only, others by during relvars only, and others by a mixture. For simplicity, however, we ignore this nicety from this point forward. We remark, however, that most of the research reported in the literature—on all aspects of temporal data, not just design issues—does seem to concentrate on the case of during or "historical" relvars only.

SINCE RELVARS ONLY

We've used the qualifier *since* several times already to refer to a relvar like SSSC_SINCE that's merely semitemporal and thereby contains "current information." To repeat, however, this latter characterization, such as it is, is actually pretty loose. The fact is, such a relvar contains not only current information as such but also, at least implicitly, information about both the past and the future, as we'll see. What's more, it also contains explicit information about the past—again as we'll see—and it might even contain explicit information about the future! So to say just that such a relvar contains "current information" is only a very rough approximation to the truth.

Be that as it may, here again, repeated from the previous section but now shown only in outline, is the definition of relvar SSSC_SINCE:

```
SSSC_SINCE { SNO , SNAME , STATUS , CITY , SINCE } KEY { SNO }
```

The predicate for this relvar, in detail, is as follows:

Ever since day SINCE,[3] *all four of the following have been true:*

a.   *Supplier SNO has been under contract.*

b.   *Supplier SNO has been named SNAME.*

---

[3] We remind you from Chapter 4 that we take expressions of the form "ever since day *d*" to mean "ever since *and not immediately before* day *d*."

c.　　*Supplier SNO has had status STATUS.*

d.　　*Supplier SNO has been located in city CITY.*

And it should be clear right away, from this formulation of the predicate, that the relvar isn't very well designed. To see why not, suppose it contains the following tuple:

SNO	SNAME	STATUS	CITY	SINCE
S1	Smith	20	London	*d04*

Suppose too that today is day 10 and that, starting from today, the status of supplier S1 is to be changed to 30, and so we replace the tuple just shown by this one:

SNO	SNAME	STATUS	CITY	SINCE
S1	Smith	30	London	*d10*

And now we've lost (among other things) the information that supplier S1 has been located in London since day 4!

Well, it should be clear from this simple example that relvar SSSC_SINCE as so far defined is incapable of representing any supplier information that predates the time of the most recent update to that supplier (speaking a little loosely). But this problem is easily fixed: We simply replace the existing "since" attribute by four such attributes, one for each of the "nonsince" attributes, thus (in outline):

```
SSSC_SINCE { SNO      ,  SNO_SINCE ,
             SNAME    ,  SNAME_SINCE ,
             STATUS   ,  STATUS_SINCE ,
             CITY     ,  CITY_SINCE }
       KEY { SNO }
```

The predicate for this revised version of SSSC_SINCE is:

Supplier SNO has been under contract ever since SNO_SINCE, has been named SNAME ever since SNAME_SINCE, has had status STATUS ever since STATUS_SINCE, and has been located in city CITY ever since CITY_SINCE.

Here's a typical tuple for this revised design:

SNO	SNO_SINCE	SNAME	SNAME_SINCE
S1	*d04*	Smith	*d04*

STATUS	STATUS_SINCE	CITY	CITY_SINCE
30	*d10*	London	*d04*

This tuple shows among other things that supplier S1 has had status 30 since day 10 but has been located in London since day 4, and so we've solved the problem.

> *Aside:* To repeat, the problem was that if we were to replace the original tuple for supplier S1 (with STATUS = 20 and SINCE = *d04*) by one with STATUS = 30 and SINCE = *d10*, then we'd lose the information that supplier S1 was previously located in London. Now, you might be thinking we could have solved that problem by changing the KEY specification for relvar SSSC_SINCE in such a way as to allow two distinct tuples to appear for supplier S1, one showing S1 with status 20 since day 4 and the other showing S1 with status 30 since day 10. But if you try to state the predicate for this revised version of the relvar, or if you try to write some queries against it, you'll quickly see why we don't seriously suggest such an approach—especially when you realize that analogous changes would presumably have to be made in connection with the SNAME and CITY attributes as well. What's more, even if we did adopt such a design and thus be able, in a sense, to deal with supplier name and status and city histories, we still wouldn't be able to deal with supplier *contract* histories. *End of aside.*

Of course, it's still the case with this revised design that the relvar can represent "current" information only—it's still just a since relvar, and the database is still merely semitemporal. Thus, for example, if on day 10 the status of supplier S1 changes to 30, and we therefore replace the tuple shown for supplier S1, with STATUS = 20 and STATUS_SINCE = *d04*, by another with STATUS = 30 and STATUS_SINCE = *d10*, then we lose the information that supplier S1 had status 20 from day 4 to day 9 inclusive. In other words, this semitemporal design can't represent historical information (other than as explained in the paragraph immediately following). However, it could still be the right design in some circumstances. In particular, it could serve as part of a combination design as discussed later in the section "Both Since and During Relvars."

Note: When we say a relvar such as SSSC_SINCE can't represent historical information, we mean it can't represent *purely* historical information—i.e., information regarding a state of affairs that held in the past but no longer does so. But if today is day 10 and the relvar states that supplier S1 has been located in London ever since day 4, then it clearly does represent historical information of a kind. Thus, it would be more accurate to say that a since relvar can't represent historical information *other than what can be inferred from the since values*. Those since values can be thought of as *explicit* historical information, and information inferred from them can be thought of as *implicit* historical information.

Further Points

A number of further points arise in connection with our revised design for relvar SSSC_SINCE, which we now proceed to discuss. First of all, of course, it's clearly not necessary to have a since attribute for *every* "nonsince" attribute in the relvar. For example, if supplier names never change, or if they do change but we're simply not interested in knowing about such changes—i.e., we're interested only in what those names happen to be at the present time—then attribute SNAME_SINCE is clearly not needed.

Second, let the SNO_SINCE value in some SSSC_SINCE tuple be d, and let the value for any of the other since attributes in that same tuple be d'; then it must be the case that $d' \geq d$.[4] In other words, we assume, reasonably enough, that if relvar SSSC_SINCE contains information regarding a contract for some supplier Sx, it doesn't contain any name, status, or city information for supplier Sx that predates the start of that contract. To put it another way: Although suppliers presumably do have a name and a status and a city before their contract starts, our database isn't concerned with such matters.

Third, although we've described SSSC_SINCE (informally, at any rate) as containing "current" information, it might nevertheless quite legitimately contain information that explicitly pertains to the future. For example, the SNO_SINCE value for some supplier Sx might be some future date d, meaning the indicated supplier *will be* placed under contract on that date in the future (in which case attribute SNO_SINCE might better be named SNO_FROM, where FROM means "effective from").

Fourth and last—and this one is important—we note that, even if it contains no information that pertains to the future explicitly, a relvar like SSSC_SINCE does necessarily contain information that pertains to the future *implicitly*. For example, if that relvar contains a tuple indicating that supplier S1 has been under contract ever since day 4, that "ever since" must be understood to be *open ended*; that is, the tuple must be understood to mean that, as far as we know, supplier S1 was, is, or will be under contract on every day from day 4 until "the last day." In other words, the associated "valid time" is, currently, the interval from day 4 to the last day. Of course, if we subsequently learn that supplier S1's contract actually terminated on some specific day, say day 25, and we update the database accordingly, the associated valid time will then become the interval [*d04:d25*].

> *Aside:* See Chapter 3 if you need to refresh your memory regarding the concept of valid time, and Chapter 17 for an extended discussion of the same concept. Here we merely

---

[4] We said at the beginning of this chapter that we would be deferring most consideration of constraints to the next two chapters. However, this particular constraint is such an obvious one that it seemed worth mentioning right away.

remind you that, strictly speaking, valid times are sets of intervals, not just individual intervals per se. In the case at hand, therefore, it would be more accurate to say the valid time is initially {[*d04*:*d99*]}—where we assume for the sake of the example that *d99* is "the last day"—and subsequently becomes {[*d04*:*d25*]} instead. Note, moreover, that because the database is merely semitemporal, this latter valid time won't actually be recorded in the database at all; rather, all information concerning supplier S1 will simply be deleted from the database when we learn the contract has terminated. More generally, in fact, any valid time that involves an interval in which the end point is anything other than "the end of time," and/or involves two or more distinct intervals, can't be represented in a database that's merely semitemporal. Again, see Chapter 17 for further discussion. *End of aside.*

DURING RELVARS ONLY

We began the previous section by examining the since, or "current," relvar SSSC_SINCE. Now we turn our attention to the during, or "historical," relvar SSSC_DURING. Note immediately, however, that (as with our earlier use of the term "current") our use of the term "historical" here is somewhat loose; clearly, a during relvar might contain explicit information pertaining to the future as well as to the past. For example, relvar SSSC_DURING might contain a tuple showing the contract for supplier Sx as extending from *di* to *dj*, where *dj* is some date in the future, and *di* might be in the future also. (And if *dj* is in the future but *di* is in the past, or is the date today, then the relvar contains current information as well.)

By way of another example, consider a relvar VACATION {EMPNO,DURING}, with predicate:

DURING denotes a maximal interval of days throughout which employee EMPNO was, is, or will be on vacation.

Here the end date probably is known, even for vacations that haven't yet ended—indeed, even for ones that haven't yet begun. So to say a during relvar contains just "historical information" is, again, only an approximation to the true state of affairs. As noted earlier, however, we find the characterization useful from an intuitive point of view, and we'll appeal to it from time to time in what follows.

Here then, repeated from the section "The Running Example Revisited" (but now shown in outline only), is the definition of relvar SSSC_DURING:

```
SSSC_DURING { SNO , SNAME , STATUS , CITY , DURING } KEY { SNO , DURING }
```

The predicate for this relvar, in detail, is as follows:

DURING denotes a maximal interval of days throughout which all four of the following were true:

a.   *Supplier SNO was under contract.*

b.   *Supplier SNO was named SNAME.*

c.   *Supplier SNO had status STATUS.*

d.   *Supplier SNO was located in city CITY.*

As in the case of the original version of relvar SSSC_SINCE in the previous section, it should be clear right away from this formulation of the predicate that relvar SSSC_DURING isn't very well designed. To see why not, suppose it contains the following tuple:

SNO	SNAME	STATUS	CITY	DURING
S2	Jones	10	Paris	[*d02*:*d04*]

Apparently, then, supplier S2 was under contract throughout the interval [*d02*:*d04*], named Jones throughout that same interval, had status 10 throughout that same interval, and was located in Paris throughout that same interval—a possible state of affairs, perhaps, but in general not a very likely one, surely; surely it would be more likely in general for the intervals during which a given supplier was under contract, had a given name, had a given status, and was located in a given city all to be different. In other words, attribute DURING (the timestamp attribute) "timestamps too much," as it were; in effect, it timestamps a combination of four separate predicates—supplier is under contract, supplier has name, supplier has status, supplier has city—instead of just a single predicate. So the obvious idea suggests itself: Why not replace the original SSSC_DURING by four separate relvars, each with its own timestamp? The relvars in question would look like this (in outline):

```
S_DURING          { SNO , DURING } KEY { SNO , DURING }

S_NAME_DURING     { SNO , SNAME , DURING } KEY { SNO , DURING }

S_STATUS_DURING   { SNO , STATUS , DURING } KEY { SNO , DURING }

S_CITY_DURING     { SNO , CITY , DURING } KEY { SNO , DURING }
```

Aside: The problems discussed in the previous section with relvar SSSC_SINCE (original version) could be characterized analogously: The timestamp attribute SINCE "timestamped too much." And we solved that problem by replacing that single SINCE attribute by four separate such attributes. Clearly, however, we can't solve the problem with relvar SSSC_DURING analogously—that is, we can't just replace the single DURING attribute by four separate such attributes (but why not?). *End of aside*.

The example thus illustrates the proposed vertical decomposition, as it applies to relvar SSSC_DURING.[5] Observe that, with respect to that decomposition, relvar S_DURING shows which suppliers were under contract when; relvar S_NAME_DURING shows which suppliers had which name when; relvar S_STATUS_DURING shows which suppliers had which status when; and relvar S_CITY_DURING shows which suppliers were located in which city when. Here are some possible sample tuples:

SNO	DURING
S2	[d01:d09]

SNO	SNAME	DURING
S2	Jones	[d01:d04]

SNO	SNAME	DURING
S2	Johns	[d05:d09]

SNO	STATUS	DURING
S2	10	[d01:d06]

SNO	STATUS	DURING
S2	15	[d07:d09]

SNO	CITY	DURING
S2	Paris	[d01:d03]

SNO	CITY	DURING
S2	Athens	[d04:d09]

Note: Of the four relvars resulting from the foregoing decomposition, relvar S_DURING in particular is, of course, the relvar on which we based a large part of our discussions in Part II of this book. In fact, though, that relvar isn't actually needed in the "during relvars only" design now under discussion. The reason is that—thanks to a certain constraint that (as we'll see in Chapter 14) will necessarily be in effect—the information contained in that relvar can always be obtained from any of the other three.[6] Nevertheless, we still prefer to include the relvar in our design, partly just for completeness, and partly because a certain degree of awkwardness and arbitrariness would occur if we didn't.

---

[5] Vertical decomposition is discussed in the literature—under the name "horizontal splitting"!—in reference [57]. The concept seems to have originated in reference [64].

[6] In other words, relvar S_DURING is redundant in the design currently under discussion. To be specific, it's subject to the constraint that its value at any time *t* is equal to the U_projection (using DURING) on {SNO,DURING} of the value of each of the other three relvars at that time *t*. Note, however, that this constraint will no longer hold when we get to the combination design to be discussed later in the chapter, in the section "Both Since and During Relvars."

A NEW NORMAL FORM

The vertical decomposition proposed in the previous section (of relvar SSSC_DURING into four separate relvars) is very reminiscent in both rationale and effect of classical normalization, and it's worth taking the time to examine the similarities in some detail. In fact, of course, vertical decomposition is exactly what classical normalization theory has always been concerned with; the decomposition operator in that theory is projection (which is a "vertical" decomposition operator by definition), and the corresponding recomposition operator is join. Indeed, the ultimate normal form with respect to classical normalization theory, fifth normal form or 5NF,[7] was originally called projection/join normal form for these very reasons [56].

Now, even before temporal data was studied, some writers—see, e.g., reference [60]— argued in favor of decomposing relvars as far as possible, instead of just as far as classical normalization would suggest. Some even argued that databases should contain binary relvars only. This latter position isn't really tenable, however. For one thing, unary relvars are sometimes needed. For another, some relvars of degree three or more simply can't be decomposed into relvars of lower degree by taking projections—or, to be more precise about the matter, they can't be so decomposed *in a nonloss way* (it's crucially important that the decomposition be nonloss, of course). By way of example, consider a ternary relvar SPJ, with attributes SNO, PNO, and JNO, representing a many to many to many relationship among suppliers, parts, and projects ("supplier SNO supplies part PNO to project JNO"). This relvar can't be nonloss decomposed into projections of lower degree in any way whatsoever.[8]

Be that as it may, the idea of decomposing relvars as far as possible is motivated by a desire for reduction to the simplest possible terms—in other words, reduction to *irreducible components*. Now, the argument in favor of such decomposition is perhaps not very strong in the case of a nontemporal relvar like the suppliers relvar from Chapter 1. However, it's much stronger in the case of a relvar like the fully temporal analog of that relvar (i.e., relvar SSSC_DURING from the previous section). Typically, a supplier's name, status, and city will vary independently over time. What's more, they'll probably vary at different rates as well. For example, it might be that a supplier's name hardly ever changes, while that same supplier's location changes occasionally and the corresponding status changes quite often—and it would be quite annoying, e.g., to have to repeat the name and city information every time the status changes (which we would have to do if we didn't do the vertical decomposition). Besides, the name history, status history, and city history of a supplier are probably each more interesting and

---

[7] It's true that fifth normal form is, as stated, the ultimate normal form with respect to classical normalization theory (but see Exercise 12.3), and it's certainly sufficient for eliminating the kind of redundancy that classical normalization is intended to eliminate. What's not true is that it's necessary for that purpose! Rather, a recently defined and strictly weaker normal form called ETNF ("essential tuple normal form") is sufficient for the purpose [30]. In practice, however, it would be extremely unusual for a relvar that's in ETNF not to be in 5NF. For the sake of the present discussion, therefore, we adopt the harmless fiction that as far as normalization as conventionally understood is concerned, 5NF is indeed the target to be aimed for.

[8] Unless a certain rather unlikely "cyclic" constraint happens to be in effect, as described in, e.g., reference [43].

more digestible concepts than the concept of a combined name / status / city history. Hence our proposed vertical decomposition.

There's another point to be made here, too. With SSSC_DURING as initially defined, we have to use a slightly nontrivial expression to get, e.g., suppliers and their city history:

```
USING ( DURING ) : SSSC_DURING { SNO , CITY , DURING }
```

(a U_projection—see Chapter 11). At the same time, the expression to get suppliers and their much less interesting combined name / status / city history is far simpler, consisting as it does of just a simple relvar reference:

```
SSSC_DURING
```

By contrast, the suggested vertical decomposition has the effect of making the more interesting queries easier to express and the less interesting ones harder. E.g., to get suppliers and their city history (more interesting):

```
S_CITY_DURING
```

And to get suppliers and their combined name / status / city history (less interesting):

```
USING ( DURING ) : S_NAME_DURING JOIN
        ( USING ( DURING ) : S_STATUS_DURING JOIN S_CITY_DURING )
```

Or (perhaps a trifle more reasonably, using an *n*-adic U_join):

```
USING ( DURING ) :
        JOIN { S_NAME_DURING , S_STATUS_DURING , S_CITY_DURING }
```

Join Dependencies and Fifth Normal Form

With the foregoing by way of motivation, we can now take a closer look at what's really going on here. First let's review the classical concept of fifth normal form (5NF), which as we said earlier is the ultimate normal form with respect to classical normalization theory. Fifth normal form is based on the concept of join dependencies, which can be defined thus:

Definition: Let *H* be a heading; then a **join dependency** (JD) with respect to *H* is an expression of the form $\circ\!\!\!\!\!\circ \{X1,X2,...,Xn\}$—pronounced "star *X1, X2, ..., Xn*"—where *X1, X2, ..., Xn* (the **components** of the JD) are subsets of *H* whose union is equal to *H*. *Note:* The phrase *JD with respect to H* can be abbreviated to just *JD* if *H* is understood. Note too that different writers use different symbols to denote a JD; we use a special kind of star ("$\circ\!\!\!\!\!\circ$"), but the "bow tie" symbol "$\bowtie$" is more often encountered in recent research literature.

Here are some examples of JDs, all of them defined in terms of the heading of the suppliers relvar from Chapter 1:[9]

```
✿ { { SNO , SNAME } , { SNO , STATUS } , { SNO , CITY } }
✿ { { SNO , SNAME , STATUS } , { SNAME , CITY } }
✿ { { SNO , SNAME , CITY } , { CITY , STATUS } }
```

Next we define what it means for a JD to be satisfied by some given relation:

Definition: Let relation r have heading H and let ✿$\{X1,X2,...,Xn\}$ be a JD, J say, with respect to H. If r is equal to the join of its projections on $X1$, $X2$,..., Xn, then r **satisfies** J; otherwise r **violates** J. *Note:* The term *join* here must be understood as referring to the n-adic version of that operator, since the JD has n components.

Note carefully that it's relations, not relvars, that satisfy or violate some given JD. For example, the relation shown as the value of relvar S in Fig. 1.1 in Chapter 1 satisfies the second of the foregoing JDs—

```
✿ { { SNO , SNAME , STATUS } , { SNAME , CITY } }
```

—and violates the third:

```
✿ { { SNO , SNAME , CITY } , { CITY , STATUS } }
```

Finally, we define what it means for a JD to hold in some given relvar:

Definition: Let relvar R have heading H and let J be a JD with respect to H. Then J **holds** in relvar R if and only if every relation that can validly be assigned to relvar R satisfies J. The JDs that hold in R are **the JDs of R**.

Note carefully that it's relvars, not relations, for which some given JD holds or not. For the suppliers relvar S from Chapter 1, for example, the first in our list of three JDs—

```
✿ { { SNO , SNAME } , { SNO , STATUS } , { SNO , CITY } }
```

—does hold, but this one (the second in our list) doesn't:

```
✿ { { SNO , SNAME , STATUS } , { SNAME , CITY } }
```

---

[9] Note very carefully that we're *not* saying here that these JDs are all satisfied by the suppliers relation shown in Fig. 1.1 (in fact, the first two are but the third isn't, as we'll see). Nor are we saying that these JDs all hold in relvar S (in fact, the first does but the second and third don't).

Taken together, what the foregoing definitions mean is that relvar R can be nonloss decomposed into its projections on $X1, X2, ..., Xn$ if and only if the JD $☆\{X1,X2,...,Xn\}$ holds in R. And now we can define fifth normal form:

> **Definition:** Relvar R is in **fifth normal form** (5NF)—also known as *projection-join normal form* (PJ/NF)—if and only if every JD of R is implied by the keys of R.

But what does it mean for a JD to be "implied by keys"? We need another definition:

> **Definition:** Let relvar R have heading H and let J be a JD with respect to H. Then J is **implied by the keys** of R if and only if every relation r that satisfies R's key constraints also satisfies J.

However, this definition, though accurate, isn't much help with the practical question of determining whether or not some given JD J is in fact implied by the keys of some given relvar R. But it turns out there's an algorithm, the *membership* algorithm, that does the job. It works like this. Let relvar R have heading H, and let $☆\{X1,X2,...,Xn\}$ be a JD, J say, with respect to H. Then:

1. If two distinct components of J both include the same key K of R, replace them in J by their union.

2. Repeat the previous step until no further replacements are possible.

At the conclusion of this process, the original JD J is implied by the keys of R if and only if the final version of J contains H as a component. (In practice, of course, we don't need to go all the way to the bitter end and compute that final version of J—we can quit as soon as a component is produced that's equal to H.)

Here's a simple example. Consider the nontemporal suppliers relvar S from Chapter 1. Here's a JD—let's call it J1—that (as we know) does hold in that relvar:

```
☆ { { SNO , SNAME } , { SNO , STATUS } , { SNO , CITY } }
```

Observe now that the components {SNO,SNAME} and {SNO,STATUS} both include the key {SNO}. Applying the membership algorithm, therefore, we can replace them by their union {SNO,SNAME,STATUS}. J1 now looks like this:

```
☆ { { SNO , SNAME , STATUS } , { SNO , CITY } }
```

Note that (a) this revised version of J1 is itself a JD with respect to the heading of relvar S, and also that (b) the JD in question does in fact hold in relvar S—two facts that together should give some insight as to how and why the membership algorithm works.

Next, the two components of this latter JD both include the key {SNO}, and so we can replace them by their union, to obtain:

```
✿ { { SNO , SNAME , STATUS , CITY } }
```

But the sole component here is the entire heading of S, and so it follows that JD J1 as originally stated is implied by the keys of relvar S.

For a greatly extended discussion of these matters and much more, please see reference [43].

U_Join Dependencies and Sixth Normal Form

Given that, in Chapter 11, we were able to define (among other things) generalized versions of the projection and join operators, which we called U_projection and U_join, respectively, you won't be surprised to learn that we can define a generalized version of join dependencies too, which we'll call U_join dependencies. Here are the relevant definitions:

Definition: Let H be a heading, and let ACL be a commalist of attribute names in which every attribute mentioned (a) is one of the attributes in H and (b) is of some interval type. Then a **U_join dependency** (U_JD) with respect to ACL and H is an expression of the form USING $(ACL) : ✿ \{X1,X2,...,Xn\}$, where $X1, X2, ..., Xn$ (the **components** of the U_JD) are subsets of H whose union is equal to H. *Note:* The phrase *U_JD with respect to ACL and H* can be abbreviated to *U_JD with respect to ACL* if H is understood; to *U_JD with respect to H* if *ACL* is understood; and to just *U_JD* if *ACL* and H are both understood.

Definition: Let relation r have heading H and let USING $(ACL) : ✿ \{X1,X2,...,Xn\}$ be a U_JD, UJ say, with respect to ACL and H. If r is U_equal to the U_join of its U_projections on $X1, X2,..., Xn$, then r **satisfies** UJ; otherwise r **violates** UJ. *Note:* The U_equality comparison, the U_join, and the U_projections mentioned in this definition must all be with respect to ACL (i.e., they must all have a prefix of the form "USING (ACL):"). Also, the term *U_join* here must be understood as referring to the n-adic version of that operator, since the U_JD has n components.

Definition: Let relvar R have heading H and let UJ be a U_JD with respect to H. Then UJ **holds** in relvar R if and only if every relation that can validly be assigned to relvar R satisfies UJ. The U_JDs that hold in R are **the U_JDs of R**.

By way of example, the following U_JD clearly holds in relvar SSSC_DURING:

```
USING ( DURING ) :
        ✿ { S_DURING , S_NAME_DURING , S_STATUS_DURING , S_CITY_DURING }
```

Explanation: Here, just for the moment, we're using the names S_DURING, etc., to refer to the corresponding U_projections, thus:

```
S_DURING
     def  USING ( DURING ) : SSSC_DURING { SNO , DURING }

S_NAME_DURING
     def  USING ( DURING ) : SSSC_DURING { SNO , SNAME , DURING }

S_STATUS_DURING
     def  USING ( DURING ) : SSSC_DURING { SNO , STATUS , DURING }

S_CITY_DURING
     def  USING ( DURING ) : SSSC_DURING { SNO , CITY , DURING }
```

What's more, of course, since the foregoing U_JD does hold, it follows that the decomposition of SSSC_DURING into these four U_projections is nonloss. So our recommended vertical decomposition is certainly safe—and, of course, it enjoys certain advantages (as we saw in the previous section), which is precisely why it's recommended.

> *Aside:* In fact, the S_DURING component in the foregoing U_JD could be dropped without loss—i.e., the resulting U_JD would still hold in SSSC_DURING—because that component is equal to the U_projection on SNO and DURING of each of the other three components (where the U_projections are, of course, each with respect to DURING).[10] It follows that we could if we liked decompose the relvar into just three projections instead of four. However, for reasons explained earlier (see the note at the very end of the section "During Relvars Only"), we prefer to keep the S_DURING projection, even though it's redundant in the foregoing sense. What's more, we'll be recommending later that we switch from the "during relvars only" design to one involving a mixture of both since and during relvars, and then S_DURING will no longer be redundant anyway[11]—at least, not in the same sense. See Chapter 14 for further explanation of this point. *End of aside*.

Note, by the way, that classical join dependencies are a special case of the generalized version (i.e., U_join dependencies) as defined above, and so we can legitimately use the same term *join dependency* to refer to both. To be specific, a classical JD is basically just that special case of a U_JD in which the USING specification mentions no attributes at all (and we'll allow that specification and colon separator to be omitted in that case). Thus, we no longer need to talk explicitly about U_JDs, as such, at all (and we no longer will, except occasionally for emphasis). Please note carefully, therefore, that throughout the rest of this chapter we'll take all references

---

[10] We made the same point earlier, in footnote 6. Note that we can say "equal" here, rather than "U_equal," because we're assuming that relvar S_DURING is kept packed on DURING. See Chapter 13 for further discussion.

[11] We touched on this point also in footnote 6.

to JDs to refer to the generalized version as described above, unless the context demands otherwise. For clarity, however, we'll occasionally make use of the explicit qualifiers *regular* (or *classical*) and *generalized*, as applicable, and we'll sometimes use the explicit U_ qualifier for the same reason.

Given all of the above, we can now define a new ("sixth") normal form:[12]

Definition: Relvar *R* is in **sixth normal form** (6NF) if and only if every JD of *R* is trivial—where a JD is **trivial** if and only if one of its components is equal to the pertinent heading in its entirety.

Note that it's immediate from the definition of "implied by keys" that a JD is certainly—in fact, trivially—implied by the pertinent keys if the JD in question is trivial. As a consequence, it's immediate from the definition of sixth normal form that every 6NF relvar is also in 5NF. (It's also immediate that a relvar is in 6NF if and only if it's *irreducible*, in the sense of that term explained earlier.) And since regular projection is a special case of U_projection and regular join is a special case of U_join, it really does make sense to think of 6NF as another level of normalization, over and above 5NF. (Indeed, it makes sense, in a way, to think of 6NF as a "tighter" version of projection/join normal form.) And that's why the name "sixth normal form" is appropriate.

Observe now that relvar SSSC_DURING isn't in 6NF, because as we saw earlier the following JD (actually a U_JD) holds—

```
USING ( DURING ) :
           ✪ { S_DURING , S_NAME_DURING , S_STATUS_DURING , S_CITY_DURING }
```

—and this JD is certainly nontrivial. However, the relvar is in 5NF, since the only JDs that hold (including the one just shown in particular) are implied by the sole key {SNO,DURING}.[13]

Aside: As noted (in effect) in an earlier aside, the nontrivial U_JD USING (DURING) : ✪{SND,STD,SCD}—where SND is an abbreviation for S_NAME_DURING, and similarly for STD and SCD—also holds in SSSC_DURING. In fact, the *classical* (also nontrivial) JD ✪{SND,STD,SCD} holds as well! That's because (a) the sole key is {SNO,DURING}; (b) as explained in Chapter 3, therefore, every attribute of the relvar is functionally dependent on {SNO,DURING}; hence, (c) the relvar can be nonloss decomposed into its (regular) projections on {SNO,SNAME,DURING}, {SNO,STATUS,DURING}, and {SNO,CITY,DURING}. Note, however, that while {SNO,DURING} would be a key for each of those projections, it wouldn't be a "U_key" (see Chapter 13.) *End of aside.*

---

[12] Sixth normal form was first defined, by the present authors, in this book's predecessor [53].

[13] The membership algorithm, defined earlier for testing whether a regular JD is implied by keys, applies to U_JDs as well.

Finally—as you must surely have been expecting—we propose that, as a general rule, a temporal relvar like SSSC_DURING that's not in 6NF should be nonloss decomposed into U_projections that are. (In our example, of course, the projection relvars S_DURING, S_NAME_DURING, S_STATUS_DURING, and S_CITY_DURING are all indeed in 6NF, as you can easily confirm for yourself.)

"THE MOVING POINT *NOW*"

Throughout our discussions prior to this point, we've assumed, reasonably enough, that history as conventionally understood starts at "the beginning of time" and continues up until the present time. In particular, we've assumed that time intervals in during relvars can stretch from any point b to any point e, where $b \leq e$ and $e \leq$ the present time.[14] However, we've also assumed that that present time is represented as some explicit value (which we've taken to be *d10*—day 10—whenever we needed to show concrete examples), and that assumption isn't reasonable at all. In particular, it suggests that whenever time marches on, so to speak, the database must be updated accordingly; in the case at hand, for example, it suggests that at midnight on day 10 every "present time" appearance of *d10* must somehow be replaced by an appearance of *d11*, instantaneously (because those appearances of *d10* didn't really mean day 10 per se, they really meant *until further notice*). A different example, involving intervals of finer granularity, might require such updates to be performed as often as every millisecond!

> *Aside:* Actually it should be obvious that using an explicit value such as *d10* to stand for *until further notice* makes no sense, because it's ambiguous. That is, there's no way to tell, in general, whether a given appearance of that value really means what it says or whether it's supposed to be understood as *until further notice*. *End of aside*.

Considerations such as the foregoing have led some writers—see, e.g., reference [19]—to propose the use of a special marker, which we'll call NOW, to denote what in Chapter 4 we called "the moving point *now*" (in other words, to stand for *until further notice*). The basic idea is to permit that special marker to appear wherever both (a) a value of the applicable point type is permitted and (b) the desired interpretation is indeed *until further notice*. Under that scheme, for example, relvar S_DURING might contain a tuple for supplier S1 with a DURING value of [*d04*:NOW] instead of [*d04*:*d10*]. (Of course, we're assuming here that the appearance of *d10* in the original interval [*d04*:*d10*] was indeed supposed to represent "the moving point *now*"—i.e., to denote *until further notice*—and not to refer to day 10 as such.)

---

[14] In other words, we've assumed that those during relvars don't contain any explicit information regarding the future (i.e., no DURING interval [*b*:*e*] is such that either *b* or *e* is in the future). Please note carefully that this assumption is *not* valid in general; we make it here only because (a) it simplifies the subsequent discussion and (b) more important, because it's safe to do so (i.e., it doesn't invalidate or materially affect in any way the conclusions to be drawn from that discussion).

Others, however (the present writers included), regard the introduction of that NOW marker as an incautious departure from sound relational principles. In particular, noting that NOW is really a variable, we observe that the approach involves the very strange—we would say logically indefensible—notion of values (interval values, in the case at hand) containing variables. In fact, the NOW construct bears some resemblance to the "null" construct of SQL, inasmuch as nulls too lead to the notion of values containing something that's not a value. The present writers among many others have long argued that nulls are and always were a huge mistake (see, e.g., references [24] and [34], also reference [90]), and we certainly don't want to repeat a mistake of such magnitude if we can help it.

By the way, note that if the DURING value in (let's assume) the unique tuple for supplier S1 in relvar S_DURING really is [*d04*:NOW], then the result of the query "When does supplier S1's contract terminate?" must be *until further notice* (i.e., "NOW"), not whatever the date happens to be today. For if the system actually evaluates that NOW at the time the query is executed and responds with (say) the value *d10*, then that response is clearly incorrect, since supplier S1's contract has in fact not yet terminated. Furthermore, if the result is indeed NOW, then that NOW must be interpreted as meaning "some indefinite point in the future," an interpretation that doesn't fit well with most people's intuitive understanding of the word *now*. What's more, if the query is issued from within some application program, then that NOW will have to be returned to some program variable—so what exactly will the value of that variable be after that NOW has been assigned to it? And what data type would that variable have to have?

Here are some further examples of the kinds of questions, arising from the notion of NOW, that you might care to ponder:

- (*The creeping delete problem.*) Let *i* be the interval [NOW:*d14*], let *t* be a tuple containing *i*, and let today be day 10. Then tuple *t* can be thought of as a kind of shorthand for five separate tuples, containing the unit intervals [*d10*:*d10*], [*d11*:*d11*], [*d12*:*d12*], [*d13*:*d13*], and [*d14*:*d14*], respectively. But when the clock reaches midnight on day 10, the first of these tuples is (in effect) automatically deleted! Likewise for day 11, day 12, and day 13 ... and what exactly happens at midnight on day 14?

- What's the result of the comparison *d10* = NOW? *Note:* Some might suggest that the result should be *unknown* ("the third truth value")—a suggestion that takes us straight back into the nulls mess, of course, a possibility we reject outright.

- What do the expressions "NOW+1" and "NOW−1" return?

- If *i1* and *i2* are the intervals [*d01*:NOW] and [*d06*:*d07*], respectively, do they meet, or overlap? Can we form their union?

- What's the result of unpacking a relation containing a tuple in which the interval attribute on which the unpacking is to be done has the value [*d04*:NOW]? In particular, does the result contain a tuple in which that attribute has the value [NOW:NOW]?

- What's the effect of assigning the interval [*d01*:NOW] to the variable I1? And then (perhaps the next day) assigning it to another variable I2? And then performing an "=" comparison on I1 and I2?

- What's the cardinality of the set {[*d01*:NOW],[*d01*:*d04*]}?

And so on (the list is far from exhaustive). We believe it's impossible to give coherent answers to questions like these; clearly, we would prefer an approach that doesn't rely on any such suspect notions as the NOW marker and values containing variables.

But, of course, if we limit ourselves to a design consisting of during relvars only, then we must put *something* in the database to represent *until further notice* when *until further notice* is really what we mean. Once again, consider the case of a supplier whose contract hasn't yet terminated. As explained in the section "Since Relvars Only," such a supplier can be regarded as having a contract that currently extends all the way into the future, right up to the very last day. Clearly, therefore, we can explicitly specify the END (DURING) value for such a supplier as the last day, and then replace that artificial value by the true value when the true value later becomes known.[15] (Of course, we're assuming here that we don't currently know when the contract will terminate. If we do know, there's no problem.) But note that this approach does mean that if "the last day" appears in the result of a query, then the user will—probably, but not necessarily (?)—have to interpret that value to mean *until further notice,* not the last day per se.

To conclude this section, we'd like to stress that the previous paragraph merely describes one possible approach to the problem of "the moving point *now*." Describing is not the same as recommending! In general, we feel it's a bad idea to record information in the database that's known to be incorrect—and, of course, an explicit statement to the effect that some contract won't terminate until "the end of time" is certainly incorrect (or, at least, so one would normally assume). In fact, recording information in the database that's known to be incorrect could be regarded as a violation of another fundamental principle: namely, the principle that tuples in the database are supposed to represent propositions we believe to be true. Don't tell lies! As already indicated, however, if our design consists of during relvars only, we might be forced to tell this particular lie on occasion—a fact that in itself might be seen as a good reason to opt for the combination design to be discussed in the section immediately following.

---

[15] So here—to spell out the obvious—we're dropping our assumption that no DURING interval [*b*:*e*] is such that either *b* or *e* is in the future.

BOTH SINCE AND DURING RELVARS

So far in this chapter, we've described two possible design approaches, one based on since relvars only and one based on during relvars only. And we've seen that both of those approaches have problems. To be specific, the first has the problem that it doesn't let us keep proper historical records, and the second has the problem that it forces us to deal with "the moving point *now*" in an unpleasantly ad hoc way. So why not combine the two approaches to get the best of both? In this section, we explore this possibility.

We begin with the observation that there's an obvious logical difference between historical and current information. To be specific, for historical information, the begin and end times are both known; for current information, by contrast, the begin time is known but the end time isn't. (Actually these claims are both somewhat oversimplified, but we'll stay with them for the time being.) And this difference suggests rather strongly that there should be two different sets of relvars, one for the current state of affairs and one for the history. (After all, there are certainly two different sets of predicates.) Here in outline is what the design for our running example will look like if we adopt this approach (remember that we're still considering suppliers only and ignoring shipments):

```
S_SINCE  { SNO ,     SNO_SINCE ,
           SNAME ,   SNAME_SINCE ,
           STATUS ,  STATUS_SINCE ,
           CITY ,    CITY_SINCE }
         KEY { SNO }

S_DURING { SNO , DURING }
         KEY { SNO , DURING }

S_NAME_DURING { SNO , SNAME , DURING }
         KEY { SNO , DURING }

S_STATUS_DURING { SNO , STATUS , DURING }
         KEY { SNO , DURING }

S_CITY_DURING { SNO , CITY , DURING }
         KEY { SNO, DURING }
```

To elaborate briefly:

■ Relvar S_SINCE is the sole since relvar. It's exactly the same as relvar SSSC_SINCE (the revised version with four "since" attributes as discussed in the section "Since Relvars Only" earlier in the chapter), except that we've abbreviated the name. *Note:* Don't confuse this new S_SINCE relvar with the relvar of the same name from Chapter 5. Also, note that this new S_SINCE relvar is in 5NF but not 6NF.

■ The relvars with DURING in their name are the during relvars, of course, and they're as discussed in the section "During Relvars Only" earlier in the chapter, except for one crucial difference: They quite definitely do *not* contain any tuples with artificial end times, to be interpreted as *until further notice* (thus, they don't violate the principle that tuples in the database are supposed to represent propositions we believe to be true). Rather, all information that would previously have been represented by such tuples is now represented by tuples in relvar S_SINCE instead.

This suggested division of temporal data into "since" and "during" pieces is the horizontal decomposition process first mentioned in the section "The Running Example" near the beginning of the chapter.[16] As you can see, that process isn't nearly as cut and dried—it's not as formal—as the vertical decomposition process discussed in earlier sections; in terms of our running example, however, you can think of it as working as follows. Suppose we start with the original fully temporal relvar SSSC_DURING from the section "The Running Example," which we assume does, in general, contain information about the current state of affairs (and the future) as well as information about the past. Then:

- First, we introduce a "since" relvar S_SINCE with an attribute for every attribute of SSSC_DURING other than the DURING attribute itself.

- Second, we associate with each attribute of S_SINCE as just defined a corresponding "since" attribute.

- Third, relvar SSSC_DURING is now to be understood as a pure "during" relvar (it won't contain tuples with artifical end times), and we can now go on to decompose that relvar vertically into 6NF projections as discussed earlier in the chapter.

Now we return briefly to those two claims, regarding the difference between historical and current information, that we said earlier in this section were slightly oversimplified. The first was that for historical information the begin and end times are both known. Sometimes, however, we don't know the end time, or possibly even the begin time, for such information; for example, we might know supplier S1 was once under contract, but not exactly when. Of course, such a state of affairs is basically just a specific example of the general (and generally vexing) problem of missing information. This isn't the place to get into a detailed discussion of that general problem;[17] instead, we content ourselves with invoking Wittgenstein's famous dictum *Wovon man nicht reden kann, darüber muss man schweigen* ("Whereof one cannot speak, thereon one must remain silent"), which we interpret to mean, in the context at hand, that another

---

[16] Horizontal decomposition is also discussed (under the name "temporal partitioning") in reference [108]. The concept seems to have originated in reference [5], and an extensive discussion appears in reference [1]. However, the primary emphasis in all of those references seems to be on physical storage issues rather than issues of logical design—for example, the title of reference [1] is "Partitioned *Storage* Structures for Temporal Databases" (emphasis added). *Note:* The literature sometimes refers to since and during information as "the current database" and "the temporal pool," respectively.

[17] A relational approach to that problem—i.e., one that (unlike SQL's nulls scheme) doesn't violate relational principles—is described in reference [27].

good general principle is that it's a bad idea to state explicitly in the database that there's something you don't know. Record only what you know!

Our second claim was that for current information the begin time is known but the end time isn't. But sometimes we do know the end time after all, even for current information—see, e.g., the VACATION example mentioned briefly in the section "During Relvars Only." In such a case, we can adopt the approach described in that section and keep during relvars only, discarding the since relvars entirely.

Considerations such as the foregoing show that the question of which design approach is best in any given situation will depend on circumstances. The combination scheme, involving both since and during relvars, is surely the most general, and is our preferred approach overall. But it's unfortunately true that the combination scheme does have the potential to complicate constraints, queries, and updates somewhat, possibly quite considerably—essentially because it'll often be the case that those constraints, queries, and updates have to span both since and during relvars. In the next four chapters, we'll explain some of those complications and offer some suggestions as to how the difficulties might be alleviated in practice.

CONCLUDING REMARKS

This chapter has been concerned rather more than most of its predecessors with temporal data specifically. The principal reason for this state of affairs is that "the moving point *now*" is a concept that applies to temporal data specifically (other kinds of data for which the concepts of previous chapters apply—the interval concept in particular—typically have nothing analogous). And it's that concept of "the moving point *now*" that led us, eventually, to our preferred approach to design as described in the previous section. To review that approach very briefly:

- We suggest that horizontal decomposition be used to separate "current" and "historical" information. Note, incidentally, that this separation is essentially the separation already found in many installations today between operational data and the data warehouse.

- We suggest that since relvars be normalized in accordance with classical normalization theory to 5NF.[18] We observe, however, that such a relvar will typically require several "since" attributes, and we've found it necessary to give a very careful interpretation for such attributes.

- We suggest that vertical decomposition be used to break during relvars down into irreducible (6NF) components.

  A couple of further points:

---

[18] Or at least ETNF.

■ All of our examples of during relvars in this chapter have involved keys that in turn involved an interval attribute. For example, the sole key for relvar S_DURING is the combination {SNO,DURING}. (That relvar happens to be all key.) But suppose suppliers never get a second chance—in other words, suppose that once a supplier's contract terminates, that supplier is never placed under contract again. Then the sole key for S_DURING would be just {SNO}, with no interval component.

■ All of our examples of during relvars have also involved at least one attribute that's *not* interval valued. But of course it's possible for a relvar to consist of, and hence to have a key that consists of, interval attributes only. As a simple example, consider a relvar BLACKOUTS with a single attribute that shows intervals during which a certain airline's frequent flyer program doesn't allow award travel.

We close this section, and this chapter, with (as promised) a brief word concerning shipments. Without going into too much detail, it should be fairly obvious that our preferred design for shipments will involve one since relvar and one during relvar, thus:

```
SP_SINCE { SNO , PNO , SINCE }
   KEY { SNO , PNO }
   FOREIGN KEY { SNO } REFERENCES S_SINCE

SP_DURING { SNO , PNO , DURING }
   KEY { SNO , PNO , DURING }
```

These relvars are already both in 6NF, and so horizontal decomposition does apply as shown, but vertical decomposition doesn't. Also, note the foreign key from SP_SINCE to S_SINCE, which reflects the fact that any supplier able to supply some part at some time must be under contract at that time. However, perhaps you can see that this constraint, though certainly necessary, is very far from being sufficient! Indeed, we'll have a lot more to say about such matters in the next two chapters.

EXERCISES

12.1 We saw in the body of the chapter that the root problem with each of the relvars SSSC_SINCE and SSSC_DURING as originally defined was that their predicates really consisted of four distinct predicates that were ANDed together. But isn't the same true of the nontemporal suppliers relvar S from Chapter 1?

12.2 Define sixth normal form (6NF). When is 6NF recommended?

12.3 We recommended in the body of the chapter that "historical" (i.e., during) relvars, at least, should usually be in 6NF. But what would it mean for a *nontemporal* relvar to be in 6NF?

12.4 Explain in your own words the horizontal and vertical decompositions described in the body of the chapter.

12.5 "Current" (i.e., since) relvars can represent information about the past and future as well as the present. Explain this remark.

12.6 "The moving point *now*" is not a value but a variable. Discuss.

12.7 Give a realistic example of a relvar consisting of interval attributes only.

12.8 Consider the following revised version of the courses-and-students database from earlier chapters (see, e.g., Exercise 6.10 in Chapter 6):

```
VAR SINCE_COURSE BASE RELATION
  { COURSENO   COURSENO ,
    CNAME      NAME ,
    AVAILABLE DATE }
  KEY { COURSENO } ;

VAR OLD_COURSE BASE RELATION
  { COURSENO          COURSENO ,
    CNAME             NAME ,
    AVAILABLE_DURING INTERVAL_DATE }
  KEY { COURSENO } ;

VAR SINCE_STUDENT BASE RELATION
  { STUDENTNO   STUDENTNO ,
    SNAME       NAME ,
    REGISTERED DATE }
  KEY { STUDENTNO } ;

VAR STUDENT_HISTORY BASE RELATION
  { STUDENTNO   STUDENTNO ,
    SNAME       NAME ,
    REG_DURING INTERVAL_DATE }
  KEY { STUDENTNO , REG_DURING } ;

VAR ENROLLMENT BASE RELATION
  { COURSENO   COURSENO ,
    STUDENTNO STUDENTNO ,
    ENROLLED   DATE }
  KEY { COURSENO , STUDENTNO }
  FOREIGN KEY { COURSENO } REFERENCES SINCE_COURSE
  FOREIGN KEY { STUDENTNO } REFERENCES SINCE_STUDENT ;
```

```
VAR COMPLETED_COURSE BASE RELATION
  { COURSENO        COURSENO ,
    STUDENTNO       STUDENTNO ,
    STUDIED_DURING  INTERVAL_DATE ,
    GRADE           GRADE }
  KEY { COURSENO , STUDENTNO } ;
```

The predicates are as follows:[19]

■ SINCE_COURSE: *Course COURSENO, named CNAME, has been available since date AVAILABLE.*

■ OLD_COURSE: *Course COURSENO, named CNAME, was available throughout interval AVAILABLE_DURING.*

■ SINCE_STUDENT: *Since student STUDENTNO, named SNAME, registered with the university on date REGISTERED.*

■ STUDENT_HISTORY: *Student STUDENTNO, named SNAME, was registered with the university throughout interval REG_DURING.*

■ ENROLLMENT: *Student STUDENTNO enrolled on course COURSENO on date ENROLLED.*

■ COMPLETED_COURSE: *Student STUDENTNO attended course COURSENO throughout interval STUDIED_DURING, achieving grade GRADE.*

No course number appears in both SINCE_COURSE and OLD_COURSE.

a. For each relvar, state whether or not it's in 6NF. If it isn't, identify any problems that might be solved by decomposing it accordingly.

b. Write a query to obtain a relation showing, for each student, the number of courses completed during each registration interval for that student.

c. Assume that for each course there are zero or more offerings, each taking place over a given interval of time. Distinct offerings of the same course can take place "back to back" or even at the same time, either partly or completely. Some offerings have already taken place; others are currently under way (but have a scheduled completion date); others are scheduled to start at some future time (but, again, have a scheduled completion date). When students enroll on a course, they must specify which offering they're enrolling for.

---

[19] In somewhat simplified form. Note in particular that all intervals involved should be understood to be maximal.

Each offering has a quota, and the number of students enrolled on that offering mustn't exceed that quota. Write the predicate and an appropriate relvar definition for a relvar COURSE_OFFERING to reflect these requirements.

d. Write a query to get STUDENTNO-DURING pairs for students who have completed at least one course, where DURING designates a maximal interval during which the specified student was attending at least one course.

ANSWERS

12.1 Yes, it does, and it's precisely for that kind of reason that (as noted in the body of the chapter) some writers have argued that even nontemporal relvars should be decomposed all the way down to irreducible components. Certainly such a decomposition is logically cleaner, in a sense. On the other hand, nontemporal relvars (and even temporal relvars, so long as they're "current" and not "historical") that are in 5NF but not 6NF don't seem to give rise to the same kinds of—or, at any rate, as many—practical problems as non6NF during relvars do, which is why we advocate the position we do: namely, 6NF for during relvars, 5NF for everything else.

12.2 Relvar *R* is in 6NF if and only if no JDs hold in *R* apart from trivial ones. Decomposition to 6NF is generally recommended if all four of the following conditions hold for *R* (which in practice they usually will, if *R* is a during relvar that isn't in 6NF already):

■ *R* has a key *K* and at least two additional attributes.

■ Those additional attributes don't include a key of *R*.

■ *K* contains an interval attribute *A*.

■ We want *R* to be kept packed on *A* (see Chapter 13).

12.3 Such a relvar is subject to no JDs at all apart from trivial ones (see the answer to the previous exercise)—but here "JDs" must be understood as purely classical ones, not the generalized U_JDs defined in the body of this chapter. Such a relvar is irreducible, in the sense that it can't be nonloss decomposed at all, other than trivially. *Note:* It's easy to see that such a relvar *R* is in 6NF if and only if it's in 5NF, is of degree *n*, and has no key of degree less than *n*-1. Observe, therefore, that:

a. Despite what we said in the body of the chapter regarding 5NF, it's really 6NF, in a sense, that's the ultimate normal form with respect to normalization as usually understood.

b. As noted in the body of the chapter, every 6NF relvar is in 5NF.

12.4 First let's consider relations, not relvars. In general, decomposition of a relation *r* is the act of deriving, from *r* and *r* alone, a collection of *n* relations *r1, r2, …, rn* such that *r1, r2, …, rn* together represent exactly the same information as *r* does (so the decomposition is *nonloss*).[20] Every relation can be "nonloss decomposed";[21] however, trivial cases where some *ri* isn't needed in the process of reconstructing *r* from *r1, r2, …, rn*—including in particular cases where some *ri* is equal to *r*—are normally not considered.

Decomposition is also usefully, and in the design context more importantly, applicable to relvars. If it's the case that, at all times, the relation assigned to relvar *R* can be nonloss decomposed in a nontrivial way, then *R* can be discarded in favor of the relvars *R1, R2, …, Rn* that correspond to the decomposition in question. Moreover:

■ If each of *R1, R2, …, Rn* has the same heading as *R* itself, then the decomposition is horizontal. In this case, the operation to derive *R1, R2, …, Rn* from *R* might be restriction, in which case the recomposition operator is union.[22] *Note:* A special form of horizontal decomposition is recommended in the temporal context, to separate "since" and "during" information. In this variation, the heading of the since relvar *SR* isn't exactly the same as the heading of the relvar *R* that's to be decomposed. To be specific, the interval valued "during" attribute of *R* is replaced in *SR* by a point valued "since" attribute, where the declared type of that "since" attribute is the point type of the interval type of the corresponding "during" attribute.[23]

■ If *R1, R2, …, Rn* all have different headings (whose union is necessarily the heading of *R*), then the decomposition is vertical. In this case, the operation to derive *R1, R2, …, Rn* from *R* is projection and the recomposition operation is join—where, in the temporal context, the terms *projection* and *join* refer to the generalized versions of those operators as

_____

[20] Be aware, however, that the term *nonloss decomposition* is usually taken to refer, informally, to vertical decomposition specifically.

[21] For some relations, however, the only possible decompositions might be trivial ones. Note in particular that *every* relation can be "nonloss decomposed," trivially, into just its identity projection.

[22] If the restriction conditions for deriving *R1, R2, …, Rn* from *R* ensure that *R1, R2, …, Rn* are pairwise disjoint, then recording the same information more than once is (desirably) avoided, and the recomposition operation becomes disjoint union.

[23] If distinct since relvars are produced for the same entity type by such a process, they can be replaced by an appropriate join.

defined in Chapter 11. *Note:* If, in every nonloss vertical decomposition of R, at least one of R1, R2, …, Rn is guaranteed always to be equal to R, then R is said to be *irreducible*.

12.5 Perhaps the best way to explain how since relvars can represent past and future information is by means of examples:

■   Past information might be represented by an attribute whose value represents the time at which a certain event took place. If it can be assumed that a certain consequential state of affairs has existed ever since that date, then present information and further past information are both implicitly represented by that same attribute. If it can be further assumed that that state of affairs will continue to exist until some date in the future, then future information is also implicitly represented. For example, an employee's date of hire indicates that the employee in question has been on the company's payroll ever since that date. If *d* is some date between the date of hire and the end of time inclusive, then the past, present, or future information that the employee was, is, or will be on the payroll on day *d* is *implicitly* represented. By contrast, the information that the employee was on the payroll on the actual date of hiring is *explicitly* represented.

■   Future information might be explicitly represented by something like a planned retirement date, representing information that on that day (explicitly) and every day after that date (implicitly) the employee will no longer be on the company's payroll.

In all cases, the since relvar in question represents our *current beliefs about* the past, present, or future (see Chapter 17 for further discussion of this point).

12.6 "The moving point *now*" is a variable precisely because it "moves"—it doesn't represent the same value at all times. If some object *x* denotes different values at different times, then that object *x* is a variable by definition. Because *now* is a variable, it's a solecism to entertain any notion of a relation (which is a value, by definition) containing it.

12.7 Here's an example of such a relvar with three interval attributes:

```
VAR RECOMMENDED_WEIGHTS BASE RELATION { HEIGHTS  INTERVAL_HEIGHT ,
                                        AGES     INTERVAL_AGE ,
                                        WEIGHTS  INTERVAL_WEIGHT }
                   KEY { HEIGHTS , AGES } ;
```

The intended interpretation is: *HEIGHTS denotes a maximal range of heights, and AGES denotes a maximal range of ages within that range of heights, such that for people whose height is in that range of heights and whose age is in that range of ages, WEIGHTS denotes the maximal range of recommended weights. Note:* We're assuming here that the relvar is kept packed on AGES within HEIGHTS. See Chapter 13 for further explanation.

12.8

a. Relvar ENROLLMENT is in 6NF, but none of the others is, and that fact can certainly lead to problems. By way of example, consider relvar STUDENT_HISTORY. It should be clear that the timestamp REG_DURING in that relvar does indeed "timestamp too much," and hence that it would be better to replace the relvar by two 6NF relvars, one showing who was registered when and one showing who had what name when. (If that were done, it might also be a good idea to add a NAME_SINCE attribute to SINCE_STUDENT, analogous to the STATUS_SINCE attribute of relvar S_SINCE.) The situation with each of the other four relvars (SINCE_COURSE, OLD_COURSE, SINCE_STUDENT, and COMPLETED_COURSE) is analogous.

b.
```
WITH ( t1 := EXTEND SINCE_STUDENT :
                    { REG_DURING :=
                        INTERVAL_DATE ( [ REGISTERED : LAST_DATE ( ) ] ) }
                                            { ALL BUT REGISTERED } ,
       t2 := t1 UNION STUDENT_HISTORY ,
       t3 := t2 JOIN COMPLETED_COURSE ,
       t4 := t3 WHERE END ( STUDIED_DURING ) ∈ REG_DURING ) :
EXTEND t4 { STUDENTNO, REG_DURING } :
                        { NUMBER_OF_COURSES_COMPLETED := COUNT ( !!t4 ) }
```

c. Predicate: *Offering* OFFERINGNO *of course* COURSENO *ran or is scheduled to run from the begin point of* DURING *to the end point of* DURING, *inclusive, and was or is restricted to* QUOTA *students.*

   Relvar definition:

```
VAR COURSE_OFFERING BASE RELATION
  { COURSENO        COURSENO ,
    OFFERINGNO      INTEGER ,
    QUOTA           INTEGER ,
    OFFERED_DURING INTERVAL_DATE }
  KEY { COURSENO , OFFERINGNO } ;
```

d.
```
( USING ( STUDIED_DURING ) :
    COMPLETED_COURSE { STUDENTNO , STUDIED_DURING } )
                            RENAME { STUDIED_DURING AS DURING }
```

Chapter 13

Database Design

II : Keys and Related Constraints

Two men say they're Jesus—one of them must be wrong.

—Dire Straits:
"Industrial Disease" (1982)

In this chapter and the next, we turn our attention to the question of the constraints that might apply to temporal data. The present chapter considers key (or "key like") constraints in particular, and Chapter 14 then addresses temporal constraints in general. Now, in Chapter 5, we saw how difficult it was, in the absence of proper interval support, even to formulate such constraints correctly; in these two chapters, we'll see how the concepts introduced in Chapters 6-11 can help to alleviate the problem, somewhat. As we'll also see, however, the solutions aren't always as straightforward as they might be. This topic is surprisingly tricky!

SIMPLIFYING THE RUNNING EXAMPLE

We assume for the purposes of this chapter that the database has been designed in accordance with the recommendations of the section "Both Since and During Relvars" in Chapter 12, and our database therefore consists of the following seven relvars:

```
S_SINCE              SP_SINCE
S_DURING             SP_DURING
S_NAME_DURING
S_STATUS_DURING
S_CITY_DURING
```

(We leave discussion of designs involving since relvars only or during relvars only to the next chapter.) With respect to the foregoing "combination" design, however, it should be clear that:

■ The attribute pairs {SNAME,SNAME_SINCE}, {STATUS,STATUS_SINCE}, and {CITY,CITY_SINCE} within the since relvar S_SINCE will all exhibit similar behavior.

■ Likewise, the during relvars S_NAME_DURING, S_STATUS_DURING, and S_CITY_DURING will also all exhibit similar behavior.

Without loss of generality, therefore, (a) we can ignore the attribute pairs {SNAME,SNAME_SINCE} and {CITY,CITY_SINCE} in relvar S_SINCE, and (b) we can ignore relvars S_NAME_DURING and S_CITY_DURING in their entirety. For the purposes of this chapter, therefore, and indeed—*please note*—for the remainder of this book (barring explicit statements to the contrary, of course), we can simplify the database still further. In other words, we can take the database to be as defined, in outline, in Fig. 13.1 below ("in outline" meaning here among other things that all constraints other than conventional KEY and FOREIGN KEY constraints have been omitted, because of course we're not yet in a position to say what those additional constraints should look like).

```
S_SINCE { SNO , SNO_SINCE , STATUS , STATUS_SINCE }
         KEY { SNO }

SP_SINCE { SNO , PNO , SINCE }
         KEY { SNO , PNO }
         FOREIGN KEY { SNO } REFERENCES S_SINCE

S_DURING { SNO , DURING }
         KEY { SNO , DURING }

S_STATUS_DURING { SNO , STATUS , DURING }
         KEY { SNO , DURING }

SP_DURING { SNO , PNO , DURING }
         KEY { SNO , PNO , DURING }
```

Fig. 13.1: Simplified database design (outline)

Here for purposes of subsequent reference are informal statements of the predicates for this simplified design. First the since relvars:

■ S_SINCE: *Supplier SNO has been under contract since SNO_SINCE and has had status STATUS since STATUS_SINCE.*

■ SP_SINCE: *Supplier SNO has been able to supply part PNO since SINCE.*

Now the during relvars:

■ S_DURING: *DURING denotes a maximal interval throughout which supplier SNO was under contract.*

■ S_STATUS_DURING: *DURING denotes a maximal interval throughout which supplier SNO had status STATUS.*

■ SP_DURING: *DURING denotes a maximal interval throughout which supplier SNO was able to supply part PNO.*

Figs. 13.2 and 13.3—which repay *very* careful study—show some sample values for these relvars.

S_SINCE

SNO	SNO_SINCE	STATUS	STATUS_SINCE
S1	*d04*	20	*d06*
S2	*d07*	10	*d07*
S3	*d03*	30	*d03*
S4	*d04*	20	*d08*
S5	*d02*	30	*d02*

SP_SINCE

SNO	PNO	SINCE
S1	P1	*d04*
S1	P2	*d05*
S1	P3	*d09*
S1	P4	*d05*
S1	P5	*d04*
S1	P6	*d06*
S2	P1	*d08*
S2	P2	*d09*
S3	P2	*d08*
S4	P5	*d05*

Fig. 13.2: Relvars S_SINCE and SP_SINCE–sample values

S_DURING

SNO	DURING
S2	[*d02:d04*]
S6	[*d03:d05*]

SP_DURING

SNO	PNO	DURING
S2	P1	[*d02:d04*]
S2	P2	[*d03:d03*]
S3	P5	[*d05:d07*]
S4	P2	[*d06:d09*]
S4	P4	[*d04:d08*]
S6	P3	[*d03:d03*]
S6	P3	[*d05:d05*]

S_STATUS_DURING

SNO	STATUS	DURING
S1	15	[*d04:d05*]
S2	5	[*d02:d02*]
S2	10	[*d03:d04*]
S4	10	[*d04:d04*]
S4	25	[*d05:d07*]
S6	5	[*d03:d04*]
S6	7	[*d05:d05*]

Fig. 13.3: Relvars S_DURING, S_STATUS_DURING, and SP_DURING–sample values

Note: The specific values shown in these figures deliberately don't correspond exactly to our usual sample values as shown in Fig. 6.1 or Fig. 9.1, though they're close. Note too that little in the present chapter depends on those specific values. As already suggested, however, a careful study of the figures should help you understand the semantics of the database in general.

Keys and Foreign Keys

The keys that apply to the database of Fig. 13.1 are as indicated in that figure, and in the case of the since relvars, at least, there's not much more to say about them. By contrast, there certainly is more to say in the case of the during relvars, and those discussions form the bulk of the rest of this chapter. As for foreign keys, in fact there's only one such in our simplified database, and that's {SNO} in the current relvar SP_SINCE, which is a foreign key referencing the sole key {SNO} in the current relvar S_SINCE:

```
FOREIGN KEY { SNO } REFERENCES S_SINCE
```

This specification, which appears as part of the definition of relvar SP_SINCE, reflects the fact that if a supplier is currently able to supply some part, then that supplier must be currently under contract. (Of course, we're appealing here to the informal notion that since relvars contain "current data" only.) As pointed out in Chapter 5, however, in connection with what was there called Constraint XST1, this foreign key constraint is insufficient by itself; what we really need is something more general, in order to enforce the constraint that *whenever* a supplier is, was, or will be able to supply some part, then that supplier is, was, or will be under contract at that same time. This more general constraint isn't a foreign key constraint as such, however, and we therefore defer further discussion of it for now. We'll come back to it in the next chapter.

We now proceed to examine, in the next several sections, three general problems that might arise in connection with temporal databases like that of Fig. 13.1, in the absence of suitable constraints: namely, the *redundancy problem*, the *circumlocution problem*, and the *contradiction problem*. (We mentioned these terms in passing in Chapter 5, as you might recall.)

Note: Relvars S_SINCE and SP_SINCE aren't discussed any further in this chapter (they're shown again in Fig. 13.4, but that's all). We'll come back to them in Chapter 14.

THE REDUNDANCY PROBLEM

Consider relvar S_STATUS_DURING. Because {SNO,DURING} is a key, a **Tutorial D** definition for that relvar might look as follows:

```
VAR S_STATUS_DURING BASE RELATION
  { SNO SNO , STATUS INTEGER , DURING INTERVAL_DATE }
    KEY { SNO , DURING } ;                /* Warning: Inadequate! */
```

As the comment indicates, however, the KEY constraint here, though it *is* logically correct, is also inadequate, in a sense. To be specific, it fails to prevent the relvar from containing (for example) both of the following tuples at the same time:

SNO	STATUS	DURING
S4	25	[d05:d06]

SNO	STATUS	DURING
S4	25	[d06:d07]

As you can see, these two tuples display a certain *redundancy*, inasmuch as the status for supplier S4 on day 6 is effectively stated twice. Clearly, it would be better if we were to replace the two tuples shown by the following single tuple:

SNO	STATUS	DURING
S4	25	[d05:d07]

Observe now that if the two original tuples were the only tuples in some relation and we were to pack that relation on DURING, we would wind up with a relation containing only the tuple just shown. Loosely speaking, therefore, we might say the tuple just shown is a "packed" tuple, obtained by packing the two original tuples on DURING ("loosely speaking" because, of course, the operation of packing really applies to relations, not tuples). So what we want to do is replace those two original tuples by that "packed" tuple. Indeed, as pointed out in Chapter 5, *not* performing that replacement—i.e., permitting both original tuples to appear—would be as bad as permitting duplicate tuples to appear, in a sense. What's more, if both original tuples did appear, the relvar would be in violation of its own predicate! Consider the tuple containing the interval [d06:d07]. That tuple says among other things that supplier S4 did *not* have status 25 on the day immediately before day 6. But then the other tuple says among other things that supplier S4 *did* have status 25 on day 5, and of course day 5 is the day immediately before day 6.[1]

THE CIRCUMLOCUTION PROBLEM

The KEY constraint shown in the previous section for S_STATUS_DURING is inadequate in another way also. To be specific, it fails to prevent the relvar from containing (for example) both of the following tuples at the same time:

---

[1] As pointed out in Chapter 5, therefore, the two original tuples don't just suffer from redundancy, they actually imply a certain contradiction. In this chapter, however, when we talk of "the contradiction problem," we're using—perhaps *usurping* is the mot juste—that term to refer specifically to the kind of situation to be discussed in the section after next. *Note:* These remarks apply also to the example to be discussed in the section "The Circumlocution Problem," mutatis mutandis.

SNO	STATUS	DURING
S4	25	*[d05:d05]*

SNO	STATUS	DURING
S4	25	*[d06:d07]*

Here there's no redundancy as such, but there's a certain *circumlocution*, inasmuch as we're taking two tuples to say what could be better said with just a single "packed" tuple (the same one as before, in fact):

SNO	STATUS	DURING
S4	25	*[d05:d07]*

In fact, not replacing the two original tuples by that single "packed" tuple would mean, again, that the relvar would be in violation of its own predicate, as you can easily confirm.

PACKED ON

Now, it should be clear that in order to avoid redundancies and circumlocutions like the ones we've been discussing, what we need to do is enforce a constraint—let's call it Constraint A— along the following lines:

- **Constraint A:** If at any given time relvar S_STATUS_DURING contains two tuples that are identical except for their DURING values *i1* and *i2*, then *i1* MERGES *i2* must be false.

Recall that MERGES is basically the logical OR of OVERLAPS and MEETS. Replacing MERGES by OVERLAPS in Constraint A gives the constraint we need to enforce in order to avoid the redundancy problem; replacing it by MEETS gives the constraint we need to enforce in order to avoid the circumlocution problem.

It should be clear too that there's a very simple way to enforce Constraint A: namely, by keeping the relvar packed at all times on DURING. We therefore propose a new PACKED ON specification, with syntax PACKED ON (*ACL*)—*ACL* standing as usual for a commalist of attribute names[2]—that can appear in a relvar definition, as here:

```
VAR S_STATUS_DURING BASE RELATION
  { SNO SNO , STATUS INTEGER , DURING INTERVAL_DATE }
    PACKED ON ( DURING )                    /* Warning: Still */
    KEY { SNO , DURING } ;                  /* inadequate!    */
```

---

[2] Of course, all of the attributes mentioned must be attributes of the relvar in question and must be interval valued (and a similar remark applies to all of the other commalists of attribute names mentioned in this chapter, unless the context demands otherwise).

The PACKED ON (DURING) specification here implies that any attempt to update the relvar in such a way that the result is *not* packed on DURING must be rejected. That is, the relvar must at all times be kept packed on DURING, and hence must at all times be identical to the result of the expression PACK S_STATUS_DURING ON (DURING)—implying among other things that this latter expression can always be replaced by the much simpler one S_STATUS_DURING, an observation that could be of interest to the optimizer. This special syntax thus suffices to solve the redundancy and circumlocution problems; in other words, it solves the problems exemplified by the constraint we referred to in Chapter 5 as Constraint XFT1.[3]

Note: An argument might possibly be made for providing two separate syntactic extensions, one for solving the redundancy problem and another for solving the circumlocution problem.[4] Indeed, we'll give an example later in this chapter of a relvar, TERM, that might be cited in support of such a position. However, we've yet to see a truly *convincing* argument for such a position; for now, therefore, our preference is to kill two birds with one stone and solve both problems at once.

THE CONTRADICTION PROBLEM

We continue to focus on relvar S_STATUS_DURING specifically. Unfortunately, the PACKED ON and KEY constraints together are still not quite adequate, because they fail to prevent the relvar from containing (for example) both of the following tuples at the same time:

SNO	STATUS	DURING
S4	10	[d04:d06]

SNO	STATUS	DURING
S4	25	[d05:d07]

Here supplier S4 is shown as having a status of both 10 and 25 on days 5 and 6 —clearly an impossible state of affairs. In other words, we have a *contradiction* on our hands; in fact, the relvar is in violation of its own predicate once again, because of course (as you'll recall) any given supplier is supposed to have exactly one status on any given day.

Note: To say any given supplier is supposed to have exactly one status on any given day is to say, more formally, that if we were to unpack S_STATUS_DURING on DURING, thereby producing a result in which every DURING value consists of a unit interval, then the functional

---

[3] Well ... it solves those problems by replacing them by another: namely, the problem of ensuring that updates don't violate the PACKED ON constraint. In Chapter 16 we'll introduce some new operators that can help with this latter task. *Note:* Analogous remarks apply to the solution we'll be proposing to the contradiction problem also (see the next two sections).

[4] We remark in passing that SQL does provide syntax that addresses—we don't say *solves!*—the redundancy problem (also the contradiction problem, in fact) but not the circumlocution problem. See Part IV for further explanation.

dependency {SNO,DURING} → {STATUS} would hold in that result. (Or, rather, it's to say the specified functional dependency would *still* hold in that result—it already holds in S_STATUS_DURING as such, of course, thanks to the specification KEY {SNO,DURING} for that relvar.) We'll have more to say regarding such matters in the next section, also in the section "Neither PACKED ON nor WHEN / THEN" later in the chapter.

WHEN / THEN

It should be clear that, in order to avoid contradictions like the ones discussed in the previous section, what we need to do is enforce a constraint—let's call it Constraint B—along the following lines:

- **Constraint B:** If at any given time relvar S_STATUS_DURING contains two tuples that have the same SNO value and different STATUS values, then their DURING values *i1* and *i2* must be such that *i1* OVERLAPS *i2* is false.

Note carefully that, as we've already seen, the fact that the relvar is kept packed on DURING isn't sufficient to enforce Constraint B. Nor, of course, is the fact that {SNO,DURING} is a key. But suppose the relvar were kept *un*packed on DURING (ignore for the moment the fact that this supposition is an impossibility, given that, as just mentioned, the relvar is actually kept packed on DURING). Then:

- All DURING values in that unpacked form would be unit intervals and would thus effectively correspond to individual time points.

- The sole key for that unpacked form would still be {SNO,DURING}, because any given supplier under contract at any given time has exactly one status at that time. In other words, as noted in the previous section, the functional dependency {SNO,DURING} → {STATUS} would still hold in that unpacked form.

- Thus, if the original relvar did contain the contradictory tuples shown earlier—

SNO	STATUS	DURING
S4	10	[d04:d06]

SNO	STATUS	DURING
S4	25	[d05:d07]

—then the unpacked form would contain (among other things) these two tuples:

SNO	STATUS	DURING
S4	10	[*d05:d05*]

SNO	STATUS	DURING
S4	25	[*d05:d05*]

And these two tuples would together violate the functional dependency {SNO,DURING} → {STATUS} that's supposed to hold in the unpacked form. Equivalently, they would violate the constraint that {SNO,DURING} is supposed to be a key for that unpacked form.

It follows that if we were to enforce the constraint that {SNO,DURING} is a key for the unpacked form UNPACK S_STATUS_DURING ON (DURING), then we'd be enforcing Constraint B a fortiori. We therefore propose another new specification, WHEN / THEN, that can appear in a relvar definition and has syntax as illustrated in this example:

```
VAR S_STATUS_DURING BASE RELATION
   { SNO SNO , STATUS INTEGER , DURING INTERVAL_DATE }
      PACKED ON ( DURING )
      WHEN UNPACKED ON ( DURING ) THEN KEY { SNO , DURING }
      KEY { SNO , DURING } ;
```

The specification WHEN UNPACKED ON (DURING) THEN KEY {SNO,DURING} implies that any attempt to update the relvar in such a way that the unpacked form of the result violates the functional dependency {SNO,DURING} → {STATUS} must be rejected. This special syntax thus suffices to solve the contradiction problem. *Note:* For reasons that should become clear later, given the WHEN / THEN specification WHEN UNPACKED ON (*ACL*) THEN KEY {*BCL*}, where *ACL* and *BCL* are both commalists of attribute names, every attribute mentioned in *ACL* must also be mentioned in *BCL*.

It follows from the foregoing discussion that the WHEN / THEN, PACKED ON, and KEY specifications are together sufficient—at last—to fix all of the problems we've been discussing in this chapter so far. However, it can't be denied that those specifications do seem to be a little clumsy, or cumbersome, in combination. In particular, the specifications WHEN UNPACKED ON (DURING) THEN KEY {SNO,DURING} and KEY {SNO,DURING}, taken together, certainly look as if they might somehow be saying the same thing twice. It therefore seems worth considering the possibility of simplifying the syntax somewhat, and we will. But there are several other topics we need to get out of the way first before we can consider such a possibility in any detail. Those topics are addressed in the next four sections. So we'll come back to the syntax issue later, in the section "Keys Revisited."

COMBINING SPECIFICATIONS

We've now met three kinds of constraints that can be specified in a relvar definition: KEY constraints, PACKED ON constraints, and WHEN / THEN constraints. At first sight, therefore, there appear to be eight possible combinations that might be specified for any given relvar. But do all of those combinations make sense?

Well, we can simplify our investigation by first stipulating—until further notice, at any rate—that at least one explicit KEY constraint is always required, since we know from Chapter 3 that every relvar certainly does have at least one key. This stipulation reduces the possibilities from eight to four. Now let R be a relvar with an interval attribute. Then we already know from previous discussions that R might need both a PACKED ON and a WHEN / THEN constraint. So the possibilities we still need to examine are:

- PACKED ON without WHEN / THEN

- WHEN / THEN without PACKED ON

- Neither PACKED ON nor WHEN / THEN

These three possibilities are the subject of the next three sections.

PACKED ON WITHOUT WHEN / THEN

It should be readily apparent without the need for detailed analysis that relvar S_DURING, with its attributes SNO and DURING, is susceptible to redundancy and circumlocution problems analogous to those discussed earlier for relvar S_STATUS_DURING. However, it's *not* susceptible to a corresponding contradiction problem. Why not? *Answer*: Because it's all key— i.e., its sole key is the attribute combination {SNO,DURING}—and so it can't possibly contain two tuples that contradict each other.[5] Thus, PACKED ON (DURING) does apply, but WHEN UNPACKED ON (DURING) THEN KEY {SNO,DURING} is unnecessary. The following thus serves as an adequate definition for this relvar:

```
VAR S_DURING BASE RELATION
  { SNO SNO , DURING INTERVAL_DATE }
    PACKED ON ( DURING )
    KEY { SNO , DURING } ;
```

So a WHEN / THEN constraint isn't needed for this relvar. However, it wouldn't be wrong to specify one, as here:

```
VAR S_DURING BASE RELATION
  { SNO SNO , DURING INTERVAL_DATE }
    PACKED ON ( DURING )
    WHEN UNPACKED ON ( DURING ) THEN KEY { SNO , DURING }
    KEY { SNO , DURING } ;
```

---

[5] At least, not in the special sense in which we're using "contradict" here.

To repeat, the WHEN / THEN constraint here isn't wrong, but it might lead to some inefficiency in implementation if the system tried to enforce it too blindly. (As we'll see in the next section, however—and as in fact should be fairly obvious—if some relvar definition does specify both WHEN ... THEN KEY {*K*} and KEY {*K*}, then enforcing the specified WHEN / THEN constraint will enforce the specified KEY constraint automatically.)

Remarks analogous to the foregoing apply to relvar SP_DURING as well and effectively dispose of that case also. Thus, the following is a possible definition for that relvar:

```
VAR SP_DURING BASE RELATION
   { SNO SNO , PNO PNO , DURING INTERVAL_DATE }
     PACKED ON ( DURING )
     KEY { SNO , PNO , DURING } ;
```

From these examples, we see that if the relvar is all key, then no WHEN / THEN is required. But it doesn't follow that if no WHEN / THEN is required, then the relvar is all key! A counterexample (relvar INFLATION) is given in the section after next, and another, perhaps slightly more convincing, is given in the answer to Exercise 13.8 at the end of the chapter.

WHEN / THEN WITHOUT PACKED ON

Suppose we're given a relvar TERM representing U.S. presidential terms, with attributes DURING and PRESIDENT and sole key {DURING}. Here's a sample value (perhaps we should say rather, here's part of the value that's current at the time of writing):

DURING	PRESIDENT
[1974:1976]	Ford
[1977:1980]	Carter
[1981:1984]	Reagan
[1985:1988]	Reagan
[1993:1996]	Clinton
[1997:2000]	Clinton
[2009:2012]	Obama

Aside: This example raises a number of points that are somewhat tangential to the main topic of this chapter but are worth mentioning in passing nonetheless. Here are some of them:

■   In practice, presidential terms are usually stated in the form of overlapping intervals—Ford, 1974-1977; Carter, 1977-1981; and so on—instead of the way we've shown them above. But the reason for this state of affairs is that the granularity of those intervals as usually stated is wrong; presidential terms really stretch from one Inauguration Day (normally a day in January) to the next, and so, e.g., Ford was president for the first few days of 1977 and Carter was president for the rest of that year.

■ President last names aren't necessarily unique—think of Roosevelt, for example, or Adams—but we choose to overlook this fact for the purposes of this chapter.

■ There are quite a few additional constraints that apply to relvar TERM, over and above the key and "key like" constraints that are the primary focus of the present chapter. For example:

    a. There's exactly one president at any given time (this is an example of what in Chapter 14 we'll be calling a *denseness* constraint).

    b. Nobody is allowed to serve as president for more than two terms (at least not since 1951, when the 22nd Amendment to the U.S. Constitution was ratified).

    c. No presidential term is allowed to exceed four years.

And so on, possibly.

We leave it as an exercise for the reader to ponder the implications of such considerations. *End of aside*.

Back to the main thread of our discussion. It should be clear that PACKED ON (DURING) must *not* be specified for relvar TERM, because (with reference to the sample value shown above) such a constraint would cause the two Reagan tuples to be packed into one and the two Clinton tuples likewise. At the same time, it should be clear that a WHEN / THEN specification *is* needed, in order to avoid the possibility that the relvar might contain, e.g., both of the following tuples at the same time:

DURING	PRESIDENT
[1985:1994]	Reagan

DURING	PRESIDENT
[1993:1996]	Clinton

In other words, without such a specification—or something equivalent to such a specification, of course—relvar TERM would be susceptible to the contradiction problem. Here then is a possible relvar definition:[6]

```
VAR TERM BASE RELATION
   { DURING INTERVAL_... , PRESIDENT NAME }
     WHEN UNPACKED ON ( DURING ) THEN KEY { DURING }
     KEY { DURING } ;
```

Several further points arise in connection with this example, however. First, note that we certainly do want to avoid the possibility that the relvar might contain, e.g., both of the following tuples at the same time:

DURING	PRESIDENT
[1993:1995]	Clinton

DURING	PRESIDENT
[1994:1996]	Clinton

(an example of the redundancy problem). At the same time, we *don't* want to avoid the possibility that the relvar might contain, e.g., both of the following tuples at the same time:

DURING	PRESIDENT
[1993:1996]	Clinton

DURING	PRESIDENT
[1997:2000]	Clinton

On the face of it, therefore, it looks as if TERM is an example of a relvar for which we might want to avoid the redundancy problem but not the circumlocution problem (a possibility touched on, briefly, earlier in the chapter).

That said, we have to say too that in our opinion the example intuitively fails, because the circumlocution it displays—if it truly is circumlocution—is intentional. To be specific, if the two Clinton tuples were to be replaced by a single packed tuple, then information would actually be lost (namely, the information that one of the DURING intervals corresponds to Clinton's first term and the other to his second). In other words, the real problem is that relvar TERM has no explicit "term number" attribute. If we introduce such an attribute, the problem goes away:

---

[6] Here and elsewhere in this chapter we use the syntax "INTERVAL_..." to denote an interval type that we don't want to get sidetracked into discussing in detail at this juncture.

DURING	PRESIDENT	TERMNO
[1974:1976]	Ford	1
[1977:1980]	Carter	1
[1981:1984]	Reagan	1
[1985:1988]	Reagan	2
[1993:1996]	Clinton	1
[1997:2000]	Clinton	2
[2009:2012]	Obama	1

(Well, the problem doesn't *entirely* go away; the relvar might still contain a pair of tuples that would better be replaced by a single tuple. For example, it might contain two tuples for Carter's single term, one with a DURING value of [1977:1978] and the other with a DURING value of [1979:1980], thus:

DURING	PRESIDENT	TERMNO
[1977:1978]	Carter	1

DURING	PRESIDENT	TERMNO
[1979:1980]	Carter	1

This state of affairs genuinely is an example of the circumlocution problem. But an exactly analogous situation could occur without the TERMNO attribute! The trouble is, before we introduced that attribute, the system couldn't tell the difference between a genuine circumlocution like this Carter example and a "false circumlocution" like the Clinton example shown earlier.)

Of course, the key constraint KEY {DURING} still holds in this revised version of relvar TERM (with its TERMNO attribute). On the face of it, however, the relvar is now susceptible to all three of our usual problems (redundancy, circumlocution, and contradiction). Redundancy would occur if the relvar were to contain, e.g., both of the following tuples at the same time:

DURING	PRESIDENT	TERMNO
[1977:1979]	Carter	1

DURING	PRESIDENT	TERMNO
[1978:1980]	Carter	1

As already noted, circumlocution would occur if the relvar were to contain, e.g., both of the following tuples at the same time:

DURING	PRESIDENT	TERMNO
[1977:1978]	Carter	1

DURING	PRESIDENT	TERMNO
[1978:1980]	Carter	1

And contradiction would occur if the relvar were to contain, e.g., both of the following tuples at the same time:

DURING	PRESIDENT	TERMNO
[1977:1980]	Carter	1

DURING	PRESIDENT	TERMNO
[1974:1977]	Ford	1

It therefore might appear as if this revised version of TERM does need both PACKED ON and WHEN / THEN, as follows:

```
VAR TERM BASE RELATION
  { DURING INTERVAL_... , PRESIDENT NAME , TERMNO INTEGER }
    PACKED ON ( DURING )
    WHEN UNPACKED ON ( DURING ) THEN KEY { DURING }
    KEY { DURING } ;
```

But observe now that there's no good reason for this relvar ever to have two distinct tuples with the same values for PRESIDENT and TERMNO. The following constraint thus applies:

```
KEY { PRESIDENT , TERMNO }
```

And this specification makes the PACKED ON specification superfluous!—not actually wrong, as it was with the original version of the relvar, but certainly unnecessary. The reason is that, since {PRESIDENT,TERMNO} is a key, packing the relvar on DURING can't possibly have any effect.[7] (More generally, the operation PACK *R* ON (*ACL*) can't possibly have any effect if *R* has a key that doesn't include the set of attributes mentioned in *ACL*. Thus, there's no point in specifying the constraint PACKED ON (*ACL*) for such a relvar.) So our final definition for relvar TERM (revised version) looks like this:

```
VAR TERM BASE RELATION
  { DURING INTERVAL ... , PRESIDENT NAME , TERMNO INTEGER }
    WHEN UNPACKED ON ( DURING ) THEN KEY { DURING }
    KEY { DURING }
    KEY { PRESIDENT , TERMNO } ;
```

In other words, relvar TERM, even with the addition of attribute TERMNO, still serves as an example of a relvar for which we would probably want to specify WHEN / THEN and not PACKED ON.

Aside: It's only fair to point out that the introduction of attribute TERMNO, while it does solve some problems, also introduces others. Obviously, there's the problem of

---

[7] Indeed, as you might have realized, the fact that {PRESIDENT,TERMNO} is a key is sufficient to avoid the redundancy and circumlocution problems—though not the contradiction problem—as described on the previous page.

guaranteeing the uniqueness of a second key. Then there's the problem of ensuring that, for a given president, a tuple with TERMNO = 2 exists only if a tuple also exists with TERMNO = 1, and ensuring moreover that BEGIN (DURING) in the tuple with TERMNO = 2, if it exists, must be greater than END (DURING) in the tuple with TERMNO = 1. For such reasons, it might be argued that the original design without TERMNO is preferable. But for definiteness we'll stay with the revised design from this point forward, barring explicit statements to the contrary. *End of aside*.

Does WHEN / THEN Imply KEY?

Here again is the definition of relvar TERM, but now with certain specifications highlighted:

```
VAR TERM BASE RELATION
   { DURING INTERVAL ... , PRESIDENT NAME , TERMNO INTEGER }
     WHEN UNPACKED ON ( DURING ) THEN KEY { DURING }
     KEY { DURING }
     KEY { PRESIDENT , TERMNO } ;
```

As noted in the section "WHEN / THEN," the highlighted specifications here certainly look as if they might be saying the same thing twice. So let's take a closer look. The WHEN / THEN specification means that if the relvar were kept unpacked on DURING, then {DURING} would still be a key. But if that relvar *were* kept unpacked on DURING, then each DURING value would be a unit interval; and if {DURING} were a key for that unpacked form, then each such unit interval would appear in that unpacked form in exactly one tuple, associated therefore with exactly one combination of PRESIDENT and TERMNO values. It follows that if we were now to (re)pack that unpacked form on DURING, any given DURING value in the result, regardless of whether it's a unit interval or not, would also appear in exactly one tuple and be associated with exactly one combination of PRESIDENT and TERMNO values. Within that result, in other words, {DURING} would certainly satisfy the key uniqueness property. And since it obviously satisfies the irreducibility property as well, it appears that the WHEN / THEN specification in this example does imply that {DURING} is a key for TERM.

   Before we try to generalize from the foregoing analysis, let's take another look at relvar S_STATUS_DURING, with definition as follows:

```
VAR S_STATUS_DURING BASE RELATION
   { SNO SNO , STATUS INTEGER , DURING INTERVAL_DATE }
     PACKED ON ( DURING )
     WHEN UNPACKED ON ( DURING ) THEN KEY { SNO , DURING }
     KEY { SNO , DURING } ;
```

This example is a little more general than the TERM example, in the following sense. Recall that in the specification WHEN UNPACKED ON (*ACL*) THEN KEY {*BCL*}, every attribute mentioned in *ACL* must also be mentioned in *BCL*. In the TERM example, *ACL* and *BCL* were identical. In the S_STATUS_DURING example, by contrast, *BCL* contains an attribute, SNO, not mentioned in *ACL*. And if we perform the same kind of analysis on S_STATUS_DURING as we did a moment ago for TERM, we'll see that the WHEN / THEN specification certainly implies that any given {SNO,DURING} value appearing in S_STATUS_DURING does appear in exactly one tuple and is associated with exactly one STATUS value. So {SNO,DURING} certainly satisfies the uniqueness property that a key for S_STATUS_DURING is required to satisfy. And since it's clear that neither {SNO} nor {DURING} by itself satisfies that property, it follows that {SNO,DURING} satisfies the irreducibility property as well, from which we can conclude that it's actually a key, and hence that the WHEN/THEN specification does imply the KEY specification.

The conclusion to be drawn from the foregoing discussion is this: If a relvar definition does specify both WHEN ... THEN KEY {*K*} and KEY {*K*}, then enforcing the specified WHEN / THEN constraint will enforce the specified KEY constraint automatically. Thus, we might reasonably invent a syntax rule to say that the KEY specification can be omitted in such a situation. We choose not to adopt such a rule, however, for reasons that should become clear in the section "Keys Revisited," later.

> *Aside:* We've seen that the answer to the question in the title of this subsection ("Does WHEN / THEN imply KEY?") is yes. But there's a sense in which the answer to the inverse question is yes, too. Suppose suppliers are subject to the (unlikely, but possible) additional constraints that (a) the status of a given supplier never changes and (b) no supplier is ever allowed to be under contract during two disjoint intervals (i.e., once a supplier's contract terminates, that supplier is never placed under contract again). Then the definition for relvar S_STATUS_DURING can be simplified to just:
>
> ```
> VAR S_STATUS_DURING BASE RELATION
>   { SNO SNO , STATUS INTEGER , DURING INTERVAL_DATE }
>     KEY { SNO } ;
> ```
>
> And the fact that SNO values are unique in this relvar clearly implies that {SNO,DURING} values are unique in the corresponding unpacked form; in other words, the constraint KEY {SNO} in this example clearly implies the constraint WHEN UNPACKED ON (DURING) THEN KEY {SNO,DURING}. *End of aside.*

One final point to close this section: Just as a relvar can have two or more keys, so a relvar can also be subject to two or more WHEN / THEN constraints. By way of example, consider the following relvar (the semantics are meant to be obvious):

```
VAR MARRIAGE BASE RELATION
  { SPOUSE1 NAME , SPOUSE2 NAME , DURING INTERVAL_... }
    PACKED ON ( DURING )
    WHEN UNPACKED ON ( DURING ) THEN KEY { SPOUSE1 , DURING }
    WHEN UNPACKED ON ( DURING ) THEN KEY { SPOUSE2 , DURING }
    KEY { SPOUSE1 , DURING }
    KEY { SPOUSE2 , DURING } ;
```

NEITHER PACKED ON NOR WHEN / THEN

Suppose we're given a relvar INFLATION representing inflation rates for a certain country during certain intervals of time. The attributes are DURING and RATE, and the sole key is {DURING}. Here's a sample value, showing that the inflation rate was 18 percent for the first three months of the year, went up to 20 percent for the next three months, stayed at 20 again for the *next* three months (but went up to 25 percent in month 7), ..., and averaged out at 20 percent for the year as a whole:

DURING	RATE
[m01:m03]	18
[m04:m06]	20
[m07:m09]	20
[m07:m07]	25
.....	..
[m01:m12]	20

Note: This relvar is perhaps not very well designed (or so it could be argued, at any rate), since it contains monthly, quarterly, and annual information all mixed together; that is, it might be better to replace it by three separate relvars. But bad or not, the design is certainly a possible one, and we'll stay with it for the sake of the discussion.

It should be clear, then, that this relvar must *not* be kept packed on DURING—i.e., PACKED ON (DURING) must not be specified—because if it were, then (in terms of the sample data shown above) the three tuples with RATE = 20 would be packed into one, and we would lose the information that the inflation rate for months 4-6 and months 7-9 was 20 percent (as it was also for the year overall). What's more, *un*packing the relvar on DURING also causes information to be lost, in general (try it on the sample data above if you don't immediately see why). We could if we like specify the following:

```
WHEN UNPACKED ON ( DURING ) THEN KEY { DURING , RATE }
```

But this specification merely says, in effect, that the result of UNPACK INFLATION ON (DURING) is all key and thus never contains any duplicate tuples, and this "constraint" is thus no constraint at all, because *no* relation ever contains any duplicate tuples.

So relvar INFLATION does seem to be an example of a relvar for which it doesn't really seem to make sense to specify either PACKED ON or WHEN / THEN. The relvar definition thus becomes simply:

```
VAR INFLATION BASE RELATION
  { DURING INTERVAL_... , RATE INTEGER }
   KEY { DURING } ;
```

In fact, this relvar is subject to none of our usual redundancy, circumlocution, and contradiction problems—or rather, to state the matter more precisely, it's impossible to tell the difference between (a) a value of the relvar that does suffer from such problems and (b) a value of the relvar that looks as if it suffers from such problems but in fact is correct and doesn't.

INFLATION vs. TERM

Now, relvar INFLATION and relvar TERM from the previous section both seem not to need a PACKED ON constraint. So how do these two relvars differ from each other? Or, rather, *do* they differ, at least in any significant respect?

Well, they certainly resemble each other inasmuch as they both have the same key, {DURING}; thus, the functional dependency {DURING} → {PRESIDENT,TERMNO} holds in TERM, and the functional dependency {DURING} → {RATE} holds in INFLATION. However, they also differ in an important respect. To be specific, suppose we unpack them both on DURING. Then:

- In the unpacked form of TERM, the functional dependency {DURING} → {PRESIDENT,TERMNO} still holds.

- In the unpacked form of INFLATION, the functional dependency {DURING} → {RATE} does *not* still hold.

Intuitively speaking, in other words, a given RATE value in relvar INFLATION is a property of the corresponding DURING interval *taken as a whole*—it's *not* a property of the individual time points that go to make up that interval. To put it another way, just because the inflation rate for, e.g., the interval [*m07*:*m09*] was 20 percent, we can't infer that the inflation rate for, e.g., the interval [*m07*:*m07*] was also 20 percent—and indeed it wasn't, according to the sample value shown.

KEYS REVISITED

Despite—or perhaps because of!—the discussions of the last few sections, it does seem likely in practice that relvars with interval attributes will often be subject to both a PACKED ON constraint and a WHEN / THEN constraint (not to mention the required KEY constraint). For that reason, it seems desirable to come up with some syntax that combines the functionality of all three. We therefore propose another shorthand; to be specific, we propose that the definition of any given relvar *R* should be allowed to contain a specification of the following form:

```
USING ( ACL ) : KEY { K }
```

Here:

- *ACL* and *K* are both commalists of attribute names, and every attribute mentioned in *ACL* must also be mentioned in *K*.

- The specification is defined to be shorthand for the combination of all three of the following:

```
PACKED ON ( ACL )
WHEN UNPACKED ON ( ACL ) THEN KEY { K }
KEY { K }
```

We refer to {*K*} here as a *U_key* for short (but see further discussion below). Using this shorthand, the definition of relvar S_STATUS_DURING, for example, might be simplified to just:

```
VAR S_STATUS_DURING BASE RELATION
  { SNO SNO , STATUS INTEGER , DURING INTERVAL_DATE }
    USING ( DURING ) : KEY { SNO , DURING } ;
```

Suppose now that the commalist of attribute names *ACL* within a given U_key specification is empty (i.e., contains no attribute names at all), thus:

```
USING ( ) : KEY { K }
```

By definition, this specification is shorthand for:

```
PACKED ON ( )
WHEN UNPACKED ON ( ) THEN KEY { K }
KEY { K }
```

So:

- First, the pertinent relvar must be kept packed on no attributes at all. But packing a relation *r* on no attributes at all simply returns *r*, so the implied PACKED ON specification has no effect.

■ Second, the pertinent relvar must be such that if it's unpacked on no attributes at all, then {*K*} is a key for the result. But unpacking a relation *r* on no attributes at all simply returns *r*, so the implied WHEN / THEN specification simply means that {*K*} is a key for the pertinent relvar, and the implied regular KEY constraint is thus redundant.

It follows that we can take a regular KEY specification of the form KEY {*K*} to be shorthand for a certain U_key specification—namely, one of the form USING ( ) : KEY {*K*}. In other words, regular KEY constraints are essentially just a special case of our proposed new syntax! Thus, if we redefine the syntax of a regular KEY specification as follows—

```
[ USING ( ACL ) : ] KEY { K }
```

—and if we allow the USING specification and colon separator to be omitted if and only if *ACL* is empty, then we no longer have any need to talk about U_keys as such at all; all keys effectively become U_keys, and we can generalize the meaning of "key" accordingly. And so we will.

Note: It's occasionally useful to refer to PACKED ON and WHEN / THEN constraints that have, and can have, no logical effect as *trivial* constraints. In particular, PACKED ON ( ) and WHEN UNPACKED ON ( ) THEN ... are both trivial in this sense. So too are:

■ PACKED ON (*ACL*), if the set of attributes of the relvar in question not included in *ACL* is a superkey for that relvar

■ WHEN ... THEN KEY {*K*}, if *K* is the entire heading of the relvar in question

Foreign U_keys

*Note: This topic is discussed in more detail in the next chapter. We include a brief and very incomplete discussion of it here only because you might feel the chapter is missing something without it. Note too—this is important!—that it's necessary to assume for the purposes of this short discussion that the database contains during relvars only, **not** a mixture of since and during relvars.*

Consider relvars S_DURING and SP_DURING, whose definitions currently look like this:[8]

```
VAR S_DURING BASE RELATION
  { SNO SNO , DURING INTERVAL_DATE }
    USING ( DURING ) : KEY { SNO , DURING } ;
```

---

[8] Specifying explicit U_keys for these two relvars means we've implicitly specified certain WHEN / THEN constraints, of course. Note, however, that these latter constraints are trivial ones, since the relvars are both all key.

```
VAR SP_DURING BASE RELATION
  { SNO SNO , PNO PNO , DURING INTERVAL_DATE }
    USING ( DURING ) : KEY { SNO , PNO , DURING } ;
```

Observe now that (as the implied WHEN / THEN constraint in fact asserts) if S_DURING were actually kept unpacked on DURING, then {SNO,DURING} would be a key for that unpacked form. Furthermore, if relvar SP_DURING were also kept unpacked on DURING, then {SNO,DURING} would be a matching foreign key in *that* unpacked form.[9] Thus, if {SNO,DURING} is regarded as a U_key for S_DURING, then {SNO,DURING} might reasonably be regarded as a matching *foreign* U_key in SP_DURING. We therefore propose another shorthand. To be specific, we propose that the definition of any given relvar *R2* should be allowed to contain a specification of the form:

```
USING ( ACL ) : FOREIGN KEY { FK } REFERENCES R1
```

As we've more or less indicated already, the semantics are that if *R1* and *R2* were both kept unpacked on the attributes specified in *ACL*, then *FK* in *R2* would be a foreign key matching the key in *R1* that's implied by the corresponding U_key definition for *R1*. We skip the details here, except to note that—as by now you should surely be expecting—regular FOREIGN KEY constraints are basically just a special case of this proposed new syntax.

PUTTING IT ALL TGETHER

We close this chapter by showing the overall effect of the syntactic simplifications discussed in the previous section on our running example (see Fig. 13.4). *Note:* We revert now to our preferred "combination" design (recall that in the subsection "Foreign U_keys" at the end of the previous section, we were assuming a design that consisted of during relvars only). Observe in particular in that combination design that, contrary to what you might have expected, relvar SP_DURING doesn't have a foreign U_key referencing S_DURING, nor do relvars S_DURING and S_STATUS_DURING have foreign U_keys referencing each other. We'll have more to say about such matters in the next chapter.

---

[9] This is where we rely on the fact that the database contains during relvars only; the claim we're making here wouldn't be valid for our preferred "combination" design (why not?).

```
S_SINCE { SNO , SNO_SINCE , STATUS , STATUS_SINCE }
         KEY { SNO }

SP_SINCE { SNO , PNO , SINCE }
          KEY { SNO , PNO }
          FOREIGN KEY { SNO } REFERENCES S_SINCE

S_DURING { SNO , DURING }
          USING ( DURING ) : KEY { SNO , DURING }

S_STATUS_DURING { SNO , STATUS , DURING }
          USING ( DURING ) : KEY { SNO , DURING }

SP_DURING { SNO , PNO , DURING }
          USING ( DURING ) : KEY { SNO , PNO , DURING }
```

Fig. 13.4: Revised version of Fig. 13.1

EXERCISES

13.1 (*This exercise subsumes Exercise 5.2 from Chapter 5.*) Explain the redundancy, circumlocution, and contradiction problems in your own words.

13.2 Explain in your own words:

a. KEY constraints

b. PACKED ON constraints

c. WHEN / THEN constraints

d. U_key constraints

13.3 Give an example of a relvar that has at least one interval attribute and requires:

a. Both a PACKED ON and a WHEN / THEN constraint

b. A PACKED ON but no WHEN / THEN constraint

c. A WHEN / THEN but no PACKED ON constraint

d. Neither a PACKED ON nor a WHEN / THEN constraint

(where by *constraint* we mean a nontrivial one throughout).

13.4 Explain how regular keys can be regarded as a special case of U_keys.

13.5 Use **Tutorial D** to formulate as many reasonable constraints as you can think of that might apply to the revised version of relvar TERM (i.e., the version with the TERMNO attribute).

13.6 Consider relvar MARRIAGE from the very end of the section "WHEN / THEN without PACKED ON" in the body of the chapter. Its definition can be simplified to:

```
VAR MARRIAGE BASE RELATION
  { SPOUSE1 NAME , SPOUSE2 NAME , DURING INTERVAL_... }
    PACKED ON ( DURING )
    USING ( DURING ) : KEY { SPOUSE1 , DURING }
    USING ( DURING ) : KEY { SPOUSE2 , DURING } ;
```

Observe now that the two U_keys here both have the same USING specification. What it would mean (if anything) for a relvar to have U_keys with different USING specifications?

13.7 Consider the revised version of courses-and-students from Exercise 12.8c in Chapter 12, with the following as an appropriate definition for relvar COURSE_OFFERING:

```
VAR COURSE_OFFERING BASE RELATION
  { COURSENO        COURSENO ,
    OFFERINGNO      INTEGER ,
    QUOTA           INTEGER ,
    OFFERED_DURING INTERVAL_DATE }
  KEY { COURSENO , OFFERINGNO } ;
```

The predicate (slightly simplified as usual) is: *Offering OFFERINGNO of course COURSENO has quota QUOTA and took place, or is scheduled to take place, during interval OFFERED_DURING.* Revise the database definition again to show all such PACKED ON, WHEN / THEN, and/or U_key constraints as you think necessary.

13.8 Suppose a given relvar has attributes A, B, and DURING, and predicate *DURING is a maximal interval of days throughout which person A was dating person B.* Assume it's possible for the interval during which A was dating B to overlap with the interval during which A was dating some distinct person B′. However, assume also that, in such a case, at least it's not allowed for the intervals in question to be identical (one does have to have *some* standards). Give an appropriate relvar definition.

ANSWERS

13.1 The redundancy, circumlocution, and contradiction problems are all problems that can arise in connection with relvars having interval attributes. We explain them in terms of relvars S_DURING and S_STATUS_DURING:

- For relvar S_DURING, the redundancy problem occurs if two or more tuples can have the same SNO value and overlapping DURING values. For example, if supplier S4 is shown in one tuple to be under contract from *d05* to *d06* and in another to be under contract from *d06* to *d07*, then the information that S4 is under contract on *d06* is represented twice.

- For relvar S_DURING again, the circumlocution problem occurs if two or more tuples can have the same SNO value and DURING values that meet or "abut." For example, if supplier S4 is shown in one tuple to be under contract from *d05* to *d05* and in another to be under contract from *d06* to *d07*, then the information that S4 is under contract from *d05* to *d07* is represented in a roundabout way, using two tuples when one would clearly be enough.

- For relvar S_STATUS_DURING, the contradiction problem—which can occur only in a relvar that has at least one nonkey attribute[10]—arises if two or more tuples can have the same SNO value, overlapping DURING values, and different STATUS values. For example, suppose supplier S4 is shown in one tuple as having status 10 from *d04* to *d06* and in another as having status 25 from *d05* to *d07*. Then supplier S1 is represented as having both status 10 and status 25 on *d05* and *d06*, thereby violating the constraint that a supplier has just one status at one time.

13.2

a. A KEY constraint specifies that a given subset of the heading of a given relvar constitutes a superkey for that relvar. The subset in question is generally assumed, but can't be guaranteed, to be a key as such (i.e., it's assumed to be irreducible). *Note:* A superkey that's not a key as such is said to be a *proper* superkey.

b. A PACKED ON constraint specifies that the relation that's the current value of the pertinent relvar at any given time must be in the specified packed form.

---

[10] A nonkey attribute is an attribute of a given relvar that isn't part of any key of that relvar. (Of course, a key attribute is an attribute of a given relvar that *is* part of some key of that relvar.)

c. A WHEN / THEN constraint specifies that a given subset of the heading of a given relvar constitutes a superkey for the specified unpacked form of that relvar. The subset in question is generally assumed, but can't be guaranteed, to be a key as such for that unpacked form (i.e., it's assumed to be irreducible).

d. A U_key constraint specifies a commalist *ACL* of attribute names and a commalist *K* of attribute names. It's shorthand for the combination of (a) the PACKED ON constraint PACKED ON (*ACL*), (b) the KEY constraint KEY {*K*}, and (c) the WHEN / THEN constraint WHEN UNPACKED ON (*ACL*) THEN KEY {*K*}.

13.3

a. S_STATUS_DURING (redundancy, circumlocution, and contradiction must all be addressed)

b. SP_DURING (contradiction can't arise)

c. TERM with no TERMNO attribute ("circumlocution"—sort of—must be permitted)

d. INFLATION

13.4 A U_key constraint specifying KEY {*K*} and an empty USING commalist is equivalent to a regular KEY constraint specifying KEY {*K*}.

13.5 The following constraints are over and above those shown explicitly in the body of the chapter.

a. No president has more than two terms:

```
CONSTRAINT C135a IS_EMPTY ( TERM WHERE TERMNO ≠ 1 AND TERMNO ≠ 2 ) ;
```

b. No presidential term lasts more than four years:

```
CONSTRAINT C135b IS_EMPTY ( TERM WHERE COUNT ( DURING ) > 4 ) ;
```

c. For a given president, a tuple with TERMNO = 2 exists only if a tuple also exists with TERMNO = 1, and BEGIN (DURING) in the tuple with TERMNO = 2, if it exists, must be greater than END (DURING) in the tuple with TERMNO = 1:

```
CONSTRAINT C135c IS_EMPTY
( ( ( TERM RENAME { DURING AS D1 , TERMNO AS T1 } ) JOIN
    ( TERM RENAME { DURING AS D2 , TERMNO AS T2 } ) )
          WHERE T1 < T2 AND BEGIN ( D2 ) ≤ END ( D1 ) ) ;
```

Note: This formulation assumes Constraint C135a is in effect.

13.6 Such a state of affairs is impossible, except in certain pathological cases (e.g., if the relvar is constrained never to contain more than one tuple). For if USING (*ACL*) ... and USING (*BCL*) ... are both specified, then—among other things—the relvar is apparently to be kept packed on both *ACL* and *BCL* at the same time.

13.7 For STUDENT_HISTORY:

```
USING ( REG_DURING ) : KEY { STUDENTNO , REG_DURING }
```

For COURSE_OFFERING:

```
USING ( OFFERED_DURING ) : KEY { COURSENO , OFFERED_DURING }
```

13.8 This is an example of a relvar for which PACKED ON applies but WHEN / THEN doesn't (even though, unlike, e.g., relvars S_DURING and SP_DURING, it's not all key). For example, the following is a possible sample value:

A	B	DURING
Amy	Bob	[*d01:d06*]
Amy	Ben	[*d04:d08*]
Ann	Bob	[*d05:d09*]

Unpacking this relation on A and DURING yields among things the following pair of tuples:

A	B	DURING
Amy	Bob	[*d05:d05*]

A	B	DURING
Amy	Ben	[*d05:d05*]

Thus, {A,DURING} is clearly not a key for the unpacked form. So here's a possible relvar definition:

```
VAR ABC BASE RELATION
  { A NAME , B NAME , DURING INTERVAL_DATE }
    PACKED ON ( A , DURING )
    KEY { A , DURING } ;
```

Note: If we assume that A is dating B at a given time if and only if B is dating A at the same time, we might want to impose a constraint on this relvar to the effect that A < B. The sample value shown above assumes such a constraint is in effect.

   As a subsidiary exercise, what changes would be required to the foregoing definition if we wanted to insist that the interval during which A was dating B didn't properly include the interval during which A was dating some distinct person B'?

Chapter 14

Database Design

III : General Constraints

You may be consistent or inconsistent,
but you shouldn't switch all the time between the two.

—Anon.

In Chapter 13, we used the during relvars from our preferred (combination) design of Fig. 13.1—relvar S_STATUS_DURING in particular—to illustrate the need for and functionality of the PACKED ON and WHEN / THEN constraints, building up to U_key specifications as a shorthand (and in particular to the realization that regular relational key specifications can be regarded as a special case of that shorthand). In the present chapter, we adopt a rather different strategy. To be specific, we stand back for a while from the specific design of Fig. 13.1 (or Fig. 13.4) and consider instead, in very general terms, *all* of the constraints that might reasonably be expected to hold in a temporal database involving suppliers and shipments.[1] Then we consider in some depth what happens to those constraints if the database contains (a) since ("current") relvars only, (b) during ("historical") relvars only, or (c) a mixture of both.

Note: Like Chapter 12 (but *not* Chapter 13), this chapter is concerned, rather more than most of its predecessors, with temporal data specifically. The principal reason for this state of affairs is that, by its very nature, temporal data often has to satisfy certain "denseness" constraints—meaning, loosely, that certain conditions have to be satisfied *at every point within* certain intervals. For example, if the database shows supplier S1 as having been under contract ever since day 4, then it must also show supplier S1 as having had some status ever since day 4, and vice versa. Such constraints don't necessarily apply to other kinds of data for which the concepts of previous chapters, such as U_keys, do apply.

We should also warn you that certain portions of this chapter might seem a little difficult, especially on a first reading. Unfortunately, the difficulties in question seem to be intrinsic. However, we do offer, in the section "Syntactic Shorthands," a few suggestions as to how it might be possible to conceal some of those difficulties from the user. Then, in the final section, we briefly discuss a few miscellaneous issues.

---

[1] We continue to ignore supplier names and cities, however.

A note on terminology: In order to avoid confusion, in what follows we'll refer to the natural language versions of the constraints we want to consider as *requirements*, and reserve the term *constraint* to mean the formulation of such a requirement in a formal language such as **Tutorial D**. We note in passing that some though not all of the requirements we'll be discussing are in fact implied by the predicates for the pertinent relvars.

THE NINE REQUIREMENTS

There are nine requirements we want to consider. They fall nicely into three groups of three. The first three are all of the form "If the database shows a given supplier as being under contract on some given day or pair of consecutive days, some other condition must also be satisfied":

- **Requirement R1:** If the database shows supplier Sx as being under contract on day d, it must contain exactly one tuple that shows that fact.

- **Requirement R2:** If the database shows supplier Sx as being under contract on days d and $d+1$, it must contain exactly one tuple that shows that fact.

- **Requirement R3:** If the database shows supplier Sx as being under contract on day d, it must also show supplier Sx as having some status on day d.

Observe that Requirement R1 has to do with avoiding redundancy and Requirement R2 with avoiding circumlocution (see Chapter 13). Requirement R3 has to do with what we referred to in the opening to this chapter as denseness.

The next three requirements are all of the form "If the database shows a given supplier as having a given status on some given day or pair of consecutive days, some other condition must also be satisfied." They bear a strong family resemblance to Requirements R1-R3, as you'll immediately see:

- **Requirement R4:** If the database shows supplier Sx as having some status on day d, it must contain exactly one tuple that shows that fact.

- **Requirement R5:** If the database shows supplier Sx as having the same status on days d and $d+1$, it must contain exactly one tuple that shows that fact.

- **Requirement R6:** If the database shows supplier Sx as having some status on day d, it must also show supplier Sx as being under contract on day d.

Requirement R4 has to do with avoiding redundancy and also contradiction (again, see Chapter 13). Requirement R5 has to do with avoiding circumlocution, and Requirement R6 has to do with denseness. Note that Requirements R3 and R6 are effectively inverses of each other.

The last three requirements are all of the form "If the database shows a given supplier as able to supply a given part on some given day or pair of consecutive days, some other condition must also be satisfied":

- **Requirement R7:** If the database shows supplier Sx as able to supply some specific part Py on day d, it must contain exactly one tuple that shows that fact.

- **Requirement R8:** If the database shows supplier Sx as able to supply the same part Py on days d and $d+1$, it must contain exactly one tuple that shows that fact.

- **Requirement R9:** If the database shows supplier Sx as able to supply some part Py on day d, it must also show supplier Sx as being under contract on day d.

Requirement R7 has to do with avoiding redundancy, Requirement R8 has to do with avoiding circumlocution, and Requirement R9 has to do with denseness. *Note:* In case you were wondering, we could simplify the phrase "some part Py" in Requirement R9 to just "some part" without changing the overall meaning. The explicit reference to Py is there purely to highlight the parallel between Requirement R9 and Requirements R7 and R8.

We offer a few further explanatory comments on these requirements. First of all, note that:

- Requirement R1 derives in part from the fact that no supplier can be under two distinct contracts at the same time.

- Requirement R4 derives in part from the fact that no supplier can have two distinct status values at the same time.

- Requirement R7 derives in part from the fact that no supplier can have two distinct "abilities to supply" the same part at the same time.

Second, note that Requirements R2, R5, and R8 can't possibly be satisfied, in general, if full vertical decomposition into 6NF hasn't been done (why not?). Note finally that analogs of the foregoing requirements will apply to any temporal database we might need to deal with—or, at least, so we conjecture. (In this connection, see Exercise 14.6 at the end of the chapter.)

SINCE RELVARS ONLY

We now consider the case of a temporal database consisting of since relvars only. The database in question—see the outline definitions in Fig. 14.1—consists essentially of the two since relvars from Fig. 13.1 (or Fig. 13.4) in Chapter 13. Note in particular that because those relvars don't involve any interval attributes, they don't involve any PACKED ON or WHEN / THEN constraints either (except for trivial ones, not shown). Sample values are shown in Fig. 14.2, a slightly modified version of Fig. 13.2 (the only changes are in the S_SINCE tuple for S4 and the SP_SINCE tuple for S4 and P5).

```
S_SINCE { SNO , SNO_SINCE , STATUS , STATUS_SINCE }
         KEY { SNO }

SP_SINCE { SNO , PNO , SINCE }
          KEY { SNO , PNO }
          FOREIGN KEY { SNO } REFERENCES S_SINCE
```

Fig. 14.1: Since relvars only

S_SINCE

SNO	SNO_SINCE	STATUS	STATUS_SINCE
S1	d04	20	d06
S2	d07	10	d07
S3	d03	30	d03
S4	d14	20	d14
S5	d02	30	d02

SP_SINCE

SNO	PNO	SINCE
S1	P1	d04
S1	P2	d05
S1	P3	d09
S1	P4	d05
S1	P5	d04
S1	P6	d06
S2	P1	d08
S2	P2	d09
S3	P2	d08
S4	P5	d14

Fig. 14.2: Since relvars only—sample values

Of course, this database is only semitemporal—it can't represent information about the past at all, apart from what might be conveyed by the "since" values. By contrast, however, it certainly can represent future information. To be specific:

- Both relvars contain implicit information regarding the future—recall the discussion toward the end of the section "Since Relvars Only" in Chapter 12, which said in effect that if (e.g.) some S_SINCE tuple shows supplier S*x* as being under contract since day *d*, then we can infer that supplier S*x* was, is, or will be under contract on every day from day *d* until "the last day" (pending future updates).

■ What's more, the relvars might contain explicit information regarding the future as well—again, recall that discussion in Chapter 12, which said in effect that (e.g.) the SNO_SINCE value for some supplier Sx might be some future date d, meaning that the indicated supplier *will be* placed under contract at that future date. Supplier S4 is a case in point in Fig. 14.2 (once again we're assuming that today is day 10, an assumption we adhere to—where it makes any difference—throughout this chapter).

We now proceed to consider what formal versions of Requirements R1-R9 might look like for this database.

Requirement R1: If the database shows supplier Sx as being under contract on day d, it must contain exactly one tuple that shows that fact.

The KEY constraint on S_SINCE takes care of this requirement. Without it, that relvar might contain (e.g.) both of the following tuples at the same time:

SNO	SNO_SINCE	. . .
S1	d04	. . .

SNO	SNO_SINCE	. . .
S1	d06	. . .

Both of these tuples show among other things that supplier S1 was under contract on day 7. If they both appeared, therefore, Requirement R1 would be violated.

Requirement R2: If the database shows supplier Sx as being under contract on days d and $d+1$, it must contain exactly one tuple that shows that fact.

The KEY constraint on S_SINCE takes care of this requirement, too. Without it, that relvar might contain (e.g.) both of the following tuples at the same time:

SNO	SNO_SINCE	. . .
S1	d04	. . .

SNO	SNO_SINCE	. . .
S1	d05	. . .

Requirement R3: If the database shows supplier Sx as being under contract on day d, it must also show supplier Sx as having some status on day d.

Given the semitemporal database of Fig. 14.1, this requirement can't be enforced. The predicate for S_SINCE (slightly simplified) is:

Supplier SNO has been under contract ever since SNO_SINCE and has had status STATUS ever since STATUS_SINCE.

Thus, it's perfectly reasonable for S_SINCE to contain a tuple in which the STATUS_SINCE value d' is greater than the SNO_SINCE value d (see, e.g., the S_SINCE tuple for supplier S1 in Fig. 14.2). And if supplier Sx is the supplier represented by that tuple, then the database shows supplier Sx as having been under contract throughout the interval $[d:d'-1]$ but does *not* show supplier Sx as having had some status throughout that interval. This latter is (typically) information about the past that can't be represented in this database.

Following on from the previous point, suppose now that the SNO_SINCE value d, in that tuple for supplier Sx, is a date in the future. Then we might reasonably want to insist that when that tuple is first inserted into the relvar, the STATUS_SINCE value must be d as well; for if it were greater than d, then Requirement R3 would be violated right away, as it were. We might even want to impose a constraint—let's call it Constraint X—to the effect that the STATUS_SINCE value, in *any* tuple, must always be equal to the associated SNO_SINCE value if this latter is a date in the future, thus (we assume here support for a niladic operator called TODAY that returns the date today):

```
CONSTRAINT X IS_EMPTY
    ( S_SINCE WHERE SNO_SINCE > TODAY ( ) AND STATUS_SINCE ≠ SNO_SINCE ) ;
```

Requirement R4: If the database shows supplier Sx as having some status on day d, it must contain exactly one tuple that shows that fact.

The KEY constraint on S_SINCE takes care of this requirement also. Without it, that relvar might contain (e.g.) both of the following tuples at the same time:

SNO	..	STATUS	STATUS_SINCE
S1	..	20	d06

SNO	..	STATUS	STATUS_SINCE
S1	..	20	d08

Indeed, it might even contain (e.g.) both of the following tuples at the same time:

SNO	..	STATUS	STATUS_SINCE
S1	..	20	d06

SNO	..	STATUS	STATUS_SINCE
S1	..	30	d06

Requirement R5: If the database shows supplier Sx as having the same status on days d and $d+1$, it must contain exactly one tuple that shows that fact.

The KEY constraint on S_SINCE takes care of this requirement as well. Without it, that relvar might contain (e.g.) both of the following tuples at the same time:

SNO	..	STATUS	STATUS_SINCE
S1	..	20	d06

SNO	..	STATUS	STATUS_SINCE
S1	..	20	d07

Requirement R6: If the database shows supplier Sx as having some status on day d, it must also show supplier Sx as being under contract on day d.

We've met this requirement before, near the end of the section "Since Relvars Only" in Chapter 12, where we observed that if the SNO_SINCE and STATUS_SINCE values in some S_SINCE tuple are d and d', respectively, then we must have $d' \geq d$. Here's the formal statement:

```
CONSTRAINT SR6 IS_EMPTY ( S_SINCE WHERE STATUS_SINCE < SNO_SINCE ) ;
```

Without this constraint, relvar S_SINCE might contain (e.g.) the following tuple:

SNO	SNO_SINCE	STATUS	STATUS_SINCE
S1	d04	20	d02

Requirement R7: If the database shows supplier Sx as able to supply some specific part Py on day d, it must contain exactly one tuple that shows that fact.

The KEY constraint on SP_SINCE takes care of this requirement. Without it, that relvar might contain (e.g.) both of the following tuples at the same time:

SNO	PNO	SINCE
S1	P1	d04

SNO	PNO_	SINCE
S1	P1	d02

Requirement R8: If the database shows supplier Sx as able to supply the same part Py on days d and $d+1$, it must contain exactly one tuple that shows that fact.

The KEY constraint on SP_SINCE takes care of this requirement, too. Without it, that relvar might contain (e.g.) both of the following tuples at the same time:

SNO	PNO	SINCE
S1	P1	*d04*

SNO	PNO_	SINCE
S1	P1	*d05*

Requirement R9: If the database shows supplier S*x* as able to supply some part P*y* on day *d*, it must also show supplier S*x* as being under contract on day *d*.

The foreign key constraint from SP_SINCE to S_SINCE takes care of part of this requirement ("any supplier able to supply some part on some day must be under contract on some day"), but we also need to ensure that the second of these "some days" doesn't precede the day when the pertinent supplier was placed under contract:

```
CONSTRAINT SR9 IS_EMPTY
          ( ( SP_SINCE JOIN S_SINCE ) WHERE SINCE < SNO_SINCE ) ;
```

(Compare and contrast Constraint XST1 in Chapter 5.) Without this constraint, S_SINCE and SP_SINCE might respectively contain (e.g.) the following tuples at the same time:

SNO	SNO_SINCE	...
S1	*d04*	...

SNO	PNO_	SINCE
S1	P*y*	*d02*

Fig. 14.3 is a completed version of Fig. 14.1 (actually the figures are identical, except for the addition in Fig. 14.3 of Constraints SR6 and SR9):

```
S_SINCE { SNO , SNO_SINCE , STATUS , STATUS_SINCE }
         KEY { SNO }

CONSTRAINT SR6 IS_EMPTY ( S_SINCE WHERE STATUS_SINCE < SNO_SINCE ) ;

SP_SINCE { SNO , PNO , SINCE }
         KEY { SNO , PNO }
         FOREIGN KEY { SNO } REFERENCES S_SINCE

CONSTRAINT SR9 IS_EMPTY
          ( ( SP_SINCE JOIN S_SINCE ) WHERE SINCE < SNO_SINCE ) ;
```

Fig. 14.3: Since relvars only—complete design

DURING RELVARS ONLY

Now we turn to the case of a temporal database consisting of during relvars only. The database in question—see the outline definitions in Fig. 14.4—consists essentially of the during relvars from Fig. 13.1 (or Fig. 13.4) in Chapter 13; however, we now show the various PACKED ON and WHEN / THEN constraints that apply to those relvars (we deliberately avoid use of the U_key shorthand for the time being). The database is fully temporal, but horizontal decomposition hasn't been done.[2] Sample values are shown in Fig. 14.5 (a considerably modified version of Fig. 13.3). *Note:* The relvars in this design can represent past and/or current and/or future information. However, we remind you from Chapter 12 that one disadvantage of such a design is that we have to use an artificial "end of time" value as the end value for any interval where the actual end time is unknown. Supplier S7 is a case in point in Fig. 14.5 (where we've assumed for the sake of the example that *d99* is "the last day").

```
S_DURING { SNO , DURING }
        PACKED ON ( DURING )
        KEY { SNO , DURING }

S_STATUS_DURING { SNO , STATUS , DURING }
        PACKED ON ( DURING )
        WHEN UNPACKED ON ( DURING ) THEN KEY { SNO , DURING }
        KEY { SNO , DURING }

SP_DURING { SNO , PNO , DURING }
        PACKED ON ( DURING )
        KEY { SNO , PNO , DURING }
```

Fig. 14.4: During relvars only

S_DURING

SNO	DURING
S2	[*d02*:*d04*]
S6	[*d03*:*d05*]
S7	[*d03*:*d99*]

S_STATUS_DURING

SNO	STATUS	DURING
S2	5	[*d02*:*d02*]
S2	10	[*d03*:*d04*]
S6	5	[*d03*:*d04*]
S6	7	[*d05*:*d05*]
S7	15	[*d03*:*d08*]
S7	20	[*d09*:*d99*]

SP_DURING

SNO	PNO	DURING
S2	P1	[*d02*:*d04*]
S2	P2	[*d03*:*d03*]
S2	P5	[*d03*:*d04*]
S6	P3	[*d03*:*d05*]
S6	P4	[*d04*:*d04*]
S6	P5	[*d04*:*d05*]
S7	P1	[*d03*:*d04*]
S7	P1	[*d06*:*d07*]
S7	P1	[*d09*:*d99*]

Fig. 14.5: During relvars only—sample values

---

[2] We note in passing that this is the state of affairs that's assumed in SQL, more or less. See Chapter 19 for further discussion.

We now proceed to consider what formal versions of Requirements R1-R9 might look like for this database.

Requirement R1: If the database shows supplier Sx as being under contract on day d, it must contain exactly one tuple that shows that fact.

The PACKED ON constraint on S_DURING takes care of this requirement. Without it, that relvar might contain (e.g.) both of the following tuples at the same time:

SNO	DURING
S2	[d02:d03]

SNO	DURING
S2	[d03:d04]

Aside: The foregoing claim re PACKED ON notwithstanding, there's a point here that might be bothering you. The database under discussion contains during relvars only. As noted in Chapter 12, therefore, the value of S_DURING at any given time is equal to the value of the U_projection using DURING of S_STATUS_DURING on SNO and DURING at the time in question;[3] in other words, S_DURING is 100 percent redundant in the design under consideration! It follows that if S_STATUS_DURING shows, implicitly, that supplier Sx is under contract on day d, then S_DURING does so too, explicitly, and Requirement R1 is thereby violated. (Analogous remarks apply to Requirement R2 also.) Well, so be it; as also noted in Chapter 12, we still prefer to include S_DURING in our design, partly just for completeness, and partly to avoid a certain degree of awkwardness and arbitrariness that would otherwise occur. In other words, the nine requirements (or those aspects of the nine requirements having to do with redundancy and circumlocution, at any rate) shouldn't necessarily be seen as inviolable rules, never to be broken; sometimes there might be good reasons not to enforce them. And here's as good a place as any to point out that redundancy per se isn't necessarily bad, anyway—it's bad only if it's not properly managed. See reference [43] for a detailed discussion of such matters. *End of aside*.

Requirement R2: If the database shows supplier Sx as being under contract on days d and $d+1$, it must contain exactly one tuple that shows that fact.

The PACKED ON constraint on S_DURING takes care of this requirement, too. Without it, that relvar might contain (e.g.) both of the following tuples at the same time:

---

[3] You might like to check for yourself that the sample values in Fig. 14.5 do satisfy this condition. As a matter of fact, we'll be *insisting* later in this section that this condition be satisfied (see the discussion of Requirements R3 and R6).

SNO	DURING
S2	[d02:d02]

SNO	DURING
S2	[d03:d04]

Requirement R3: If the database shows supplier S*x* as being under contract on day *d*, it must also show supplier S*x* as having some status on day *d*.

Suppliers are shown as being under contract in S_DURING and as having some status in S_STATUS_DURING. Requirement R3 implies that every tuple pairing supplier S*x* with day *d* in the unpacked form of S_DURING must also appear in the unpacked form of the projection of S_STATUS_DURING on SNO and DURING (both unpackings being done on DURING, of course). Hence the following constraint must hold:

```
CONSTRAINT DR3 USING ( DURING ) :
            S_DURING ⊆ S_STATUS_DURING { SNO , DURING } ;
```

Without this constraint, S_DURING might contain, e.g., just the tuple for supplier S7 shown on the left below, while at the same time S_STATUS_DURING contains, e.g., just the tuple for supplier S7 shown on the right below:

SNO	DURING
S7	[d03:d99]

SNO	STATUS	DURING
S7	20	[d09:d99]

As we saw in the previous chapter, however, to say Constraint DR3 holds is to say a certain *foreign U_key* constraint is in effect. In other words, we could if we like replace that constraint by the following specification:

```
USING ( DURING ) :
        FOREIGN KEY { SNO , DURING } REFERENCES S_STATUS_DURING
```

(part of the definition of relvar S_DURING).

We'll have more to say regarding Requirement R3 and Constraint DR3 (or its foreign U_key equivalent) when we discuss Requirement R6, later in this section.

Requirement R4: If the database shows supplier S*x* as having some status on day *d*, it must contain exactly one tuple that shows that fact.

The PACKED ON and WHEN / THEN constraints on S_STATUS_DURING take care of this requirement. Without PACKED ON, that relvar might contain (e.g.) both of the following tuples at the same time:

SNO	STATUS	DURING
S7	15	[d03:d06]

SNO	STATUS	DURING
S7	15	[d05:d08]

And without WHEN / THEN, the relvar might contain (e.g.) both of the following tuples at the same time:

SNO	STATUS	DURING
S7	15	[d03:d06]

SNO	STATUS	DURING
S7	20	[d05:d08]

Requirement R5: If the database shows supplier S*x* as having the same status on days *d* and *d*+1, it must contain exactly one tuple that shows that fact.

The PACKED ON constraint on S_STATUS_DURING takes care of this requirement as well. Without it, that relvar might contain (e.g.) both of the following tuples at the same time:

SNO	STATUS	DURING
S7	15	[d03:d06]

SNO	STATUS	DURING
S7	15	[d07:d08]

Requirement R6: If the database shows supplier S*x* as having some status on day *d*, it must also show supplier S*x* as being under contract on day *d*.

As noted in the section "The Nine Requirements," Requirement R6 is effectively the inverse of Requirement R3. Thus, the following specification takes care of matters:

```
USING ( DURING ) : FOREIGN KEY { SNO , DURING } REFERENCES S_DURING
```

(part of the definition of relvar S_STATUS_DURING). Without this constraint, S_DURING might contain, e.g., just the tuple for supplier S7 shown on the left below, while at the same time S_STATUS_DURING contains, e.g., just the tuple for supplier S7 shown on the right below:

SNO	DURING
S7	[d10:d99]

SNO	STATUS	DURING
S7	20	[d09:d99]

So S_DURING and S_STATUS_DURING each have a foreign U_key referencing the other.

Alternatively, we could define an explicit constraint (DR6), identical to Constraint DR3 but with a "⊇" operator in place of the "⊆" operator, thus:

```
CONSTRAINT DR6 USING ( DURING ) :
          S_DURING ⊇ S_STATUS_DURING { SNO , DURING } ;
```

And then we could combine the two explicit constraints like this:

```
CONSTRAINT DR36 USING ( DURING ) :
          S_DURING = S_STATUS_DURING { SNO , DURING } ;
```

This last (Constraint DR36) is an example of what might be called a *U_equality dependency*. (Equality dependencies as such—i.e., without that "U_"—are discussed in reference [43].)

Note: Constraint DR6 implies that when information regarding a new contract is first entered into the database, a tuple to say the pertinent supplier is under contract must be inserted into S_DURING *and* a tuple to say the supplier has some particular status must be inserted into S_STATUS_DURING (see the discussion of *multiple assignment* in Chapter 16). What's more, the DURING values in those two tuples must be the same; the begin point must be the date when the supplier was or will be placed under contract, and the end point will be the corresponding date of termination or—perhaps more likely—an artificial "end of time" marker.

Requirement R7: If the database shows supplier S*x* as able to supply some specific part P*y* on day *d*, it must contain exactly one tuple that shows that fact.

The PACKED ON constraint on SP_DURING takes care of this requirement. Without it, that relvar might contain (e.g.) both of the following tuples at the same time:

SNO	PNO	DURING
S2	P1	[*d02:d03*]

SNO	PNO	DURING
S2	P1	[*d03:d04*]

Requirement R8: If the database shows supplier S*x* as able to supply the same part P*y* on days *d* and *d*+1, it must contain exactly one tuple that shows that fact.

The PACKED ON constraint on SP_DURING takes care of this requirement, too. Without it, that relvar might contain (e.g.) both of the following tuples at the same time:

SNO	PNO	DURING
S2	P1	[*d02:d02*]

SNO	PNO	DURING
S2	P1	[*d03:d04*]

Requirement R9: If the database shows supplier S*x* as able to supply some part P*y* on day *d*, it must also show supplier S*x* as being under contract on day *d*.

The foreign U_key constraint

```
USING ( DURING ) : FOREIGN KEY { SNO , DURING } REFERENCES S_DURING
```

—part of the definition of SP_DURING—takes care of this requirement (compare and contrast Constraint XFT3 in Chapter 5). Without this constraint, SP_DURING might contain the tuple for supplier S7 shown on the right below, while at the same time S_DURING contains the tuple for supplier S7 shown on the left below:

SNO	DURING
S7	[d10:d99]

SNO	PNO	DURING
S7	P1	[d09:d99]

To complete this section, Fig. 14.6 shows a revised version of the original design from Fig. 14.4. Observe that we do now make use of the U_key and foreign U_key shorthands. Observe too, more interestingly, that the figures (Figs. 14.4 and 14.6, that is) are essentially identical!— the differences between them are merely cosmetic. In other words, in the case of a design consisting of during relvars only, the U_key and foreign U_key constraints are together sufficient, in and of themselves, to take care of the nine requirements.[4]

```
S_DURING { SNO , DURING }
        USING ( DURING ) : KEY { SNO , DURING }
        USING ( DURING ) : FOREIGN KEY { SNO , DURING }
                                    REFERENCES S_STATUS_DURING

S_STATUS_DURING { SNO , STATUS , DURING }
        USING ( DURING ) : KEY { SNO , DURING }
        USING ( DURING ) : FOREIGN KEY { SNO , DURING }
                                    REFERENCES S_DURING

SP_DURING { SNO , PNO , DURING }
        USING ( DURING ) : KEY { SNO , PNO , DURING }
        USING ( DURING ) : FOREIGN KEY { SNO , DURING }
                                    REFERENCES S_DURING
```

Fig. 14.6: During relvars only—complete design

---

[4] As we'll see in Part IV of this book, SQL takes advantage of this state of affairs. (Well ... it goes some way toward doing so, at any rate.)

BOTH SINCE AND DURING RELVARS

Now we turn to the case of a temporal database consisting of a mixture of since and during relvars (refer to Fig. 14.7):

```
S_SINCE { SNO , SNO_SINCE , STATUS , STATUS_SINCE }
        KEY { SNO }

SP_SINCE { SNO , PNO , SINCE }
        KEY { SNO , PNO }
        FOREIGN KEY { SNO } REFERENCES S_SINCE

S_DURING { SNO , DURING }
        PACKED ON ( DURING )
        KEY { SNO , DURING }

S_STATUS_DURING { SNO , STATUS , DURING }
        PACKED ON ( DURING )
        WHEN UNPACKED ON ( DURING ) THEN KEY { SNO , DURING }
        KEY { SNO , DURING }

SP_DURING { SNO , PNO , DURING }
        PACKED ON ( DURING )
        KEY { SNO , PNO , DURING }
```

Fig. 14.7: Both since and during relvars

Fig. 14.7 is basically a repeat of Fig. 13.4 from Chapter 13, except that we now show all applicable PACKED ON and WHEN / THEN constraints explicitly (as in the previous section, we deliberately avoid use of the U_key shorthand for the time being). Sample values (copied from Figs. 13.2 and 13.3) are shown in Fig. 14.8. Note in particular that all of the DURING values in that figure are genuine values; we no longer need those artificial "end of time" markers that we had to use in the "during relvars only" design in the previous section.

S_SINCE

SNO	SNO_SINCE	STATUS	STATUS_SINCE
S1	d04	20	d06
S2	d07	10	d07
S3	d03	30	d03
S4	d04	20	d08
S5	d02	30	d02

SP_SINCE

SNO	PNO	SINCE
S1	P1	d04
S1	P2	d05
S1	P3	d09
S1	P4	d05
S1	P5	d04
S1	P6	d06
S2	P1	d08
S2	P2	d09
S3	P2	d08
S4	P5	d05

Fig. 14.8: Both since and during relvars—sample values (Part 1 of 2)

```
S_DURING

┌──────┬───────────────┐
│ SNO  │    DURING     │
├──────┼───────────────┤
│ S2   │   [d02:d04]   │
│ S6   │   [d03:d05]   │
└──────┴───────────────┘


S_STATUS_DURING

┌──────┬────────┬───────────────┐
│ SNO  │ STATUS │    DURING     │
├──────┼────────┼───────────────┤
│ S1   │   15   │   [d04:d05]   │
│ S2   │    5   │   [d02:d02]   │
│ S2   │   10   │   [d03:d04]   │
│ S4   │   10   │   [d04:d04]   │
│ S4   │   25   │   [d05:d07]   │
│ S6   │    5   │   [d03:d04]   │
│ S6   │    7   │   [d05:d05]   │
└──────┴────────┴───────────────┘
```

```
SP_DURING

┌──────┬──────┬───────────────┐
│ SNO  │ PNO  │    DURING     │
├──────┼──────┼───────────────┤
│ S2   │  P1  │   [d02:d04]   │
│ S2   │  P2  │   [d03:d03]   │
│ S3   │  P5  │   [d05:d07]   │
│ S4   │  P2  │   [d06:d09]   │
│ S4   │  P4  │   [d04:d08]   │
│ S6   │  P3  │   [d03:d03]   │
│ S6   │  P3  │   [d05:d05]   │
└──────┴──────┴───────────────┘
```

Fig. 14.8 cont.: Both since and during relvars—sample values (Part 2 of 2)

We now proceed to consider what formal versions of Requirements R1-R9 might look like for this database. It's only fair to warn you, however, that some of those requirements are going to be a little more awkward to deal with than they were previously, precisely because the corresponding constraints are going to have to refer to since and during relvars taken in combination.

Requirement R1: If the database shows supplier S*x* as being under contract on day *d*, it must contain exactly one tuple that shows that fact.

As noted in the section "The Nine Requirements," Requirement R1 has to do with avoiding redundancy—specifically, redundancy within or across S_SINCE and S_DURING, given the database of Fig. 14.7. Now, the KEY constraint on S_SINCE guarantees that S_SINCE by itself can't violate the requirement, and the PACKED ON constraint on S_DURING guarantees that S_DURING by itself can't violate it, either (as indeed we saw in the previous two sections). What we need, therefore, is an additional constraint to ensure that those two relvars don't *both* show supplier S*x* as being under contract on the same day:

```
CONSTRAINT BR1 IS_EMPTY
   ( ( S_SINCE JOIN S_DURING ) WHERE SNO_SINCE < POST ( DURING ) ) ;
```

Without this constraint, S_SINCE and S_DURING might respectively contain (e.g.) the following tuples at the same time:

SNO	SNO_SINCE	. . .
S1	*d04*	. . .

SNO	DURING
S1	[*d06:d08*]

Both of these tuples show among other things that supplier S1 was under contract on day 7.[5]

Requirement R2: If the database shows supplier S*x* as being under contract on days *d* and *d*+1, it must contain exactly one tuple that shows that fact.

Requirement R2 has to do with avoiding circumlocution, within and across S_SINCE and S_DURING, and the analysis that follows thus parallels, somewhat, the one just given for Requirement R1. First, the KEY constraint on S_SINCE guarantees that S_SINCE by itself can't violate the requirement, and the PACKED ON constraint on S_DURING guarantees that S_DURING by itself can't violate it, either. What we need, therefore, is an additional constraint to ensure that if S_SINCE shows supplier S*x* as being under contract since day *d*, then S_DURING doesn't show supplier S*x* as being under contract on the day immediately before that day *d*:

```
CONSTRAINT BR2 IS_EMPTY
     ( ( S_SINCE JOIN S_DURING ) WHERE SNO_SINCE = POST ( DURING ) ) ;
```

Without this constraint, S_SINCE and S_DURING might respectively contain (e.g.) the following tuples at the same time:

SNO	SNO_SINCE	. . .
S1	*d04*	. . .

SNO	DURING
S1	[*d01:d03*]

We now observe that Constraints BR1 and BR2 obviously can, and probably should, be combined into a single constraint as follows:

```
CONSTRAINT BR12 IS_EMPTY
     ( ( S_SINCE JOIN S_DURING ) WHERE SNO_SINCE ≤ POST ( DURING ) ) ;
```

Requirement R3: If the database shows supplier S*x* as being under contract on day *d*, it must also show supplier S*x* as having some status on day *d*.

---

[5] Constraint BR1 is the first of many in this chapter in which the expression POST (DURING) appears. At the risk of pointing out the obvious, therefore, we think it worth stating explicitly that those expressions are all *safe*, in the sense that they'll never cause POST to be invoked on some DURING value for which the end point is "the end of time."

This requirement has to do with denseness. Now, the relvars that show a given supplier as being under contract on a given day are S_SINCE and S_DURING; while the relvars that show a given supplier as having a given status on a given day are S_SINCE (again) and S_STATUS_DURING. Thus, the easiest way to think about Requirement R3 in this context is as follows—and this kind of thinking is going to apply to certain of the other requirements too (to Requirements R6 and R9, to be specific):

■ With respect to the property of being under contract, imagine information from S_SINCE and S_DURING being combined in a single relvar S_DURING′ (that relvar will look just like S_DURING in the "during relvars only" case).

■ With respect to the property of having some status, imagine information from S_SINCE and S_STATUS_DURING being combined in a single relvar S_STATUS_DURING′ (that relvar will look just like S_STATUS_DURING in the "during relvars only" case).

■ Then there'll be a foreign U_key from S_DURING′ to S_STATUS_DURING′ that says that every {SNO,DURING} value appearing in the unpacked form of S_DURING′ on DURING must also appear in the unpacked form of S_STATUS_DURING′ on DURING.

So here's a possible formulation:[6]

```
CONSTRAINT BR3
    WITH ( t1 := EXTEND S_SINCE : { DURING := INTERVAL_DATE
                                    ( [ SNO_SINCE : LAST_DATE ( ) ] ) } ,
           t2 := t1 { SNO , DURING } ,
           t3 := t2 UNION S_DURING ,
           t4 := EXTEND S_SINCE : { DURING := INTERVAL_DATE
                                    ( [ STATUS_SINCE : LAST_DATE ( ) ] ) } ,
           t5 := t4 { SNO , STATUS , DURING } ,
           t6 := t5 UNION S_STATUS_DURING ,
           t7 := t6 { SNO , DURING } ) :
    USING ( DURING ) : t3 ⊆ t7 ;
```

Without this constraint, it would be possible for S_SINCE to contain (e.g.) the tuple shown on the left below, while at the same time the unpacked form of S_STATUS_DURING on DURING did *not* contain tuples of the form shown on the right below:

---

[6] In this formulation, *t3* is S_DURING′ and *t6* is S_STATUS_DURING′. It's interesting to note, incidentally, that the foreign U_key shorthand as such isn't much help with this particular constraint. Perhaps there's scope here for generalizing a little further and defining yet another shorthand, at a slightly higher level of abstraction. Reference [41] discusses such a possibility, albeit in the nontemporal context only (but the proposals of that reference could presumably be extended to take care of the temporal case as well).

SNO	SNO_SINCE	STATUS	STATUS_SINCE
S1	*d04*	20	*d06*

SNO	STATUS	DURING
S1	*st4*	[*d04:d04*]

SNO	STATUS	DURING
S1	*st5*	[*d05:d05*]

Incidentally, the (unspecified) STATUS value *st5* in the tuple for supplier S1 and interval [*d05:d05*] here can't possibly be 20, thanks to Constraint BR5 (see later).

There are several further points to be made in connection with Requirement R3 and Constraint BR3. First of all, suppose information regarding some specific contract is represented in S_SINCE and not S_DURING (in other words, we're talking about a current or future contract that has no history yet). Then Requirement R3 implies that the SNO_SINCE and STATUS_SINCE values in the pertinent S_SINCE tuple must be equal.

Second, Requirement R3 also implies that every supplier number appearing in S_DURING must also appear in S_STATUS_DURING (if a supplier has some contract history, that supplier must certainly have some status history):[7]

```
CONSTRAINT BR3X S_DURING { SNO } ⊆ S_STATUS_DURING { SNO } ;
```

Constraint BR3X is an example of an inclusion dependency [10]. We mentioned such dependencies in passing in Chapter 5; as noted in that chapter, they can be regarded as a generalization of referential constraints. Some syntactic shorthand for expressing them might be useful in practice.

Third, although (as we've just said) every supplier number appearing in S_DURING must also appear in S_STATUS_DURING, note carefully that the converse is false. To be specific, suppose there's some supplier who (a) is currently under contract, (b) has never previously had a contract, and (c) has changed status since coming under contract. Then that supplier will be represented in S_STATUS_DURING but not in S_DURING. And so now we've taken care of a small piece of unfinished business from Chapter 12, where we said that S_DURING was strictly redundant in the design consisting of during relvars only but not in the combination design.[8] Well, now we can see why this is so. To be specific, S_DURING isn't guaranteed in the latter case to be such that its value is always equal to the U_projection, using DURING, of the value of S_STATUS_DURING on SNO and DURING at the time in question.

---

[7] But the same is obviously true if we have historical relvars only—so why didn't we mention this point in the previous section?

[8] At least, not in the same sense. But in fact it *is* redundant, inasmuch as its value at any given time can always be obtained from relvars S_STATUS_DURING and S_SINCE taken in combination. As in the "during relvars only" design, however, we still prefer to include S_DURING in our design, partly just for completeness, and partly to avoid a certain degree of awkwardness and arbitrariness that would otherwise occur.

Fourth, observe that Constraint BR3 as stated contains two interval selector invocations in which the end time is specified as "the last day"—note the LAST_DATE ( ) invocations—and then goes on to ask (in effect) for certain relations containing such intervals to be unpacked. Naturally, we hope the implementation will be smart enough not to materialize the unpacked relations in question! See Appendix E for further discussion of such matters.

Finally, to jump ahead of ourselves for a moment: As noted a couple of times previously in this chapter, Requirement R6 is effectively the inverse of Requirement R3. As a consequence, a suitable formulation of the constraint ("Constraint BR6") needed to take care of Requirement R6 can be obtained from Constraint BR3 by simply replacing the "⊆" operator in the last line by a "⊇" operator. However, it obviously makes sense to combine the two constraints by using "=" instead, as follows (note the revised constraint name):

```
CONSTRAINT BR36
    WITH ( t1 := EXTEND S_SINCE : { DURING := INTERVAL_DATE
                                    ( [ SNO_SINCE : LAST_DATE ( ) ] ) } ,
           t2 := t1 { SNO , DURING } ,
           t3 := t2 UNION S_DURING ,
           t4 := EXTEND S_SINCE : { DURING := INTERVAL_DATE
                                    ( [ STATUS_SINCE : LAST_DATE ( ) ] ) } ,
           t5 := t4 { SNO , STATUS , DURING } ,
           t6 := t5 UNION S_STATUS_DURING ,
           t7 := t6 { SNO , DURING } ) :
    USING ( DURING ) : t3 = t7 ;
```

Requirement R4: If the database shows supplier S*x* as having some status on day *d*, it must contain exactly one tuple that shows that fact.

Requirement R4 has to do with avoiding redundancy and contradiction, within or across S_SINCE and S_STATUS_DURING. The KEY constraint on S_SINCE and the PACKED ON and WHEN / THEN constraints on S_STATUS_DURING are sufficient to guarantee that neither of those relvars can violate this requirement by itself. But we need to add:

```
CONSTRAINT BR4 IS_EMPTY
    ( ( S_SINCE JOIN S_STATUS_DURING { SNO , DURING } )
                    WHERE STATUS_SINCE < POST ( DURING ) ) ;
```

Without this constraint, S_SINCE and S_STATUS_DURING might respectively contain (e.g.) the following tuples at the same time:

SNO	SNO_SINCE	STATUS	STATUS_SINCE
S1	*d04*	20	*d04*

SNO	STATUS	DURING
S1	20	[*d04:d06*]

They might even contain (e.g.) the following tuples at the same time:

SNO	SNO_SINCE	STATUS	STATUS_SINCE
S1	*d04*	20	*d04*

SNO	STATUS	DURING
S1	10	[*d04:d06*]

Requirement R5: If the database shows supplier S*x* as having the same status on days *d* and *d*+1, it must contain exactly one tuple that shows that fact.

Requirement R5 has to do with avoiding circumlocution, within and across S_SINCE and S_STATUS_DURING. Again the KEY constraint on S_SINCE and the PACKED ON constraint on S_STATUS_DURING are relevant. In addition, we need:

```
CONSTRAINT BR5 IS_EMPTY
    ( ( S_SINCE JOIN S_STATUS_DURING )
            WHERE STATUS_SINCE = POST ( DURING ) ) ;
```

Without this constraint, S_SINCE and S_STATUS_DURING might respectively contain (e.g.) the following tuples at the same time:

SNO	SNO_SINCE	STATUS	STATUS_SINCE
S1	*d04*	20	*d06*

SNO	STATUS	DURING
S1	20	[*d05:d05*]

Exercise: As we saw earlier, it made sense to combine Constraints BR1 and BR2 into a single constraint, BR12; so why don't we do something similar with constraints BR4 and BR5?

Requirement R6: If the database shows supplier S*x* as having some status on day *d*, it must also show supplier S*x* as being under contract on day *d*.

This requirement, which has to do with denseness, has already been taken care of under the discussion of Requirement R3 above. However, we give an example of a violation of the requirement that could occur if Constraint BR36 weren't in effect. Without that constraint, S_STATUS_DURING might contain (e.g.) the following tuple—

SNO	STATUS	DURING
S1	*st*	[*d04:d04*]

—while at the same time neither S_SINCE nor S_DURING contains a tuple showing supplier S1 as being under contract on day 4.

Observe, incidentally, that (contrary to what might have intuitively been expected):

■ It's not the case that {SNO,DURING} in S_STATUS_DURING is a foreign U_key referencing {SNO,DURING} in S_DURING. (In fact we effectively already know this—see the discussion under Requirement R3 above—but the point bears repeating.)

■ It's not even the case that every SNO value appearing in S_STATUS_DURING must also appear in S_DURING. (In fact we know this too—again, see the discussion under Requirement R3 above.) However, it's at least true that every SNO value appearing in S_STATUS_DURING must also appear in either S_DURING or S_SINCE, and possibly in both.

Both of these points are illustrated by the sample values in Fig. 14.8.

Requirement R7: If the database shows supplier Sx as able to supply some specific part Py on day d, it must contain exactly one tuple that shows that fact.

Requirement R7 has to do with avoiding redundancy, within or across SP_SINCE and SP_DURING. The KEY constraint on SP_SINCE and the PACKED ON constraint on SP_DURING are sufficient to guarantee that neither of those relvars can violate this requirement by itself. But we need to add:

```
CONSTRAINT BR7 IS_EMPTY
    ( ( SP_SINCE JOIN SP_DURING ) WHERE SINCE < POST ( DURING ) ) ;
```

Without this constraint, SP_SINCE and SP_DURING might respectively contain (e.g.) the following tuples at the same time:

SNO	PNO	SINCE
S1	P1	*d04*

SNO	PNO	DURING
S1	P1	[*d06:d08*]

Requirement R8: If the database shows supplier Sx as able to supply the same part Py on days d and d+1, it must contain exactly one tuple that shows that fact.

Requirement R8 has to do with avoiding circumlocution, within or across SP_SINCE and SP_DURING. Again the KEY constraint on SP_SINCE and the PACKED ON constraint on SP_DURING are relevant. In addition, we need:

```
CONSTRAINT BR8 IS_EMPTY
    ( ( SP_SINCE JOIN SP_DURING ) WHERE SINCE = POST ( DURING ) ) ;
```

Without this constraint, SP_SINCE and SP_DURING might respectively contain (e.g.) the following tuples at the same time:

SNO	PNO_	SINCE
S1	P1	*d04*

SNO	PNO	DURING
S1	P1	[*d01:d03*]

Constraints BR7 and BR8 can be combined as follows:

```
CONSTRAINT BR78 IS_EMPTY
    ( ( SP_SINCE JOIN SP_DURING ) WHERE SINCE ≤ POST ( DURING ) ) ;
```

Requirement R9: If the database shows supplier S*x* as able to supply some part P*y* on day *d*, it must also show supplier S*x* as being under contract on day *d*.

This requirement has to do with denseness. In fact, it's quite similar in structure to Requirement R6, which in turn was somewhat similar to Requirement R3. We therefore skip the detailed analysis here and simply state the constraint:

```
CONSTRAINT BR9
    WITH ( t1 := EXTEND S_SINCE : { DURING := INTERVAL_DATE
                                    ( [ SNO_SINCE : LAST_DATE ( ) ] ) } ,
        t2 := t1 { SNO , DURING } ,
        t3 := t2 UNION S_DURING ,
        t4 := EXTEND SP_SINCE : { DURING := INTERVAL_DATE
                                    ( [ SINCE : LAST_DATE ( ) ] ) } ,
        t5 := t4 { SNO , DURING } ,
        t6 := SP_DURING { SNO , DURING } ,
        t7 := t5 UNION t6 ) :
    USING ( DURING ) : t3 ⊇ t7 ;
```

Without this constraint, SP_DURING might contain (e.g.) the following tuple—

SNO	PNO	DURING
S1	P1	[*d04:d04*]

—while at the same time neither S_SINCE nor S_DURING contains a tuple showing supplier S1 as being under contract on day 4.

To complete this section, Fig. 14.9 shows a revised version of the original design from Fig. 14.7. Observe that we do now make use of the "U_key" shorthand.

```
S_SINCE { SNO , SNO_SINCE , STATUS , STATUS_SINCE } KEY { SNO }

SP_SINCE { SNO , PNO , SINCE } KEY { SNO , PNO }
         FOREIGN KEY { SNO } REFERENCES S_SINCE

S_DURING { SNO , DURING } USING ( DURING ) : KEY { SNO , DURING }

S_STATUS_DURING { SNO , STATUS , DURING }
         USING ( DURING ) : KEY { SNO , DURING }

SP_DURING { SNO , PNO , DURING }
         USING ( DURING ) : KEY { SNO , PNO , DURING }

CONSTRAINT BR12 IS_EMPTY
   ( ( S_SINCE JOIN S_DURING ) WHERE SNO_SINCE ≤ POST ( DURING ) ) ;

CONSTRAINT BR36
   WITH ( t1 := EXTEND S_SINCE : { DURING := INTERVAL_DATE
                                   ( [ SNO_SINCE : LAST_DATE ( ) ] ) } ,
          t2 := t1 { SNO , DURING } ,
          t3 := t2 UNION S_DURING ,
          t4 := EXTEND S_SINCE : { DURING := INTERVAL_DATE
                                   ( [ STATUS_SINCE : LAST_DATE ( ) ] ) } ,
          t5 := t4 { SNO , STATUS , DURING } ,
          t6 := t5 UNION S_STATUS_DURING ,
          t7 := t6 { SNO , DURING } ) :
   USING ( DURING ) : t3 = t7 ;

CONSTRAINT BR3X S_DURING { SNO } ⊆ S_STATUS_DURING { SNO } ;

CONSTRAINT BR4 IS_EMPTY
   ( ( S_SINCE JOIN S_STATUS_DURING { SNO , DURING } )
                   WHERE STATUS_SINCE < POST ( DURING ) ) ;

CONSTRAINT BR5 IS_EMPTY
   ( ( S_SINCE JOIN S_STATUS_DURING )
             WHERE STATUS_SINCE = POST ( DURING ) ) ;

CONSTRAINT BR78 IS_EMPTY
   ( ( SP_SINCE JOIN SP_DURING ) WHERE SINCE ≤ POST ( DURING ) ) ;

CONSTRAINT BR9
   WITH ( t1 := EXTEND S_SINCE : { DURING := INTERVAL_DATE
                                   ( [ SNO_SINCE : LAST_DATE ( ) ] ) } ,
          t2 := t1 { SNO , DURING } ,
          t3 := t2 UNION S_DURING ,
          t4 := EXTEND SP_SINCE : { DURING := INTERVAL_DATE
                                   ( [ SINCE : LAST_DATE ( ) ] ) } ,
          t5 := t4 { SNO , DURING } ,
          t6 := SP_DURING { SNO , DURING } ,
          t7 := t5 UNION t6 ) :
   USING ( DURING ) : t3 ⊇ t7 ;
```

Fig. 14.9: Both since and during relvars—complete design

SYNTACTIC SHORTHANDS

From the discussions and examples in this chapter so far, it certainly seems that the design with both since and during relvars gives rise to the most complicated constraints. Nevertheless, we still regard that design as our preferred one in general. In this section, therefore, we make good on our promise from the beginning of the chapter (our promise, that is, to try to conceal some of that complication from the user) by looking for ways of making it a little easier to specify all of the constraints that seem to be needed with that particular design.

We begin by observing that—as is well known, of course—the KEY and FOREIGN KEY specifications used in regular (i.e., nontemporal) relvar definitions are essentially just shorthand for constraints that can be expressed, albeit more longwindedly, using the general "constraint language" portion of any relationally complete language such as **Tutorial D**. However, the shorthands in question are extremely useful ones: Quite apart from the fact that they save us a lot of writing, they also effectively serve *to raise the level of abstraction*, by allowing us to talk in terms of certain "bundles" of concepts that seem to fit together very naturally. (As a bonus, they also pave the way for more efficient implementation.) And it's our belief that analogous shorthands can be defined to provide similar benefits in the temporal case, as we now show.

Before we get into details, however, we should make it clear that we're far more concerned in this book with getting the foundations right than we are with purely syntactic matters. Thus, the remarks in what follows should be seen mainly as "notes toward" the kind of shorthands we believe ought to be feasible in practice. Certainly the concrete syntax needs further work.

Now, it's indeed the case that we can observe some abstract structure in Fig. 14.9 that looks as if it would be applicable to temporal databases in general. To be specific, we can make the following observations regarding the design of Fig. 14.9:

1. Each of the since ("current") relvars concerns certain "entities" and specifies certain "properties" of those entities.

2. Within each such since relvar, the entities are identified by a set K of key attributes and the properties are specified by other attributes (as usual).[9] Some of those since relvars also have foreign keys that reference other since relvars (again as usual).

3. Within each such since relvar, each property has an associated "since" attribute, and so does the key. Within any given tuple, no "since" attribute has a value less than that of the "since" attribute associated with the key.

4. Given any specific since relvar, each property also has an associated during ("historical") relvar, and so does the key. Each such during relvar consists of:

---

[9] We assume for simplicity here that each such relvar has just one key, which we refer to in the remainder of the discussion simply as *the* key. Some refinements will be required to our tentative syntax proposals in order to cater for the possibility of since relvars with two or more keys.

a.   A set of attributes *K* corresponding to the key of the pertinent since relvar

b.   Attribute(s) corresponding to the pertinent property (except for the during relvar associated with the key of the since relvar, to which this paragraph b. doesn't apply)

c.   A "during" attribute

5.   Each of those during relvars is subject to the constraint that the combination of *K* and DURING is a U_key.

6.   Each combination of a property (or the key) in a since relvar together with the corresponding during relvar is subject to certain constraints that are implied by Requirements R1-R9 (or by whatever analogs of those requirements apply to the temporal database we happen to be dealing with), and the general form of those constraints is as illustrated in Fig. 14.9.

We therefore propose a set of syntactic extensions along the following lines.

■   First of all, we propose some syntax for specifying that, within a given since relvar, some specified attribute *B* is the "since" attribute corresponding to some specified set of attributes *A*. For example (note the highlighted text):

```
VAR S_SINCE BASE RELATION
  { SNO          SNO ,
    SNO_SINCE     DATE SINCE_FOR { SNO } ,
    STATUS        INTEGER ,
    STATUS_SINCE  DATE SINCE_FOR { STATUS } }
  KEY { SNO } ;

VAR SP_SINCE BASE RELATION
  { SNO          SNO ,
    PNO          PNO ,
    SINCE DATE SINCE_FOR { SNO , PNO } }
  KEY { SNO , PNO }
  FOREIGN KEY { SNO } REFERENCES S_SINCE ;
```

Now the system knows that SNO_SINCE and STATUS_SINCE are the "since" attributes for {SNO} and {STATUS}, respectively, in relvar S_SINCE, and SINCE is the "since" attribute for {SNO,PNO} in relvar SP_SINCE. It also knows for each of those relvars which "since" attribute is associated with the key, and in the case of S_SINCE it knows that the constraint

```
IS_EMPTY ( S_SINCE WHERE STATUS_SINCE < SNO_SINCE )
```

is required to hold.

- Next, we propose some syntax for specifying the during relvar corresponding to a given "since" attribute. For example (again note the highlighted text):

```
VAR S_SINCE BASE RELATION
   { SNO            SNO ,
     SNO_SINCE      DATE SINCE_FOR { SNO } HISTORY_IN ( S_DURING ) ,
     STATUS         INTEGER ,
     STATUS_SINCE DATE SINCE_FOR { STATUS }
                                       HISTORY_IN ( S_STATUS_DURING ) }
   KEY { SNO } ;

VAR SP_SINCE BASE RELATION
   { SNO    SNO ,
     PNO    PNO ,
     SINCE DATE SINCE_FOR { SNO , PNO } HISTORY_IN ( SP_DURING ) }
   KEY { SNO , PNO }
   FOREIGN KEY { SNO } REFERENCES S_SINCE ;
```

Now the system knows that relvars called S_DURING, S_STATUS_DURING, and SP_DURING must be defined. In fact, those definitions might even be automated (since the system certainly knows what their structure must be), but for explanatory purposes we show them explicitly here:

```
VAR S_DURING BASE RELATION
   { SNO      SNO ,
     DURING INTERVAL_DATE }
   USING ( DURING ) : KEY { SNO , DURING } ;

VAR S_STATUS_DURING BASE RELATION
   { SNO      SNO ,
     STATUS INTEGER ,
     DURING INTERVAL_DATE }
   USING ( DURING ) : KEY { SNO , DURING } ;

VAR SP_DURING BASE RELATION
   { SNO      SNO ,
     PNO      PNO ,
     DURING INTERVAL_DATE }
   USING ( DURING ) : KEY { SNO , PNO , DURING } ;
```

We conjecture that the foregoing specifications taken together should be sufficient for the system to infer Constraints BR12, BR36, BR3X, BR4, BR5, BR78, and BR9 for itself, thereby avoiding any need for those constraints to be stated explicitly.[10]

---

[10] In this connection, however, see footnote 6 in Chapter 15.

CONCLUDING REMARKS

We conclude this chapter with a few miscellaneous observations.

- In conventional databases, relvars are sometimes "dropped" (meaning the relvar in question is deleted entirely, and there's now no information regarding the relvar in question in the database catalog). In the temporal context, however, it seems unlikely that a during relvar would ever be dropped, since the whole point of the database is to maintain historical records.[11] By contrast, a since relvar might perhaps be dropped, but it would probably be necessary to move all of the information it contains to appropriate during relvars first. For obvious reasons, moreover, dropping either kind of relvar is likely to require a lot of revision to existing constraints.

- Another operation that's sometimes performed in conventional databases is that of adding a new attribute to an existing relvar. In a temporal database, adding a new attribute to a during relvar seems to make little sense, because—given our recommendations regarding sixth normal form, at any rate—each such relvar represents the history of just one "property," more or less by definition. By contrast, adding a new attribute to a since relvar might make sense, but (a) the new attribute would probably need an accompanying new "since" attribute, and (b) it would probably need an accompanying new during relvar as well. New constraints would also be required.

- Third, we note that constraints in general do change over time (though the particular kinds of constraints we've been discussing in this chapter are perhaps less susceptible to change than most). As a consequence, a temporal database might contain data that satisfies some constraint that was in effect when the data was entered into the database but fails to satisfy some revised version of that constraint that's in effect now. One implication is that constraints themselves might need to include temporal components ("valid times," in fact—see Chapters 4 and 17). A further and possibly more serious implication is that the database catalog might itself need to be treated as a temporal database. However, further discussion of such possibilities is beyond the scope of this book.

Finally, we began this chapter by describing the nine requirements, all of which stated in effect that certain conditions *must* hold in any temporal database involving suppliers and shipments. Subsequently, however, we saw that it might sometimes be acceptable to violate certain of those requirements after all (see the discussion of Requirement R1 in the section "During Relvars Only"). Thus, where the requirements generally say that some condition *must* be satisfied, it might perhaps be better if they said that, other things being equal, the condition in

---

[11] Perhaps we should say rather that it would seem *unwise* to drop such a relvar. We all know the problem of discovering we need something we threw away only yesterday.

question *should preferably* be satisfied. At any rate they should generally be understood in this light.

EXERCISES

14.1 What's a denseness constraint?

14.2 We said in the section "The Nine Requirements" that Requirements R2, R5, and R8 can't possibly be satisfied, in general, if full vertical decomposition into 6NF hasn't been done. Why not?

14.3 In the design consisting of during relvars only, S_DURING is such that its value at any given time is equal to the value of the U_projection, using DURING, of S_STATUS_DURING on {SNO,DURING} at that same time. So shouldn't a constraint be stated to that effect?

14.4 (*Repeated from the body of the chapter.*) With reference to the section "Both Since and During Relvars," we said it's a logical consequence of Requirement R3 that every supplier number appearing in S_DURING must also appear in S_STATUS_DURING (see Constraint BR3X). But we also pointed out that the same was obviously true with the "during relvars only" design; so why didn't we mention the point when we were discussing this latter design?

14.5 With reference to Fig. 14.9:

a. Why isn't {SNO,DURING} in SP_DURING defined to be a foreign U_key (using DURING) referencing S_DURING?

b. Among other things, Requirement R3 clearly implies that if t is a tuple in S_SINCE, and if the SNO_SINCE and STATUS_SINCE values in t are d and d', respectively, then it must be the case that $d \leq d'$. Does Constraint BR36 take care of this requirement?

c. (*Repeated from the body of the chapter.*) We saw it made sense to combine Constraints BR1 and BR2 into a single constraint (BR12), so why didn't we do something similar with constraints BR4 and BR5?

14.6 State analogs of the nine requirements in a form (natural language only) that applies to the courses-and-students database from Exercise 13.7 in Chapter 13.

14.7 Given your answer to Exercise 14.6:

a. Show the corresponding formal constraints.

b.   What SINCE_FOR and HISTORY_IN specifications, if any, would you add to the database definition?

14.8 The database definition from Exercise 13.7 in Chapter 13 really needs to be extended still further to allow us to record, in connection with an enrollment, the particular offering to which that enrollment is assigned. State whatever additional natural language requirements you can think of that might arise in connection with such an extension. Also make the corresponding changes to the **Tutorial D** definition of the database.

14.9 In the body of the chapter we mentioned a niladic operator called TODAY that returns the date today. Care needs to be taken, however, if such an operator is referenced within an integrity constraint. Why?

ANSWERS

14.1 A denseness constraint is a constraint to the effect that some condition $c1$ must be satisfied throughout every interval throughout which some other condition $c2$ is satisfied. For example, $c1$ might be "supplier Sx is under contract" and $c2$ "supplier Sx is able to supply some part."

14.2 Loosely, because a during relvar that's not in 6NF will display some redundancy (see, e.g., relvar SSSC_DURING in Chapter 12). A more formal answer follows. First, Requirements R2, R5, and R8 are all requirements to the effect that the database mustn't contain more than one tuple representing a certain proposition. A fortiori, therefore, no relvar must do so, either. Now, a relvar R that's not in 6NF is, by definition, one whose predicate can be expressed as a conjunction (AND) of two or more predicates; thus, if t is a tuple in such a relvar R, then t must represent some true proposition of the form $p1$ AND $p2$, where $p1$ and $p2$ are propositions ($p1 \neq p2$). Now let the proposition $p1$ AND $p3$ ($p2 \neq p3$) also be true and be capable of representation by a tuple t' that could appear in R. By *The Closed World Assumption*, then, that tuple t' must in fact appear in R. Thus, proposition $p1$ is represented by more than one tuple in the database, thereby violating one of the specified requirements.

14.3 Yes, but it is—either in the form of constraint DR36, q.v., or in the form of the two foreign U_keys, one from each of the relvars to the other.

14.4   Because the constraint in question (a hypothetical "Constraint DR3X") is subsumed by Constraint DR3.

14.5

a. Because a supplier number can appear in SP_DURING without appearing in S_DURING (in other words, a supplier with no contract history can nevertheless have a shipment history). A fortiori, therefore, an {SNO,DURING} value can appear in the unpacked form of SP_DURING on DURING without simultaneously appearing in the unpacked form of S_DURING on DURING.

b. Assuming various other constraints in the figure are also enforced, yes, it does.

c. Because Requirement R4 has to do merely with the supplier having *some* status value on some day, while Requirement R5 has to do with the supplier having *the same* status value on consecutive days.

14.6 The courses-and-students analog actually consists of 22 requirements, as follows (note the numbering):

1. If the database shows course Cx as being available on day *d*, it must contain exactly one tuple that shows that fact.

2. If the database shows course Cx as being available on days *d* and *d*+1, it must contain exactly one tuple that shows that fact.

3. If the database shows course Cx as being available on day *d*, it must also show course Cx as having some name on day *d*.

4. If the database shows course Cx as having some name on day *d*, it must contain exactly one tuple that shows that fact.

5. If the database shows course Cx as having the same name on days *d* and *d*+1, it must contain exactly one tuple that shows that fact.

6. If the database shows course Cx as having some name on day *d*, it must also show course Cx as being available on day *d*.

7. If the database shows student STx as being registered on day *d*, then it must contain exactly one tuple that shows that fact.

8. If the database shows student STx as being registered on days *d* and *d*+1, it must contain exactly one tuple that shows that fact.

9. If the database shows student STx as being registered on day *d*, it must also show student Sx as having some name on day *d*.

10. If the database shows student STx as having some name on day *d*, it must contain exactly one tuple that shows that fact.

11. If the database shows student STx as having the same name on days *d* and *d*+1, it must contain exactly one tuple that shows that fact.

12. If the database shows student STx as having some name on day *d*, it must also show student STx as being registered on day *d*.

13. If the database shows student STx as being enrolled on course Cx on day *d*, it must contain exactly one tuple that shows that fact.

14. If the database shows student STx as being enrolled on course Cx on days *d* and *d*+1, it must contain exactly one tuple that shows that fact.

15. If the database shows student STx as being enrolled on course Cx on day *d*, it must also show student STx as being registered on day *d*.

16. If the database shows student STx as being enrolled on course Cx on day *d*, it must also show course Cx as being available on day *d*.

17. If the database shows student STx as having achieved grade *g* on course Cx on day *d*, it must contain exactly one tuple that shows that fact.

18. If the database shows offering *o* of course Cx as taking place on day *d*, it must contain exactly one tuple that shows that fact.

19. If the database shows offering *o* of course Cx as taking place on days *d* and *d*+1, it must contain exactly one tuple that shows that fact.

20. If the database shows offering *o* of course Cx as having quota *q* on day *d*, it must contain exactly one tuple that shows that fact.

21. If the database shows offering *o* of course C*x* as having quota *q* on days *d* and *d*+1, it must contain exactly one tuple that shows that fact.

22. If the database shows offering *o* of course C*x* as taking place on day *d*, it must also show C*x* as being available on day *d*.

14.7

a. The following solutions follow the numbering in the answer to the previous exercise.

1. The key specifications for CURRENT_COURSE and OLD_COURSE partly cater for this requirement, but we also need:

```
CONSTRAINT X147R1 IS_EMPTY
    ( ( CURRENT_COURSE { COURSENO , AVAILABLE } JOIN
             OLD_COURSE { COURSENO , AVAILABLE_DURING } )
                        WHERE AVAILABLE < POST ( AVAILABLE_DURING ) ) ;
```

However, the fact that {COURSENO} is a key for OLD_COURSE strongly suggests that old courses are never revived, in which case the following simplification of Constraint X147R1 would cater for that requirement as well as the current one:

```
CONSTRAINT X147R1S IS_EMPTY
    ( CURRENT_COURSE { COURSENO } JOIN OLD_COURSE { COURSENO } ) ;
```

2. The key specifications for CURRENT_COURSE and OLD_COURSE partly cater for this requirement. If Constraint X147R1S is defined, then no additional constraint is needed. Otherwise, the requirement could be catered for by:

```
CONSTRAINT X147R2 IS_EMPTY
    ( ( CURRENT_COURSE { COURSENO , AVAILABLE } JOIN
            OLD_COURSE { COURSENO , AVAILABLE_DURING } )
      WHERE AVAILABLE = POST ( AVAILABLE_DURING ) ) ;
```

Constraints X147R1 and X147R2 could be combined as follows:

```
CONSTRAINT X147R1&2 IS_EMPTY
    ( ( CURRENT_COURSE { COURSENO , AVAILABLE } JOIN
            OLD_COURSE { COURSENO , AVAILABLE_DURING } )
      WHERE AVAILABLE ≤ POST ( AVAILABLE_DURING ) ) ;
```

3. No additional constraint is needed. The requirement is catered for by the headings of CURRENT_COURSE and OLD_COURSE.

4. Constraint X147R1 and the key specifications for CURRENT_COURSE and OLD_COURSE cater for this requirement.

5. Constraint X147R1&2 and the key specifications for CURRENT_COURSE and OLD_COURSE cater for this requirement.

6. No additional constraint is needed. The requirement is catered for by the headings of CURRENT_COURSE and OLD_COURSE.

7. The requirement is partly catered for by the specifications of {STUDENTNO} as a key for CURRENT_STUDENT and USING (REG_DURING) : {STUDENTNO,REG_DURING} as a U_key for STUDENT_HISTORY. But we also need:

```
CONSTRAINT X147R7 IS_EMPTY
    ( ( CURRENT_STUDENT { STUDENTNO , REGISTERED } JOIN
        STUDENT_HISTORY { STUDENTNO , REG_DURING } )
                        WHERE REGISTERED < POST ( REG_DURING ) ) ;
```

8. The requirement is partly catered for by the specifications of {STUDENTNO} as a key for CURRENT_STUDENT, USING (REG_DURING) : {STUDENTNO,REG_DURING} as a U_key for STUDENT_HISTORY, and Constraint X147R7. But we also need:

```
CONSTRAINT X147R8 IS_EMPTY
    ( ( CURRENT_STUDENT { STUDENTNO , REGISTERED } JOIN
        STUDENT_HISTORY { STUDENTNO , REG_DURING } )
                        WHERE REGISTERED = POST ( REG_DURING ) ) ;
```

Constraints X147R7 and X147R8 could be combined as follows:

```
CONSTRAINT X147R7&8 IS_EMPTY
 ( ( CURRENT_STUDENT { STUDENTNO , REGISTERED } JOIN
     STUDENT_HISTORY { STUDENTNO , REG_DURING } )
                     WHERE REGISTERED ≤ POST ( REG_DURING ) ) ;
```

9. No additional constraint is needed. The requirement is catered for by the headings of CURRENT_STUDENT and STUDENT_HISTORY.

10. Constraint X147R7, the key specification for CURRENT_STUDENT, and the U_key specification for STUDENT_HISTORY together cater for this requirement.

11. Constraint X147R7&8, the key specification for CURRENT_STUDENT, and the U_key specification for STUDENT_HISTORY together cater for this requirement.

12. No additional constraint is needed. The requirement is catered for by the headings of CURRENT_STUDENT and STUDENT_HISTORY.

13. The key specifications for ENROLLMENT and COMPLETED_COURSE partly cater for this requirement, but something equivalent to the following is also needed:

```
CONSTRAINT X147R13 IS_EMPTY
( ( ENROLLMENT        { COURSENO , STUDENTNO , ENROLLED } JOIN
    COMPLETED_COURSE { COURSENO , STUDENTNO , STUDIED_DURING } )
                   WHERE ENROLLED < POST ( STUDIED_DURING ) ) ;
```

14. The key specifications for ENROLLMENT and COMPLETED_COURSE partly cater for this requirement, but we also need:

```
CONSTRAINT X147R14 IS_EMPTY
   ( ( ENROLLMENT JOIN COMPLETED_COURSE )
               WHERE ENROLLED = POST ( STUDIED_DURING ) ) ;
```

Constraints X147R13 and X147R14 could be combined as follows:

```
CONSTRAINT X147R13&14 IS_EMPTY
   ( ( ENROLLMENT JOIN COMPLETED_COURSE )
               WHERE ENROLLED ≤ POST ( STUDIED_DURING ) ) ;
```

15. The foreign key constraint from ENROLLMENT to CURRENT_STUDENT partly caters for this requirement, but we also need:

```
CONSTRAINT X147R15 IS_EMPTY
   ( ( ENROLLMENT JOIN CURRENT_STUDENT ) WHERE REGISTERED > ENROLLED )
   AND WITH
   ( t1 := EXTEND CURRENT_STUDENT : { DURING := INTERVAL_DATE
                                    ( [ REGISTERED : LAST_DATE ( ) ] ) }
                                       { STUDENTNO , DURING } ,
     t2 := t1 UNION ( STUDENT_HISTORY RENAME { REG_DURING AS DURING } )
                                       { STUDENTNO , DURING } ,
     t3 := ( COMPLETED_COURSE RENAME { STUDIED_DURING AS DURING } )
                                       { STUDENTNO , DURING } ) :
     USING ( DURING ) : t3 ⊂ t2 ;
```

16. The foreign key constraint from ENROLLMENT to CURRENT_COURSE partly caters for this requirement, but we also need:

```
CONSTRAINT X147R16 IS_EMPTY
   ( ( ENROLLMENT JOIN CURRENT_COURSE ) WHERE AVAILABLE > ENROLLED )
   AND WITH
   ( t1 := EXTEND CURRENT_COURSE : { DURING :=  INTERVAL_DATE
                                    ( [ AVAILABLE : LAST_DATE ( ) ] ) }
                                          { COURSENO , DURING } ,
      t2 := t1 UNION ( OLD_COURSE RENAME { AVAILABLE_DURING AS DURING } )
                                          { COURSENO , DURING } ) ,
      t3 := ( COMPLETED_COURSE RENAME ( STUDIED_DURING AS DURING ) )
                                          { COURSENO , DURING } ) :
   USING ( DURING ) : t3 ⊆ t2 ;
```

17. The key specification for COMPLETED_COURSE caters for this requirement.

18. The key specification for COURSE_OFFERING caters for this requirement.

19. The key specification for COURSE_OFFERING caters for this requirement.

20. The key specification for COURSE_OFFERING caters for this requirement.

21. The key specification for COURSE_OFFERING caters for this requirement.

22. The requirement could be catered for by the following:

```
CONSTRAINT X147R22 WITH
   ( t1 := EXTEND CURRENT_COURSE : { DURING := INTERVAL_DATE
                                    ( [ AVAILABLE : LAST_DATE ( ) ] ) }
                                          { COURSENO , DURING } ,
      t2 := T1 UNION ( OLD_COURSE RENAME ( AVAILABLE_DURING AS DURING ) )
                                          { COURSENO , DURING } ) ,
      t3 := ( OFFERING RENAME ( OFFERED_DURING AS DURING ) )
                                          { COURSENO , DURING } ) :
USING ( DURING ) : t3 ⊆ t2 ;
```

b. Add to the specification of AVAILABLE in CURRENT_COURSE:

```
SINCE_FOR { COURSENO , NAME }
HISTORY_IN ( OLD_COURSE )
```

Add to the specification of REGISTERED in CURRENT_STUDENT:

```
SINCE_FOR { STUDENTNO , NAME }
HISTORY_IN ( STUDENT_HISTORY )
```

Add to the specification of ENROLLED in ENROLLMENT:

```
SINCE_FOR { COURSENO , STUDENTNO }
HISTORY_IN ( COMPLETED_COURSE )
```

Note: These last additions are perhaps a little suspect—the ENROLLED attribute represents the date on which the student enrolled for some offering of the course, not the date on which that student's study of that course started.

14.8 The requirement to record on which particular offering a student enrolls on could be addressed by adding an OFFERINGNO attribute to both of the relvars ENROLLMENT and COMPLETED_COURSE. The STUDIED_DURING attribute of COMPLETED_COURSE is probably now redundant, since the start of a student's study presumably coincides with the start of the offering. However, the end of a student's study might be considered to be earlier than the end of the offering in the case of dropouts, in which case perhaps STUDIED_DURING should be replaced by a COMPLETED_ON attribute of type DATE. The following new natural language requirement arises:

23. If the database shows student S*x* as having enrolled on offering *o* of course C*y* on day *d*, it must also show offering *o* of course C*y* as starting to take place on or after day *d*. (Presumably it's not permitted for a student to enroll on an offering that has already started, and might even have finished.)

Requirement 16 no longer applies.

Requirement 23 could be catered for by this:

```
CONSTRAINT X148R23 IS_EMPTY
    ( ( ENROLLMENT JOIN COURSE_OFFERING )
                WHERE ENROLLED > BEGIN ( OFFERED_DURING ) ) ;
```

If COMPLETED_ON is added to COMPLETED_COURSE, then the following new natural language requirement arises:

24. If the database shows student S*x* as having completed offering *o* of course C*y* on day *d*, it must also show offering *o* of course C*y* as starting to take place on or after day *d* and finishing before or on day *d*.

Requirement 24 could be catered for as follows:

```
CONSTRAINT X148R24 IS_EMPTY
    ( ( ENROLLMENT JOIN COURSE_OFFERING )
                WHERE COMPLETED_ON ∈ OFFERED_DURING ) ;
```

14.9 Let *D* be a variable of type DATE, and consider the boolean expression *D* > TODAY ( ). Observe that this expression could evaluate to TRUE on some given day and FALSE on the next, even if the value of *D* remains unchanged between the two evaluations. Thus, an integrity constraint that involves such an expression—or the checking implied by such a constraint, rather—could succeed on one day and fail on the next, even if the database hasn't changed in the interim.

Chapter 15

Q u e r i e s

Fools ask questions that wise men cannot answer.

—17th century proverb

In this chapter we consider the question—unfortunately a somewhat nontrivial one—of what's involved in formulating queries on a temporal database. We base most of our examples and discussions on the various versions of the suppliers-and-shipments database described in Chapter 12; we also assume throughout that the constraints discussed in the last two chapters are in effect, and we make tacit use of that assumption in certain of our query formulations. *Note:* We continue to ignore supplier names and cities until further notice.

THE TWELVE QUERIES

Of course, we've seen many examples of queries in this book already, especially in Chapters 7-11. However, most of those earlier examples were intended primarily to illustrate the functionality of some specific operator; also, they all involved during or "historical" relvars specifically, or at any rate relvars (or relations) with interval attributes. In this chapter, by contrast, we want to concentrate on how we might formulate a variety of arguably more realistic queries on a more complete database. For purposes of future reference, we list below the queries we'll be considering.

Query Q1: Get the status of supplier S1 on day *dn*.

Query Q2: Get pairs of supplier numbers such that the indicated suppliers were assigned their current status on the same day.

Query Q3: Get supplier numbers for suppliers currently able to supply both part P1 and part P2.

Query Q4: Get supplier numbers for suppliers not currently able to supply both part P1 and part P2.

Query Q5: Get supplier numbers for suppliers currently able to supply some part who have changed their status since they most recently became able to supply some part.

Query Q6: Get intervals during which at least one supplier was under contract.

Query Q7: Suppose the result of Query Q6 is kept as a relvar BUSY. Use BUSY to get intervals during which no supplier was under contract at all.

Query Q8: Get supplier numbers for suppliers currently under contract who also had an earlier contract.

Query Q9: Get SNO-PARTS-DURING triples such that the indicated supplier was able to supply the indicated range of parts during the indicated interval.

Query Q10: Suppose the result of Query Q9 is kept as a relvar S_PARTS_DURING. Use S_PARTS_DURING to get SNO-PNO-DURING triples such that the indicated supplier was able to supply the indicated part during the indicated interval.

Query Q11: Given relvar TERM, with attributes DURING, PRESIDENT, and TERMNO, and both {DURING} and {PRESIDENT,TERMNO} as keys, get DURING-PRESIDENT pairs such that the indicated president held office throughout the indicated interval.

Query Q12: Given relvar TERM as in Query Q11, get pairs of presidents who held office in the same year (in the sense that, e.g., Ford and Carter held office in the same year, because Ford's term ended when Carter's began, on January 20th, 1977).

Incidentally, it's worth noting that certain of these queries—Queries Q6, Q7, and Q9, for example—can be handled only rather clumsily (possibly not at all, in some cases) in certain of the other temporal database approaches described in the literature. The reason is that the approaches in question typically violate *The Information Principle* (see Chapter 4) by treating timestamps in general, and interval timestamps in particular, as special in some way, instead of representing them by regular relational attributes. See reference [29] for further discussion.

The structure of the chapter is as follows. Following these preliminary remarks, the next three sections show what the sample queries might look like on a database involving (a) since ("current") relvars only, (b) during ("historical") relvars only, or (c) a mixture of both. The final section then considers the possibility of providing a collection of predefined views in order to simplify the formulation of certain kinds of queries, thereby making the user's life a little easier than it otherwise might be.

SINCE RELVARS ONLY

As just indicated, in this section we limit our attention to a version of the database that contains since or "current" relvars only. Fig. 15.1, a copy of Fig. 14.3, shows the database definition (in outline), pertinent constraints included. We remind you that this database can't represent information about the past at all, other than whatever might be conveyed by the "since" values; on the other hand, it can definitely represent future information (certainly implicitly, and possibly explicitly as well). Refer to Fig. 14.2 in Chapter 14 for some sample values.

```
S_SINCE { SNO , SNO_SINCE , STATUS , STATUS_SINCE }
         KEY { SNO }

CONSTRAINT SR6 IS_EMPTY ( S_SINCE WHERE STATUS_SINCE < SNO_SINCE ) ;

SP_SINCE { SNO , PNO , SINCE }
         KEY { SNO , PNO }
         FOREIGN KEY { SNO } REFERENCES S_SINCE

CONSTRAINT SR9 IS_EMPTY
         ( ( SP_SINCE JOIN S_SINCE ) WHERE SINCE < SNO_SINCE ) ;
```

Fig. 15.1: Since relvars only

Perhaps we should explain at the outset that some of the query formulations in this section aren't really very temporal in nature (after all, the database itself is only semitemporal). Part of the point, though, is to pave the way for the discussion of fully temporal databases in later sections. Also, we ignore Queries Q11 and Q12, since they assume the existence of a fully temporal relvar (namely, TERM) and thus aren't in the spirit of a merely semitemporal database like that of Fig. 15.1.

Query Q1: Get the status of supplier S1 on day *dn*.

First we remind you that if some S_SINCE tuple says supplier S*x* has had (or will have) status *st* from day *d* onward, we interpret that tuple as meaning that supplier S*x* had, has, or will have status *st* on every day from day *d* until "the last day." It follows that Query Q1 can be answered from the database of Fig. 15.1 if and only if (a) S_SINCE contains a (necessarily unique) tuple for supplier S1 and (b) the STATUS_SINCE value in that tuple is less than or equal to *dn*. Here then is a suitable formulation:

```
( S_SINCE WHERE SNO = SNO ( 'S1' ) AND STATUS_SINCE ≤ dn ) { STATUS }
```

If this expression yields an empty result, it means that either (a) S_SINCE contains no tuple for S1 or (b) S_SINCE does contain a tuple for S1 but the STATUS_SINCE value in that tuple is greater than *dn*. Both of these possibilities mean the query can't be answered, because the information isn't in the database.

Note: We're assuming in this example—and we'll continue to assume throughout the rest of the chapter—that results are always required in relational form, even when (as in the present case) a simple scalar result might serve the purpose.

Query Q2: Get pairs of supplier numbers such that the indicated suppliers were assigned their current status on the same day.

The first point to make here is that the natural language version of this query ought really to be stated in terms of suppliers who were *or will be* assigned their current status on the same day; also, the qualifier "current" has to be understood as meaning *current at the time in question.* For simplicity, however, we'll ignore such refinements for the most part, both in this example and throughout the remainder of this chapter (in our natural language statements, that is, but not, of course, in their formal counterparts).

Observe next that a given supplier has a current status if and only if there exists a tuple for that supplier in S_SINCE—and if such a tuple does exist, then the STATUS_SINCE value in that tuple gives the date when that current status was assigned to that supplier. Hence:

```
WITH ( t1 := S_SINCE { SNO , STATUS_SINCE } ,
       t2 := t1 RENAME { SNO AS XNO } ,
       t3 := t1 RENAME { SNO AS YNO } ,
       t4 := t2 JOIN t3 ,
       t5 := t4 WHERE XNO < YNO ) :
t5 { XNO , YNO }
```

Note: Line 5 here requests a restriction of *t4* to just those tuples where supplier number XNO is less than supplier number YNO. Well, we've seen this trick before, in Chapter 2 and elsewhere; the idea is to eliminate pairs of supplier numbers of the form (*x,x*) and to guarantee that the pairs (*x,y*) and (*y,x*) don't both appear. Of course, the operator "<" must be defined for type SNO in order for this trick to work.

Query Q3: Get supplier numbers for suppliers currently able to supply both part P1 and part P2.

A formulation of this query is straightforward:

```
WITH ( t1 := ( SP_SINCE WHERE PNO = PNO ( 'P1' ) ) { SNO } ,
       t2 := ( SP_SINCE WHERE PNO = PNO ( 'P2' ) ) { SNO } ) :
t1 JOIN t2
```

We could replace JOIN in the last line here by INTERSECT if we liked.

Query Q4: Get supplier numbers for suppliers not currently able to supply both part P1 and part P2.

A formulation of this query is easily obtained by extending the formulation for Query Q3 slightly:

```
WITH ( t1 := ( SP_SINCE WHERE PNO = PNO ( 'P1' ) ) { SNO } ,
       t2 := ( SP_SINCE WHERE PNO = PNO ( 'P2' ) ) { SNO } ,
       t3 := t1 JOIN t2 ) :
S_SINCE { SNO } MINUS t3
```

Query Q5: Get supplier numbers for suppliers currently able to supply some part who have changed their status since they most recently became able to supply some part.

Suppliers who are currently able to supply some part are represented in SP_SINCE, and the date when they most recently became able to do so can also be obtained from that relvar. Furthermore, the date when they acquired their current status—i.e., the date of their most recent status change, in effect—is given in S_SINCE. Hence:

```
WITH ( t1 := EXTEND SP_SINCE { SNO } :
                     { MRC := MAX ( !!SP_SINCE , SINCE ) } ,
       t2 := S_SINCE JOIN t1 ,
       t3 := t2 WHERE STATUS_SINCE > MRC ) :
t3 { SNO }
```

Query Q6: Get intervals during which at least one supplier was under contract.

Given only the semitemporal database of Fig. 15.1, the best attempt we can make at answering this query is just to say that if the earliest SNO_SINCE date in relvar S_SINCE is *d*, then at least one supplier is under contract on every day from *d* to "the last day" (inclusive):

```
RELATION { TUPLE { DURING INTERVAL_DATE
                 ( [ MIN ( S_SINCE , SNO_SINCE ) : LAST_DATE ( ) ] ) } }
```

Explanation: The expression overall here is a relation selector invocation of the form RELATION {TUPLE {DURING INTERVAL_DATE ([*b*:*e*])}}; it returns a relation with just one attribute, called DURING, and just one tuple. The expression within the outermost set of braces is a tuple selector invocation; it denotes the sole tuple in that single-tuple relation. That tuple in turn has just one component, called DURING. The DURING value in that tuple is specified by means of the interval selector invocation INTERVAL_DATE ([*b*:*e*]), where the *b* value is obtained by means of an invocation of the aggregate operator MIN—returning the minimum value of attribute SNO_SINCE within relvar S_SINCE—and the *e* value is obtained by means of an invocation of LAST_DATE.

However, there's a problem with the foregoing formulation. In fact, that formulation will suffice, just so long as we can be sure that S_SINCE is nonempty. If it *is* empty, however, then (as explained in reference [45]) the MIN invocation will raise an exception—or, at least, so we assume for present purposes.[1] So if we can't assume S_SINCE is nonempty, a more complicated formulation becomes necessary:

```
WITH ( t1 := EXTEND S_SINCE { } :
                   { EARLIEST := MIN ( S_SINCE , SNO_SINCE ) } ,
       t2 := EXTEND t1 : { DURING := INTERVAL_DATE
                                   ( [ EARLIEST : LAST_DATE ( ) ] ) } ) :
t2 { DURING }
```

Explanation: The first step here extends the projection of S_SINCE on no attributes. That projection is either TABLE_DUM or TABLE_DEE—TABLE_DUM if S_SINCE is empty, TABLE_DEE otherwise [25]. If it's TABLE_DUM, then *t1* is empty too (and the MIN operator is never invoked);[2] otherwise, *t1* contains just one tuple. And if *t1* is empty, so is *t2*, and so is the overall result; otherwise, *t2* (like *t1*) contains just one tuple, and so does the overall result.

Query Q7: Suppose the result of Query Q6 is kept as a relvar BUSY. Use BUSY to get intervals during which no supplier was under contract at all.

If we can assume BUSY is nonempty, then it'll actually contain just one tuple, and the following formulation will suffice:

```
RELATION { TUPLE { DURING INTERVAL_DATE
   ( [ FIRST_DATE ( ) : PRE ( DURING FROM ( TUPLE FROM BUSY ) ) ] ) } }
```

Explanation: Again the overall expression here is a relation selector invocation of the form RELATION {TUPLE {DURING INTERVAL_DATE ([*b*:*e*])}}; thus, it returns a relation with one attribute, called DURING, and one tuple. The sole DURING value within that relation is specified by means of an interval selector invocation of the form INTERVAL_DATE ([*b*:*e*]), where the *b* value is obtained by means of an invocation of FIRST_DATE and the *e* value is the date immediately preceding the begin point of the sole DURING value in BUSY. *Note:* See Chapter 2 if you need to refresh your memory regarding the meaning of expressions like DURING FROM (TUPLE FROM BUSY).

This time, however, there are two problems with the formulation as shown. In fact, that formulation will suffice so long as we can be sure that (a) BUSY is nonempty *and* (b) the sole interval it contains doesn't have "the beginning of time" as its begin point (it will, of course, have "the end of time" as its end point). Here by contrast is a more complicated formulation that works correctly in all cases:

---

[1] Actually there's some debate over what should happen if an aggregate operator like MIN is invoked on an empty argument. A discussion of that debate would be out of place in this book, however; see, e.g., reference [45] if you want more details.

[2] Note, however, that even if it's empty, *t1* still has just one attribute, called EARLIEST.

```
USING ( DURING ) : RELATION { TUPLE { DURING INTERVAL_DATE
                               ( [ FIRST_DATE ( ) : LAST_DATE ( ) ] ) } }
             MINUS BUSY
```

This expression makes use of a U_MINUS operation. However, we would certainly prefer that the implementation not physically materialize the results of the two UNPACKs implied by that operation—especially in the case of the left operand, since the unpacked form of that operand contains a tuple for every day from the beginning of time to the end of time inclusive! (See Appendix E for a discussion of implementation matters in general.) An alternative but ugly formulation that explicitly avoids such possible inefficiencies is:

```
CASE
   WHEN IS_EMPTY ( BUSY ) THEN
        RELATION { TUPLE { DURING INTERVAL_DATE
                         ( [ FIRST_DATE ( ) : LAST_DATE ( ) ] ) } }
   WHEN IS_EMPTY ( BUSY WHERE BEGIN ( DURING ) > FIRST_DATE ( ) ) THEN
        RELATION { DURING INTERVAL_DATE } { }
   ELSE RELATION { TUPLE { DURING INTERVAL_DATE
                     ( [ FIRST_DATE ( ) :
                         PRE ( DURING FROM ( TUPLE FROM BUSY ) ) ] ) } }
END CASE
```

Query Q8: Get supplier numbers for suppliers currently under contract who also had an earlier contract.

Given only the semitemporal database of Fig. 15.1, this query can't be answered (in fact, it can't even be formulated), because the information isn't in the database.

Query Q9: Get SNO-PARTS-DURING triples such that the indicated supplier was able to supply the indicated range of parts during the indicated interval.

The result of this query will look like—more precisely, it'll be of the same type as—relvar S_PARTS_DURING from the section "A More Searching Example" in Chapter 6 (see Fig. 6.2). Here's a possible formulation:

```
WITH ( t0 := EXTEND SP_SINCE :
             { PARTS  := INTERVAL_PNO ( [ PNO : PNO ] ) ,
               DURING := INTERVAL_DATE ( [ SINCE : LAST_DATE ( ) ] ) } ) :
USING ( PARTS , DURING ) : t0 { SNO , PARTS , DURING }
```

Note the use of (a) multiple EXTEND and (b) U_projection in this example.

Query Q10: Suppose the result of Query Q9 is kept as a relvar S_PARTS_DURING. Use S_PARTS_DURING to get SNO-PNO-DURING triples such that the indicated supplier was able to supply the indicated part during the indicated interval.

```
WITH ( t1 := UNPACK S_PARTS_DURING ON ( PARTS ) ,
         t2 := EXTEND t1 : { PNO := POINT FROM PARTS } ) :
USING ( DURING ) : t2 { ALL BUT PARTS }
```

Note the use of POINT FROM here to extract the single point from a unit interval.

DURING RELVARS ONLY

Now we turn our attention to a version of the database that contains during or "historical" relvars only. Fig. 15.2, a copy of Fig. 14.6, shows the database definition. The database is fully temporal, but horizontal decomposition hasn't been done; thus, the database can represent information about the future as well as the past, but typically has to use artificial "end of time" values to mark the end of any interval whose true end point is currently unknown. Refer to Fig. 14.5 in Chapter 14 for some sample values.

```
S_DURING { SNO , DURING }
        USING ( DURING ) : KEY { SNO , DURING }
        USING ( DURING ) : FOREIGN KEY { SNO , DURING }
                                    REFERENCES S_STATUS_DURING

S_STATUS_DURING { SNO , STATUS , DURING }
        USING ( DURING ) : KEY { SNO , DURING }
        USING ( DURING ) : FOREIGN KEY { SNO , DURING }
                                    REFERENCES S_DURING

SP_DURING { SNO , PNO , DURING }
        USING ( DURING ) : KEY { SNO , PNO , DURING }
        USING ( DURING ) : FOREIGN KEY { SNO , DURING }
                                    REFERENCES S_DURING
```

Fig. 15.2: During relvars only

Query Q1: Get the status of supplier S1 on day *dn*.

This one is straightforward:

```
( S_STATUS_DURING WHERE SNO = SNO ( 'S1' ) AND dn ∈ DURING ) { STATUS }
```

Note that this formulation works even if *dn* is a date in the future. Of course, the result will be empty if supplier S1 isn't represented in the database at all.

Query Q2: Get pairs of supplier numbers such that the indicated suppliers were assigned their current status on the same day.

A supplier will have some current status if and only if there's a tuple for that supplier in S_STATUS_DURING with a DURING value that encompasses the date today, in which case the

STATUS and BEGIN (DURING) values in that tuple will give that supplier's current status and the date when that current status was assigned. So:

```
WITH ( t1 := S_STATUS_DURING WHERE TODAY ( ) ∈ DURING ,
       t2 := ( EXTEND t1 : { D := BEGIN ( DURING ) } ) { SNO , D } ,
       t3 := t2 RENAME { SNO AS XNO } ,
       t4 := t2 RENAME { SNO AS YNO } ,
       t5 := t3 JOIN t4 ,
       t6 := t5 WHERE XNO < YNO ) :
t6 { XNO , YNO }
```

As in Chapter 14, we're assuming the availability here of a niladic operator called TODAY that returns today's date.

Query Q3: Get supplier numbers for suppliers who were able to supply both part P1 and part P2 at the same time.

Here we've revised the query slightly to make it a little more typical of a fully temporal database as such; to be specific, we've replaced "suppliers currently able" by "suppliers who were able [*i.e., to supply both parts*] at the same time." Here's a suitable formulation:

```
WITH ( t1 := ( SP_DURING WHERE PNO = PNO ( 'P1' ) ) { SNO , DURING } ,
       t2 := ( SP_DURING WHERE PNO = PNO ( 'P2' ) ) { SNO , DURING } ,
       t3 := USING ( DURING ) : t1 JOIN t2 ) :
t3 { SNO }
```

Query Q4: Get supplier numbers for suppliers who were never able to supply both part P1 and part P2 at the same time.

Again we've revised the query slightly. Here's a suitable formulation:

```
WITH ( t1 := ( SP_DURING WHERE PNO = PNO ( 'P1' ) ) { SNO , DURING } ,
       t2 := ( SP_DURING WHERE PNO = PNO ( 'P2' ) ) { SNO , DURING } ,
       t3 := USING ( DURING ) : t1 JOIN t2 ) :
S_DURING { SNO } MINUS t3 { SNO }
```

Query Q5: Get supplier numbers for suppliers who, while they were under some specific contract, changed their status since they most recently became able to supply some part under that contract.

Once again we've revised the original query; what's more, the revised version is now quite complicated. In particular, note the requirement that both specified events (changing status, becoming able to supply some part) must have occurred while the same contract was in effect. This requirement accounts for the restriction operations in lines 3 and 6 below.

```
WITH ( t1 := ( S_STATUS_DURING RENAME { DURING AS X } ) { SNO , X } ,
       t2 := t1 JOIN S_DURING ,
       t3 := t2 WHERE X ⊆ DURING ,
       t4 := ( SP_DURING RENAME { DURING AS Y } ) { SNO , Y } ,
       t5 := t4 JOIN t3 ,
       t6 := t5 WHERE Y ⊆ DURING ,
       t7 := EXTEND t6 { SNO , DURING } :
                      { BXMAX := MAX ( !!t6 , BEGIN ( X ) ) ,
                        BYMAX := MAX ( !!t6 , BEGIN ( Y ) ) } ,
       t8 := t7 WHERE BXMAX > BYMAX ) :
t8 { SNO }
```

Query Q6: Get intervals during which at least one supplier was under contract.

```
USING ( DURING ) : S_DURING { DURING }
```

Or, more straightforwardly, just:

```
PACK S_DURING { DURING } ON ( DURING )
```

Query Q7: Suppose the result of Query Q6 is kept as a relvar BUSY. Use BUSY to get intervals during which no supplier was under contract at all.

```
USING ( DURING ) : RELATION { TUPLE { DURING INTERVAL_DATE
                                    ( [ FIRST_DATE ( ) : LAST_DATE ( ) ] ) } }
              MINUS BUSY
```

This formulation is identical to the "best" formulation given for this query in the previous section.

Query Q8: Get supplier numbers for suppliers currently under contract who also had an earlier contract.

```
WITH ( t1 := ( S_DURING WHERE TODAY ( ) ∈ DURING ) { SNO } ,
       t2 := ( S_DURING WHERE TODAY ( ) > END ( DURING ) ) { SNO } ) :
t1 JOIN t2
```

Query Q9: Get SNO-PARTS-DURING triples such that the indicated supplier was able to supply the indicated range of parts during the indicated interval.

```
WITH ( t0 := EXTEND SP_DURING :
                    { PARTS := INTERVAL_PNO ( [ PNO : PNO ] ) } ) :
USING ( PARTS , DURING ) : t0 { SNO , PARTS , DURING }
```

Query Q10: Suppose the result of Query Q9 is kept as a relvar S_PARTS_DURING. Use S_PARTS_DURING to get SNO-PNO-DURING triples such that the indicated supplier was able to supply the indicated part during the indicated interval.

```
WITH ( t1 := UNPACK S_PARTS_DURING ON ( PARTS ) ,
       t2 := EXTEND t1 : { PNO := POINT FROM PARTS } ) :
USING ( DURING ) : t2 { ALL BUT PARTS }
```

This expression is identical to its counterpart in the previous section.

Query Q11: Given relvar TERM, with attributes DURING, PRESIDENT, and TERMNO, and both {DURING} and {PRESIDENT,TERMNO} as keys, get DURING-PRESIDENT pairs such that the indicated president held office throughout the indicated interval.

```
PACK TERM { DURING , PRESIDENT } ON ( DURING )
```

Query Q12: Given relvar TERM as in Query Q11, get pairs of presidents who held office in the same year (in the sense that, e.g., Ford and Carter held office in the same year, because Ford's term ended when Carter's began—namely, on January 20th, 1977).

```
WITH ( t1 := TERM RENAME { DURING AS D1 , PRESIDENT AS P1 } ,
       t2 := TERM RENAME { DURING AS D2 , PRESIDENT AS P2 } ,
       t3 := ( t1 JOIN t2 ) WHERE P1 ≠ P2 AND END ( D1 ) = PRE ( D2 ) ) :
t3 { P1 , P2 }
```

BOTH SINCE AND DURING RELVARS

In this section, we consider a version of the database containing both since and during relvars. This version, which we refer to as the combination design, keeps "current" information in the since relvars and "historical" information in the during relvars. Fig. 15.3, an edited version of Fig. 14.7, shows the database definition, including some but not all of the pertinent constraints. Refer to Fig. 14.8 in Chapter 14 for some sample values.

```
S_SINCE { SNO , SNO_SINCE , STATUS , STATUS_SINCE }
        KEY { SNO }

SP_SINCE { SNO , PNO , SINCE }
        KEY { SNO , PNO }
        FOREIGN KEY { SNO } REFERENCES S_SINCE

S_DURING { SNO , DURING }
        USING ( DURING ) : KEY { SNO , DURING }

S_STATUS_DURING { SNO , STATUS , DURING }
        USING ( DURING ) : KEY { SNO , DURING }

SP_DURING { SNO , PNO , DURING }
        USING ( DURING ) : KEY { SNO , PNO , DURING }
```

Fig. 15.3: Both since and during relvars

In contrast to the version of the database discussed in the previous section ("During Relvars Only"), it's important to understand that:

■ No during relvar in this version of the database contains any interval with an artificial "end of time" marker as its end value.

■ Some of the information in those during or "historical" relvars might in fact concern current or even future contracts.

The queries that follow are identical in their natural language form to their counterparts from the previous section. Because of the foregoing bullet points, however, the corresponding formal expressions are sometimes different. Also, we ignore Queries Q7 and Q10-Q12, because the formal versions of those queries are identical to their counterparts in the previous section.

Query Q1: Get the status of supplier S1 on day *dn*.

The difficulty here is that we don't know, in general, whether the answer to the query is to be found in S_SINCE or S_STATUS_DURING. Hence:

```
WITH ( t1 := S_SINCE WHERE SNO = SNO ( 'S1' ) ) ,
       t2 := EXTEND t1 : { DURING :=
                   INTERVAL_DATE ( [ STATUS_SINCE : LAST_DATE ( ) ] } ,
       t3 := t2 { STATUS , DURING } ,
       t4 := S_STATUS_DURING WHERE SNO = SNO ( 'S1' ) ,
       t5 := t4 { STATUS , DURING } ,
       t6 := t3 UNION t5 ) :
( t6 WHERE dn ∈ DURING ) { STATUS }
```

An alternative formulation, involving in effect an explicit test to see which relvar contains the desired information, might look like this:

```
WITH ( t := TUPLE FROM ( S_SINCE WHERE SNO = SNO ( 'S1' ) ) ,
       s := STATUS FROM t ,
       d := STATUS_SINCE FROM t ) :
IF dn ≥ d THEN RELATION { TUPLE { STATUS s } }
          ELSE ( S_STATUS_DURING WHERE SNO = SNO ( 'S1' )
                                 AND dn ∈ DURING ) { STATUS }
END IF
```

Note: This is the first time we've seen code in this book in which the assignments in a WITH specification have been anything other than relational assignments as such (to be specific, the assignment to *t* here is a tuple assignment and the assignments to *s* and *d* are scalar assignments). More to the point, note that—unlike the first formulation above—this alternative formulation of the query relies on the strong, and in general unwarranted, assumption that there's a tuple for supplier S1 in relvar S_SINCE. The first formulation is to be preferred.

For interest, we show yet another possible formulation of this query, one that (like the one we showed first) doesn't rely on the existence of a tuple for supplier S1 in relvar S_SINCE:

```
WITH ( t0 := S_SINCE WHERE SNO = SNO ( 'S1' ) ) :
IF IS_NOT_EMPTY ( t0 )
    THEN t0 { STATUS }
    ELSE ( S_STATUS_DURING WHERE SNO = SNO ( 'S1' )
                        AND dn ∈ DURING ) { STATUS }
END IF
```

Query Q2: Get pairs of supplier numbers such that the indicated suppliers were assigned some status on the same day.

Here we've revised the query slightly in order to illustrate another complication that arises from the combination design. The complication is this: S_SINCE might show some supplier S*x* as having been assigned some *current* status on some given day *d*, while S_STATUS_DURING shows some distinct supplier S*y* as having been assigned some *historical* status on that same day *d*. (Analogous remarks apply to Queries Q3-Q6 as well, as we'll see.) Hence:

```
WITH ( t1 := ( EXTEND S_STATUS_DURING :
                   { STATUS_SINCE := BEGIN ( DURING ) } )
                                   { SNO , STATUS_SINCE } ,
        t2 := t1 UNION S_SINCE { SNO , STATUS_SINCE } ,
        t3 := t2 RENAME { SNO AS XNO } ,
        t4 := t2 RENAME { SNO AS YNO } ,
        t5 := t3 JOIN t4 ,
        t6 := t5 WHERE XNO < YNO ) :
t6 { XNO , YNO }
```

Query Q3: Get supplier numbers for suppliers who were able to supply both part P1 and part P2 at the same time. (This isn't the original version of this query but the revised version from the section "During Relvars Only.")

```
WITH ( t1 := ( EXTEND SP_SINCE : { DURING :=
                   INTERVAL_DATE ( [ SINCE : LAST_DATE ( ) ] ) } )
                                   { SNO , PNO , DURING } ,
        t2 := SP_DURING UNION t1 ,
        t3 := ( t2 WHERE PNO = PNO ( 'P1' ) ) { SNO , DURING } ,
        t4 := ( t2 WHERE PNO = PNO ( 'P2' ) ) { SNO , DURING } ,
        t5 := USING ( DURING ) : t3 JOIN t4 ) :
t5 { SNO }
```

Query Q4: Get supplier numbers for suppliers who were never able to supply both part P1 and part P2 at the same time. (This isn't the original version of this query but the revised version from the section "During Relvars Only.")

```
WITH ( t1 := ( EXTEND SP_SINCE : { DURING :=
                     INTERVAL_DATE ( [ SINCE : LAST_DATE ( ) ] ) } )
                                         { SNO , PNO , DURING } ,
       t2 := SP_DURING UNION t1 ,
       t3 := ( t2 WHERE PNO = PNO ( 'P1' ) ) { SNO , DURING } ,
       t4 := ( t2 WHERE PNO = PNO ( 'P2' ) ) { SNO , DURING } ,
       t5 := USING ( DURING ) : t3 JOIN t4 ) :
t2 { SNO } MINUS t5 { SNO }
```

Query Q5: Get supplier numbers for suppliers who, while they were under some specific contract, changed their status since they most recently became able to supply some part under that contract. (This isn't the original version of this query but the revised version from the section "During Relvars Only.")

```
WITH ( t1  := ( EXTEND S_SINCE : { DURING :=
                     INTERVAL_DATE ( [ SNO_SINCE : LAST_DATE ( ) ] ) } )
                                         { SNO , DURING } ,
       t2  := t1 UNION S_DURING ,
       t3  := ( EXTEND S_SINCE : { DURING :=
                     INTERVAL_DATE ( [ STATUS_SINCE : LAST_DATE ( ) ] ) } )
                                         { SNO , STATUS , DURING } ,
       t4  := t3 UNION S_STATUS_DURING ,
       t5  := ( EXTEND SP_SINCE : { DURING :=
                     INTERVAL_DATE ( [ SINCE : LAST_DATE ( ) ] ) } )
                                         { SNO , PNO , DURING } ,
       t6  := t5 UNION SP_DURING ,
       t7  := ( t4 RENAME { DURING AS X } ) { SNO , X } ,
       t8  := t7 JOIN t2 ,
       t9  := t8 WHERE X ⊆ DURING ,
       t10 := ( t6 RENAME { DURING AS Y } ) { SNO , Y } ,
       t11 := t10 JOIN t9 ,
       t12 := t11 WHERE Y ⊆ DURING ,
       t13 := EXTEND t12 { SNO , DURING } :
                   { BXMAX := MAX ( !!t12 , BEGIN ( X ) ) ,
                     BYMAX := MAX ( !!t12 , BEGIN ( Y ) ) } ,
       t14 := t13 WHERE BXMAX > BYMAX ) :
t14 { SNO }
```

Query Q6: Get intervals during which at least one supplier was under contract.

```
WITH ( t1 := EXTEND S_SINCE : { DURING :=
                     INTERVAL ( [ SNO_SINCE : LAST_DATE ( ) ] ) } ,
       t2 := t1 { SNO , DURING } UNION S_DURING ) :
USING ( DURING ) : t2 { DURING }
```

Query Q8: Get supplier numbers for suppliers currently under contract who also had an earlier contract.

```
( S_SINCE JOIN S_DURING ) { SNO }
```

Query Q9: Get SNO-PARTS-DURING triples such that the indicated supplier was able to supply the indicated range of parts during the indicated interval.

```
WITH ( t1 := EXTEND SP_SINCE :
                { PARTS  := INTERVAL_PNO ( [ PNO : PNO ] ) ,
                  DURING := INTERVAL_DATE ( [ SINCE : LAST_DATE ( ) ] ) } ,
         t2 := t1 { SNO , PARTS , DURING } ,
         t3 := EXTEND SP_DURING :
                { PARTS := INTERVAL_PNO ( [ PNO : PNO ] ) } ,
         t4 := t3 { SNO , PARTS , DURING } ) :
USING ( PARTS , DURING ) : t2 UNION t4
```

VIEWS CAN HELP

It's undeniable that several of the query formulations shown in the previous section were fairly complicated: more complicated, in all likelihood, than some users will be prepared to deal with. Yet the database we were discussing in that section made use of what we repeatedly said in previous chapters was our preferred design! In this section, we explore the possibility of making life a little easier for the user by predefining a suitable collection of views (also known as *virtual relvars*) for such a database.

Broadly speaking, the views we have in mind have the effect of conceptually undoing the horizontal and vertical decompositions described in Chapter 12. Of course, it's important to understand that the decompositions are indeed only *conceptually* undone; the relvars that result do have the effect of making certain queries easier to state, but they don't contravene the design recommendations of Chapter 12. Indeed, what we're proposing here is a perfectly standard technique. For example, given the original nontemporal version of the suppliers-and-shipments database from Chapter 1, we might well define the join of suppliers and shipments as a view in order to simplify the formulation of certain queries, even though such a view would violate well known principles of normalization.[3]

Unfortunately, our running example is a little too simple to illustrate the foregoing ideas properly, so we need to extend that example slightly. Let's therefore bring supplier city information back into the picture by (a) reinstating attributes CITY and CITY_SINCE in relvar S_SINCE and (b) reinstating relvar S_CITY_DURING, with its attributes SNO, CITY, and DURING, thus:[4]

```
S_SINCE { SNO ,    SNO_SINCE ,
          STATUS , STATUS_SINCE ,
          CITY ,   CITY_SINCE }
        KEY { SNO }
```

---

[3] In fact it wouldn't even be in second normal form. See reference [43] if you need an explanation of this point.

[4] We won't actually be referring to these attributes or this relvar in any of our sample queries, but they do help to make the process of defining the views a little more realistic (especially in the case of the view we'll be calling S").

```
S_CITY_DURING { SNO , CITY , DURING }
      USING ( DURING ) : KEY { SNO , DURING }
```

Providing sample data values for these two relvars is left as an exercise.

Now we can explain the views we have in mind. First, we define four views S_DURING', S_STATUS_DURING', S_CITY_DURING', and SP_DURING' that effectively combine current and historical information, thereby undoing the original horizontal decompositions:[5]

```
VAR S_DURING' VIRTUAL
  ( S_DURING UNION
    ( EXTEND S_SINCE :
        { DURING := INTERVAL_DATE ( [ SNO_SINCE : LAST_DATE ( ) ] ) } )
                                                 { SNO , DURING } ) ... ;

VAR S_STATUS_DURING' VIRTUAL
  ( S_STATUS_DURING UNION
    ( EXTEND S_SINCE :
        { DURING := INTERVAL_DATE ( [ STATUS_SINCE : LAST_DATE ( ) ] ) } )
                                            { SNO , STATUS , DURING } ) ... ;

VAR S_CITY_DURING' VIRTUAL
  ( S_CITY_DURING UNION
    ( EXTEND S_SINCE :
        { DURING := INTERVAL_DATE ( [ CITY_SINCE : LAST_DATE ( ) ] ) } )
                                            { SNO , CITY , DURING } ) ... ;

VAR SP_DURING' VIRTUAL
  ( SP_DURING UNION
    ( EXTEND SP_SINCE :
        { DURING := INTERVAL_DATE ( [ SINCE : LAST_DATE ( ) ] ) } )
                                            { SNO , PNO , DURING } ) ... ;
```

Next, we define a view S″ that effectively combines supplier contract, status, and city information, thereby undoing the original vertical decomposition:

```
VAR S'' VIRTUAL
  ( USING ( DURING ) : S_STATUS_DURING' JOIN S_CITY_DURING' ) ... ;
```

Note: There's no need to include S_DURING' in the U_join here, because the unpacked form of S_DURING' on DURING is equal to both:

a. The unpacked form on DURING of the projection on SNO and DURING of S_STATUS_DURING', and

---

[5] The **Tutorial D** syntax for defining a view was illustrated in Chapter 3. More to the point, it might be possible to provide these view definitions automatically, much as the relvar definitions discussed in the section "Syntactic Shorthands" in Chapter 14 might be provided automatically. For example, recall the specifications SINCE_FOR and HISTORY_IN from Chapter 14; for definiteness, consider the case in which these specifications are associated with attribute STATUS_SINCE specifically. Then we might imagine a further extension to those specifications of the form COMBINED_IN (S_STATUS_DURING'), which would cause the system to define a view with the specified name and requisite structure automatically.

b. The unpacked form on DURING of the projection on SNO and DURING of S_CITY_DURING'.

Thus, no information would be added—or lost—if S_DURING' were included.

For completeness, let's also define a view SP" that effectively does for shipments what S" does for suppliers:

```
VAR SP'' VIRTUAL ( SP_DURING' ) ... ;
```

(Since shipments were in fact never vertically decomposed in the first place, views SP" and SP_DURING' are identical, of course.)

Fig. 15.4 shows the structure, in outline, of all of these views. Note the U_key specifications in particular.[6] As an exercise, you might like to try stating the corresponding predicates (for all of the views in the figure). You might also like to think about any foreign U_key relationships that might exist among those views.

```
S_DURING' { SNO , DURING }
        USING ( DURING ) : KEY { SNO , DURING }

S_STATUS_DURING' { SNO , STATUS , DURING }
        USING ( DURING ) : KEY { SNO , DURING }

S_CITY_DURING' { SNO , CITY , DURING }
        USING ( DURING ) : KEY { SNO , DURING }

SP_DURING' { SNO , PNO , DURING }
        USING ( DURING ) : KEY { SNO , PNO , DURING }

S'' { SNO , STATUS , CITY , DURING }
        USING ( DURING ) : KEY { SNO , DURING }

SP'' { SNO , PNO , DURING }
        USING ( DURING ) :  KEY { SNO , PNO , DURING }
```

Fig. 15.4: Structure of the views

We now proceed to reconsider Queries Q1-Q10 in terms of these views (Queries Q11 and Q12 remain unchanged, of course).

Query Q1: Get the status of supplier S1 on day *dn*.

---

[6] Unlike SQL, **Tutorial D** does allow KEY and FOREIGN KEY specifications on view definitions, so it would seem reasonable to allow U_key and foreign U_key specifications also. But we would also hope (with respect to keys and U_keys, at least) that the system would be able to infer such specifications for itself, without having to be told them explicitly. Note, however, that spelling out those specifications explicitly—i.e., explicitly stating the U_key and foreign U_key constraints for the views—could serve as a very user friendly way of stating all of the constraints needed by the combination design, as described in the section "Both Since and During Relvars" in Chapter 14. (Of course, we would prefer it if the system could infer those constraints for itself, as we conjectured it could in the section "Syntactic Shorthands" in that same chapter.)

This one is now very easy:

```
( S'' WHERE SNO = SNO ( 'S1' ) AND dn ∈ DURING ) { STATUS }
```

Note: We could have specified relvar S_STATUS_DURING' in place of relvar S"—it would make no difference to the result.

Query Q2: Get pairs of supplier numbers such that the indicated suppliers were assigned some status on the same day. (This is the version of the query we discussed in connection with the combination design.)

```
WITH ( t1 := ( EXTEND S_STATUS_DURING' : { D := BEGIN ( DURING ) } )
                                                   { SNO , D } ,
       t2 := t1 RENAME { SNO AS XNO } ,
       t3 := t1 RENAME { SNO AS YNO } ,
       t4 := t2 JOIN t3 ,
       t5 := t4 WHERE XNO < YNO ) :
t6 { XNO , YNO }
```

This expression is very similar to the one shown for this query in the section "Both Since and During Relvars," except that (a) the reference to relvar S_STATUS_DURING has been replaced by one to relvar S_STATUS_DURING' and (b) there's now no explicit reference to relvar S_SINCE at all. Observe in particular that, by contrast with what we had to do in that previous section, there's now no need to give special attention to current information.

Query Q3: Get supplier numbers for suppliers who were able to supply both part P1 and part P2 at the same time. (This the revised version of the query we discussed in the sections "During Relvars Only" and "Both Since and During Relvars.")

```
WITH ( t1 := ( SP'' WHERE PNO = PNO ( 'P1' ) ) { SNO , DURING } ,
       t2 := ( SP'' WHERE PNO = PNO ( 'P2' ) ) { SNO , DURING } ,
       t3 := USING ( DURING ) : t1 JOIN t2 ) :
t3 { SNO }
```

This expression is considerably simpler than the one shown in the previous section; in fact, it's essentially identical—as is only to be expected—to the one shown in the section "During Relvars Only." A similar remark applies to Queries Q4-Q6 (also to Query Q9), and we therefore omit detailed consideration of those cases. So let's move on to Query Q7.

Query Q7: Suppose the result of Query Q6 is kept as a relvar BUSY. Use BUSY to get intervals during which no supplier was under contract at all.

The views obviously don't help with this query (the formulation remains as it was before, in the sections "During Relvars Only" and "Both Since and During Relvars").

Query Q8: Get supplier numbers for suppliers currently under contract who also had an earlier contract.

This query is actually *harder* to express using the views than it was before (as a comparison of the formulations in the previous two sections should lead you to expect).

Query Q10: Suppose the result of Query Q9 is kept as a relvar S_PARTS_DURING. Use S_PARTS_DURING to get SNO-PNO-DURING triples such that the indicated supplier was able to supply the indicated part during the indicated interval.

As with Query Q7, the views don't help with this query (the formulation remains as it was in the section "During Relvars Only").

EXERCISES

Write **Tutorial D** expressions for the following queries on the version of the courses-and-students database from Exercise 13.7 in Chapter 13.

15.1 Get the maximum grade ever achieved by student ST1 on any course.

15.2 Get student numbers for students currently enrolled on both course C1 and course C2.

15.3 Get student numbers for students not currently enrolled on both course C1 and course C2.

15.4 Get intervals during which at least one course was being offered.

15.5 Get intervals during which no course was being offered at all.

ANSWERS

15.1 `WITH ( t0 := COMPLETED_COURSE WHERE STUDENTNO = STUDENTNO ( 'ST1' ) ) :`
`     EXTEND t0 { } : { MAXG := MAX ( !!t0 , GRADE ) }`

15.2 `WITH ( t1 := ( ENROLLMENT WHERE COURSENO = COURSENO ( 'C1' ) )`
`                                          { STUDENTNO } ,`
`            t2 := ( ENROLLMENT WHERE COURSENO = COURSENO ( 'C2' ) )`
`                                          { STUDENTNO } ) :`
`     t1 JOIN t2`

15.3 Let *r* be the relation denoted by the expression given as the solution to Exercise 15.2. Then:

```
CURRENT_STUDENT { STUDENTNO } MINUS r
```

15.4 USING (OFFERED_DURING) : COURSE_OFFERING { OFFERED_DURING }

15.5 USING { OFFERED_DURING } :
    RELATION { TUPLE { OFFERED_DURING INTERVAL_DATE
                                   ([FIRST_DATE ( ) : LAST_DATE ( )]) } }
                  MINUS COURSE_OFFERING { OFFERED_DURING }

Chapter 16

Updates

Change is inevitable ... Change is constant.

—Benjamin Disraeli (speech, 1867)

In Chapter 15 we examined what we called the "somewhat nontrivial question" of formulating queries against a temporal database; now we turn our attention to the even more nontrivial question of formulating updates against such a database. As usual, we base most of our examples and discussions on the various versions of the suppliers-and-shipments database described in Chapter 12, and we assume the integrity constraints discussed in Chapters 13 and 14 are in effect. In contrast to the previous chapter, however, we make no attempt to use the same examples on every version of the database; indeed, it wouldn't really be feasible to do so, for reasons that should become apparent as we proceed.

We remind you that, in accordance with normal convention, we use the term *update* in lower case to refer to the explicit relational assignment operator and all of the syntactic variants thereof (INSERT, D_INSERT, DELETE, I_DELETE, and UPDATE), considered collectively; when we want to refer to the UPDATE operator as such, we set it in all caps as just shown. We also call out a couple of points that we didn't bother to state explicitly in earlier chapters but are in fact implicit in the very nature of the relational model:

- It doesn't really make sense to talk in terms of updating individual tuples—we ought really always to talk in terms of updating *sets* of tuples (though the set in question might be of cardinality one, of course, or even zero).

- In fact, it doesn't really make sense to talk in terms of updating tuples (or even sets of tuples) anyway, because tuples, like relations, are values, and by definition values can't be updated. What we really mean when we talk of updating tuple *t1* to *t2* (say), within some relvar *R*, is that we're *replacing* tuple *t1* in *R* by some other tuple *t2*. And even that kind of talk is still imprecise!—what we *really* mean is that we're replacing the relation *r1* that's the current value of *R* by some other relation *r2*. Analogous remarks apply as well to phrases such as "updating attribute *A*" (within some tuple or tuples).

Despite the foregoing, we'll continue to talk much of the time in terms of updating individual tuples, and even updating individual attributes within tuples—the practice is convenient—but it must be understood that such talk is really only shorthand, and rather sloppy shorthand at that.

The structure of the chapter is as follows. Following this brief introduction, the next section considers databases consisting of since relvars only. The next three sections then consider databases consisting of during relvars only; the first discusses U_updates, the second PORTION specifications, and the third multiple assignment. The next section then considers the case of a database that contains both kinds of relvars. The final section offers a few closing remarks; in particular, like the final section in the previous chapter, it briefly considers the possibility of providing a collection of predefined views, with the aim of simplifying the formulation of certain operations that might otherwise seem dauntingly complex.

SINCE RELVARS ONLY

In this section we address the comparatively straightforward case of updates on a version of the database that contains just the "current" relvars S_SINCE and SP_SINCE. Fig. 16.1, a copy of Fig. 14.2 from Chapter 14, shows some sample values; we'll base our examples on those specific values, where it makes any difference. We remind you that this database can't represent information about the past at all, other than what might be conveyed by the "since" values; however, it can represent future information—certainly implicitly, and possibly explicitly as well. Refer to Fig. 14.3 in Chapter 14 if you need to remind yourself of the constraints that apply to this database.

S_SINCE

SNO	SNO_SINCE	STATUS	STATUS_SINCE
S1	d04	20	d06
S2	d07	10	d07
S3	d03	30	d03
S4	d14	20	d14
S5	d02	30	d02

SP_SINCE

SNO	PNO	SINCE
S1	P1	d04
S1	P2	d05
S1	P3	d09
S1	P4	d05
S1	P5	d04
S1	P6	d06
S2	P1	d08
S2	P2	d09
S3	P2	d08
S4	P5	d14

Fig. 16.1: Since relvars only—sample values

One general remark that's worth making right away is the following: Given that a database is essentially a collection of propositions (see Chapter 1)—more precisely, propositions we currently believe to be true ones—a good way to think about updating in general is to think in terms of adding, removing, and replacing such propositions, instead of thinking, as we more usually do, in terms of adding, removing, and replacing tuples. (This remark applies to the entire chapter, not just to the present section.) This shift in emphasis can be helpful in understanding what's really going on, especially when we reach later sections of the chapter where, as already indicated, some of the examples unfortunately start to get quite complicated.

Given the foregoing, it might help to begin our discussions in this section by stating the predicates for relvars S_SINCE and SP_SINCE once again:

- S_SINCE: *Supplier SNO has been under contract since SNO_SINCE and has had status STATUS since STATUS_SINCE.*

- SP_SINCE: *Supplier SNO has been able to supply part PNO since SINCE.*

The propositions we'll be considering in the rest of this section are all instantiations of one or other of these predicates. (Actually, since the examples in this section all have to with relvar S_SINCE specifically, they'll all be instantiations of the first predicate specifically.)

Perhaps we should add that, like the queries in the section "Since Relvars Only" in the previous chapter (and for much the same reasons), the updates to be discussed in the present section aren't particularly temporal in nature. In fact, it turns out there's not much to say about those updates anyway; updating a database that's merely semitemporal turns out not to differ in any major respect from updating a database that isn't temporal at all, as we'll see.

Update U1: Add a proposition to show that supplier S9 has just been placed under contract, starting today, with status 15.

```
INSERT S_SINCE
        RELATION { TUPLE { SNO            SNO ( 'S9' ) ,
                           SNO_SINCE      TODAY ( ) ,
                           STATUS         15 ,
                           STATUS_SINCE   TODAY ( ) } } ;
```

This INSERT statement effectively adds to the database the proposition "Supplier S9 has been under contract since day *dc* and has had status 15 since day *ds*," where *dc* and *ds* are both whatever the date happens to be today. (As in previous chapters, we assume the availability of a niladic operator called TODAY that returns the date today.)

Update U2: Remove the proposition showing that supplier S5 is under contract.

```
DELETE S_SINCE WHERE SNO = SNO ( 'S5' ) ;
```

This DELETE statement effectively removes from the database the proposition "Supplier S5 has been under contract since day *dc* and has had status *st* since day *ds*," where *dc*, *st*, and *ds* are whatever the SNO_SINCE, STATUS, and STATUS_SINCE values happen to be in the current tuple for supplier S5.

Update U3: Replace the proposition showing that supplier S1 was placed under contract on day 4 by one showing that the same supplier was placed under contract on day 3 instead.

```
UPDATE S_SINCE WHERE SNO = SNO ( 'S1' ) : { SNO_SINCE := d03 } ;
```

As explained in Chapter 3, this UPDATE statement is shorthand for:

```
S_SINCE := ( S_SINCE WHERE NOT ( SNO = SNO ( 'S1' ) ) )
             UNION
           ( EXTEND ( S_SINCE WHERE SNO = SNO ( 'S1' ) ) :
                                      { SNO_SINCE := d03 } ) ;
```

Thus, the effect is (a) to remove the proposition "Supplier S1 has been under contract since day 4 (and has had some specific status *st* since some specific day *ds*)" and then (b) to add the proposition "Supplier S1 has been under contract since day 3 (and has had that same status *st* since that same day *ds*)." The only difference between these two propositions is in the SNO_SINCE value, of course, and the desired result is thereby achieved.

DURING RELVARS ONLY I: U_UPDATES

In this section and the next two, we consider updates on a version of the database consisting of just the "historical" relvars S_DURING, S_STATUS_DURING, and SP_DURING. Fig. 16.2, a copy of Fig. 14.5, shows some sample values for these relvars; we'll base our examples on those specific values, where it makes any difference. The database is fully temporal, but horizontal decomposition hasn't been done; thus, the database can represent information about the future as well as the past, but typically has to use artificial "end of time" values (*d99* in Fig. 16.2) to mark the end of any interval whose true end point is currently unknown. Refer to Fig. 14.6 in Chapter 14 if you need to remind yourself of the constraints—specifically, the U_key and foreign U_key constraints—that apply to this database. Here are the applicable predicates:

- S_DURING: *DURING denotes a maximal interval throughout which supplier SNO was under contract.*

- S_STATUS_DURING: *DURING denotes a maximal interval throughout which supplier SNO had status STATUS.*

- SP_DURING: *DURING denotes a maximal interval throughout which supplier SNO was able to supply part PNO.*

For simplicity, however, we'll focus in this section and the next (on PORTION specifications) on relvar SP_DURING almost exclusively.

S_DURING

SNO	DURING
S2	[d02:d04]
S6	[d03:d05]
S7	[d03:d99]

S_STATUS_DURING

SNO	STATUS	DURING
S2	5	[d02:d02]
S2	10	[d03:d04]
S6	5	[d03:d04]
S6	7	[d05:d05]
S7	15	[d03:d08]
S7	20	[d09:d99]

SP_DURING

SNO	PNO	DURING
S2	P1	[d02:d04]
S2	P2	[d03:d03]
S2	P5	[d03:d04]
S6	P3	[d03:d05]
S6	P4	[d04:d04]
S6	P5	[d04:d05]
S7	P1	[d03:d04]
S7	P1	[d06:d07]
S7	P1	[d09:d99]

Fig. 16.2: During relvars only—sample values

U_INSERT

Update U4: Add the proposition "Supplier S2 was able to supply part P4 on day 2."

The following INSERT is sufficient:

```
INSERT SP_DURING
        RELATION { TUPLE { SNO     SNO ( 'S2' ) ,
                           PNO     PNO ( 'P4' ) ,
                           DURING INTERVAL_DATE ( [ d02 : d02 ] ) } } ;
```

However, suppose the proposition to be added had specified part P5 instead of P4. Then we couldn't just insert the corresponding tuple into SP_DURING (even though we're indeed just trying to add a proposition to the database, logically speaking). Because if we did, that relvar would then contain the following two tuples—

SNO	PNO	DURING
S2	P5	[d02:d02]

SNO	PNO	DURING
S2	P5	[d03:d04]

—and thus would no longer be packed on DURING, and would thereby violate the PACKED ON constraint on that relvar.

In order to address this problem, we introduce a generalized form of INSERT—another shorthand, of course—which we call U_INSERT:

Definition: Let relation *r* and relvar *R* be of the same type *T*, and let *ACL* be a commalist of attribute names in which every attribute mentioned (a) is one of type *T*'s component attributes and (b) is of some interval type. Then the update operator invocation

```
USING ( ACL ) : INSERT R r
```

denotes the **U_INSERT** (with respect to *ACL*) of *r* into *R*, and it's defined to be shorthand for the following explicit assignment:

```
R := USING ( ACL ) : R UNION r
```

In other words, the update works by (a) unpacking (on *ACL*) both *r* and the relation that's the current value of *R*, (b) forming the union of those two unpacked relations, (c) packing the result of the previous step on *ACL*, and finally (d) assigning that packed result to *R*. Points arising:

■ The qualification "with respect to *ACL*" (on the phrase "U_INSERT of *r* into *R*") can be omitted if the commalist *ACL* is understood. *Note:* An analogous remark applies to all of the operators to be defined in this section; thus, we won't bother to keep repeating the point but will instead let this one paragraph do duty for all.

■ If *ACL* is empty, then the USING specification and the colon separator can be omitted, and the U_INSERT reduces to a regular INSERT. *Note:* Again an analogous remark applies to all of the operators we'll be defining in this section and we won't keep repeating the point, again letting this one paragraph do duty for all.

■ We pointed out in Chapter 13 that PACKED ON constraints solve certain problems—basically, the problems of redundancy and circumlocution—by replacing them by another problem: namely, the problem of ensuring that updates don't violate those constraints. We also said we'd be introducing some operators later that can help to simplify this latter task. Well, the operators in question are, of course, precisely U_INSERT and the other new update operators to be described in the present chapter.

■ With respect to U_INSERT specifically: As you can see, that operator is defined in terms of U_UNION, just as regular INSERT is defined in terms of regular UNION. As a consequence, U_INSERT can have the arguably counterintuitive effect of decreasing the cardinality of the target relvar. Developing an example to illustrate this point is left as an exercise.

■ Of course, we can and do additionally define a "disjoint" version of U_INSERT ("disjoint U_INSERT"). The syntax is as for U_INSERT, except that D_INSERT appears in place of INSERT; likewise, the expansion is as for U_INSERT, except that D_UNION appears in place of UNION. The semantics should thus be obvious, and we omit further details here.

To return to Update U4, the following formulation will suffice regardless of whether the specified part number P*y* is P4 or P5:[1]

```
USING ( DURING ) :
INSERT SP_DURING
        RELATION { TUPLE { SNO      SNO ( 'S2' ) ,
                           PNO      PNO ( 'Py' ) ,
                           DURING INTERVAL_DATE ( [ d02 : d02 ] ) } } ;
```

Now, a regular INSERT can always fail on a key constraint violation. Analogously, of course, a U_INSERT can fail on a U_key violation.[2] Well ... it can't fail on a PACKED ON violation, thanks to the way it's defined; however, it can certainly fail on a WHEN / THEN violation, though only if relvar *R* and relation *r* have at least one nonkey attribute. For example, given the sample values of Fig. 16.2, the following U_INSERT fails in just such a way—

```
USING ( DURING ) :
INSERT S_STATUS_DURING
        RELATION { TUPLE { SNO      SNO ( 'S2' ) ,
                           STATUS 20 ,
                           DURING INTERVAL_DATE ( [ d04 : d06 ] ) } } ;
```

—because the unpacked form of S_STATUS_DURING on DURING already contains (among other things) a tuple saying supplier S2 has status *10* on day 4.

Of course, U_INSERTs can violate other kinds of constraints, too. In particular, they can fail on a foreign U_key (referential constraint) violation. For example, given the sample values of Fig. 16.2, the following U_INSERT fails in just such a way—

```
USING ( DURING ) :
INSERT SP_DURING
        RELATION { TUPLE { SNO      SNO ( 'S2' ) ,
                           PNO      PNO ( 'P4' ) ,
                           DURING INTERVAL_DATE ( [ d01 : d03 ] ) } } ;
```

—because supplier S2 wasn't under contract on day 1.

Note: For the remainder of this chapter, we won't bother to discuss possible integrity constraint violations unless there's some special point to be made in connection with them.

---

[1] But what if it's P1 or P2? Or P3?

[2] So can a regular INSERT, of course.

U_DELETE

Update U5: Remove the proposition "Supplier S6 was able to supply part P3 from day 3 to day 5" (in other words, after the specified removal has been performed, the database shouldn't show supplier S6 as supplying part P3 on any of days 3, 4, or 5).

Before we consider what's involved in achieving the desired effect here, we should take a moment to think about why we might ever want to remove a proposition from a fully temporal database anyway. After all, the database is supposed to contain historical records—so once a given proposition *p* has been represented in the database, isn't that proposition a historical record that should be kept in the database "forever"?

Well, this discussion takes us straight into the realm of valid time vs. transaction time (see Chapter 4). If the database did once say some proposition *p* was true, then that state of affairs— i.e., the fact that it said so—is certainly a matter of historical record. What's more, that historical record should indeed be kept "forever," with a transaction time to indicate just when the database did say so (i.e., that *p* was true). However, proposition *p* as such is *not* a matter of history; if we subsequently find it's false—perhaps we made a mistake originally and it shouldn't have been represented in the database in the first place—then we should definitely remove it.

We'll return to such matters and discuss them in much more depth in Chapter 17. For now, let's just consider how to achieve the desired effect in the particular case at hand. In fact, the following DELETE will suffice:

```
DELETE SP_DURING WHERE SNO = SNO ( 'S6' ) AND PNO = PNO ( 'P3' )
                 AND DURING = INTERVAL_DATE ( [ d03 : d05 ] ) ;
```

But suppose the proposition to be removed had specified the interval from day 4 (instead of day 3) to day 5. Then the corresponding DELETE—

```
DELETE SP_DURING WHERE SNO = SNO ( 'S6' ) AND PNO = PNO ( 'P3' )
                 AND DURING = INTERVAL_DATE ( [ d04 : d05 ] ) ;
```

—will have no effect (it certainly won't delete anything), because there *is* no tuple in relvar SP_DURING for supplier S6 and part P3 with DURING = [*d04:d05*]. Clearly, therefore, we need another shorthand:

Definition: Let *R* be a relvar and let *ACL* be a commalist of attribute names in which every attribute mentioned (a) is one of *R*'s component attributes and (b) is of some interval type. Then the update operator invocation

```
USING ( ACL ) : DELETE R WHERE bx
```

denotes a **U_DELETE WHERE** (with respect to *ACL* and *bx*) on *R*, and it's defined to be shorthand for the following explicit assignment:

```
R := USING ( ACL ) : R WHERE NOT ( bx )
```

As you can see, this operator is defined in terms of U_restriction, just as—as we saw in Chapter 3—regular DELETE WHERE is defined in terms of regular restriction.[3] In other words, the update works by (a) unpacking the current value of *R* on *ACL*, (b) forming the relation with body consisting of those tuples of that unpacked relation that satisfy the condition NOT (*bx*), (c) packing the result of the previous step on *ACL*, and finally (d) assigning that packed result to *R*. In the example, therefore, the desired effect can be achieved as follows:

```
USING ( DURING ) :
DELETE SP_DURING WHERE SNO = SNO ( 'S6' ) AND PNO = PNO ( 'P3' )
                  AND DURING ⊆ INTERVAL_DATE ( [ d04 : d05 ] ) ;
```

Note that the "=" comparison on DURING in the original (incorrect) formulation has become a "⊆" comparison in this latter formulation. That's because after SP_DURING has been unpacked on DURING, the DURING reference in the WHERE condition is a reference to a unit interval specifically. The following alternative formulation might make this point a little more clearly (the difference is in the last line):

```
USING ( DURING ) :
DELETE SP_DURING WHERE SNO = SNO ( 'S6' ) AND PNO = PNO ( 'P3' )
                  AND POINT FROM DURING ∈ INTERVAL_DATE ( [ d04 : d05 ] ) ;
```

Either way, the effect on SP_DURING, given the sample values of Fig. 16.2, is as shown here (the change is in the highlighted tuple):

SNO	PNO	DURING
S2	P1	[d02:d04]
S2	P2	[d03:d03]
S2	P5	[d03:d04]
S6	*P3*	**[d03:d03]**
S6	P4	[d04:d04]
S6	P5	[d04:d05]
S7	P1	[d03:d04]
S7	P1	[d06:d07]
S7	P1	[d09:d99]

Note: As you can see, U_DELETE WHERE is really a kind of UPDATE (in the example, it "updates" just one tuple)—but calling it a DELETE seems preferable, intuitively speaking. Also, as you might expect, such an operation can have the arguably counterintuitive effect of

---

[3] Actually these remarks aren't quite accurate, because the boolean expression *bx* isn't limited to being a restriction condition as defined in Chapter 2 but instead can be arbitrarily complex. However, we choose to overlook this point of detail here.

increasing the cardinality of the target relvar. Developing an example to illustrate this point is left as an exercise.

By the way, you might be thinking that removing propositions can never cause a PACKED ON constraint to be violated, and hence that the final PACK step in the U_DELETE WHERE definition (caused by the USING (*ACL*) specification) is unnecessary. In fact, this conjecture is correct in the specific example just discussed, because the initial unpacking and subsequent repacking are both done on the basis of a single attribute; but it's not correct, in general, if the unpacking and repacking are done on the basis of two attributes or more. By way of example, consider relvar S_PARTS_DURING once again (see the section "A More Searching Example" in Chapter 6). Suppose that relvar has the following relation as its current value:[4]

SNO	PARTS	DURING
S1	[P1:P2]	[*d01*:*d03*]
S1	[P3:P3]	[*d01*:*d02*]

Note that this relation is packed on (DURING,PARTS), in that order, as you can easily confirm.[5] Now consider the following U_DELETE WHERE:

```
USING ( PARTS , DURING ) :
DELETE S_PARTS_DURING WHERE DURING ⊆ INTERVAL_DATE ( [ d01 : d02 ] ) ;
```

Let's work through this update in detail. First of all, the preliminary UNPACK on (PARTS,DURING) gives:

SNO	PARTS	DURING
S1	[P1:P1]	[*d01*:*d01*]
S1	[P1:P1]	[*d02*:*d02*]
S1	[P1:P1]	[*d03*:*d03*]
S1	[P2:P2]	[*d01*:*d01*]
S1	[P2:P2]	[*d02*:*d02*]
S1	[P2:P2]	[*d03*:*d03*]
S1	[P3:P3]	[*d01*:*d01*]
S1	[P3:P3]	[*d02*:*d02*]

Removing the tuples whose DURING value is included in the interval [*d01*:*d02*] gives:

---

[4] As with Fig. 6.2 in Chapter 6 (and for essentially the same reasons), the relation shown here as the current value of the relvar is certainly incomplete; however, this fact doesn't materially affect the subsequent discussion.

[5] Is it also packed on (PARTS,DURING), in that order?

SNO	PARTS	DURING
S1	[P1:P1]	[*d03*:*d03*]
S1	[P2:P2]	[*d03*:*d03*]

And this relation certainly does violate the constraint PACKED ON (DURING,PARTS) (and the constraint PACKED ON (PARTS,DURING) too, come to that). So it needs to be packed to just:

SNO	PARTS	DURING
S1	[P1:P2]	[*d03*:*d03*]

U_DELETE bis

So much for U_DELETE WHERE. But we can additionally define a "U_" version of deletes of the form DELETE *R r*, thus:

Definition: Let relation *r* and relvar *R* be of the same type *T*, and let *ACL* be a commalist of attribute names in which every attribute mentioned (a) is one of type *T*'s component attributes and (b) is of some interval type. Then the update operator invocation

```
USING ( ACL ) : DELETE R r
```

denotes the **U_DELETE** (with respect to *ACL*) of *r* from *R*, and it's defined to be shorthand for the following explicit assignment:

```
R := USING ( ACL ) : R MINUS r
```

As you can see, this operator is defined in terms of U_MINUS instead of U_restriction. By way of example, consider the following U_DELETE statement, which has the effect of removing the proposition "Supplier S6 was able to supply part P3 from day 4 to day 5" (the modified form of Update U5 discussed earlier):

```
USING ( DURING ) :
DELETE SP_DURING
        RELATION { TUPLE { SNO SNO ( 'S6' ) , PNO PNO ( 'P3' ,
                           DURING INTERVAL_DATE ( [ d04 : d05 ] } } ;
```

Note that this statement is indeed of the form USING (*ACL*) : DELETE *R r*. In accordance with the foregoing definition, then, what happens is this:

■ The relation *r1* that's the current value of SP_DURING is unpacked on DURING. Call the result *u1*.

■ The relation *r2* that results from evaluation of the expression

```
RELATION { TUPLE { SNO SNO ( 'S6' ) , PNO PNO ( 'P3' ,
                   DURING INTERVAL_DATE ( [ d04 : d05 ] } }
```

is also unpacked on DURING. Call the result *u2*.

■ The difference *u1* MINUS *u2* is formed, the result is packed on DURING, and *that* result is then assigned to SP_DURING.

And it's easy to see that the overall effect is the same as for the U_DELETE_WHERE formulation from the previous subsection:

```
USING ( DURING ) :
DELETE SP_DURING WHERE SNO = SNO ( 'S6' ) AND PNO = PNO ( 'P3' )
                AND POINT FROM DURING ∈ INTERVAL_DATE ( [ d04 : d05 ] ) ;
```

Two final points to close this subsection:

■ We can and do additionally define an "included" version of this second kind of U_DELETE operator ("included U_DELETE"). The syntax is as for U_DELETE—not U_DELETE WHERE, please note—except that I_DELETE appears in place of DELETE; likewise, the expansion is as for U_DELETE, except that I_MINUS appears in place of MINUS. The semantics should thus be obvious, and we omit further details here.

■ Because operations of the form USING (*ACL*) : DELETE *R* WHERE *bx* are so much more commonly used in practice than ones of the form USING (*ACL*) : DELETE *R r*, from this point forward we'll take the shorthand name "U_DELETE" to refer to the first form rather than the second (barring explicit statements to the contrary, of course).

U_UPDATE

Update U6: Replace the proposition "Supplier S2 was able to supply part P5 from day 3 to day 4" by the proposition "Supplier S2 was able to supply part P5 from day 2 to day 4" (the only difference is in the interval begin point).

The question of why we might ever want to replace a proposition is analogous to the question of why we might ever want to remove one (see the discussion of Update U5 above). Be that as it may, the following UPDATE will suffice in the particular case at hand:

```
UPDATE SP_DURING WHERE SNO = SNO ( 'S2' ) AND PNO = PNO ( 'P5' )
                 AND DURING = INTERVAL_DATE ( [ d03 : d04 ] ) :
              { DURING := INTERVAL_DATE ( [ d02 : d04 ] ) } ;
```

Aside: We remark in passing that reference [52] would allow the attribute assignment in the last line here to be expressed thus—

```
BEGIN ( DURING ) := d02
```

—meaning, loosely, that the BEGIN point of the interval is to be set to *d02* while the END point is left unchanged. In the same kind of way, the assignment (e.g.)

```
END ( DURING ) := d07
```

would mean, loosely, that the END point of the interval is to be set to *d07* while the BEGIN point is left unchanged.[6] In these examples, BEGIN (DURING) and END (DURING) are behaving as what reference [52] calls pseudovariables (or pseudovariable references, rather). In general, a pseudovariable reference is an operational expression appearing where a variable reference would normally be expected—in particular, in the target position within an assignment operation. For further details, see reference [52]. *End of aside*.

   Back to the example. Suppose now that the requirement had been to replace the proposition "Supplier S2 was able to supply part P5 on day 3" by the proposition "Supplier S2 was able to supply part P5 on day 2" (observe that now we're talking about individual days, not intervals). Then the corresponding update—

```
UPDATE SP_DURING WHERE SNO = SNO ( 'S2' ) AND PNO = PNO ( 'P5' )
                 AND DURING = INTERVAL_DATE ( [ d03 : d03 ] ) :
              { DURING := INTERVAL_DATE ( [ d02 : d02 ] ) } ;
```

—will have no effect (it certainly won't update anything), because there *is* no tuple in relvar SP_DURING for supplier S2 and part P5 with DURING = [*d03*:*d03*]. So we need another shorthand:

Definition: Let *R* be a relvar and let *ACL* be a commalist of attribute names in which every attribute mentioned (a) is one of *R*'s component attributes and (b) is of some interval type. Then the update operator invocation

```
USING ( ACL ) : UPDATE R WHERE bx : { attribute assignments }
```

---

[6] Actually, as mentioned in passing in Chapter 6, reference [52] would probably use THE_BEGIN and THE_END in these assignments instead of just BEGIN and END as such.

denotes a **U_UPDATE** (with respect to *ACL*) on *R*, and it's defined to be shorthand for the following explicit assignment:

```
WITH ( t1 := UNPACK R ON ( ACL ) ,
       t2 := t1 WHERE NOT ( bx ) ,
       t3 := t1 MINUS t2 ,
       t4 := EXTEND t3 : { attribute assignments } ,
       t5 := t2 UNION t4 ) :
R := PACK t5 ON ( ACL )
```

Here then is a U_UPDATE statement to replace the proposition "Supplier S2 was able to supply part P5 on day 3" by the proposition "Supplier S2 was able to supply part P5 on day 2":

```
USING ( DURING ) :
UPDATE SP_DURING WHERE SNO = SNO ( 'S2' ) AND PNO = PNO ( 'P5' )
                 AND DURING = INTERVAL_DATE ( [ d03 : d03 ] ) :
                 { DURING := INTERVAL_DATE ( [ d02 : d02 ] ) } ;
```

But there's another way to do this update, a way that some might find more intuitively pleasing than the foregoing U_UPDATE formulation. Which brings us to the next section.

DURING RELVARS ONLY II: PORTION SPECIFICATIONS

The alternative solution to the problem discussed at the end of the previous section involves a *PORTION* specification on UPDATE. But PORTION can be used with DELETE, too, and it suits our purposes better to discuss that case first.

PORTION DELETE

Update U7 (*modified version of Update U5*): Remove the proposition "Supplier S6 was able to supply part P3 from day 4 to day 5."

In the previous section we gave the following formulation of this update:

```
USING ( DURING ) :
DELETE SP_DURING WHERE SNO = SNO ( 'S6' ) AND PNO = PNO ( 'P3' )
                 AND DURING ⊆ INTERVAL_DATE ( [ d04 : d05 ] ) ;
```

But here's another formulation that works just as well (note the highlighted text, and note in particular that this statement isn't a U_DELETE as such):[7]

---

[7] On the other hand, it certainly does involve some preliminary unpacking and subsequent repacking, as we'll see.

```
DELETE SP_DURING WHERE SNO = SNO ( 'S6' ) AND PNO = PNO ( 'P3' ) :
         PORTION { DURING { INTERVAL_DATE ( [ d04 : d05 ] ) } } ;
```

In order to explain how this statement works, we offer the following preliminary definition:

Definition (*first version*): Let *R* be a relvar, let *A* be an attribute of *R* of some interval type *T*, and let *ix* be an expression denoting an interval of type *T*. Then the update operator invocation

```
DELETE R WHERE bx : PORTION { A { ix } }
```

denotes a **PORTION DELETE** on *R*, and it's defined to be shorthand for the following explicit assignment:

```
WITH ( t1 := R WHERE ( bx ) AND A OVERLAPS ( ix ) ,
       t2 := R MINUS t1 ,
       t3 := UNPACK t1 ON ( A ) ,
       t4 := t3 WHERE NOT ( A ⊆ ( ix ) ) ,
       t5 := t2 UNION t4 ) :
R := PACK t5 ON ( A )
```

We leave it as an exercise to check the example given above against this definition. By the way, observe that in this definition we have an example—the first we've seen since Chapter 2—of WITH being used on a statement as opposed to an expression.

Now, relvars can have any number of interval attributes, of course—they aren't limited to just one. So it seems reasonable, within the PORTION portion of a PORTION DELETE on relvar *R*, to allow interval expressions to be specified for any subset of relvar *R*'s interval attributes. Here's an example, expressed in terms of relvar S_PARTS_DURING once again (again, see the section "A More Searching Example" in Chapter 6 if you need to refresh your memory):

```
DELETE S_PARTS_DURING :
    PORTION { PARTS { INTERVAL_PNO ( [ PNO ( 'P2' ) : PNO ( 'P4' ) ] ) } ,
              DURING { INTERVAL_DATE ( [ d03 : d05 ] ) } } ;
```

(Examples like this one show why those outer braces are necessary in a PORTION specification.) The intent here,loosely, is to delete tuples from the unpacked form of S_PARTS_DURING whose PARTS value is in the range [P2:P4] **and** whose DURING value is in the range [*d03*:*d05*] (and then to pack the result, of course). Here's the definition:

Definition (*second version*): Let *R* be a relvar, let *A1*, *A2*, ..., *An* be interval attributes of *R*, of types *T1*, *T2*, ..., *Tn*, respectively, and let *ix1*, *ix2*, ..., *ixn* be expression denoting intervals of types *T1*, *T2*, ..., *Tn*, respectively. Then the update operator invocation

```
DELETE R WHERE bx :
       PORTION { A1 { ix1 } , A2 { ix2 } , ..., An { ixn } } ;
```

denotes a **PORTION DELETE** on *R*, and it's defined to be shorthand for the following explicit assignment:

```
WITH ( t1 := R WHERE ( bx ) AND A1 OVERLAPS ( ix1 )
                            AND A2 OVERLAPS ( ix2 )
                            ................
                            AND An OVERLAPS ( ixn ) ,
       t2 := R MINUS t1 ,
       t3 := UNPACK t1 ON ( A1 , A2 , ..., An ) ,
       t4 := t3 WHERE NOT ( A1 ⊆ ( ix1 ) OR
                            A2 ⊆ ( ix2 ) OR
                            ............
                            An ⊆ ( ixn ) ) ,
       t5 := t2 UNION t4 ) :
R := PACK t5 ON ( A1 , A2 , ..., An )
```

As an exercise, try working through the PORTION DELETE on S_PARTS_DURING shown above, using some sample data of your own invention.

Next, it also seems reasonable, within the PORTION portion of a PORTION DELETE on relvar *R*, to allow two or more interval expressions to be specified for each interval attribute.[8] Here's a simple example, this time reverting to our familiar relvar SP_DURING:

```
DELETE SP_DURING WHERE SNO = SNO ( 'S7' ) :
                 PORTION { DURING { INTERVAL_DATE ( [ d04 : d06 ] ) ,
                                    INTERVAL_DATE ( [ d12 : d99 ] ) } } ;
```

(Examples like this one show why those inner braces are necessary in a PORTION specification.) The intent here, loosely, is to delete tuples for supplier S7 from the unpacked form of SP_DURING whose DURING value is in the range [*d04*:*d06*] *or* in the range [*d12*:*d99*] (and then to pack the result, of course). Here's the result, given the sample values of Fig. 16.2:

SNO	PNO	DURING
S2	P1	[*d02*:*d04*]
S2	P2	[*d03*:*d03*]
S2	P5	[*d03*:*d04*]
S6	P3	[*d03*:*d05*]
S6	P4	[*d04*:*d04*]
S6	P5	[*d04*:*d05*]
S7	*P1*	[*d03*:*d03*]
S7	*P1*	[*d07*:*d07*]
S7	*P1*	[*d09*:*d11*]

---

[8] IXSQL [76,79], which is the source of the PORTION idea in general, didn't actually support this possibility.

And here's the definition, expressed for simplicity in terms of just one interval attribute:

Definition (*third version*): Let *R* be a relvar, let *A* be an attribute of *R* of some interval type *T*, and let each of *ix1*, *ix2*, ..., *ixn* be an expression denoting an interval of type *T*. Then the update operator invocation

```
DELETE R WHERE bx : PORTION { A { ix1 , ix2 , ... , ixn } }
```

denotes a **PORTION DELETE** on *R*, and it's defined to be shorthand for the following explicit assignment:

```
WITH ( t1 := R WHERE ( bx ) AND ( A OVERLAPS ( ix1 ) OR
                                   A OVERLAPS ( ix2 ) OR
                       ...............
                                   A OVERLAPS ( ixn ) ) ,
       t2 := R MINUS t1 ,
       t3 := UNPACK t1 ON ( A ) ,
       t4 := t3 WHERE NOT ( A ⊆ ( ix1 ) AND
                            A ⊆ ( ix2 ) AND
                    ............
                            A ⊆ ( ixn ) ) ,
       t5 := t2 UNION t4 ) :
R := PACK t5 ON ( A )
```

Extending this definition to cover the case of more than one interval attribute—in effect, combining the second and third definitions above—is left as another exercise. Note, however, that (in general, and speaking somewhat loosely) the commas within the inner braces represent OR, while the other commas represent AND.

PORTION UPDATE

Update U8 (*modified version of Update U6*): Replace the proposition "Supplier S2 was able to supply part P5 on day 3" by the proposition "Supplier S2 was able to supply part P5 on day 2."

```
UPDATE SP_DURING WHERE SNO = SNO ( 'S2' )
                 AND   PNO = PNO ( 'P5' ) :
    PORTION { DURING { INTERVAL_DATE ( [ d03 : d03 ] ) } } :
    { DURING := INTERVAL_DATE ( [ d02 : d02 ] ) } ;
```

How this example works should be intuitively obvious, but spelling out the semantics of the general case (i.e., UPDATE with a PORTION specification in general) we leave as another exercise for the reader. We content ourselves here with offering some further examples.

Update U9 (*modified version of Update U8*): Replace the proposition "Supplier S2 was able to supply part P5 on day 3" by the proposition "Supplier S2 was able to supply part P5 on day 2"—

but do so only if the interval containing day 3 during which supplier S2 was able to supply part P5 is at least seven days long.

This example is plainly somewhat contrived, but it serves our purpose here. The point about it is this: Clearly, we need to check whether the specified interval is indeed at least seven days long before we do any unpacking (after unpacking, of course, every interval will be just one day long). And that's what this formulation does:

```
UPDATE SP_DURING WHERE SNO = SNO ( 'S2' )
                 AND    PNO = PNO ( 'P5' )
                 AND    d03 ∈ DURING
                 AND    COUNT ( DURING ) ≥ 7 :
       PORTION { DURING { INTERVAL_DATE ( [ d03 : d03 ] ) } } :
     { DURING := INTERVAL_DATE ( [ d02 : d02 ] ) } ;
```

Update U10: Replace every proposition of the form "Supplier S*x* was able to supply part P8 during interval *i*" by one of the form "Supplier S*x* was able to supply part P9 during interval *i*"— but only if interval *i* overlaps [*d05*:*d08*], and then perform the replacement only for that part of interval *i* that overlaps [*d02*:*d06*].

Again this example is highly contrived, of course, but here's a suitable formulation:

```
UPDATE SP_DURING WHERE PNO = PNO ( 'P8' )
                 AND    DURING OVERLAPS INTERVAL_DATE ( [ d05 : d08 ] ) :
       PORTION { DURING { INTERVAL_DATE ( [ d02 : d06 ] ) } } :
     { PNO := PNO ( 'P9' ) } ;
```

Observe in this example that it's not the interval as such that's being updated.

Update U11: Replace the proposition "Supplier S1 was under contract from day 4 to day 8 inclusive" by the proposition "Supplier S2 was under contract from day 6 to day 7 inclusive."

Now, it might well be argued that this example is not merely contrived but goes beyond the bounds of reasonableness, since *no term* in the new proposition is the same as its counterpart in the old one![9] (After all, the idea of updating a tuple in such a way that every component is changed is usually looked at a trifle askance, even in a nontemporal database.) Be that as it may, here's a possible formulation:

```
UPDATE S_DURING WHERE SNO = SNO ( 'S1' ) :
       PORTION { DURING { INTERVAL_DATE ( [ d04 : d08 ] ) } } :
     { SNO := SNO ( 'S2' ) ,
       DURING := INTERVAL_DATE ( [ d06 : d07 ] ) } ;
```

---

[9] *Term* is being used here in a slightly technical sense.

If before this UPDATE relvar S_DURING looks like this—

SNO	DURING
S1	[*d03*:*d10*]
S2	[*d02*:*d05*]

—then after the UPDATE it looks like this:

SNO	DURING
S1	[*d03*:*d03*]
S1	[*d09*:*d10*]
S2	[*d02*:*d07*]

Two final points to close this section:

■ First, we've considered PORTION in connection with the regular DELETE and UPDATE operators but not with their "U_" counterparts U_DELETE and U_UPDATE. Whether this latter possibility makes sense or could be useful is a matter that requires further investigation.

■ Second, we've considered PORTION in connection with update operators, but a PORTION version of restrict could be useful too (more useful, possibly, than U_restrict, as a matter of fact). E.g., given the sample value shown for S_DURING in Fig. 16.2, the expression

```
S_DURING PORTION { DURING { INTERVAL_DATE ( [ d05 : d08 ] ) } }
```

would yield:

SNO	DURING
S6	[*d05*:*d05*]
S7	[*d05*:*d08*]

DURING RELVARS ONLY III: MULTIPLE ASSIGNMENT

Now we turn our attention to the question of updating S_DURING and S_STATUS_DURING (as noted earlier, examples in the previous two sections mostly dealt just with SP_DURING). First we remind you of the design of the relevant portions of the database:

```
S_DURING { SNO , DURING }
        USING ( DURING ) : KEY { SNO , DURING }
        USING ( DURING ) : FOREIGN KEY { SNO , DURING }
                                    REFERENCES S_STATUS_DURING

S_STATUS_DURING { SNO , STATUS , DURING }
        USING ( DURING ) : KEY { SNO , DURING }
        USING ( DURING ) : FOREIGN KEY { SNO , DURING }
                                    REFERENCES S_DURING
```

Note in particular that each of these relvars has a foreign U_key that references the other: The one in S_STATUS_DURING reflects the fact that any supplier that has some status at some time must be under contract at that time, and the one in S_DURING reflects the fact that any supplier under contract at some time must have some status at that time (recall the discussion of denseness constraints in Chapter 14).

Update U12 (*same as Update U1*): Add proposition(s) to show that supplier S9 has just been placed under contract, starting today, with status 15.

The following code will suffice:

```
INSERT S_DURING RELATION { TUPLE
    { SNO    SNO ( 'S9' ) ,
      DURING INTERVAL_DATE ( [ TODAY ( ) : LAST_DATE ( ) ] ) } } ,

INSERT S_STATUS_DURING RELATION { TUPLE
    { SNO    SNO ( 'S9' ) ,
      STATUS 15 ,
      DURING INTERVAL_DATE ( [ TODAY ( ) : LAST_DATE ( ) ] ) } } ;
```

Explanation: Clearly, we need two INSERTs here; the target relvars are S_DURING and S_STATUS_DURING, respectively, and the set of tuples to be inserted—actually a singleton set—is denoted by a simple relation selector invocation in each case. Note carefully, however, that the two INSERTs are separated by a comma, not a semicolon, and are thereby bundled into a single statement. That statement in turn is essentially just syntactic shorthand for an explicit *multiple assignment* that looks like this (again note the comma separator):

```
S_DURING := S_SINCE UNION RELATION { TUPLE
    { SNO    SNO ( 'S9' ) ,
      DURING INTERVAL_DATE ( [ TODAY ( ) : LAST_DATE ( ) ] ) } } ,

S_STATUS_DURING := S_SINCE UNION RELATION { TUPLE
    { SNO    SNO ( 'S9' ) ,
      STATUS 15 ,
      DURING INTERVAL_DATE ( [ TODAY ( ) : LAST_DATE ( ) ] ) } } ;
```

As we saw in Chapter 3, the semantics are as follows:

■ First, the source expressions on the right sides of the individual assignments are evaluated.

■ Second, those individual assignments are executed.

■ Last, any applicable constraints are checked.

Observe in particular that, precisely because the source expressions are all evaluated before any of the individual assignments are executed, none of those individual assignments can depend on the result of any other, and so the sequence in which they're executed is irrelevant.[10] In the example, the net effect is thus that S_DURING and S_STATUS_DURING are updated "simultaneously"—i.e., both relvars are updated as part of the same statement execution. Note that indeed both updates *must* be part of the same statement execution, for at least the following two reasons:

■ First, as already noted, each of the relvars has a foreign U_key referencing the other; thus, if either was updated without the other, a referential constraint violation would occur.

■ Second, we need to guarantee that the two invocations of TODAY both return the same value.

Update U13: Remove all proposition(s) showing supplier S7 as being under contract.

Again a multiple assignment is needed:

```
DELETE SP_DURING WHERE SNO = SNO ( 'S7' ) ,

DELETE S_STATUS_DURING WHERE SNO = SNO ( 'S7' ),

DELETE S_DURING WHERE SNO = SNO ( 'S7' ) ;
```

(The first comma here could be replaced by a semicolon, but the second mustn't be.) Here's the expansion in terms of explicit assignment:

```
SP_DURING          :=    SP_DURING WHERE NOT ( SNO = SNO ( 'S7' ) ) ,

S_STATUS_DURING    :=    S_STATUS_DURING WHERE NOT ( SNO = SNO ( 'S7' ) ) ,

S_DURING           :=    S_DURING WHERE NOT ( SNO = SNO ( 'S7' ) ) ;
```

---

[10] With the following important exception (previously noted in Chapter 3): Repeated assignments to the same target are effectively executed in sequence as written.

Update U14 (*similar to Update U2, but note the different wording*): Supplier S7's current contract has just been terminated. Update the database accordingly.

```
UPDATE S_DURING WHERE SNO = SNO ( 'S7' )
                AND TODAY ( ) ∈ DURING :
   { END ( DURING ) := TODAY ( ) } ,

UPDATE S_STATUS_DURING WHERE SNO = SNO ( 'S7' )
                       AND TODAY ( ) ∈ DURING :
   { END ( DURING ) := TODAY ( ) } ,

UPDATE SP_DURING WHERE SNO = SNO ( 'S7' )
                 AND TODAY ( ) ∈ DURING :
   { END ( DURING ) := TODAY ( ) } ;
```

Note the use of syntax that assigns directly to END (DURING) in this example (we explained this syntax in an aside in the discussion of Update U6 in the section "During Relvars I: U_updates," earlier in the chapter). More important, note that the "removal" of certain propositions here is being done by means of UPDATE operations! (The propositions in question all have to do with the notion that supplier S7 is under contract until "the last day.") Indeed, it's often the case in a fully temporal database that there's no simple correspondence between (a) adding or removing or replacing propositions and (b) adding or removing or replacing tuples. Several examples in the next section will illustrate this same point.

Here for interest is an explicit assignment—in fact, a multiple assignment—that's equivalent to the first (only) of the three foregoing UPDATE operations:

```
WITH ( t := S_DURING WHERE SNO = SNO ( 'S7' ) AND TODAY ( ) ∈ DURING ) :
DELETE S_DURING t ,
INSERT S_DURING ( EXTEND t : { END ( DURING ) := TODAY ( ) } ) ;
```

We remark in passing that this latter multiple assignment shows very clearly that an UPDATE in general can be thought of as a DELETE followed by an INSERT on the same target. We'll make use of this fact several times in the section immediately following.

BOTH SINCE AND DURING RELVARS

Now we turn to our preferred version of the database, which contains a mixture of since and during relvars. This version, which we refer to as the combination design, keeps "current" information in the since relvars and "historical" information in the during relvars. Fig. 16.3, a copy of Fig. 14.8, shows some sample values; we'll base our examples on those specific values, where it makes any difference. Refer to Fig. 14.9 in Chapter 14 if you need to remind yourself of the constraints that apply to this database. Here are the applicable predicates (in simplified form once again):

■ S_SINCE: *Supplier SNO has been under contract since SNO_SINCE and has had status STATUS since STATUS_SINCE.*

■ SP_SINCE: *Supplier SNO has been able to supply part PNO since SINCE.*

■ S_DURING: *DURING denotes a maximal interval throughout which supplier SNO was under contract.*

■ S_STATUS_DURING: *DURING denotes a maximal interval throughout which supplier SNO had status STATUS.*

■ SP_DURING: *DURING denotes a maximal interval throughout which supplier SNO was able to supply part PNO.*

S_SINCE

SNO	SNO_SINCE	STATUS	STATUS_SINCE
S1	*d04*	20	*d06*
S2	*d07*	10	*d07*
S3	*d03*	30	*d03*
S4	*d04*	20	*d08*
S5	*d02*	30	*d02*

SP_SINCE

SNO	PNO	SINCE
S1	P1	*d04*
S1	P2	*d05*
S1	P3	*d09*
S1	P4	*d05*
S1	P5	*d04*
S1	P6	*d06*
S2	P1	*d08*
S2	P2	*d09*
S3	P2	*d08*
S4	P5	*d05*

S_DURING

SNO	DURING
S2	[*d02:d04*]
S6	[*d03:d05*]

SP_DURING

SNO	PNO	DURING
S2	P1	[*d02:d04*]
S2	P2	[*d03:d03*]
S3	P5	[*d05:d07*]
S4	P2	[*d06:d09*]
S4	P4	[*d04:d08*]
S6	P3	[*d03:d03*]
S6	P3	[*d05:d05*]

S_STATUS_DURING

SNO	STATUS	DURING
S1	15	[*d04:d05*]
S2	5	[*d02:d02*]
S2	10	[*d03:d04*]
S4	10	[*d04:d04*]
S4	25	[*d05:d07*]
S6	5	[*d03:d04*]
S6	7	[*d05:d05*]

Fig. 16.3: Both since and during relvars–sample values

Update U15: Add the proposition "Supplier S4 has been able to supply part P4 since day 10."

The following INSERT will suffice:

```
INSERT SP_SINCE RELATION { TUPLE { SNO    SNO ( 'S4' ) ,
                                    PNO    PNO ( 'P4' ) ,
                                    SINCE d10 } } ;
```

But suppose the proposition to be added had specified day 9 instead of day 10; given the sample values shown in Fig. 16.3, the corresponding INSERT would then have failed on a violation of Constraint BR78 (actually on the "BR8" portion of that constraint—see Fig. 14.9 in Chapter 14). That constraint, to remind you, is intended to enforce the requirement that if the database shows supplier Sx as able to supply the same part Py on days d and $d+1$, it must contain exactly one tuple that shows that fact. In the case at hand, if the INSERT were permitted, relvars SP_SINCE and SP_DURING would then contain the following tuples, respectively, and would thereby violate the constraint:

SNO	PNO	SINCE
S4	P4	$d09$

SNO	PNO	DURING
S4	P4	[$d04$:$d08$]

To add that revised proposition, therefore, what we need to do is the following:

- Delete the tuple from SP_DURING for S4 and P4 with DURING = [$d04$:$d08$].

- Insert a tuple into SP_SINCE for S4 and P4 with SINCE = $d04$.

Also, of course, these two updates need to be performed "at the same time." The following code (a multiple assignment) will thus suffice:

```
DELETE SP_DURING WHERE SNO = SNO ( 'S4' )
                 AND   PNO = PNO ( 'P4' )
                 AND   DURING = [d04:d08] ,

INSERT SP_SINCE RELATION { TUPLE { SNO    SNO ( 'S4' ) ,
                                   PNO    PNO ( 'P4' ) ,
                                   SINCE d04 } } ;
```

Observe now that the code just shown is, of course, specific to a certain specific update and a certain specific set of existing values in the database. Here by contrast is generic code that will effectively add the proposition "Supplier Sx has been able to supply part Py since day d" to the database, regardless of the specific values of S*x* and P*y* and *d* and regardless of the specific values currently existing in the database:

```
WITH ( temp := SP_DURING WHERE
                SNO = Sx AND PNO = Py AND d ≤ POST ( DURING ) ) :
CASE
   WHEN IS_EMPTY ( temp )
      THEN INSERT SP_SINCE
           RELATION { TUPLE { SNO Sx , PNO Py , SINCE d } } ;
   ELSE
      DELETE SP_DURING temp ,
      INSERT SP_SINCE RELATION { TUPLE
         { SNO Sx , PNO Py , SINCE MIN ( temp , BEGIN ( DURING ) ) } } ;
END CASE ;
```

Points arising:

■ Of course, we're not suggesting that users should actually have to write code like that just shown. For one thing, it might be possible to perform such generic updates using a set of appropriately defined views (see the final section in this chapter). But our primary concern here is, as always, with fundamental concepts and principles, not so much with details of concrete syntax and the like.

■ If a tuple for supplier S*x* and part P*y* already exists in relvar SP_SINCE, the code will fail on a key constraint violation; if no tuple for supplier S*x* exists in relvar S_SINCE, it will fail on a foreign key constraint violation. In practice, the code should be extended to take care of such possibilities appropriately.

■ Note that the code still works even if the value *d* isn't just (as it was in our "day 9" version of Update U15) the immediate successor of the end point of the most recent interval shown for S*x* and P*y* in SP_DURING but is in fact a point within that interval, or even a point within some earlier interval for that same supplier and part.

■ Finally, although not necessary in the case at hand, in general such generic code might need to use U_INSERT and U_DELETE (or DELETE PORTION) operations instead of the regular INSERT and DELETE operations shown.

Update U16: After today, supplier S1 will no longer be able to supply part P1. Update the database accordingly.

The value shown for SP_SINCE in Fig. 16.3 shows that supplier S1 has been able to supply part P1 since day 4. Given this state of affairs, the following code will suffice:

```
INSERT SP_DURING RELATION { TUPLE { SNO SNO ( 'S1' ) , PNO PNO ( 'P1' ) ,
       DURING INTERVAL_DATE ( [ d04 : TODAY ( ) ] ) } } ,

DELETE SP_SINCE WHERE SNO = SNO ( 'S1' ) AND PNO = PNO ( 'P1' ) ;
```

Here's code for the general case—i.e., generic code to update the database to reflect the fact that supplier S*x* has been able to supply part P*y* since day *d* but after today will no longer be able to do so:

```
WITH ( temp := SP_SINCE WHERE SNO = Sx AND PNO = Py ) :
IF IS_NOT_EMPTY ( temp ) THEN
    INSERT SP_DURING RELATION { TUPLE
        { SNO Sx , PNO Py , DURING INTERVAL_DATE
            ( [ SINCE FROM ( TUPLE FROM temp ) : TODAY ( ) ] ) } } ,
    DELETE SP_SINCE temp ;
END IF ;
```

Note: To return to Update U16 per se, we were making a tacit assumption in connection with that example that the original proposition—"Supplier S1 was able to supply part P1 since day 4"—was in fact true (or, rather, we believed it was true). But suppose we find we made a mistake, and the SP_SINCE tuple for S1 and P1 with SINCE = *d04* should never have been in that relvar in the first place. Then we would need to perform an appropriate DELETE on SP_SINCE *without* performing a corresponding INSERT on SP_DURING:

```
DELETE SP_SINCE WHERE SNO = SNO ( 'S1' ) AND PNO = PNO ( 'P1' ) ;
```

Analogous remarks apply to other updates also: If the reason for the update is simply to correct an earlier mistake, then it might be inappropriate, or incorrect, to perform "simultaneous updates" on other relvars. For definiteness, we assume in our examples that such simultaneous updates are both appropriate and necessary—but exactly what's appropriate and necessary in any given situation will, of course, depend on circumstances.

Update U17:   Replace the proposition "Supplier S2 has been able to supply part P1 since day 8" by the proposition "Supplier S2 has been able to supply part P1 since day 7."

Given the sample values of Fig. 16.3, the following UPDATE will suffice:

```
UPDATE SP_SINCE WHERE SNO = SNO ( 'S2' ) AND PNO = PNO ( 'P1' ) :
    { SINCE := d07 } ;
```

But suppose the new SINCE value had been day 5, not day 7. Given those same sample values (i.e., as shown in Fig. 16.3), then the corresponding UPDATE would have failed on a violation of Constraint BR78 (actually on the "BR8" portion of that constraint—see Fig. 14.9 in Chapter 14). For if the UPDATE were permitted, relvars SP_SINCE and SP_DURING would then contain the following tuples, respectively, and would thereby violate the constraint:

SNO	PNO	SINCE
S2	P1	*d05*

SNO	PNO	DURING
S2	P1	[*d02:d04*]

Thus, what we need to do is as follows:

```
DELETE SP_DURING WHERE SNO = SNO ( 'S2' ) AND PNO = PNO ( 'P1' )
                                     AND END ( DURING ) = d04 ,

UPDATE SP_SINCE WHERE SNO = SNO ( 'S2' ) AND PNO = PNO ( 'P1' ) :
                                     { SINCE := d02 } ;
```

More generally, here's code that will effectively replace the proposition "Supplier Sx has been able to supply part Py since day d" by the proposition "Supplier Sx has been able to supply part Py since day d'":

```
WITH ( temp := SP_DURING WHERE
                   SNO = Sx AND PNO = Py AND d ≤ POST ( DURING ) ) :
CASE
   WHEN IS_EMPTY ( temp )
      THEN UPDATE SP_SINCE WHERE SNO = Sx AND PNO = Py :
           { SINCE := d' } ;
   ELSE
      DELETE SP_DURING temp ,
      UPDATE SP_SINCE WHERE SNO = Sx AND PNO = Py :
           { SINCE := MIN (temp , BEGIN ( DURING ) ) } ;
END CASE ;
```

As you can see, this code is very similar to the generic "insert" code shown earlier under Update U10, except that the two INSERTs in that code have been replaced by UPDATEs. Note, however, that the code does assume a tuple for supplier Sx and part Py currently exists in relvar SP_SINCE. Extending the code appropriately to avoid reliance on such an assumption is left as an exercise.

We conclude this section with the following observations. First, we've considered attempts to change the SINCE component of an SP_SINCE tuple (loosely speaking), but not attempts to change either the SNO or the PNO component. We leave it as a further exercise to determine that considerations essentially similar to those already discussed apply in these cases too. If you want to try this exercise, we suggest you consider the following examples (expressed as usual in terms of the sample values shown in Fig. 16.3):

a. Replace the PNO component of the SP_SINCE tuple for S4 and P5 by P4.

b. Replace the SNO component of the SP_SINCE tuple for S1 and P4 by S4.

Second, we've considered updates affecting relvars SP_SINCE and SP_DURING but not ones affecting S_SINCE, S_DURING, or S_STATUS_DURING. However, the behavior of these latter relvars with respect to updating in general doesn't differ significantly from that of relvars SP_SINCE and SP_DURING. The details are left as another exercise.

VIEWS CAN HELP

It's clear from the discussions in the foregoing sections that updating a temporal database has the potential to be a seriously complicated matter. Among other things, we've seen that it rarely seems to be possible to talk straightforwardly in terms of adding, removing, or replacing tuples, as we usually (albeit informally) do; rather, it seems to make more sense to talk in terms of adding, removing, or replacing propositions. And we've also seen in particular that if the database involves a mixture of since and during relvars, then:

a. It's often impossible to talk about just one of INSERT, DELETE, and UPDATE in isolation—often, an update involves, e.g., an INSERT on one relvar and a DELETE on another.

b. It's also often impossible to talk about updating since or during relvars in isolation—often, since and during relvars need to be updated simultaneously.

So can we provide some syntactic shorthands to make life a little less daunting for the user in this potentially complex area? We believe the answer to this question is *yes*. To be specific, we believe the automatic provision of views as discussed in the section "Views Can Help" in Chapter 15 can help with updates, just as it can with queries.[11] We content ourselves with a single example, making use of view S_STATUS_DURING' (see Chapter 15 for a definition of that view).

Update U18: Supplier S1's status has just changed to 25. Update the database accordingly.

```
UPDATE S_STATUS_DURING' WHERE SNO = SNO ( 'S1' ) :
PORTION { DURING { INTERVAL_DATE ( [ TODAY ( ) : LAST_DATE ( ) ] ) } } :
                                      { STATUS := 25 } ;
```

Suppose that, prior to the foregoing update, view S_STATUS_DURING' contains the following "current" tuple (possibly other tuples as well) for supplier S1:

---

[11] Of course, we're assuming here that the system under consideration does allow views to be updated. See reference [44] for a discussion of view updating in general.

SNO	STATUS	DURING
S1	20	[*d04:d99*]

Suppose too that today is day 10. After the update, then, the relvar—that is, the view—will contain the following *two* tuples (possibly others as well) for supplier S1:

SNO	STATUS	DURING
S1	20	[*d04:d09*]
S1	25	[*d10:d99*]

(More precisely, the underlying base relvars, S_SINCE and S_STATUS_DURING, will have been updated in such a way as to cause these two tuples both to appear in the view.)

We conjecture that a mechanism along the lines of that sketched above should be sufficient for the system to be able to conceal from the user much of the complexity described in earlier sections (in the section "Both Since and During Relvars" in particular).

EXERCISES

16.1 In the body of the chapter we described "U_" versions of various shorthands for relational assignment—INSERT, DELETE, and so on—but we never mentioned a "U_" version of explicit relational assignment as such. Why not?

16.2 Using the version of the courses-and-students database from Exercise 13.7 in Chapter 13, give realistic examples (in natural language) of updates that might be required on that database. Be sure to show examples that will require (a) multiple assignment; (b) U_INSERT or U_DELETE or U_UPDATE operations; (c) PORTION specifications.

16.3 Given your answer to Exercise 16.2, write suitable **Tutorial D** statements to perform the specified updates.

16.4 How might views help with Exercise 16.3?

16.5 Here again is the sample "PORTION restrict" from the body of the chapter:

```
S_DURING PORTION { DURING { INTERVAL_DATE ( [ d05 : d08 ] ) } }
```

Give an equivalent expression not using PORTION.

ANSWERS

16.1 Consider a hypothetical assignment of the form:

```
USING ( ACL ) : R := r ;
```

Presumably, this statement would have to be defined to be shorthand for:

```
R := PACK ( UNPACK r ON ( ACL ) ) ON ( ACL ) ;
```

And, of course, this latter reduces to just:

```
R := PACK r ON ( ACL ) ;
```

A shorthand therefore seems hardly worth defining (though we could obviously define one anyway, if desired).

16.2 Here are five examples (note the numbering):

1. New courses C542 ("**Tutorial D**") and C543 ("Temporal Databases") became available on June 1st, 2013.

2. Currently available courses C193 ("SQL") and C203 ("Object Oriented Databases") were discontinued at the end of their most recent offering.

3. Student ST21, Hugh Manatee, not currently registered with the university, *was* registered from October 1st, 2011, to June 30th, 2012, but the database doesn't show that fact.

4. Student ST19 changed her name to Anna Marino on November 18th, 2012.

5. For each student currently shown as having unregistered on July 31st, 2011, for each day of that registration period that falls between that date and the beginning of the year, the record is to show an asterisk appended to the student's name (bearing in mind that some students had asterisks appended to their names for some periods in 2010, too).

16.3

```
1. INSERT CURRENT_COURSE
        RELATION { TUPLE { COURSENO COURSENO ( 'C542' ) ,
                           CNAME NAME ( 'Tutorial D' ) ,
                           AVAILABLE DATE ( '2013/06/01' ) } ,
                   TUPLE { COURSENO COURSENO ( 'C543' ) ,
                           CNAME NAME ( 'Temporal Databases' ) ,
                           AVAILABLE DATE ( '2013/06/01' ) } } ;

2. WITH ( SQL_OO := CURRENT_COURSE WHERE COURSENO = COURSENO ( 'C193' )
                                   OR COURSENO = COURSENO ( 'C203' ) ) :
   DELETE CURRENT_COURSE SQL_OO ,
   INSERT OLD_COURSE
       ( EXTEND SQL_OO : { AVAILABLE_DURING := INTERVAL_DATE
           ( [ AVAILABLE FROM ( TUPLE FROM ( ‼COURSE_OFFERING ) ) :
             MAX ( ‼COURSE_OFFERING , END ( OFFERED_DURING ) ) ] ) )
                                { COURSENO , CNAME , AVAILABLE_DURING } ;
```

Note: The foregoing code assumes a course being discontinued always had at least one offering. Extending it to take care of the possibility of this assumption being invalid is left as a subsidiary exercise.

```
3. USING ( REG_DURING ) :
   INSERT STUDENT_HISTORY RELATION { TUPLE
       { STUDENTNO   STUDENTNO ( 'ST21' ) ,
         SNAME       NAME ( 'Hugh Manatee' ) ,
         REG_DURING INTERVAL_DATE ( [ DATE ( '2011/10/01' ) :
                                      DATE ( '2012/06/30' ) ] ) } } ;

4. UPDATE CURRENT_STUDENT WHERE STUDENTNO = STUDENTNO ( 'ST19' ) AND
                               REGISTERED ≤ DATE ( '2012/11/18' ) AND
                               SNAME ≠ NAME ( 'Anna Marino' ) :
                 { SNAME := NAME ( 'Anna Marino' ) ,
                   REGISTERED := DATE ( '2002/11/18' ) } ,
   INSERT STUDENT_HISTORY
   ( EXTEND CURRENT_STUDENT WHERE STUDENTNO = STUDENTNO ( 'ST19' ) AND
                               REGISTERED < DATE ( '2012/11/18' ) AND
                               SNAME ≠ NAME ( 'Anna Marino' ) :
       { REG_DURING :=
         INTERVAL_DATE ( [ REGISTERED : DATE ( '2002/11/17' ) ] ) } )
                                { ALL BUT REGISTERED } ,
   USING ( REG_DURING ) :
   UPDATE STUDENT_HISTORY WHERE STUDENTNO = STUDENTNO ( 'ST19' ) AND
                             DATE ( '2012/11/18' ) ≤ POINT FROM REG_DURING :
       { SNAME := NAME ( 'Anna Marino' ) } ;
```

Note: The first of the three individual updates in this multiple assignment replaces any existing tuple for student ST19 in CURRENT_STUDENT by a tuple reflecting that student's new name and the date from which that new name became effective (except that, in the special case where the putative new name is in fact the same as the old one, no change is made to that relvar). The second update adds a tuple to STUDENT_HISTORY in the case where student ST19 had been registered with the university since some time before the date on which her name was changed, reflecting the fact that for a time she was registered under her old name. The third replaces any existing tuples showing student ST19 as having been registered on or after November 18th, 2012, by a set of tuples correctly reflecting the change of name on that date.

5.
```
UPDATE STUDENT_HISTORY WHERE END ( REG_DURING ) = DATE ( '2011/07/31' ) :
   PORTION { REG_DURING { INTERVAL_DATE ( [ DATE ( '2011/01/01' ) :
                                            DATE ( '2011/07/31' ) ] ) } } :
              { SNAME := NAME ( CHAR ( SNAME ) || '*' ) } ;
```

16.4 Suppose we could combine relvars CURRENT_HISTORY and STUDENT_HISTORY into a view called STUDENT_PAST_OR_PRESENT. Then part 4 of the answer to Exercise 16.3 could be simplified to just:

4.
```
USING ( REG_DURING ) :
UPDATE STUDENT_PAST_OR_PRESENT
       WHERE STUDENTNO = STUDENTNO ( 'ST19' )
       AND DATE ( '2012-11-18' ) ≤ POINT FROM REG_DURING :
     { SNAME := NAME ( 'Anna Marino' ) } ;
```

16.5
```
WITH ( i := INTERVAL_DATE ( [ d05 : d08 ] ) ) ,
       t := S_DURING WHERE DURING OVERLAPS i ) :
   EXTEND t : { DURING := DURING INTERSECT i }
```

Chapter 17

Logged Time
and Stated Time

"Why, sometimes I've believed
as many as six impossible things before breakfast."
—The White Queen, in Lewis Carroll:
Through the Looking-Glass and What Alice Found There (1871)

In this chapter, we take a much closer look at two concepts we first encountered in Chapter 4, *valid time* and *transaction time*. We begin by briefly reviewing some of the ideas originally introduced in connection with those concepts in that earlier chapter.

A QUICK REVIEW

Consider the following simple example. Suppose our usual relvar S_DURING currently contains just this single tuple for supplier S2:

SNO	DURING
S2	[d02:d04]

Then we might say, loosely, that the valid time for the proposition "Supplier S2 was under contract" is the interval from day 2 to day 4.

Suppose further that the foregoing tuple exists in the database, in relvar S_DURING, from time *t1* to time *t2* (only). Then we might say, again loosely, that the transaction time for the proposition "Supplier S2 was under contract from day 2 to day 4" is the interval from *t1* to *t2*.

Points arising from this example:

■ Valid times refer to *something we currently believe to be true* (we currently believe the interval during which "Supplier S2 was under contract" was day 2 to day 4). By contrast, transaction times refer to *when the database said something was true* (the interval during which the database said "Supplier S2 was under contract from day 2 to day 4" was *t1* to *t2*).

■ As the previous bullet item clearly indicates, the two "somethings" in question are, in general, different—that is, they're two different propositions.

■ Valid times and transaction times are both, more precisely, *sets* of intervals. In the example, the valid time for the proposition "Supplier S2 was under contract" is the set of intervals {[*d02*:*d04*]}. And if relvar S_DURING currently shows that supplier S2 was additionally under contract from day 6 to day 9 (but not at any other time), then the valid time for the proposition "Supplier S2 was under contract" would be the set of intervals {[*d02*:*d04*], [*d06*:*d09*]}. However, when the set of intervals constituting some particular valid time or transaction time contains just one interval, we often say—for simplicity, albeit rather sloppily—that the valid time or transaction time in question is just that single interval as such.

■ Valid times are updatable, because they represent our beliefs about history, and beliefs can change. By contrast, transaction times represent history as such; hence, they're not updatable, because history as such is immutable.

■ When we say valid times represent our "beliefs about" history, we mean those beliefs are *ones we hold right now* ... and, of course, what we believe right now can refer to something in the past and/or the present and/or the future. For example, we might believe right now that supplier S2 *was* under contract from day 2 to day 4, in the past; or we might believe right now that supplier S2 *is* under contract right now, in the present; or we might believe right now that supplier S2 *will be* under contract from day 20 to day 40, in the future. Thus, we take the term *history*, in such phrases as "belief(s) about history," to include the present and/or future, as applicable, unless the context demands otherwise.

■ By contrast, transaction times can refer only to the past. That is, we can't possibly say that *at some future time* the database will say something was true.[1] Nor, strictly speaking, can we even sensibly say that *right now* the database says something is true, because by definition "right now" is always at least a little bit later in time than when we most recently looked to see what the database in fact does say.[2]

■ For obvious reasons, transaction times also can't refer to a time in the past earlier than the time when the proposition they apply to was added to the database.

---

[1] At least, if we do say such a thing, we can't possibly be certain that what we're saying is true.

[2] As the physicist John Bell once observed: "We have no access to the past. We have only our memories and records." (Quoted in *The End of Time* by Julian Barbour, Cambridge University Press, 1999.)

■ Finally, observe that all of the "times" we've been dealing with in this book prior to the present chapter (with the exception of those few introductory remarks in Chapter 4) have been valid times specifically.

All of that being said, we now remind you that, as noted in Chapter 4, there's quite a lot more to be said about these concepts; hence the present chapter. Indeed, as the title of the chapter itself suggests, one of the things we want to do is propose some alternative terms for the concepts, and we'll do that in the "Terminology" section, later. However, we need to discuss a lot of material of a more fundamental nature first.

One final preliminary remark: The notion of transaction time applies to every relvar in the database (obviously enough).[3] By contrast, the notion of valid time applies only to temporal relvars, because—by definition—temporal relvars are the only ones with "valid time" attributes. The rest of this chapter explains just what we mean when we say that either of these two concepts "applies to" some particular relvar!

A CLOSER LOOK

Note: The discussions in this section are unavoidably a little complicated, which is why we've left them to this late stage in the book. Caveat lector.

Again assume relvar S_DURING contains just this one tuple for supplier S2:

SNO	DURING
S2	[d02:d04]

Assume as before that:

a. This tuple represents the proposition—let's call it *p*—"Supplier S2 was under contract from day 2 to day 4." In other words, it tells us that the interval from day 2 to day 4 is the valid time for the proposition—let's call it *q*—"Supplier S2 was under contract."

b. The tuple exists in the database from time *t1* to time *t2* only. In other words, the transaction time for proposition *p* is the interval from *t1* to *t2*.

---

[3] In fact it makes sense to extend that notion to apply to *any relation that can be derived from* the relvars in the database. See the answer to Exercise 17.4 at the end of the chapter.

Please observe now—important!—that proposition *p* ("Supplier S2 was under contract from day 2 to day 4") does *not* logically imply proposition *q* ("Supplier S2 was under contract"). Rather, it implies the proposition "Supplier S2 was under contract *at some time*."[4] Now, if you find what we've just said a little difficult to understand, we frankly wouldn't blame you; but here's a different example that might make the point more clearly. Let *x* be the proposition "All politicians are corrupt this year." Then proposition *x* does *not* imply the proposition *y* "All politicians are corrupt": certainly not in logic, and possibly not in informal discourse either. (Even if the latter proposition *y* is in fact true, we still can't conclude as much, logically, from the truth of proposition *x* alone.)

To return to proposition *p*: We've said that (a) proposition *p* doesn't imply the proposition "Supplier S2 was under contract" but that (b) what it does imply is the proposition "Supplier S2 was under contract at some time," or (a little more formally) "There exists a time *t* such that supplier S2 was under contract at time *t*." And while an argument might be made from common sense that this latter proposition surely does imply that supplier S2 was under contract, such an argument wouldn't be a valid *logical* argument. *In fact, proposition q ("Supplier S2 was under contract") isn't represented in the database at all, neither explicitly nor implicitly.*

> *Aside:* To say some proposition is represented implicitly is to say that (a) no tuple representing that proposition appears in the database explicitly, but that (b) such a tuple can be derived in some way from those tuples that do appear explicitly. For example, a tuple representing the proposition "Supplier S2 was under contract on day 3" can be derived from the tuple representing the proposition "Supplier S2 was under contract from day 2 to day 4." Thus, if the latter proposition is represented explicitly, then the former proposition is also represented, but implicitly. *End of aside.*

Now, given that, as we've said, the valid time for proposition *q* is the interval [*d02:d04*], it makes sense to say the valid time for any proposition that's implied by *q*—i.e., that can be derived from *q*—is also [*d02:d04*]. For example, since [*d02:d04*] is indeed the valid time for *q* ("Supplier S2 was under contract"), then it's also the valid time for the proposition "There exists some supplier SNO such that supplier SNO was under contract."

The net of the discussion so far is this: Valid times apply, typically, to propositions that aren't represented in the database at all!—neither explicitly nor implicitly. *We recommend that you make sure you understand this point before reading any further.*

———— ♦♦♦♦♦ ————

---

[4] The following might help here. Recall the nontemporal suppliers relation depicted in Fig. 1.1 in Chapter 1. That relation contains among other things the tuple (S1,Smith,20,London). Therefore, the projection of that relation on all but CITY contains among other things the tuple (S1,Smith,20). But the proposition corresponding to this latter tuple isn't "Supplier S1 is named Smith and has status 20"; rather, it's "Supplier S1 is named Smith and has status 20 *and is located somewhere*." The situation in this example is precisely analogous to the situation under discussion in the main text here.

Back to the example. Observe now that the statement "The transaction time for proposition *p* is the interval from *t1* to *t2*" is itself a proposition and can thus be represented as a tuple, like this (using X_DURING to denote transaction time):

SNO	DURING	X_DURING
S2	[d02:d04]	[t1:t2]

This tuple, involving as it does two distinct timestamps, one representing valid time and the other transaction time, is an example of what's sometimes called in the literature a "bitemporal tuple." Note carefully, however, that the DURING timestamp (valid time) in that tuple applies to one proposition and the XDURING timestamp (transaction time) in that tuple applies to another, *different* proposition. As the example suggests, therefore, a bitemporal tuple can be thought of (yet again somewhat loosely) as showing the transaction time *tt* for the valid time *vt* for some proposition *q*. See the section "Logged Times" for further discussion.

Now we turn to an example that in some ways is simpler than the ones we've been considering so far. Suppose some relvar in the database contains the following tuple:

FIGURE	NO_OF_SIDES
Triangle	3

The intended interpretation is, of course, "Triangles have three sides." Note in particular that this proposition— let's call it *z*—has no valid time component at all. But we can certainly think of it as having a valid time! To be precise, it's certainly the case that we believe right now that proposition *z* is true right now in the present, always was true in the past, and always will be true in the future. Implicitly, therefore, the valid time for *z* is *always* (i.e., "all of time," or in other words the interval from the beginning of time to the end of time, inclusive).[5] And precisely because the valid time is indeed "all of time," there's no point in saying so explicitly, by means of an explicit timestamp in the database. Turning this statement around, it's reasonable to say that, in general, a proposition that's represented in the database without an explicit valid time has an implicit valid time of "always."[6]

---

[5] Alternatively, we could say proposition *z* is *independent of time*.

[6] Don't be misled here: The fact that a given proposition has a valid time of "always" *doesn't* mean the proposition in question is, was, and always will be true—it means only that *we believe right now that* the proposition in question is, was, and always will be true. In other words, it's not impossible that some future change in the state of affairs could cause us to modify that belief. For example, consider the proposition "The angles of a triangle add up to 180 degrees." This proposition might well be represented in the database at some time with a valid time of "always". But suppose we then discover that triangles laid out on the surface of the Earth, instead of in a plane, have angles that add up to more than 180 degrees. Then our beliefs have changed, and something must therefore be done to the database to reflect that fact.

Aside: Here's another example to illustrate the same point. Suppose we want to record the values of various "universal constants"—π, φ, e, c, and so on—in the database; in other words, we want to record propositions of the form "The value of universal constant *u* is *v*." Then it should be clear that, again, explicit valid times make little sense for such propositions. *End of aside*.

Observe next that *every* proposition that has ever been recorded in the database, regardless of whether it has or had an explicit valid time, certainly has a transaction time. For example, if the tuple corresponding to proposition *z*—"Triangles have three sides"—is recorded in the database from time *t1* to time *t2* (only), then the transaction time for the proposition "*z* is, was, and always will be true" is the interval from *t1* to *t2*.

Given the foregoing, again consider the following "bitemporal tuple" (let's call it *bt*):

SNO	DURING	X_DURING
S2	[d02:d04]	[t1:t2]

Just to remind you, the proposition (let's call it *b*) represented by this tuple is "The transaction time for proposition *p* is the interval from *t1* to *t2*," where proposition *p* in turn is the proposition "Supplier S2 was under contract from day 2 to day 4."

Suppose now that tuple *bt* itself currently appears in the database (which, as we'll see later, in the section "Logged Times," it certainly might do). Then the corresponding proposition *b* has a valid time and a transaction time. The valid time is, implicitly, "always" (certainly it has no explicit valid time). What about the transaction time? Well, presumably tuple *bt* was—at least conceptually (again see the section "Logged Times")—inserted into the database at some time *t*;[7] and if tuple *bt* does indeed, as stated, currently appear in the database, and if it has done so ever since time *t*, then the transaction time for proposition *b* is clearly the interval from time *t* to whatever the time happens to be right now. (Recall that transaction times can't refer to the future, so there's no question of saying the transaction time is the interval from time *t* to "the end of time.")

With the foregoing examples and discussion providing the necessary intuitive underpinnings, we can now—at last—offer some reasonably precise definitions:

Definition: The **transaction time** for a proposition *p* is the set of times *t* such that, according to what the database stated at time *t*, *p* was true. Note that proposition *p* (a) must have been represented in the database at some time, either explicitly or implicitly, and (b) can itself refer to the past and/or present and/or future.

---

[7] Note that *t* can't be less than *t2* (why?).

Definition: The **valid time** for a proposition q is the set of times t such that, according to what the database currently states (which is to say, according to our current beliefs), q is, was, or will be true at time t. Note that proposition q itself probably isn't represented in the database, either explicitly or implicitly (though it might be).

In a nutshell:

- Transaction times are the times in the past when *the database said* we believed something is, was, or will be true.

- Valid times are the times (past and/or present and/or future) when, *according to what we believe right now*, something is, was, or will be true.

Furthermore, we assume for convenience and definiteness that (a) the transaction time for a given proposition p consists of a set of intervals, and that set is effectively kept in packed form; (b) the valid time for a given proposition q likewise consists of a set of intervals, and that set also is effectively kept in packed form. *Note:* By "effectively kept in packed form" here, we mean that if the set of intervals in question is presented to the user by means of an interval valued attribute A within some relation r, then r is packed on A.

THE DATABASE AND THE LOG

Following on from the definitions and explanations of the previous section, we now observe that there's a significant operational difference between valid times and transaction times, a difference that can be characterized informally as follows:

Valid times are kept in the database, transaction times are kept in the log.

We believe this informal characterization can be a great aid to clear thinking in this potentially confusing area, and we therefore elaborate on it in this section.

First of all, then, note that a database is really a *variable*; the operation of "updating the database" causes the current value of that variable to be replaced by another value. The values in question are *database values*, and the variable is a *database variable*. In other words, the logical difference discussed in Chapter 3 between relation values and relation variables (relvars) applies to databases as well, mutatis mutandis. Here's a lightly edited but pertinent quote from reference [52]:

> The first version of this document drew a distinction between database values and database variables, analogous to the distinction between relation values and relation variables. It also introduced the term *dbvar* as shorthand for *database variable*. While we still believe this distinction to be a valid one, we found it had

little direct relevance to other aspects of these proposals. We therefore decided, in the interests of familiarity, to revert to more traditional terminology.

Now this bad decision has come home to roost! With hindsight, it would have been much better to "bite the bullet" and adopt the more logically correct terms *database value* and *database variable* (or dbvar), despite their lack of familiarity.[8]

But there's another way to think about the foregoing. To be specific, a database update can be thought of, not so much as replacing the current database value by another such value, but rather as deriving a "new" database value from the "old" one (thereby making that new value the current value), *while at the same time keeping the old value around in the system as well.* The "old" database value is, of course, the one that was current immediately prior to the update in question. It follows that the overall database can be thought of as a *sequence* or *stack* of database values, where each such value is timestamped with the time of the update that produced it, and the complete sequence or stack is ordered chronologically.[9] The most recent value in the sequence is, of course, the current one—it's the database as it appears right now. And the only kind of update operation we can apply to the overall database, conceptually speaking, is the one that takes the current database value and derives from it a new such value, which then becomes current in turn.

What's more, that sequence of database values can usefully be thought of as a *log*; after all, it's effectively an abstract or idealized version of the recovery log as implemented in real systems, providing as it does a full historical record of every update that has ever been performed on the database. And the most recent log entry—i.e., the most recent database value in the chronological sequence of such values—provides a record of our current beliefs.[10]

Note: In real systems, of course, log entries typically refer to updates at the level of (e.g.) disk pages, not at the level of the entire database. This state of affairs doesn't materially affect the discussion, however. Also, we remark in passing that the well known concept of *point in time recovery* can be seen as a process that makes use of the actual *physical* log, together with a backup copy of the database, to (re)construct one of the database values that make up our hypothetical *imaginary* log.

By way of illustration, we return to the example from the section "Valid Time vs. Transaction Time" in Chapter 4, in which a tuple showing supplier S1 as being under contract during some interval was inserted into the database at time *t1* and replaced at time *t2*, and that replacement tuple was then deleted at time *t3*. Let *t2′* and *t3′* be the timestamps of the log entries—i.e., the database values—immediately preceding those for times *t2* and *t3*, respectively.

---

[8] A much more detailed discussion of these ideas and some of the issues they raise can be found in reference [44].

[9] Compare the discussion in the section "The Underlying Intuition" in Chapter 11. Note, however, that the sequences discussed in that chapter were timestamped with valid times, whereas the sequence we're discussing here is timestamped with transaction times.

[10] In other words, "the database is not the database—the log is the database, and the database is just an optimized access path to the most recent version of the log." The thought expressed by this aphorism is a piece of folklore that has been circulating in the database community for a long time. It appears to have its origin in a paper by Schueler [100].

Clearly, then, the log entries for times *t1* to *t2'* will contain the original tuple, while those for times *t2* to *t3'* will contain the replacement tuple, and those from time *t3* onward will contain no corresponding tuple at all. (We assume for simplicity that no tuple showing supplier S1 as being under contract appeared in the database either before time *t1* or after time *t3*.) The transaction times for the applicable propositions can thus clearly be obtained from the timestamps associated with the pertinent log entries.

What about the valid times? By now, it should be clear that these times don't correspond to log entry timestamps at all. Indeed, as we saw in the section "A Closer Look," if *q* is a proposition to which the concept of valid time applies, we don't keep *q* as such in the database; rather, we keep *p*, the corresponding *timestamped extension* of *q*, in the database. And the timestamps in such timestamped extensions, which denote the applicable valid times, are represented by means of attribute values in the usual relational way. Hence, *current* valid times—by which we mean, by definition, those times we currently believe to be valid—always appear in the current value of the database, which always corresponds, again by definition, to the most recent entry in the log.

We now proceed to consider a number of further points that arise in connection with the idea that "the log is the real database." *Note:* Some of these points have been touched on or at least hinted at previously in this chapter, but it still seems worthwhile to bring them together and spell them out explicitly here.

- As noted earlier, a proposition *p* might have a transaction time consisting of several discrete intervals—from *t1* to *t2*, then from *t3* to *t4*, then from *t5* to *t6*, and so on (where *t1*, *t2*, etc., are all distinct). That is, times *t1*, *t3*, *t5*, etc., correspond to updates that caused a representation of *p* to appear in the database (either implicitly or explicitly), while times *t2*, *t4*, *t6*, etc., correspond to updates that caused that representation to disappear again.

- Likewise, a proposition *q* might have a current valid time that consists of several discrete intervals. Here, however, the intervals concerned are simply values that currently appear in the database (or are implied by such values). To repeat an earlier example, suppose relvar S_DURING currently contains just the following two tuples for supplier S2:

SNO	DURING
S2	[d02:d04]

SNO	DURING
S2	[d06:d09]

Then the current valid time for the proposition "Supplier S2 was under contract" is the set of intervals {[*d02:d04*], [*d06:d09*]}.

- As our examples and definitions have clearly indicated—note in particular the fact that the definitions are asymmetric—if *p* is a proposition to which the concept of transaction time applies and *q* is a proposition to which the concept of valid time applies, then *p* and *q* are typically not the same proposition. Certainly it seems to be hard to find a *nontrivial* proposition that has both a nontrivial associated transaction time and a nontrivial associated valid time.

- You might be surprised to learn that, in some respects, valid times are less interesting than transaction times. Why so? Well, we've seen that valid times are represented by means of attributes in the usual relational way. They can thus certainly be queried. Moreover, when such attributes appear in relvars—as opposed to relations—they can of course be updated as well as queried (loosely speaking); thus, valid times can be changed to reflect changing beliefs. In principle, therefore, valid time attributes aren't significantly different from attributes of any other kind, at least insofar as their ability to participate in queries and updates (and constraints) is concerned.

  What about transaction times? Well, if transaction times really are based on log entry timestamps as suggested above, then it should be clear that, unlike valid times, they're maintained by the system, not by users. Indeed, we pointed out earlier that transaction times are nonupdatable, meaning that (of course) they certainly can't be updated by users. However, users do need to be able to query them; for example, we might want to ask— perhaps for audit purposes—"When if ever did the database say that supplier S2 was under contract on day 4?" We might want to reference them in constraints, too.

  At least two problems arise immediately from this requirement. First, of course, the system doesn't really maintain the log in the form we've been describing (i.e., as a timestamped sequence of database values); as a consequence, it's highly unlikely that the system will allow us to formulate queries against the database value at some arbitrary past time *t* directly. Second, even if we could formulate such a query, the corresponding timestamp *t* isn't represented as part of that database value as such but is, rather, a kind of tag that's associated with that value; as a consequence, we still couldn't formulate a query—at least, not a relational query—that references that timestamp directly.

  For such a query even to be expressible, therefore, the relevant timestamps, along with the information they timestamp, (a) will have to be made available in standard relational form and (b) will have to be made part of the current database value. (They must be made part of the current database value specifically, because, in a sense, the current database value is the only one that "really exists"; certainly it's the only one that can be directly queried.)[11] The section "Logged Times," later, offers some suggestions as to how these requirements (a) and (b) might be satisfied in practice.

- It follows from all of the above that—despite what we said in this connection earlier—the imaginary log we've been talking about is best thought of not as an abstraction of the usual recovery log, but rather as an *audit trail*. After all, its purpose is essentially to serve as a history of update events and to allow questions to be asked later about what was done to the

---

[11] As already pointed out, in effect, in footnote 2.

database when, and such questions are certainly questions of an auditing nature and have little to do with recovery.

■ We've been talking as if updates take effect on the database at the instant at which they're executed. But that's not what happens in practice; in practice, updates are effectively applied only if and when the relevant transaction reaches a successful termination (commit point). It follows that the transaction time *instant*—i.e., the time point—corresponding to a particular update isn't exactly the time of the update operation per se but is, logically, the time of the corresponding COMMIT operation (suggesting among other things that several distinct updates might all be associated with the same transaction time instant). This state of affairs has a variety of implications and ramifications—some of which aren't immediately obvious—but the details are beyond the scope of this chapter. See Exercise 19.9 in Chapter 19 (and the answer to that exercise) for further discussion.

TERMINOLOGY

We've now discussed the valid time and transaction time concepts at some length. As indicated in Chapter 4, however, we don't much care for the conventional terminology in this area—as we said in that chapter, the meanings of the terms can hardly be said to "leap off the page," as it were—and we'd like to try to come up with some better terms if possible. Such is the purpose of the present section.

First, regarding valid time, we have to say we find little need to refer to the concept at all, precisely because we regard valid times as essentially just regular data. Indeed, as you must surely have noticed, we hardly used the term at all in Chapters 5-16, even though the concept underpinned almost all of the discussions in those chapters.[12] These facts notwithstanding, we'd still like to find a term that captures, better than "valid time" does, the essence of what's really going on, in order that we might have a good term to use on those rare occasions when we do need to refer to the concept explicitly. As for transaction time, here we definitely do need to refer to the concept by name from time to time—pun intended—and so we'd definitely like to find a better term.[13]

It's not worth discussing here all of the various alternatives we considered and subsequently discarded. Suffice it to say that, as the title of this chapter suggests, we finally settled on the terms *logged time* and *stated time* (for transaction time and valid time, respectively). Thus, to repeat the definitions:

---

[12] We speculate that it's precisely because the approach to temporal data espoused in so much of the literature—even to some extent in the SQL standard—is, at best, less than fully relational, that the term *valid time* (or some equivalent term) occurs in that literature so ubiquitously.

[13] We're not alone in finding the terms *transaction time* and *valid time* unsatisfactory, incidentally. For example, the SQL standard uses the perhaps slightly more reasonable terms *system time* and *application time*, respectively. And IBM's DB2 product agrees with the standard with regard to system time, but uses *business time* in place of application time.

Definition: The **logged time** for a proposition *p* is the set of times *t* such that, according to what the database stated at time *t*, *p* was true.

Definition: The **stated time**—sometimes *currently* stated time, for emphasis—for a proposition *q* is the set of times *t* such that, according to what the database currently states (which is to say, according to our current beliefs), *q* is, was, or will be true at time *t*.

However, it's only fair to warn you that our preferred terms aren't used much (or at all!) in the temporal database literature in general. Indeed, by way of a kind of postscript to everything we've been saying in this chapter so far, we briefly consider some definitions from the literature of the concepts we've been discussing. The definitions in question are taken from a document titled, in part, "The Consensus Glossary of Temporal Database Concepts" [62]:

- "The *valid time* of a fact is the time when the fact is true in the modeled reality."

- "A database fact is stored in a database at some point in time, and after it is stored, it is current until it is logically deleted. The *transaction time* of a database fact is the time when the fact is current in the database and may be retrieved."

Here's our own gloss on these glossary definitions. First, the term *fact*, which is mentioned several times, doesn't itself appear in the glossary; in ordinary English, however, facts are usually taken to be true by definition. Indeed, a "false fact" is a contradiction in terms, and so, in the definition of valid time, "when the fact is a fact" might perhaps be more apt than "when the fact is true." (But of course *the fact is a fact* is a tautology.) Also, it's not clear whether any distinction is intended—and if so, what the distinction might be—between the term *fact*, unqualified (mentioned in the definition of valid time), and the term *database fact* (mentioned in the definition of transaction time).

Second, the term *the modeled reality* (also not in the glossary) presumably means what in such contexts is more usually referred to as "the real world."[14] "Valid time" thus apparently means the time when the "fact" was actually true in the real world, not, as we claimed earlier, the time when it was true according to our current beliefs. But if this interpretation is correct, it's not clear why the term is being defined at all. (We can operate only in terms of what we believe to be true, not in terms of any kind of "absolute" truth, and the definition seems to be saying that valid time does have something to do with some kind of absolute truth.)

Third, the term *current* (in the transaction time definition) seems to be used in a very strange way. Surely it would be more usual to say that something is "current in the database" if and only if that something was part of the current database value; yet this interpretation is certainly not—it *can't* be—what's intended in the transaction time definition.

---

[14] Or does it perhaps mean not, as normal English usage would have it, "the reality that's being modeled" but, rather, "the modeled version of reality"?

Fourth, reference [62] elsewhere says this:

■   "[The] transaction-time lifespan refers to the time when the database object is current in the database."

Presumably the term *database object* here is meant as a synonym for what was previously called a database fact (?). But what about *transaction time* and *transaction-time lifespan*? Are these terms also synonyms of each other? If they are, then why there are two different terms? And if they aren't, what's the difference between them?

   All in all, it seems to us that the definitions in reference [62] simply serve to reinforce our earlier contention that the notions of valid time and transaction time need *very* careful explanation, as well as (preferably) more carefully chosen names. And, of course, the provision of such an explanation and such names has been our aim in this chapter, up to this point. In particular, we feel bound to say that, in our opinion, it's very hard to come up with such an explanation and such names without first facing up to the idea that a database—more specifically, a database *value*—is essentially a collection of true propositions, instead of trying to rely on undefined and fuzzy concepts like "database facts" or "database objects."

LOGGED TIMES

Now, we pointed out earlier that even though users can't update logged times, they certainly must be able to query them. We also pointed out that this requirement implies that:

a. Logged times must be made available (along with the data they refer to) in standard relational form, and

b. They must be made available as part of the current database value.

In this section, we describe one possible way of achieving these objectives in a user friendly fashion.

   Essentially, what we propose is that if *R* is a database relvar, then the definition of *R* should be allowed to contain a request for the automatic provision and maintenance of an auxiliary relvar that gives the logged time history for that relvar *R*. For example (note the highlighted text):

```
VAR S_DURING BASE RELATION
   { SNO     SNO ,
     DURING  INTERVAL_DATE }
   USING ( DURING ) : KEY { SNO , DURING }
   LOGGED_TIMES_IN ( S_DURING_LOG ) ;
```

The effect of the LOGGED_TIMES_IN specification is to cause the system to provide a relvar called S_DURING_LOG (the "logged time relvar" for S_DURING) with attributes SNO,

DURING, and—let's agree—X_DURING, and with tuples that together represent the logged times for all of the tuples that have ever appeared, explicitly or implicitly, in S_DURING. (We'll explain that "explicitly or implicitly" a little later in this section.) For example, suppose today is day 75. Then Fig. 17.1 shows a possible value for S_DURING, together with a possible corresponding value for S_DURING_LOG. *Note:* We've numbered the tuples in the logged time relvar S_DURING_LOG for purposes of subsequent explanation.

S_DURING

SNO	DURING
S2	[d02:d04]
S6	[d03:d05]

S_DURING_LOG

	SNO	DURING	X_DURING
1	S2	[d02:d04]	[d04:d07]
2	S2	[d02:d04]	[d10:d20]
3	S2	[d02:d04]	[d50:d75]
4	S6	[d02:d05]	[d15:d25]
5	S6	[d03:d05]	[d26:d75]
6	S1	[d01:d01]	[d20:d30]
7	S1	[d05:d06]	[d40:d50]

Fig. 17.1: Relvars S_DURING and S_DURING_LOG–sample values

Explanation:

- First of all, S_DURING currently says among other things that supplier S2 was under contract from day 2 to day 4. Tuple 1 of S_DURING_LOG tells us that S_DURING also said the same thing at an earlier time, from day 4 to day 7. Tuple 2 of S_DURING_LOG tells us that relvar S_DURING said the same thing again at another earlier time, from day 10 to day 20.

  Aside: In a more realistic example, of course, the granularity for X_DURING intervals would almost certainly be, not days, but (for example) microseconds; moreover, no X_DURING interval would ever have an end value exactly equal to "the time right now." (The most it could ever be is something just slightly earlier than "the time right now.") We choose to ignore such details here in the interest of simplicity. *End of aside*.

- Tuple 3 of S_DURING_LOG tells us that S_DURING has been saying that same thing—i.e., that supplier S2 was under contract from day 2 to day 4—from day 50 to the present day (i.e., day 75). Now, in Chapter 12, in the section "The Moving Point *Now*," we argued that representing the present day in the database by an actual value like *d75* was a bad idea.[15] In particular, we pointed out that it implied that all of those *d75*'s would somehow

---

[15] That is, it's a bad idea if that value doesn't actually denote the present day but is meant to be interpreted as *until further notice*.

have to be replaced by *d76*'s on the stroke of midnight on day 75. However, those arguments don't apply in the present situation, because:

a.　Relvar S_DURING_LOG doesn't actually need to exist at all times—it's sufficient for the system to materialize it when it's referenced in some query (and even then it surely shouldn't be necessary to materialize it in its entirety). In other words, a helpful way to think of S_DURING_LOG is as a *view*—but it's not a view that's defined in terms of other relvars in the database; rather, it's a view that's defined in terms of the log. Furthermore, of course, the definition of that view in terms of the log is provided by the system, not by some human user.

b.　Relvar S_DURING_LOG is updatable by the system but not by ordinary users. Thus, the process of replacing all of those *d75*'s by *d76*'s on the stroke of midnight on day 75 is carried out by the system, not by some user (and, of course, that process is probably never carried out *physically* at all).

c.　In any case, the proposition "From day 50 to day 75, the database said that supplier S2 was under contract from day 2 to day 4" is true! Certainly we mustn't use the artificial "end of time" trick in connection with logged times that we do sometimes use in connection with stated times, because (e.g.) the proposition "From day 50 to *the end of time*, the database said that supplier S2 was under contract from day 2 to day 4" is false. (Recall once again that logged times can never refer to the future.)

■　S_DURING also currently says that supplier S6 was under contract from day 3 to day 5. By contrast, tuple 4 of S_DURING_LOG tells us that S_DURING said previously (from day 15 to day 25) that supplier S6 was under contract from *day 2* to day 5; however, tuple 5 of S_DURING_LOG tells us that ever since day 26, relvar S_DURING has been saying that supplier S6 was under contract from *day 3* to day 5.

■　Finally, S_DURING currently has nothing to say about supplier S1 at all. However, tuple 6 of S_DURING_LOG tells us that S_DURING did say from day 20 to day 30 that supplier S1 was under contract, on day 1 only; likewise, tuple 7 tells us that S_DURING also said from day 40 to day 50 that supplier S1 was under contract from day 5 to day 6. (We deduce that all information regarding supplier S1 was deleted from relvar S_DURING on day 31 and again on day 51, presumably because it was discovered to be incorrect.)

Let's summarize what we've learned so far. First, let *R* be a regular relvar, and let *R'* be the associated logged time relvar. Let *R* have interval attributes *A1*, *A2*, ..., *An* (only), possibly with other attributes (not interval valued) as well. Then:

■ The heading of *R'* consists of the heading of *R* extended with an interval attribute called X_DURING.

■ For every tuple *t* that has ever appeared in the fully unpacked form of *R*—see the note immediately following this paragraph for an explanation of what we mean by "fully unpacked" in this context—*R'* effectively contains *m* distinct tuples for some *m* > 0. Each such tuple consists of tuple *t* extended with an X_DURING value, such that the transaction time for *t* (or, rather, for the proposition represented by *t*) is precisely the set containing just those *m* X_DURING values. *R'* is kept packed on (*A1,A2,...,An,*X_DURING). By the way, observe that the packing of *R' must* be done on attribute X_DURING last, as indicated.

    Note: The "fully unpacked form of *R*" referred to in the foregoing paragraph is the result of UNPACK *R* ON (*A1,A2,...,An*). When we said earlier that *R'* gives the logged times for all of the tuples that have ever appeared explicitly *or implicitly* in *R*, what we were referring to was *the set of all tuples t such that t has appeared at some time in that fully unpacked form.*

■ Finally, if the constraint USING (*A1,A2,...,An*) : KEY {*K*} holds in *R*, then the constraint USING (*A1,A2,...,An,*X_DURING) : KEY {*K,*X_DURING} holds in *R'*.

As a basis for a second example, we turn to our usual relvar S_SINCE:

```
VAR S_SINCE BASE RELATION
  { SNO            SNO ,
    SNO_SINCE      DATE ... ,
    STATUS         INTEGER ,
    STATUS_SINCE DATE ... }
  KEY { SNO }
  LOGGED_TIMES_IN ( S_SINCE_LOG ) ;
```

Fig. 17.2 shows some sample values. We leave a detailed examination of that figure to you, except that:

■ First, we remind you that we're assuming that today is day 75.

■ Second, we draw your attention to the S_SINCE_LOG tuple for supplier S2 in which the SNO_SINCE and S_STATUS_SINCE values are both *d07*, while the X_DURING value is [*d06:d75*]. What does this combination of values imply? (*Answer:* On day 6, a tuple was inserted into relvar S_SINCE to say supplier S2 would be placed under contract on day 7— a date in the future, at the time of the INSERT.)

S_SINCE

SNO	SNO_SINCE	STATUS	STATUS_SINCE	...
S1	d04	20	d06	...
S2	d07	10	d07	...
S3	d03	30	d03	...
S4	d04	20	d08	...
S5	d02	30	d02	...

S_SINCE_LOG

SNO	SNO_SINCE	STATUS	STATUS_SINCE	...	X_DURING
S1	d04	15	d04	...	[d04:d05]
S1	d04	20	d06	...	[d06:d75]
S2	d02	5	d02	...	[d01:d02]
S2	d02	10	d03	...	[d03:d04]
S2	d07	10	d07	...	[d06:d75]
S3	d03	30	d03	...	[d03:d75]
S4	d04	10	d04	...	[d04:d04]
S4	d04	25	d05	...	[d05:d07]
S4	d04	20	d08	...	[d08:d75]
S5	d02	30	d02	...	[d02:d75]
S6	d03	5	d03	...	[d03:d04]
S6	d03	7	d05	...	[d05:d05]

Fig. 17.2: Relvars S_SINCE and S_SINCE_LOG–sample values

QUERIES INVOLVING LOGGED TIME

In this final section of the chapter, we consider a few sample queries involving the logged time relvars S_SINCE_LOG and S_DURING_LOG.

Query X1: When if ever did the database say that supplier S6 was under contract on day 4?

Assume for the sake of this first example that we know the supplier we're interested in, supplier S6, isn't currently under contract. Thus, if that supplier was ever under contract at all, it was definitely in the past; in particular, the information that the supplier was under contract on day 4, if currently thought ever to have been true, will appear in S_DURING. Of course, it won't still appear in S_DURING if it was previously thought to be true but was subsequently discovered not to be, because in that case the pertinent tuple(s) will have been deleted. Either way, however, the pertinent logged time information will certainly be present in S_DURING_LOG. So let's take a look at the sample value for S_DURING_LOG in Fig. 17.1. Here's what we get if we restrict that sample value to just the tuples showing supplier S6 as being under contract on day 4:

SNO	DURING	X_DURING
S6	[*d02*:*d05*]	[*d15*:*d25*]
S6	[*d03*:*d05*]	[*d26*:*d75*]

So here's a suitable formulation of the query:

```
WITH ( t1 := S_DURING_LOG WHERE SNO = SNO ( 'S6' ) AND d04 ∈ DURING ) :
USING ( X_DURING ) : t1 { X_DURING }
```

And here's the result:

X_DURING
[*d15*:*d75*]

Query X2: When if ever did the database say that supplier S2 was under contract on day 4?

The query has the same form as Query X1—the only difference is in the supplier number. But this time let's assume we don't know whether the supplier we're interested in is currently under contract;[16] thus, the information we want (or some of it, at any rate) might be in S_SINCE_LOG. Let's assume also that we don't know whether that supplier ever had a previous contract, so the information we want (or, again, some of it) might be in S_DURING_LOG. Given the relation shown as a sample value for S_SINCE_LOG in Fig. 17.2, here's what we get if we restrict that relation to just the tuples showing supplier S2 as being under contract on day 4:

SNO	SNO_SINCE	STATUS	STATUS_SINCE	...	X_DURING
S2	*d02*	5	*d02*	...	[*d01*:*d02*]
S2	*d02*	10	*d03*	...	[*d03*:*d04*]

And given the relation shown as a sample value for S_DURING_LOG in Fig. 17.1, here's what we get if we restrict *that* relation to just the tuples showing supplier S2 as being under contract on day 4:

---

[16] Considerations of this kind tend to suggest that the COMBINED_IN syntax, mentioned briefly in Chapter 15 in connection with regular relvars, could be useful in connection with logged time relvars too.

SNO	DURING	X_DURING
S2	[d02:d04]	[d04:d07]
S2	[d02:d04]	[d10:d20]
S2	[d02:d04]	[d40:d75]

So here's a possible formulation of the query:

```
WITH ( t1 := S_SINCE_LOG WHERE SNO = SNO ( 'S2' ) AND d04 ≥ SNO_SINCE ,
       t2 := t1 { X_DURING } ,
       t3 := S_DURING_LOG WHERE SNO = SNO ( 'S2' ) AND d04 ∈ DURING ,
       t4 := t3 { X_DURING } ) :
USING ( X_DURING ) : t2 UNION t4
```

And if the sample values for S_SINCE_LOG and S_DURING_LOG are the actual values,[17] then here's the result:

X_DURING
[d01:d07]
[d10:d20]
[d40:d75]

Query X3: On day 8, what did the database say was supplier S2's term of contract?

Note that this query treats logged time as the known value (namely, day 8) and stated time as the unknown and is thus the inverse of the previous examples, in a sense. Here's a suitable formulation:

```
WITH ( t1 := S_SINCE_LOG WHERE SNO = SNO ( 'S2' ) AND d08 ∈ X_DURING ,
       t2 := EXTEND t1 : { DURING :=
                                INTERVAL_DATE ( [ SNO_SINCE : d99 ] ) } ,
       t3 := t2 { DURING } ,
       t4 := S_DURING_LOG WHERE SNO = SNO ( 'S2' ) AND d08 ∈ X_DURING ,
       t5 := t4 { DURING } ) :
USING ( DURING ) : t3 UNION t5
```

EXERCISES

17.1 Consider Fig. 17.2 again. Explain in your own words how to interpret that figure.

---

[17] Actually they can't be (see Exercise 17.2).

17.2 Are the sample values in Figs. 17.1 and 17.2 mutually consistent?

17.3 Instead of having just one logged time relvar for S_SINCE as in Fig. 17.2, might it have made more sense to have separate logged time relvars for (a) the projection of S_SINCE on SNO and SNO_SINCE and (b) the projection of S_SINCE on SNO, STATUS, and STATUS_SINCE? If so, why?

17.4 Following on from Exercise 17.3, might it make sense to allow the user to request automatic provision of a logged time relvar for an *arbitrary* projection (in particular, one not including a key) of an *arbitrary* relvar R (in particular, one that includes no interval attributes)? If so, why? What syntactic extensions might be needed to the proposals described in this chapter in order to permit such requests to be specified?

17.5 Would there be any point in requesting a logged time relvar for the *nullary* projection of some relvar R (i.e., the projection of R on no attributes at all)? If so, why? Again, what syntactic extensions (if any) might be needed in order to permit such requests to be specified?

ANSWERS

17.1 Relvar S_SINCE in Fig. 17.2 represents current beliefs concerning suppliers under contract right now (or possibly in the future): when their contracts started, what their current status values are, and when those current status values were assigned. The predicate for S_SINCE is:

> *Supplier SNO has been under contract ever since day SNO_SINCE (and not on the day immediately before that day) and has had status STATUS ever since day STATUS_SINCE (and not on the day immediately before that day).*

Relvar S_SINCE_LOG in Fig. 17.2 is a record of the contents of S_SINCE from the time of creation of this latter relvar up to the time right now (i.e., up to the present day, since we're assuming, rather unrealistically, a granularity of one day).[18] It contains just enough information to enable the value of S_SINCE on any particular day in that interval to be reconstructed. The predicate for S_SINCE_LOG is:

---

[18] Note that S_SINCE_LOG presumably continues to exist even if S_SINCE is dropped—a fact that suggests that it might be intuitively preferable not to bundle together the creation of the two relvars, as our proposed LOGGED_TIMES_IN syntax does, but rather to create them separately. For further discussion of this possibility, see the answer to Exercise 17.4.

X_DURING denotes a maximal interval throughout which relvar S_SINCE contained a tuple stating that supplier SNO had been under contract ever since day SNO_SINCE and had had status STATUS ever since day STATUS_SINCE.[19]

See the answer to Exercise 17.3 below for further discussion.

17.2 The sample values in Figs. 17.1 and 17.2 aren't mutually consistent. A detailed explanation follows.

Consider Fig. 17.2. Using the names "S_SINCE" and "S_SINCE_LOG" to denote the relations shown as values of the relvars with those names in that figure, we now show that at least those two relations are consistent with each other. First, let *r* be the result of S_SINCE_LOG WHERE END (X_DURING) = *d75* and let *s* be the result of S_SINCE JOIN *r*. Then the result of *s* {ALL BUT X_DURING} is equal to both S_SINCE and *r* {ALL BUT X_DURING}, indicating that:

a. Every tuple in S_SINCE is equal to the projection of some tuple of *r* on all but X_DURING.[20] Thus, wherever S_SINCE shows some information as being current, that information is indeed shown in S_SINCE_LOG as being currently recorded in S_SINCE.

b. The projection of every tuple in *r* on all but X_DURING is equal to some tuple of S_SINCE. Thus, wherever S_SINCE_LOG shows information as being currently recorded in S_SINCE, that information is indeed currently recorded in S_SINCE.

The only tuples not yet considered are those in result of S_SINCE_LOG MINUS *r*. As these tuples represent information that was recorded in S_SINCE on days in the past, they can't possibly fail to be consistent with the other tuples shown in S_SINCE in Fig. 17.2.

The same argument, mutandis mutatis, can be used to show that the sample values shown for S_DURING and S_DURING_LOG in Fig. 17.1 are also mutually consistent.

Further, the values of S_DURING and S_SINCE shown in Figs. 17.1 and 17.2, respectively, are also mutually consistent. The S_DURING value shows supplier S2 as having been under contract on days 2, 3, and 4 but not on days 1 or 5, which is consistent with that supplier having been under contract ever since day 7 but not on day 6, as shown in S_SINCE. Similarly, that same S_DURING value shows supplier S6 as having been under contract on days 3, 4, and 5 but

---

[19] Two points here: First, we're relying on our usual understanding of *ever since* as meaning *ever since and not immediately before*; second, we ought really to say X_DURING denotes a maximal interval *of days* (or, more realistically, of microseconds, or nanoseconds, or whatever the applicable granularity happens to be).

[20] We're appealing here to the fact that although (by definition) projection is an operator that applies to relations, it obviously makes sense to talk in terms of projections of individual tuples; in other words, we can "overload" the relational projection operator and define a version that works for tuples as well. Analogous remarks apply to certain other relational operators also. See, e.g., reference [45] for further discussion.

not on days 2 or 6, which is consistent with that supplier not currently being under contract, as shown by omission by S_SINCE. (Note the appeal to *The Closed World Assumption* here.)

So far, so good. However, it's easy to see that the value of S_DURING_LOG in Fig. 17.1 isn't consistent with the value of S_SINCE_LOG in Fig. 17.2. For example, consider tuple 7 in S_DURING_LOG. It shows among other things that on day 40 S_DURING stated that supplier S1 had been under contract on days 5 and 6 but not on days 4 or 7. But "the second tuple" in S_SINCE_LOG (if you'll pardon the phrase) has it that on day 40 S_SINCE stated that supplier S1 had been under contract ever since day 4, contradicting the information that S1 was not under contract on days 4 or 7. In other words, if we're to believe the information currently shown in S_SINCE_LOG and S_DURING_LOG, then the database must have been in an inconsistent state on day 40.

17.3 Yes, it probably does make better sense. Take a look at the predicate for that relvar (i.e., relvar S_SINCE_LOG) as stated in the answer to Exercise 17.1. It should be clear from that predicate that the timestamp X_DURING "timestamps too much," and hence that S_SINCE_LOG isn't in 6NF, and hence that it probably ought to be decomposed into 6NF projections. For example, if we restrict the sample value shown for the relvar in Fig. 17.2 to just the tuples for supplier S1, we get this result—

SNO	SNO_SINCE	STATUS	STATUS_SINCE	...	X_DURING
S1	d04	15	d04	...	[d04:d05]
S1	d04	20	d06	...	[d06:d75]

—which tells us twice that the database once said supplier S1 was under contract on day 4. In other words, relvar S_SINCE_LOG suffers from redundancy.[21]

Further, those same two tuples for supplier S1 mean the relvar also suffers from circumlocution. To be specific, the relvar is taking two tuples to say what could have been said in one: namely, that supplier S1 was under contract from day 4 to day 75. (By the way, both of these problems (i.e., redundancy and circumlocution) mean that relvar S_SINCE_LOG is in violation of its own predicate!)

Now, it might be argued that because it's the system that takes all responsibility for the maintenance of S_SINCE_LOG, any "update anomalies"—see reference [43]—arising from the failure to normalize to 6NF are of no real consequence. (We'd certainly need to tidy up the predicate, though.) But failure to decompose to 6NF, while it does make certain queries

---

[21] Of course, the root problem here is that relvar S_SINCE itself isn't in 6NF. If we were to decompose it into projections (one on SNO and SNO_SINCE and the other on SNO, STATUS, and STATUS_SINCE), each with its own logged time relvar, then the problem under discussion would go away (despite the fact that the second of these projections would still not be in 6NF).

(basically those requiring joins) easier, doesn't make *all* the difficult ones easier, and it does make what should be easy ones harder (see the section "Queries Involving Logged Time" in the body of the chapter).

17.4 First, it clearly does make sense to let the user request a logged time relvar for a relvar without any interval attributes—S_SINCE_LOG (for relvar S_SINCE) is a case in point. For an example of a logged time relvar for an arbitrary projection of such a relvar, consider one for the projection of S_SINCE on STATUS (let's call it STATUS_LOG). STATUS_LOG would show, for each status value that has ever been assigned to any supplier, the continuous intervals during which it was stated by the database as being assigned to at least one supplier. But that information can easily be derived from S_SINCE_LOG, anyway; thus, it would make sense to ask for automatic provision of STATUS_LOG only if not all of the more detailed information provided by S_SINCE_LOG is required.

As for a syntactic extension, here are some pertinent observations. The LOGGED_TIMES_IN syntax proposed in the body of the chapter appears as part of the definition of some relvar *R*, and the corresponding logged time relvar is thus implicitly associated with *R* as such. Now, if we want it to be associated with some projection of *R*—in particular, a projection that doesn't retain some key of R—then we might as well let it be associated with some arbitrary relational expression.[22] But then a drastic alteration to the syntax proposed in the chapter would be needed. To be specific, instead of a LOGGED_TIMES_IN option on a relvar definition, what would be needed would be a separate definition for the logged time relvar as such, perhaps as in this example:

```
VAR SUPPLIER_EXISTENCE_LOG BASE RELATION
   { X_DURING INTERVAL_DATE }
   USING ( X_DURING ) : KEY { X_DURING }
   LOGGED_TIMES_FOR ( S_SINCE { } UNION S_DURING { } ) ;
```

The intent here is to define a logged time relvar showing intervals during which the database has acknowledged the existence at some time of at least one supplier under contract (every X_DURING value in SUPPLIER_EXISTENCE_LOG represents an interval throughout which it was the case that relvars S_SINCE and S_DURING weren't both empty). In general, the attributes of such a relvar will be the single specified one (X_DURING in the example), which must be of some temporal interval type, together with those of the result of the LOGGED_TIMES_FOR expression.

---

[22] Indeed, such a feature could be extremely useful. Consider the (fairly nontrivial!) query "When if ever did the database say some supplier could supply all of the parts supplied?" The answer to this query is precisely the logged time for *rx*, where *rx* is a relational expression denoting suppliers able to supply all parts supplied.

Note that such a logged time relvar (*R'*, say) would permit the result of the LOGGED_TIMES_FOR expression as it would have been on any given day *d* to be obtained by evaluating an expression of the following form:

```
( R' WHERE d ∈ X_DURING ) { ALL BUT X_DURING }
```

17.5 The answer to Exercise 17.4 includes an example of a logged time relvar for the union of two nullary projections.

Chapter 18

P o i n t   a n d   I n t e r v a l   T y p e s

R e v i s i t e d

Second thoughts are best.

—late 16th century proverb

It's time to take care of some unfinished business. In Chapter 6, we said every interval type involves an underlying point type, and a point type is essentially just a type that has a successor function. Here's the pertinent text from that chapter (irrelevant material omitted):

A given type *T* is usable as a point type if all of the following are defined for it:

■ A *total ordering*, according to which the operator ">" (greater than) is defined for every pair of values *v1* and *v2* of type *T*, such that if *v1* and *v2* are distinct, exactly one of the expressions *v1* > *v2* and *v2* > *v1* returns TRUE and the other returns FALSE

■ Niladic *first* and *last* operators, which return the smallest and largest value of type *T,* respectively, according to the aforementioned ordering

■ Monadic *next* and *prior* operators, which return the successor (if it exists) and predecessor (if it exists), respectively, of any given value of type *T* according to the aforementioned ordering

However, it turns out that there's a lot more to be said on the topic of point types in general (and therefore on the associated topic of interval types as well); hence the present chapter. Unfortunately, it also turns out that a great deal of groundwork needs to be laid, and a large number of implications and ramifications need to be explored, before we can really get to the substance of some of the issues. Thus, if you find it seems to be taking a long time for the true significance of the chapter to emerge, we just have to ask you to be patient; that true significance will—we hope—emerge eventually.

ORDERED vs. ORDINAL

Our first point is this: As you might have noticed, that definition from Chapter 6 gives a list of conditions that are certainly *sufficient* for a type *T* to be usable as a point type—but are they all *necessary*? In what follows, we'll show (eventually) that the answer to this question is *no*. But first things first. We begin by drawing a distinction between ordered and ordinal types:

> **Definition:** An **ordered type** is a type for which a total ordering is defined. In other words, an ordered type is a type *T* such that the expression *v1* > *v2* is defined for all pairs of values *v1* and *v2* of type *T*, returning TRUE if and only if *v1* follows *v2* with respect to the applicable ordering.

> **Definition:** An **ordinal type** is an ordered type for which certain additional operators are defined: *first*, *last*, *next*, *prior*, and possibly others.

> In **Tutorial D**, for example:

- Type INTEGER is an ordinal type. In fact, we can say more specifically that any given type is an ordinal type if and only if it's isomorphic to type INTEGER.

- By contrast, type RATIONAL ("rational numbers") is an ordered type but not an ordinal one, because if *p/q* is a rational number, then—in mathematics at least, if not in computer arithmetic—there's no rational number that can be said to be "next" in numerical order, immediately following *p/q*.[1]

Given these definitions, we can now say that all of the types, apart from interval types, that we'll be discussing in this chapter—until further notice, at any rate—will be ordinal types specifically. For simplicity, therefore, from this point forward we'll take the unqualified term *type* to mean an ordinal type specifically, where it makes any difference (unless the context demands otherwise, of course).

Now, in Chapter 6, we made a crucial assumption: to be specific, we assumed the successor function for a given point type was unique (in other words, if *T* is a point type, then *T* has exactly one successor function). However, we also said this assumption was a very strong one, and we gave the example of a type, "calendar dates," for which we might want to consider two distinct successor functions, "next day" and "next year." (In fact, we might want to consider many different successor functions for this type: "next day," "next business day," "next week," "next

---

[1] Of course, if by *type* here we mean a type that's supported by some actual implementation of some actual programming language, then every such type is necessarily finite. Thus, if that type is also ordered—as, e.g., type RATIONAL is—then (at least in principle) it can be made to be "isomorphic to type INTEGER." We choose to overlook this point of detail in this book.

month," "next year," "next century," and so on.) And we promised to come back to this issue later. Now it's time to do so.[2]

It turns out that the key to the problem we're trying to solve is the notion of *type inheritance*. We therefore begin with a section—unfortunately but inevitably a little on the lengthy side—describing the salient features of that concept.

TYPE INHERITANCE

A robust, rigorous, and formal model of type inheritance (*inheritance* for short) is presented in references [51-52], and it's that model we'll be following here. *Note:* We mention this point right away because several different approaches to inheritance are described in the literature (and implemented, in some cases, in commercial products and languages), yet we find at least some of those approaches to be logically questionable. This isn't the place to get into details; please just be aware that the approach described in the present book differs in certain important respects from approaches described elsewhere in the literature.

Consider the type "calendar dates" once again. In contrast to earlier chapters, assume this type is *not* built in (this assumption allows us to illustrate a number of ideas explicitly that might otherwise have to be implicit). Also, let's agree to call this type not DATE but DDATE, in order to emphasize the fact that it denotes dates that are accurate to the day. Of course, DDATE is an ordinal type; its values are ordered chronologically, and the successor function is basically "next day," or in other words just "add one day." We'll give a definition for this operator (also for the associated *first*, *last*, *next*, and *prior* operators) in the next section, "Point Types Revisited," but here's a definition for the type as such:

```
TYPE DDATE POSSREP DPRI { DI INTEGER CONSTRAINT DI ≥ 1 AND DI ≤ N } ;
```

Explanation:

- Type DDATE has a possible representation called DPRI ("DDATE possible representation as integers") that says that any given DDATE value can possibly be represented by a positive integer called DI.

- The CONSTRAINT portion of the POSSREP specification constrains type DDATE to be such that values of DI must lie in the range [1:N], where N is some large integer (we leave the actual value of N unspecified here to avoid irrelevancies).

Please refer to Chapter 1 if you need to refresh your memory regarding either possible representations (*possreps* for short) in general or type constraints in particular.

---

[2] Actually, we're going to discover eventually that our assumption of a unique successor function isn't too wide of the mark after all. But we're going to have to cover a lot of groundwork first.

Now, we saw in Chapter 1 that every type requires (a) an equals operator and (b) for each declared possrep, a selector operator and a set of THE_ operators (actually just one THE_ operator, in the case at hand). Here are definitions of those operators for type DDATE. *Note:* The implementation code for the equals operator, at least, can and probably should be provided automatically by the system. We show it here explicitly for pedagogic reasons.

```
OPERATOR DPRI ( DI INTEGER ) RETURNS DDATE ;
   /* code to return the DDATE value corresponding */
   /* to the given integer DI                      */
END OPERATOR ;

OPERATOR THE_DI ( DD DDATE ) RETURNS INTEGER ;
   /* code to return the integer corresponding */
   /* to the given DDATE value DD               */
END OPERATOR ;

OPERATOR "=" ( DD1 DDATE , DD2 DDATE ) RETURNS BOOLEAN ;
   RETURN ( THE_DI ( DD1 ) = THE_DI ( DD2 ) ) ;
END OPERATOR ;
```

The selector operator DPRI allows the user to specify, or select, a required DDATE value by providing the appropriate positive integer. (You can think of it as an operator for converting a positive integer to a DDATE value, if you like.) For example, the DPRI invocation

```
DPRI ( 59263 )
```

returns whatever DDATE value—i.e., whatever date in the calendar, accurate to the day— happens to be 59,263rd in the overall ordering of such values. However, what's clearly missing here is a more user friendly way of specifying such DDATE values. So let's extend the type definition to add a second possrep, thus:

```
TYPE DDATE POSSREP DPRI { DI INTEGER CONSTRAINT DI ≥ 1 AND DI ≤ N }
           POSSREP DPRC { DC CHAR    CONSTRAINT ................. } ;
```

The CONSTRAINT specification for possrep DPRC (details of which are omitted here for simplicity) constitutes another constraint on values of type DDATE; it consists of a probably rather complicated expression that constrains such values to be such that they can possibly be represented by—let's assume—character strings of the form *yyyy/mm/dd*, where *yyyy* is an unsigned positive integer in the range [0001:9999],[3] *mm* is an unsigned positive integer in the range [01:12], *dd* is an unsigned positive integer in the range [01:31], and the overall *yyyy/mm/dd* string abides by the usual calendar rules. Of course, every value of type DDATE has both a

---

[3] In practice it would be better not to limit the range of years in such a manner, so that BCE dates—i.e., dates before the start of the common era—and dates after 9999 CE could both be supported; we assume the range we do here (i.e., [0001:9999]) purely for definiteness and simplicity. It would also be nice in literals to allow insignificant leading zeros to be omitted.

DPRI representation and a DPRC representation, a fact that implies among other things that every DPRI value must be representable as a DPRC value and vice versa.

We also need a selector and a THE_ operator corresponding to the DPRC possrep:

```
OPERATOR DPRC ( DC CHAR ) RETURNS DDATE ;
    /* code to return the DDATE value corresponding */
    /* to the given yyyy/mm/dd string DC            */
END OPERATOR ;

OPERATOR THE_DC ( DD DDATE ) RETURNS CHAR ;
    /* code to return the yyyy/mm/dd string corresponding */
    /* to the given DDATE value DD                        */
END OPERATOR ;
```

Now the user can write, e.g.,

```
DPRC ( '2013/07/20' )
```

to specify a certain date—July 20th, 2013, in the example—and

```
THE_DC ( d )
```

to obtain the character string representation of a given DDATE value *d*.

Note: In practice, we would surely want to define numerous additional operators in connection with type DDATE: one to return the year corresponding to a given DDATE value, another to return the month, another to return the year and month in the form of a *yyyy/mm* string, another to return the day of the week, various arithmetic operators (e.g., to return the date *n* days before or after a specified date), and many others. We omit detailed discussion of such operators here, since they're irrelevant to our main purpose.

To get back to that main purpose, then: We can use type DDATE to illustrate the concept of type inheritance by observing that sometimes we're not interested in dates that are accurate all the way to the day. For example, sometimes accuracy to the month is all that's required—the day within the month is irrelevant. Equivalently, we might say that, for certain purposes, we're interested only in those values of type DDATE that happen to correspond to (let's agree) the first of the month—just as, e.g., when we count in tens, we're interested only in those numbers that happen to correspond to the first of each successive sequence of ten integers (10, 20, 30, etc.).

Now, if we're interested only in a subset of the values that make up some type *T*, then by definition we're dealing with a *subtype*—call it *T'*—of type *T*. In a geometric system, for example, we might have two types called RECTANGLE and SQUARE, with the obvious semantics; and since every square is certainly a rectangle, albeit a special case, we can say that (a) every value of type SQUARE is also a value of type RECTANGLE, and hence that (b) type SQUARE is a subtype of type RECTANGLE. Here's a definition:

Definition: Type T' is a **subtype** of type T if and only if every value of type T' is also a value of type T (i.e., the set of values of type T' is a subset of the set of values of type T).

Points arising:

- Every type is a subtype of itself (because every set is a subset of itself).

- If T' is a subtype of T and T'' is a subtype of T', then T'' is a subtype of T.

- If T' is a subtype of T and there's at least one value of T that's not a value of T', then T' is a *proper* subtype of T (thus, although T itself is a subtype of T, it's not a proper one).

- If T' is a subtype of T, then T is a *supertype* of T' (and T is a *proper* supertype of T' if and only if T' is a proper subtype of T).

So, to continue with our example, let's define a type MDATE that's a proper subtype of type DDATE, where MDATE denotes dates that are accurate only to the month, not the day:

```
TYPE MDATE IS DDATE CONSTRAINT FIRST_OF_MONTH ( DDATE )
     POSSREP MPRI { MI = THE_DI ( DDATE ) }
     POSSREP MPRC { MC = SUBSTR ( THE_DC ( DDATE ) , 1 , 7 ) } ;
```

Explanation:

- Type MDATE is defined to be a subtype of type DDATE, thanks to the specification IS DDATE.

- In fact, a DDATE value is an MDATE value if and only if the DDATE value corresponds to the first of the month, thanks to the CONSTRAINT specification. (We've assumed the existence of an operator called FIRST_OF_MONTH that takes a value of type DDATE and returns TRUE if that value does indeed correspond to the first of the pertinent month, FALSE otherwise.)

- Like type DDATE, type MDATE has two possreps, MPRI and MPRC, each of which is derived, in the manner specified, from the corresponding possrep for type DDATE. MPRC in particular allows us to think of MDATE values as if they were character strings of the form *yyyy/mm*. (In practice, we'd probably want to define yet another possrep for type MDATE, namely "month number," again derived in some way from some possrep for type DDATE. We omit further consideration of this possibility for simplicity.)

Here now are the necessary selector and THE_ operators for type MDATE as just defined:

```
OPERATOR MPRI ( MI INTEGER ) RETURNS MDATE ;
    /* code to return the MDATE value corresponding   */
    /* to the given integer MI (which must correspond */
    /* in turn to the first of the month)             */
END OPERATOR ;

OPERATOR THE_MI ( MD MDATE ) RETURNS INTEGER ;
    /* code to return the integer corresponding */
    /* to the given MDATE value MD              */
END OPERATOR ;

OPERATOR MPRC ( MC CHAR ) RETURNS MDATE ;
    /* code to return the MDATE value corresponding */
    /* to the given yyyy/mm string MC               */
END OPERATOR ;

OPERATOR THE_MC ( MD MDATE ) RETURNS CHAR ;
    /* code to return the yyyy/mm string corresponding */
    /* to the given MDATE value MD                     */
END OPERATOR ;
```

We've now defined type MDATE as a proper subtype of type DDATE (see the simple *type hierarchy* in Fig. 18.1). What are the implications of this fact? Probably the most important is the phenomenon known as *value substitutability*, which in the case at hand means that *wherever the system expects a value of type DDATE, we can always substitute a value of type MDATE instead* (because MDATE values *are* DDATE values). In particular, therefore, if *Op* is an operator that applies to DDATE values in general, we can always apply *Op* to an MDATE value specifically.[4] For example, the operators "=", THE_DI, and THE_DC defined above for values of type DDATE all apply to values of type MDATE as well (they're *inherited* by type MDATE from type DDATE). Of course, the converse is false—operators specifically defined for values of type MDATE don't apply to values of type DDATE (in general), because DDATE values aren't MDATE values (again in general). We'll see some examples in the next section.

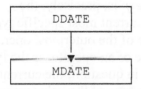

Fig. 18.1: A simple type hierarchy

It follows from the foregoing that, e.g., the following code fragment is valid:

---

[4] The operator *Op* is thus *polymorphic* (see the remarks on this subject in Chapters 1 and 7). In other words, value substitutability implies polymorphism—*inclusion* polymorphism, to be specific (other kinds exist, as noted in Chapter 7). *Note:* Inclusion polymorphism is so called on the grounds that, e.g., the set of MDATE values is *included in* the set of DDATE values.

```
VAR I INTEGER ;
VAR MDX MDATE ;
VAR DDX DDATE ;

I := THE_DI ( MDX ) ;
IF MDX = DDX THEN ... END IF ;
/* etc., etc., etc. */
```

For simplicity, let's assume for the remainder of this section that the type hierarchy contains just types DDATE and MDATE and no others. Given that assumption, let's take a closer look at the fundamental operations of *assignment* (":=") and *equality comparison* ("="). First, assignment. Consider the following example:

```
VAR DDX DDATE ;

DDX := MPRC ( '2013/09' ) ;
```

In the assignment here, the target variable on the left side is declared to be of type DDATE, but the source expression on the right side denotes a value of type MDATE. However, the assignment is valid, thanks to value substitutability. And after the assignment, of course, the variable contains a DDATE value that happens to satisfy the type constraint for type MDATE (to be specific, it contains the value DPRC ('2013/09/01'), which is in fact an MDATE value). We can therefore say that, while the *declared* type of variable DDX is (as stated) DDATE, the current *most specific* type—i.e., the type of the current value of that variable—is MDATE. (That current value is of type DDATE as well, of course, because MDATE values *are* DDATE values. Thus, a given value has, in general, several types. As noted in Chapter 1, however, it always has exactly one most specific type.)

Now, it's important to understand that the distinction we're discussing here, between declared and current most specific types, applies not just to variable references but in fact to expressions in general. In other words, every expression has both a declared type and a current most specific type. To be specific, the declared type of an expression *exp* is, precisely, the declared type of the outermost operator involved in *exp*; likewise, the current most specific type of that same expression *exp* is, precisely, the current most specific type of the outermost operator invocation involved in the evaluation of *exp*.[5] *Note:* The declared type of an operator is the type named in the RETURNS specification in the definition of the operator in question; the current most specific type of an invocation of that operator is the most specific type of the value returned by the invocation in question.

To continue with the code fragment shown above, suppose the following assignment is now executed:

```
DDX := DPRC ( '2012/10/17' ) ;
```

---

[5] If the expression consists of a simple variable reference, that operator is basically just "return the value of this variable," and the declared type and most specific type of the expression are just the declared type and most specific type of the variable in question (as we've more or less said already).

The current most specific type of variable DDX is now DDATE again, because the expression on the right side is of most specific type DDATE (i.e., it's "only" of type DDATE, not type MDATE).

One more example:

```
DDX := DPRC ( '2000/11/01' ) ;
```

Here the DPRC invocation on the right side actually returns a value of type not just DDATE but MDATE, because the value in question satisfies the "first of month" constraint for type MDATE. We refer to this effect as *specialization by constraint*, on the grounds that the result of the DPRC invocation is "specialized" to type MDATE, precisely because it does satisfy the type constraint for type MDATE. And after the assignment, of course, the current most specific type of variable DDX is MDATE, too.

To generalize from the foregoing examples, let V be a variable of declared type T and let T' be a proper subtype of T. Then:

■ If the current most specific type of V is T and a value v of most specific type T' is assigned to V, the current most specific type of V becomes T' (as we've just seen). This effect is a logical consequence of the phenomenon we call specialization by constraint, as already explained.

■ Conversely, if the current most specific type of V is T' and a value v of most specific type T is assigned to V, the current most specific type of V becomes T. We refer to this effect as *generalization by constraint*, on the grounds that the current most specific type of V is "generalized" to type T—it's established as T because the value v satisfies the type constraint for T and not for any proper subtype of T.

We note in passing that it's precisely in this area (specialization by constraint and generalization by constraint) that the inheritance model we advocate [51-52] departs most obviously from other approaches described in the literature.

Be that as it may, you can see from the foregoing examples that it's a rule regarding assignment that the most specific type of the source value can be any subtype (not necessarily a proper subtype, of course) of the declared type of the target variable. What about equality comparisons? In the absence of subtyping and inheritance, the comparison $v1 = v2$ would require the comparands $v1$ and $v2$ to be of the same type, T say. Thanks to value substitutability, however, we can substitute a value of any subtype of T for $v1$ and a value of any subtype of T for $v2$. It follows that for the comparison $v1 = v2$ to be legitimate, it's necessary and sufficient that the most specific types of the comparands have a common supertype. Of course, the comparison will give true if and only if $v1$ and $v2$ are in fact the same value (implying in particular, therefore, that they're of the same most specific type).

POINT TYPES REVISITED

Of course, there's a lot more that could be said about type inheritance in general, but what we've said so far should suffice for the purposes of this chapter (for the time being, at any rate). Now let's get back to point types as such. Now, it's clear that type DDATE from the previous section can be made to meet all of the requirements for such a type if we want it to (and we do)—we can certainly define a total ordering based on a ">" operator for values of the type, and we can certainly define the necessary "first," "last," "next," and "prior" operators as well. In fact, **Tutorial D** allows a type definition to state explicitly that the type in question is an ordinal type, as in this example (note the highlighted text):

```
TYPE DDATE ORDINAL
    POSSREP DPRI { DI INTEGER CONSTRAINT DI ≥ 1 AND DI ≤ N }
    POSSREP DPRC { DC CHAR     CONSTRAINT ................ } ;
```

The ORDINAL specification implies that ">", "first," "last," "next," and "prior" operators must all be explicitly defined for the type (a real language might require the names of those operators to be specified as part of the ORDINAL specification). Here are some possible definitions for those operators:

```
OPERATOR ">" ( DD1 DDATE , DD2 DDATE ) RETURNS BOOLEAN ;
    RETURN ( THE_DI ( DD1 ) > THE_DI ( DD2 ) ) ;
END OPERATOR ;

OPERATOR FIRST_DDATE ( ) RETURNS DDATE ;
    RETURN DPRI ( 1 ) ;
END OPERATOR ;

OPERATOR LAST_DDATE ( ) RETURNS DDATE ;
    RETURN DPRI ( N ) ;
END OPERATOR ;

OPERATOR NEXT_DDATE ( DD DDATE ) RETURNS DDATE ;
    RETURN DPRI ( THE_DI ( DD ) + 1 ) ;
END OPERATOR ;

OPERATOR PRIOR_DDATE ( DD DDATE ) RETURNS DDATE ;
    RETURN DPRI ( THE_DI ( DD ) - 1 ) ;
END OPERATOR ;
```

Type DDATE now meets the sufficiency requirements for a point type. Note carefully, however, that the "first," "last," "next," and "prior" operators are named FIRST_DDATE, LAST_DDATE, NEXT_DDATE, and PRIOR_DDATE, respectively.[6] Although we did follow

---

[6] By the way, what happens if, e.g., NEXT_DDATE is invoked on "the last day"? *Answer:* The DPRI selector invocation fails on a type constraint violation.

this style of naming in earlier chapters ("FIRST_*T*," etc., where *T* is the name of the pertinent point type), we never really explained it properly, but now we need to, and we will.

Consider type MDATE. As we know, MDATE is a proper subtype of DDATE; thus, since DDATE is an ordinal type, we can regard MDATE as an ordinal type too, if we want to (and again we do want to, because we want to use type MDATE as a point type). So we need to define associated ">", "first," "last," "next," and "prior" operators for type MDATE. The ">" operator is inherited from type DDATE. So too are the operators NEXT_DDATE and so on; however, those operators are *not* the "next" (etc.) operators we need for type MDATE! For example, given the MDATE value August 1st, 2015, the operator NEXT_DDATE will return the date of the next day (August 2nd, 2015), not the date of the next month (September 1st, 2015). Thus, we need some new operators for type MDATE:

```
OPERATOR FIRST_MDATE ( ) RETURNS MDATE ;
   RETURN MPRI⁻ ( op ( 1 ) ) ;
   /* op ( 1 ) computes the integer possible representation */
   /* —presumably 1—for the first day of the first month    */
END OPERATOR ;

OPERATOR LAST_MDATE ( ) RETURNS MDATE ;
   RETURN MPRI⁻ ( op ( N ) ) ;
   /* op ( N ) computes the integer possible representation */
   /* for the first day of the last month                   */
END OPERATOR ;

OPERATOR NEXT_MDATE ( MD MDATE ) RETURNS MDATE ;
   RETURN MDATE ( THE_MI ( MD ) + incr ) ;
   /* incr is 28, 29, 30, or 31, as applicable */
END OPERATOR ;

OPERATOR PRIOR_MDATE ( MD MDATE ) RETURNS MDATE ;
   RETURN MDATE ( THE_MI ( MD ) - decr ) ;
   /* decr is 28, 29, 30, or 31, as applicable */
END OPERATOR ;
```

And now we can see why the "first," "last," "next," and "prior" operators for a given type *T* have to be named FIRST_*T*, LAST_*T*, NEXT_*T*, and PRIOR_*T*, respectively. For example, given the MDATE value August 1st, 2015, the operator NEXT_DDATE returns August 2nd, 2015 (as we already know); by contrast, the operator NEXT_MDATE returns September 1st, 2015. NEXT_DDATE and NEXT_MDATE are thus clearly different operators.

Aside: An alternative approach would be to call both NEXT_DDATE and NEXT_MDATE simply "NEXT" and provide two different *implementation versions* of that "NEXT" operator, using the mechanism—mentioned briefly in Chapters 7 and 8 and again in Chapter 17—called *overloading*. The expression NEXT (*exp*) would then cause the MDATE or DDATE implementation to be invoked according as to whether the type of *exp* was MDATE or just DDATE. (*Note:* The phrase "the type of *exp*" here could mean either the declared type or the most specific type, depending on factors beyond the scope of the present discussion.) However, such a scheme would do rather serious damage to an important prescription of our inheritance model—in terms of the DDATE and MDATE example, it could imply that there'd be no way to apply the DDATE version of NEXT to a value of type MDATE—and we therefore reject it. *End of aside*.

NUMERIC POINT TYPES

Now we'd like to shift gears, as it were, and talk about the implications of the ideas discussed in this chapter so far for certain types that differ in kind, somewhat, from the calendar types DDATE and MDATE we've concentrated on prior to this point. To be specific, there are some languages—SQL is one—that support a variety of system defined NUMERIC types (where "numeric" really means fixed point decimal numbers, such 43.7 or −6.9). For example, the following is a legal SQL variable definition:

```
DECLARE V NUMERIC ( 5 , 2 ) ;
```

Values of the specific numeric type illustrated here—i.e., NUMERIC(5,2)—are decimal numbers with precision five and scale factor two. In other words, those values are precisely the following:

```
-999.99 , -999.98 , ... , -000.01 , 000.00 , 000.01 , ... , 999.99
```

In general, the *precision* for a given numeric type specifies the total number of decimal digits,[7] and the *scale factor* specifies the position of the assumed decimal point, in the string of digits denoting any given value of the type in question, where:

■ A nonnegative scale factor q means the decimal point is assumed to be q decimal places to the left of the rightmost decimal digit of such a string of digits.

■ By contrast, a negative scale factor $-q$ means the decimal point is assumed to be q decimal places to the right of the rightmost decimal digit of such a string of digits.

Note, therefore, that the precision and scale factor between them serve as an a priori constraint on values of the type; in effect, they constitute the applicable type constraint.

---

[7] Actually there's some confusion in the literature over the term *precision*. The definition given here is in accordance with the one given in *The Facts on File Dictionary of Mathematics* (Market House Books Ltd., New York, 1999) and with Java and PL/I usage. Other writers use the term to mean what we prefer to call the *scale factor*; this second interpretation is in accordance with the definition given in *The McGraw-Hill Dictionary of Mathematics* (McGraw-Hill, New York, 1994) and with C++ and sometimes (but not always!) SQL usage.

Aside: Observe that NUMERIC isn't a type as such; instead, it's a type generator. Specific numeric types such as NUMERIC(5,2) are obtained by invoking that type generator with arguments representing the desired precision and scale factor. *End of aside.*

We need to stress the fact that values of type NUMERIC(p,q) should be thought of as being denoted by strings of digits with an *assumed* decimal point. What this means is that if v is such a value, then v can be thought of in terms of a p-digit integer, n say; however, that p-digit integer n must be interpreted as denoting the value $v = n * (10^{-q})$. The multiplier 10^{-q} is the *scale* defined by the scale factor q (e.g., for NUMERIC(5,2), the scale is one hundredth).[8] Observe that, by definition, every value of the type is evenly divisible by the scale (i.e., dividing the value in question by the scale always leaves a zero remainder). We note that the concept of scale can reasonably be applied to the examples of the previous section as well; for type DDATE it's one day, for type MDATE it's one month.

Note: From this point forward, we adopt the usual conventions regarding the omission of insignificant leading and trailing zeros in numeric literals. Thus, we might say more simply that the values of type NUMERIC(5,2) are:

```
-999.99 , -999.98 , ... , -.01 , 0 , .01 , ... , 999.99
```

Fig. 18.2 gives several examples of NUMERIC types, with the corresponding scale and a symbolic picture of a typical value (ignoring the possible prefix minus sign) in each case.

Type	Scale	Picture
NUMERIC(4,1)	1/10	*xxx.x*
NUMERIC(3,1)	1/10	*xx.x*
NUMERIC(4,2)	1/100	*xx.xx*
NUMERIC(3,0)	1	*xxx.*
NUMERIC(3,-2)	100	*xxx*00.
NUMERIC(3,5)	1/100000	.00*xxx*

Fig. 18.2: Examples of numeric types

Points arising:

■ Real languages usually provide a system defined type called INTEGER; indeed, we've been assuming the existence of just such a type throughout this book. However, we can now see that INTEGER is effectively just another spelling for NUMERIC(p,0) for some

---

[8] And yes, there's confusion over the term *scale* too. The definition given here is in accordance with that given in *The Facts on File Dictionary of Mathematics* (more or less). PL/I, although it agrees with our definition of the term *scale factor*, uses *scale* to refer instead to the distinction between fixed and floating point. SQL sometimes (but not always!) uses *scale* to mean *scale factor*. Also, *scale* is sometimes used as a synonym for *base* or *radix*.

particular (system defined) precision *p*. *Note:* While every value of type INTEGER is certainly an integer, of course, it's not the case that type INTEGER is the only type whose values are all integers. In fact, every type of the form NUMERIC(*p,q*) for which *q* is negative also has values that are all integers (see the next bullet item).

■ If the scale factor *q* is negative, least significant digits of the integer part of the number are missing. Those missing digits are assumed to be zeros. By way of example, values of type NUMERIC(3,−2) are:

```
-99900 , -99800 , ... , -100 , 0 , 100 , ... , 99900
```

All of these values are numbers—in fact, integers—that are evenly divisible by one hundred, which is the scale.

Incidentally, we can use this example to highlight the important difference between a literal and a value (the concepts are indeed often confused—see, e.g., reference [11]). As explained in Chapter 1, a literal is *not* a value but is, rather, a symbol that denotes a value. Thus, e.g., the symbol 99900 is a literal that might on the face of it be thought of as denoting a value of type NUMERIC(5,0), not NUMERIC(3,−2). However, the value in question does happen to satisfy the type constraint for values of type NUMERIC(3,−2), which is, as we'll see in a moment, actually a subtype of NUMERIC(5,0). Conceptually, therefore, specialization by constraint comes into play—at compile time, in fact—and the literal thus does indeed denote a value of type NUMERIC(3,−2). Similarly, the literal 5.00 actually denotes a value of type INTEGER. See the discussion of multiple inheritance later in this section for further discussion.

■ If the scale factor *q* is greater than the precision *p*, most significant digits of the fractional part of the number are missing. Again, those missing digits are assumed to be zeros. By way of example, values of type NUMERIC(3,5) are:

```
-0.00999 , -0.00998 , ... , -0.00001 , 0.0 , 0.00001 , ... , 0.00999
```

(Here we do show the zero integer part preceding the decimal point, just for explicitness.) All of these values are numbers that are evenly divisible by one hundred thousandth, which is the scale.

Now, it's surely obvious that any of these NUMERIC types can be used as a point type, and we'll examine that possibility in a few moments. However, there's an important issue that needs to be addressed first, as follows:

■ Consider the types NUMERIC(3,1) and NUMERIC(4,1). It should be clear that every value of type NUMERIC(3,1) is a value of type NUMERIC(4,1) as well[9]—to be specific, a value of type NUMERIC(4,1) for which the leading digit in the integer part happens to be zero. It follows that NUMERIC(3,1) is a proper subtype of NUMERIC(4,1), and so we can (for example) assign a value of the former type to a variable that's declared to be of the latter type.

■ Now consider the types NUMERIC(3,1) and NUMERIC(4,2). It should also be clear that every value of type NUMERIC(3,1) is a value of type NUMERIC(4,2) as well[10]—to be specific, a value of type NUMERIC(4,2) for which the trailing digit in the fractional part happens to be zero. It follows that NUMERIC(3,1) is a proper subtype of NUMERIC(4,2) as well.

■ Observe now that neither of NUMERIC(4,1) and NUMERIC(4,2) is a subtype of the other; for example, 999.9 is a value of the first type that's not a value of the second, while 99.99 is a value of the second type that's not a value of the first. And so we see that type NUMERIC(3,1) has two distinct proper supertypes, neither of which is a subtype of the other. It follows that here we're dealing with *multiple inheritance*—i.e., a form of inheritance in which a given type can have *n* proper supertypes, none of which is a subtype of any other, for some $n > 1$. (By contrast, the form of inheritance discussed earlier in this chapter was, tacitly, what's called *single* inheritance only. Of course, single inheritance is just a degenerate special case of multiple inheritance.)

Thus, we need to digress again for a moment in order to extend the ideas presented earlier for single inheritance to deal with the possibility of multiple inheritance.

Multiple Inheritance

Consider the case of numeric types once again. Assume for definiteness and simplicity that the maximum precision the system supports is 3 (the minimum, of course, is 1) and the maximum and minimum scale factors are 4 and −4, respectively. Then Fig. 18.3 shows the corresponding *type lattice*—a simple type hierarchy will obviously no longer suffice—for the entire range of valid numeric types. (For space reasons, we abbreviate the type name "NUMERIC(p,q)" throughout that figure to just "p,q".) The figure should be more or less self-explanatory, except for the two types LUB and GLB shown at the top and bottom of the lattice, respectively, which we now explain:

---

[9] The converse is false, of course.

[10] Again the converse is false.

- Type LUB ("least upper bound") contains all possible NUMERIC values and is a proper supertype of every other type in the figure.[11]

- Type GLB ("greatest lower bound"), by contrast, is a type that contains just the single value zero; it's a proper subtype of every other type in the figure.

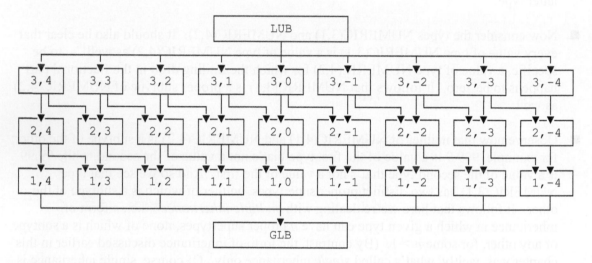

Fig. 18.3: A simple type lattice

What extensions are needed to our model of inheritance as sketched earlier in order to deal with situations like the one illustrated in Fig. 18.3? It turns out that—at least so far as we're concerned in the present book—not many extensions are needed at all. In fact, the only one we need consider here is this:

- If types *T1* and *T2* overlap (i.e., have at least one value in common), then they must have both:

  a. A common supertype *T*, and

  b. A common subtype *T'* (the *intersection type* for *T1* and *T2*) such that every value that's of both type *T1* and type *T2* is in fact a value of type *T'*.

(Actually the foregoing statement is both simpler and more complicated than it really needs to be—simpler, because among other things it needs to be generalized to deal with three or more

---

[11] In fact type LUB (a) contains no value that's not a value of one of its proper subtypes and is therefore (b) an example of what our inheritance model refers to as a *dummy type*. It might be used, for example, as the type of a parameter in the definition of some operator—e.g., an "absolute value of" operator, ABS—that's meant to apply to all possible numeric values.

overlapping types; more complicated, because if the proper groundwork is laid first, it can be stated much more elegantly and precisely. See reference [51] for further discussion.)

Observe now that the foregoing rule is certainly satisfied in Fig. 18.3. For example, consider the types NUMERIC(2,1) and NUMERIC(2,0). These two types do overlap—for example, they have the value 9 in common. And:

a. They do have a common supertype, NUMERIC(3,1).

b. They also have a common subtype, NUMERIC(1,0), such that a value is of both the specified types if and only if it's a value of that common subtype.[12]

The foregoing rule regarding overlapping types can be regarded as a rule that type lattices like that in Fig. 18.3 are required to obey in order to be well formed. And, assuming the type lattice we have to deal with is indeed well formed in this sense, we can now say that:

■ Our previous rule regarding assignment remains unchanged: namely, the most specific type of the source must be some subtype of the declared type of the target.

■ What's more, our previous rule for equality comparison remains unchanged, too: The most specific types of the comparands must have a common supertype. However, this latter rule now has an extended interpretation. For example, it's possible that a comparison between a NUMERIC(2,1) value and a NUMERIC(2,0) value might give true—but only if the values in question are in fact both of the corresponding intersection type NUMERIC(1,0) (and are both the same value, of course).

Point Types Continued

Now let's get back to the main topic of this chapter. Clearly, all of the various numeric types we've been discussing can be used as point types—they all have a total ordering, and "first," "last," "next," and "prior" operators can obviously be defined for all of them. However, they differ in one significant respect from types DDATE and MDATE as discussed earlier, inasmuch as the definitions of the "first" (etc.) operators are all effectively *implied* by the applicable precision and scale—the precision implies the definitions of the "first" and "last" operators, and the scale implies the definitions of the "next" and "prior" operators. For example, consider the type NUMERIC(3,1), which consists of the following values (in order):

```
-99.9 , -99.8 , ... , -0.1 , 0 , 0.1 , ... , 99.9
```

---

[12] Of course, NUMERIC(3,1) isn't the only common supertype in this particular example (though it does happen to be the only one apart from LUB). Likewise, NUMERIC(1,0) isn't the only common subtype, either, though it does happen to be the only one apart from GLB.

Clearly, the "first" operator here returns −99.9, the "last" operator returns 99.9, the "next" operator is "add one tenth," and the "prior" operator is "subtract one tenth."

> *Aside:* To be consistent with our earlier remarks regarding operator naming, the foregoing operators ought by rights to be named FIRST_NUMERIC(3,1), LAST_NUMERIC(3,1), NEXT_NUMERIC(3,1), and PRIOR_NUMERIC(3,1), respectively! Quite apart from the question as to whether such names are even syntactically legal, we'd be the first to admit that they're clumsy and ugly. However, as we've said elsewhere in this book, we're concerned here not so much with matters of concrete syntax, but rather with the question of getting the conceptual foundations right. And conceptually, yes, the "first," "last," "next," and "prior" operators for type NUMERIC(3,1) really are different from the corresponding operators for (e.g.) type NUMERIC(4,2), and they do need different names. (If they need names at all, that is—but they might not. For example, the expression NEXT_NUMERIC(3,1) (*exp*), where *exp* is of declared type NUMERIC(3,1), will clearly return the same result as the expression *exp* + 0.1. Thus, the conventional "+" operator might be all we need here.[13] Note too that even though the declared type of the expression *exp* + 0.1 will probably be just LUB, the result it returns at run time will certainly be of type NUMERIC(3,1)—and possibly some proper subtype thereof—thanks to specialization by constraint.) *End of aside*.

Other Scales

In effect, what we've been claiming in our discussion so far is this: To say a certain NUMERIC type has a certain precision and scale is really just a shorthand way of saying we have a type that (a) is usable as a point type, (b) has values that are numbers, and (c) has certain specific "first," "next," etc., operators. We now observe, however, that this shorthand—what we might call "the NUMERIC(p,q) shorthand"—works *only if the desired scale is a power of ten*. But other scales are certainly possible, and perhaps desirable, even with types that are essentially numeric in nature. We now briefly consider this possibility.

By way of a simple example, suppose we want a point type consisting of even integers—which is to say, an ordinal type for which (a) the values are (let's agree) the integers −99998, −99996, ..., −2, 0, 2, ..., 99998, and (b) the "first," "next," etc., operators are as suggested by this sequence (i.e., the "first" operator returns −99998, the "next" operator is "add two," and so on). No NUMERIC(p,q) shorthand is capable of expressing these requirements. Instead, therefore, we need to define an explicit subtype, perhaps as follows:

```
TYPE EVEN_INTEGER ORDINAL
        IS INTEGER CONSTRAINT MOD ( INTEGER , 2 ) = 0 ... ;
```

---

[13] Overloading again! But we're all very used to the idea that "+" is overloaded, even if we're not used to describing the situation in such terms.

MOD here ("modulo") is, let's assume, an operator that takes two integer operands and returns the remainder that results after dividing the first by the second. (The reference to the type name "INTEGER" in the CONSTRAINT specification is meant to stand for an arbitrary value of type INTEGER.)

The "=" and ">" operators for EVEN_INTEGER are inherited from type INTEGER. As for the "first" (etc.) operators, they might be defined as follows:

```
OPERATOR FIRST_EVEN_INTEGER ( ) RETURNS EVEN_INTEGER ;
   RETURN -99998 ;
END OPERATOR ;

OPERATOR LAST_EVEN_INTEGER ( ) RETURNS EVEN_INTEGER ;
   RETURN 99998 ;
END OPERATOR ;

OPERATOR NEXT_EVEN_INTEGER ( I EVEN_INTEGER ) RETURNS EVEN_INTEGER ;
   RETURN I + 2 ;
END OPERATOR ;

OPERATOR PRIOR_EVEN_INTEGER ( I EVEN_INTEGER ) RETURNS EVEN_INTEGER ;
   RETURN I - 2 ;
END OPERATOR ;
```

Aside: Actually we've taken some rather considerable liberties in these operator definitions. The fact is that, e.g., the expression in the RETURN statement in the definition of FIRST_EVEN_INTEGER ought really to be, not just the literal −99998 as shown, but rather an expression of the form TREAT_AS_EVEN_INTEGER (−99998). However, detailed discussion of this point would take us much further away from our main topic than we care to go here; thus, we've adopted certain simplifications in order to avoid a detailed discussion of a subject that's not very relevant to our main purpose.[14] For further discussion and explanation, see reference [51]. *End of aside.*

In the same kind of way, we might define, e.g., a point type where the scale is calendar quarters and the "next" operator is "add three months," or a point type where the scale is decades and the "next" operator is "add ten years" (and so on).

GRANULARITY REVISITED

We now turn our attention to the concept of granularity. Recall from Chapter 4 that this term refers, informally, to the "size" of the individual points, or equivalently the size of the gap

---

[14] In case you're interested, however, the essence of the matter is that we surely can't expect the *compiler* to recognize that the integer literal −99998 actually denotes a value of the *user defined* type EVEN_INTEGER.

between adjacent points, for the point type in question. Fig. 18.4 lists the various point types we've been considering in this chapter so far, with (a) their scales as previously discussed and also with (b) their corresponding granularities.

Point type	Scale	Granularity
DDATE	1 day	1 day
MDATE	1 month	1 month
NUMERIC(5,2)	1/100	1/100
NUMERIC(4,1)	1/10	1/10
NUMERIC(3,1)	1/10	1/10
NUMERIC(4,2)	1/100	1/100
NUMERIC(3,0)	1	1
NUMERIC(3,-2)	100	100
NUMERIC(3,5)	1/100000	1/100000
EVEN_INTEGER	2	2

Fig. 18.4: Sample point types with their scales and granularities

Now, you might have noticed that we didn't mention the term *granularity* in previous sections of this chapter at all. One major reason for that omission is that, in all of the examples discussed in this chapter so far, the granularity is identical to the corresponding scale, as Fig. 18.4 clearly shows. For those types, therefore, the term is simply redundant; it's just another term for a concept for which a better term already exists (not to mention the fact that *scale* is formally defined, while—*pace* references [6] and [62]—*granularity* seems not to be). However, a more important reason for the omission is that there are some point types for which the concept of granularity doesn't apply. We'll give an example in a few moments. First, however, we want to consider a different example, involving a user defined type called HEIGHT. Here's the definition:

```
TYPE HEIGHT POSSREP HIPR { HI INTEGER CONSTRAINT HI > 0 AND HI ≤ 120 } ;
```

Type HEIGHT is meant to represent person heights. Legal values are as follows:

```
HIPR ( 1 ) , HIPR ( 2 ) , ... , HIPR ( 120 )
```

These values are meant to denote heights in inches (we're assuming nobody is under one inch or over ten feet tall). Clearly, the granularity is one inch. Or is it? Surely we might equally well say it's two half-inches, or one twelfth of a foot—or even 2.54 centimeters, or 25.4 millimeters, or any of many, many other possibilities. Thus, we see that, in general, granularity requires some associated *unit of measure* (not necessarily unique) in order for it to make sense.

Of course, while there might be many different ways, some of which might be more user friendly than others, of stating what the granularity actually is in any given situation, those different ways must all be logically equivalent to one another—which is just as well, in fact, since the concept of units of measure has no formal part to play in a type definition. Indeed, reference [52] argues that, as a general rule, types and units should generally not be in any kind of one to one correspondence. That is, instead of having (e.g.) one type representing heights in inches and another representing heights in centimeters, it would be better to have just one HEIGHT type with two distinct possreps, one for inches and one for centimeters. But now we're beginning to stray too far from our main topic once again. To return to that topic, we now show (as promised) an example of a point type for which the granularity concept doesn't seem to apply at all:

```
TYPE RICHTER ORDINAL
     POSSREP RPR { R NUMERIC ( 3 , 1 ) CONSTRAINT R > 0.0 } ;
```

Type RICHTER is meant to represent points on the Richter scale. Legal values are as follows:

```
RPR ( 0.1 ) , RPR ( 0.2 ) , ... , RPR ( 1.0 ) ,
RPR ( 1.1 ) , RPR ( 1.2 ) , ... ,
............................. , RPR ( 99.9 )   /* help! */
```

As is well known, however, the Richter scale is not linear but logarithmic to base 10.[15] As a consequence, it makes little sense to talk about the concept of "granularity" in this context at all—the gaps between one RICHTER value and the next aren't of constant size.[16] So what this example demonstrates is that there's a logical difference between scale and granularity:

■ Scale is, as already stated, a formal concept; essentially, it's the basis of the definition of the successor function ("next").

■ Granularity, by contrast, is an informal concept only; it helps to explain at an intuitive level what a certain point type is supposed to represent. However, it does tacitly assume that the point type in question involves evenly spaced values.

In other words, the tacit model underlying the concept of granularity seems to be something like the following:

■ We're given a linear axis (e.g., "the timeline") with certain points marked on it.

■ Those marked points are the only ones of interest—there are no accessible points "between" adjacent points on the axis. To put it another way, measurements along the axis

---

[15] For the record, if p and p' are adjacent points on the scale (e.g., 4.1 and 4.2, respectively), then a magnitude p' earthquake has a "shaking amplitude" approximately 1.26 times greater than a magnitude p earthquake. An earthquake measuring, say, 5.0 on the Richter scale has a ten times greater shaking amplitude than one measuring 4.0.

[16] Actually the same could be said of type MDATE, since different months are of different lengths.

are discrete, not continuous (they always correspond to one of the marked points, there are no "half measures").

- Those points of interest are assumed to be evenly spaced along the axis. That is, if *p1* and *p2* are any two adjacent points, then the size *g* of the gap between *p1* and *p2*—which must be measured, be it noted, by going outside the model—is always the same.

- That constant value *g* is the granularity. Furthermore, it corresponds to the scale, in the sense that *g* is what must be "added" to any given point to get to the next.

But the RICHTER example shows that the even spacing assumption isn't always valid. For type RICHTER, scale makes sense, but granularity does not. More generally, whenever granularity makes sense, then scale does too, but the converse is false.

We now consider one last example of a point type in order to show that, not only does granularity not always apply, but scale doesn't always apply either:

```
TYPE PRIME ORDINAL IS INTEGER CONSTRAINT ... ;
```

Values of type PRIME are (let's agree) prime numbers, starting with two; the CONSTRAINT specification, details of which are omitted for simplicity, presumably consists of a reference to some operator that determines, for any given positive integer *p*, whether *p* is in fact prime.

Now, prime numbers are certainly not regularly spaced, so the concept of granularity doesn't apply. What's more, there's no obvious scale, either! And yet PRIME is clearly usable as a point type—">" is obviously applicable, and we can define suitable "first" (etc.) operators, thus:

```
OPERATOR FIRST_PRIME ( ) RETURNS PRIME ;
   RETURN 2 ;
END OPERATOR ;

OPERATOR LAST_PRIME ( ) RETURNS PRIME ;
   RETURN N ;        /* N = the largest representable prime */
END OPERATOR ;

OPERATOR NEXT_PRIME ( P PRIME ) RETURNS PRIME ;
   /* code to compute the prime immediately following P */
END OPERATOR ;

OPERATOR PRIOR_PRIME ( P PRIME ) RETURNS PRIME ;
   /* code to compute the prime immediately preceding P */
END OPERATOR ;
```

So PRIME is an example of a type that's certainly usable as a point type and yet has no scale (and a fortiori no granularity).[17]

To summarize: The concept of granularity (a) isn't formally defined, (b) doesn't always apply, and (c) seems to be identical to the concept of scale when it does apply. Given this state of affairs, it seems a little strange that the concept has received so much attention in the literature—especially since, as noted in Chapter 4, there seems to be a certain amount of confusion surrounding the concept anyway; for example, it's sometimes taken to be the same as *precision* (!). By way of a second example (i.e., of apparent confusion), you might like to meditate on the following definition from reference [62]. Italics are as in the original.

> [The] *timestamp granularity* is the size of each chronon in a timestamp interpretation. For example, if the timestamp granularity is one second, then the duration of each chronon in the timestamp interpretation is one second (and vice versa) ... If the context is clear, the modifier "timestamp" may be omitted.

Note: The concept of "timestamp interpretation" is defined elsewhere in the same document thus:

> [The] *timestamp interpretation* gives the meaning of each timestamp bit pattern in terms of some time-line clock chronon (or group of chronons).

(The term *chronon* was discussed briefly in Chapter 4.)

INTERVAL TYPES REVISITED

In Chapter 6, we defined an interval type to be, specifically, a *generated* type of the form INTERVAL_T, where T is a point type. Like all generated types, therefore, interval types have certain generic operators associated with them: specifically, interval selectors, BEGIN and END, PRE and POST, POINT FROM, "∈" and "∋", COUNT, Allen's operators, and interval UNION, INTERSECT, and MINUS. In this section, we consider some of the implications of the ideas discussed so far in this chapter on these operators.

We begin our investigation by noting that if T is a point type and T' is a proper subtype of T, then INTERVAL_T' is *not* a subtype of INTERVAL_T. Why not? Because intervals of type INTERVAL_T' aren't intervals of type INTERVAL_T. Indeed, even if intervals i and i', of types INTERVAL_T and INTERVAL_T' respectively, have the same begin and end points b and e, they're not the same interval, because they have different sets of contained points (except in the special case where $b = e$, meaning the interval in question is a unit interval). For example, take T and T' as INTEGER and EVEN_INTEGER, respectively, and consider $i = [2:6]$ and $i' = [2:6]$; then i contains the integers 2, 3, 4, 5, and 6, while i' contains just the even integers 2, 4, and 6.

---

[17] Perhaps we might say it does have a scale but the scale in question is *nonuniform*. But the concept of a nonuniform scale doesn't seem very useful.

Note: Even in that special case where *b* = *e*, intervals *i* and *i'* are still not the same interval, precisely because they're of different types. For example, the operator invocations POST(*i*) and POST(*i'*) will give different results, even in this special case (unless *e* happens to be the last value of both types *T* and *T'*, of course, in which case the POST invocations are both undefined).

One important consequence of the foregoing is that the type of a given interval can't be inferred from the type of its begin and end points. It follows that—as indeed we already know from earlier chapters—interval selectors do need that "_*T*" qualifier, just as the "first" and "next" (etc.) operators do. Here are a couple of examples:

```
INTERVAL_INTEGER       ( [2:6] )
INTERVAL_EVEN_INTEGER  ( [2:6] )
```

The general format—assuming, as usual, closed:closed notation just for definiteness—is INTERVAL_*T* ([*b*:*e*]), where *b* and *e* are values of type *T* and *b* ≤ *e*.

A more general consequence is as follows. We've seen in particular that if *T'* is a proper subtype of *T*, then INTERVAL_*T'* isn't a subtype of INTERVAL_*T*. In fact, if *IT* is the interval type INTERVAL_*T*, then in general there's *no* interval type of the form INTERVAL_*T'*—let's call it *IT'*—that's a proper subtype of *IT*. For suppose, conversely, that such a type *IT'* does in fact exist. Let *i'* = [*b'*:*e'*] be an interval of type *IT'* such that *b'* ≠ *e'*. Since *IT'* is a subtype of *IT*, *i'* must be an interval of type *IT* as well. But even if *b'* and *e'* happen to be values of type *T*, *i'* can't possibly be an interval of type *IT*, because its contained points are determined by the successor function for *T'*, which by definition is distinct from the successor function for *T*. Contradiction!

Note: The remarks in the foregoing paragraph are broadly true, but there are some minor exceptions that we should at least mention in passing:

■ First, if *T'* is empty—see the answer to Exercise 6.5 in Chapter 6—then *IT'* is a subtype of all possible interval types; in fact, it's a *proper* subtype of all of them except for *IT'* itself. However, *IT'*, like *T'*, is empty in this case (it contains no intervals).

■ Second, if *T'* is a singleton type whose sole value is a value of type *T*—again see the answer to Exercise 6.5 in Chapter 6—then *IT'* is a subtype of *IT* after all, but it contains just one interval (necessarily a unit interval, of course).

■ Third (and perhaps more important than the previous two possibilities), it might be possible to define a type *IT'* that *is* a proper subtype of *IT*—for example, *IT'* might be defined to consist of just those intervals of type *IT* that happen to be unit intervals—but if *T* contains at least two points, then such a type *IT'* can't be defined by means of the interval type generator. Thus, it wouldn't be a type (a generated type, that is) of the form INTERVAL_*T'* as such. Please note, therefore, that (as we've more or less said already) when we use the term *interval type* in this book, we always mean, specifically, a type that's produced by some invocation of the INTERVAL type generator.

Next, we observe that intervals are of course values; like all values, therefore, they carry their type around with them, so to speak. Thus, if *i* is an interval, it can be thought of as carrying around with it a kind of flag that announces "I'm an interval of type INTERVAL_INTEGER" or "I'm an interval of type INTERVAL_EVEN_INTEGER" or "I'm an interval of type INTERVAL_DDATE" (etc., etc.). In fact, if we ignore the minor exceptions identified above, we can reasonably say that every interval carries exactly one type with it, and so we can speak unambiguously of *the* type of any given interval. (That type is of course the most specific type of the interval in question, but in effect it's the least specific type too, and indeed the declared type of any expression denoting it as well.)

Now consider the operator POST, which, given the interval *i* = [*b*:*e*], returns the immediate successor *e*+1 of the end point *e* of *i*. Now, the type of the argument *i* here is known and well defined; hence the applicable successor function is known as well, and so there's no need for POST to involve any kind of *_T* qualifier. Thus, the following is a valid POST invocation:

```
POST ( INTERVAL_INTEGER ( [2:6] ) )
```

The result, of course, is 7. By contrast, the POST invocation

```
POST ( INTERVAL_EVEN_INTEGER ( [2:6] ) )
```

returns 8, not 7.

It should be clear that remarks analogous to the foregoing apply equally to PRE, BEGIN, END, and indeed to all of the other generic interval operators, because the applicable successor function, when needed, is always known. In other words, the *only* interval operators that require that *_T* qualifier are interval selectors. (In fact, of course, interval selectors differ in kind from the other operators mentioned, inasmuch as their operands are points, not intervals. In this respect, they resemble the operators "first," "last," "next," and "prior," all of which take operands that are points, and all of which do need that *_T* qualifier.)

Allen's Operators Revisited

Suppose we're given three point types *T*, *T1*, and *T2*, such that *T1* and *T2* are distinct proper subtypes of *T*. To make the example a little more concrete, take *T* to be INTEGER, and take *T1* and *T2* to be "integers that are multiples of two" and "integers that are multiples of three," respectively.[18] Now let *p1* be a value (point) of type *T1* and let *p2* be a value of type *T2*. As we already know, then, the comparison

```
p1 = p2
```

---

[18] We deliberately choose a pair of types *T1* and *T2* that overlap, in the sense that they have values in common.

is certainly legal, and might even give TRUE (e.g., suppose *p1* and *p2* are both 18). Moreover, the comparison

```
p1 > p2
```

is also legal—at least, it would be unreasonable to define ">" in such a way as to make it not so—and of course it might give TRUE as well (e.g., suppose *p1* is 14 and *p2* is 9).

Given the foregoing state of affairs, let's see whether it makes any sense to generalize Allen's operators accordingly. For brevity, let's agree to use the shorthand names *IT*, *IT1*, and *IT2* to denote the interval types INTERVAL_T, INTERVAL_T1, and INTERVAL_T2, respectively. Then:

- Let *i1* = [*b1:e1*] be an interval of type *IT1*. Define *j1* = [*b1:e1*] to be the unique interval of type *IT* with the same begin and end points as *i1*. For example, if *b1* and *e1* are 2 and 6, respectively, then *i1* contains just the points 2, 4, and 6, while *j1* contains the points 2, 3, 4, 5, and 6.

- Similarly, let *i2* = [*b2:e2*] be an interval of type *IT2*, and define *j2* = [*b2:e2*] to be the unique interval of type *IT* with the same begin and end points as *i2*.

Now let *Op* denote any of Allen's operators apart from "="; then we can define *i1 Op i2* to be logically equivalent to *j1 Op j2*—though whether we'd really want to do so is another matter! Anyway, let's see how this proposed definition works out for each of the operators in turn:

- *Inclusion:* Let *i1* and *i2* be [4:8] and [3:12], respectively. Then *i1* ⊂ *i2* is true, and so of course are *i1* ⊆ *i2*, *i2* ⊃ *i2*, and *i2* ⊇ *i2*. Note, however, that (e.g.) *i1* ⊂ *i2* does *not* mean in this context that every point in *i1* is also a point in *i2*, a state of affairs that might immediately give us pause ... Do we really want to go down this path? Well, let's overlook such reservations and continue, at least for now.

- *BEFORE and AFTER:* Let *i1* and *i2* be [4:6] and [9:18], respectively. Then *i1* BEFORE *i2* is true, and so of course is *i2* AFTER *i1*.

- *OVERLAPS:* Let *i1* and *i2* be [4:10] and [9:18], respectively. Then *i1* OVERLAPS *i2* and *i2* OVERLAPS *i1* are both true—despite the fact that *i1* and *i2* have no points in common!

- *MEETS:* Let *i1* and *i2* be [4:8] and [9:18], respectively. Then *i1* MEETS *i2* and *i2* MEETS *i1* are both true.

- *MERGES:* As usual, *i1* MERGES *i2* is true if and only if *i1* OVERLAPS *i2* is true or *i1* MEETS *i2* is true (but OVERLAPS and MEETS now have extended definitions).

■ *BEGINS and ENDS:* Let *i1* and *i2* be [6:10] and [6:18], respectively. Then *i1* BEGINS *i2* is true. Similarly, let *i1* and *i2* be [14:18] and [6:18], respectively. Then *i2* ENDS *i1* is true.

It follows from all of the above that we can generalize the interval union, intersection, and difference operators as well (again, if we want to):

■ *UNION:* The definition remains unchanged—*i1* UNION *i2* is defined if and only if *i1* MERGES *i2* is true, in which case it returns [MIN{*b1,b2*}:MAX{*e1,e2*}]. Note, however, that the result is of type *IT*, not *IT1* or *IT2*. For example, let *i1* and *i2* be [4:10] and [9:18], respectively; then *i1* UNION *i2* is [4:18], containing the following points:

```
4 , 5, 6 , 7 , 8 , 9 , 10 , 11 , 12 , 13 , 14 , 15 , 16 , 17 , 18
```

■ *INTERSECT:* Again the definition remains unchanged—*i1* INTERSECT *i2* is defined if and only if *i1* OVERLAPS *i2* is true, in which case it returns [MAX{*b1,b2*}:MIN{*e1,e2*}]. Again, however, that the result is of type *IT*, not *IT1* or *IT2*. For example, let *i1* and *i2* be [4:10] and [9:18], respectively; then *i1* INTERSECT *i2* is [9:10], containing just the following points:

```
9 , 10
```

■ *MINUS:* Yet again the definition remains effectively unchanged—*i1* MINUS *i2* is defined if and only if (a) *i1* OVERLAPS *i2* is false (in which case *i1* MINUS *i2* reduces to simply *i1*), or (b) *j1* (not *i1*) contains either *b2* or *e2* but not both, or (c) exactly one of *i2* BEGINS *i1* and *i2* ENDS *i1* is true. Once again, however, the result is of type *IT*, not *IT1* or *IT2*. For example, let *i1* and *i2* be [4:10] and [9:18], respectively; then *i1* MINUS *i2* is [4:8], containing just the following points:

```
4 , 5 , 6 , 7 , 8
```

Finally, recall that the all important PACK operator is defined in terms of interval union and intersection, and so it follows that PACK too can be generalized along the foregoing lines. (So of course can UNPACK.) We leave the specifics as something for you to think about, if you're interested. Our own feeling, though, for what it's worth, is that these various generalized definitions—starting with interval inclusion and continuing with OVERLAPS, MEETS, and so on—display so much in the way of anomalous behavior that it would be better not to support them after all.

CONCLUDING REMARKS

In this chapter, we've examined, among many other things, type inheritance, both single and multiple—at least insofar as that concept applies to point and interval types—and the associated notions of ordering, precision, scale, successor function, and granularity. These various concepts, though distinct, are very much interwoven; in fact, they're interwoven in rather complicated ways, and it can sometimes be quite difficult to say just where the demarcations lie. What we've tried to do is pin down the distinctions among them (the concepts, that is) as precisely as possible, and thereby shed some light on a subject on which much of the existing literature seems to be very confusing—not to say confused.

EXERCISES

18.1 Define in your own terms:

a. Substitutability

b. Specialization by constraint

c. Generalization by constraint

18.2 What do you understand by the term *multiple inheritance*?

18.3 Let CHAR(*n*) denote a type whose values are character strings of at most *n* characters. Does CHAR(*n*) make sense as a point type?

18.4 Define a point type called MONEY, with the obvious semantics. Give definitions for all associated selectors and THE_ operators, also for the successor function and related operators (FIRST_MONEY, NEXT_MONEY, etc.).

18.5 Extend your answer to Exercise 18.4 to incorporate the necessary support for two distinct monetary scales, one expressed in terms of (say) dollars and the other in terms of cents.

ANSWERS

18.1

a. *Substitutability* is a term used in connection with operator invocations. It refers to the substitution of arguments, in the invocation in question, for the parameters of the operator in question. Let *Op* be an operator, let *P* be a parameter to *Op*, and let *P* be of declared type *T*. Further, let *P* not be subject to update. Then *The Principle of Value Substitutability* allows the argument (a value) substituted for *P* in any given invocation of *Op* to be of any subtype of *T*.

Suppose now that *P* is subject to update (so the corresponding argument expression is required to be a variable reference specifically). A *Principle of Variable Substitutability*, analogous to *The Principle of Value Substitutability*, would say that wherever an argument variable of type *T* is expected, a variable of any proper subtype of *T* is also permitted. In that case, it would be permitted, for example, to assign a value of type RECTANGLE to a variable of declared type SQUARE. Since rectangles generally aren't squares, such an assignment should clearly fail at run time, if not at compile time. For such reasons, a *Principle of Variable Substitutability* isn't normally adopted. *Note:* Object oriented languages typically do, however, allow such "variable substitutability" for certain special kinds of variables known as *objects*. They do so, somewhat suspectly, by not allowing invocations of update operators on such variables to give rise to a change of most specific type. One consequence of this approach is that if you define an "object class" called SQUARE, you must be prepared to deal with the fact that objects of that class might not correspond to squares in the real world but only to rectangles (because adjacent sides are of different lengths).

b. *Specialization by constraint* is the phenomenon whereby the result *x* of evaluating an expression of declared type *T* might have types *T1*, *T2*, ..., *Tn* in addition to type *T*, by virtue of the fact that each of *T1*, *T2*, ..., *Tn* is a proper subtype of *T* such that *x* satisfies the constraint that defines the values constituting that subtype.

c. *Generalization by constraint* is the phenomenon whereby the result *x* of evaluating an expression to be assigned to variable *V* of declared type *T* might cause the most specific type of *V*—necessarily a subtype of *T*—to be some proper supertype of the most specific type of the value being replaced by *x*.

18.2 *Multiple inheritance* is a term denoting the possibility that a type might have two or more distinct immediate supertypes—where type *T* is an *immediate* supertype of type *T'* if and only if it's a proper supertype of *T'* and there's no type *T"*, distinct from both *T* and *T'*, such that *T* is a proper supertype of *T"* and *T"* is a proper supertype of *T'*. *Note:* If and only if *T* is an immediate supertype of *T'* , then *T'* is an immediate subtype of *T*.

18.3   Let the characters in the character set from which strings of type CHAR(*n*) are drawn be totally ordered, with *lc* as the least character in that ordering and *gc* as the greatest, and let string comparisons be done in the usual way, character by character from left to right. Then

FIRST_CHAR(*n*) is the empty string and LAST_CHAR(*n*) is the string consisting of *n* occurrences of the character *gc*. For a given string *s* ≠ LAST_CHAR(*n*), of length *ls*, NEXT_CHAR(*s*) could be defined as follows:

Case 1: When *ls* < *n*, then *s* concatenated with *lc*.

Case 2: When *ls* = *n* and the rightmost character of *s* isn't *gc*, then the string formed by replacing that rightmost character by its immediate successor.

Case 3: When *ls* = *n* and the rightmost *k* characters of *s* are all *gc*, then the string consisting of the leftmost *ls* − (*k* + 1) characters of *s* followed by the character that's the immediate successor of the (*ls* − *k*)th character of *s*.

Therefore CHAR(*n*) is usable as a point type.[19] But does it make any *sense* as a point type? Possibly, and intervals such as INTERVAL_CHAR(30) (['Darwen':'Date']) might have some useful application. However, counterintuitive results might arise from the fact that, for example, 'Daszzzzzzzzzzzzzzzzzzzzzzzzzzzz' is a string in that interval.

Have you heard the one about the person who, looking in the bookstore for a book on hypnotism, discovered and bought the one titled *Guide to Hypnotism*? Disappointment ensued when she discovered she had purchased Volume 6 of a certain encyclopedia.

18.4
```
TYPE MONEY ORDINAL POSSREP DOLLARS_AND_CENTS { D_AND_C NUMERIC(9,2) } ;

    OPERATOR DOLLAR_AND_CENTS ( D_AND_C NUMERIC(9,2) ) RETURNS MONEY ;
        /* code to return the MONEY value corresponding */
        /* to the given NUMERIC(9,2) value D_AND_C      */
    END_OPERATOR ;

    OPERATOR THE_D_AND_C ( AMOUNT MONEY ) RETURNS NUMERIC(9,2) ;
        /* code to return the NUMERIC(9,2) value corresponding */
        /* to the given MONEY value AMOUNT                      */
    END OPERATOR ;

    OPERATOR "=" ( A1 MONEY , A2 MONEY ) RETURNS BOOLEAN ;
        RETURN ( THE_D_AND_C ( A1 ) = THE_D_AND_C ( A2 ) ) ;
    END OPERATOR ;

    OPERATOR ">" ( A1 MONEY , A2 MONEY ) RETURNS BOOLEAN ;
        RETURN ( THE_D_AND_C ( A1 ) > THE_D_AND_C ( A2 ) ) ;
    END OPERATOR ;

    OPERATOR FIRST_MONEY ( ) RETURNS MONEY ;
        RETURN DOLLARS_AND_CENTS ( -9999999.99 ) ;
    END OPERATOR ;
```

---

[19] By contrast, **Tutorial D**'s type CHAR is *not* so usable, because values of that type have no defined upper bound *n* on their length.

```
   OPERATOR LAST_MONEY ( ) RETURNS MONEY ;
      RETURN DOLLARS_AND_CENTS ( 9999999.99 ) ;
   END OPERATOR ;

   OPERATOR NEXT_MONEY ( AMOUNT MONEY ) RETURNS MONEY ;
      RETURN DOLLARS_AND_CENTS ( THE_D_AND_C ( AMOUNT ) + 0.01 ) ;
   END OPERATOR ;

   OPERATOR PRIOR_MONEY ( AMOUNT MONEY ) RETURNS MONEY ;
      RETURN DOLLARS_AND_CENTS ( THE_D_AND_C ( AMOUNT ) - 0.01 ) ;
   END OPERATOR ;
```

18.5
```
   TYPE CMONEY ORDINAL POSSREP DOLLARS_AND_CENTS { D_AND_C NUMERIC(9,2) } ;

   OPERATOR DOLLARS_AND_CENTS ( D_AND_C NUMERIC(9,2) ) RETURNS CMONEY ;
      /* code to return the CMONEY value corresponding */
      /* to the given NUMERIC(9,2) value D_AND_C        */
   END_OPERATOR ;

   OPERATOR THE_D_AND_C ( AMOUNT CMONEY ) RETURNS NUMERIC(9,2) ;
      /* code to return the NUMERIC(9,2) value corresponding */
      /* to the given CMONEY value AMOUNT                     */
   END_OPERATOR ;

   OPERATOR "=" ( A1 CMONEY , A2 CMONEY ) RETURNS BOOLEAN ;
      RETURN ( THE_D_AND_C ( A1 ) = THE_D_AND_C ( A2 ) ) ;
   END_OPERATOR ;

   OPERATOR ">" ( A1 CMONEY , A2 CMONEY ) RETURNS BOOLEAN ;
      RETURN ( THE_D_AND_C ( A1 ) > THE_D_AND_C ( A2 ) ) ;
   END_OPERATOR ;

   OPERATOR FIRST_CMONEY ( ) RETURNS CMONEY ;
      RETURN DOLLARS_AND_CENTS ( -9999999.99 ) ;
   END_OPERATOR ;

   OPERATOR LAST_CMONEY ( ) RETURNS CMONEY ;
      RETURN DOLLARS_AND_CENTS ( 9999999.99 ) ;
   END_OPERATOR ;

   OPERATOR NEXT_CMONEY ( AMOUNT CMONEY ) RETURNS CMONEY ;
      RETURN DOLLARS_AND_CENTS ( THE_D_AND_C ( AMOUNT ) + 0.01 ) ;
   END_OPERATOR ;

   OPERATOR PRIOR_CMONEY ( AMOUNT CMONEY ) RETURNS CMONEY ;
      RETURN DOLLARS_AND_CENTS ( THE_D_AND_C ( AMOUNT ) - 0.01 ) ;
   END_OPERATOR ;

   TYPE DMONEY ORDINAL IS CMONEY
      CONSTRAINT MOD ( CMONEY , 1.00 ) = 0.00
      POSSREP DOLLARS { D = THE_D_AND_C ( CMONEY ) } ;
```

Note: The constraint here requires the "cents" portion to be zero.

```
OPERATOR DOLLARS ( D_AND_C NUMERIC(7,0) ) RETURNS DMONEY ;
   /* code to return the DMONEY value corresponding */
   /* to the given NUMERIC(7,0) value D_AND_C       */
END_OPERATOR ;

OPERATOR THE_D_AND_C ( AMOUNT MONEY ) RETURNS NUMERIC(7,0) ;
   /* code to return the NUMERIC(7,0) value corresponding */
   /* to the given MONEY value AMOUNT                      */
END_OPERATOR ;

OPERATOR FIRST_DMONEY ( ) RETURNS DMONEY ;
   RETURN DOLLARS ( -9999999.00 ) ;
END_OPERATOR ;
```

Note: The "cents" portion of the argument to DOLLARS has to be zero, of course, as dictated by the type constraint for type DMONEY.

```
OPERATOR LAST_DMONEY ( ) RETURNS DMONEY ;
   RETURN DOLLARS ( 9999999.00 ) ;
END_OPERATOR ;

OPERATOR NEXT_DMONEY ( AMOUNT DMONEY ) RETURNS DMONEY ;
   RETURN DOLLARS ( THE_D ( AMOUNT ) + 1.00 ) ;
END_OPERATOR ;

OPERATOR PRIOR_DMONEY ( AMOUNT DMONEY ) RETURNS DMONEY ;
   RETURN DOLLARS ( THE_D ( AMOUNT ) - 1.00 ) ;
END_OPERATOR ;
```

Part IV

SQL SUPPORT

This is the final part of the main body of the book. It consists of just one rather lengthy chapter. In it, we examine the relevant features of the SQL standard and see how they measure up against all of the various concepts and techniques we've been describing in earlier parts of the book. By the way, do please note that we use the term *SQL* to mean the standard version of that language exclusively, not some proprietary dialect (barring explicit statements to the contrary). In particular, we follow the standard in assuming the pronunciation "ess cue ell," not "sequel," thereby saying things like *an* SQL table, not *a* SQL table.

Chapter 19

The SQL Standard

Standards are always out of date.
That's what makes them standards.

—Alan Bennett:
Forty Years On (1969)

Temporal database support was added to the SQL standard in the 2011 edition of that standard ("SQL:2011"—see reference [61]). In this chapter, we examine that support in some detail, and we analyze and assess it from the point of view of our own approach to temporal data as described in Parts II and III of this book. But we might as well give the game away right up front: While SQL's temporal features might reasonably be described as a step—possibly, in some respects, even a fairly large step—in the right direction, they nevertheless fail in all too many ways to solve (or, in some cases, even attempt to solve) all of the problems we identified in Parts II and III of this book.

We use the structure of earlier parts of this book as a loose organizing principle for the discussions that follow. In other words, we'll cover SQL's temporal features in a sequence that parallels, more or less, the sequence in which we described their counterparts in the chapters in earlier parts of the book. Recall, however, that Chapters 1-3 were basically just a refresher course on the relational model, and Chapters 4 and 5 were concerned merely with setting the scene, as it were; we didn't really start to get into our preferred approach to the problem until we reached Chapter 6, on intervals, and so that's where we'll start now.

PERIODS

SQL doesn't support intervals. In their place, it supports what it calls *periods*—but those periods aren't values in their own right (i.e., there are no period *types*); instead, they consist of explicit FROM-TO value pairs (typically pairs of column values, if we're talking about periods that happen to be represented within SQL tables specifically).[1] Note, moreover, that those periods are quite specifically temporal in nature; SQL has nothing corresponding to the general purpose

---

[1] Two points here: First, SQL couldn't call its periods intervals even if it wanted to, because it already uses the term *interval* to mean something else (actually a duration, such as 3 hours or 90 days). Second, in this chapter (and for obvious reasons) we use the SQL terms *table*, *row*, *column*, etc., not their relational counterparts, at least when we're discussing SQL specifically.

interval abstraction as described in earlier chapters. So an SQL version of the suppliers-and-shipments database—the first, simplest (?), but still fully temporal form—from Part II of this book might look as shown in Fig. 19.1.

S_FROM_TO

SNO	DFROM	DTO
S1	d04	d99
S2	d02	d05
S2	d07	d99
S3	d03	d99
S4	d04	d99
S5	d02	d99

SP_FROM_TO

SNO	PNO	DFROM	DTO
S1	P1	d04	d99
S1	P2	d05	d99
S1	P3	d09	d99
S1	P4	d05	d99
S1	P5	d04	d99
S1	P6	d06	d99
S2	P1	d02	d05
S2	P1	d08	d99
S2	P2	d03	d04
S2	P2	d09	d99
S3	P2	d08	d99
S4	P2	d06	d10
S4	P4	d04	d09
S4	P5	d05	d99

Fig. 19.1: SQL version of suppliers and shipments—sample values

Fig. 19.1 is basically a repeat of Fig. 5.3 from Chapter 5, except that:

■ We've renamed the "from" and "to" columns DFROM and DTO, respectively (D for during). *Note:* FROM and TO as such are reserved words in SQL and so can't be used as column names without being enclosed in what the standard calls double quotes (in other words, quotation marks). As for the tables themselves, we've named them S_FROM_TO and SP_FROM_TO as in Chapter 5, in order to stress the point that they do indeed have explicit "from" and "to" columns instead of a single "during" column.

■ We've replaced all of those *d10* "end of time" markers by the slightly more reasonable value *d99*. *Note:* As far as SQL is concerned, the actual end of time is DATE '9999-12-31' and the beginning of time is DATE '0001-01-01' (both values given here in the form of DATE literals, which by definition are accurate to the day—though SQL does also support finer granularities, of course, as we'll see later). Throughout this chapter, therefore, references to *d99* should be taken as denoting "the last day" as understood by SQL (i.e., December 31st, 9999).

■ As we've said, an SQL period is denoted by an explicit pair of "from" and "to" values, not by a single interval value. As a consequence, SQL has to specify the intended interpretation for such value pairs, and it plumps for the closed:open interpretation; that is, the "from" value denotes the first point contained in the period, and the "to" value denotes the point immediately following the last point contained in the period. For this reason, we've increased all of the "to" values in the figure (other than those "end of time" markers) by one day.

■ Following on from the previous point, however, there's a serious oddity here. Precisely because periods in SQL do use the closed:open interpretation, there's no way "the end of time" can actually be contained in such a period! If, as in Fig. 19.1, we specify a "to" value of *d99*, then the last day that's actually contained in the period in question is *d98*, which of course isn't "the end of time." On the other hand, we can't specify a "to" value of *d100*, because *d100* isn't legal as a DATE value in SQL.[2] To put the point another way, no "from" value can ever be equal to *d99*, and SQL has no way of representing the fact that some state of affairs holds on day *d99*.

Perhaps we should take a moment to consider SQL's rationale for not supporting period types as such. The following quote is taken from reference [65]:

Many treatments of temporal databases introduce a period data type,[3] defined as an ordered pair of two datetime values ... SQL:2011 has not taken this route. Adding a new data type to the SQL standard (or to an SQL product) is a costly venture because of the need to support the new data type in the tools and other software packages that form the ecosystem surrounding SQL. For example, if a period type were added to SQL, then it would have to also be added to the stored procedure language, to all database APIs such as JDBC, ODBC, and .NET, as well as to the surrounding technology such as ETL products, replication solutions, and others. There must also be some means of communicating period values to host languages that do not support period as a native data type, such as C or Java. These factors can potentially slow down the adoption of a new type for a long time.

But note the consequences of adopting this position. Among other things, it appears to mean that "the ecosystem surrounding SQL" simply has no knowledge or understanding of the temporal aspects of SQL databases. What are the implications of this state of affairs? For example, does it mean a natural language front end won't be able to handle temporal queries? And in any case, don't essentially the same arguments apply to user defined types, too—in fact, to all possible user defined types? Are we to conclude that the set of system defined types in SQL is cast in concrete and can never change?[4]

Anyway, here's the SQL definition—i.e., the CREATE TABLE statement—for table S_FROM_TO:

---

[2] What we mean here, of course, is that SQL's DATE type doesn't include a value representing January 1st, 10000; hence, DATE '10000-01-01' isn't a legal DATE literal in SQL.

[3] That "period data type" would more correctly be "period type generator."

[4] But of course it does change. For example, several new system defined types—type BOOLEAN among them—first appeared in the 1999 edition of the standard ("SQL:1999").

```
CREATE TABLE S_FROM_TO
     ( SNO    SNO  NOT NULL ,
       DFROM DATE NOT NULL ,
       DTO    DATE NOT NULL ,
       PERIOD FOR DPERIOD ( DFROM , DTO ) ,
       UNIQUE ( SNO , DPERIOD WITHOUT OVERLAPS ) ) ;
```

Explanation:

■ Table S_FROM_TO is, of course, a base table, in SQL terms. For simplicity, we'll adopt the convention throughout this chapter that the term *table*, unqualified, means a base table specifically, unless the context demands otherwise.

■ The PERIOD FOR specification defines columns DFROM and DTO to be the boundary columns for a period called DPERIOD. Note very carefully that DPERIOD itself is *not* a column. However, period names are allowed to appear in just one context where column references are permitted: They can be used as *period references* within certain boolean expressions, typically within a WHERE clause (see the discussion of Allen's operators, later in this section).[5]

■ The columns that are paired in a PERIOD FOR specification must both be of the same data type—either DATE, as in the example, or some SQL timestamp type such as TIMESTAMP(6).[6] As already indicated, therefore, SQL's periods are specifically temporal in nature; there's no support for intervals (or periods, rather) involving integers, or heights, or money values, or indeed anything else at all.

■ It follows from the previous point that the only point types supported in SQL are dates and SQL-style timestamps. For simplicity, throughout what follows we'll concentrate on type DATE only and ignore the other possibilities (i.e., we'll assume from this point forward that periods are always measured in days specifically), until further notice. Now, we saw in Chapter 6 that a point type requires niladic *first* and *last* operators and monadic *next* and *prior* operators. For type DATE, invocations of the *first* and *last* operators can be represented by literals denoting "the first day" and "the last day," respectively, as we've already seen. As for *next* (the successor function), the operator for adding one day suffices. Here's a simple example (note the syntax):[7]

```
DFROM + INTERVAL '1' DAY
```

---

[5] They can also appear in UNIQUE and FOREIGN KEY specifications (see the section "Database Design") and FOR PORTION OF specifications (see the section "Updates"), but not where column references as such can appear.

[6] Details of SQL date and timestamp types as such are beyond the scope of this book. If you want to know more, we refer you to either reference [47] or the SQL standard itself [61].

[7] The subexpression INTERVAL '1' DAY here is actually an example of an SQL interval literal (see footnote 1).

Prior is analogous, of course.

■ As already noted, SQL's periods implicitly use the closed:open interpretation, as in, e.g., [*d02,d05*). The PERIOD FOR specification in the definition of table S_FROM_TO effectively reflects this state of affairs by guaranteeing that, within any row of that table, the value of DFROM will always be less than that of DTO. More generally, in fact, SQL will enforce the constraint for *any* period, no matter how or where it's specified (in a table definition or elsewhere), that the "from" value is strictly less than the "to" value.[8] *Note:* The expression [*d02,d05*) isn't meant to be actual SQL syntax (we'll explain that actual syntax when we get to "period selectors," later in this section). However, it's at least true, as the example suggests, that SQL uses a comma, not a colon, as a separator.

■ Period DPERIOD in the example represents what SQL calls *application time*, which is the SQL term for valid time. (Recall from Chapter 17 that our own preferred term for this concept is *stated time*. In this chapter, however, we'll stay with the SQL term.)

■ No SQL table can ever have more than one application time period. Now, this rule is perhaps not *too* unreasonable, given that—as we effectively saw in Chapter 12, in the section "During Relvars Only"—it usually wouldn't make sense for a table to have more than one, anyway (though it might).[9] Observe, however, that the table in question had probably better be in 6NF—for otherwise the application time period will probably be "timestamping too much," as we put it in that discussion in Chapter 12. Note, therefore, that converting a nontemporal design into a satisfactory temporal analog will typically involve rather more than just adding an application time period to each nontemporal table (as indeed we also saw in Chapter 12).

■ We defer detailed explanation of the UNIQUE specification to the next section ("Database Design").[10] However, we remark that—regardless of whether WITHOUT OVERLAPS is specified—UNIQUE (SNO,DPERIOD...) effectively defines, not a key as such, but rather a proper superkey (see the answer to Exercise 13.2a in Chapter 13).

For completeness, we also show an SQL definition for table SP_FROM_TO:

---

[8] Except, arguably, for the case of the period specified by the time points *t1* and *t2* in FOR SYSTEM_TIME BETWEEN *t1* AND *t2* (see the section "System Time," later), where the closed:closed interpretation applies.

[9] Here repeated from Chapter 6 is an example where it does make sense: namely, relvar EMP, with attributes ENO, PRIMARY, and SECONDARY, where PRIMARY and SECONDARY show the intervals of time during which employee ENO received his or her primary and secondary education, respectively. See also Exercise A.3 in Appendix A.

[10] We could have used an SQL PRIMARY KEY specification in place of that UNIQUE specification, but we omit discussion of SQL's primary keys as such in this chapter because (as noted in Chapter 3) we prefer to downplay the idea of making one of possibly several keys primary, meaning it's somehow "more equal than all the others."

```
CREATE TABLE SP_FROM_TO
     ( SNO   SNO  NOT NULL ,
       PNO   PNO  NOT NULL ,
       DFROM DATE NOT NULL ,
       DTO   DATE NOT NULL ,
       PERIOD FOR DPERIOD ( DFROM , DTO ) ,
       UNIQUE ( SNO , PNO , DPERIOD WITHOUT OVERLAPS ) ,
       FOREIGN KEY ( SNO , PERIOD DPERIOD )
               REFERENCES S_FROM_TO ( SNO , PERIOD DPERIOD ) ) ;
```

The only new feature here is the FOREIGN KEY specification, an explanation of which we also defer to the next section ("Database Design").

"Period Selectors"

Since SQL has no period types, it also has no period variables. A fortiori, therefore, it has no period variable references, nor more generally does it have period expressions—i.e., expressions that return a period value—of any kind. It does, however, have a construct that might be thought of as a kind of "period selector" operator, and, as a special case of that construct, it does support a kind of "period literal." However, these constructs can appear in just two contexts—they can appear in a FOR PORTION OF specification, which we'll be discussing in the section "Updates" later, and they can also appear in a "period predicate" (which is a special kind of boolean expression), where they can be used to denote an operand, or both operands, to one of Allen's operators. The syntax is PERIOD (f,t), where f and t are expressions both of the same type, either DATE or some timestamp type.

> *Aside:* Don't be confused by this syntax: As already stated, SQL implicitly uses the closed:open interpretation, so the syntax PERIOD (f,t) denotes what would more conventionally be represented as $[f,t)$, or in closed:closed notation$[f,t-1]$. In this chapter, for reasons of explicitness and (we hope) clarity, we'll occasionally make use of $[f,t)$ as an abbreviation for PERIOD (f,t). *End of aside.*

Here then is a simple SQL query against table S_FROM_TO:

```
SELECT DISTINCT SNO
FROM   S_FROM_TO
WHERE  PERIOD ( DFROM , DTO ) OVERLAPS
       PERIOD ( DATE '2012-12-01' , DATE '2013-01-01' )
```

Observe that the OVERLAPS operands in this example are denoted by constructs—SQL calls them *period predicands*—that do look something like hypothetical "period selector" invocations, and the second in particular does look something like a hypothetical "period literal."

Note: In the common special case where a period predicand denotes a period that's explicitly defined to be part of some SQL table, the corresponding period name can be used in place of the corresponding "period selector." Thus, the foregoing SQL query might be simplified slightly to:

```
SELECT  DISTINCT SNO
FROM    S_FROM_TO
WHERE   DPERIOD OVERLAPS
        PERIOD ( DATE '2012-12-01' , DATE '2013-01-01' )
```

Period Operators

In Chapter 7, we discussed the following operators on intervals: BEGIN and END; PRE and POST; POINT FROM; and "∈" and "∋". So let p be an SQL period predicand, and let the FROM-TO pair denoted by p be $[f,t)$. Then the following table shows how analogs of those operators, applied to p, can be expressed in SQL:

Operator	SQL analog	
BEGIN	f	
END	t - '1' DAY	
PRE	f - '1' DAY	
POST	t	
POINT FROM	no direct support	/* see below */
∈	no direct support	/* see below */
∋	p CONTAINS x	/* see below */

For POINT FROM, of course, we can write simply f (or t - '1' DAY), but it's our responsibility to ensure the period in question does indeed contain just one day (no exception will be raised if it doesn't). As for "∈", the hypothetical expression "$x \in p$" can always be recast as p CONTAINS x (where x is any SQL expression that evaluates to a value of the applicable point type). Note carefully, however, that the point t is explicitly *not* contained in the period $[f,t)$.

Allen's Operators

As the sample query shown earlier suggests, the SQL syntax for invoking one of Allen's operators (*Op*, say) takes the usual infix form:

```
p1 Op p2
```

Let $[f1,t1)$ and $[f2,t2)$ be the FROM-TO pairs corresponding to the period predicands $p1$ and $p2$, respectively. Then the following table shows how Allen's operators can be expressed in SQL:

Operator	SQL analog
equality	*p1* EQUALS *p2*
includes	*p1* CONTAINS *p2*
properly includes	*no direct support*
is included in	*no direct support*
is properly included in	*no direct support*
BEFORE	*p1* PRECEDES *p2*
AFTER	*p1* SUCCEEDS *p2*
OVERLAPS	*p1* OVERLAPS *p2*
MEETS	*p1* IMMEDIATELY PRECEDES *p2* OR
	p1 IMMEDIATELY SUCCEEDS *p2*
MERGES	*no direct support*
BEGINS	*no direct support*
ENDS	*no direct support*

Points arising:

■ Note that SQL uses the same keyword, CONTAINS, to denote both "∋" and "⊇" (in other words, CONTAINS is overloaded).

■ It's a little odd that certain of the SQL expressions shown are actually longer (sometimes quite a bit longer) than the expressions they're explicitly defined to be "shorthand" for. For example, *p1* PRECEDES *p2* simply means $t1 \leq f2$, and *p1* IMMEDIATELY PRECEDES *p2* simply means $t1 = f2$. It's also odd that PERIOD $(f1,t1)$ = PERIOD $(f2,t2)$ is illegal, and yet $(f1,t1) = (f2,t2)$ is not only legal but means exactly the same as PERIOD $(f1,t1)$ EQUALS PERIOD $(f2,t2)$.

■ Of course, the cases where SQL has no direct support can always be worked around—but it's a pity that MERGES in particular has to be treated in this fashion. Here for the record is an SQL analog (not the only one possible, but perhaps the most obvious) of *p1* MERGES *p2*:

```
p1 OVERLAPS p2 OR
p1 IMMEDIATELY PRECEDES p2 OR
p1 IMMEDIATELY SUCCEEDS p2
```

Finally, in Chapter 7 we also defined an interval COUNT operator and interval UNION, INTERSECT, and MINUS operators. SQL has no counterparts to the last three. As for COUNT, it can be simulated by simply subtracting the applicable *from* value from the corresponding *to* value. For example, given the period [4,11), the corresponding count is 11 − 4 = 7. *Note:* We're pretending here for simplicity that SQL supports periods whose contained values are integers. In practice, of course, those contained points will be SQL datetime values; thus, the expression *to* − *from* will return an SQL-style interval (i.e., a duration), which will then have to be cast to the desired integer value, thus: CAST ((*to* − *from*) AS INTEGER).

PACK, UNPACK, and U_ Operators

SQL has no support for the PACK and UNPACK operators—unfortunately a rather serious omission! A fortiori, therefore, it also has no support for the generalized relational operators (U_join and the rest, also the U_ comparisons) described in Chapter 11. It also has no support for the U_update operators (U_INSERT and the rest) described in Chapter 16.

DATABASE DESIGN

Our discussions in the previous section tacitly assumed a "fully temporal" design. And the reason for that assumption was that, frankly, there's not much to be said—at least, not much of real interest, and certainly not much from a purely SQL perspective—about an SQL design that's merely semitemporal. Just for the record, however, SQL can of course use its existing DATE and TIMESTAMP data types as a basis for defining semitemporal tables. Here's a simple example. It's an SQL version of the design consisting of relvars S_SINCE and SP_SINCE from Chapter 14 (see Figs. 14.1 and 14.3 in that chapter). Note the SQL versions of Constraints SR6 and SR9 in particular.

```
CREATE TABLE S_FROM
     ( SNO          SNO      NOT NULL ,
       SNO_FROM     DATE     NOT NULL ,
       STATUS       INTEGER  NOT NULL ,
       STATUS_FROM  DATE     NOT NULL ,
       UNIQUE ( SNO ) ) ;

CREATE TABLE SP_FROM
     ( SNO      SNO  NOT NULL ,
       PNO      PNO  NOT NULL ,
       SP_FROM DATE NOT NULL ,
       UNIQUE ( SNO , PNO ) ,
       FOREIGN KEY ( SNO ) REFERENCES S_FROM ( SNO ) ) ;

CREATE ASSERTION SR6 CHECK ( NOT EXISTS
     ( SELECT * FROM S_FROM
       WHERE   STATUS_FROM < SNO_FROM ) ) ;

CREATE ASSERTION SR9 CHECK ( NOT EXISTS
     ( SELECT * FROM SP_FROM NATURAL JOIN S_FROM
       WHERE   SP_FROM < SNO_FROM ) ) ;
```

Now let's consider a fully temporal SQL design—a "historical tables only" design, in effect—for suppliers and shipments. Of course, we've already seen SQL definitions for tables S_FROM_TO and SP_FROM_TO, but now let's bring supplier status history back into the picture, so that the complete database definition looks as shown in Fig. 19.2. Sample values are shown in Fig. 19.3, an edited version of Fig. 14.5 from Chapter 14.

```
CREATE TABLE S_FROM_TO
     ( SNO    SNO   NOT NULL ,
       DFROM  DATE  NOT NULL ,
       DTO    DATE  NOT NULL ,
       PERIOD FOR DPERIOD ( DFROM , DTO ) ,
       UNIQUE ( SNO , DPERIOD WITHOUT OVERLAPS ) ,
       FOREIGN KEY ( SNO , PERIOD DPERIOD )
                 REFERENCES S_STATUS_FROM_TO ( SNO , PERIOD DPERIOD ) ) ;

CREATE TABLE S_STATUS_FROM_TO
     ( SNO     SNO     NOT NULL ,
       STATUS  INTEGER NOT NULL ,
       DFROM   DATE    NOT NULL ,
       DTO     DATE    NOT NULL ,
       PERIOD FOR DPERIOD ( DFROM , DTO ) ,
       UNIQUE ( SNO , DPERIOD WITHOUT OVERLAPS ) ,
       FOREIGN KEY ( SNO , PERIOD DPERIOD )
                 REFERENCES S_FROM_TO ( SNO , PERIOD DPERIOD ) ) ;

CREATE TABLE SP_FROM_TO
     ( SNO    SNO   NOT NULL ,
       PNO    PNO   NOT NULL ,
       DFROM  DATE  NOT NULL ,
       DTO    DATE  NOT NULL ,
       PERIOD FOR DPERIOD ( DFROM , DTO ) ,
       UNIQUE ( SNO , PNO , DPERIOD WITHOUT OVERLAPS ) ,
       FOREIGN KEY ( SNO , PERIOD DPERIOD )
                 REFERENCES S_FROM_TO ( SNO , PERIOD DPERIOD ) ) ;
```

Fig. 19.2: Historical tables only—SQL definitions

S_FROM_TO

SNO	DFROM	DTO
S2	d02	d05
S6	d03	d06
S7	d03	d99

S_STATUS_FROM_TO

SNO	STATUS	DFROM	DTO
S2	5	d02	d03
S2	10	d03	d05
S6	5	d03	d05
S6	7	d05	d06
S7	15	d03	d09
S7	20	d09	d99

SP_FROM_TO

SNO	PNO	DFROM	DTO
S2	P1	d02	d05
S2	P2	d03	d04
S2	P5	d03	d05
S6	P3	d03	d06
S6	P4	d04	d05
S6	P5	d04	d06
S7	P1	d03	d05
S7	P1	d06	d08
S7	P1	d09	d99

Fig. 19.3: Historical tables only—sample values

Note: The sample values shown in Fig. 19.3 aren't meant to correspond in any particular way to the ones shown in Fig. 19.1.

Now let's concentrate for the moment on table S_STATUS_FROM_TO. Here again is the UNIQUE specification for that table:

```
UNIQUE ( SNO , DPERIOD WITHOUT OVERLAPS )
```

In a nutshell, what this specification does is prevent the table from suffering from the redundancy and contradiction problems described in Chapters 13 and 14. (Note, however, that it doesn't prevent it from suffering from the circumlocution problem.) More precisely, what it says is this:

(*Expansion*)[11] Let row *r* in table S_STATUS_FROM_TO have SNO, STATUS, DFROM, and DTO values *sno*, *st*, *df*, and *dt*, respectively. Derive from that row *n* distinct rows, one for each DATE value *d* such that $df \leq d < dt$; each such derived row contains the SNO value *sno*, the STATUS value *st*, and one of those *n* DATE values, *d*. Let *T* be a table containing all such derived rows for all such rows *r* (and nothing else besides), and let D be the column of *T* that contains those DATE values *d*. Then no two rows of that table *T* have the same (SNO,D) value.

The UNIQUE specifications for S_FROM_TO and SP_FROM_TO are analogous, except that for those two tables the contradiction problem doesn't—in fact, can't—arise.

Now, you might be thinking from the foregoing that WITHOUT OVERLAPS is equivalent to our PACKED ON constraint, but it isn't, not quite (precisely because it doesn't address the circumlocution problem), and the tables are thus not necessarily kept in packed form.[12] Alternatively, you might be thinking it's equivalent to our WHEN / THEN constraint, but again it isn't. To see why not, consider what happens if S_STATUS_FROM_TO contains two rows for supplier S1 and status 20, one with period [*d04,d08*) and the other with period [*d06,d10*). Then the UNPACK implied by WHEN / THEN wouldn't give rise to a uniqueness constraint violation but would simply eliminate the duplicates (for days 6 and 7) implied by these two rows (i.e., WHEN / THEN addresses the contradiction problem, not the redundancy problem). By contrast, the same thing does *not* happen—i.e., a uniqueness constraint violation *would* occur—with WITHOUT OVERLAPS (check the "expansion" algorithm above).

We turn now to the FOREIGN KEY specifications. Here again is the specification for the foreign key from S_STATUS_FROM_TO to S_FROM_TO:

```
FOREIGN KEY ( SNO , PERIOD DPERIOD )
          REFERENCES S_FROM_TO ( SNO , PERIOD DPERIOD )
```

---

[11] The term *expansion* here derives from the term used in the standard itself [61] to describe this process—it's not a reference to the EXPAND operator from Chapter 8.

[12] In other words, we might say, loosely, that SQL supports WITHOUT OVERLAPS rather than WITHOUT MERGES, and WITHOUT MERGES would have been preferable.

Incidentally, note the tiny syntactic inconsistency here: The FOREIGN KEY specification uses the explicit keyword PERIOD, twice, but the "target" UNIQUE specification doesn't use it at all—indeed, it would fail on a syntax error if it did. Note also that referential actions such as cascade delete aren't allowed in connection with foreign key specifications like the one shown.

Anyway, what the foregoing foreign key specification says is this: If we perform (a) the expansion process described above on S_STATUS_FROM_TO and (b) the analogous process on S_FROM_TO, then (c) the combination of SNO and the column D containing the DATE values produced in that expansion, in the expanded form of S_STATUS_FROM_TO, will be a regular foreign key referencing the corresponding columns in the expanded form of S_FROM_TO. In other words, if some row in S_STATUS_FROM_TO contains the period [*f*,*t*), then there must be one or more rows in S_FROM_TO with the same supplier number and with periods that when merged—when packed together, in fact—include that same period [*f*,*t*).[13]

The foreign key specifications for S_FROM_TO and SP_FROM_TO are analogous, of course.

The net of the foregoing discussions is this: While SQL doesn't exactly support U_keys or foreign U_keys as such, it does support constructs of a somewhat similar nature. As a consequence, it manages to take care of six of "the nine requirements" from Chapter 14 in a fairly economical way, syntactically speaking. (The three it doesn't take care of are R2, R5, and R8, or in other words the ones that have to do with circumlocution.) So that's a definite plus. But there are some negatives as well:

- First, each of S_FROM_TO and S_STATUS_FROM_TO has a foreign key that references the other. As a consequence, the tables must be kept "in synch," as it were. Now, the operator we used for such purposes in Chapter 16 was multiple assignment (multiple *relvar* assignment, to be specific). Unfortunately, however, SQL has no direct support for such an operator, and the task of keeping those SQL tables in synch is thus not entirely straightforward. See the discussion of Updates U12, U13, and U14 in the section "Updates," later, for further explanation.

- Second, SQL doesn't support PACK and UNPACK, and so the user's job of making sure the various KEY and FOREIGN KEY constraints aren't violated is rather more difficult than it might otherwise be. In other words, keeping the tables in packed form, assuming that's what's wanted, is at least partly the user's problem—a problem that isn't made any easier by the fact that, as noted previously, SQL also fails to support the U_update operators (U_INSERT in particular).

---

[13] Note the phrase "one or more rows," however. We can't replace that phrase by "exactly one row," because there's no guarantee that S_FROM_TO is kept in packed form. Thus, for example, S_STATUS_FROM_TO might have a row for supplier S1 with period [*d04*,*d11*), while S_FROM_TO has two rows for supplier S1, one with period [*d04*,*d07*) and one with period [*d07*,*d11*).

QUERIES

Let's consider some of the sample queries from Chapter 15 and see how they might look in SQL, using the design of Fig. 19.2 and (where applicable) the sample values of Fig. 19.3. To be specific, we'll consider Queries Q1-Q3, Q5, Q6-Q7, and Q9.

Query Q1: Get the status of supplier S1 on day *dn*, together with the associated period (this is a slightly modified version of Query Q1 from Chapter 15).

```
SELECT  STATUS , DFROM , DTO
FROM    S_STATUS_FROM_TO
WHERE   SNO = SNO ( 'S1' )
AND     DPERIOD CONTAINS dn
```

This one is straightforward, in part because the WITHOUT OVERLAPS specification for table S_STATUS_FROM_TO is sufficient to guarantee that there'll be at most one row in that table that satisfies the condition in the WHERE clause. Note, however, that that WHERE clause makes it look as if that table has a column called DPERIOD, which of course it doesn't. More to the point, the result table doesn't either; in fact, the whole notion that columns DFROM and DTO together define an SQL-style period *doesn't apply* to that result table. (It's relevant to point out that the SELECT clause doesn't mention DPERIOD, as such, at all; instead, it mentions—it *has* to mention—the boundary columns DFROM and DTO.) Thus, while table S_STATUS_FROM_TO does have an associated "application time," the result table doesn't. *Application time periods don't "carry through" operational expressions*.

Now, this kind of situation is exactly what's to be expected of a language in which certain constructs are treated as special cases (instead of as what some writers like to call "first class objects") and well established language design principles such as orthogonality [35] are ignored. Be that as it may, the full consequences of such a situation aren't immediately clear, but here's one obvious one. Consider the following expression:

```
SELECT STATUS , DFROM , DTO
FROM ( SELECT *
       FROM   S_STATUS_FROM_TO ) AS POINTLESS
WHERE  SNO = SNO ( 'S1' )
AND    DPERIOD CONTAINS dn
```

This expression certainly looks as if it ought to be logically equivalent to the one shown previously, and indeed it would be, if DPERIOD were just a column name. In fact, however, it fails on a syntax error—the table denoted by the subquery in the FROM clause doesn't have a column, or indeed anything at all, called DPERIOD.[14] You might like to meditate on some of

---

[14] We could avoid that syntax error by replacing the reference to DPERIOD in the last line by the "period selector invocation," or period predicand, PERIOD (DFROM,DTO).

the implications of this state of affairs. For example, what happens if we use the expression SELECT * FROM S_STATUS_FROM_TO to define a view? Does that view inherit the period DPERIOD? *Answer*: No, it doesn't (because if it did, it could only be thanks to still more special casing—special casing on top of special casing, in fact).

By the way, the fact that periods don't carry through operational expressions is actually a logical consequence of what we earlier called the "not *too* unreasonable" rule that no SQL table can have more than one application time period, together with the rather less reasonable way that SQL has chosen to denote such periods—essentially, by representing what ought to be a general purpose construct in a special case way. For if periods did carry through such expressions, then the result of, e.g., a join might have two such periods (or, more generally, n such periods for some arbitrary $n > 1$), thereby violating that "not too unreasonable" rule.

Query Q2: Get pairs of supplier numbers such that the indicated suppliers were assigned their current status on the same day.

```
WITH t1 AS ( SELECT SNO , DFROM
             FROM   S_STATUS_FROM_TO
             WHERE  DPERIOD CONTAINS CURRENT_DATE ) ,
     t2 AS ( SELECT SNO AS XNO , DFROM
             FROM   t1 ) ,
     t3 AS ( SELECT SNO AS YNO , DFROM
             FROM   t1 ) ,
     t4 AS ( SELECT XNO , YNO
             FROM   t2 NATURAL JOIN t3 )
SELECT XNO , YNO FROM t4 WHERE XNO < YNO
```

For an explanation of the logic underlying the foregoing formulation, see Chapter 15. By the way, note the use here of (and syntax for) SQL's WITH construct. Note also the reference to the SQL "system variable"—also known as a *datetime value function*—CURRENT_DATE.

Query Q3: Get supplier numbers for suppliers who were able to supply both part P1 and part P2 at the same time.

```
SELECT DISTINCT t1.SNO
FROM    SP_FROM_TO AS t1 , SP_FROM_TO AS t2
WHERE   t1.SNO = t2.SNO
AND     t1.PNO = PNO ( 'P1' )
AND     t2.PNO = PNO ( 'P2' )
AND     t1.DPERIOD OVERLAPS t2.DPERIOD
```

Observe that we have to express this query, in part, in terms of an explicit invocation of one of Allen's operators (OVERLAPS, in the case at hand), because SQL doesn't support the higher level "U_" abstractions such as U_join.

Query Q5: Get supplier numbers for suppliers who, while they were under some specific contract, changed their status since they most recently became able to supply some part under that contract.

```
WITH t1 AS ( SELECT SNO , DFROM AS FX , DTO AS TX
             FROM   S_STATUS_FROM_TO ) ,
     t2 AS ( SELECT SNO , FX , TX , DFROM , DTO
             FROM   t1 NATURAL JOIN S_FROM_TO ) ,
     t3 AS ( SELECT SNO , FX , TX , DFROM , DTO
             FROM   t2
             WHERE  PERIOD ( DFROM , DTO ) CONTAINS
                                           PERIOD ( FX , TX ) ) ,
     t4 AS ( SELECT SNO , DFROM AS FY , DTO AS TY
             FROM   SP_FROM_TO ) ,
     t5 AS ( SELECT SNO , FX , TX , DFROM , DTO , FY , TY
             FROM   t4 NATURAL JOIN t3 ) ,
     t6 AS ( SELECT SNO , FX , TX , DFROM , DTO , FY , TY
             FROM   t5
             WHERE  PERIOD ( DFROM , DTO )
                                 CONTAINS PERIOD ( FY , TY ) ) ,
     t7 AS ( SELECT SNO , ( SELECT MAX ( FX )
                            FROM   t6 AS tt6
                            WHERE  tt6.SNO = t6.SNO
                            AND    tt6.DFROM = t6.DFROM
                            AND    tt6.DTO = t6.DTO ) AS BXMAX ,
                          ( SELECT MAX ( FY )
                            FROM   t6 AS tt6
                            WHERE  tt6.SNO = t6.SNO
                            AND    tt6.DFROM = t6.DFROM
                            AND    tt6.DTO = t6.DTO ) AS BYMAX
             FROM   t6 )
SELECT SNO FROM t7 WHERE BXMAX > BYMAX
```

Exercise: Does the formulation shown above assume that tables SP_FROM_TO and S_STATUS_FROM_TO are kept packed on DPERIOD? And should any of those SELECT clauses specify DISTINCT?

Query Q6: Get periods during which at least one supplier was under contract.

```
SELECT DISTINCT DFROM , DTO
FROM   S_FROM_TO
```

Of course, the result here won't be properly packed, in general, even if table S_FROM_TO is kept packed on DPERIOD. Now, we saw in Chapter 8 that PACK (at least in its simple "COLLAPSE" form) can be defined in terms of FORALL, EXISTS, "∈", FIRST, LAST, PRE, and POST—and since all of these constructs can at least be simulated in SQL, it follows that it must be possible to write an SQL expression that, given an SQL table, returns a packed version of that table. Like us, however, you probably wouldn't like to have to write such an expression, and we're not even going to try.

Note: Remarks somewhat analogous to the foregoing would apply to an SQL version of Query A, the query we used in Chapter 5 and elsewhere to demonstrate the desirability of supporting a "temporal projection" operator.

Query Q7: Suppose the result of Query Q6 is kept as a table BUSY. Use BUSY to get periods during which no supplier was under contract at all.

Let ETERNITY be the result of the following expression:

```
SELECT  TEMP.*
FROM    ( VALUES ( DATE '01-01-01' , DATE '9999-12-31' ) )
        AS TEMP ( DFROM , DTO )
```

Conceptually, then (and speaking rather loosely), what we need to do is unpack ETERNITY, unpack BUSY, form the difference between the two unpacked results in that order, and then pack that difference. The details are left as an exercise.[15]

Note: Remarks somewhat analogous to the foregoing would apply to an SQL version of Query B, the query we used in Chapter 5 and elsewhere to demonstrate the desirability of supporting a "temporal difference" operator.

Query Q9: Get (SNO,*pf,pt,df,dt*) quintuples such that supplier SNO was able to supply all parts with part numbers in the range [*pt,pf*) throughout the time period [*df,dt*).

SQL provides essentially no features at all to help with queries like this one. Note in particular that (a) the query involves nontemporal "periods" (or intervals)—namely, ranges of part numbers—and (b) the result ought by rights to involve two distinct "periods" (or intervals).

UPDATES

Now we consider some of the update examples from Chapter 16 (though we deliberately treat them here in a somewhat different order). Our first example (Update U12) involves just tables S_FROM_TO and S_STATUS_FROM_TO, not SP_FROM_TO.

Update U12: Add proposition(s) to show that supplier S9 has just been placed under contract, starting today, with status 15.

Tentative formulation:

---

[15] This is meant to be a joke. Apologies if you think it not in the best of taste.

```
INSERT INTO S_FROM_TO ( SNO , DFROM , DTO )
       VALUES ( SNO ( 'S9' ) , CURRENT_DATE , DATE '9999-12-31' ) ;

INSERT INTO S_STATUS_FROM_TO ( SNO , STATUS , DFROM , DTO )
       VALUES ( SNO ( 'S9' ) , 15 , CURRENT_DATE , DATE '9999-12-31' ) ;
```

Well, there are two problems here. The first is that each of the tables has a foreign key that references the other, and so they really need to be updated "simultaneously." But SQL doesn't support multiple assignment on tables. Somewhat unfortunately, therefore, what we have to do is wrap the two updates up into a transaction and defer the constraint checking to some later time (COMMIT time at the latest). *Note:* Actually, SQL has no explicit support for *single* table assignment, let alone support for the multiple version that we'd like here. Of course, it does support the INSERT, DELETE (etc.), shorthands, but again only in "single assignment" form.

The second problem is those two CURRENT_DATE references. In order to guarantee that both of the inserted rows wind up containing the exact same DFROM value, we ought really to "code defensively" by (a) assigning the value of CURRENT_DATE to some local variable (X, say) before doing either of the INSERTs, and then (b) replacing those separate references to CURRENT_DATE in those two INSERT statements by references to X instead.

Update U13: Remove all proposition(s) showing supplier S7 as being under contract.

Again several updates are needed, and they need to be wrapped up into a transaction (though again we won't bother to show the transaction details):

```
DELETE FROM SP_FROM_TO WHERE SNO = SNO ( 'S7' ) ;

DELETE FROM S_STATUS_FROM_TO WHERE SNO = SNO ( 'S7' ) ;

DELETE FROM S_FROM_TO WHERE SNO = SNO ( 'S7' ) ;
```

Note that (with reference to the sample values shown in Fig. 19.3), some of the rows we're deleting here represent current beliefs about past states of affairs.

Update U14: Supplier S7's current contract has just been terminated. Update the database accordingly.

```
SET X = CURRENT_DATE ;
SET Y = X + INTERVAL '1' DAY ;

UPDATE S_FROM_TO
SET    DTO = Y
WHERE  SNO = SNO ( 'S7' )
AND    DPERIOD CONTAINS X ;
```

```
UPDATE S_STATUS_FROM_TO
SET    DTO = Y
WHERE  SNO = SNO ( 'S7' )
AND    DPERIOD CONTAINS X ;

UPDATE SP_FROM_TO
SET    DTO = Y
WHERE  SNO = SNO ( 'S7' )
AND    DPERIOD CONTAINS X ;
```

Note the slight trickiness arising here in connection with the new DTO values.[16] Once again these statements ought really all to be wrapped up into a transaction, of course.

Update U4: Add the proposition "Supplier S2 was able to supply part P4 on day 2."

```
INSERT INTO SP_FROM_TO ( SNO , PNO , DFROM , DTO )
        VALUES ( SNO ( 'S2' ) , PNO ( 'P4' ) , d02 , d03 ) ;
```

But suppose the proposition had specified part P5 instead of P4. Then if we were to insert just the corresponding row into SP_FROM_TO, that table would contain the following two rows—

SNO	PNO	DFROM	DTO
S2	P5	*d02*	*d03*

SNO	PNO	DFROM	DTO
S2	P5	*d03*	*d05*

—and thus would no longer be properly packed, even if it was so before. Now, when we were faced with this problem in Chapter 16, we fixed it by defining a new operator, called U_INSERT. But SQL has no support for "U_" operators of any kind, and so the problem is simply passed back to the user.

Update U5: Remove the proposition "Supplier S6 was able to supply part P3 from day 3 to day 5, inclusive" (in other words, after the specified removal has been performed, the database shouldn't show supplier S6 as supplying part P3 on any of days 3, 4, or 5).

```
DELETE
FROM   SP_FROM_TO
WHERE  SNO = SNO ( 'S6' )
AND    PNO = PNO ( 'P3' )
AND    DPERIOD EQUALS PERIOD ( d03 , d06 ) ;
```

---

[16] That particular trickiness could be avoided by replacing the three UPDATE statements by three statements of the form DELETE FROM *t* FOR PORTION OF DPERIOD FROM X TO DATE '9999-12-31' (where *t* is S_FROM_TO, S_STATUS_FROM_TO, or SP_FROM_TO, as applicable). We'll be discussing FOR PORTION OF specifications in a few moments, under Update U5.

Now, this formulation does happen to work, because SP_FROM_TO does happen to contain a row satisfying exactly the specified conditions. But consider the following modified version of the example. Suppose the proposition to be removed had been "Supplier S7 was able to supply part P1 from day 4 to day 11." Then the corresponding DELETE—

```
DELETE
FROM    SP_FROM_TO
WHERE   SNO = SNO ( 'S7' )
AND     PNO = PNO ( 'P1' )
AND     DPERIOD EQUALS PERIOD ( d04 , d12 ) ;
```

—will have no effect. However, SQL does support a FOR PORTION OF clause on DELETE (referencing, specifically, the application time period), such that the desired removal in the example can be effected thus:

```
DELETE
FROM    SP_FROM_TO FOR PORTION OF DPERIOD FROM d04 TO d12
WHERE   SNO = SNO ( 'S7' )
AND     PNO = PNO ( 'P1' ) ;
```

The FOR PORTION OF clause applies, in effect, to the table identified by the table reference in the immediately preceding FROM clause.[17] It provides a limited version of the functionality provided by PORTION as described in Chapter 16. The general syntax is:

```
FOR PORTION OF p FROM t1 TO t2
```

Here *p* is the name of the application time period and *t1* and *t2* are expressions denoting values of the applicable SQL datetime type. Thus, what happens in the example—conceptually, at any rate[18]—is this:

1. Let table *t1* contain just those rows of SP_FROM_TO that satisfy the boolean expression in the WHERE clause (i.e., the rows for supplier S7 and part P1).

2. Let table *t2* contain just those rows of *t1* that satisfy the boolean expression DPERIOD OVERLAPS [*d04,d12*].

---

[17] In SQL, therefore, the PORTION clause appears before the WHERE clause, while in **Tutorial D** it's the other way around (speaking *very* loosely in both cases). Given the semantics, q.v., the latter seems to make more intuitive sense.

[18] We say "conceptually" because the procedure as we describe it talks in terms of packing and unpacking certain tables, and of course SQL doesn't actually support such operators. (Technically speaking, in fact, the tables in question don't even have any periods, as such, to serve as a basis for doing that packing and unpacking anyway, since periods don't carry through operational expressions.) By the way, the procedure in question also accounts for the following delightful statement in the SQL standard [61]: "[The] primary effect of a <delete statement: searched> that [specifies] FOR PORTION OF on a base table *T* is to insert zero, one, or two new rows into *T* for each row that is deleted from *T*."

3. Let table *t3* contain just one row: namely, some row from *t2*.

4. Let table *t4* be the result of unpacking *t3* on DPERIOD.

5. Let table *t5* be the result of removing from *t4* all rows whose DPERIOD values (which are all "unit periods," of course) are included in [*d04,d12*).

6. Let table *t6* be the result of packing *t5* on DPERIOD.

7. Let table *t7* be the result of replacing *t3*, in SP_FROM_TO, by *t6*.

8. Repeat Steps 3-7 for each row of *t2* in turn.

Let's see how this procedure works out in detail for the case at hand:

- *t1* consists of the following three rows (we've labeled them for future reference):

x1

SNO	PNO	DFROM	DTO
S7	P1	*d03*	*d05*

x2

SNO	PNO	DFROM	DTO
S7	P1	*d06*	*d08*

x3

SNO	PNO	DFROM	DTO
S7	P1	*d09*	*d99*

- *t2* is the same as *t1*.

- Let *t3* be the table containing just row *x1*. Then unpacking *t3* produces a table *t4* containing just two rows, for [*d03,d04*) and [*d04,d05*), and removing the rows whose DPERIOD values are included in [*d04,d12*) produces a table *t5* containing just one row, for [*d03,d04*). Packing *t5* then produces *t6*, which is identical to *t5* in this case. Thus, the effect of this step is to replace *x1* in SP_FROM_TO by a row for [*d03,d04*).

- Next, let *t3* be the table containing just row *x2*. Then unpacking *t3* produces a table *t4* containing just two rows, for [*d06,d07*) and [*d07,d08*), and removing the rows whose DPERIOD values are included in [*d04,d12*) produces an empty table *t5*. Packing *t5* produces *t6*, which is also empty. Thus, the effect of this step is simply to remove *x2* from SP_FROM_TO.

■ Next, let *t3* be the table containing just row *x3*. Then unpacking *t3* produces a table *t4* containing 90 rows, for [*d09,d10*), [*d10,d11*), ..., and [*d98,d99*). Removing the rows whose DPERIOD values are included in [*d04,d12*) produces a table *t5* containing all except the first three of these 90 rows. Packing *t5* produces *t6*, which contains just one row, for [*d12,d99*]. Thus, the effect of this step is to replace *x3* in SP_FROM_TO by a row for [*d12,d99*).

So the final value of SP_FROM_TO is as follows (the only change is, of course, in the highlighted rows, i.e., the ones for supplier S7 and part P1):

SNO	PNO	DFROM	DTO
S2	P1	*d02*	*d05*
S2	P2	*d03*	*d04*
S2	P5	*d03*	*d05*
S6	P3	*d03*	*d06*
S6	P4	*d04*	*d05*
S6	P5	*d04*	*d06*
S7	***P1***	***d03***	***d04***
S7	***P1***	***d12***	***d99***

By the way, suppose we now execute the following INSERT (which can be regarded, a trifle loosely, as the inverse of the foregoing DELETE):

```
INSERT INTO SP_FROM_TO ( SNO , PNO , DFROM , DTO )
        VALUES ( SNO ( 'S7' ) , PNO ( 'P1' ) , d04 , d12 ) ;
```

Here's the result (showing the rows for S7 and P1 only, for simplicity):

SNO	PNO	DFROM	DTO
. .	. .	. . .	. . .
S7	P1	*d03*	*d04*
S7	***P1***	***d04***	***d12***
S7	P1	*d12*	*d99*

The point about this example, of course, is that the three rows for S7 and P1 in the result are *not* automatically packed together into one.

Note finally that FOR PORTION OF can be used with UPDATE as well as DELETE. The specifics are essentially as for the DELETE case, and we omit the details here, except to note that—in contrast to PORTION UPDATE as discussed in Chapter 16—the SET clause in such an UPDATE isn't allowed to assign to either the "from" or the "to" column of the application time period.

SYSTEM TIME

In addition to application time, SQL also supports *system time*, which is the SQL term for transaction time. (Our own preferred term for this concept is *logged time*, as you'll probably recall; in this chapter, however, we'll stay with the SQL term.) Now, you'll probably also recall that the approach we proposed to this issue in Chapter 17 involved having separate logged time relvars, automatically maintained by the DBMS as—in effect—views of the system log. But SQL doesn't do anything like that. Instead, it allows tables to have an explicit *system time period* (at most one such per table), instead of or as well as an explicit application time period. Note, therefore, that *any* table—any base table, that is—can have a system time period, regardless of whether or not it's a historical table in the sense in which we've been using this latter term in this chapter so far.[19] For simplicity, therefore, let's begin by looking at an example of a "nonhistorical" table with a system time period. To be specific, let's suppose for the sake of the example that we want to keep system time information, but not application time information, for suppliers and their status values. Then instead of S_STATUS_FROM_TO, we might define a table XS_STATUS_FROM_TO that looks like this:

```
CREATE TABLE XS_STATUS_FROM_TO
     ( SNO    SNO      NOT NULL ,
       STATUS INTEGER NOT NULL ,
       XFROM  TIMESTAMP(12) GENERATED ALWAYS AS ROW START NOT NULL ,
       XTO    TIMESTAMP(12) GENERATED ALWAYS AS ROW END   NOT NULL ,
       PERIOD FOR SYSTEM_TIME ( XFROM , XTO ) ,
       UNIQUE ( SNO ) ,
       FOREIGN KEY ( SNO ) REFERENCES XS_FROM_TO ( SNO ) )
       WITH SYSTEM VERSIONING ;
```

Explanation:

■ Observe first that table XS_STATUS_FROM_TO has just two "regular" columns, SNO and STATUS. These are the only columns users can update directly (see the subsection "Updates on System-Versioned Tables" below).

■ The system time period—which, as usual in SQL, uses the closed:open interpretation—has the required name SYSTEM_TIME. The PERIOD FOR SYSTEM_TIME specification defines columns XFROM and XTO—which for the sake of the example we've defined to

---

[19] But the table in question had better be in 6NF, for otherwise that system time period will probably be "timestamping too much" once again.

be of type TIMESTAMP(12), meaning times that are accurate to the picosecond—to be the boundary columns for that period.

■ The specifications GENERATED ALWAYS AS ROW START (on XFROM) and GENERATED ALWAYS AS ROW END (on XTO) are required. That's because values of those columns aren't assigned by explicit user updates in the usual way but are instead assigned automatically by the system (again, see the subsection "Updates on System-Versioned Tables" below).

■ The specification WITH SYSTEM VERSIONING is actually optional, but we'll treat it as required until further notice. Note, however, that if it appears, then PERIOD FOR SYSTEM_TIME must be specified as well.

■ The remaining specifications are discussed in the next subsection but one, "UNIQUE and FOREIGN KEY Specifications for System-Versioned Tables."

Updates on System-Versioned Tables

Regardless of whether or not it has an application time period, a table for which WITH SYSTEM VERSIONING is specified is called a *system-versioned* table. Consider the system-versioned table XS_STATUS_FROM_TO. When it's first defined, that table is empty, of course. Suppose we now execute the following INSERT statement:

```
INSERT INTO XS_STATUS_FROM_TO ( SNO , STATUS )
       VALUES ( SNO ( 'S1' ) , 20 ) ;
```

Further, suppose this INSERT statement is executed at time *t02* by the system clock.[20] Then the row that's actually inserted looks like this:

SNO	STATUS	XFROM	XTO
S1	20	*t02*	*t99*

Observe, therefore, that the user does *not*—in fact, *must* not—specify explicit values to be inserted into columns XFROM and XTO; instead, the system automatically inserts the timestamp *t02* in the XFROM position and "the end of time" timestamp *t99* in the XTO position. *Note:*

---

[20] The standard (reference [61]) doesn't actually mention the system clock; instead, it just says there's something called *the transaction timestamp*, which (a) is required to remain constant throughout the life of the transaction in question, (b) is used as the source for those XFROM and XTO values, and (c) is presumably distinct for distinct transactions, though the standard doesn't actually seem to come out and say as much anywhere. In the example being considered here, therefore, it's necessary to assume that the INSERT, UPDATE, and DELETE statements are each part of a separate transaction. See Exercise 19.9 at the end of the chapter for further discussion.

Here and elsewhere in this chapter we use *t99* to denote the maximum value of type TIMESTAMP(12). For the record, the actual SQL value would be:

```
TIMESTAMP '9999-12-31 23:59:59.999999999999'
```

Now suppose we execute the following UPDATE statement:

```
UPDATE XS_STATUS_FROM_TO
SET    STATUS = 25
WHERE  SNO = SNO ( 'S1' ) ;
```

Further, suppose this UPDATE statement is executed at time *t06* by the system clock. After the UPDATE, then, the table looks like this:

SNO	STATUS	XFROM	XTO
S1	25	*t06*	*t99*
S1	20	*t02*	*t06*

In other words, the UPDATE in this example does two things:

- It inserts a new row for supplier S1 with STATUS value 25, XFROM value *t06*, and XTO value *t99*.

- It also replaces the old row for supplier S1 by a new row that's identical to that old row except that the XTO value is *t06* instead of *t99*.

  Aside: Suppose the "new" STATUS value happens to be the same as the "old" one (i.e., suppose the SET clause in the UPDATE specified STATUS = 20 instead of STATUS = 25). Then a new row will still be inserted, with the result that the table overall will no longer be packed on SYSTEM_TIME, even if it was so before. *End of aside.*

Finally, suppose we subsequently execute the following DELETE statement:

```
DELETE
FROM   XS_STATUS_FROM_TO
WHERE  SNO = SNO ( 'S1' ) ;
```

Further, suppose this DELETE statement is executed at time *t45* by the system clock. After the DELETE, then, the table looks like this:

SNO	STATUS	XFROM	XTO
S1	25	*t06*	*t45*
S1	20	*t02*	*t06*

In other words, the DELETE doesn't actually delete anything; instead, it simply replaces the XTO value in the "current row" for supplier S1 by *t45*. *Note:* The current row for supplier S1 is, of course, the row for supplier S1 in which the XTO value is *t99* (see the next subsection for further discussion). After the DELETE, there's no current row for supplier S1 at all.

Observe now that current rows are the only ones that can be updated[21]—once a "historical" row gets into the table (see the subsection immediately following), it's there forever, and it never changes (though of course it can be queried, as we'll see).

To sum up: The system time columns in a system-versioned table are effectively invisible as far as update operations are concerned—they're maintained entirely, and of course desirably, by the system, not the user, and there's no way the user can assign values to those columns directly. Note the following also:

- Let *C* be a contract for some supplier S*x*.

- Let *xcf* and *xct* be the minimum XFROM value in table XS_STATUS_FROM_TO for contract *C* and the maximum XTO value in table XS_STATUS_FROM_TO for contract *C*, respectively.

- Let *t* be an arbitrary time such that $xcf \leq t < xct$.

- Then table XS_STATUS_FROM_TO contains exactly one row for supplier S*x* in which the system time period contains that value *t*.

In other words, XS_STATUS_FROM_TO contains the total status history for contract *C*, without any redundancy or gaps (though not necessarily without circumlocution).

UNIQUE and FOREIGN KEY Specifications for System-Versioned Tables

Every row in a system-versioned table is either a current row or a historical row. If as in our example the system time end column is called XTO, then a current row is, as already indicated, a row in which the XTO value is "the end of time." A historical row is a row that's not current.

---

[21] As a consequence, DELETE and UPDATE on a table with system time don't need (and don't allow) a FOR PORTION OF clause that references the system time period.

Observe now that the UNIQUE and FOREIGN KEY specifications in the table definition for a system-versioned table apply to the current rows only. In other words, in the case of table XS_STATUS_FROM_TO:

- The specification UNIQUE (SNO) says there's at most one current row in that table at any given time for a given supplier number.

- The specification FOREIGN KEY (SNO) REFERENCES XS_FROM_TO (SNO) says that for every current row in the table at any given time, there's exactly one current row in table XS_FROM_TO with the same supplier number.[22] In fact, of course, there'll be a foreign key specification on XS_FROM_TO that "goes the other way" as well, thanks to our usual denseness requirements: For every current row in XS_FROM_TO at any given time, there'll be exactly one current row in XS_STATUS_FROM_TO with the same supplier number.

Now, the foregoing rules are perhaps reasonable, given that historical rows are never updated and can therefore never violate any constraints.[23] At the same time, however, they do seem a little questionable ... What's really going on here is this: A system-versioned table like XS_STATUS_FROM_TO is really a kind of shorthand for a combination of two separate tables, one current and one historical. And it might be clearer to make this fact explicit, somewhat along the lines suggested in Chapters 12-15 in connection with our own "preferred approach" to design (though there we were talking about application time, not system time). Then there'd be no need to play the foregoing kinds of games with SQL's existing UNIQUE and FOREIGN KEY syntax. On the other hand, making the separation explicit might make certain queries more complex, unless the system provides some appropriate shorthands.

> *Aside:* IBM's DB2 product, which does make the separation explicit, shows what such shorthands might look like in practice. By the way, it's worth noting that there could be certain administrative advantages to making the separation explicit. For example, it might be desirable to have two different indexes, one on the current table and one on the historical table; or it might be desirable to be able to carry out recovery operations on the two tables separately. But these are pragmatic issues, of course, having to do with the way the implementation in question happens to be designed. Ideally, therefore, they should have no bearing on what the user interface looks like. *End of aside.*

---

[22] Of course, we're assuming the existence here of another system-versioned table, XS_FROM_TO, with the obvious definition and semantics.

[23] More precisely, they can never violate any constraints that were in effect at the time they appeared in the table.

Queries on System-Versioned Tables

By default, queries on a system-versioned table apply only to the current rows (i.e., they behave as if the historical rows simply weren't there). Thus, if table XS_STATUS_FROM_TO contains just two rows right now, as follows—

SNO	STATUS	XFROM	XTO
S1	25	*t06*	*t99*
S1	20	*t02*	*t06*

—then the query

```
SELECT  STATUS
FROM    XS_STATUS_FROM_TO
WHERE   SNO = SNO ( 'S1' )
```

returns the following result:[24]

STATUS
25

To query historical rows, or more generally to query both current and historical rows, we can qualify the pertinent table reference (in the FROM clause) by a "FOR SYSTEM_TIME ..." specification, as in this example:

```
SELECT  STATUS , XFROM , XTO
FROM    XS_STATUS_FROM_TO FOR SYSTEM_TIME AS OF t04
WHERE   SNO = SNO ( 'S1' )
```

Result (see further explanation below):

STATUS	XFROM	XTO
20	*t02*	*t06*

---

[24] The absence of any double underlining in this result and the next is *not* a mistake [25].

Note that this result does have XFROM and XTO columns (of course), but it doesn't have a system time period as such—like application time periods, system time periods don't "carry through" operational expressions.

The following FOR SYSTEM_TIME options are supported (*t*, *t1*, and *t2* are expressions denoting timestamps):

- FOR SYSTEM_TIME AS OF *t*

  Selects rows whose system time period contains *t*.

- FOR SYSTEM_TIME FROM *t1* TO *t2*

  Selects rows whose system time period overlaps the closed:open period [*t1*:*t2*).

- FOR SYSTEM_TIME BETWEEN *t1* AND *t2*

  Selects rows whose system time period overlaps the closed:closed period [*t1*:*t2*].

The semantics are as indicated.[25] Observe that FOR SYSTEM_TIME can be thought of as providing a kind of FOR PORTION OF functionality, albeit for queries instead of updates. (On the other hand, FOR SYSTEM_TIME is used to qualify a specific reference to a specific table—typically within a FROM clause within a SELECT expression—whereas FOR PORTION OF is used, in effect, to qualify a DELETE or UPDATE statement as such.) Omitting the FOR SYSTEM_TIME specification entirely is equivalent to specifying FOR SYSTEM_TIME AS OF CURRENT_TIMESTAMP.

Tables with System Time but without WITH SYSTEM VERSIONING

Finally, recall that WITH SYSTEM VERSIONING is in fact optional. However, a table with system time for which WITH SYSTEM VERSIONING isn't specified doesn't really support much by way of "transaction time history" at all (at least, not as that term is usually understood), even though it does have a system time period. Certainly the rows in such a table are all current ones—there aren't any historical rows. Thus, INSERT on such a table behaves just as it does for a system-versioned table; UPDATE does change the system start time in affected rows but doesn't insert any "history" rows; and DELETE simply removes affected rows, again without inserting any "history" rows. In consequence, every row in such a table contains (a) a system

---

[25] In fact, FOR SYSTEM_TIME specifications are explicitly defined to be shorthand for certain boolean expressions, referencing the boundary columns of the system time period as appropriate, that logically belong in the WHERE clause (indeed, users could simply write out those boolean expressions in the WHERE clause for themselves, if they wanted to). But it does seem a little odd that SQL seems to think such specifications are useful in connection with system time periods but not application time periods. (We note in passing that IBM's DB2 product does support them for the latter as well as the former.) By the way: What happens in the case of BETWEEN if the timestamps represented by *t1* and *t2* are the beginning and end of time, respectively?

start time indicating when that row was last updated (or inserted) and (b) a system end time that's always equal to "the end of time."

BITEMPORAL TABLES

An SQL table can have both an application time period and a system time period. Everything we've said in previous sections regarding tables with just one of the two applies equally to such "bitemporal tables," mutatis mutandis (note, however, that *bitemporal table* isn't an official SQL term). Here by way of example are definitions for bitemporal versions (with system versioning) of tables S_FROM_TO and S_STATUS_FROM_TO:

```
CREATE TABLE BS_FROM_TO
     ( SNO   SNO  NOT NULL ,
       DFROM DATE NOT NULL ,
       DTO   DATE NOT NULL ,
       PERIOD FOR DPERIOD ( DFROM , DTO ) ,
       UNIQUE ( SNO , DPERIOD WITHOUT OVERLAPS ) ,
       FOREIGN KEY ( SNO , PERIOD DPERIOD )
          REFERENCES BS_STATUS_FROM_TO ( SNO , PERIOD DPERIOD ) ,
       XFROM  TIMESTAMP(12) GENERATED ALWAYS AS ROW START NOT NULL ,
       XTO    TIMESTAMP(12) GENERATED ALWAYS AS ROW END   NOT NULL ,
       PERIOD FOR SYSTEM_TIME ( XFROM , XTO ) )
       WITH SYSTEM VERSIONING ;

CREATE TABLE BS_STATUS_FROM_TO
     ( SNO    SNO      NOT NULL ,
       STATUS INTEGER NOT NULL ,
       DFROM  DATE    NOT NULL ,
       DTO    DATE    NOT NULL ,
       PERIOD FOR DPERIOD ( DFROM , DTO ) ,
       UNIQUE ( SNO , DPERIOD WITHOUT OVERLAPS ) ,
       FOREIGN KEY ( SNO , PERIOD DPERIOD )
               REFERENCES BS_FROM_TO ( SNO , PERIOD DPERIOD ) ,
       XFROM  TIMESTAMP(12) GENERATED ALWAYS AS ROW START NOT NULL ,
       XTO    TIMESTAMP(12) GENERATED ALWAYS AS ROW END   NOT NULL ,
       PERIOD FOR SYSTEM_TIME ( XFROM , XTO ) )
       WITH SYSTEM VERSIONING ;
```

Now let's focus on just BS_STATUS_FROM_TO, for definiteness. When it's first defined, that table is empty, of course. Suppose we now execute the following INSERT statement:

```
INSERT INTO BS_STATUS_FROM_TO ( SNO , STATUS , DFROM , DTO )
       VALUES ( SNO ( 'S2' ) , 5 , d02 , d05 ) ;
```

Further, suppose this INSERT statement is executed at time *t11*. Then the row that's actually inserted looks like this:

SNO	STATUS	DFROM	DTO	XFROM	XTO
S2	5	d02	d05	t11	t99

Now suppose we execute the following UPDATE statement at time *t22* (note the FOR PORTION OF specification):

```
UPDATE BS_STATUS_FROM_TO
FOR     PORTION OF DPERIOD FROM d03 TO d04
SET     STATUS = 10
WHERE   SNO = SNO ( 'S2' ) ;
```

After this UPDATE, the table looks like this:

SNO	STATUS	DFROM	DTO	XFROM	XTO
S2	5	d02	d05	t11	t22
S2	5	d02	d03	t22	t99
S2	10	d03	d04	t22	t99
S2	5	d04	d05	t22	t99

Now suppose we execute the following DELETE statement at time *t33* (again note the FOR PORTION OF specification):[26]

```
DELETE
FROM    BS_STATUS_FROM_TO
FOR     PORTION OF DPERIOD FROM d03 TO d05
WHERE   SNO = SNO ( 'S2' ) ;
```

Now the table looks like this:

SNO	STATUS	DFROM	DTO	XFROM	XTO
S2	5	d02	d05	t11	t22
S2	5	d02	d03	t22	t99
S2	10	d03	d04	t22	t33
S2	5	d04	d05	t22	t33

Finally, we execute the following DELETE statement at time *t44*:

---

[26] For simplicity we ignore the fact that the specified DELETE would actually violate the foreign key constraint from BS_FROM_TO to BS_STATUS_FROM_TO.

```
DELETE
FROM    BS_STATUS_FROM_TO
WHERE   SNO = SNO ( 'S2' ) ;
```

Then the final version of the table looks like this:

SNO	STATUS	DFROM	DTO	XFROM	XTO
S2	5	d02	d05	t11	t22
S2	5	d02	d03	t22	t44
S2	10	d03	d04	t22	t33
S2	5	d04	d05	t22	t33

SUMMARY AND ASSESSMENT

In this final section, we briefly summarize the features of our own approach to temporal data as described in Parts II and III of this book and show in each case whether SQL supports the feature in question (and if so, how). We also offer some occasional comments regarding that SQL support.

Database Design

In Chapter 12, we described three broad approaches to design: since relvars only, during relvars only, or a mixture, with the mixture being our preference. SQL effectively assumes the second approach—at least, it provides no direct support for the third, though there's nothing to stop us from adopting such a scheme if we want to. Of course, as explained in Chapter 12, that second approach inevitably entails dealing with "the moving point *now*" in some ad hoc kind of way, and we've seen that SQL agrees with us in using explicit "end of time" markers for that purpose.

We also recommended strongly in Chapter 12 that during relvars be in 6NF. Of course, designing relvars (or tables) to be in some particular normal form is indeed a design matter, not a matter of legislation, so SQL quite rightly has nothing to say on the issue. But it's hard to escape the impression that SQL's temporal features were expressly designed on the basis of an assumption that converting a nontemporal database into a temporal analog could and should be done by simply adding timestamp columns to existing tables (in which case it's quite likely that those resulting temporal tables won't be in 6NF). For example, consider this extract from reference [65]:

> The choice of returning current ... rows as the default [*i.e., from a query on a system-versioned table*] ... helps with ... database migration in that applications running on non system-versioned tables would continue to work and produce the same results when those tables are converted to system-versioned tables.

And this from the same source:

> One of the advantages of the SQL:2011 approach over an approach based on the period data type is that it allows existing databases ... to take advantage of the SQL:2011 extensions more easily. Ever since DBMSs have been on the scene, users have been building their own solutions for handling temporal data as part of their application logic ... It would be very expensive for users invested in such solutions to replace them with a solution that uses a single column of [some] period type.

Well, we've given our reasons elsewhere (see, e.g., reference [29]) for being somewhat skeptical regarding the kinds of scenarios being envisaged here; indeed, we explained in some detail in Chapter 12 why doing temporal database design by simply adding a timestamp attribute to a relvar without one wasn't, in general, a very good idea.

In Chapter 13, we proposed the PACKED ON, WHEN /THEN, U_key, and foreign U_key constraints for temporal relvars. SQL has features that provide some but not all of the functionality of these constraints. To be specific:

a. WITHOUT OVERLAPS on an SQL UNIQUE specification can be used to prevent redundancy and contradiction, though not circumlocution.

b. The UNIQUE and FOREIGN KEY specifications, if used in connection with tables with an application time period (and if used appropriately, of course), are almost equivalent to analogous U_key and foreign U_key specifications.

But keeping tables in fully packed form, assuming that's what's desired, is the user's responsibility. (Well, so it is in our proposals too—but then we provide various features, such as U_INSERT, that are explicitly intended to help the user in this regard. SQL doesn't, not really.)

We also proposed some syntactic shorthands in Chapter 14—basically the SINCE_FOR and HISTORY_IN specifications—to simplify the process of defining the relvars in our preferred approach. SQL has nothing analogous. Of course, it doesn't *need* anything corresponding to HISTORY_IN, because it doesn't do horizontal decomposition anyway. But something analogous to SINCE_FOR could be useful.

We also mentioned the possibility of another syntactic shorthand in Chapters 15 and 16—basically some kind of a COMBINED_IN specification—to simplify the process of querying and updating the relvars by undoing the decompositions involved in our preferred approach. Again SQL has nothing analogous. Of course, it doesn't really need anything for undoing horizontal decomposition, because, to say it again, it doesn't really do horizontal decomposition in the first place. But undoing vertical decomposition is another matter.

Feature List

We now present a list of the various features of our overall approach and their SQL counterparts (where such exist), together with some brief commentary where appropriate. Please note, however, that we most definitely do *not* want this list to be used as a basis for any kind of "checklist" evaluation (not of SQL per se, and not of anything else, either). We do think it can serve as a convenient framework for structuring discussion, but it's not meant to serve as a basis for any kind of scoring scheme. We're not interested in scoring schemes.

Note: Of course, many of the features we show below as "missing" in SQL do have various workarounds; thus, a *no* in the SQL column should usually—though not always!—be taken to mean only "no *direct* support."

Feature	SQL:2011 analog
intervals (values)	periods (but value pairs, not values)
interval type generator and interval types	*no* — periods aren't "first class objects" and can't be used orthogonally
no particular interval style forced by the system	periods always closed:open
"automatic" enforcement of "from" < "to" (in closed:open terms)	*yes*
nontemporal intervals	temporal periods only
any ordinal type usable as a point type	DATE and TIMESTAMP types only
successor function (NEXT_*T*)	*yes* — e.g., *d* + INTERVAL '1' DAY
PRIOR_*T*	*yes* — e.g., *d* – INTERVAL '1' DAY
FIRST_*T*	*yes*[27] — e.g., DATE '0001–01–01'
LAST_*T*	*yes*[28] — e.g., DATE '9999–12–31'
interval attribute reference	period name (but only in certain boolean expressions and FOR PORTION OF clauses)

---

[27] Though it's worth noting that SQL requires the user to know the actual value, which FIRST_*T* doesn't. (A similar remark applies to LAST_*T*, of course.)

[28] But no "from" value can ever be equal to this value—i.e., SQL is incapable of representing the fact that some state of affairs holds at "the end of time."

interval selector invocation (including interval literals)	period predicand (but only in certain boolean expressions and FOR PORTION OF clauses)
BEGIN	*yes* —"from" (column reference)
END	*yes* — e.g.,"to" – INTERVAL '1' DAY
PRE	*yes* — e.g., "from" – INTERVAL '1' DAY
POST	*yes* — "to" (column reference)
POINT FROM	*no*
"∈"	*no*
"∋"	CONTAINS (but care needed over "to")
"=" (Allen)	EQUALS
"⊆"	*no*
"⊂"	*no*
"⊇"	CONTAINS (note the overloading)
"⊃"	*no*
BEFORE	PRECEDES
AFTER	SUCCEEDS
OVERLAPS	OVERLAPS
MEETS	*no*[29]
MERGES	*no*

---

[29] Of course, MEETS can be expressed in terms of IMMEDIATELY PRECEDES and IMMEDIATELY SUCCEEDS, as we already know. A similar remark applies to MERGES also.

BEGINS	*no*
ENDS	*no*
COUNT	"to" – "from" (but result must be cast to type INTEGER)
UNION	*no*
INTERSECT	*no*
MINUS	*no*
relvars with two or more interval attributes	*no* — except for the special case of a bitemporal table
derived relations with intervals	*no*
EXPAND and COLLAPSE	*no*
PACK and UNPACK on one attribute	*no*
PACK and UNPACK on any number of attributes	*no*
"automatic" packing of query results	*no*
updating beliefs about the past	*yes*
U_ operators (U_join, etc.)	*no*
U_ comparisons	*no*
interval-only relations	*yes*
"Queries A and B" (see, e.g., Chapter 11)	intolerably clumsy

"nine requirements" (see Chapter 14)	prevent redundancy and contradiction: *yes* prevent circumlocution: *no* denseness: *yes* (but needs deferred checking)
multiple relvar assignment	*no*
U_update operators	*no*
PORTION (single interval)	*yes*
PORTION (two or more intervals)	*no*
stated time	application time (base tables only)
logged time	system time[30] (base tables only; explicitly part of the table in question)
LOGGED_TIMES_IN (see Chapter 17)	*no*
"automatic" packing of logged time query results	*no*
more than one successor function (as in, e.g., DDATE vs. MDATE)	*yes* — e.g., d + INTERVAL '1' DAY vs. d + INTERVAL '1' MONTH (but one point type, not two)
numeric point types (as in, e.g., NUMERIC(p,q))	*no*
cyclic point types (see Appendix A)	*no*

To all of the above, we'd like to add the following.

- Our own approach is truly general purpose. It's based on a widely applicable abstraction, the interval. What's more, it conforms 100 percent to relational principles. The only places where time as such shows up in our approach are in connection with (a) design

---

[30] But see Exercise 19.8.

specifics—but then, as previously noted, design considerations are largely orthogonal to relational model considerations anyway—and (b) logged times, as described in Chapter 17.

■ SQL's approach, by contrast, is quite definitely specific to temporal data as such (as indeed the very term *period* strongly suggests). The concept of time is all pervasive. Partly as a consequence of this state of affairs, SQL also violates certain rather important principles: *The Assignment Principle*, certainly (see Chapter 3); *The Information Principle*, at least arguably[31] (see Chapter 4); and *The Principle of Interchangeability* (of views and base relvars—see reference [44]). It also suffers from a variety of ad hoc limitations: e.g., the limitation of at most two (rather special) periods per table, and the limitation of periods to base tables specifically (this latter is the source of the violation of *The Principle of Interchangeability*, of course).

EXERCISES

19.1 Given table XS_STATUS_FROM_TO as defined in the body of the chapter, what does the expression SELECT * FROM XS_STATUS_FROM_TO evaluate to?

19.2 What are the predicates for S_STATUS_FROM_TO and XS_STATUS_FROM_TO?

19.3 Here repeated from Exercise 2.2 in Chapter 2 are **Tutorial D** definitions for the three relvars in the original version of the courses-and-students database:

```
VAR COURSE BASE RELATION
   { COURSENO   COURSENO ,
     CNAME      NAME ,
     AVAILABLE  DATE }
   KEY { COURSENO } ;

VAR STUDENT BASE RELATION
   { STUDENTNO  STUDENTNO ,
     SNAME      NAME ,
     REGISTERED DATE }
   KEY { STUDENTNO } ;

VAR ENROLLMENT BASE RELATION
   { COURSENO   COURSENO ,
     STUDENTNO  STUDENTNO ,
     ENROLLED   DATE }
   KEY { COURSENO , STUDENTNO }
   FOREIGN KEY { COURSENO } REFERENCES COURSE
   FOREIGN KEY { STUDENTNO } REFERENCES STUDENT ;
```

---

[31] This particular observation might not apply to SQL:2011 as such, but it certainly does apply to IBM's DB2 product, on which the design of SQL:2011 is allegedly based [97]. (Or is it the other way around? See reference [89].) *Note:* The reason it applies to DB2 is that DB2's temporal support includes a notion of "hidden columns."

Observe now that although we didn't say as much in Chapter 2, this database is actually semitemporal. Give CREATE TABLE statements for a fully temporal SQL analog.

19.4 (*Based on Exercises 15.2-15.5 in Chapter 15.*) Given your answer to Exercise 19.3, write SQL queries for the following:

a. Get student numbers for students currently enrolled on both course C1 and course C2.

b. Get student numbers for students not currently enrolled on both course C1 and course C2.

c. Get intervals during which at least one course was being offered.

d. Get intervals during which no course was being offered at all.

19.5 (*Based on the answer to Exercise 16.2 in Chapter 16.*) Given your answer to Exercise 19.3, write SQL updates for the following:

a. New courses C542 ("**Tutorial D**") and C543 ("Temporal Databases") became available on June 1st, 2013.

b. Currently available courses C193 ("SQL") and C203 ("Object Oriented Databases") were discontinued at the end of May this year (2013).

c. Student ST21, Hugh Manatee, not currently registered with the university, *was* registered from October 1st, 2011, to June 30th, 2012, but the database doesn't show that fact.

d. Student ST19 changed her name to Anna Marino on November 18th, 2012.

19.6 Let BSP_FROM_TO be a system-versioned bitemporal analog of table SP_FROM_TO from the body of the chapter. Give a suitable CREATE TABLE statement.

19.7 Using the bitemporal table BS_FROM_TO as defined in the body of the chapter, write SQL queries for the following:

a. When if ever did the database say that supplier S2 was under contract on day 4?

b. On day 8, what did the database say was supplier S2's term of contract?

19.8 In the body of the chapter, we saw that current rows in tables with system time have a system time period in which the "to" value is represented by "the end of time" (*t99* in examples).

But *system time* is just SQL's term for transaction time or—our preferred term—logged time, and we saw in Chapter 17 that, by definition, transaction times can never refer to the future. How do you reconcile this state of affairs?

19.9 Our explanation of system time (also known as transaction time or—our preferred term— logged time) in the body of the chapter referred to the system clock. However, we did also say, in a footnote, that the standard doesn't actually mention this concept—it merely says there's something called *the transaction timestamp*, which is required to remain constant throughout the life of the transaction in question and is used for the purpose of timestamping rows in tables with system time. How do you think transaction timestamps might be implemented in a real system?

ANSWERS

19.1 It evaluates to that restriction of the table that contains current rows only. Note, therefore, that the usual definition, to the effect that SELECT * FROM *T* returns table *T* in its entirety, is no longer applicable. Perhaps even more counterintuitively, the expression TABLE *T* can no longer be said to denote table *T* (!). *Note:* In case you're unfamiliar with this latter SQL construct—i.e., an expression of the form TABLE *T*—we should explain that it's defined to be shorthand for SELECT * FROM *T*. (At least, that's what the standard says; however, it would probably be more correct to say it's shorthand for a parenthesized version of this latter expression, thus: (SELECT * FROM *T*).)

19.2 We don't have a good answer to this exercise. In fact, we seriously doubt whether a good answer even exists. The essence of the problem is this: Although the tables in question are guaranteed to be free of redundancy (and of course contradiction), they're *not* guaranteed to be free of circumlocution. To illustrate the point, let's focus on table S_STATUS_FROM_TO, for definiteness. Here then is the obvious first attempt at a predicate—let's call it *P*—for that table:

> *Supplier SNO had status STATUS throughout the period ("period p") from day DFROM to the day that's the immediate predecessor of day DTO, inclusive.*

Note that we can't extend this predicate by adding *and not throughout any period that properly includes period p*, precisely because the table isn't guaranteed to be kept packed on DPERIOD.
>   Now, Fig. 19.3 shows S_STATUS_FROM_TO as containing a row—let's call it row *r*— indicating that supplier S7 had status 15 throughout the period [*d03,d09*). However, there are numerous ways of splitting up that period [*d03,d09*) into smaller, nonoverlapping periods. Here are just a few of them:

- $[d03,d04)$ $[d04,d05)$ $[d05,d06)$ $[d06,d07)$ $[d07,d08)$ $[d08,d09)$
- $[d03,d05)$ $[d05,d06)$ $[d06,d07)$ $[d07,d08)$ $[d08,d09)$
- $[d03,d04)$ $[d04,d06)$ $[d06,d07)$ $[d07,d08)$ $[d08,d09)$
- $[d03,d06)$ $[d06,d08)$ $[d08,d09)$
- $[d03,d07)$ $[d07,d09)$

And so on. It follows that it would be possible, without violating the WITHOUT OVERLAPS constraint on S_STATUS_FROM_TO, to replace row *r* by several distinct rows, and to do so, moreover, in several different ways. And every such replacement row—call it *r'*—would represent a true instantiation of predicate *P!* So predicate *P* can't possibly be right. Why not? Well, recall *The Closed World Assumption* from Chapter 3. That assumption, translated into SQL terms, says that row *r* appears in table *T* at time *t* **if and only if** *r* satisfies the predicate for *T* at time *t* (emphasis added). In the case at hand, however, table S_STATUS_FROM_TO clearly isn't going to contain all of those possible rows *r'* at the same time, and so predicate *P* clearly isn't sufficient, in and of itself, to pin down just which rows do or don't appear in that table at any given time.

Here's another predicate we might consider (let's call it *P'*):

Supplier SNO had status STATUS throughout the period ("period p") from day DFROM to the day that's the immediate predecessor of day DTO, inclusive, and hence—but only implicitly—throughout every period properly included in period p.

But predicate *P'* doesn't do the job either. To be specific, it's true—as it was with the previous attempt, predicate *P*—that if row *r* appears in the table, then row *r* necessarily satisfies this predicate; conversely, however, it *isn't* true that if row *r* satisfies this predicate, then row *r* necessarily appears in the table.

To sum up: It seems to be the case that certain real world situations can be represented by the same SQL table—table S_STATUS_FROM_TO, in the case at hand—in more than one way. This state of affairs begins to look like a rather serious violation of relational principles. To put it another way, avoiding circumlocution seems to be even more important than we originally thought, and SQL tables, precisely because they don't avoid it, seem to be less than fully respectable, relationally speaking.[32]

19.3 In contrast to earlier exercises and answers having to do with this database (see, e.g., Exercise 12.8c in Chapter 12), we choose to go for a pure 6NF design here.

---

[32] The same criticism would apply to relvars in **Tutorial D**, of course, if they permitted the same kind of circumlocution.

```
CREATE TABLE COURSE_FROM_TO
    ( COURSENO COURSENO NOT NULL ,
      DFROM    DATE     NOT NULL ,
      DTO      DATE     NOT NULL ,
      PERIOD FOR AVAILABLE ( DFROM , DTO ) ,
      UNIQUE ( COURSENO , AVAILABLE WITHOUT OVERLAPS ) ,
      FOREIGN KEY ( COURSENO , PERIOD AVAILABLE )
         REFERENCES COURSE_NAME_FROM_TO ( COURSENO , PERIOD NAMED ) ) ;

CREATE TABLE COURSE_NAME_FROM_TO
    ( COURSENO COURSENO NOT NULL ,
      CNAME    NAME     NOT NULL ,
      DFROM    DATE     NOT NULL ,
      DTO      DATE     NOT NULL ,
      PERIOD FOR NAMED ( DFROM , DTO ) ,
      UNIQUE ( COURSENO , NAMED WITHOUT OVERLAPS ) ,
      FOREIGN KEY ( COURSENO , PERIOD NAMED )
         REFERENCES COURSE_FROM_TO ( COURSENO , PERIOD AVAILABLE ) ) ;

CREATE TABLE STUDENT_FROM_TO
    ( STUDENTNO STUDENTNO NOT NULL ,
      DFROM     DATE      NOT NULL ,
      DTO       DATE      NOT NULL ,
      PERIOD FOR REGISTERED ( DFROM , DTO ) ,
      UNIQUE ( STUDENTNO , REGISTERED WITHOUT OVERLAPS ) ,
      FOREIGN KEY ( STUDENTNO , PERIOD REGISTERED )
         REFERENCES STUDENT_NAME_FROM_TO ( STUDENTNO , PERIOD NAMED ) );

CREATE TABLE STUDENT_NAME_FROM_TO
    ( STUDENTNO STUDENTNO NOT NULL ,
      SNAME     NAME      NOT NULL ,
      DFROM     DATE      NOT NULL ,
      DTO       DATE      NOT NULL ,
      PERIOD FOR NAMED ( DFROM , DTO ) ,
      UNIQUE ( STUDENTNO , NAMED WITHOUT OVERLAPS ) ,
      FOREIGN KEY ( STUDENTNO , PERIOD NAMED )
         REFERENCES STUDENT_FROM_TO ( STUDENTNO , PERIOD REGISTERED ) );

CREATE TABLE ENROLLMENT_FROM_TO
    ( COURSENO   COURSENO  NOT NULL ,
      STUDENTNO  STUDENTNO NOT NULL ,
      DFROM      DATE      NOT NULL ,
      DTO        DATE      NOT NULL ,
      PERIOD FOR ENROLLMENT ( DFROM , DTO ) ,
      UNIQUE ( COURSENO , STUDENTNO , ENROLLMENT WITHOUT OVERLAPS ) ,
      FOREIGN KEY ( COURSENO , PERIOD ENROLLMENT )
         REFERENCES COURSE_FROM_TO ( COURSENO , PERIOD AVAILABLE ) ,
      FOREIGN KEY ( STUDENTNO , PERIOD ENROLLMENT )
         REFERENCES STUDENT_FROM_TO ( STUDENTNO , PERIOD REGISTERED ) );
```

19.4

a. ```
    WITH t1 AS (SELECT STUDENTNO
                 FROM   ENROLLMENT_FROM_TO
                 WHERE COURSENO = COURSENO ('C1') AND DTO = d99) ,
         t2 AS (SELECT STUDENTNO
                 FROM   ENROLLMENT_FROM_TO
                 WHERE COURSENO = COURSENO ('C2') AND DTO = d99)
    SELECT STUDENTNO FROM t1 NATURAL JOIN t2
    ```

   *Note:* The expression DTO = *d99* in the definitions of *t1* and *t2* here could be replaced by ENROLLMENT CONTAINS CURRENT_DATE if desired.

b.  The problem statement is ambiguous!  We interpret the requirement to be "Get student numbers for students *currently enrolled on at least one course, but* not currently enrolled on both course C1 and course C2."  Let the result of evaluating the expression given as the answer to part a. above be assigned to table *Ta*.  Then the following will suffice:

    ```
    SELECT STUDENTNO FROM ENROLLMENT_FROM_TO WHERE DTO = d99
    EXCEPT
    SELECT STUDENTNO FROM Ta
    ```

   Note that there won't be any duplicate student numbers in the result here (why not?).

c. ```
    SELECT DISTINCT DFROM , DTO
    FROM   COURSE_FROM_TO
    ```

   But the result here almost certainly won't be in packed form. Do you have a good way to fix this problem? If so, we'd like to hear about it. You can contact us via the publisher.

d. This one is even worse, and would remain so even if we could figure out a way to get the result in part c. into packed form. *No solution provided*.

19.5

a. ```
    INSERT INTO COURSE_FROM_TO (COURSENO , DFROM , DTO)
           VALUES (COURSENO ('C542') ,
                              DATE '2013-06-01' , DATE '9999-12-31') ,
                  (COURSENO ('C543') ,
                              DATE '2013-06-01' , DATE '9999-12-31') ;

    INSERT INTO COURSE_NAME_FROM_TO (COURSENO , CNAME , DFROM , DTO)
           VALUES (COURSENO ('C542') , NAME ('Tutorial D') ,
                              DATE '2013-06-01' , DATE '9999-12-31') ,
                  (COURSENO ('C543') , NAME ('Temporal Databases') ,
                              DATE '2013-06-01' , DATE '9999-12-31') ;
    ```
    ```

Of course, these two INSERTs really need to be done as part of the same transaction. An analogous remark applies to the answers to parts b.-d. also.

b.
```
UPDATE COURSE_FROM_TO
SET    DTO = DATE '2013-05-31'
WHERE  DTO = DATE '9999-12-31'
AND    COURSENO IN ( COURSENO ( 'C193' ) , COURSENO ( 'C203' ) ) ;

UPDATE COURSE_NAME_FROM_TO
SET    DTO = DATE '2013-05-31'
WHERE  DTO = DATE '9999-12-31'
AND    COURSENO IN ( COURSENO ( 'C193' ) , COURSENO ( 'C203' ) ) ;
```

We assume for simplicity here that table ENROLLMENT_FROM_TO doesn't show any students as currently enrolled on either of these courses.

c.
```
INSERT INTO STUDENT_FROM_TO ( STUDENTNO , DFROM , DTO )
       VALUES ( STUDENTNO ( 'ST21' ) ,
                        DATE '2011-10-01' , DATE '2012-06-30' ) ;

INSERT INTO STUDENT_NAME_FROM_TO ( STUDENTNO , SNAME , DFROM , DTO )
       VALUES ( STUDENTNO ( 'ST21' ) , NAME ( 'Hugh Manatee' ) ,
                        DATE '2011-10-01' , DATE '2012-06-30' ) ;
```

d.
```
UPDATE STUDENT_NAME_FROM_TO
SET    DTO = DATE '2012-11-18'
WHERE  STUDENTNO = STUDENTNO ( 'ST19' )
AND    NAMED CONTAINS DATE '2012-11-18' ;

INSERT STUDENT_NAME_FROM_TO ( STUDENTNO , SNAME , DFROM , DTO )
VALUES ( STUDENTNO ( 'ST19' ) ,
         NAME ( 'Anna Marino' ) , DATE '2012-11-18' ,
           ( SELECT MIN ( DTO ) FROM STUDENT_NAME_FROM_TO
             WHERE STUDENTNO = STUDENTNO ( 'ST19' )
             AND   NAMED CONTAINS DATE '2012-11-18' ) ;
```

Note: This solution assumes the database currently shows student ST19 as having some name on November 18th, 2012.

19.6
```
CREATE TABLE BSP_FROM_TO
      ( SNO    SNO   NOT NULL ,
        PNO    PNO   NOT NULL ,
        DFROM DATE NOT NULL ,
        DTO    DATE NOT NULL ,
        PERIOD FOR DPERIOD ( DFROM , DTO ) ,
        UNIQUE ( SNO , PNO , DPERIOD WITHOUT OVERLAPS ) ,
        FOREIGN KEY ( SNO , PERIOD DPERIOD )
                REFERENCES BS_FROM_TO ( SNO , PERIOD DPERIOD ) ,
        XFROM  TIMESTAMP(12) GENERATED ALWAYS AS ROW START NOT NULL ,
        XTO    TIMESTAMP(12) GENERATED ALWAYS AS ROW END   NOT NULL ,
        PERIOD FOR SYSTEM_TIME ( XFROM , XTO ) ,
        UNIQUE ( SNO , PNO ) )
        WITH SYSTEM VERSIONING ;
```

19.7

a.
```
SELECT XFROM , XTO
FROM   BS_FROM_TO
FOR    SYSTEM_TIME BETWEEN t01 AND t99
WHERE  SNO = SNO ( 'S2' )
AND    DPERIOD CONTAINS d04
```

For simplicity we use *t01* and *t99* here to denote the first and last value, respectively, of type TIMESTAMP(12). The result is guaranteed to be free of redundancy but not necessarily free of circumlocution.

b.
```
SELECT DFROM , DTO
FROM   BS_FROM_TO
FOR    SYSTEM_TIME BETWEEN t01 AND t99
WHERE  SNO = SNO ( 'S2' )
AND    SYSTEM_TIME CONTAINS d08
```

19.8 The situation here is analogous to that described in Chapter 12 in connection with during relvars only and "the moving point *now*." The point is, those appearances of *t99* in current rows don't really mean the end of time as such—rather, they stand for *until further notice*. However, SQL has no direct way of saying something is true "until further notice"; thus, it has to resort to that "end of time" trick,[33] much as we had to do for "valid" or stated time in a design consisting of during relvars only. As noted in Chapter 12, however, such tricks effectively mean we're recording in the database something we *know* is false—a practice that's logically incorrect, and hence somewhat hard to condone.

---

[33] Which (as you might recall) is something we said in Chapter 17 we certainly mustn't do!

19.9 There are several interconnected issues involved here, and a good way to explain them, or at least air them, is by means of a series of questions and answers—a kind of dialog between a hypothetical student and teacher, as follows.

Student: First of all, why do we need this transaction timestamp notion at all? Why can't we just timestamp updates with the system clock reading, as suggested in the body of the chapter? Surely that would be the obvious approach. Is there something wrong with it?

Teacher: Well, imagine the following scenario. You start a transaction on Monday. Your transaction updates some row *r* on Wednesday,[34] so—assuming we do use the system clock— the pertinent timestamp is Wednesday. On Friday, your transaction successfully completes (i.e., commits). Meanwhile, I submit a query on row *r* on Thursday, and I see the version of *r* that was current before your transaction ran. (I can't see your updated version, because your transaction hasn't committed yet.) Then I submit the same query on Saturday—and now I do see your updated version of *r*. What's more, I see now that your updated version of *r* came into being on Wednesday, *before* I ran my query on Thursday! So why didn't I see that version on Thursday?

Student: But wait a minute. Surely, when my transaction updates *r* on Wednesday, I get an exclusive lock on *r*. So when you try to access *r* on Thursday, you're trying to get at least a shared lock on *r*, and so you'll have to wait. And when my transaction commits, you'll come out of the wait state, but then you'll see my updated version of *r*. Isn't that right?

Teacher: Yes, it's right in principle, so long as the DBMS we're talking about is one that uses locking for concurrency control and abides by all of the protocols normally associated with locking. But it might not be! The SQL standard nowhere mentions locking as such, and indeed there are concurrency control schemes that don't use it. For example, there's a scheme called *multiversion read* (MVR). Under MVR, if I ask to see a row *r* that you already have update access to, then I'm given access to a previously committed version of that row (in our example, that would be the version of *r* as it was last Sunday). In other words, the system makes it look as if my transaction actually ran before yours.

Student: But isn't that approach a little suspect? It looks to me as if there's something inconsistent going on. On Thursday, you're going to make some business decision on the basis of incorrect information—to be specific, on the basis of row *r* having the value on Thursday that you saw on Thursday. What are you going to do on Saturday when you discover that row *r*

---

[34] We assume for simplicity throughout this dialog that it does make sense to talk in terms of updating individual rows.

actually had a different value on Thursday? I mean, the ATM machine might have dispensed hard cash on Thursday ... and you can't call it back on Saturday, can you?

Teacher: I can't answer that.

Student: All right, let's go back to locking. It seems to me there are other problems too, even with locking. Suppose we don't use the system clock; suppose instead that, since updates don't "really" happen until they're committed, we use commit time as the transaction timestamp. One obvious difficulty springs to mind immediately: namely, at the time when an update is requested inside the transaction, we don't know what the commit time is going to be. So what's the transaction timestamp, within a given transaction, for a row that has been updated in that transaction and not yet committed, because the transaction hasn't yet finished?[35]

Teacher: Good point! Perhaps we might use the transaction start time, instead of commit time, for the transaction timestamp?

Student: All right ... So suppose I update the same row twice in the same transaction. If we use the same timestamp for both updates, how can I see, within that same transaction, the update history for that row? I mean an update history that does reflect both of those updates?

Teacher: I give up.

---

[35] It's pertinent to mention here that the SQL standard [61] explicitly requires the transaction timestamp to be determined *before* the transaction in question does any updating. Here's the actual text from the standard: "The transaction timestamp is set by an SQL-implementation before any SQL-data change statement executes in that transaction and, once set, remains unchanged during that SQL-transaction." So it seems that the transaction timestamp, whatever it is, can't possibly be commit time.

APPENDIXES

There are six appendixes:

A. Cyclic Point Types

B. Is Ordinality Necessary?

C. Generalizing PACK and UNPACK

D. A **Tutorial D** Grammar

E. Implementation Considerations

F. References and Bibliography

Appendix A and Appendix B discuss further possible extensions to, or variations on, the point type concept, together with certain implications of such variations for the corresponding interval types. Appendix C considers the possibility of generalizing the PACK and UNPACK operators to deal with sets (or relations) that contain something other than intervals. Appendix D provides an abbreviated grammar for **Tutorial D**. Appendix E discusses a variety of transformation laws and algorithms for implementing the various operators described in the body of the book (especially in Chapters 9-11). Appendix F provides an annotated list of bibliographic references.

Appendix A

Cyclic Point Types

What goes around comes around.

—late 20th century catchphrase

All of the intervals [b:e] discussed in the body of this book were required—in fact, defined—to satisfy the condition $b \leq e$. And yet intervals that appear to violate this condition are quite common in everyday life. For example, someone doing shiftwork might be required to work from 11:00 pm to 7:00 am, or a restaurant might be open each week from Thursday to Tuesday. The intervals in these two examples are based on what might be called *wraparound* or *cyclic* point types—to be specific, "time of day" and "day of week," respectively, with the obvious semantics in each case. Such types share with modular arithmetic the property that the available values can be thought of as points arranged around the circumference of a circle, such that every value has both a successor and a predecessor, and there's no first or last value. So the question is: To what extent can the ideas discussed in the body of the book for regular—or what might be called *linear*—point types be made to work for cyclic types? Indeed, can they be made to work at all? Investigating this issue is the purpose of this appendix.

THE WEEKDAY EXAMPLE

For definiteness, let's focus on the weekday example (see Fig. A.1).

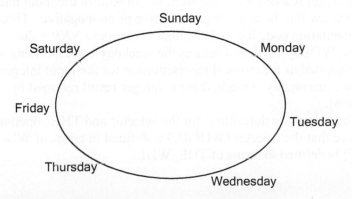

Fig. A.1: Days of the week as a cyclic type

Here then is a possible type definition, or at least the beginnings of such a definition, for type WEEKDAY:

```
TYPE WEEKDAY
    POSSREP WDPRI { WDI INTEGER CONSTRAINT WDI ≥ 0 AND WDI ≤ 6 }
    POSSREP WDPRC { WDC CHAR CONSTRAINT WDC = 'Sun' OR WDC = 'Mon'
                              OR WDC = 'Tue' OR WDC = 'Wed'
                              OR WDC = 'Thu' OR WDC = 'Fri'
                              OR WDC = 'Sat' } ;
```

As you can see, we've defined two possible representations ("possreps") for this type—one, WDPRI, as an integer WDI in the range [0:6], and the other, WDPRC, as a character string WDC with values 'Sun', 'Mon', etc. *Note:* For the rest of this appendix we'll refer to individual days, much of the time, by those shorthand names Sun, Mon, etc. Also, we'll take Sunday to be day 0, Monday to be day 1, and so on.

Here now are the selector definition and associated THE_ operator definition for possrep WDPRI (in outline only—coding details are omitted, since they presumably reference whatever the physical representation for weekdays might be, and such matters are irrelevant to our main purpose in this appendix):

```
OPERATOR WDPRI ( WDI INTEGER ) RETURNS WEEKDAY ;
    /* code to return the WEEKDAY value corresponding */
    /* to the given integer WDI                       */
END OPERATOR ;

OPERATOR THE_WDI ( WD WEEKDAY ) RETURNS INTEGER ;
    /* code to return the integer corresponding */
    /* to the given WEEKDAY value WD            */
END OPERATOR ;
```

By definition, the WDPRI selector takes an integer as input and returns a weekday. However, it turns out to be convenient, for reasons we'll see later, not to require the input integer WDI to fall in the range [0:6] but to allow it to be any integer, negative or nonnegative. Thus, we assume the first thing the implementation code for WDPRI does is compute *NNR* = the nonnegative remainder after dividing WDI by 7;[1] then it returns the weekday corresponding to *NNR*. The value *NNR* here can be regarded as a canonical representation for the input integer WDI. *Note:* By contrast, we assume, reasonably enough, that the integer result returned by THE_WDI *is* always in the range [0:6].

Turning to possrep WDPRC, here now are definitions for the selector and THE_ operator associated with that possrep. Observe that the selector (WDPRC) is defined in terms of WDPRI and the THE_operator (THE_WDC) is defined in terms of THE_WDI.

---

[1] E.g., the nonnegative remainder after dividing −17 by 7 is +4, because −17 = (−3)*7 + 4; thus, "day −17" = day 4 = Thursday. (By contrast, the negative remainder is −3, because −17 = (−2)*7 − 3.)

```
OPERATOR WDPRC ( WDC CHAR ) RETURNS WEEKDAY ;
    RETURN CASE
        WHEN WDC = 'Sun' THEN WDPRI ( 0 )
        WHEN WDC = 'Mon' THEN WDPRI ( 1 )
        WHEN WDC = 'Tue' THEN WDPRI ( 2 )
        WHEN WDC = 'Wed' THEN WDPRI ( 3 )
        WHEN WDC = 'Thu' THEN WDPRI ( 4 )
        WHEN WDC = 'Fri' THEN WDPRI ( 5 )
        WHEN WDC = 'Sat' THEN WDPRI ( 6 )
    END CASE ;
END OPERATOR ;

OPERATOR THE_WDC ( WD WEEKDAY ) RETURNS CHAR ;
    RETURN CASE
        WHEN THE_WDI ( WD ) = 0 THEN 'Sun'
        WHEN THE_WDI ( WD ) = 1 THEN 'Mon'
        WHEN THE_WDI ( WD ) = 2 THEN 'Tue'
        WHEN THE_WDI ( WD ) = 3 THEN 'Wed'
        WHEN THE_WDI ( WD ) = 4 THEN 'Thu'
        WHEN THE_WDI ( WD ) = 5 THEN 'Fri'
        WHEN THE_WDI ( WD ) = 6 THEN 'Sat'
    END CASE ;
END OPERATOR ;
```

Of course, we also need the "=" operator:

```
OPERATOR "=" ( WD1 WEEKDAY , WD2 WEEKDAY ) RETURNS BOOLEAN ;
    RETURN ( THE_WDI ( WD1 ) = THE_WDI ( WD2 ) ) ;
END OPERATOR ;
```

Note: This last definition could and probably should be provided automatically by the system. We show it explicitly for pedagogic reasons.

WEEKDAY AS A POINT TYPE

So is WEEKDAY a valid point type? Well, intervals of the form "Wednesday to Friday" or "Friday to Monday" certainly make good intuitive sense. But in Chapter 18 we said point types were supposed to be ordinal types, and WEEKDAY doesn't fit the definition of an ordinal type, because there's no first value of the type and no last. On the other hand, values of the type are certainly ordered; we all know that, e.g., Friday comes after Thursday. So there's an ordering all right, but that ordering isn't linear but *cyclic*,[2] meaning that when we've cycled through all the values we start again (Sunday follows immediately after Saturday).

How do such considerations affect our usual notions of point types and interval types? Well, here's a definition, paraphrased from Chapter 18, of what it means to be an ordinal type:

---

[2] The more usual term in mathematics would be *periodic*. For obvious reasons, however, this latter term would be likely to cause confusion, especially in an SQL context.

Definition: An **ordinal type** is a type *T* such that (a) the expression *v1* > *v2* is defined for all pairs of values *v1* and *v2* of type *T*, returning TRUE if and only if *v1* follows *v2* with respect to the pertinent ordering, and (b) certain additional operators are required: *first*, *last*, *next*, *prior*, and possibly others.

First of all, then, does ">" apply to values of type WEEKDAY? Well, there seem to be two ways we might define such an operator:

■ We could define *v1* > *v2* to be true if and only if THE_WDI (*v1*) > THE_WDI (*v2*) is true, so that Sat > Fri > ... > Mon > Sun. This definition doesn't seem very useful, since (among other things) it would apparently outlaw intervals like [Fri:Mon].

■ We could define *v1* > *v2* to be true if and only if *v1* follows *v2* according to the cyclic ordering. This definition seems even more useless than the previous one, since it implies that ">" would be indistinguishable from "≠" (*v1* > *v2* would be true if and only if *v1* ≠ *v2* was also true).

So if WEEKDAY is going to be usable as a point type, it seems we're going to have to find a way to make it be so without relying on a ">" operator as such.

Second, as already noted, type WEEKDAY has no "first" and "last" operators. But it does have successor and predecessor functions. Here are the definitions:[3]

```
OPERATOR NEXT_WEEKDAY ( WD WEEKDAY ) RETURNS WEEKDAY ;
   RETURN WDPRI ( THE_WDI ( WD ) + 1 ) ) ;
END OPERATOR ;

OPERATOR PRIOR_WEEKDAY ( WD WEEKDAY ) RETURNS WEEKDAY ;
   RETURN WDPRI ( THE_WDI ( WD ) - 1 ) ) ;
END OPERATOR ;
```

What's more, these functions, unlike their counterparts for ordinal types, never fail.

So let's invent some syntax for indicating that a given type is a cyclic type—perhaps as indicated here (note the highlighted text):

```
TYPE WEEKDAY CYCLIC ... ;
```

We interpret the CYCLIC specification as implying that:

■ A niladic cardinality operator must be defined, which returns the number *N* of values in the type (*N* is 7, of course, in the case of type WEEKDAY). A real language might require the

---

[3] It's in these definitions that we rely on the fact that the integer that's the input to WDPRI doesn't have to lie in the range [0:6].

name of that operator—COUNT_WEEKDAY, say—to be stated as part of the CYCLIC specification.[4]

■ Monadic "next" and "prior" operators must also be defined, and they must be isomorphic to "add one" and "subtract one," respectively, in arithmetic modulo *N*. A real language might require the names of those operators—NEXT_WEEKDAY and PRIOR_WEEKDAY, in our running example—to be stated as part of the CYCLIC specification.

THE CORRESPONDING INTERVAL TYPE

Now let's see if we can make sense of an interval type of the form INTERVAL_WEEKDAY. Values of this type, if they do make sense, will be intervals of the form $[b:e]$, where b and e are both values of type WEEKDAY. What happens to the associated operators?

First we define the necessary interval selector operator, as follows: The selector invocation INTERVAL_WEEKDAY ($[b:e]$), where b and e are values of type WEEKDAY, returns the interval consisting of the sequence b, $b+1$, ..., e, such that no weekday appears more than once in that sequence.[5] That is, starting at day b, we trace our steps around the cyclic ordering until we meet day e for the first time, and then we stop (so no interval is ever more than seven days in length). Here are some examples:

```
INTERVAL_WEEKDAY ( [ WDPRC('Mon') : WDPRC('Fri') ] )
INTERVAL_WEEKDAY ( [ WDPRC('Fri') : WDPRC('Mon') ] )
INTERVAL_WEEKDAY ( [ WDPRC('Wed') : WDPRC('Wed') ] )
INTERVAL_WEEKDAY ( [ WDPRC('Wed') : WDPRC('Tue') ] )
```

The first three of these examples are straightforward: They denote the five-day interval from Monday to Friday, the four-day interval from Friday to Monday, and the unit (one-day) interval consisting of just Wednesday, respectively. The fourth example deserves a closer look, however. On the face of it, of course, it simply denotes the seven-day interval from Wednesday to Tuesday—but that interval is slightly special, in that it contains all possible values of the underlying point type; in other words, it's what we might call (for the purposes of this appendix, at any rate) a *universal interval*. The obvious question arises: If, e.g., [Sun:Sat] and [Thu:Wed]—to adopt an obvious shorthand notation—are two such intervals, but with different begin and end points, are they equal or not?

We answer this question in the negative. Certainly there's an intuitive distinction, and indeed a pragmatically useful distinction, to be drawn between, e.g., the interval [Sun:Sat] and the interval [Thu:Wed]. Of course, it's true that these intervals do both contain the same set of

---

[4] Don't confuse this operator with the operator COUNT (without a _*T* suffix), which returns the cardinality of an interval.

[5] Other styles—open:closed, closed:open, open:open—can be supported too, of course; we assume closed:closed here just to be definite. Note too that the expression "$b+1$" in this sentence must be understood to mean "$b+1$ modulo 7" (and a similar remark applies to such expressions elsewhere in this appendix).

points; however, those points appear in a different sequence with respect to the intervals in which they appear. (All universal intervals of type INTERVAL_WEEKDAY consist of some cyclic permutation of the sequence Sun, Mon, Tue, Wed, Thu, Fri, Sat, of course.)[6]

Further Operators

The BEGIN, END, PRE, POST, POINT FROM, "∈", "∋", and COUNT operators are all straightforward and require no further discussion here.

ALLEN'S OPERATORS

Allen's operators do apply to intervals where the underlying point type is cyclic, but some of the definitions need revision. Let $i1 = [b1:e1]$ and $i2 = [b2:e2]$ be two such intervals (both defined, of course, over the same point type). Then:

Equals: This operator is unaffected: that is, $i1 = i2$ is true if and only if $b1 = b2$ and $e1 = e2$ are both true. Observe that this definition is consistent with our earlier statement to the effect that universal intervals such as, e.g., [Sun:Sat] and [Thu:Wed] are different intervals.

Inclusion: The "⊆", "⊂", "⊇", and "⊃" operators do apply, but their definitions need to be stated somewhat differently, as follows. Consider, e.g., the intervals $i1 = $ [Fri:Mon] and $i2 = $ [Sun:Sat]. Clearly, every point in $i1$ is also a point in $i2$. Equally clearly, it seems unreasonable to say $i1$ is included in $i2$, because even though the set of points in $i1$ is a subset of the set of points in $i2$, the *sequence* of points in $i1$ isn't a *subsequence* of the sequence of points in $i2$. The following definition is motivated by such considerations. Consider the process of examining the set of points $b2, b2+1, b2+2, ..., e2$—i.e., the set of points in $i2$—in sequence according to the cyclic ordering. Then $i1 \subseteq i2$ is true if and only if, as we perform this process, we encounter both $b1$ and $e1$ and we do *not* encounter $e1$ before $b1$. (So if $i1 \subseteq i2$, then every point p that appears in $i1$ also appears in $i2$. However, the converse isn't necessarily true. That is, the fact that every point p that appears in $i1$ also appears in $i2$ does *not* imply that $i1 \subseteq i2$.)

　　　The operators "⊂", "⊇", and "⊃" are then defined in terms of "⊆" in the usual way: $i1 \subset i2$ is true if and only if $i1 \subseteq i2$ and $i1 \neq i2$ are both true; $i2 \supseteq i1$ is true if and only if $i1 \subseteq i2$ is true; $i2 \supset i1$ is true if and only if $i1 \subset i2$ is true.

---

[6] A cyclic permutation of a given sequence of values is the sequence obtained by shifting every value n places along, with wraparound, for some specified nonnegative integer n. For example, if $n = 3$, the sequence obtained from Sun, Mon, Tue, Wed, Thu, Fri, Sat is the sequence Wed, Thu, Fri, Sat, Sun, Mon, Tue.

Examples:

```
[Tue:Thu] ⊏ [Mon:Fri]  :  TRUE
[Sat:Wed] ⊐ [Sun:Mon]  :  TRUE
[Mon:Fri] ⊒ [Thu:Sat]  :  FALSE
[Thu:Tue] ⊑ [Mon:Fri]  :  FALSE
```

Note the last of these in particular; as we examine the set of points Mon, Tue, Wed, Thu, Fri, we do encounter both Thu and Tue, but we do so "the wrong way round," as it were (we get to the end point Tue before the begin point Thu). For similar reasons, neither of the universal intervals [Mon:Sun] and [Tue:Mon] is considered to be included in the other.

BEFORE and AFTER: These operators also apply, but the definitions need to be stated a little differently, as follows: *i1* BEFORE *i2* is true if and only if, in the cyclic ordering starting from *b1*, (a) *e1* is encountered before *b2* and (b) *e2* is encountered before *b1* is encountered a second time. Note that it follows from this definition that *i2* BEFORE *i1* is true if and only if *i1* BEFORE *i2* is true (!). It also follows that *i1* BEFORE *i2* is true if and only if *i1* and *i2* are disjoint—i.e., there's no point *p* that appears in both *i1* and *i2*. Also, *i2* AFTER *i1* is true if and only if *i1* BEFORE *i2* is true (so in fact the operators BEFORE and AFTER are one and the same, both reducing to simply NOT OVERLAPS, or DISJOINT).
   Examples:

```
[Tue:Wed]  BEFORE  [Fri:Sat]  :  TRUE
[Fri:Sat]  BEFORE  [Tue:Wed]  :  TRUE
[Tue:Wed]  AFTER   [Fri:Sat]  :  TRUE
[Fri:Sat]  AFTER   [Tue:Wed]  :  TRUE
[Tue:Fri]  BEFORE  [Wed:Sat]  :  FALSE
```

OVERLAPS: The simplest way to define this operator is simply to say that *i1* OVERLAPS *i2* is true if and only if *i1* and *i2* aren't disjoint—i.e., if and only if there exists at least one point *p* that appears in both *i1* and *i2*. Equivalently, *i1* OVERLAPS *i2* is true if and only if *i1* BEFORE *i2* is false. Note, however, that *i1* can overlap *i2* at both ends, as it were (see, e.g., the fifth example below), something that can't happen with ordinal point types.
   Examples: The following pairs of intervals overlap:

```
[Tue:Thu]  and  [Wed:Fri]
[Tue:Thu]  and  [Mon:Wed]
[Tue:Thu]  and  [Mon:Tue]
[Tue:Thu]  and  [Fri:Wed]
[Thu:Tue]  and  [Mon:Fri]
```

The following, by contrast, don't—i.e., they're disjoint:

```
[Tue:Thu]  and  [Sat:Sun]
[Tue:Thu]  and  [Fri:Sun]
[Tue:Thu]  and  [Sun:Mon]
```

MEETS: The original definition from Chapter 7 remains unchanged: *i1* MEETS *i2* is true if and only if *b2* = *e1*+1 is true or *b1* = *e2*+1 is true (and *i2* MEETS *i1* is true if and only if *i1* MEETS *i2* is true). Note, however, that *i1* can meet *i2* at both ends, as it were, something that can't happen with ordinal point types; note also that *i1* can meet *i2* at one end and overlap it at the other, again something that can't happen with ordinal point types.

Examples: The following pairs of intervals meet:

```
[Tue:Thu]  and  [Fri:Sat]
[Tue:Thu]  and  [Sun:Mon]
[Tue:Thu]  and  [Fri:Wed]
```

(The last pair don't just meet, they also overlap.) By contrast, the following don't meet:

```
[Tue:Thu]  and  [Sat:Sat]
[Tue:Thu]  and  [Sat:Sun]
```

MERGES: The original definition from Chapter 7 remains unchanged: *i1* MERGES *i2* is true if and only if *i1* OVERLAPS *i2* is true or *i1* MEETS *i2* is true. Here's an example of a pair of intervals that *don't* "merge" in this sense:

```
[Mon:Wed]  and  [Fri:Sat]
```

BEGINS and ENDS: The original definitions from Chapter 7 remain unchanged: (a) *i1* BEGINS *i2* is true if and only if *b1* = *b2* and *e1* ∈ *i2* are both true; (b) *i1* ENDS *i2* is true if and only if *e1* = *e2* and *b1* ∈ *i2* are both true.

Examples:

```
[Tue:Wed]  BEGINS  [Tue:Sat]  : TRUE
[Tue:Fri]  BEGINS  [Tue:Thu]  : FALSE
[Tue:Wed]  ENDS    [Sun:Wed]  : TRUE
[Fri:Mon]  ENDS    [Sat:Mon]  : FALSE
```

UNION, INTERSECT, AND MINUS

Again let *i1* and *i2* be intervals defined over the same point type. Now, we saw in Chapter 7 that:

- *i1* UNION *i2* is defined if and only if *i1* MERGES *i2* is true.

- *i1* INTERSECT *i2* is defined if and only if *i1* OVERLAPS *i2* is true.

■ *i1* MINUS *i2* is defined if and only if (a) *i1* and *i2* are disjoint, or (b) *i1* contains either *b2* or *e2* but not both, or (c) exactly one of *i2* BEGINS *i1* and *i2* ENDS *i1* is true.

But in that chapter, of course, the underlying point type was an ordinal type. As a consequence, we were able to define the foregoing operators in terms of the auxiliary operators MAX and MIN, and these latter operators in turn were defined in terms of ">". If UNION, INTERSECT, and MINUS are to apply to intervals over cyclic point types, therefore, we need to come up with some different definitions, since ">" is no longer available to us. We propose the following. First, let *PT* be the cyclic point type in question, and let *i1* = [*b1*:*e1*] and *i2* = [*b2*:*e2*], where *b1*, *e1*, *b2*, and *e2* are values of type *PT*. Then we can define UNION, INTERSECT, and MINUS as follows.

UNION: Consider the expression *i1* UNION *i2*, where, as before, *i1* MERGES *i2* is true (the expression is undefined otherwise). The easiest way to define the semantics of this expression seems to be by means of a short pseudocode algorithm, as follows.[7]

> *Aside:* It would be nice to come up with an alternative, nonalgorithmic (i.e., nonprocedural) definition; unfortunately, it seems to be quite difficult to do so. Perhaps there's a way to generalize MAX and MIN so that the original definition from Chapter 7 still works. Of course, it's true that when it's defined, *i* = *i1* UNION *i2* contains exactly the points that appear in *i1* or *i2* or both, but it seems to be quite difficult to distinguish nonalgorithmically between the case where BEGIN(*i*) = BEGIN(*i1*) and the case where BEGIN(*i*) = BEGIN(*i2*), and similarly for END(*i*) = END(*i1*) vs. END(*i*) = END(*i2*). Analogous remarks apply to INTERSECT and MINUS also (see later). *End of aside.*

■ Starting at the point *b1*, trace around the cyclic ordering until one of the points {*b2*, *e1*, *e2*} is reached.

■ Let "*p* ≽ *q*" mean either that *p* and *q* coincide or that *q* is encountered before *p* when tracing around the cyclic ordering starting at some specified point.

■ Let "first *p* such that *p* ≽ *q*" mean whichever of the points {*b1*,*b2*,*e1*,*e2*} is encountered first when tracing around the cyclic ordering starting at *q*.[8]

Then we have:

---

[7] You might find it helpful to draw a sketch of the various cases as you work through the algorithm.

[8] Insofar as the present appendix is concerned, however, *q* will never be *e1* (except perhaps if that point coincides with one of the others), and the first *p* such that *p* ≽ *q* will never be *b1* (again, except perhaps if that point coincides with one of the others).

```
IF i1 NOT MERGES i2 THEN error (undefined) END IF ;
CASE ;
    WHEN first p such that p ⩾ b1 is b2 THEN
        CASE ;
            WHEN first p such that p ⩾ b2 is e1 THEN RETURN [b1:e2] ;
            WHEN first p such that p ⩾ b2 is e2 THEN RETURN [b1:e1] ;
        END CASE ;
    WHEN first p such that p ⩾ b1 is e1 THEN
        CASE /* i1 MEETS i2 must be true */ ;
            WHEN b2 = e1+1 THEN RETURN [b1:e2] ;
            WHEN b1 = e2+1 THEN RETURN [b2:e1] ;
        END CASE ;
    WHEN first p such that p ⩾ b1 is e2 THEN
        CASE ;
            WHEN first p such that p ⩾ e2 is b2 THEN RETURN [b1:b1-1] ;
            WHEN first p such that p ⩾ e2 is e1 THEN RETURN [b2:e1] ;
        END CASE ;
END CASE ;
```

Here are some examples:

```
[Mon:Wed] UNION [Fri:Sat] : undefined
[Mon:Thu] UNION [Tue:Fri] = [Mon:Fri]
[Tue:Fri] UNION [Mon:Thu] = [Mon:Fri]
[Mon:Thu] UNION [Sat:Tue] = [Sat:Thu]
[Thu:Sat] UNION [Mon:Thu] = [Mon:Sat]
[Sat:Sat] UNION [Sat:Sat] = [Sat:Sat]
[Tue:Fri] UNION [Sat:Tue] = [Sat:Fri]
[Tue:Fri] UNION [Sat:Mon] = [Tue:Mon]
[Sat:Mon] UNION [Tue:Fri] = [Sat:Fri]
```

Note: As the last two examples demonstrate, the algorithm isn't guaranteed to produce the same result for *i1* UNION *i2* and *i2* UNION *i1* in the special case where *i1* and *i2* between them contain all of the available values. (Both results are universal intervals, of course—i.e., they both contain all of the available values—but in general they begin at different points.) Clearly it would be preferable not to lose the commutativity of union, and so the algorithm needs a small adjustment to fix this problem.[9]

INTERSECT: Now consider the expression *i1* INTERSECT *i2*. As before, *i1* OVERLAPS *i2* must be true; note, however, that this requirement, though necessary, isn't sufficient for the expression to be defined. To be specific, we mustn't have the intervals overlapping each other at both ends, as it were (unless at least one of the intervals in question is a universal interval). Thus, with the same notation and initial conditions as for UNION above, we have:

---

[9] Of course, it's at least always true (as previously noted) that when it's defined, *i* = *i1* UNION *i2* does contain exactly the points that appear in either or both of *i1* and *i2*.

```
IF i1 NOT OVERLAPS i2 THEN error (undefined) END IF ;
IF i1 overlaps i2 at both ends¹⁰
    AND COUNT(i1) ≠ COUNT_WEEKDAY ( )
    AND COUNT(i2) ≠ COUNT_WEEKDAY ( )
THEN error (undefined) END IF ;
CASE ;
    WHEN first p such that p ≽ b1 is b2 THEN
        CASE ;
            WHEN first p such that p ≽ b2 is e1 THEN RETURN [b2:e1] ;
            WHEN first p such that p ≽ b2 is e2 THEN RETURN [b2:e2] ;
        END CASE ;
    WHEN first p such that p ≽ b1 is e1 THEN
        /* i1 ⊂ i2 must be true */ RETURN [b1:e1] ;
    WHEN first p such that p ≽ b1 is e2 THEN
        CASE ;
            WHEN first p such that p ≽ e2 is b2 THEN
                /* e1 = b1-1 must be true */ RETURN [b2:e2] ;
            WHEN first p such that p ≽ e2 is e1 THEN
                                              RETURN [b1:e2] ;
        END CASE ;
END CASE ;
```

Here are some examples (all of which use the same input intervals as their union example counterpart shown earlier, except for the last two, which had no such counterparts):

```
[Mon:Wed] INTERSECT [Fri:Sat] :  undefined
[Mon:Thu] INTERSECT [Tue:Fri] =  [Tue:Thu]
[Tue:Fri] INTERSECT [Mon:Thu] =  [Tue:Thu]
[Mon:Thu] INTERSECT [Sat:Tue] =  [Mon:Tue]
[Thu:Sat] INTERSECT [Mon:Thu] =  [Thu:Thu]
[Sat:Sat] INTERSECT [Sat:Sat] =  [Sat:Sat]
[Tue:Fri] INTERSECT [Sat:Tue] =  [Tue:Tue]
[Tue:Fri] INTERSECT [Sat:Mon] :  undefined
[Sat:Mon] INTERSECT [Tue:Fri] :  undefined
[Thu:Wed] INTERSECT [Sat:Fri] =  [Sat:Fri]
[Sat:Fri] INTERSECT [Thu:Wed] =  [Thu:Wed]
```

Note: As the last two examples demonstrate, the algorithm isn't guaranteed to produce the same result for *i1* INTERSECT *i2* and *i2* INTERSECT *i1* in the special case where *i1* and *i2* are both universal intervals.[11] As in the case of UNION, therefore, the algorithm needs a small adjustment to fix this problem.

MINUS: Now consider the expression *i1* MINUS *i2*. This expression is certainly defined if any of the following is the case (as before):

---

[10] We state this condition here only informally, for simplicity. Basically what it means, however, is this: Tracing around the cyclic ordering starting at *b1*, we encounter the points *e2*, then *b2*, then *e1*, in that order. In practice, defining a new comparison operator ("DOUBLE OVERLAPS"?) might be desirable.

[11] Of course, it's at least always true that when it's defined, *i* = *i1* INTERSECT *i2* does contain exactly the points that appear in both *i1* and *i2*.

a. *i1* and *i2* are disjoint.

b. *i1* contains either *b2* or *e2* but not both.

c. Exactly one of *i2* BEGINS *i1* and *i2* ENDS *i1* is true.

But there's another possibility too—the operator is also defined if:

d. *i1* and *i2* overlap at both ends (so long as *i2* isn't a universal interval, of course).

Thus, with the same notation and initial conditions as for UNION and INTERSECT above, we have:

```
IF COUNT ( i2 ) = COUNT_WEEKDAY ( ) THEN error (undefined) END IF ;
IF i1 OVERLAPS i2
   AND NOT ( b2 ∈ i1 XOR e2 ∈ i1 ) /* XOR = exclusive OR */
   AND NOT ( i2 BEGINS i1 XOR i2 ENDS i1 )
   AND NOT ( i1 overlaps i2 at both ends )
THEN error (undefined) END IF ;
CASE ;
   WHEN first p such that p ≽ b1 is e1 THEN RETURN [b1:e1] ;
   WHEN first p such that p ≽ b1 is b2 THEN
      CASE ;
         WHEN first p such that p ≽ b2 is e1 THEN
                                          RETURN [b1:b2-1] ;
         WHEN first p such that p ≽ b2 is e2 THEN
                                          RETURN [e2+1:b2-1] ;
      END CASE ;
   WHEN first p such that p ≽ b1 is e2 THEN
      CASE ;
         WHEN first p such that p ≽ e2 is e1 THEN
                                          RETURN [e2+1:e1] ;
         WHEN first p such that p ≽ e2 is b2 THEN
                                          RETURN [e2+1:b2-1] ;
      END CASE ;
END CASE ;
```

Here are some examples, most of which use the same input intervals as their intersection example counterpart shown earlier:[12]

---

[12] Note that at least it's always true that when it's defined, *i = i1* MINUS *i2* does contain exactly the points that appear in *i1* and not in *i2*.

```
[Mon:Wed] MINUS [Fri:Sat] = [Mon:Wed]
[Mon:Thu] MINUS [Tue:Fri] = [Mon:Mon]
[Tue:Fri] MINUS [Mon:Thu] = [Fri:Fri]
[Mon:Thu] MINUS [Sat:Tue] = [Wed:Thu]
[Thu:Sat] MINUS [Mon:Thu] = [Fri:Sat]
[Sat:Sat] MINUS [Sat:Sat] : undefined
[Tue:Fri] MINUS [Sat:Tue] = [Wed:Fri]
[Tue:Fri] MINUS [Sat:Mon] = [Tue:Fri]
[Sat:Mon] MINUS [Tue:Fri] = [Sat:Mon]
[Tue:Sun] MINUS [Sat:Wed] : [Thu:Fri]
[Sat:Fri] MINUS [Thu:Wed] : undefined
[Tue:Thu] MINUS [Thu:Fri] = [Tue:Wed]
```

PACK AND UNPACK

Given that union and intersection can both be defined for intervals over cyclic point types, so too can the PACK and UNPACK operators. For example, suppose we're given a relation *r* that looks like this:

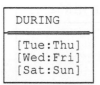

```
┌─────────────┐
│ DURING      │
╞═════════════╡
│ [Tue:Thu]   │
│ [Wed:Fri]   │
│ [Sat:Sun]   │
└─────────────┘
```

Then the packed and unpacked forms of *r* look like this (packed on the left, unpacked on the right):

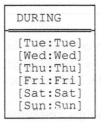

```
┌─────────────┐      ┌─────────────┐
│ DURING      │      │ DURING      │
╞═════════════╡      ╞═════════════╡
│ [Tue:Sun]   │      │ [Tue:Tue]   │
└─────────────┘      │ [Wed:Wed]   │
                     │ [Thu:Thu]   │
                     │ [Fri:Fri]   │
                     │ [Sat:Sat]   │
                     │ [Sun:Sun]   │
                     └─────────────┘
```

Overall, therefore, we conclude that:

a. Cyclic types such as WEEKDAY are indeed valid as point types.

b. Such types behave normally, except that FIRST_*T* and LAST_*T* don't apply and NEXT_*T* and PRIOR_*T* never fail.

c. The corresponding interval types also behave more or less normally, except that we don't—actually we *can't*—require the begin point to be less than or equal to the end point, and certain operators need somewhat revised definitions.

d. The conditions stated previously in Chapters 6 and 18 for a type to be usable as a point type are sufficient but not all necessary.

EXERCISES

A.1   Define "time of day," with a scale of one hour, as a cyclic point type. Include all necessary associated operator definitions.

A.2   Given that *i1* and *i2* denote intervals over the "time of day" point type, fill in the blanks in the following table:

i1	*i2*	*i1* UNION *i2*	*i1* INTERSECT *i2*	*i1* MINUS *i2*
[09:17]	[11:21]			
[08:12]	[12:16]			
[21:07]	[05:11]			
[09:18]	[05:14]			
[05:14]	[05:14]			
[09:15]	[11:14]			
[09:15]	[09:12]			
[09:12]	[13:17]			
[09:12]	[15:17]			
[09:12]	[09:15]			
[06:18]	[18:06]			

Note: We assume for simplicity here that intervals over the "time of day" point type are expressed in the form [*xx:yy*], where *xx* and *yy* are two-digit integers in the range [00:23] and denote time points accurate to the hour on the 24-hour clock.

A.3   Certain commercial enterprises (e.g., shops, restaurants) are open for business only at certain times on certain days (e.g., Monday to Friday, 9:00 am to 5:00 pm). Design a database to represent such information. What are some of the considerations that might influence your design?

ANSWERS

A.1
```
TYPE TOD CYCLIC POSSREP HOUR { H INTEGER CONSTRAINT 0 ≤ H AND H ≤ 23 } ;

OPERATOR HOUR ( H INTEGER ) RETURNS TOD ;
    /* code to return the TOD value corresponding */
    /* to the given integer H                     */
END OPERATOR ;
```

By definition, the HOUR selector takes an integer and returns a time of day accurate to the hour. We assume the argument corresponding to the parameter H is any integer. Thus, we assume the implementation code for HOUR computes *NNR* = the nonnegative remainder after dividing H by 24 and then returns the time of day corresponding to *NNR*.

```
OPERATOR THE_H ( T WEEKDAY ) RETURNS INTEGER ;
    /* code to return the integer corresponding */
    /* to the given TOD value T                 */
END OPERATOR ;
```

The integer value returned by THE_H is always in the range [00:23].

```
OPERATOR "=" ( T1 TOD ,T2 TOD ) RETURNS BOOLEAN ;
    RETURN ( THE_H ( T1 ) = THE_H ( T2 ) ) ;
END OPERATOR ;

OPERATOR NEXT_TOD ( T TOD ) RETURNS TOD ;
    RETURN HOUR ( THE_H ( T ) + 1 ) ) ;
END OPERATOR ;

OPERATOR PRIOR_TOD ( T TOD ) RETURNS TOD ;
    RETURN HOUR ( THE_H ( T ) - 1 ) ) ;
END OPERATOR ;
```

A.2

i1	*i2*	*i1* UNION *i2*	*i1* INTERSECT *i2*	*i1* MINUS *i2*
[09:17]	[11:21]	[09:21]	[11:17]	[09:10]
[08:12]	[12:16]	[08:16]	[12:12]	[08:11]
[21:07]	[05:11]	[21:11]	[05:07]	[21:04]
[09:18]	[05:14]	[05:18]	[09:14]	[15:18]
[05:14]	[05:14]	[05:14]	[05:14]	*undefined*
[09:15]	[11:14]	[09:15]	[11:14]	*undefined*
[09:15]	[09:12]	[09:15]	[09:12]	[13:15]
[09:12]	[13:17]	[09:17]	*undefined*	[09:12]
[09:12]	[15:17]	*undefined*	*undefined*	[09:12]
[09:12]	[09:15]	[09:15]	[09:12]	*undefined*
[06:18]	[18:06]	[06:05]	*undefined*	[07:17]

A.3   The exercise is open ended, so this answer is necessarily only partial. Consider a relvar *R* with attributes *CE* (commercial enterprise), *D* (interval of days), and *H* (interval of hours). The general case is: *CE* is open for business only on selected days (e.g., weekdays), and during different hours on different days (e.g., Thursday is early closing day), and during two or more disjoint intervals on at least some days (e.g., Mondays 9:00 am to 12:30 pm, 2:00 pm to 5:00 pm, closed for lunch 12:30 pm to 2:00 pm). In this general case, relvar *R* is all key. If *CE* is open for business during different hours on different days but not during two or more disjoint intervals on any given day, then relvar *R* has key {*CE,D*}. If *CE* is open for business for the same hours every day it's open, then again relvar *R* has key {*CE,D*}, but now the functional dependency {*CE*} → {*H*} holds, and *R* isn't in 6NF (in fact, it isn't even in 2NF). And so on ... E.g., what if *CE* is open for business every day of the year except for certain national holidays?

As a subsidiary exercise, try writing the predicates for the various aforementioned cases.

Appendix B

Is Ordinality Necessary?

*The ordinality of a table relationship is a message
the designer uses to identify two facts about the relationship.*

—*www.cs.kent.edu/~wfan/link/dbapre/dbatest/54903f.htm*

Throughout the bulk of this book, we've assumed that the point types over which intervals are defined must be ordinal types specifically. In other words, we've assumed that any such point type—call it T—must be "isomorphic to type INTEGER," meaning that:

1. A total ordering exists—i.e., the operator ">" is defined for every pair of values of type T.

2. A first and a last value of type T, denoted FIRST_T ( ) and LAST_T ( ), respectively, exist with respect to that ordering.

3. A successor function, denoted NEXT_T (p) and returning the (unique) immediate successor of p with respect to that ordering, is defined for every value p of type T except for $p =$ LAST_T ( ). Moreover—we didn't bother to spell these assumptions out before, but now we feel it desirable to do so—(a) if $p1 \neq p2$ then NEXT_T ($p1$) $\neq$ NEXT_T ($p2$), and (b) there's exactly one value of type T, viz., FIRST_T ( ), that's not the successor of any p.

Properties 2 and 3 here are what distinguish an ordinal type from one that's merely ordered. Let's agree to refer to those two properties, taken together, as *ordinality*. Now, if ordinality applies to type T, then it's clear that every interval of type INTERVAL_T consists of a finite sequence of discrete points. But what would happen if ordinality failed to hold? Would it be possible to build an approach to intervals based on a point type for which, say, LAST_T ( ) is undefined? Alternatively, would it be possible to build such an approach based on a point type for which NEXT_T (p) is undefined? Note that questions like these do seem worth exploring, because many languages do support types that are ordered but not ordinal.[1] For example, consider the **Tutorial D** types RATIONAL and CHAR. Both of these types are ordered, and yet **Tutorial D** has no explicit support for LAST_RATIONAL ( ), NEXT_RATIONAL (p),

---

[1] As noted in Chapter 18, if by *types* here we mean types that are supported by some actual implementation of some actual programming language, then every such type is necessarily finite. So if such a type is ordered, it can (at least in principle) be made "isomorphic to type INTEGER," in which case it will effectively be an ordinal type after all. We choose to overlook this point of detail here.

LAST_CHAR ( ), or NEXT_CHAR (*p*). As a consequence, a **Tutorial D** implementation is free not to provide such operators, and—according to the proposals discussed in the body of the book—types RATIONAL and CHAR would then not be usable as point types, a state of affairs that has certainly been criticized by some.

So let's see, first, what happens if we drop property 2 but keep property 3. By way of illustration, consider what happens if type *T* is INTEGER. For that type, it would be quite usual for a language to support NEXT_*T* (*p*)—if only in the form "*p*+1"—and yet not support either FIRST_*T* ( ) or LAST_*T* ( ).[2] But let's consider the general case:

- With regard to FIRST_*T* ( ), we observe that nothing in Parts II and III of this book depended on support for that operator (apart from that operator FIRST_*T* ( ) itself, of course).

- With regard to LAST_*T* ( ), by contrast, we did effectively make use of that operator in our "during relvars only" designs, and we also used it in certain relational expressions (i.e., in certain queries and view definitions)—that is, we frequently made use of intervals of the form [*d*:LAST_*T* ( )], to be interpreted as "from day *d* until further notice." *Note:* Here, of course, we're assuming that *T* is a temporal type specifically.

Thus, dropping LAST_*T* ( ) would appear to militate strongly in favor of our horizontal decomposition approach to temporal database design (so, good!). However, certain "temporal" queries, and in particular our proposed COMBINED_IN views, won't work any longer, and some other solution will have to be found to the issues those queries and views address. But these are hardly insuperable problems.

We turn now to the possibility of dropping property 3 but keeping property 2. Here there's rather more to say (and rather more to be investigated), inasmuch as we did propose several operators in Parts II and III of this book that depended on—or at least were defined in terms of—that successor function NEXT_*T* (*p*) that's now no longer available.

Aside: Dropping property 3—that is, dropping the assumption that a successor function exists—isn't usually referred to in the literature in such terms; instead, it's usually described as "adopting the continuity assumption," on the grounds that a point type for which no successor function exists behaves like the real number line (which is certainly continuous), and hence that intervals defined on such a point type behave like sections of that line. Note that time in particular certainly feels as if it were continuous in this sense;[3] so adopting the continuity assumption, if it were possible, might well be more intuitively attractive, at least in this particular context. We claim, however, that continuity as such

---

[2] SQL is a case in point; as noted in Chapter 19, SQL doesn't really support FIRST_*T* ( ) or LAST_*T* ( ) as such—instead, users have to write out the corresponding literals.

[3] We realize not everyone agrees with this assertion.

isn't really the issue; in fact, it seems to us a complete red herring. To see why, it's sufficient to consider just the rational numbers,[4] which resemble the reals in that they're what the mathematicians call "everywhere dense," but differ from the reals in that they don't form a continuum. In other words, the rationals have no successor function—if *p* is a rational number, there's no rational number *p'* that can be considered the immediate successor of *p*—even though, to repeat, they don't form a continuum as such. Note too that any interval defined over the rational numbers will in fact contain an infinite number of points (except for the special case of a unit interval, of course).

Now, we're not suggesting here that a point type consisting of all rational numbers might, or even could, actually be supported. However, you might find it helpful to interpret what follows in terms of a hypothetical "rational numbers" point type (containing, therefore, an infinite number of point values), and hypothetical intervals defined over that hypothetical point type. *End of aside.*

Before we go any further, we should make it clear that we're certainly not alone in assuming the existence of a successor function—essentially all of the temporal database literature does the same thing. Nor have we seen a concrete language proposal based on the idea that such an assumption be dropped. We therefore confine ourselves in the remainder of this appendix to what we hope are a few pertinent remarks.

■ *With regard to points*: As already indicated, the comparison operators ("=", ">", etc.) all still work, of course, but NEXT_*T* (*p*) and PRIOR_*T* (*p*) make no sense. By contrast, FIRST_*T* ( ) and LAST_*T* ( ) do make sense—in temporal terms, they return "the beginning of time" and "the end of time," respectively.

■ *With regard to intervals*: COUNT clearly no longer applies. By contrast, Allen's operators do apply, but any definition of such an operator that previously depended on the existence of a successor function will obviously have to be revised. Consider MEETS, for example. We can never validly say that, e.g., intervals *i1* = [*b1*:*e1*] and *i2* = [*b2*:*e2*]—both expressed using closed:closed notation, observe—meet, because we can never validly say either that *b2* is the immediate successor of *e1* or that *b1* is the immediate successor of *e2*. A similar though somewhat more complicated remark applies if both intervals are expressed using open:open notation. By contrast, if *i1* uses closed notation at its end and *i2* uses open notation at its beginning, or the other way around, then it does make sense to say of *i1* and *i2* either that they meet or that they don't. To be specific (and for the record), two intervals meet if and only if they take one of the following forms:

---

[4] And here we really do mean rational numbers as defined in mathematics, not just values of **Tutorial D**'s RATIONAL type.

$[b:p]$	and	$(p:e]$	$[b:p)$	and	$[p:e]$
$[b:p]$	and	$(p:e)$	$[b:p)$	and	$[p:e)$
$(b:p]$	and	$(p:e]$	$(b:p)$	and	$[p:e]$
$(b:p]$	and	$(p:e)$	$(b:p)$	and	$[p:e)$

We now observe that the foregoing discussion of MEETS touches on a potentially serious anomaly. In Chapter 6, we said the four notations—closed:closed, closed:open, open:closed, open:open—constituted four different possible representations for intervals, implying among other things that those notations were effectively interchangeable. However, we did also point out, in a footnote, that the interval [*b*:*e*] can't be represented in either open:closed or open:open notation if *b* is "the beginning of time," nor can it be represented in either closed:open or open:open notation if *e* is "the end of time." And we went on to say that the closed:closed notation is actually the only one that's capable of representing all possible intervals. In other words, if we assume reliance on a successor function, then the closed:closed notation is really the only one that's one hundred percent valid as a possible representation—a state of affairs that accounts in part for our favoring it throughout Parts II and III of this book, of course.

Now, given that Parts II and III of this book did assume support for a successor function, the fact that the other three notations were subject to the slight weaknesses just explained was perhaps not all that significant. But it's not at all clear that the same remains true if that assumption is dropped. For suppose we do drop it. Then:

■ First of all, none of the intervals [*b*:*e*), (*b*:*e*], and (*b*:*e*) has an exact closed:closed equivalent. In other words, there are intervals—in fact, an infinite number of them, at least in principle—that can't be represented in closed:closed notation.

■ At the same time, the interval [*b*:*e*] has no exact equivalent in any of the other three notations. Thus, there are also intervals—again, an infinite number of them, in principle— that can be represented only in closed:closed notation. *Note:* As a particularly important special case of the foregoing, intervals of the form [*p*:*p*]—that is, unit intervals—can be represented only in closed:closed notation.

■ In fact, the situation is even worse than just indicated. First, each of the four notations is capable of representing (in principle) an infinite number of intervals that can't be represented at all in any of the other three. Second, any given interval is in fact capable of representation in just one of the four notations!

It follows that we can never validly say that an expression using any particular one of the four notations denotes the same interval as one using any of the other three. The full implications of this state of affairs are unclear, to say the least, but it does seem at any rate that *none* of the four can truly be said by itself to constitute a valid possible representation for intervals, absent a successor function. Thus, it looks as if the user is going to have to be extremely careful in choosing the appropriate notation to use in any particular situation, absent such a function; in fact, the user is probably going to be forced into adopting a kind of "mix and match" approach, instead of choosing just one notation and sticking with it as we did most of the time in Parts II and III of this book. What makes matters worse is that every interval will then to have to carry with it some indication as to the notation used to express it; moreover, the system will then have to remember, somehow, which particular notation was used on each particular occasion.

Aside: Alternatively, we could say—as SQL does,[5] in effect, even though SQL does assume the existence of a successor function—that just one of the four notations is supported. In that case, the notation in question would have to be either closed:open or open:closed, if MEETS is to be supported. But then certain intervals wouldn't be expressible at all; in particular, we'd lose the concept of unit intervals altogether!—since, as we've seen, unit intervals can be expressed only using closed:closed notation. *End of aside*.

Well, let's soldier on ... Let's consider closed:open notation, just to be definite. Then the operators BEGIN (*i*) and POST (*i*) are available, but the operators PRE (*i*) and END (*i*) aren't. Of course, if *i* is the interval [*b*:*e*), then the point *e* is given by POST (*i*); however, that point isn't actually contained in *i* and is thus not truly the end point of that interval, at least not in the sense in which that term was defined in Chapter 6.

Next, regardless of which notation we consider, the UNPACK operator is no longer available. (Why not?) This loss appears to be a matter of some concern, at least at first sight. Although UNPACK is perhaps not all that useful in its own right, our "U_" operators are all defined in terms of it (and so is PACK, if the packing is done on more than one attribute); thus, we would need to revisit all of those operators to see if we could redefine them in such a way as to avoid having to rely on UNPACK. What's more, we would then have to ensure that those redefined operators were all implementable.

Stop Press: Shortly before completion of the final draft of this book, we were made aware of some recent work by Erwin Smout [102]. In that reference, Smout shows that PACK and the U_ operators—or most of them, at any rate[6]—can indeed be defined without appealing to UNPACK. Now, we do believe our definition, using UNPACK, is easier to understand from a conceptual point of view; but given Smout's definition, it does seem that some limited support for intervals over nonordinal types could be provided *alongside* support for intervals over ordinal types as described in the body of the book. See the annotation to reference [102] in Appendix F for further discussion.

---

[5] In fact, as SQL *must* do (see Chapter 19).

[6] Unfortunately the jury is still out regarding U_restrict and U_extend, and when it will come back remains to be seen. Our discussion of these operators in Appendix E is relevant here.

The foregoing remarks notwithstanding, we certainly don't want to discard reliance on a successor function altogether, for the following reasons among others:

■ First, we've seen that certain operators—e.g., COUNT (*i*)—that can be defined when a successor function exists can't be defined when it doesn't (other than as discussed under "One final point" below). Note in particular that not having to depend on some specific notation—closed:open, for example—does convey significant advantages.

■ Second, nobody has yet been able to show us any *useful* operators that can be defined if we discard the successor function and not if we don't.

It seems, then, that there's nothing to lose, and much to gain, by assuming the successor function exists.

One final point: It has been suggested that it might be possible to make operators that depend on a successor function work even if no such function is defined for the point type in question. The idea is that the desired scale—and thereby the desired successor function, in effect—could be specified explicitly when the operator in question is invoked. For example, let *i* be a temporal interval, and let the underlying temporal point type be ordered but not ordinal. Then we've seen that, e.g., the expression COUNT (*i*) makes no sense. However, if we define *j* to be the expression—

```
INTERVAL_DDATE ( [ CAST_TO_DDATE ( BEGIN ( i ) ) ,
                    CAST_TO_DDATE ( POST  ( i ) ) ] )
```

—then the expression COUNT (*j*) clearly does make sense. *Explanation*: The CAST invocations each effectively convert their argument to a time point that's accurate to the day. The overall interval selector invocation *j* thus effectively converts the interval *i* to one whose contained points are discrete and accurate to the day, and thereby effectively specifies the pertinent scale and successor function.

Our response to the foregoing is as follows: If the assumption that there's no successor function means having to replace all corresponding intervals by ones for which such a function does apply every time we want to perform certain important operations on them, then there seems little point in adopting that assumption in the first place. Indeed, if we're correct in saying that adopting that assumption brings with it no useful operators that are unavailable otherwise, then a language that makes that assumption would be isomorphic to one that doesn't, and the entire argument reduces to a mere matter of syntax. However, we note that not having to specify the scale explicitly every time we want to perform any of the otherwise undefined operations would surely save a great deal of writing.

Appendix C

Generalizing PACK and UNPACK

All generalizations are dangerous
(often quoted in the form *All generalizations are false*).
—Alexandre Dumas *fils* (attrib.)

In Chapter 8, we introduced the operators EXPAND and COLLAPSE and considered their effect on sets of intervals specifically. But we did also note the point in passing that there's no reason why those operators shouldn't be generalized to work on other kinds of sets, and indeed there might be good reasons to do so. In this appendix, we briefly investigate this possibility. Recall from Chapter 10, however, that EXPAND and COLLAPSE—meaning, specifically, the unary relation versions of those operators—are really special cases of UNPACK and PACK, respectively; thus, the discussions in this appendix can and will be framed in terms of UNPACK and PACK instead of EXPAND and COLLAPSE as such. For simplicity, however, we'll pretend as we did throughout most of Chapter 8—barring explicit statements to the contrary— that the operands to those operators are just sets and not, as they really ought to be, unary relations. Among other things, this pretense should help make the pictures we'll be drawing to illustrate the ideas a little easier to understand.

SETS OF RELATIONS

Let X be a set of relations all of the same type RT. Then we define UNPACK (X) and PACK (X) as follows:

- UNPACK (X) returns a set Y of relations of type RT, such that (a) each relation in Y is of cardinality one and (b) a relation containing tuple t appears in Y if and only if a relation containing tuple t appears in X. Note in particular, therefore, that if X is empty, then Y is empty also. (What happens if X contains just one relation and that relation is empty?)

- PACK (X) returns a set Y containing exactly one relation of type RT: namely, the union of all of the relations in X.[1] Note in particular, therefore, that if X is empty, then Y contains just the empty relation of type RT, and if X contains just one relation r, then Y also contains

---

[1] In other words, PACK for a set of relations is basically just *aggregate union* (see, e.g., reference [42] or reference [50]).

just that one relation *r*. (Refer to Chapter 2 if you need to refresh your memory regarding unions of just one relation and unions of no relations at all.)

Fig. C.1 shows a sample set of relations and the corresponding unpacked and packed forms of that set.

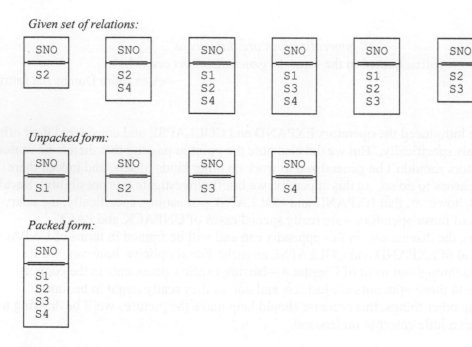

Fig. C.1: Unpacking and packing a set of relations (example)

SETS OF SETS

In similar fashion we can define UNPACK and PACK for sets of sets. Let *ST* be some set type,[2] and let *X* be a set of sets all of type *ST*. Then:

■ UNPACK (*X*) returns a set *Y* of sets of type *ST*, such that (a) each set in *Y* is of cardinality one and (b) a set containing the value *v* appears in *Y* if and only if a set containing the value *v* appears in *X*. *Note:* If *X* is empty, then *Y* is empty also. What happens if *X* contains just one set and that set is empty?

---

[2] The term *set type* hasn't been defined or previously used in this book, but its meaning is surely obvious. Analogous remarks apply to the term *bag type* in the next two sections.

■ PACK (*X*) returns a set *Y* containing exactly one set of type *ST*: namely, the union of all of the sets in *X*. (If *X* is empty, then *Y* contains just the empty set of type *ST*, and if *X* contains just one set *s*, then *Y* also contains just that one set *s*.)

Fig. C.2 gives an example (compare Fig. C.1).

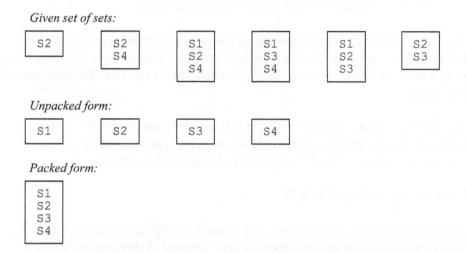

Fig. C.2: Unpacking and packing a set of sets (example)

SETS OF BAGS

We can also, albeit somewhat less satisfactorily, define UNPACK and PACK for sets of bags.[3] Let *X* be a set of bags all of the same type *BT*. Then:

■ UNPACK (*X*) returns a set *Y* of bags of type *BT*, such that (a) each bag in *Y* is of cardinality one and (b) a bag containing the value *v* appears in *Y* if and only if a bag containing the value *v* appears in *X*. *Note carefully that each bag in Y is in fact a set, and furthermore that (by definition, since Y is a set) no bag in Y appears more than once.*

■ PACK (*X*) returns a set *Y* containing exactly one bag of type *BT*: namely, the union of all of the bags in *X*.

At this point, however, we run into a problem. What exactly do we mean by "the union of all of the bags in *X*"? It turns out that if *A* and *B* are bags, then there are three different

---

[3] Recall from Chapter 2 that a *bag*, also known as a *multiset*, is like a set but permits duplicates.

interpretations that might be given to the natural language expression "the union of *A* and *B*"—i.e., there are three different union operators that can apply to bags [39]:

■ The first is the regular *set union* operator, which returns a result—in fact, a set—in which the value *v* appears exactly once if and only if it appears in *A* or *B* or both at least once. In SQL terms, this is the UNION DISTINCT operator (more or less).

■ The second is what might be called the *union plus* operator, which returns a result—a bag—in which the value *v* appears exactly *n* times if and only if it appears exactly *a* times in *A* and exactly *b* times in *B* and *n* = *a*+*b*. In SQL terms, this is the UNION ALL operator (again, more or less).

■ The third is the true *bag union* operator as such [39], which returns a result—again a bag—in which the value *v* appears exactly *n* times if and only if it appears exactly *a* times in *A* and exactly *b* times in *B* and *n* = MAX {*a*,*b*}. SQL doesn't support this operator.

So which union should we use in "bag PACK"?

■ If it's the regular set union, the resulting bag will contain no duplicates (in fact, it'll be a set). In a sense, therefore, information—specifically, "amount of duplication" information—represented by the original set of bags will be lost (in general).

■ On the other hand, if it's one of the other two unions, then one unfortunate consequence is that the expressions PACK (*X*) and PACK (UNPACK (*X*)) will produce different results (again in general).

To illustrate these matters, let *X* contain just two bags, one containing just one occurrence of the supplier number S1 and nothing else, and the other containing just two occurrences of the supplier number S1 and nothing else. Then:

■ UNPACK (*X*) returns a set containing just one bag (actually a set) containing just one occurrence of S1.

■ PACK (UNPACK (*X*)) thus also returns a set containing just one bag (actually a set) containing just one occurrence of S1—and we get this same result no matter which union we use in the definition of PACK.

■ However, PACK (*X*) returns three different results, depending on which kind of union we use:

- (*Set union*) PACK (*X*) returns the same result as PACK (UNPACK (*X*)): namely, a set containing just one bag containing just one occurrence of S1. (But therefore the "amount of duplication" information—i.e., the fact that S1 appeared once in one bag and twice in the other in the original set of bags *X*—has been lost. Of course, the same observation applies to UNPACK (*X*) also in this example.)

- (*Union plus*) PACK (*X*) returns a set containing just one bag containing three occurrences of S1. This result is different from the result of PACK (UNPACK (*X*)) (see above).

- (*Bag union*) PACK (*X*) returns a set containing just one bag containing two occurrences of S1. This result is also different from the result of PACK (UNPACK (*X*)) (see above).

From the foregoing analysis, it follows that, while we certainly can define UNPACK and PACK operators for sets of bags if we want to, on the whole it looks as if it might not be a good idea to do so. Moreover, analogous remarks apply to sets of lists and sets of arrays and, more generally, to sets involving *any* kind of "collection," if individual collections of the kind in question can contain distinct elements with the same value.

BAGS: A DIGRESSION

This appendix overall is concerned primarily with various kinds of sets; however, the discussions of the previous section ("Sets of Bags") remind us that some languages—SQL among them—support bags in addition to or in place of sets, and the case of bags as opposed to sets is thus perhaps worth some brief consideration as well. Now, bags can of course contain elements of many different kinds (integers, tuples, intervals, relations, and so on). In this appendix, however, we limit our attention to the cases of (a) bags whose contained elements are sets—the inverse, in a sense, of the case examined in the previous section—and (b) bags whose contained elements are themselves bags in turn.

Bags of Sets

Let *X* be a bag of sets, all of the same type *ST*. Then:

- UNPACK (*X*) returns a bag *Y* of sets of type *ST*, such that (a) each set in *Y* is of cardinality one and (b) a set containing the value *v* appears in *Y* exactly *n* times if and only if that value *v* appears in exactly *n* sets in *X*.

- PACK (*X*) returns a bag *Y* containing exactly one set of type *ST*: namely, the set union of all of the sets in *X*. (Since by definition the elements in *X* are sets specifically, the only kind of union that makes sense here is, of course, regular set union.)

By way of illustration, let *X* contain just three sets, one containing just the supplier number S1, one containing just the supplier numbers S1 and S2, and one being empty. Then:

- UNPACK (*X*) returns a bag containing just three sets, two containing just S1 and one containing just S2.

- PACK (UNPACK (*X*)) returns a bag (actually a set) containing just one set, containing just S1 and S2.

- PACK (*X*) returns the same result as PACK (UNPACK (*X*)).

It follows that if we support bags at all, we can certainly define PACK and UNPACK for the particular case of bags whose contained elements are sets, if we want to.

Bags of Bags

Now we turn our attention to the case of bags whose contained elements are bags themselves—despite the fact that (in accordance with the remarks at the end of the section "Sets of Bags") it's our belief that support for UNPACK and PACK on such a construct might be a little unwise. Be that as it may, let *X* be a bag of bags all of the same type *BT*. Then:

- UNPACK (*X*) returns a bag *Y* of bags of type *ST*, such that (a) each bag in *Y* is of cardinality one and (b) a bag containing the value *v* appears in *Y* exactly *n* times if and only if that value *v* appears a total of *n* times in the "union plus" of all of the bags in *X*.

- PACK (*X*) returns a set *Y* containing exactly one bag of type *BT*: namely, the union of all of the bags in *X*—but again, as in the section "Sets of Bags," we have three choices as to what might be meant by the term "union" here.

Development of examples to illustrate the foregoing definitions is left as an exercise.

OTHER KINDS OF SETS

What about sets (or possibly bags) of values that aren't collections?—for example, a set of integers or a set of tuples? Without going into details, suffice it to say that we've investigated this question, and we believe PACK and UNPACK should both be defined just to return their input in such cases.

EFFECT ON "PACK AND UNPACK ON"

Chapters 9 and 10 described in great detail what we might call "the PACK and UNPACK ON" operators—i.e., versions of PACK and UNPACK that pack or unpack a given relation on the basis of some interval attribute (Chapter 9), or more generally on the basis of some number of such attributes (Chapter 10). So what about packing or unpacking a relation on the basis of an attribute of some other type? In this section, we consider just one example of this possibility; to be specific, we show what's involved in packing a relation on a single attribute, but one that's relation valued instead of interval valued (an unpack analog of the example is left as an exercise). Fig. C.3 shows such a relation; let's call it r. Note the redundancy in that relation—for example, it shows supplier S2 paired with part P3 twice. Note that it also shows supplier S3 paired with no parts at all.

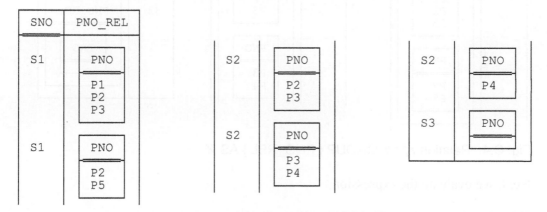

Fig. C.3: A relation with a relation valued attribute (RVA)

From the definition of the PACK operator in Chapter 9, we have the following as the expansion for the expression PACK r ON (PNO_REL):[4]

```
WITH ( r1 := r GROUP { PNO_REL } AS X ,
       r2 := EXTEND r1 : { X := COLLAPSE ( X ) } ) :
r2 UNGROUP X
```

Let's consider this expansion one step at a time.

---

[4] And here for clarity we retain the reference to COLLAPSE as such, instead of replacing it by PACK.

1. First, we evaluate the expression

```
r GROUP { PNO_REL } AS X
```

The result is shown in Fig. C.4. Observe that not only does that result have an attribute, *X*, that's relation valued (as is always the case with the result of a GROUP operation), but the relations that are values of that attribute have a single attribute, PNO_REL, that's relation valued in turn. In other words, there's a kind of "double nesting" going on here—the result is a relation that contains relations that contain relations.

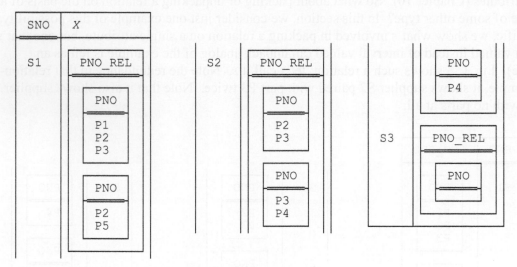

Fig. C.4: Relation *r1* = *r* GROUP { PNO_REL } AS *X*

2. Next, we evaluate the expression

```
EXTEND r1 : { X := COLLAPSE ( X ) }
```

The result, *r2*, is shown in Fig. C.5.

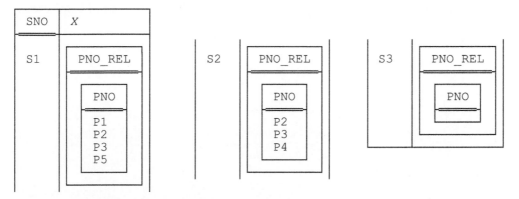

Fig. C.5: Relation *r2* = EXTEND *r1*: {*X* = COLLAPSE (*X*)}

3. Finally, we evaluate the expression

```
r2 UNGROUP X
```

The result is shown in Fig. C.6. Note that the net effect is to eliminate all of the redundancies that were present in the original relation *r*. The parallels with packing a relation on an interval valued attribute should be obvious.

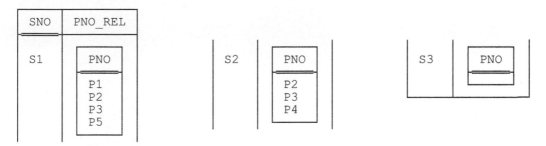

Fig. C.6: Overall result of PACK *r* ON (PNO_REL)

Appendix D

A Tutorial D Grammar

I never use a big, big D—

—W. S. Gilbert:
HMS Pinafore (1878)

This appendix gives for purposes of reference a simple BNF grammar for **Tutorial D** relational expressions and assignments (only). The grammar is derived from the comprehensive version given in reference [50] but additionally takes account of image relations, which aren't mentioned in that reference.[1] *Note:* For space reasons, certain of the syntactic categories mentioned in this grammar have names that are slightly abbreviated compared to their counterparts in the body of the book (e.g., *<relation selector>* instead of *<relation selector invocation>*). Also, the following are deliberately omitted:

- Aspects of the language not used in this book

- Definitional operations, such as those used to define base relvars, views, and constraints

- Nonrelational expressions, including aggregate operator invocations in particular

- Everything proposed in this book for dealing with intervals and related matters

Also, the grammar is simplified in certain respects. In particular, it makes no attempt to say where image relations can and can't be used, nor does it pay any attention to operator precedence. (As a result of this latter point, certain constructs permitted by the grammar—for example, the expression *r1* MINUS *r2* MINUS *r3*—are potentially ambiguous. Additional rules are needed to resolve such issues, but such rules are omitted here. Of course, parentheses and/or WITH specifications can always be used to guarantee a desired order of evaluation anyway.)

A few further points of detail:

---

[1] The website *www.thethirdmanifesto.com* contains the most recent version of reference [50]. It also gives information regarding a variety of existing **Tutorial D** implementations, as well as other projects related to *The Third Manifesto* as such (see reference [52]). See also *http://dbappbuilder.sourceforge.net/rel.html*, which provides access to free downloads for *Rel*, a prototype implementation of **Tutorial D** by Dave Voorhis.

■ All syntactic categories of the form *<... name>* are assumed to be *<identifier>*s and are defined no further in this appendix.

■ Although the category *<bool exp>* is left undefined, it might help to recall that a relational comparison in particular is a special case.

■ As always, all of the various commalists mentioned are allowed to be empty.

Note: Please don't be confused by the fact that, in accordance with normal convention, we use brackets "[" and "]" in this grammar to enclose optional material. (In the body of the book, of course, brackets were used in interval selector invocations and were thus part of the language as such, not part of the metalanguage.) By contrast, we depart from normal convention in that braces "{" and "}" in the grammar stand for themselves—i.e., they're symbols in the language being defined, not, as they usually are, symbols of the metalanguage. To be specific, braces are used in the grammar below to enclose commalists of items when the commalist in question is intended to denote a set of some kind—implying in particular that (a) the order in which the items appear within that commalist is immaterial, and further that (b) if an item appears within that commalist more than once, it's treated as if it appeared just once.

Expressions

```
<relation exp>
    ::=    <with exp> | <nonwith exp> | ( <relation exp> )

<with exp>
    ::=    WITH ( <temp assign commalist> ) : <relation exp>
```

Note: A *<temp assign>* is syntactically identical to a *<relation assign>*, except that an introduced "temporary" name can appear wherever a *<relvar name>* can appear.[2]

```
<nonwith exp>
    ::=    <image relation ref> | <relation op> | ( <relation op> )

<image relation ref>
    ::=    !!<relvar name> | !!( <relation exp> ) | ( <image relation ref> )

<relation op>
    ::=    <relation selector> | <monadic op> | <dyadic op> | <n-adic op>

<relation selector>
    ::=    RELATION [ <heading> ] { <tuple exp commalist> }
         | TABLE_DUM | TABLE_DEE
```

---

[2] Actually a *<temp assign>* doesn't have to be a relational assignment specifically, but we make no attempt to include the nonrelational case in the simplified grammar in this appendix.

Note: In the first *<relation selector>* format, the optional *<heading>* must be specified if the *<tuple exp commalist>* is empty. TABLE_DUM and TABLE_DEE are shorthand for the *<relation selector>*s RELATION { } { } and RELATION { } { TUPLE { }}, respectively.

```
<heading>
    ::=    { <attribute commalist> }

<attribute>
    ::=    <attribute name> <type name>

<monadic op>
    ::=    <relvar name> | <rename> | <where> | <project> | <extend>
         | <wrap> | <unwrap> | <group> | <ungroup>

<rename>
    ::=    <relation exp> RENAME { <renaming commalist> }

<renaming>
    ::=    <attribute name> AS <attribute name>

<where>
    ::=    <relation exp> [ WHERE <bool exp> ]

<project>
    ::=    <relation exp> { [ ALL BUT ] <attribute name commalist> }

<extend>
    ::=    EXTEND <relation exp> : { <attribute assign commalist> }

<wrap>
    ::=    <relation exp> WRAP { [ ALL BUT ] <attribute name commalist> }
                                        AS <attribute name>

<unwrap>
    ::=    <relation exp> UNWRAP <attribute name>

<group>
    ::=    <relation exp> GROUP { [ ALL BUT ] <attribute name commalist> }
                                        AS <attribute name>

<ungroup>
    ::=    <relation exp> UNGROUP <attribute name>

<attribute assign>
    ::=    <attribute name> := <exp>
```

Note: An alternative form of *<attribute assign>*, syntactically identical to a *<relation assign>* except that the pertinent *<attribute name>* (a) can appear wherever a *<relvar name>* is allowed and (b) must appear in place of the target *<relvar name>* (in both cases, within that *<attribute assign>*), is also supported if the attribute in question is relation valued. The same goes for tuple valued attributes, mutatis mutandis.

```
<dyadic op>
    ::=    <relation exp> <dyadic op name> <relation exp>

<dyadic op name>
    ::=    UNION | D_UNION | INTERSECT | MINUS | I_MINUS
           | JOIN | TIMES | MATCHING | NOT MATCHING

<n-adic op>
    ::=    <n-adic op name> { <relation exp commalist> }

<n-adic op name>
    ::=    UNION | D_UNION | INTERSECT | JOIN | TIMES

<relation comp>
    ::=    <relation exp> <relation comp op> <relation exp>

<relation comp op>
    ::=    = | ≠ | ⊆ | ⊂ | ⊇ | ⊃
```

Assignments

```
<relation assignment>
    ::=    [ WITH ( <temp assign commalist> ) : ]
                              <relation assign commalist> ;

<relation assign>
    ::=    <relvar name> := <relation exp>
        | <insert> | <d_insert>| <delete> | <i_delete>| <update>

<insert>
    ::=    INSERT <relvar name> <relation exp>

<d_insert>
    ::=    D_INSERT <relvar name> <relation exp>

<delete>
    ::=    DELETE <relvar name> <relation exp>
        | DELETE <relvar name> [ WHERE <bool exp> ]

<i_delete>
    ::=    I_DELETE <relvar name> <relation exp>

<update>
    ::=    UPDATE <relvar name> [ WHERE <bool exp> ] :
                              { <attribute assign commalist> }
```

Appendix E

Implementation Considerations

There are only two qualities in the world:
efficiency and inefficiency.

—George Bernard Shaw:
John Bull's Other Island (1907)

Our primary aim in this book has been to show how the relational model can be used to address the problem of temporal data management or, more generally, any problem for which the interval abstraction is applicable. In other words, our concern has been with getting the underlying theory right. In this appendix, by contrast, we take a look at the pragmatic issue of implementation—though we should say immediately that some of the ideas we'll be discussing are still somewhat logical, not physical, in nature, and are thus still model issues in a way. To be specific, we'll be considering among other things certain transformation laws (which we'll refer to as just *transforms* for short) that apply to certain of the relational operators—PACK and UNPACK in particular—and those transforms can certainly be regarded as characteristics of, or logical consequences of, the underlying model. We'll also sketch the details of certain implementation algorithms for all of those operators.

Of course, we make no claim that what follows is the last word on the matter. Indeed, it wouldn't be the last word even if we were to expand it to include all of our own thoughts on the subject. New and better techniques are constantly being invented in this field as in others, and we welcome the possibility of innovations on the part of other workers in this area.

PACK AND UNPACK

We begin by listing some simple transforms that apply to the PACK and UNPACK operators in particular (with additional commentary in certain cases). Let r be an arbitrary relation. Then:

1. PACK r ON ( ) $\equiv$ r
2. UNPACK r ON ( ) $\equiv$ r

Now let r have interval attributes $A1, A2, ..., An$ ($n \geq 1$), and let ACL be a commalist of attribute names containing just those names $A1, A2, ..., An$ in sequence as shown. Then:

3. PACK (PACK *r* ON (ACL)) ON (ACL)   ≡ PACK *r* ON (ACL)

4. PACK (UNPACK *r* ON (ACL)) ON (ACL) ≡ PACK *r* ON (ACL)

5. UNPACK (UNPACK *r* ON (ACL)) ON (ACL) ≡ UNPACK *r* ON (ACL)

6. UNPACK (PACK *r* ON (ACL)) ON (ACL)   ≡ UNPACK *r* ON (ACL)

   Now let *BCL* be an arbitrary permutation of *ACL*. Then:

7. UNPACK *r* ON (ACL) ≡ UNPACK *r* ON (BCL)

Note that an analogous transform does *not* apply to PACK, in general.

   Next, recall from Chapter 10 that PACK *r* ON (*ACL*) for *n* > 1 is defined to require a preliminary *UNPACK r* ON (*ACL*). In other words:

   PACK *r* ON (ACL) ≡
       PACK (... (PACK (PACK *r'* ON (A1)) ON (A2)) ...) ON (An)

where *r'* is

   UNPACK *r* ON (A1 , A2 , ..., An)

However, there's no need to do the preliminary UNPACK on *A1*. In other words, the following is another valid transform:

8. PACK *r* ON (ACL) ≡
       PACK (... (PACK (PACK *r''* ON (A1)) ON (A2)) ...) ON (An)

where *r''* is

   UNPACK *r* ON (A2 , ..., An)

As an important special case of Transform 8, we can ignore the implicit initial UNPACK entirely when packing on just a single attribute (as in fact we already know).

   Now let *r* be a relation with an interval attribute *A*, and let *B* be all of the attributes of *r* apart from *A*. Let *r1, r2, ..., rk* be a partitioning of *r* on *B*—i.e., a grouping of the tuples of *r* into distinct sets (*partitions*) *r1, r2, ..., rk* such that (a) all *B* values in partition *ri* are the same and (b) *B* values in partitions *ri* and *rj* (*i* ≠ *j*) are different. Then, using the *n*-adic form of D_UNION ("disjoint union"), we have:

9. PACK *r* ON (A) ≡ D_UNION { PACK *r1* ON (A) ,
                                  PACK *r2* ON (A) ,
                                  ....   ,
                                  PACK *rk* ON (A) }

```
10.  UNPACK r ON ( A )  ≡  D_UNION { UNPACK r1 ON ( A ) ,
                                     UNPACK r2 ON ( A ) ,
                                     .........           ,
                                     UNPACK rk ON ( A ) }
```

We'll make use of Transform 9 in particular in our discussion of the SPLIT operator, later. We close the present discussion by observing that if

a. *r* is a relation with an interval attribute *A* and *B* is all of the attributes of *r* apart from *A* (as for Transforms 9 and 10 above), and

b. *r* is represented in storage by a stored file *f* such that there's a one to one correspondence between the tuples of *r* and the stored records of *f*, and

c. *f* is sorted in "BEGIN (*A*) within *B*" order,

then PACK *r* ON (*A*) and UNPACK *r* ON (*A*) can both be implemented in a single pass over *f*. The PACK case is particularly important, and we therefore offer some further comments in connection with it.

Suppose we're processing that stored file *f* in "BEGIN (*A*) within *B*" order. Consider a particular *B* value *b*; by definition, all stored records having *B* = *b* will be grouped together. Therefore, when we're processing that particular group of stored records, as soon as we encounter one whose *A* value neither meets nor overlaps the *A* value from the immediately preceding record, we can emit an output record (and similarly when we reach the end of the entire group). The PACK implementation can thus be *pipelined*—i.e., the result can be computed "one tuple at a time" (more correctly, one record at a time), and there's no need for the invoker to wait for the entire result to be materialized before carrying out further work.

The foregoing observations are pertinent to many of the implementation algorithms to be discussed in the sections to follow. In particular, those observations imply that whenever such an algorithm talks about inserting a tuple into some result that's being built up gradually, it might be possible for the implementation to return just the tuple in question—or the record, rather—to the invoker; thus, the overall result (usually representing some relation in some unpacked form) might never need to be physically materialized in its entirety.

In addition to the foregoing considerations, if *f* is indeed sorted on *B* as suggested, then that fact permits an obvious and efficient implementation for the operation of partitioning *r* on *B*. This point is worth making explicitly because several of the algorithms to be discussed in the sections that follow make use of such partitioning.

———— ◆◆◆◆◆ ————

The various U_ operators discussed in Chapter 11 are all defined in terms of PACK and UNPACK. An efficient implementation of these latter operators is thus highly desirable. We now take a closer look at this issue.

PACK

The basic problem with PACK from an implementation standpoint is that it's defined in terms of a preliminary series of *UN*PACKs, and UNPACK has the potential to be extremely expensive in execution, in terms of both space and time. Following reference [76], therefore, we now proceed to show how:

a. Certain of those preliminary UNPACKs can be "optimized away" entirely, and

b. Others can be replaced internally by a more efficient operator called SPLIT.

It's convenient to begin by introducing an operator that we'll call PACK′ ("pack prime"). Informally, PACK′ is the same as PACK, except that it doesn't do the preliminary unpacking that's required by the formal definition of PACK as such. (In our implementation algorithms, therefore, we'll take care to use PACK′ in place of PACK only when we know it's safe to do so—in particular, when we know the input relation is appropriately unpacked already.) Here first is the definition of PACK′ when the packing is to be done on the basis of just a single attribute:[1]

```
PACK'  r ON ( A )  ≡
       WITH ( r1 := r GROUP { A } AS X ,
              r2 := EXTEND r1 : { X := COLLAPSE ( X ) } ) :
       r2 UNGROUP Y
```

This definition is identical to the one we gave for the regular PACK operator in Chapter 9, where we were concerned with packing on the basis of a single attribute only. In other words, PACK′ is identical to PACK if the packing is on the basis of a single attribute—naturally, since no preliminary unpacking is necessary when packing on the basis of just one attribute, as we already know.

Next, we define PACK′ on attributes $A1, A2, ..., An$ ($n > 1$), in that order, thus:

```
PACK'  r ON ( A1 , A2 , ... , An )  ≡
PACK' ( ... ( PACK' ( PACK' r ON ( A1 ) ) ON ( A2 ) ) ... ) ON ( An )
```

---

[1] As in Appendix C, for clarity we retain the reference to COLLAPSE in this expansion instead of replacing it by PACK.

Here's an example. Consider Fig. E.1, which shows a sample value for relvar S_PARTS_DURING—a relvar that, as you'll recall from Chapter 6 and elsewhere, has two interval attributes, PARTS and DURING.[2] We've labeled the tuples in the figure for purposes of subsequent reference. Observe that the relation in the figure does involve certain redundancies; for example, tuples *x3* and *x4* both tell us among other things that supplier S1 was able to supply part P06 on day *d08*.

	SNO	PARTS	DURING
x1	S1	[P01:P02]	[*d01:d04*]
x2	S1	[P04:P09]	[*d01:d04*]
x3	S1	[P06:P10]	[*d03:d08*]
x4	S1	[P01:P08]	[*d07:d10*]
x5	S2	[P15:P20]	[*d01:d10*]
x6	S3	[P01:P05]	[*d10:d15*]
x7	S3	[P01:P05]	[*d16:d20*]
x8	S3	[P05:P10]	[*d25:d30*]

Fig. E.1: Relvar S_PARTS_DURING—sample value

Of course, we can eliminate those redundancies—also any circumlocutions that might be present—by replacing the current value of S_PARTS_DURING by the result of evaluating the following expression (which uses PACK, not PACK′, please note):

```
PACK S_PARTS_DURING ON ( PARTS , DURING )
```

Given the relation shown in Fig. E.1, the result is shown in Fig. E.2.

	SNO	PARTS	DURING
y1	S1	[P01:P02]	[*d01:d04*]
y2	S1	[P04:P09]	[*d01:d02*]
y3	S1	[P04:P10]	[*d03:d04*]
y4	S1	[P06:P10]	[*d05:d06*]
y5	S1	[P01:P10]	[*d07:d08*]
y6	S1	[P01:P08]	[*d09:d10*]
y7	S2	[P15:P20]	[*d01:d10*]
y8	S3	[P01:P05]	[*d10:d20*]
y9	S3	[P05:P10]	[*d25:d30*]

Fig. E.2: Packing the relation of Fig. E.1 on (PARTS,DURING)

---

[2] Two points here: First, most of the discussions in this appendix are expressed in terms of packing and unpacking on exactly two attributes, for definiteness. However, those discussions all extend gracefully to the case of *n* attributes for arbitrary *n* (see references [80-81]); in particular, they apply to the important special case *n* = 1, a case that's much easier to deal with in practice, as we'll see. Second, as with Fig. 6.2 in Chapter 6 (and for essentially the same reasons), the "sample value" shown for relvar S_PARTS_DURING in Fig. E.1 is actually incomplete; however, this fact doesn't materially affect the subsequent discussion.

Next, we note that (thanks to Transform 4) the foregoing PACK expression is logically equivalent to this longer one:

```
PACK
    ( UNPACK S_PARTS_DURING ON ( DURING , PARTS ) )
ON ( PARTS , DURING )
```

Note: We've deliberately specified the attributes in the sequence DURING then PARTS (for the UNPACK) and PARTS then DURING (for the PACK), for reasons that'll become clear in just a moment. Of course, the sequence makes no difference anyway in the case of UNPACK.

We now observe that the argument to PACK in the foregoing longer expression is guaranteed to be appropriately unpacked, and we can therefore safely replace that PACK by PACK′ instead, thus:

```
PACK′
    ( UNPACK S_PARTS_DURING ON ( DURING , PARTS ) )
ON ( PARTS , DURING )
```

This expression in turn is logically equivalent to:

```
WITH ( t1 := UNPACK S_PARTS_DURING ON ( DURING ) ,
       t2 := UNPACK t1 ON ( PARTS ) ,
       t3 := PACK′ t2 ON ( PARTS ) ) :
PACK′ t3 ON ( DURING )
```

However, we can replace *t2* by *t1* in the third step here (dropping the second step entirely), thanks to the following identity:

```
PACK′ ( UNPACK t1 ON ( PARTS ) ) ON ( PARTS ) ≡ PACK′ t1 ON ( PARTS )
```

(This identity is clearly valid, because (a) PACK′ is identical to PACK if the operation is performed on the basis of a single attribute, and (b) we know from Transform 4 that the identity that results if we replace PACK′ by PACK on both sides is valid.) So the overall expression can be simplified to just:

```
WITH ( t1 := UNPACK S_PARTS_DURING ON ( DURING ) ,
       t3 := PACK′ t1 ON ( PARTS ) ) :
PACK′ t3 ON ( DURING )
```

So we've succeeded in optimizing away one of the UNPACKs, and the operation is thus more efficient than it was before.

Can we get rid of the second UNPACK as well? Well, we've already indicated that the answer to this question is *yes*, but the details are a little more complicated than they were for the first one. Basically, the idea is to avoid unpacking "all the way," as it were (i.e., unpacking all the way down to unit intervals); instead, we "unpack" (or *split*, rather) only as far as is truly necessary—which is to say, down only to certain *disjoint subintervals*. The effect is to produce a result with (in general) fewer tuples than a full UNPACK would produce; however, that result is still such as to allow us "to focus on the information content ... without having to worry about the many different ways in which that information might be bundled together into clumps," as we put it in Chapter 8.

By way of example, consider tuple *x3* from Fig. E.1:

	SNO	PARTS	DURING
x3	S1	[P06:P10]	[*d03:d08*]

This tuple can be split into the following three tuples (note the tuple labels):

	SNO	PARTS	DURING
x31	S1	[P06:P10]	[*d03:d04*]

	SNO	PARTS	DURING
x32	S1	[P06:P10]	[*d05:d06*]

	SNO	PARTS	DURING
x33	S1	[P06:P10]	[*d07:d08*]

Of course, tuples *x31-x33* together represent the same information as the original tuple *x3* did.

Why exactly would we want to split tuple *x3* in the way just shown? In order to answer this question, consider first the relation—let's call it *X*—that's the restriction of the relation in Fig. E.1 to just the tuples for supplier S1:

	SNO	PARTS	DURING
x1	S1	[P01:P02]	[*d01:d04*]
x2	S1	[P04:P09]	[*d01:d04*]
x3	S1	[P06:P10]	[*d03:d08*]
x4	S1	[P01:P08]	[*d07:d10*]

Note that the tuple to be split, tuple *x3*, has DURING value *i* = [*d03:d08*]. Intuitively speaking, then, we split tuple *x3* the way we did because:

■ Interval *i* consists of the six points *d03*, *d04*, *d05*, *d06*, *d07*, and *d08*.

■ Of these six, the four points *d03*, *d04*, *d07*, and *d08* (only) are boundary points—i.e., begin or end points—for the DURING value in at least one tuple in *X*.

■ Those boundary points divide interval *i* into precisely the subintervals [*d03:d04*], [*d05:d06*], and [*d07:d08*]. Hence the indicated split.

Here then is our general algorithm for splitting all of the tuples in some given relation. *Note:* We'll state and illustrate the algorithm initially with reference to the simple relation *X* shown above, containing just the tuples for supplier S1 (i.e., tuples *x1-x4*) from Fig. E.1; then we'll extend the algorithm to deal with an arbitrary relation, using the relation in Fig. E.1 as the basis for an extended example.

Step 1: Create an ordered list *L* consisting of all points *p* such that *p* is equal to either *b* or *e*+1 for some DURING value [*b:e*] in *X*. In our example, *L* is the list

```
d01 , d03 , d05 , d07 , d09 , d11
```

Step 2: Let *x* be some tuple in *X*. Create an ordered list *Lx* consisting of all points *p* from *L* such that $b \leq p \leq e+1$, where [*b:e*] is the DURING value in *x*. For example, in the case of tuple *x3*, *Lx* is the list

```
d03 , d05 , d07 , d09
```

Step 3: For every consecutive pair of points *b* and *e* appearing in *Lx*, produce a tuple obtained from tuple *x* by replacing the DURING value in *x* by the interval [*b:e*−1]. For tuple *x3*, this step yields the three tuples *x31-x33* shown earlier. We say that tuple *x3* has been *split with respect to the points in L.*

If we now repeat Steps 2 and 3 for every tuple in *X* and construct a relation containing all and only the tuples thus produced, we obtain the relation *Y* shown in Fig. E.3. We'll express this fact for the purposes of this appendix by saying that *Y* is obtained by evaluating the expression

```
SPLIT X ON ( DURING ) PER L
```

In other words, we'll assume for the purposes of this appendix that we have available to us an operator called SPLIT whose syntax is SPLIT *r* ON (*A*) PER *L*, where *r* is a relation, *A* is an interval attribute of *R*, and *L* is a list of values of the point type underlying the interval type of attribute *A*.

	SNO	PARTS	DURING
x11	S1	[P01:P02]	[*d01:d02*]
x12	S1	[P01:P02]	[*d03:d04*]
x21	S1	[P04:P09]	[*d01:d02*]
x22	S1	[P04:P09]	[*d03:d04*]
x31	S1	[P06:P10]	[*d03:d04*]
x32	S1	[P06:P10]	[*d05:d06*]
x33	S1	[P06:P10]	[*d07:d08*]
x41	S1	[P01:P08]	[*d07:d08*]
x42	S1	[P01:P08]	[*d09:d10*]

Fig. E.3: Relation *Y* = SPLIT *X* ON (DURING) PER *L*

And now the expression

```
PACK' Y ON ( PARTS , DURING )
```

gives us all of the tuples to be found for supplier S1 in the result of packing S_PARTS_DURING on (PARTS, DURING)—in other words, tuples *y1-y6* as shown in Fig. E.2—without performing any UNPACKs, as such, at all.

> *Aside:* The foregoing algorithm does have the slightly unfortunate effect in the example of first splitting tuple *x1* into tuples *x11* and *x12* and then recombining those two tuples to obtain tuple *x1* again—or tuple *y1*, rather, as it's labeled in Fig. E.2. It would be possible to revise the algorithm in such a way as to avoid such unnecessary splitting and recombining, but care would be needed to ensure that the revisions did in fact decrease the overall execution time and not increase it. We omit further discussion of this possibility here. *End of aside.*

To complete our discussion of SPLIT: Clearly, in order to split every tuple in the original S_PARTS_DURING relation, what we need to do is partition that relation on attribute SNO (in our example, we obtain three partitions, one for each of suppliers S1, S2, and S3), and then repeat Steps 1-3 above with each partition in turn taking on the role of *X*.

Having explained SPLIT, we can now present an efficient algorithm for implementing PACK—PACK, not PACK'—in terms of SPLIT on a relation *r* with two interval attributes *A1* and *A2*. Let *B* be all of the attributes of *r* apart from *A1* and *A2*. Then:

Step 1: Initialize *result* to empty.

Step 2: Partition *r* on *B*. Let the resulting partitions be *r1, r2, ..., rk*.

Step 3: Execute the following:

```
do for each ri ( i = 1 , 2 , ... , k ) ;
   if COUNT ( ri ) = 1 then result := result D_UNION ri ;
                         else do Steps 4 and 5 ;
end do ;
```

Step 4: Create an ordered list L consisting of all points p such that p is equal to either $b =$ BEGIN $(A2)$ or $e+1 =$ POST $(A2)$ for some $A2$ value $[b:e]$ in ri.

Step 5: Execute the following:

```
WITH ( t1 := SPLIT ri ON ( A2 ) PER L ,
       t2 := PACK' t1 ON ( A1 ) ,
       t3 := PACK' t2 ON ( A2 ) ) :
result := result D_UNION t3 ;
```

We observe that, in comparison with an implementation involving explicit UNPACKS, the foregoing algorithm (a) is considerably faster and (b) requires substantially less space, because it's applied to each partition of the original relation separately. Additional implementation techniques, such as the use of suitable indexes (on the final result as well as on the original relation and intermediate results), can be used to improve execution time still further. Details of such additional techniques are beyond the scope of this appendix, however. *Note:* The foregoing remarks also apply, mutatis mutandis, to the algorithms we'll be presenting in later sections for U_UNION, U_MINUS, and so on. We won't repeat them in those later sections, however, letting this one paragraph do duty for all.

We close this discussion by observing that the implementation algorithm for PACK becomes *much* simpler in the important special case in which the packing is done on the basis of just a single attribute, because in that case no splitting or unpacking is needed at all. That is, if r is a relation with an interval attribute A and B is all of the attributes of r apart from A, then we can implement PACK r ON (A) by simply implementing PACK' r ON (A). And if r is represented in storage by a stored file f such that there's a one to one correspondence between the tuples of r and the stored records of f, then an efficient way to implement PACK' r ON (A) is to sort f into "BEGIN (A) within B" order and then perform the packing in a single pass over f, as noted earlier in this section.

UNPACK

Again let r be a relation with two interval attributes $A1$ and $A2$ and let B be all of the attributes of r apart from $A1$ and $A2$. Consider the expression:

```
UNPACK r ON ( A1 , A2 )
```

The first thing we do is PACK (yes, pack) *r* on (*A1*,*A2*), using the efficient implementation for PACK described above. Let *r'* be the result of this step. Then we execute the following pseudocode algorithm:

```
result := empty ;
do for each tuple t ∈ r' ;
   do for each p1 ∈ ( A1 FROM t ) ;
      do for each p2 ∈ ( A2 FROM t ) ;
         insert tuple { A1 [p1:p1] , A2 [p2:p2] , B ( B FROM t ) }
                 into result ;
      end do ;
   end do ;
end do ;
```

Of course, we're assuming here that materialization of the unpacked form of *r* on (*A1*,*A2*) is actually required. In practice, it's to be hoped that various transforms can be used to optimize away the need for such materialization, in which case it'll be sufficient to perform just the preliminary PACK step. In other words, it might not be necessary to produce the unpacked form at all, if (as will usually be the case) the result of the original UNPACK is to be passed as an argument to some operator *Op* and the desired overall result can be obtained by applying *Op* (or some other operator *Op'*) directly to *r'* (= PACK *r* ON (*A1*,*A2*)) instead of *r*. In particular, it should *never* be necessary to materialize the result of unpacking a relation on the basis of just one attribute, except in the unlikely case in which the user explicitly requests the result of such materialization—to be displayed, for instance.

A GRAPHICAL REPRESENTATION

The graphical representation introduced in Chapter 10 in connection with the notion of packing relations on two (or more?) attributes can be used to illustrate certain of the ideas discussed in the previous section, and some readers might find such illustrations helpful. Consider once again the relation *X* from a few pages back, which contained just the tuples *x1-x4* (the ones for supplier S1) from Fig. E.1:

	SNO	PARTS	DURING
x1	S1	[P01:P02]	[*d01:d04*]
x2	S1	[P04:P09]	[*d01:d04*]
x3	S1	[P06:P10]	[*d03:d08*]
x4	S1	[P01:P08]	[*d07:d10*]

Fig. E.4 shows a graphical representation of the PARTS and DURING components of the four tuples in this relation. The redundancy, or overlap, among those tuples—indicated by darker shading—is very obvious from that figure.

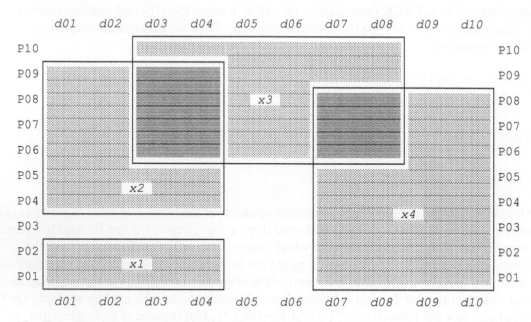

Fig. E.4: Graphical representation of tuples *x1-x4*

Fig. E.5 shows a similar graphical representation for the corresponding "packed tuples" *y1-y6* from Fig. E.2. Here it's obvious that the overlaps have disappeared.

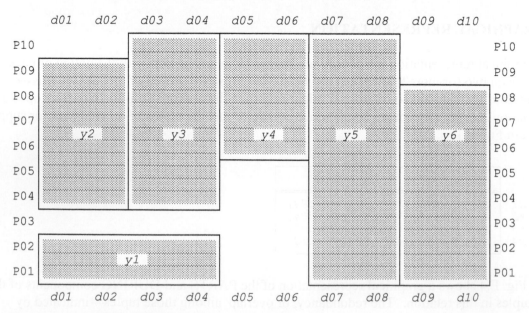

Fig. E.5: Graphical representation of tuples *y1-y6*

In like manner, for supplier S3,[3] figures analogous to Figs. E.4 and E.5 would show that:

a. Tuples *x6* and *x7* (see Fig. E.1) correspond to adjacent—not overlapping—rectangles (*adjacent* here meaning, more precisely, that the right edge of the rectangle for *x6* and the left edge of the rectangle for *x7* exactly coincide).

b. Packing those two tuples yields tuple *y8* (see Fig. E.2), corresponding to a single combined rectangle.

Now recall the following expression which, given the relation of Fig. E.1 as input, yields the relation of Fig. E.2 as output:

```
WITH ( t1 := UNPACK S_PARTS_DURING ON ( DURING ) ,
       t2 := UNPACK t1 ON ( PARTS ) ,
       t3 := PACK' t2 ON ( PARTS ) ) :
PACK' t3 ON ( DURING )
```

Figs. E.6, E.7, and E.8 show graphical representations of *t1*, *t2*, and *t3*, respectively (tuples for supplier S1 only in every case). As for the result of the overall expression, we've already seen the graphical representation for that (for supplier S1, at least) in Fig. E.5.

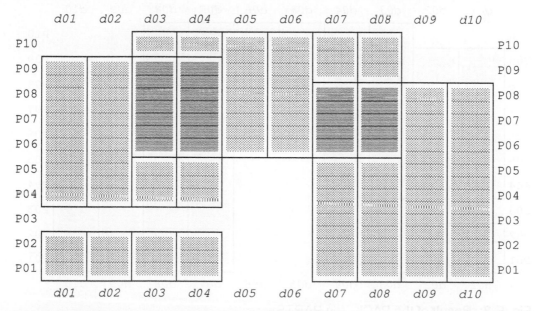

Fig. E.6: Result of the first UNPACK (on DURING)

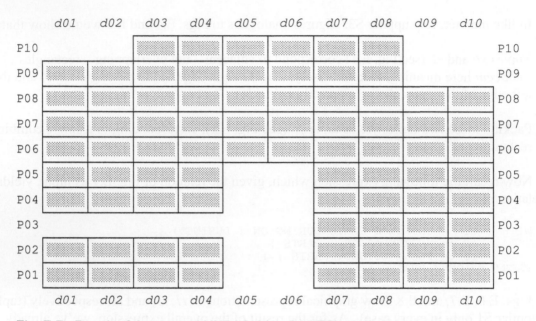

Fig. E.7: Result of the second UNPACK (on PARTS)

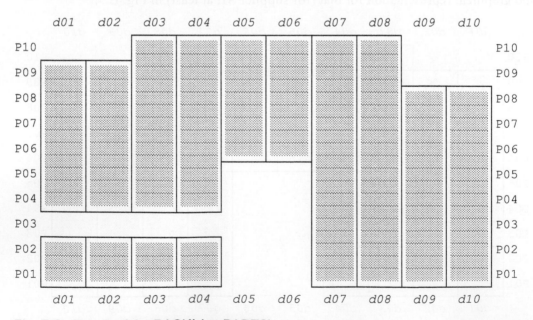

Fig. E.8: Result of the PACK′ (on PARTS)

Finally, if once again *X* is the relation containing tuples *x1-x4* only and *L* is the list *d01*, *d03*, *d05*, *d07*, *d09*, *d11*, then Fig. E.9 is a graphical representation of the result of the expression

```
SPLIT X ON ( DURING ) PER L
```

(see Fig. E.3).

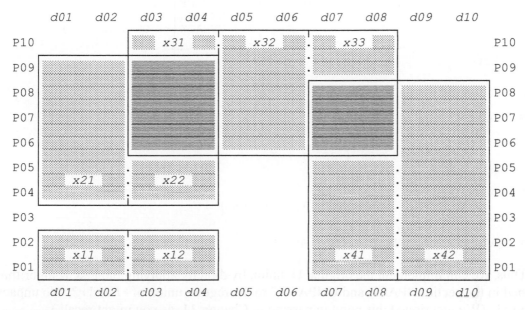

Fig. E.9: Result of splitting *x1-x4*

ALGEBRAIC OPERATORS

Now we turn our attention to the "U_" operators (U_union and the rest). All of these operators are defined to do a preliminary UNPACK on their relation operand(s); as always, however, we want to avoid actually having to perform those UNPACKs if we possibly can. Fortunately, there are several transforms and algorithms available to help us in this connection, which we now proceed to describe.[4]

---

[4] Avoiding unpacking seems to be impossible only in connection with certain U_restricts and U_extends, q.v. These exceptions aren't too worrying, however, since they don't seem very useful and thus aren't likely to be used much in practice. (As a matter of fact, most cases where it does seem that U_restrict in particular might be useful can easily be reformulated to avoid use of U_restrict as such anyway.) What's more, even where unpacking can't be avoided, pipelining can help—i.e., the packing process will usually be able to process comparatively small numbers of tuples at a time, to yield one tuple in the packed form. Thus, the unpacking and subsequent (re)packing can be done piecemeal, thus saving memory space if not CPU time.

U_UNION

First of all, it's easy to see that UNPACK distributes over regular UNION:

```
UNPACK ( r1 UNION r2 ) ON ( ACL )  ≡  ( UNPACK r1 ON ( ACL ) )
                                       UNION
                                       ( UNPACK r2 ON ( ACL ) )
```

Hence we have:

```
    USING ( ACL ) : r1 UNION r2

def
 ≡  PACK
        ( ( UNPACK r1 ON ( ACL ) )
            UNION
          ( UNPACK r2 ON ( ACL ) ) )
     ON ( ACL )

 ≡  PACK
        ( UNPACK ( r1 UNION r2 ) ON ( ACL ) )
     ON ( ACL )

 ≡  PACK ( r1 UNION r2 ) ON ( ACL )
```

Thus, we can implement the original U_union by directly applying the PACK algorithm described in the section "PACK and UNPACK" to the regular union of *r1* and *r2*. No unpacking is required. (We mentioned this point in passing in Chapter 11, as you might recall.)

We can improve matters still further—in particular, we can avoid actually materializing the union of *r1* and *r2*—by means of the following algorithm (a modified version of the PACK algorithm discussed earlier). Let *r1* and *r2* each have interval attributes *A1* and *A2* and let *B* be all of the attributes apart from *A1* and *A2* in each. Then:

Step 1: Initialize *result* to empty.

Step 2: Let *r* be the result of *r1* UNION *r2* (but see the note following Step 5). Partition *r* on *B* into *z1*, *z2*, ..., *zk*.[5]

Step 3: For each *zi* (*i* = 1, 2, ..., *k*), do Steps 4 and 5.

Step 4: Create an ordered list *L* consisting of all points *p* such that *p* is equal to either BEGIN (*A2*) or POST (*A2*) for some *A2* value in *zi*.

Step 5: Execute the following:

---

[5] We refer to the partitions here as *z1*, *z2*, etc., instead of (as elsewhere) *r1*, *r2*, etc., merely in order to avoid confusion with the original relations *r1* and *r2*.

```
WITH ( t1 := SPLIT zi ON ( A2 ) PER L ,
        t2 := PACK' t1 ON ( A1 ) ,
        t3 := PACK' t2 ON ( A2 ) ) :
result := result D_UNION t3 ;
```

Note: Although Step 2 above refers explicitly to *r* as the union of *r1* and *r2*, there's no need to check for appearances of the same tuple in both *r1* and *r2*, as the invocations of PACK' in Step 5 will eliminate any duplicates. In fact, there's no need for *r* to be physically materialized at all; instead, the implementation can simply perform a search on *r1* and *r2* to find the tuples that belong to any given partition *zi* (indeed, Steps 4 and 5 effectively do just that). In this connection, we remind you that sorting can be useful in the implementation of partitioning.

Further improvements are possible. In particular, Step 5 can sometimes be simplified to just

```
result := result D_UNION zi ;
```

For example, suppose relations *r1* and *r2* are as shown in Fig. E.10 (note that they're both restrictions of the relation in Fig. E.1), and consider, e.g., tuple *x5*. Since that tuple has an SNO value that appears in *r1* and not *r2*, it can be inserted directly into the result without any need for the SPLIT and the two PACK' operations. In appropriate circumstances, it should be possible to insert sets containing any number of tuples directly into the result in this manner.

r1	SNO	PARTS	DURING
x1	S1	[P01:P02]	[*d01*:*d04*]
x2	S1	[P04:P09]	[*d01*:*d04*]
x4	S1	[P01:P08]	[*d07*:*d10*]
x5	S2	[P15:P20]	[*d01*:*d10*]
x6	S3	[P01:P05]	[*d10*:*d15*]

r2	SNO	PARTS	DURING
x3	S1	[P06:P10]	[*d03*:*d08*]
x7	S3	[P01:P05]	[*d16*:*d20*]
x8	S3	[P05:P10]	[*d25*:*d30*]

Fig. E.10: Relations *r1* and *r2*

This brings us to the end of our discussion of U_UNION. We've considered this operator in some detail in order to give some idea as to the range of implementation and optimization possibilities that might be available in general. In our discussions of the other operators below, we won't usually try to be so comprehensive.

U_MINUS

Consider the expression

```
USING ( A1 , A2 ) : r1 MINUS r2
```

where *r1* and *r2* are as for U_UNION above. Here's the implementation algorithm:

Step 1: Initialize *result* to empty.

Step 2: Partition *r1* on *B* into *r11, r12, ..., r1h.* For each *r1i* (*i* = 1, 2, ..., *h*), define *r2i* as *r2* MATCHING *r1i*{*B*} (thus, *r2i* consists of all *r2* tuples with the same *B* value as the tuples in *r1i*).

Step 3: For each *i* (*i* = 1, 2, ..., *h*), do Steps 4 and 5.

Step 4: Create an ordered list *L1* consisting of all points *p1* such that *p1* is either BEGIN (*A1*) or POST (*A1*) for some *A1* value in *r1i* UNION *r2i*. Also, create an ordered list *L2* consisting of all points *p2* such that *p2* is either BEGIN (*A2*) or POST (*A2*) for some *A2* value in *r1i* UNION *r2i*.

Step 5: Execute the following:

```
WITH ( t1 := SPLIT r1i ON ( A1 ) PER L1 ,
       t2 := SPLIT t1  ON ( A2 ) PER L2 ,
       t3 := SPLIT r2i ON ( A1 ) PER L1 ,
       t4 := SPLIT t3  ON ( A2 ) PER L2 ,
       t5 := t2 MINUS t4 ,
       t6 := PACK' t5 ON ( A1 ) ,
       t7 := PACK' t6 ON ( A2 ) ) :
result := result D_UNION t7 ;
```

U_INTERSECT

U_INTERSECT is a special case of U_JOIN, and the same techniques apply. See the subsection immediately following.

U_JOIN

We observe first that—as we saw in Exercise 11.3 in Chapter 11—U_JOIN can be defined without any explicit reference to UNPACK at all, as follows (we assume for simplicity that the packing and unpacking is to be done on the basis of a single attribute *A*):

```
USING ( A ) : r1 JOIN r2  ≡
      WITH ( t1 := r1 RENAME { A AS X } ,
             t2 := r2 RENAME { A AS Y },
             t3 := t1 JOIN t2 ,
             t4 := t3 WHERE X OVERLAPS Y ,
             t5 := EXTEND t4 : { A := X INTERSECT Y } ,
             t6 := T5 { ALL BUT X , Y } ) :
      PACK t6 ON ( A )
```

We now exploit the ideas underlying the foregoing definition in the following algorithm for implementing the expression

```
USING ( A1 , A2 ) : r1 JOIN r2
```

We assume that *r1* has attributes *A*, *B*, *A1*, and *A2*; *r2* has attributes *A*, *C*, *A1*, and *A2*; and *A1* and *A2* are interval attributes.

Step 1: Initialize *result* to empty.

Step 2: Execute the following pseudocode algorithm:

```
let a be an A value that appears both in some tuple ∈ r1
                                 and in some tuple ∈ r2 ;
do for each such a ;
   do for each tuple t1 ∈ r1 with A = a ;
      do for each tuple t2 ∈ r2 with A = a ;
      with ( a11 := A1 FROM t1 , a21 := A2 FROM t1 ,
             a12 := A1 FROM t2 , a22 := A2 FROM t2 ) :
         if a11 OVERLAPS a12 AND a21 OVERLAPS a22
         then insert tuple
            { A a , B ( B FROM t1 ) , C ( C FROM t2 ) ,
              A1 ( a11 INTERSECT a12 ) , A2 ( a21 INTERSECT a22 ) }
              into result ;
         end if ;
      end do ;
   end do ;
end do ;
```

Step 3: Using the PACK algorithm described earlier, execute the following:

```
result := PACK result ON ( A1 , A2 ) ;
```

Note: If the U_JOIN is performed on the basis of just a single attribute and the input relations *r1* and *r2* are already packed on that attribute, then Step 3 here is unnecessary.

U_project

The expression

```
USING ( ACL ) : r { BCL }
```

is defined to be equivalent to

```
PACK ( ( UNPACK r ON ( ACL ) ) { BCL } ) ON ( ACL )
```

However, there's no need to perform the initial UNPACK shown in this definition. In other words, the foregoing expression can be further simplified to just

```
PACK ( r { BCL } ) ON ( ACL )
```

Thus, the implementation algorithm is:

Step 1: Initialize *result* to empty.

Step 2: Execute the following pseudocode algorithm:

```
do for each tuple t ∈ r ;
    add tuple t { BCL } to result ;
end do ;
```

Step 3: Execute the following:

```
result := PACK result ON ( ACL ) ;
```

Points arising:

- In practice we would expect the "add tuple" statement in Step 2 to be subject to pipelining, whereby the added tuple is immediately input to the next step—in this case Step 3.

- As a consequence, *result* in Step 2 must be understood as a bag of tuples, not a relation, because it might contain duplicates (but any such duplicates will be removed by the PACK in Step 3).

- Note, therefore, that we've taken the liberty in Step 3 of applying a relational operator, PACK, to something that isn't necessarily a relation.

- Finally, note also the use of tuple projection ("*t* {*BCL*}") in Step 2.

U_restrict

The expression

```
USING ( ACL ) : r WHERE bx
```

is defined to be equivalent to

```
PACK ( ( UNPACK r ON ( ACL ) ) WHERE bx ) ON ( ACL )
```

   In the (unusual) special case where *bx* mentions no attribute in *ACL*, this latter expression can be simplified to just

```
PACK ( r WHERE bx ) ON ( ACL )
```

The implementation algorithm for this simple case is immediate:

```
WITH ( t1 := r WHERE bx ) : PACK t1 ON ( ACL )
```

Furthermore, if relation *r* is already packed on *ACL*, the PACK step is unnecessary.
   More usually, of course, *bx* will mention at least one attribute in *ACL*, and such cases appear to pose a significant challenge to our aim of avoiding materialization of unpacked forms. We illustrate the problem by considering the simple case where *bx* is nothing more than a comparison between an attribute *A* in *ACL* and a literal. Bear in mind the important point that within *bx* the attribute reference *A* denotes a unit interval.
   Consider the following example of a U_restriction:

```
USING ( A ) : r WHERE A ⊆ [b:e]
```

This U_restriction is logically equivalent to the following U_JOIN:

```
USING ( A ) : r JOIN RELATION { TUPLE { A [b:e] } }
```

And we've already seen shown that U_JOIN can be implemented without unpacking. But it does seem rather a challenge to expect an implementation that recognizes the foregoing equivalence to do the same thing for all expressions that happen to be equivalent to that U_JOIN invocation. By way of illustration, note that all of the following are equivalent to $A \subseteq [b:e]$:

- $[b:e] \supseteq A$

- POINT FROM $A \in [b:e]$

- $[b:e] \ni$ POINT FROM A

- $A \geq b$ AND $A \leq e$

■ $b \leq A$ AND $A \leq e$

And so on (note in particular that POINT FROM *i*, BEGIN (*i*) and END (*i*) are all equivalent when *i* is a unit interval).

When *bx* contains logical connectives, we can find equivalent expressions using relational counterparts of those connectives. For example, negation suggests MINUS, or (perhaps better) its generalization NOT MATCHING. Thus we have:

■ USING (A) : *r* WHERE NOT (A ⊆ [*b*:*e*])
  ≡
  USING (A) : *r* NOT MATCHING RELATION { TUPLE { A [*b*:*e*] } }

■ USING (A) : *r* WHERE A ⊆ [*b1*:*e1*] OR A ⊆ [*b2*:*e2*]
  ≡
  USING (A) : *r* JOIN (RELATION { TUPLE { A [*b1*:*e1*] } }
                       UNION
                       RELATION { TUPLE { A [*b2*:*e2*] } })
  ≡
  USING (A) : *r* JOIN RELATION { TUPLE { A [*b1*:*e1*] } ,
                                    TUPLE { A [*b2*:*e2*] } }

■ USING (A1 , A2) : *r* WHERE A1 ⊆ [*b1*:*e1*] AND A2 ⊆ [*b2*:*e2*]
  ≡
  USING (A1 , A2) : *r* JOIN RELATION { TUPLE { A1 [*b1*:*e1*] ,
                                                  A2 [*b2*:*e2*] } }

As you can see, these various alternative formulations are really no more complicated than the U_restrictions they correspond to; thus, users might not complain if they're forced to use them themselves (for performance reasons) when the implementation fails to rise to the aforementioned challenge.

We close this subsection by noting an example where the final PACK step isn't needed:

USING (A1 , A2) : *r* WHERE A1 = A2

Before reading on, you might like to try verifying this claim for yourself. *Explanation*: Let *s* be the result of (UNPACK *r* ON (*A1*,*A2*)) WHERE *A1* = *A2* and let *B* be all of the attributes of *s* apart from *A1* and *A2*. Let tuples *t1* and *t2* of *s* be such that *B* FROM *t1* = *B* FROM *t2* and *A1* FROM *t1* = *A1* FROM *t2*. Then it follows from the stated WHERE condition that *t1* and *t2* are the same tuple. Thus, *t1* can't be "merged" with any other tuples in the packing process, and the fact that *s* = PACK *s* ON (*A1*,*A2*) follows immediately.

By the way, the foregoing example isn't completely unrealistic. Suppose *A1* represents stated time intervals and *A2* logged time intervals; then relation *s* tells us the times at which the database's record was in synch with our beliefs at those times. For example, if *r* is the relvar S_DURING_LOG (see the section "Logged Times" in Chapter 17), then a tuple for supplier S1 in *s* would be telling us that throughout the unit interval [*d*:*d*] the database said we believed S1 was under contract throughout that same unit interval [*d*:*d*]. However, we'd surely prefer to see the *maximal* intervals throughout which the database and our beliefs were in synch. Such a result could be obtained by means of an expression of the form:

```
USING ( A1 , A2 ) : r JOIN ( r { ALL BUT A1 } RENAME { A2 AS A1 } )
```

And we know how to implement U_JOIN without unpacking.

U_EXTEND

The expression

```
USING ( ACL ) : EXTEND r : { B := exp }
```

is defined to be equivalent to

```
PACK
    ( EXTEND ( UNPACK r ON ( ACL ) ) : { B := exp } )
ON ( ACL )
```

In the special case where *exp* mentions no attribute in *ACL*, this expression can be simplified to just

```
PACK ( EXTEND r : { B := exp } ) ON ( ACL )
```

The implementation algorithm for this simple case is immediate:

```
WITH ( t1 := EXTEND r : { B := exp } ) : PACK t1 ON ( ACL )
```

Furthermore, if relation *r* is already packed on *ACL*, the PACK step is unnecessary.
    In fact, the foregoing observations also apply when *exp* mentions just one of the attributes in *ACL*. For example, in

```
USING ( A ) : EXTEND r : { LA := COUNT ( A ) }
```

the USING specification is completely redundant—the expression reduces to just

```
PACK ( EXTEND r : { LA := 1 } ) ON ( A )
```

And if relation *r* is already packed on *ACL*, then (as before) the PACK step is unnecessary.

Aside: Actually it's quite difficult to come up with examples any more complicated than the one just shown. For example, consider:

```
WITH ( A2 := [d03:d07] ,
       r2 := r1 WHERE A1 MERGES A2 ) :
USING ( A1 ) : EXTEND r2 : { XA := A1 UNION A2 }
```

If *A1* = [*d01:d02*] in some tuple of *r2*, then one of the resulting assignments to XA becomes XA := [*d01:d01*] UNION [*d03:d07*], which fails. If evaluation does succeed, however, then the same result can be achieved by replacing the U_EXTEND invocation by PACK (EXTEND *r2* : { XA := *A1* UNION *A2* }) ON (*A1*). *End of aside.*

However, when we consider examples where *exp* mentions two or more attributes in *ACL*, we run into difficulties. For one thing, it remains the case that genuinely useful examples don't readily come to mind; for another, the simple but contrived examples that do come to mind seem to be such that unpacked form can't be completely avoided. For example, let relation *s* be the result of

```
USING ( A1 , A2 ) : EXTEND r : { TV := ( A1 = A2 ) }
```

If, in some tuple *t* of *s*, TV = TRUE, then the values of *A1* and *A2* in *t* are the same unit interval and *t* thus appears in the unpacked form of *s*. For consider, if *t* is the tuple {*A1* [*d02:d02*], *A2* [*d02:d02*], TV TRUE}, then *s* can't contain a tuple {*A1* [*d02:d02*], *A2* [*dx:dx*], TV TRUE}, where *dx* ≠ *d02* and [*dx:dx*] MERGES [*d02:d02*]. For that reason, there's a certain amount of unavoidable unpacking involved in the following pseudocode algorithm.

Step 1: Initialize *t1* to empty.

Step 2: Execute the following:

```
do for each tuple t ∈ ( r WHERE A1 OVERLAPS A2 ) :
   do for each point p in ( A1 FROM t ) INTERSECT ( A2 FROM t ) :
      u := tuple { A1 [p:p], A2 [p:p], B B } ;
      if NOT ( u ∈ t1 )
      then
         add u to t1 ;
   end do ;
end do ;
```

Step 3: Execute the following:

```
result := WITH ( t2 := USING ( A1 , A2 ) : r MINUS t1 ,
                 t3 := EXTEND t1 : { TV := TRUE } ,
                 t4 := EXTEND t2 : { TV := FALSE } ) :
          t3 D_UNION t4 ;
```

No final PACK is needed here because *t1* and *t2* are both in packed form, from which it follows that *t3* and *t4* are also in packed form, and therefore, because they're disjoint, so is *result*. However, *t1*, materialized in Step 2, is in unpacked form.

U_GROUP

It's easiest to explain the implementation of U_GROUP in terms of a concrete example. Let the current value of relvar SP_DURING be as follows:

SNO	PNO	DURING
S1	P1	[d01:d05]
S1	P2	[d03:d08]
S1	P3	[d04:d10]

Consider the expression:

```
USING ( DURING ) : SP_DURING GROUP { PNO } AS PNO_REL
```

This expression is defined to be equivalent to:

```
PACK
    ( UNPACK SP_DURING ON ( DURING ) ) GROUP { PNO } AS PNO_REL )
ON ( DURING )
```

Here then is the implementation algorithm:

Step 1: Initialize *result* to empty.

Step 2: Partition SP_DURING on SNO. In the example, this step yields a single partition, for supplier S1.

Step 3: For each resulting partition *p*, do Steps 4 to 6 below.

Step 4: Split the tuples in *p*. For the single partition in the example (for supplier S1), this step yields:

SNO	PNO	DURING
S1	P1	[d01:d02]
S1	P1	[d03:d03]
S1	P1	[d04:d05]
S1	P2	[d03:d03]
S1	P2	[d04:d05]
S1	P2	[d06:d08]
S1	P3	[d04:d05]
S1	P3	[d06:d08]
S1	P3	[d09:d10]

Step 5: Apply the specified grouping, to yield *px*, say. In the example, this step yields—

SNO	PNO_REL	DURING
S1	*pr1*	[d01:d02]
S1	*pr2*	[d03:d03]
S1	*pr3*	[d04:d05]
S1	*pr4*	[d06:d08]
S1	*pr5*	[d09:d10]

—where relations *pr1*, *pr2*, *pr3*, *pr4*, and *pr5* are as follows:

pr1		*pr2*		*pr3*		*pr4*		*pr5*

PNO
P1

PNO
P1
P2

PNO
P1
P2
P3

PNO
P2
P3

PNO
P3

Step 6: `result := result D_UNION ( PACK px ON ( DURING ) ) ;`

U_UNGROUP

The implementation algorithm for U_UNGROUP is very similar to that for U_GROUP, except that no splitting is needed in Step 4 and (of course) UNGROUP is used instead of GROUP in Step 5. We omit the details here.

U_comparisons

First we consider "U_=". The expression

```
USING ( ACL ) : r1 = r2
```

is defined to be equivalent to

```
( UNPACK r1 ON ( ACL ) ) = ( UNPACK r2 ON ( ACL ) )
```

Here's the implementation algorithm:

```
WITH ( t1 := PACK r1 ON ( ACL ) ,
       t2 := PACK r2 ON ( ACL ) ) :
t1 = t2
```

Note: The two PACKs here are correct—they're not typographical errors for UNPACK. Turning now to "U_⊆", the expression

```
USING ( ACL ) : r1 ⊆ r2
```

is defined to be equivalent to

```
( UNPACK r1 ON ( ACL ) ) ⊆ ( UNPACK r2 ON ( ACL ) )
```

which is in turn equivalent to

```
IS_EMPTY ( USING ( ACL ) : r1 MINUS r2 )
```

And we know how to implement U_MINUS without unpacking. As for "U_⊇", the expression USING (*ACL*) : *r1* ⊇ *r2* is of course equivalent to USING (*ACL*) : *r2* ⊆ *r1*.

UPDATE OPERATORS

We assume throughout this section that relvar R has heading $\{A,B,A1,A2\}$ and key $\{A,A1,A2\}$, where $A1$ and $A2$ are interval attributes and B is all of the attributes of R apart from A, $A1$, and $A2$. We further assume that R is subject to the U_key constraint USING ($A1,A2$): KEY $\{A,A1,A2\}$, and hence in particular that the value of R is packed on ($A1,A2$) at all times.

Intuitively, the basic idea with respect to all three of U_INSERT, U_DELETE, and U_UPDATE is that it's not necessary to unpack (or split, rather) and subsequently repack *all* of the tuples involved in the operation—it's sufficient to split and repack just those tuples that are relevant, as we'll see.

U_INSERT

Let the set of tuples to be inserted into R be the tuples in relation r.

Step 1: If *R* and *r* together contain distinct tuples *t1* and *t2* such that

```
( ( A FROM t1 ) = ( A FROM t2 ) ) AND
( ( A1 FROM t1 ) OVERLAPS ( A1 FROM t2 ) ) AND
( ( A2 FROM t1 ) OVERLAPS ( A2 FROM t2 ) )
```

then signal error: *WHEN / THEN constraint violation.* (Of course, U_INSERTs, U_DELETEs, and U_UPDATEs can all fail on a variety of constraint violations. We don't show the code to deal with such errors in general, but we do mention WHEN / THEN constraints, in connection with U_INSERT in particular, because of their fundamental nature—also because they're conceptually easy to deal with.)

Step 2: Partition *r* on {*A,B*}. For each resulting partition *pr*, do Steps 3 to 5.

Step 3: Let *t1* be a tuple of *R* such that there exists some tuple *t2* in *pr* such that

```
( ( A FROM t1 ) = ( A FROM t2 ) ) AND
( ( B FROM t1 ) = ( B FROM t2 ) ) AND
( ( A1 FROM t1 ) MEETS ( A1 FROM t2 ) OR
  ( A2 FROM t1 ) MEETS ( A2 FROM t2 ) )
```

Let *r1* be the set of all such tuples *t1*.

Step 4: Delete all tuples of *r1* from *R*.

Step 5: Let *r2* be the result of USING (*A1,A2*): *r1* UNION *pr*. Insert all tuples of *r2* into *R*. Note that no key uniqueness checking will be needed in this step.

U_DELETE

We deliberately don't consider the completely general case here, but limit ourselves to U_DELETEs of the following "almost completely general" form:

```
USING ( A1 , A2 ) : DELETE R WHERE A1 ⊆ a1
                               AND   A2 ⊆ a2
                               AND  ( bx ) ) ;
```

Step 1: Let *r1* be the set of all tuples *t1* of *R* satisfying

```
( ( A1 FROM t1 ) OVERLAPS a1 ) AND
( ( A2 FROM t1 ) OVERLAPS a2 ) AND
( bx )
```

Step 2: Let tuple *t1* of *r1* be as follows:

```
TUPLE { A a , B b , A1 i1 , A2 i2 }
```

Let *r2* be the set of all tuples *t2* of the form

```
TUPLE { A a , B b , A1 ( i1 INTERSECT a1 ) , A2 ( i2 INTERSECT a2 ) }
```

Step 3: Let *r3* be the result of

```
USING ( A1 , A2 ) : r1 MINUS r2
```

Step 4: Delete all tuples of *r1* from *R*.

Step 5: Use the algorithm for U_INSERT to insert the tuples of *r3* into *R*.

Note: As we saw in Chapter 16, PORTION DELETE is often likely to be preferred over U_DELETE. As some commercial implementations already support an SQL version of this operator (see Chapter 19), however, we see no need to present an implementation algorithm here.

U_UPDATE

We deliberately don't consider the completely general case here, but limit ourselves to U_UPDATEs of the "almost completely general" form:

```
USING ( A1 , A2 ) : UPDATE R WHERE A1 ⊆ a1
                                AND    A2 ⊆ a2
                                AND    ( bx ) :
                    { attribute assignments } ;
```

The following algorithm is very similar to that for U_DELETE:

Step 1: Let *r1* be the set of all tuples *t1* of *R* satisfying

```
( ( A1 FROM t1 ) OVERLAPS a1 ) AND
( ( A2 FROM t1 ) OVERLAPS a2 ) AND
( bx )
```

Step 2: Let tuple *t1* of *r1* be as follows:

```
TUPLE { A a , B b , A1 i1 , A2 i2 }
```

Let *r2* be the set of all tuples *t2* of the form

```
TUPLE { A a , B b , A1 ( i1 INTERSECT a1 ) , A2 ( i2 INTERSECT a2 ) }
```

Step 3: Let *r3* be the result of

```
USING ( A1 , A2 ) : r1 MINUS r2
```

Step 4: Let *r2'* be that relation that results from applying the specified attribute assignments to *r2*.

Step 5: Delete all tuples of *r1* from *R*.

Step 6: Use the algorithm for U_INSERT to insert the tuples of *r3* into *R*.

Step 7: Use the algorithm for U_INSERT to insert the tuples of *r2'* into *R*.

Note: The remark concerning PORTION DELETE at the end of the previous subsection applies to PORTION UPDATE also, mutatis mutandis.

A FINAL REMARK

The UNPACK operator is a crucial conceptual component of our approach to the management of interval data in general and temporal data in particular. But UNPACK has been criticized in the literature on the grounds that it necessarily entails poor performance. We hope the discussions in this appendix will help to lay such criticisms to rest. To say it again, UNPACK is a crucial *conceptual* component of our approach—but it's only a conceptual component. We don't want unpackings per se ever to be physically performed if we can possibly avoid them; and in this appendix we've shown how they can usually be avoided.

Appendix F

References and Bibliography

You will find it a very good practice always to verify your references, sir.
—Martin Joseph Routh
(from John William Burgon: *Memoir of Dr. Routh*, 1878)

This appendix provides a consolidated and mostly annotated list of references for the entire book. If a reference isn't annotated, it usually means it's discussed (or at least mentioned, along with some indication as to its content) at some earlier point in the book.

1. Ilsoo Ahn and Richard T. Snodgrass: "Partitioned Storage Structures for Temporal Databases," *Information Systems 13*, No. 4 (1988).

   The partitioning referred to in the title of this paper is akin to our idea of horizontal decomposition. As the title suggests, however, the emphasis in the paper is more on the use of such decomposition as a technique for *physical* design. (To quote reference [108]: "Temporal partitioning is ... in the domain of physical design.")

2. James F. Allen: "Maintaining Knowledge about Temporal Intervals," *CACM 26*, No. 11 (November 1983).

   The source of Allen's operators (see Chapter 7). For purposes of reference, we give below a complete list of the operators from Allen's paper, together with our own and SQL's analogs of those operators. *Note:* The "*i*" in ALLEN's operators *mi, oi, di, si*, and *fi* stands for *inverse*. (The *m, o*, and *d* operators in particular—unlike our analogs of those operators—aren't commutative; thus, if, e.g., *m* is pronounced *meets*, then *mi* might reasonably be pronounced *is met by*, or just *met by*.) Observe that Allen has no direct analog of our MERGES operator, nor of "⊂" or "⊃", nor of the negated forms (NOT OVERLAPS, etc.) of any of our other operators.

Allen operator (example)	Operator name	Our analog	SQL analog
i1 = i2	equal	i1 = i2	p1 EQUALS p2
i1 < i2	before	i1 BEFORE i2	p1 PRECEDES p2
i1 > i2	after	i1 AFTER i2	p1 SUCCEEDS p2
i1 m i2	meets	i1 MEETS i2	see Chapter 19
i1 mi i2	met by	i2 MEETS i1	see Chapter 19
i1 o i2	overlaps	i1 OVERLAPS i2	p1 OVERLAPS p2
i1 oi i2	overlapped by	i2 OVERLAPS i1	p2 OVERLAPS p1
i1 d i2	during	i2 ⊆ i1	p1 CONTAINS p2
i1 di i2	contains	i2 ⊇ i1	p2 CONTAINS p1
i1 s i2	starts	i1 BEGINS i2	
i1 si i2	started by	i2 BEGINS i1	
i1 f i2	finishes	i1 ENDS i2	
i1 fi i2	finished by	i2 ENDS i1	

Aside: Reference [76] gives the following somewhat more extensive list of operators and helpful explanatory diagram:

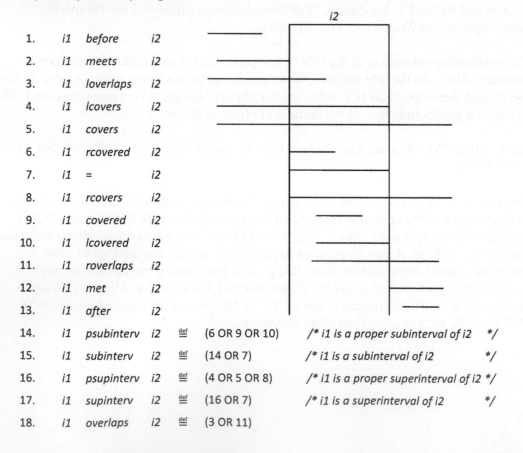

1. i1 *before* i2
2. i1 *meets* i2
3. i1 *loverlaps* i2
4. i1 *lcovers* i2
5. i1 *covers* i2
6. i1 *rcovered* i2
7. i1 *=* i2
8. i1 *rcovers* i2
9. i1 *covered* i2
10. i1 *lcovered* i2
11. i1 *roverlaps* i2
12. i1 *met* i2
13. i1 *after* i2
14. i1 *psubinterv* i2 ≝ (6 OR 9 OR 10)   /* i1 is a proper subinterval of i2   */
15. i1 *subinterv* i2 ≝ (14 OR 7)   /* i1 is a subinterval of i2   */
16. i1 *psupinterv* i2 ≝ (4 OR 5 OR 8)   /* i1 is a proper superinterval of i2 */
17. i1 *supinterv* i2 ≝ (16 OR 7)   /* i1 is a superinterval of i2   */
18. i1 *overlaps* i2 ≝ (3 OR 11)

19.	*i1*	*cp*	*i2*	≝	(3 OR 4 OR . . . OR 11) /* *i1 has common points with i2* */
20.	*i1*	*merges*	*i2*	≝	(19 OR 2 OR 12)
21.	*i1*	*precedes*	*i2*	≝	(1 OR 2 OR 3 OR 4 OR 5 OR 6)
22.	*i1*	*prequals*	*i2*	≝	(21 OR 7) /* *i1 precedes or equals i2* */
23.	*i1*	*follows*	*i2*	≝	(8 OR 9 OR 10 OR 11 OR 12 OR 13)
24.	*i1*	*folequals*	*i2*	≝	(23 OR 7) /* *i1 follows or equals i2* */
25.	*i1*	*adjacent*	*i2*	≝	(2 OR 12)

We leave it as an exercise to interpret these operators in terms of the operators defined in Chapter 7. *End of aside*.

3. Khaled K. Al-Taha, Richard T. Snodgrass, and Michael D. Soo: "Bibliography on Spatiotemporal Databases," *ACM SIGMOD Record 22*, No. 1 (March 1993).

Here's a lightly edited extract from the preamble to this bibliography: "Only recently have issues concerning the simultaneous support of both space and time in databases been considered. While this new area of research was presaged by Thrift's observation in 1977 that time could be considered to be an additional dimension in a two- or three-dimensional space [Thrift 1977], little was done until Nikos Lorentzos's and Gail Langran's doctoral dissertations [Langran 1989A, Lorentzos 1988]." To elaborate briefly: Reference [Thrift 1977] is N. Thrift: "An Introduction to Time Geography," in *Concepts in Modern Geography 13*, Geo-Abstracts Ltd., London, U.K. (1977); reference [Langran 1989A] is G. Langran: "Time in Geographic Information Systems," Ph.D. Dissertation, University of Washington (1989); reference [Lorentzos 1988] is our reference [67].) It's particularly interesting to see that the authors of this bibliography are here on record as agreeing that "time is just another dimension"—a position we agree with, though we haven't used the term *dimension* (in this context) much in the present book.

4. Gad Ariav: "A Temporally Oriented Data Model," *ACM TODS 11*, No. 4 (December 1986).

The approach described in this paper differs from just about every other in the literature (with the possible exception of reference [17]). In effect, it timestamps entire relations, instead of individual attributes—more precisely, individual attribute values—or individual tuples (see the annotation to reference [18]). An algebra and an SQL extension are defined. However, the algebra is incomplete (only three operators are defined), and the author states explicitly that further work is needed.

5. J. Ben-Zvi: "The Time Relational Model," Ph.D. Dissertation, Computer Science Department, University of California at Los Angeles (1982).

Ben-Zvi was one of the earliest workers in the temporal database field. A useful brief summary of his ideas and contributions can be found in a short paper by Gadia [59].

6. Claudio Bettini, Curtis E. Dyreson, William S. Evans, Richard T. Snodgrass, and X. Sean Wang: "A Glossary of Time Granularity Concepts," in reference [55].

This paper is an attempt to inject some rigor into the granularity issue. It's intended as a formal addendum to reference [62].

7. Michael H. Böhlen: "Temporal Database System Implementations," *ACM SIGMOD Record 24*, No. 4 (December 1995).

A survey of 13 implemented systems, with a high level analysis of system features supported (or not, as the case may be). The following observations regarding the systems examined are worthy of note: "Transaction time support is negligible ... The focus is on queries. Updates, rules, and integrity constraints are neglected ... Temporal database design has barely found its way into products." (Of course, the paper is rather old by now, and this last sentence is no longer as true as it used to be.)

8. Michael H. Böhlen, Christian S. Jensen, and Richard T. Snodgrass: "Temporal Statement Modifiers," *ACM TODS 25*, No. 4 (December 2000).

Among other things this paper defines ATSQL, an SQL-based temporal language that's similar in spirit to TSQL2 [105-106].

9. Michael H. Böhlen, Richard T. Snodgrass, and Michael D. Soo: "Coalescing in Temporal Databases," Proc. 22nd Int. Conf. on Very Large Data Bases, Mumbai (Bombay), India (September 1996).

The operation of *coalescing* is analogous, more or less, to our PACK operation. This paper presents a set of algebraic transformation rules for expressions involving such coalescing and investigates approaches to the implementation of such expressions.
    As an aside, we note that the PACK operator and the related UNPACK operator are known by a variety of names in the literature.[1] Reference [98] calls them CONTRACT and EXPAND, respectively. The previous edition of reference [37] called them COALESCE and UNFOLD. PACK has also been called COMPRESS [94]. And reference [70] (as well

---

[1] Actually this remark isn't quite accurate, because much of the literature defines the operators, whatever they might be called, in terms of "relations" with "hidden attributes" (see Chapter 4). By contrast, our PACK and UNPACK operators are defined in terms of relations as such, in which by definition all attributes have explicit names and can—and in fact must—be referenced by those names, and those names only.

as several others by Lorentzos and various coauthors) defines a pair of operators called FOLD and UNFOLD, but those operators aren't quite the same as our PACK and UNPACK; loosely, FOLD "packs" a set of *points* into a set of intervals, and UNFOLD "unpacks" a set of intervals into a set of points (the same paper uses NORMALIZE—originally spelled NORMALISE—for what we call PACK). Finally, there's at least one paper in the literature (namely, reference [95]) that uses PACK and UNPACK to mean something quite different: namely, operators that are akin, somewhat, to the regular GROUP and UNGROUP operators of relational algebra.

10. Marco A. Casanova, Ronald Fagin, and Christos H. Papadimitriou: "Inclusion Dependencies and Their Interaction with Functional Dependencies," Proc. 1st ACM SIGACT-SIGMOD Symposium on Principles of Database Systems, Los Angeles, Calif. (March 1982).

The origin of the concept of inclusion dependencies (INDs). The paper provides a sound and complete set of inference rules for such dependencies.

11. R. G. G. Cattell and Douglas K. Barry (eds.): *The Object Data Standard: ODMG 3.0.* San Francisco, Calif.: Morgan Kaufmann (2000).

12. James Clifford: "A Model for Historical Databases," Proc. Workshop on Logical Bases for Data Bases, Toulouse, France (December 1982).

See reference [13], also the annotation to reference [18].

13. James Clifford and Albert Croker: "The Historical Relational Data Model (HRDM) Revisited," in reference [110].

Revises and extends the proposals of reference [12].

14. James Clifford, Albert Croker, and Alexander Tuzhilin: "On Completeness of Historical Relational Query Languages," *ACM TODS 19*, No. 1 (March 1994).

A quote: "In this paper we define *temporally grouped* and *temporally ungrouped* historical data models and propose two notions of *historical relational completeness*, analogous to Codd's notion of relational completeness, one for each type of model" (italics in the original). The paper additionally considers to what extent various approaches described in the literature satisfy the proposed completeness criteria. The approaches in question are HRDM [13], Gadia's approach [58], TQuel [104], and Lorentzos's approach [68].

15. J. Clifford and A. Rao: "A Simple General Structure for Temporal Domains," in reference [96].

Proposes a formalism for defining a variety of temporal point types, associated interval types, and operators on values of those types.

16. J. Clifford and A. Tuzhilin (eds.): *Recent Advances in Temporal Databases* (Proc. Int. Workshop on Temporal Databases, Zurich, Switzerland, September 17th-18th, 1995). New York, N.Y.: Springer-Verlag (1995).

17. James Clifford and David S. Warren: "Formal Semantics for Time in Databases," *ACM TODS 8*, No. 2 (June 1983).

Describes an approach based on the idea that any given relvar (our term) can be thought of as a sequence of timestamped relations, where the timestamps in question correspond to logged time points (not intervals) as discussed in Chapter 17. The major contribution of the paper is a formal definition of the approach in terms of intensional logic.

18. James Clifford and Abdullah Uz Tansel: "On An Algebra for Historical Relational Databases: Two Views," Proc. ACM SIGMOD Int. Conf. on Management of Data, Austin, Tex. (May 1985).

In the first part of this paper, Clifford proposes an algebra for dealing with "temporal relations" in which attribute values can be relations and the tuples within those inner relations can be timestamped with time points representing stated (i.e., valid) time. In the second part, Tansel proposes another algebra in which the timestamps are intervals rather than points (see also references [109] and [111]). *Note:* Timestamping tuples within values of relation valued attributes is known, loosely, as "timestamping attributes"; it's contrasted with "timestamping tuples," which refers to the idea of timestamping tuples in the *containing* instead of the *contained* relation, an idea that seems to have originated in reference [12]. The approach we advocate in the present book is somewhat akin to "timestamping tuples," except that the "timestamps" in question are actually part of the tuples in question; in other words, they're represented by means of relational attributes in the usual way. Also, of course, a given tuple in our approach can contain any number of such "timestamps."

19. James Clifford, Curtis Dyreson, Tomás Isakowitz, Christian S. Jensen, and Richard T. Snodgrass: "On the Semantics of 'Now' in Databases," *ACM TODS 22*, No. 2 (June 1997).

Presents arguments in favor of allowing database tuples to contain the variable referred to in Chapter 12 as "the NOW marker" (and several other similar variables as well). To quote: "This article ... provides a formal basis for defining the semantics of databases with variables ... [It] demonstrates that existing variables, such as *now* and *until changed*, are indispensable [*sic*] in databases. It also ... introduces new *now-relative* and *now-relative indeterminate* [variables]." *Note:* The term *variable* here doesn't refer to our relation variables (relational databases always contain variables of that kind, of course); rather, it refers to "the NOW marker" and other similar constructs.

20. E. F. Codd: "Derivability, Redundancy, and Consistency of Relations Stored in Large Data Banks," IBM Research Report RJ599 (August 19th, 1969). Republished in *ACM SIGMOD Record 38*, No. 1 (March 2009).

Codd's very first published paper on the relational model.

21. E. F. Codd: "A Relational Model of Data for Large Shared Data Banks," *CACM 13*, No. 6 (June 1970). Republished in *Milestones of Research—Selected Papers 1958-1982 (CACM 25th Anniversary Issue)*, *CACM 26*, No. 1 (January 1983) and elsewhere.

A revised and extended version of reference [20]. The major technical difference between the two is that reference [20] permits relation valued attributes while reference [21] prohibits them.

22. E. F. Codd: "Relational Completeness of Data Base Sublanguages," in Randall Rustin (ed.), *Data Base Systems:* Courant Computer Science Symposia 6. Englewood Cliffs, N.J.: Prentice-Hall (1972).

23. E. F. Codd and C. J. Date: "Much Ado about Nothing," in C. J. Date, *Relational Database Writings 1991-1994*. Reading, Mass.: Addison-Wesley (1995).

Codd was probably the best known advocate of nulls and many-valued logics as a basis for dealing with missing information. This article contains the text of a debate between Codd and one of the present authors on the subject.

24. Hugh Darwen (writing as Andrew Warden): "Into the Unknown," in C. J. Date, *Relational Database Writings 1985-1989*. Reading, Mass.: Addison-Wesley (1990).

25. Hugh Darwen: "The Nullologist in Relationland," in C. J. Date and Hugh Darwen, *Relational Database Writings 1989-1991*. Reading, Mass.: Addison-Wesley (1992).

26. Hugh Darwen: "Valid Time and Transaction Time Proposals: Language Design Aspects," in reference [55].

Among other things, this paper advocates the language design principle known as *syntactic substitution*: "A language definition should start with a few judiciously chosen primitive operators ... Subsequent development is [done], where possible, by defining new operators in terms of ... previously defined [ones]. Most importantly, syntactic substitution does not refer to an imprecise principle such as might be expressed as "*A* is something like, possibly very like, *B*," where *A* is some proposed new syntax and *B* is some expression using previously defined operators. If *A* is close in meaning to *B* but cannot be specified by true syntactic substitution, then we have a situation that is disagreeable and probably unacceptable, in stark contrast to true syntactic substitution, which can be very agreeable and acceptable indeed."

27. Hugh Darwen: "The Decomposition Approach," in C. J. Date and Hugh Darwen, *Database Explorations: Essays on The Third Manifesto and Related Topics.* Bloomington, Ind.: Trafford Publishing (2010). *Note:* This paper is based on an earlier presentation by Darwen titled "How to Handle Missing Information Without Using Nulls," the slides for which can be found at *www. thethirdmanifesto.com* (May 9th, 2003; revised May 16th, 2005).

28. Hugh Darwen: *An Introduction to Relational Database Theory.* Frederiksberg, Denmark: Ventus (2012). Free download available at *http://bookboon.com.*

29. Hugh Darwen and C. J. Date: "An Overview and Analysis of Proposals Based on the TSQL2 Approach," in C. J. Date, *Date on Database: Writings 2000-2006.* Berkeley, Calif.: Apress (2006).

Of previously published proposals for dealing with the temporal database problem, TSQL2 [105-106] is probably the best known, and several other proposals, including in particular those of reference [107], have been based on it. This paper provides an overview and critical analysis of such proposals, comparing and contrasting them with the approach advocated in the present book.

30. Hugh Darwen, C. J. Date, and Ronald Fagin: "A Normal Form for Preventing Redundant Tuples in Relational Databases," Proc. 15th Int. Conf. on Database Theory, Berlin, Germany (March 26th-29th, 2012).

31. Hugh Darwen, Mike Sykes, et al.: "Concerns about the TSQL2 Approach to Temporal Databases," Kansas City, Mo. (May 1996); *ftp://sqlstandards.org/SC32/WG3/Meetings/ MCI_1996_05_KansasCity_USA/mci071.ps.* (This is an internal working document, not generally available at the time of writing.)

A precursor to reference [32], criticizing among other things the notion of "temporal upward compatibility" advocated in reference [107] (also in reference [8]). Briefly, temporal upward compatibility means it should be possible to convert an existing nontemporal database into a temporal one by just "adding temporal support," thereby allowing existing nontemporal applications to run unchanged against the now temporal database. See reference [29] for further discussion.

32. Hugh Darwen, Mike Sykes, et al.: "On Proposals for Valid-Time and Transaction-Time Support," Madrid, Spain (January 1997); *ftp://sqlstandards.org/SC32/WG3/Meetings/ MAD_1997_01_Madrid_ESP/mad146.ps*. (This is an internal working document, not generally available at the time of writing.)

A response to reference [107].

33. C. J. Date: "Dates and Times in IBM SQL: Some Technical Criticisms," in *Relational Database Writings 1985-1989*. Reading, Mass: Addison-Wesley (1990).

We include this reference merely to draw attention to the fact that the support in IBM's DB2 product for datetime data types—not to be confused with its temporal support— differs significantly, in both syntax and semantics, from that of the SQL standard [61]. For a detailed tutorial on this latter, see reference [47].

34. C. J. Date: "NOT Is Not "Not"! (Notes on Three-Valued Logic and Related Matters)," in *Relational Database Writings 1985-1989*. Reading, Mass: Addison-Wesley (1990).

35. C. J. Date: "A Note on Orthogonality," in *Relational Database Writings 1994-1997*. Reading, Mass: Addison-Wesley (1998).

36. C. J. Date: "Encapsulation Is a Red Herring," *Database Programming & Design 12,* No. 9 (September 1998).

37. C. J. Date: *An Introduction to Database Systems* (8th edition). Boston, Mass.: Addison-Wesley (2004).

38. C. J. Date: "On the Notion of Logical Difference"; "On the Logical Difference Between Model and Implementation"; and "On the Logical Differences Between Types, Values, and Variables," all in *Date on Database: Writings 2000 2006*. Berkeley, Calif.: Apress (2006).

39. C. J. Date: "The Theory of Bags: An Investigative Tutorial," in *Logic and Databases: The Roots of Relational Theory*. Victoria, B.C.: Trafford Publishing (2007).

40. C. J. Date: "Image Relations," in C. J. Date and Hugh Darwen, *Database Explorations: Essays on The Third Manifesto and Related Topics*. Bloomington, Ind.: Trafford Publishing (2010).

41. C. J. Date: "Inclusion Dependencies and Foreign Keys," in C. J. Date and Hugh Darwen, *Database Explorations: Essays on The Third Manifesto and Related Topics*. Bloomington, Ind.: Trafford Publishing (2010).

42. C. J. Date: *SQL and Relational Theory: How to Write Accurate SQL Code* (2nd edition). Sebastopol, Calif.: O'Reilly Media (2012).

43. C. J. Date: *Database Design and Relational Theory: Normal Forms and All That Jazz*. Sebastopol, Calif.: O'Reilly Media (2012).

44. C. J. Date: *View Updating and Relational Theory: Solving the View Update Problem*. Sebastopol, Calif.: O'Reilly Media (2013).

45. C. J. Date: *Relational Theory for Computer Professionals: What Relational Databases Are Really All About*. Sebastopol, Calif.: O'Reilly Media (2013).

46. C. J. Date: *The New Relational Database Dictionary* (to appear).

This reference is the third in a series. The first was titled simply *The Relational Database Dictionary* (O'Reilly, 2006). The second was titled *The Relational Database Dictionary, Extended Edition* (Apress, 2008).

47. C. J. Date and Hugh Darwen: *A Guide to the SQL Standard* (4th edition). Reading, Mass.: Addison-Wesley (1997).

A comprehensive tutorial on SQL:1992, this book also contain details of the Call Level Interface feature CLI (added to the standard in 1995), the Persistent Stored Modules feature PSM (added in 1997), and a few features that became part of SQL:1999. *Note:* Although the book is now quite old, most of what it has to say is still applicable to the current version of the standard, SQL:2011 [61].

48. C. J. Date and Hugh Darwen: "Multiple Assignment," in C. J. Date, *Date on Database: Writings 2000-2006*. Berkeley, Calif.: Apress (2006).

49. C. J. Date and Hugh Darwen: "*The Third Manifesto*," in *Database Explorations: Essays on The Third Manifesto and Related Topics*. Bloomington, Ind.: Trafford Publishing (2010).

See the annotation to reference [52].

50. C. J. Date and Hugh Darwen: "**Tutorial D**," in *Database Explorations: Essays on The Third Manifesto and Related Topics*. Bloomington, Ind.: Trafford Publishing (2010).

See the annotation to reference [52].

51. C. J. Date and Hugh Darwen: "The Inheritance Model" and "The Inheritance Model: What Was Changed and Why," in *Database Explorations: Essays on The Third Manifesto and Related Topics.* Bloomington, Ind.: Trafford Publishing (2010).

52. C. J. Date and Hugh Darwen: *Databases, Types, and the Relational Model: The Third Manifesto* (3rd edition). Boston, Mass.: Addison-Wesley (2007).

This book introduces and explains *The Third Manifesto,* a precise though somewhat formal definition of the relational model and a supporting type theory (including a comprehensive model of type inheritance—see reference [51]). Note that the *Manifesto* as such constitutes just one comparatively short chapter in the book (twelve pages, out of a total of well over 500). The book also contains a definition of the language **Tutorial D**. (Please observe that **Tutorial D** isn't part of the *Manifesto* as such but is merely one possible language that can be used to illustrate and explain the ideas of the *Manifesto*.) *Note:* Upgraded definitions of both the *Manifesto* itself and **Tutorial D** can be found in references [49] and [50], respectively. The most recent versions can be found at the website *www.thethirdmanifesto. com*, which also gives information regarding a variety of existing **Tutorial D** implementations, as well as other projects related to the *Manifesto*.

53. C. J. Date, Hugh Darwen, and Nikos A. Lorentzos: *Temporal Data and the Relational Model.* San Francisco, Calif.: Morgan Kaufmann (2003).

The present book's predecessor.

54. Christina Davies, Brian Lazell, Martin Hughes, and Leslie Cooper: "Time Is Just Another Attribute—Or at Least Another Dimension," in reference [16].

To quote: "[The] flexibility and simplicity of the relational model are too valuable to be jettisoned without good reason ... [A] much stronger case must be made against the unextended relational model before it is rejected or modified for temporal applications." (We agree strongly with these remarks.) The paper presents three case studies and identifies some limitations of TSQL2 [105-106]. It also argues that if SQL is to be extended, then the extensions in question should not be limited to temporal intervals only.

55. Opher Etzion, Sushil Jajodia, and Suryanarayana Sripada (eds.): *Temporal Databases: Research and Practice.* New York, N.Y.: Springer-Verlag (1998).

This book is an anthology giving "the state of the temporal database art" as of about 1997. It's divided into four major parts, as follows:

1. Temporal Database Infrastructure
2. Temporal Query Languages
3. Advanced Applications of Temporal Databases
4. General Reference

Several of the references listed in this appendix—in particular reference [26]—are included in this book.

56. Ronald Fagin: "Normal Forms and Relational Database Operators," Proc. 1979 ACM SIGMOD Int. Conf. on Management of Data, Boston, Mass. (May/June 1979).

This paper, which is the one that introduced projection/join normal form (also known as 5NF), is the definitive reference on what might be called classical normalization theory.

57. Shashi K. Gadia and Jay H. Vaishnav: "A Query Language for a Homogeneous Temporal Database," Proc. 4th ACM SIGACT-SIGMOD Symposium on Principles of Database Systems, Portland, Ore. (March 1985).

Sketches a language for dealing with "temporal relations" in which, as in reference [18], attributes can be relation valued and tuples within those inner relations can be timestamped (see also reference [58]). The timestamps are sets of intervals in packed form, and they represent stated times, not logged times. The term *homogeneous* in the paper's title refers to the restriction that—as the paper itself puts it—"the temporal domain within a tuple does not vary from one attribute to another ... [As a consequence,] there are several weaknesses in the model. For example, ... information about persons, their parents and dates of birth [can't be represented in the same relation]."

58. Shashi K. Gadia: "A Homogeneous Relational Model and Query Languages for Temporal Databases," *ACM TODS 13*, No. 4 (December 1988).

A more formal and complete treatment of the model underlying the proposals of reference [57].

59. Shashi K. Gadia: "Ben-Zvi's Pioneering Work in Relational Temporal Databases," in reference [110].

60. Patrick Hall, John Owlett, and Stephen Todd: "Relations and Entities," in G. M. Nijssen (ed.), *Modelling in Data Base Management Systems.* Amsterdam, Netherlands: North-Holland (1976).

61. International Organization for Standardization (ISO): *Database Language SQL,* Document ISO/IEC 9075:2011 (2011).

The current version, or edition, of the SQL standard ("SQL:2011").

62. Christian S. Jensen and Curtis E. Dyreson (eds.): "The Consensus Glossary of Temporal Database Concepts—February 1998 Version," in reference [55].

This glossary follows on from, and subsumes, two earlier ones which appeared in *ACM SIGMOD Record 21*, No. 3 (September 1992) and *ACM SIGMOD Record 23*, No. 1 (March 1994), respectively. We strongly agree with the article's opening remarks: "A technical language is an important infrastructural component of any scientific community. To be effective, such a language should be well defined, intuitive, and agreed upon." The authors then go on to give, not just their own preferred terms and definitions as such, but also discussions of alternative terms, justifications for their preferences, and so forth. Note, however, that several terms and concepts discussed in the present book seem to have no counterpart in this glossary, the following among them:

- Point types
- Ordinal types
- Cyclic types
- Successor functions (NEXT_*T*), etc.
- Interval types and the interval type generator
- BEGIN, END, PRE, POST, and POINT FROM
- Allen's operators
- Interval UNION, INTERSECT, and MINUS
- EXPAND and COLLAPSE
- Equivalence (for sets of intervals)
- "The moving point *now*"

63. Christian S. Jensen, Richard T. Snodgrass, and Michael D. Soo: "Extending Existing Dependency Theory to Temporal Databases," *IEEE Transactions on Knowledge and Data Engineering 8*, No. 4 (August 1996).

This paper is one of many to define "temporal" versions of certain familiar relational concepts: specifically (in the case at hand), temporal functional dependencies, temporal primary keys, and temporal normal forms. However, the definitions in question all rely on an assumption that timestamps aren't represented by regular relational attributes.

64. S. Jones and P. J. Mason: "Handling the Time Dimension in a Data Base," Proc. Int. Conf. on Data Bases, Aberdeen, Scotland (July 1980). London, U.K.: Heyden & Son (1980).

One of the very earliest proposals (possibly *the* earliest).

65. Krishna Kulkarni and Jan-Eike Michels: "Temporal Features in SQL:2011," *ACM SIGMOD Record 41*, No. 3 (September 2012).

66. Mark Levene and George G. Loizou: *A Guided Tour of Relational Databases and Beyond.* London, U.K.: Springer-Verlag (1999).

Includes one chapter (Chapter 7, "Temporal Relational Databases") on temporal matters. Section 4 of that chapter ("A Historical Relational Algebra") discusses Lorentzos's work as described in references [68] and [70].

67. Nikos A. Lorentzos: "A Formal Extension of the Relational Model for the Representation and Manipulation of Generic Intervals," Ph.D. Dissertation, Birkbeck College, University of London, U.K. (August 1988).

The approach to temporal data described and advocated in the present book has its origins in Lorentzos's research as reported in his PhD dissertation (as well as in numerous subsequent publications by Lorentzos and other researchers; see, e.g., references [68], [70], and [76]). As far as we're aware, Lorentzos's dissertation was (a) the first to propose the interval abstraction as such; (b) the first, or one of the first, to propose a truly relational approach to the problem; and (c) the first to propose the idea that temporal support should be at least partly just a special case of support for intervals in general. (We note in passing that reference [89] effectively supports these claims.)

Note: We need to say something regarding the use of the term *extension* in the title of this reference. That term refers primarily to the introduction of:

a. A generic interval data type (or rather, as we would now say, an interval type generator), along with

b. A variety of new operators that can be applied to relations with attributes of some interval type.

As explained in Chapter 4, however, the question of which types and type generators are supported is orthogonal to the question of support for the relational model as such. And support for "new operators" is part of (and is implied by) support for "new types." In other words, features a. and b. above can certainly be regarded as an extension to *something*, but they're not an extension to the relational model. It's this fact that enables us to claim, legitimately, that our approach to temporal database issues is a truly relational one and involves no changes or extensions to the classical relational model.

　　Remarks analogous to the foregoing apply equally to the titles of several other references in this appendix—for example, references [70] and [74]—and we won't bother to repeat them every time, instead letting the foregoing paragraphs do duty for all.

68. Nikos A. Lorentzos and R. G. Johnson: "TRA: A Model for a Temporal Relational Algebra," in reference [96].

　　This paper and reference [69], which overlap somewhat, were the first to discuss the FOLD and UNFOLD operators (predecessors of PACK and UNPACK, respectively). Significantly, the paper includes an example of a relation with two distinct "valid time" attributes, something the SQL standard wouldn't permit. It also discusses what it calls "periodic" (i.e., cyclic) temporal data, such as hours of the day. *Note:* Despite the reference in the paper's title to "a temporal relational algebra," the authors are careful to state explicitly that they're not proposing any "new elementary relational algebra operations." In other words, their "temporal relational algebra" is just the classical relational algebra, enhanced (as in the present book) with certain useful shorthands.

69. Nikos A. Lorentzos and R. G. Johnson, "Extending Relational Algebra to Manipulate Temporal Data," *Information Systems 13*, No. 3 (1988).

　　See the annotation to reference [68].

70. Nikos A. Lorentzos: "The Interval-Extended Relational Model and Its Application to Valid-Time Databases," in reference [110].

71. Nikos A. Lorentzos: "DBMS Support for Time and Totally Ordered Compound Data Types," *Information Systems 17*, No. 5 (September 1992).

　　In this book we've discussed the nature of interval types at considerable length, but we've said comparatively little about the nature of the point types in terms of which those interval types are defined. This paper and reference [72] address this latter issue. In essence, they propose a new type generator that would allow users to define temporal point types that almost certainly wouldn't be available as system defined types. An example might be time points measured in terms of week and day numbers (e.g., "week 5, day 2"). Another might be time points measured using a cesium-based atomic clock, in which the time unit is 1/9,192,631,770th of a second (such a point type is needed in certain scientific applications). Nontemporal point types (e.g., weights measured in stones, pounds, and ounces) can also be defined by means of the proposed type generator. *Note:* Alternative proposals for dealing with some of these matters—in particular, with the question of units and granularity—can be found in Chapter 18 of the present book, also in reference [52].

72. Nikos A. Lorentzos: "DBMS Support for Nonmetric Measurement Systems," *IEEE Transactions on Knowledge and Data Engineering 6*, No. 6 (December 1994).

See the annotation to reference [71].

73. Nikos A. Lorentzos and Hugh Darwen: "Extension to SQL2 Binary Operations for Temporal Data" (invited paper), Proc. 3rd HERMIS Conf., Athens, Greece (September 26th-28th, 1996).

This paper extends the work described in reference [76]. It proposes the addition of analogs of certain of our "U_" operators to "SQL2" (i.e., the SQL:1992 standard); to be specific, it discusses what we would now call U_JOIN, U_UNION, U_INTERSECT, and U_MINUS, and gives examples in each case.

74. Nikos A. Lorentzos and R. G. Johnson, "An Extension of the Relational Model to Support Generic Intervals," in Joachim W. Schmidt, Stefano Ceri, and Michel Missikoff (eds.), *Extending Database Technology*. New York, N.Y.: Springer-Verlag (1988).

This paper was the first to show that temporal data management is actually a special case of a more general problem: namely, that of supporting a "generic interval type" (what we would now call an interval type generator), together with operators to deal with relations that include interval data.

75. Nikos A. Lorentzos and Vassiliki J. Kollias: "The Handling of Depth and Time Intervals in Soil Information Systems," *Comp. Geosci. 15*, 3 (1989).

Defines a set of operators for dealing with data related to changes in the composition of soil with depth and the way those changes themselves change with time. *Note:* We include this reference here primarily as a concrete example of an application area in which at least some of the pertinent intervals are nontemporal ones specifically.

76. Nikos A. Lorentzos and Yannis G. Mitsopoulos: "IXSQL: An Interval Extension to SQL," Proc. Int. Workshop on an Infrastructure for Temporal Databases, Arlington, Tex. (June 14th-16th, 1993).

An informal presentation of the ideas discussed more formally in reference [79].

77. Nikos A. Lorentzos and Yannis Manolopoulos: "Efficient Management of 2-Dimensional Interval Relations," Proc. 5th DEXA Int. Conf., Athens, Greece (September 1994), in D. Karagiannis (ed)., *Lecture Notes in Computer Science 856*. New York, N.Y.: Springer-Verlag (1994).

The source of the SPLIT operator described in Appendix E of the present book (in fact, Appendix E is heavily based on ideas first presented in this paper). *Note:* The term *2-dimensional interval relation* in the title of this paper refers to relations with two distinct interval attributes, not to relations with a single attribute whose values are two-dimensional intervals.

78. Nikos A. Lorentzos and Yannis Manolopoulos: "Functional Requirements for Historical and Interval Extensions to the Relational Model," *Data and Knowledge Engineering 17* (1995).

Identifies a number of criteria that support for interval (and therefore temporal) data should satisfy. Two broad approaches to the problem are described, "nested" and "nonnested." The authors show that all of the approaches intended for temporal data in particular can in fact be used for interval data in general. They then proceed to evaluate all known approaches in terms of the criteria identified in the paper.

79. Nikos A. Lorentzos and Yannis G. Mitsopoulos: "SQL Extension for Interval Data," *IEEE Transactions on Knowledge and Data Engineering 9*, No. 3 (May/June 1997).

Describes IXSQL, "an *Interval Extension* to *SQL*." IXSQL is based on the operators of the conventional relational algebra, together with two additional operators, FOLD and UNFOLD (predecessors of PACK and UNPACK, respectively). As its name suggests, the language is explicitly intended for the management of interval data —though it's important to note that in fact it supports both interval and noninterval data in the same uniform way. Since the paper also shows that temporal data is just a special case of interval data in general, it follows that IXSQL actually supports both temporal and nontemporal data in that same uniform fashion. See also reference [76] and, for a further extension of the IXSQL approach, reference [119].

80. Nikos A. Lorentzos, Alexandra Poulovassilis, and Carol Small: "Implementation of Update Operators for Interval Relations," *BCS Comp. J. 37*, No. 3 (1994).

Describes optimized implementation algorithms for operations on relations with two or more interval attributes (see Appendix E).

81. Nikos A. Lorentzos, Alexandra Poulovassilis, and Carol Small: "Manipulation Operations for an Interval-Extended Relational Model," *Data and Knowledge Engineering 17* (1995).

This paper is a more formal version of reference [80]. Complexity and simulation results are included.

82. Nikos A. Lorentzos, Nektaria Tryfona, and Jose R. Rios Viqueira: "Relational Algebra for Spatial Data Management," Proc. Int. Workshop on Integrated Spatial Databases: Digital Images and GIS, Portland, Maine (June 14th-16th, 1999).

This paper presents initial results from the research described in more detail in reference [84].

83. N. A. Lorentzos and J. R. R. Viqueira: "On a Spatio-Temporal Relational Model Based on Quanta," in M. Koubarakis et al (eds.), *Spatiotemporal Databases: The Chorochronos Approach—Lecture Notes in Computer Science 2520.* New York, N.Y.: Springer-Verlag (2003).

See reference [119].

84. N. A. Lorentzos and J. R. R. Viqueira: "Relational Formalism for the Management of Spatial Data," *BCS Comp. J. 49*, No. 1 (January 2006).

This paper defines spatial data types in terms of "spatial quanta" and further generalizes the FOLD and UNFOLD operators of IXSQL [79] to make them applicable to spatial data. Additional operators based on FOLD, UNFOLD, and existing relational operators are also defined, such that the complete set of operators thus made available fully supports the management of spatial data. The new operators are also applicable to conventional data and have considerable practical interest. See also references [84] and [119].

85. N. A. Lorentzos, J. R. Rios Viqueira, and N. Tryfona: "Quantum-Based Spatial Extension to the Relational Model," in Dimitrios I. Fotiadis and Stavros D. Nikolopoulos (eds.), *Advances in Informatics.* Singapore: World Scientific Publishing (2000).

86. N. A. Lorentzos, C. P. Yialouris, and A. B. Sideridis: "Time-Evolving Rule-Based Knowledge Bases," *Data and Knowledge Engineering 29*, No. 3 (1999).

This paper applies the relational operators defined in reference [79] to support temporal knowledge, meaning knowledge that changes over time.

87. V. Lum et al.: "Designing DBMS Support for the Temporal Dimension," Proc. ACM SIGMOD Int. Conf. on Management of Data, Boston, Mass. (June 1984).

This early paper recognizes the need for supporting both logged times and stated times, but proposes that only logged times be given special treatment by the system—stated times are to be dealt with by means of regular attributes in the usual way. The paper gives numerous reasons as to why an implementation that doesn't give special internal treatment to logged times won't perform well. Special storage structures and access methods are proposed to address such problems.

88. N. G. Martin, S. B. Navathe, and R. Ahmed: "Dealing with Temporal Schema Anomalies in History Databases," Proc. 13th Int. Conf. on Very Large Data Bases, Brighton, U.K. (September 1987).

> To quote from the abstract: "Because history databases do not discard data, they cannot discard outdated database schemas. Thus, in any proposal for a practical history database system, some method must be provided for accessing data [described by] outdated, yet historically valid, schemas." *Note:* We touched on this kind of problem very briefly at the end of Chapter 14.

89. Robert Matchett: "Temporal Tables in DB2," *IBM Data Magazine* (April 2012).

90. David McGoveran: "Nothing from Nothing" (in four parts), in C. J. Date, Hugh Darwen, and David McGoveran, *Relational Database Writings 1994-1997*. Reading, Mass.: Addison-Wesley (1998).

> Part I of this paper explains the crucial role of logic in database systems. Part II shows why that logic must be two-valued logic (2VL) specifically, and why attempts to use three-valued logic (3VL) in this context are misguided. Part III examines the problems that three-valued logic (3VL) is supposed to solve. Finally, Part IV describes a set of pragmatic solutions to those problems—including in particular some recommended database design approaches—that don't involve 3VL.

91. E. McKenzie and R. Snodgrass: "Supporting Valid Time: An Historical Algebra," Tech. Report TR87-008, Dept. of Computer Science, University of North Carolina, Chapel Hill, N.C. (1987).

> Defines an algebra for the management of valid time (called stated time in the present book). A *historical relation* must have at least one valid time attribute (though the attribute in question is apparently not a regular attribute as such). Values of such an attribute are sets of time points (e.g., the set {*d01,d02,d03,d04,d08,d09,d10*}). Tuples that are identical except possibly for their valid time component are said to be "value equivalent"; relations aren't allowed to contain distinct but value equivalent tuples. The existing operators of the

relational algebra are adjusted in such a way as to enforce this requirement. New operators are also defined.

92. Edwin McKenzie and Richard Snodgrass: "Extending the Relational Algebra to Support Transaction Time," Proc. ACM SIGMOD Int. Conf. on Management of Data, San Francisco, Calif. (May 1987).

This paper provides a formalization of the concept of transaction time (called logged time in the present book) in terms of denotational semantics. The fundamental observation is that, as explained in Chapter 17, a database is really a variable; an update causes one value of that variable to be replaced by another, and the complete set of such values over time can be thought of as a chronologically ordered sequence. (Actually, the paper talks in terms of individual relations rather than the database as a whole, but the foregoing remarks are still applicable, mutatis mutandis.) The paper proposes extending the relational algebra to include an update operator called *rollback*.[2]

Note: In the introduction, the paper says that in "Codd's relational algebra ... the relations ... model the current reality as is currently best known." We believe we've shown in the present book how "Codd's relational algebra" can be used to deal with all kinds of temporal data, not just "the current reality" but past and future states of affairs as well.

93. L. Edwin McKenzie, Jr., and Richard T. Snodgrass: "Evaluation of Relational Algebras Incorporating the Time Dimension in Databases," *ACM Comp. Surv. 23*, No. 4 (December 1991).

To quote from the abstract: "In this paper we survey extensions of the relational algebra [to support queries on temporal databases] ... We identify 26 criteria that provide an objective basis for evaluating temporal algebras ... Twelve time-oriented algebras are summarized and then evaluated against the criteria." *Note:* Another approach to evaluating alternative temporal proposals can be found in reference [78].

94. Shamkant B. Navathe and Rafi Ahmed: "Temporal Extensions to the Relational Model and SQL," in reference [110].

Proposes a scheme in which intervals are represented by distinct "begin" and "end" attributes (i.e., the interval [b:e] is represented by distinct attributes with values b and e, respectively—more or less as in the SQL standard, in other words, except that SQL uses the closed:open interpretation). As for the relational operators: Projection remains unchanged. Restriction is extended to support interval comparisons such as OVERLAPS

---

[2] Note that the relational algebra as classically understood (and as described in Chapter 2) consists by definition of read-only operators exclusively.

(expressed in the proposed SQL extension by means of a WHEN clause). Four distinct joins are defined, two giving a result with one pair of begin/end attributes and two giving a result with two such pairs. Finally, four new restriction-like operators are defined that involve only the begin and end attributes.

95. G. Özsoyoglu, Z. M. Özsoyoglu, and V. Matos: "Extending Relational Algebra and Relational Calculus with Set-Valued Attributes and Aggregate Functions," *ACM TODS 12*, No. 4 (December 1987).

96. C. Rolland, F. Bodart, and M. Leonard (eds.): *Temporal Aspects in Information Systems.* Amsterdam, Netherlands: North-Holland (1988).

97. Cynthia Saracco, Matthias Nicola, and Lenisha Gandhi: "A Matter of Time: Temporal Data Management in DB2 10" (April 2012), *http://www.ibm.com/developerworks/data/library/techarticle/dm1204db2temporaldata/.*

98. N. L. Sarda: "Algebra and Query Language for a Historical Data Model," *BCS Comp. J. 33*, No. 1 (February 1990).

This reference, along with reference [99], appeared shortly after reference [68] (and they do resemble this latter reference, somewhat). It—i.e., reference [98]—defines a "temporal relational algebra" consisting of Codd's original operators plus two more whose functionality resembles that of FOLD and UNFOLD as defined in reference [68].

99. N. L. Sarda: "Extension to SQL for Historical Databases," *IEEE Transactions on Knowledge and Data Engineering 2*, No. 2 (February 1990).

Applies the ideas of the reference [98] to SQL specifically.

100. B.-M. Schueler: "Update Reconsidered," in G. M. Nijssen (ed.), *Architecture and Models in Data Base Management Systems.* Amsterdam, Netherlands: North-Holland (1977).

The source of the important idea, or shift in perspective, to the effect that "the log is the real database" (see Chapter 17). Schueler argues forcefully that destructive overwriting operations—i.e., UPDATE and DELETE operations as conventionally understood—should be outlawed. Instead, every item in the database should be thought of as a chronologically ordered stack: The top entry in the stack represents the current value of the item, and previous values are represented by entries lower down; thus, an INSERT or UPDATE places a new entry on the top of the stack and pushes all existing entries one place down. (We're being deliberately vague here as to what exactly an "item" might consist of.) Each entry is timestamped, and all entries are accessible at all times. Schueler claims that such a scheme would dramatically simplify the structure of the system with respect to recovery, auditability, locking, archiving, understandability, and usability—not to mention the purely temporal issues that are the focus of the present book—and hence reduce system costs and improve system functionality in a variety of important ways.

101. Arie Shoshani and Kyoji Kawagoe: "Temporal Data Management," Proc. 12th Int. Conf. on Very Large Data Bases, Kyoto, Japan (August 1986).

Sketches another nonrelational "temporal data model." The model in question is motivated by research into scientific and statistical databases, which typically contain sets of measurements (e.g., results of experiments). The basic data object is the *time sequence*, which is a chronologically ordered sequence of <*time*:*value*> pairs for some given *surrogate* (where the surrogate in question denotes some entity). For example, the time sequence <2012:130>, <2013:138>, <2014:142> might represent the weight of some given person on three consecutive birthdays.

102. Erwin Smout: "Could Packing Be Specified in Terms of Closed-Open Interval Semantics Without Having to Commit to Granularity?", *http://www.thethirdmanifesto.com/papers.html/ packing-without-granularity.pdf* (to appear). *Note:* A draft of this paper dated January 14th, 2014 was offered as a contribution to the email discussion forum *ttm@thethirdmanifesto.com*, and the remarks that follow are based on that draft.

The formalism on which the approach to temporal data discussed in the body of this book is based assumes that a successor function ("NEXT_*T*") always exists. As we know from Appendix B, however, that assumption has been the subject of some criticism. The present reference [102] shows that such an assumption might in fact be unnecessary. In other words, it presents an alternative formalism, one that (in effect) assumes that point types are ordered but not necessarily ordinal. In outline, what it does is this: First, it defines an interval as a pair of values, FROM and TO (necessarily of the same ordered type), such that FROM < TO (intervals are thus explicitly assumed to be in closed:open form). It then defines what it means for two such intervals to be equal, to meet, or to overlap, in all cases avoiding any reliance on a successor function. Using these operators, it then defines PACK—not UNPACK!—and various U_ operators (U_join, etc.). It also gives a precise definition of packed form (here called packed normal form),[3] and algorithms for achieving that packed form.

    We continue to believe that the UNPACK operator and unpacked form are conceptually useful tools for explaining our approach to temporal data in an intuitive fashion. It is, however, extremely interesting, and indeed encouraging, to note that those tools might not be totally necessary as a logical underpinning for that approach.

---

[3] Something we didn't do in the body of the book, incidentally.

103. Richard Snodgrass and Ilsoo Ahn: "A Taxonomy of Time in Databases," Proc. ACM SIGMOD Int. Conf. on Management of Data, Austin, Tex. (May 1985).

The source of the terms *transaction time*, *valid time*, and *user defined time*. *Note:* Transaction time and valid time were discussed at length in the present book, but "user defined time" wasn't mentioned. This latter term is used in the present reference to refer to temporal values and attributes that are "not interpreted by the DBMS"; examples might be date of birth, date of last salary increase, and time of arrival. Observe, however, that in the approach to temporal databases advocated in the present book, transaction times and valid times are also—like all other values and attributes!—"not interpreted by the DBMS."

104. Richard Snodgrass: "The Temporal Query Language TQuel," *ACM TODS 12*, No. 2 (June 1987). See also Richard Snodgrass: "An Overview of TQuel," in reference [110].

TQuel was a version of the Ingres language QUEL, extended to support temporal data. This paper describes the TQuel language and a prototype implementation.

105. R. T. Snodgrass et al.: "TSQL2 Language Specification," *ACM SIGMOD Record 23*, No. 1 (March 1994).

106. Richard T. Snodgrass (ed.): *The TSQL2 Temporal Query Language*. Norwell, Mass.: Kluwer Academic Publishers (1995). *Note:* A new edition of this book was published by Springer in 2012.

The definitive reference on the TSQL2 language. The following quote from a Kluwer brochure gives a sense of the book's scope: "A consensus effort of eighteen temporal database experts has resulted in a new temporal database query language, TSQL2, which is upwardly compatible with the international standard [i.e., SQL:1992].[4] TSQL2 provides comprehensive support for temporal applications. No other temporal query language covers as much ground. TSQL2 was designed to be compatible with existing database design and implementation methodologies. The complete specification of the language is included. TSQL2 is also an effective platform for teaching temporal database concepts, eliminating the need to constantly switch between incompatible language proposals." See also references[8], [105], [107], and [108], and (for an alternative point of view) references [29] and [54].

---

[4] Note, however, that TSQL2 differs considerably from the temporal features of SQL:2011 as described in Chapter 19 of the present book.

107. Richard T. Snodgrass, Michael H. Böhlen, Christian S. Jensen, and Andreas Steiner: "Adding Valid Time to SQL/Temporal" and "Adding Transaction Time to SQL/Temporal," Madrid, Spain (January 1997); *ftp://sqlstandards.org/SC32/WG3/Meetings/ MAD_1997_01_Madrid_ESP/mad146.ps.* (This is an internal working document, not generally available at the time of writing.)

These two papers together constitute a TSQL2-based proposal for incorporating temporal functionality into the SQL standard [i.e., SQL:1992]. They were originally submitted to the January 1997 meeting of the ISO committee JTC1/SC21/WG3 Database Languages rapporteur group, but were subsequently withdrawn. See also reference [31].

108. Richard T. Snodgrass: *Developing Time-Oriented Database Applications in SQL.* San Francisco, Calif.: Morgan Kaufmann (2000).

This book uses TSQL2 [105-106] as a basis for explaining in generic terms how to implement temporal applications and databases in SQL:1992 (in other words, using SQL DBMSs that have no built in temporal support at all, apart from SQL's standard datetime types or something analogous). It also includes product specific information and suggestions for several different commercially available (but, at least in 2000 when the book appeared, nontemporal) products: Microsoft Access and SQL Server, IBM DB2 Universal Database, Oracle8 Server, Sybase SQL Server, and UniSQL.

109. Abdullah U. Tansel: "Adding Time Dimension to Relational Model and Extending Relational Algebra," *Information Systems 11*, No. 4 (1986).

This paper can be seen as a more formal version of material from reference [18]. See also reference [112].

110. Abdullah Uz Tansel, James Clifford, Shashi Gadia, Sushil Jajodia, Arie Segev, and Richard Snodgrass (eds.): *Temporal Databases: Theory, Design, and Implementation.* Redwood City, Calif.: Benjamin/Cummings (1993).

This book is a collection of papers. It's divided into four parts, as follows:

1. Extensions to the Relational Data Model
2. Other Data Models
3. Implementation
4. General Language and Other Issues in Temporal Databases

Several of the other references mentioned in this appendix are included in this book.

111. A. U. Tansel and L. Garnett: "Nested Historical Relations," Proc. ACM SIGMOD Int. Conf. on Management of Data, Portland, Ore. (June 1989).

See the annotation to references [18] and [112].

112. Abdullah Uz Tansel and Erkan Tin: "Expressive Power of Temporal Relational Query Languages and Temporal Completeness," in reference [55].

The idea of trying to define some notion of "temporal completeness" seems like a worthy objective (in this connection, see also references [14] and [114]). This paper proposes that a temporal query language (a) should be relationally complete [22] but (b) should also support interval selectors and the "point ∈ interval" operator (to use the terminology of the present book). The paper then evaluates a number of proposed approaches with respect to these criteria.

113. David Toman: "Point-Based Temporal Extensions of SQL and Their Efficient Implementation," in reference [55].

As its title suggests, this paper proposes an extension to SQL based on time points instead of intervals. Some interesting questions are raised concerning implementation. Answers to those questions could be relevant to languages based on intervals too, because the unit intervals resulting from UNPACK are effectively isomorphic to points, in a sense.

114. Alexander Tuzhilin and James Clifford: "A Temporal Relational Algebra as a Basis for Temporal Relational Completeness," Proc. 16th Int. Conf. on Very Large Data Bases, Brisbane, Australia (August 1990).

To quote from the abstract: "We define a temporal algebra that is applicable to *any* temporal relational data model ... We show that this algebra has the expressive power of a safe temporal calculus ... We propose [this] temporal algebra ... and the equivalent temporal calculus as ... alternative [bases for defining] temporal relational completeness."

115. J. W. van Roessel: "Conceptual Folding and Unfolding of Spatial Data for Spatial Queries," in V. B. Robinson and H. Tom (eds.), *Toward SQL Database Extensions for Geographic Information Systems*. National Institute of Standards and Technology Report NISTIR 5258, Gaithersburg, Md. (1993).

This reference uses Lorentzos's FOLD and UNFOLD operators (predecessors of PACK and UNPACK, respectively) as the basis for defining an approach to dealing with spatial data. See also reference [116].

116. J. W. van Roessel: "An Integrated Point-Attribute Model for Four Types of Areal GIS Features," Proc. 6th Int. Symp. on Spatial Data Handling, Edinburgh, U.K. (September 5th-9th, 1994).

117. Costas Vassilakis: "Design and Optimized Implementation of a System for the Management of Historical Data," Department of Informatics, University of Athens, Greece (October 1995).

Describes some research based on Lorentzos's FOLD and UNFOLD operators [67-68].

118. Costas Vassilakis, Nikos Lorentzos, and Panagiotis Georgiadis: "Implementation of Transaction and Concurrency Control Support in a Temporal DBMS," *Information Systems 23*, No. 5 (1998).

Identifies transaction management problems (and describes solutions to those problems) in a temporal DBMS implemented as a separate software layer on top of a conventional DBMS. For example, an operator such as PACK, if implemented in such a separate layer, might map to a sequence of several operations—possibly including operations to write intermediate results into the database—at the level of the underlying DBMS.

119. J. R. R. Viqueira and N. A. Lorentzos: "SQL Extension for Spatio-Temporal Data," *VLDB Journal 16*, No. 2 (April 2007).

The work described in this paper is based on previous research reported in references [79] and [84]. It formalizes an SQL extension for the management of spatiotemporal data (see reference [3])—which is to say, spatial data that evolves with respect to time—and shows how a single set of relational operators can be made to apply uniformly to conventional, temporal, interval, spatial, and spatiotemporal data.

120. Yu Wu, Sushil Jajodia, and X. Sean Wang: "Temporal Database Bibliography Update," in reference [55].

This paper is one in a cumulative series. Earlier contributions are as follows (in reverse chronological sequence):

■ Vassilis J. Tsotras and Anil Kumar: "Temporal Database Bibliography Update," *ACM SIGMOD Record 25*, No. 1 (March 1996).

■ Nick Kline: "An Update of the Temporal Database Bibliography," *ACM SIGMOD Record 22*, No. 4 (December 1993).

- Michael D. Soo: "Bibliography on Temporal Databases," *ACM SIGMOD Record 20*, No. 1 (March 1991).

- Robert B. Stam and Richard T. Snodgrass: "A Bibliography on Temporal Databases," *Data Engineering Bulletin 11*, No. 4 (December 1988).

- Edwin McKenzie: "Bibliography: Temporal Databases," *ACM SIGMOD Record 15*, No. 4 (December 1986).

- A. Bolour, T. L. Anderson, L. J. Dekeyser, and Harry K. T. Wong: "The Role of Time in Information Processing: A Survey," *ACM SIGMOD Record 12*, No. 3 (April 1982).

See also reference [3].

121. Y. Zhang: "Multi-Temporal Database Management with a Visual Query Interface," Ph.D. Dissertation, Department of Computer and Systems Services, Royal Institute of Technology and Stockholm University, Sweden (October 1997).

Zhang's dissertation is based on Lorentzos's FOLD and UNFOLD operators [67-68].

Index

For alphabetization purposes, (a) differences in fonts and case are ignored; (b) quotation marks are ignored; (c) other punctuation symbols—hyphens, underscores, parentheses, etc.—are treated as blanks; (d) numerals precede letters; (e) blanks precede everything else.

Printed and bound by CPI Group (UK) Ltd, Croydon, CR0 4YY

03/10/2024

01040322-0005